TABLE OF CONTENTS

To Order A Copy Of This Book, Please Mail To:

Author/Publisher
Michael A. Blaugher
124 East Foster Parkway
Fort Wayne, IN 46806-1730
260/744-1020
E-mail: airmuseums@aol.com • www.aircraftmuseums.com

Quantity Discounts Available.

W9-AAK-143

Museum Codes:

Adm	=	Admission	**Int'l**	=	International	**RoY**	=	Rest of Year
Appt	=	Appointment	**Jr**	=	Junior	**ES**	=	Easter
Ave	=	Avenue	**Mi**	=	Miles	**T**	=	Thanksgiving
Blvd	=	Boulevard	**PA**	=	Public Affairs	**C**	=	Christmas
CAF	=	Confederate Air Force	**POB**	=	Post Office Box	**N**	=	New Years
Dir	=	Director	**Pres**	=	President	**D**	=	Day
Dr	=	Drive	**St**	=	Street	**E**	=	Eve
Exec	=	Executive	**Snr**	=	Senior Citizen	**L**	=	Labor
						M	=	Memorial

All aircraft are stated by their Type, Model and Series

Aircraft Status Codes:

Flyable	**(F)**
Static Indoor Display	**(D)**
Storage	**(S)**
Replica	**(REP)**
Restoration Project	**(P)**
Static Outdoor Display	**(O)**
On Loan	**(L)**

Military Codes:
AFB = Air Force Base
ANG = Air National Guard
ARB = Air Reserve Base
NAS = Naval Air Station

22nd Edition Released February 2004
1st Edition: April 1987
ISBN: 0-9749772-0-9
ISSN: 1074-9675

Front Cover, Top Photo by: Alice McCormick, Exec Assistant -
The Aviation Museum of Kentucky, Lexington, KY
Front Cover, Bottom Left Photo by: Tom Leunig
Front Cover, Bottom Right Photo by: Mike & Kim Schoenau,
Owners, Aero Dogs, Tulare, CA (See Restaurant Section)
Back Cover, Top Photos by: Larry Ford
Back Cover, Bottom Photos by: William Hatcher

All information is based on letter responses I received from to 01/20/04.

Due to constant changes any information in this book may not be correct.
For current information call or Mail the museum. Some Air Force Bases
may not allow civilians on the base unless you get a pass.
Check ahead for the bases you plan to visit.

ALABAMA

Ardmore - Alabama Welcome Center, 26865 I-65, 35739, 256-423-3891
AL / TN Border, Saturn I Apollo

Birmingham - Southern Museum of Flight, 4343 73rd St N, 35206-3642,
205-833-8226, Fax 836-2439, Tue-Sat 9:30-4:30, Sun 1-4, Adm Adult $3
Snrs & Child $2 Child Uner 4 Free, Dir: Bud Warner, Library, Gift Shop,
Refurbishing Shop and Theater. www.southernmuseumofflight.org,
Halls A-D = HA-HD, Storage = S, On Loan = L, Antrium = A

A-4J(TA) Cockpit	HB	F-105F	SL	Piel-Emeraude	S
A-7E	SL	F-102A(TF)	SL	Pitts Special	A
A-12	SL	F-106	SL	PL-4A	S
AT-6G	HC	F-111A	S	PT-19 Project	S
Aero Commander 680	S	Foker D-7 Project	S	R4D-6Q	S
Aeronca 11AC	HB	Forney Ercoupe F-1	HB	Rand KR-1	HB
Aeronca K	S	Great Lakes 2T-1A-2	HC	RC-3	HC
Aeronca Sedan Floats	S	H-1(UH)	SL	Rotorway Helicopter	HB
BD-4	S	H-6(OH)	SL	Rotec Rally	S
BD-5B	S	H-54B(CH)	SL	Rutan Vari-Eze	HB
Beagle B.206	S	Harrison Mini-Mack	HB	Sonerai II-T	S
Bensen Gyrocopter	A	Huff-Daland Duster	HC	Sport Fury	S
BT-13B	SL	J-3 Project	SL	Starduster	S
Bushby Mustang II	HB	Link Trainer	HB	Stinson SR-5	S
Cumulus Glider	S	Longwing Eaglerock	HB	Stinson 10-A	S
Curtiss D.5 Rep	HC	MiG-15	SL	T-33A	SL
F-4N	SL	MiG-21	SL	T-37B	SL
F-84F 2ea	SL	Mitchell B-10 Buzzard	HB	TG-4A	S
F-86F	SL	Monerai S Glider	HB	Vari-Viggen	
F-101	SL	Mooney Mite M.18	HB		

Evergreen - Middleton Airport, 334-578-1274, Stewart Flying Service
334-578-4905, 35747   FJ-3   T-28C

Huntsville - Alabama Space & Rocket Center, 1 Tranquility Base, Off I-565 Between
I-65 and US 231, 35805-3370, 800-633-7280, 256-837-3400, Daily 9-5 Except:
Memorial-Labor Day, Daily 8-7, Closed TD, CD, Adm Adult $9, Child $6,
Curator: Edward Buckbee; http://info.uah.edu/huntsville/tourist/space-center.html
Quick 1910,   A-12,   V-1 & V-2 Rockets Spacecraft

Aviation Challenge, 1 Tranquility Base, 35805-3371, 888-364-3483
Aviation Camps for Grades 4-12 & Adult, One Week of: Land/Water Survival,
Principals and Simulator Flight Basics, From $399-899, Static Displays Include:
Www.dogfite.com

AH-1	F-14	MiG-17
F-4	F-111	YAV-8B Harrier II

U.S. Space Camp, 1 Tranquility Base, 35805-3371, 800-637-7223
Space Camp for Grades 4-12 & Adult, One Week of: Space Training & Missions
From $399-899,Static Displays Include: SR-71, Apollo 16, Saturn V, Space Shuttle
www.spacecamp.com

Redstone Arsenal, Gate 9, Martin Rd and Mills Rd, Base Pass Needed

AH-1F	AH-64A	ACH-47A	UH-1M

Mobile - Battleship Memorial Park, POB 65, 2701 Battleship Parkway, 36601,
Between Exit 27&30, 334-433-2703, Daily 8-Sunset, Closes 4pm Oct-March,
6pm April-Sept, Closed CD, Adm Adult $10, Child 6-12 $5, Under 6 Free, Gift Shop,
Breakfast $14-18, Lunch $16-18, Dinner $24-27, www.ussalabama.com

A-12 Cygnus 938	F-16A(GF)	HU-16E	M-4 Tank
A-4L	F-86L	OS2U	M-26 Tank
F4U-7	F-8G(RF)	P-51D(F)	M-48AL Tank
B-25J	F4B-4 Rep	SBD-3	M-42A1 Tank
B-52D	F4U-7	UH-1B	M-60A1 Tank
C-47D(VC)	F9F-5P	YF-17(F/A-18)	T-55 Tank Iraqi
CH-21B	H-1B(UH)	USS ALABAMA	PBR Gun Boat
F-105B-IRE	H-19	USS DRUM Submarine	ICBM
F-4C	HH-52A	M-75 APC	

Montgomery - Gunter AFB, 36114, 334-279-1110, Mon-Fri 8-4, Closed Holidays
C-47B,   GAM-72

Maxwell AFB, Chennault Circle, 36112-5000, 334-293-2017, 3800
ABW/PA, Air University, Daily 7-6, Free Adm

B-25J"Poopsie"	F-4C	F-100C	F-105D	T-38A
B-52D	F-86L"Chris"	F-101C(RF)	T-38A	

2

Ozark - Alabama Aviation & Technical College, US Hwy 231S, 36361,
334-774-5113,   Lear Jet 25

US Army Aviation Museum, Fort Rucker, Bldg 617, POB 620610,
36362-0610, 334-255-4443, Mon-Fri 9-4,Sat-Sun 12-4 Free Adm, Closed TD,
CE, CD, NE, ND, Gift Shop 598-9465, www.armyavnmuseum.org,

Bldg 600X		Bldg 600X		Bldg 600X		Bldg 600X	
AX-6	13	H-23B(OH)	0	L-6	7	T-28A	9
Bell 207	0	H-23C(OH)	7	L-13A	7	T-34A(YT)	S
C-7A(YC)	0	H-23F(OH)	9	L-15A(YL)	9	T-37A	
C-45H	C	H-25A	0	L-16A	0	T-39A	S
C-45J(UC)	C	H-26A(XH)	0	L-17A	7	T-41B	7
C-47A	0	H-30(YH)	8	L-17B		T-42	C
C-121A(VC)	C	H-32(YH)	7	L-18C	7	TG-3	13
C-126(LC)	0	H-34A(CH)	0	L-19A	7,S	U-1A	9
CL-475	8	H-34A(VCH)	8	L-19D(TL)		U-3A	S
DH 1A	0	H-37B(CH)	0	L-20A	7	U-4A	S
E-5A(YE)	7	H-39A(XH)	8	L-21A(TL)	8	U-6A(YU)	0
F-51D	9	H-40H(XH)	7	L-200A	9	U-8A	S
H-1	77	H-41A(YH)	7	MI-4	S	U-8G	S
H-1F (AH)		H-47A(ACH)		Nieuport 28C-1		U-9A	C
H-1G (AH)	0	H-51A(XH)		O-3G1(XAO)	13	U-9A(YU)	S
H-1J (AH)		H-55A(TH)	777	O-3A(YO)	0	U-9D(NRU)	C
H-1B (UH)	GG	H-56A(AH)	0	O-3BR(YHO)	0	U-10(YU)	8
H-1H (UH)	8	H-58A(OH)	GG	OV-1A(YO)	9	U-10A	S
H-1M (UH)	G	H-61 (UH)	13	OV-1B	C	U-21(YU)	9
H-1D(YUH)	0	H-61A(YUH)		OV-1C	C	V-1 (XV)	9
H-4A (OH)	8	H-63 (YAH)		P-2E (AP)	C	V-3A (XV)	
H-5A (OH)	7	H-64 (AH)		P-9 (AO)	9	V-5B (XV)	S
H-6A (OH)	78	H-64A(YAH)	0	P-51		V-6A (XV)	
H-6A(YOH)	0	H-347(CH)	S	PT-17		VZ-3RY	9
H-13B(OH)	77	J-3	0	QH-50C	13	VZ-ZAP	0
H-13E(OH)	0	JN-4D		QQ-50	13	X-14	7
H-13T(TH)	0	L-1A	9	R-4B	0	X-26B	9
H-18 (XH)	7	L-2A	9	R-5	9	XROE-1	0
H-19C	0	L-3A	7	R-9B (XR)	8		
H-19D(UH)	9	L-4B	0,7	RU-8D	0		
H-21C(CH)	0	L-5	0	S-60	13		
H-23A(OH)	0	L-5G	0	SE-5A			

DRONES: Fairchild Dragonfly   13 Philco-Ford Prairie II 0
         Lockheed Aquilla   0 Lockheed Test Bed   13
         N.V.   0 McDonnell Douglas Mark II

Tuskegee - General Daniel "Chappie" James Airman's & Industrial Museum,
Air Tuskegee, Flight Field, 1727 Airport Rd, 36083-2813, 3 Mi N of City,
334-724-0602,   F9F

Tuskegee Airmen National Historic Site, 1616 Chappie James Ave, 36803,
I-85 exit 38, Go 1 Mi S on Hwy 81, SE on Hwy 199 (Chappie James Ave)
www.nps.gov/tuai, Artifacts

ALASKA

Anchorage - Alaska Aviation Heritage Museum, 4721 Aircraft Dr, Lake Hood, 99502,
800-770-5325, 907-248-5325, Fax 248-6391, May 1-Oct 1, Daily 9-6,
RoY 9-6 Closed Sun,Adm Adult $5, Theater, Gift Shop, www.alaskaairmuseum.com

American Pilgram 100B	Grumman G-44 Widgeon	Stearman C2B
AT-19	Hamilton Metalplane H47	Stinson 108
Bellanca Sr Pacemaker Fus	J2F-6	Stinson SR-9 CM
Bellanca Pacemaker CH-300	K1-84 Keystone Loening	Stinson SR
C-45H	L-5 Stinson Sentinel	Stinson A Trimotor
C-45F(UC)	Noordyn Norseman	T-50
Curtiss Robin	P-40E (P)=project	Travelair S6000B Floats (P)
DWC	PBY-5A	UH-1H
Fairchild FC2W Frame	S-43 (Nose Only)	Waco UIC
Fairchild 24G	Spartan Executive	Waco YKC Floats
Ford 5-AT Wreckage	Spencer Aircar	

Kulis ANG Base Museum, 6000 Air Guard Rd, 99502-1998, 907-249-1176,

AT-6D	C-47A	F-86A	C-123J	F-80	T-33A

Elmendorf AFB, 3rd Wing Grp Info Mana, HQ 21ST TFW/PA 99506, 907-552-5755,
CRC: Sgt, Matthew T Fast, F-4C   F-102A   T-33A

Fairbanks - Alaskaland Pioneer Air Museum, 2300 Airport Way, 99701,
907-451-0037, 452-2969, Mail: Interior & Arctic Alaska Aeronautical Museum,
POB 70437, 99707-0437, Memorial-Labor Day, Daily 11-9, Open Holidays
Adm $2 For All, www.akpub.com/akttt/aviat.html

B-10	MX Quicksilver	Rutan Vari-eze
Baking Duce II (F.M.1)	C-64A Mk.IV	Stinson SR-5 Jr
C-45F(UC)	Pereira S.P. 3	V-77/AT-19
Fairchild 24J	PT-22 (ST3KR)	UH-1H
Fokker Super Universal Frame	Raven S-50	
HO45	Rotorway 133	

3

Healy - Denali Wings, Box 254, 99743, 907-683-2245,   Ford Tri-Motor

Wasilla - Museum of Alaska Transportation & Industry, 99687, POB 870646, 99687
   907-376-1211, Mem - Labor Day Mon-Sat 10-6, Winter Tue-Sat 8-4, Adm Adult $3,
   Student $1.50, Family $7, Gift Shop, Train Museum, www.museumofalaska.org
   Bowers Model A   JB-2

C-47A	H-21B(CH)	F-102A	K-84	Stinson SR
C-123J	D.W.C.	HH-5	L-6A	Waco

Whitehorse - Yukon Transportation Museums, 30 Electra Cresent, Y1A-6E6,
   867-668-4792, Fax 633-5547, Mon-Sun, May 14-Aug 31, 10-6, Sep 1-9, 12-4
   Adm Adult $4.25, Senior(55+)$3.25, Student $3.25, Child(6-12)$2, Family $9
   Gift Shop, www.yukontransportmuseum.homestead.com/files/ytmuseum1.html, DC-3

ARIZONA

Apache Jct - American Legion Post 27, 1880 Apache Trail, 480-982-0220, T-33A

Coolidge - Coolidge Municipal Airport, E Kenilworth, 85228, 520-723-9169,
   5 Mi SE of City,   MiG-15 (15ea)

Ft Huachuca - Huachuca Museum Society, Boyd & Grierson St, POB 766, 85613-6000,
   PA: 520-458-4716, Mon-Fri 9-4, Sat-Sun 1-4,Free Adm, OV-1D, RC-121G

Gila Bend - Gila Bend AF AUX, 520-683-6200,   F-105D   T-33A

Grand Canyon - Grand Canyon National Park Airport, 928-638-2407,
   6 Miles S of city. AN-2 Russian Antonov, P-47

   Planes of Fame, Grand Canyon Valle Airport, 86023, 520-635-1000,
   Hwy 64 & 180 Junction, Mail: HCR 34 Box B, Valle Williams, AZ, 86046,
   Daily 9-6, Closed TD, CD, Adm Adult $5.00, Child 5-12 $1.95,
   Under 5 Free, Constellation Tour $3.00, Gift Shop
   D = Indoors,   O = Outdoors,   F = Flyable,   S = Storage

AT-6G	GAM-54	RP-5ARP-76B
Bede BD-5Vee (D,S)	HA-112	Rutan Long-EZ
Bf 109G-10/U4 (D)	KD6D-2	Schmitt Commuter (D,S)
Bristol F2.b (F)Rep	L-19A (F)	Siemens-Schuckert D.IV (S)Rep
C-121A(VC) (F)	MiG-15 (O,S)	Spitfire MK V
Curtiss Robin	MWM-74	T-6G
DH 100 Mk III	MXY-7 (D)	T-33A (S)
F-84B (S)	P-51D (F)	TM-61
F-86L Cockpit	PT-17Pitts S-2B (S)	US Navy Bat
F11F-1 (O,S)	Q-5	
Ford 5-AT (S)	RB-26C	

Green Valley - Titan Missile Museum, 85714, I-19 Exit 69, Take Duval Mine
   Rd West, Go 1/10 Mi past La Canada, Nov 1-April 30 Daily, May 1-Oct 31 Wed-Sun 9-5,
   Last Tour 4pm Closed TD, CD, 520-625-7736,791-2929, Adm Adult $6, Military $5
   Child 10-17 $3, Under 10 Free, Pima Air Museum & Titan Missile Museum $10,
   www.pimaair.org, Titan II Missile Silo # 571-7,   UH-1F

   Williams AFB, 85240-5000, PA: 520-635-8200, 82 FTW/DOOB

F-86E	P-80A	T-33A	T-38A(QT)

Mesa - CAF - Arizona Wing & Museum, 2017 N Greenfield Rd, Falcon Field, Sky Harbor Airport
   85215, Mail: POB 2969, 85214, 480-924-1940, 981-1945, Daily 10-4, Adm Adult $5
   Child Under 14 $2.50, Child Under 5 Free, Gift Shop, www.arizonawingcaf.org

A-26C	B-25	C-54	O-2A
AF-2S (Project)	C-45	Mig-15	SNJ
B-17G	C-47	N2S-5	T-33

   Goss Hawk Unlimited (Restoration Facility), 4636 Fighter Aces Dr, 85215, 480-396-9644,
   Fax Same, Mail: POB 20455, 85277-0455, www.gosshawkunlimited.com,
   email: gosshawkunl@aol.com, Projects: Fw 190-D13   P-63C   P-63E

   Marsh Aviation Co, 5060 Falcon Dr, 85215, 480-832-3770, Fax: 985-2840,
   Firefighting Fleet of S-2F1T & S2R Air Tankers

Phoenix - Deer Valley Airport, 702 W Deer Valley Rd, at 7th Ave, 85027, 623-869-0975

AT-6(3ea)	C-123K	F-8K	MiG-15

   Luke AFB(afres), 85309-5000, PA: 623-856-6011, Daily 7:30-4, Tours Fri 9-1,

AT-6	F-84F	F-102A	HU-16E
F-4N	F-86F	F-104C	T-33A
F-15B	F-100C	HH-34J	

   Global Aeronautical Museum, 12448 N 29th Ave, 85029

   Phoenix ANG, Sky Harbor Int'l Airport, 97218-2797, 623-288-5611,   F-104C

Prescott - Embry-Riddle Aeronautical University, 3200 Willow Creek Rd,
   86301-3720, 928-776-3728, North of Bookstore,   F-104

4

Scottsdale - Constellation Group, 15111 N Hayden Rd, #160-190, 602-443-3967,
    Fax: 443-0623,   C-121A(MATS L-749)

Tucson - Pima Air & Space Museum, 6000 E. Valencia Rd, 85706, 520-574-0462, 574-9658,
    Daily 9-5, No Adm After 4pm, Adm Adult $9.75, Sr $8.75, Child 7-12 $6
    Under 7 Free, Closed CD, Snack Bar, Gift Shop 618-4815,
    www.pimaair.org/, e-mail:pimaair@azstarnet.com

A-4C	C-118A(VC)	FireFly 7 Balloon	P2V
A-6E	C-119C	FJ-4B(AF-1E)	P2V-7 (AP-2H)
A-7D (LTV)	C-119 Fire Fight	Flagor SkyScooter	P.Airwave 69 Kiss
A-7E	C-121A	Fleet Model 1	PBM-5A
A-10A	C-121T(RC)	Fw 44-J	Pentecost Hoppicopter
A-26A	C-123B	GNAT	PGM-17(DSV-2C)
A-101	C-123B Fire Fight	H-1F(UH)	Pitts Special S1
A3D-1(YEA-3A)	C-123K	H-1H(UH)	PQ-14 Drone
A4D-2N	C-124C	H-1M(UH)	PT-17 (2 ea)
AD-5N1(A1-G)	C-130A	H-3F(HH)	PT-19
ADM-20C	C-130D	H-5G(R-5)	PT-22
Aerosport Quail	C-131F 2ea	H-19B(UH)	PT-26
AF-2S	C-133B	H-21C	PV-2
AGM-12	C-135J(EC)	H-34C(VH)	QH-50C/DSN-3
AGM-28A	Cessna 120	H-37B(CH)	Quickie
AIM-4	Cessna 150L	H-43F(HH)	R-4B
AIR-21	Cessna 310	H-52(HH) (S-62)	R5O-5
AQM-34L Drone	CG-4A	H-52A(HH)	RA-5C
AQM-34Q Drone	Cruisair 14-13-2	H-54A(HH)	RB-1
AT-6B	CT-39A	H-55A(TH) 4ea	RNF
AT-7	CW 15-C Sedan	Harvard Mk.IV	S2F-1 (2 ea)
AT-9A	D-16	Hiller Flying	SBD-4
AT-11	D-21	Platform	SE-210
AV-8C	DC-7B	HO3S-1G	SM-68
B-17G(PB-1G)	DHC-1	Homebuilt	SNB-5(UC-45)
B-18B	Drone	HTL-7(TH-13N)	SNB-5
B-23(UC-67)	E-1B	HU-16A (SA-16)	Spad XIII Rep7/8
B-24J	Easy Riser	HUP-2	SR-71A
B-25J	Ercoupe 415-C	HUP-3 (H-25A)	Star Bumble Bee
B-26C(EDB)	F-4C	Hyper Light Hg	Sud Caravelle
B-29(TB)	F-4E(NF)	Icarus Hg	Swallow A
B-377SG 201	F-4J(YF)	J-2	T-28C
B-45A	F-9J(RF)	J-4A	T-29A
B-47A	F-14A	J4F-2	T-33A
B-47E(EB)	F-15A	JRS-1/S-43	T-37B
B-50J(KB)	F-84B	KD6G-2	T-38
B-52A	F-84C (2 EA)	L-2M	T2V (T-1A)
B-52D	F-84F(RF)	L-3B	TBM-3
B-52G	F-86H	L-5B	TF-9J
B-57D(RB)	F-86L	L-6	TG-3A
B-57E	F-89J	L-23D (U-8)	TG-6A
B-57F(WB)	F-84F	Lark 95	TH-55A
B-58A	F-94C	Learjet 23	TV-2(T-33B)
B-66D(WB)	F-100C	LGM-25C	U-3A(L-27A)
BC-12D	F-101B	Long EZ	U-6A
Bede 4	F-101C(RF)	MC-4C	U-11A(UO-1)
Bede 5	F-101H(RF)	MGM 109 Missile	UC-36(L-10A)
Bede 5J	F-102A(TF)	MiG-15 bis	UC-45J(SNB-2C)
Beech D-18S	F-102A	MiG-15 UTI	UC-78B(T-50)
BGM 109G	F-104D	MiG-17 PFC	UH-12C
Boeing 707-720	F-105D	MiG-17 PFD	VC-137B
Bonanza N-35	F-105G (2 EA)	MiG-21 PF	VC-140B
Bowers Fly Baby	F-106A	MM-2 Mustang II	Vickers 744
BT-13A	F-107A	MQM-33	VP-1
C-14(YC)	F-111E	MQM-57 Drone	VT-29B
C-15(YC)	F11F-1A (F-11A)	N22S Nomad	Waco RNS
C-45J(YC)	F3D-2 (TF-10B)	N3N	Waco ZKS-6
C-46D 2ea	F3H-2 (F-3B)	NA-64	Waco UPF-7
C-47	F4D-1(F-6A)	O-2A	Wright Flyer Rep
C-47B	F4U-4	OH-43D	X-15A-2
C-54D(DC-4)	F7F-3N	OQ-3 Drone	XJL-1
C-69 (L-049)	F8U-1 (F-8A)	Osprey 2	YC-125A
C-78(UC)	F9F-4	OV-1C	YO-3A
C-82A	F9F-8	OV-10D	YQM-98A Drone
C-97G(KC)	FA-330	P-63E	Zugvogel III-B
C-97G	Falcon II	P-80B	
C-117D (R4D-8)			

390th Memorial Museum, 6000 E Valencia Rd, on the grounds of Pima Air & Space Museum
POB 15087, 85708-0087, 520-574-0462, 574-0287, 9-5 Daily, Closed CD, ND, Admission Charged
www.390th.org/ B-17G

American Legion Post 109, 15921 S Houghton Rd, 84747, 520-762-5652, F-4E

AMARC=Aerospace Maintenance and Regeneration Center (Boneyard)
Tours Only, Contact: Lynda McWilliams at Pima Air & Space Museum: 520-574-0462
48 Hours Prior, Tickets & Departure at Pima Air Museum Gift Shop(9:30, 11, 12:30, 2, 3:30),
Closed Major Holidays, Adm Adult $5, Snrs/Mil $3.50, 17 & Under $3, Schools $2,
Photo ID Required, Containing of 4926 Aircraft in 2600 Acres of Outdoor Storage,

139 Patrol Planes	570 Trainers
426 Cargo Planes	1142 Ground Attack Jets
562 Helicopters	2087 Jet Fighter

Davis-Monthan AFB, NCOIC, Public Affairs, 836 AD/PA, 85707-5000, 520-228-4717
Appt Only, PA: Keith Ylvisaker, 748-3900, http://dm.af.mil/amarc/default.htm

A-7D	B-52D	CH-3C	F-100F	OV-10A
A-10A	C-130A	F-4N	F-105D	U-2C

Hamilton Aviation, 6901 S Park Ave, 85706, 520-294-3481,
Convair 580 (2 each) Outside Airport

Specialized Aircraft, HU-16 (4ea)

Tucson ANG, Tucson Int'l Airport, 85734, 520-573-2210, HU-16 (2ea)

A-7D	F-84F	F-100D	F-102A

Western Int'l HU-16

Winslow - Meteor Crater, 928-289-2362, 20 Miles W of Winslow Off I-40,
Mail: Meteor Crater Enterprises, Inc, POB 0070,Flagstaff, 86002-0070,
(May 15 -Sept 15) 6-6, Remaining 8-5, Adm Adult $7, Sr $6, Child 6-17 $2,
5 & Under Free, 71 Space RV Park, 520-289-4002, 1 Mi Wide/570 Ft Deep Crater
www.meteorcrater.com, e-mail: info@meteorcrater.com, Apollo Space Capsule

Yuma - Marine Corps Air Station, 85369-5001, 928-341-2011,
PA Chief: C.A.Demar Community Relations: Judy Yeadon, 2275,

A-4	F-4(2ea)	AV/8A

ARKANSAS
Eureka Springs - Aviation Cadet Museum, 542 CR 2073, 72632, 479-253-5008
www.aviationcadet.com

Fayetteville - Arkansas Air Museum, 4290 S School Ave, Drake Field, US 71
72701, 479-521-4947, Mon-Fri, Sun 11-4:30,Sat 10-4:30, Closed TD, CD, ND, Adm Adult $2,
Child 6-18 $1, Under 6 Free, Curator: John C Kalagias, Restoration Viewing,
Gift Shop Mon-Tue, Theater, www.arkairmuseum.org

A-4C	DGA 11	L-16	Stinson Junior S
AT-6G	DGA 18K	Neiuport 28C	TravelAir Model 4000
Curtiss CW-1	Globe Swift	PT-17	
DC-3 Cockpit Proj	H-1S(AH)H-1H(UH)	SE.5A	
DGA 6			

Fort Smith - Ebing ANG Base, 188TH TFG, Ft Smith Municipal Airport, 72906,

479-648-5271,	F-4	RF-84

Little Rock - Aerospace Education Center, 3301 E. Roosevelt Rd, 72201, 501-371-0331,
376-4232 Gift Shop, IMAX Theater, www.aerospaced.org,

Link	Wright Flyer	Headwind JD-HWL-7
Sopwith Camel F-1	Apollo CM	Bell Eagle Eye
Command Aire 5-C-3	Adventura	

All Flags Heritage Park, Camp Robinson Army Reserve Base,
PA: Lt Col Lashbrook 501-212-5020, F-104, USAF & Army Aircraft Displayed

Little Rock AFB, 314 TAW/HO, 72099-5000, 501-988-3131,
Wing Historian: Sgt. John G Schmidl

B-47E	C-119J	F-4C(RF)	H-1M(UH)
B-57C	C-130A	F-84(RF)	T-33A
C-47	C-131A(HC)	F-101C(RF)	M-60 Tank

Pine Bluff - CAF Razorback Wing, Grider Field, Sat-Sun, www.cafark.org,

A-26	BT-13	L-3	PT-19	SNJ
AT-6	C-45	PT-17	PT-26	

Pocahontas - Pocahontas Mncpl Airport, US Hwy 67, A-7, Sikorsky Heliocopter

Rogers - Rogers Municipal Airport, Carter Field, 479-631-1626, F-101B

Springdale - CAF Blackhawk Squadron, Squadron Leader: Robert A Bell,
Route 8, Box 264, 72764, 479-756-8302

Ozark Military Museum, POB 1766, Springdale Mncpl Airport, 72765
479-422-0208, Historian Mike Eckels email: skyhawk2@tcac.net
Several Military: Aircraft, Vehicles and Artillery

Walnut Ridge - Walnut Ridge Army Flying School Museum, 2 Sky Watch Dr,
Walnut Ridge, AR 72476, 870-886-7357 or 870-886-3859,
www.walnutridge-aaf.com/museum.htm, H-1(AH), Link Trainer, SNB/JNB Trainer

CALIFORNIA

Alameda - Alameda Naval Air Station, 1000 Cmdr Dr, 510-xxx-xxxx, Sn Brn, 94501, A-4, A-7

Atwater - Aviation Challenge, 3600 B St, 95301, 888-MACHONE, 209-726-0156,
Located at Castle AFB, Aviation Camps for Grades 4-12 & Adult, One Week of:
Land/Water Survival, Principals and Simulator Flight Basics, From $399-899,
Www.aviationchallenge.net,

Castle Air Museum, POB 5050 Santa Fe, 95301, 209-723-2178, Adjacent To Castle AF
On Santa Fe Rd Off HWY 99, Gift Shop 723-2182, Restaurant 723-2177
Memorial-Labor Day 9-5, Remaining 10-4, Closed: ES, TD, CD, ND, Adm Adult $7,
Child 8-16 $5, Active & 7 & Under Free, Seniors $5, Curator Jack R Gotcher,
www.elite.net/castle-air/index.htm, email cam@elite.net, (S) = Storage

A-26B	BT-13	F-86H	KC-97L
AGM-28B	C-45A	F-89J	PT-17 (S)
AT-6	C-46D	F-100(CF)	PT-22
B.2 Avro Vulcan	C-47A	F-101B	PT-23 (S)
B-17G	C-54E(R5D)(S)	F-104D	O-2A
B-18A	C-56	F-105B	SA-16 (S)
B-23	C-60B(L-18C)(S)	F-106	SR-71A
B-24M	C-78(VC) (S)	F-111A(FB)	T-33A
B-25J	C-119C	GAM-63	T-34(YT)
B-26B (S)	C-123K	HH-43B	TG-3
B-29A(B-50)	C-131A(HC)	HU-16B	U-3A
B-36H(RB)	C-135A(KC)	L-4 (S)	UC-78
B-45A	CG-4 (S)	L-5E (S)	WB-50D
B-47E	F-4	L-13 (S)	VH-13H (S)
B-52D	F-80B	L-21A (S)	U-6A(L-20A)(S)
B-57E(EB)	F-84F	KAQ-1	

Bishop - Inyo National Forest, 798 N Main St, 93514, 760-873-2529, TA-4B, Train

Burbank - Producers Air Force, 1 Orange Grove Terrace, 91501,
Contact: Chuck Hood,
Replica's From Movies For Sale: F-5, F-6, F-15, F-16

Calistoga - Calistoga Gliderport (Next to "Nance's Hot Springs"), 1546
Lincoln Ave, 707-942-5000, Daily 9-5, Gift Shop, Glider Ride For One $79
For 20 Min, $110 For 30 Min, Ride For Two $110 For 20 Min, $150 For
30 Min, Occasional Bi-Plane Ride In A Travel-Air or Waco Classic,
Contact: John Marchesini, Schweizer 2-32, 3 Place (4 ea)
Schweizer 2-33, 2 Place (2 ea)
Schweizer SGS-126B, 1 Place (3 ea)

Camarillo - WWII Aviation Museum, CAF Southern California Wing,
Camarillo Airport, 455 Aviation Dr, 93010, 805-482-0064, Formerly Oxnard AFB,
Daily 10-4, Adm Adult $5, Child 13-18, Child Under 13 $1,
Couples $5, Child 10-116 $1, Under 10 Free, Dir: Dave Long

A6M-3 (P)	C-131 (T-29)	P-38	YAK-3
B-25J (P)	F6F-5	P-51	
C-46F (2ea)	F8F-2	SNJ-4 (P)	
C-121C	Fairchild 24	SNJ-5Spitfire	

Constellation Historical Society, Global Aeronautical Foundation,
POB 2617, Camarillo Airport, Contact: Wayne Jones, EC-121C

Chino - Planes of Fame (See Next Page)

Corona - CAF Inland Empire Squadron, Municipal 909-736-2289, L-4, SNJ-5

El Cajon - CAF Air Grp 1, Flying Field Museum, Gillespie Field, 1935 N Marshall
Ave, 92020, 619-448-4505, Sat 8-4, www.p82.org

AT-6	FM-2	L-5	SNJ
AV-8A	J-2	P-82	UC-78B

El Cajon
San Diego Aerospace Museum, Gillespie Field, 335 Kenney St, 92020, 619-234-8291
Mon, Wed, Fri 8-3, Free Adm, Restoration Facility, www.aerospacemuseum.org

A-4C	AV-8A	F4B-4	P-51D
A-6E	F-8J	Great Lakes T2-1A	Pietenpol Air Camper
A-7B	F-14A	H-1B(UH)	Ryan 147T Drone
AGM-129 Missile	F-16N	L-2B	SBD (3/4 Scale)
AT-6	F-86F	L-19	Sopwith Pup
Atlas Missile	F-102A	Mutual Blackbird	

El Centro - El Centro Naval Air Facility, 92243-5000, 760-339-2524,
8 Miles W of City, N of I-8, A-4 A-7D, F-18A

Chino - The Air Museum "Planes of Fame", WWII Cal-Aero Field, 7000 Merrill
Ave, Box 17, 91710, 909-597-3722, 597-3514, Daily 9-5, Closed TD, CD,
Adm Adult $8.95, Child 5-12 $1.95, Under 5 Free, Gift Shop, Pres: Steven J Hinton
"Fighter Rebuilders" Restoration Facility, Curator: Edward T Maloney
www.planesoffame.org, Rep=Replica, F=Flyable, S=Static,
RF=Restore to Fly, RS=Restore to Static, ST=Storage,

S	A-4B	F	F6F-5K	F	P-12E/F4B-3
ST	A-37	S	F7F-3N	F	P-26A
ST	A6M5	R	F8F-1	F	P-38J-20-LO
F	A6M5		F8F-2	S	P-39N-5-BE
	AD-4N		F8U-1	F	P-40N
RS	Aichi D3A2 Val Rep	S	F9F-5P	F	P-47G
F	AN-2	S	FJ-3		P-51A
S	Apollo Module Rep	S	FM-2(F4F)	F	P-51D
R	Apollo CM		Fokker DR.1	RF	P-59A(YP)
F	AT-12A/2PA		Fokker D VII		P-63
S	B-17G		Formula 1 Racer	S	P-80A
F	B-25J	S	FR-1 Ryan		P-84F
F	B-26C(RB)		G4M1		PB4Y
S	B-50A Fuse	S	GAM-54		PQ-14/TDC-2
RS	Ba-349		H-1 Racer	F	PT-17
	Bensen B-8M	S	H-23		PT-19
	Blaty Orion	ST	H-34		PV-2
S	Bristol F2.b Rep	F	HA-1112		R3C-2
RF	BT-15 Val		HD-1	S	Ric Jet RJ-4
ST	C-45/SNB		Hurricane Mk X	S	Rider R-4 Rep
	Cessna 210	RS	He-100	S	Rider R-5 8-Ball
	Chanute Hang Glider	S	He 162A-1		RP-5A
F	Convair 240(C-131B)	S	Horten Ho.IV	S	RP-76B Drone
	Cricket NC-12	RF	Howard 250	S	RP-54D Drone
S	CSM/Escape Tower		J2F-6	S	Rutan Long-Easy
ST	Curtiss Pusher	S	J2M3	S	Rutan Quickie 2
S	D-558-II	S	J8M1		S-S D.IV
F	DH 100 Mk.VI	S	KD6D-2		S&N Flying Wing
ST	DC-3 Cockpit		L-5G		Schmidt Helio
S	Deperdussin Racer	F	L-13A	F	SBD-5
S	DGA-5		L-17	F	SNJ-5
S	Discoverer Capsule	S	L-18(C-60)	RF	Spitfire Mk.IXe
S	Easy Riser H.G.	S	LeBel VTO	RS	T-2A Rockwell
	F-14A		Lilenthal	S	T-33
	F-26		LK-10	F	TBM-3
	F-80		Lockheed Q-5	S	TM-61
S	F-84F		Luscombe Silvaire		TS-11
S	F-84K(RF)		M-39	F	TV-2
	F-86F	S	Me 108		Ultralight
S	F-86LFuselage	S	Me 163B Rep	S	V-1(Fi-103)
S	F-86H(QF)	R	Mercury Capsule		Williams W-7
RS	F-89J	S	MiG-15		X-1
RT	F-89J	S	MiG-17		X-2 Rep
S	F-100D	RF	Miles/Atwood Rep		X-7
S	F-102A		MQM-74	S	Yak-18
	F-10	S	MXY-7	ST	Yak-11
S	F-105B	F	N9M-B Flying Wing	S	Yak-11
F	F3F-2		Nieuport 28C		
	F4U-1A		O-47		
	F6F-3				

Yanks Air Museum, Chino Airport West Side, 7000 Merrill Ave, N Side of Airport
909-597-1734, Mon-Fri 8-3, Free Adm, By Appt, Curator Ron Blondell,
R=Restoration; A=Awaiting Restoration; www.yanksair.com

A-4B (A)	C-47A (A)	HU-1 (A)	P-51D-10
A-4E (A)	E-2 (A)	JN-4D	P-63C
American Eagle A-1	EA-6B (A)	KD6G-2 Drone	PT-26 (A)
AQM-37A Drone	Ercoupe 415-D (A)	KDB-1 Drone	SB2C-3 (A)
B1 Mahoney Ryan	F-4C (2ea) (A)	L-5 (A)	SBD-4 (2 ea)
B-25J (R)	F-4J	LP-3	SNJ-5
Bell 47D1	F-14A	MC-1	Stearman 4D
BQM-126A Drone	F-14A (A)	Mig 27 Drone	Stearman Bull
BT-13B	F-80C (A)	M-S Salaman	T-33A (A)
Bruner-Winkle Bird	F-105	N3N-3(3 ea)	T-37 (A)
Bruner-Winkle Sparrow	F4U-4B (R)	O-52	T-38A (A)
C-40 (R)	F6F-5	Ohka 11 (A)	T-50 (UC-78)
C-43(UC)	FJ-1 (A)	OS2U-3 (A)	TBF-1 (A)
C-46 (A)	FM-2	P-38L	TDU-25B Drone
Cessna AW	G-1B(YG)	P-39N-0	Thomas Pidgeon (R)
CG-4A (A)	G-6 (A)	P-40E	YPT9B Clooudboy
Curtiss Robin C-1(R)	H-3(CH)	P-47D	
Curtiss Robin	H-3E(CH) (A)	P-47M	
C-47 (R)	H-34 (A)	P-51A-1	

Fairfield - Travis Air Force Museum, Bldg 80, Burgan Blvd, 4535-5000, I-80
to Airbase Parkway Exit, East to Main Gate, Right on Burgan Blvd, Mail:
POB 1565, 707-424-5605, Mon-Sat 9-4, Closed Federal Holidays, Adm Free,
Airpark Open Daily Dawn till Dusk, www.travis.amc.af.mil/
Indoor Museum = *

A-26K	C-119	F-102A	Link Trainer *
AT-11 (P)*	C-124C	F-104A	O-2A
B-29 *	C-131E	F-105D	PT-19 *
B-52D	C-140A	Gonzales *	T-28 *
BT-13 *	CT-39A	H-21B	T-39A
C-45H	F-4C	H-34(VC)	U-3A
C-54	F-84F	L-4 *	
C-56	F-86L	L-5 *	
C-118A(C-54Q)	F-101B	LC-126A	

Firebaugh - The Heritage Eagles Museum, Eagle Field, 11163 North Eagle Av
93622, www.b25.net/museum,   B-25

Fresno - Fresno ANG, Fresno Air Terminal, 93727-2199, 559-454-5100,
26th NORAD Region & Air Div; 194th FIS, 144th FIW,

F-4	F-86L	F-106A	T-33A
F-86A	F-102A	P-51D	

Fountain Valley - Twin Beech Assoc, Mail: POB 8186, 92728-8186, Pres:
Enrico Bottieri 714-964-4864, Historian Robert Parmerter 607-638-9343

Fullerton - Air Combat USA, 230 N Dale Pl, Mail: POB 2726, 92833-2524,
800-522-7590 714-522-7590, Fly Laser Dog Fights in the SIAI Marchetti
SF260, $695 Phase I/II, $1295 Full Day Training & 2 Flight Missions &
G-1 Jacket, See Offerings for List of 18 Participating Cities.

Hawthorne - Western Museum of Flight, 12016 Prairie Ave, 90250,310-332-6228
Fax: 664-6778, Tue-Sun 10-3, Adm Adult $3, Child $2, Dir: Darrell McNeal.
www.wmof.com/welcome.htm

A-4A	F-5A	Radioplane RP-5A	T-51R-5190 Engine
AT-6E(XA)	Gyrocopter	Radioplane RP-76	V-12 Engine
DH 82	JB-1	Rogallo Wing	
F-14A	Montgomery	A-1020 Engine	
F-17(YF)	Glider	GR-1820-G205 Engine	
F-20 Fuse	Northrop KD2R-5	J-79-GE-3A Engine	
F-23(YF)	O-3A(YO)	R-985-AN-1 Engine	

Hayward - Vintage Air Museum, Field Bud Aviation, 20301 Skywest Dr, 94544
510-782-9063

C-3 (2ea)	PA-12	Stearman 4CM-1
Cessna 180	PA-23-250	Stearman Stock
DH 89 Project	Ryan STA	Travel Air 4000

Hemet - Ryan School of Aeronautics Museum, 4280 Waldon Weaver Rd,
Mail: 5001 W Florida Ave # 176, 92545-3823, 909-658-2716, Thur-Sun 10-3
Closed Major Holidays, Free Adm, Gift Shop, Theater, Artifacts

Imperial - Pioneer's Museum, 373 E Aten Rd, 92251, 760-352-3211
F-14   M-60 Tank

Inyo - Inyo National Park, TA-4B, K30 N Gauge Train

Inyokern - US Aviation Museum, Pacific Coast Division, 1300 Airport Rd, 93527,
760-377-0012, www.come.to/usam, Founder Tony Mazzolini

A-4	B-29 Project 2ea	F-35
A-7	F-4	F-86

Lancaster - Antelope Valley College, Aviation Dept, 3041 W Ave, 93536
661-722-0615, D-558-2 Skyrocket #3

Constellation Historical Society, 104 East Ave, K4 Suite G,
93535, 661-945-2093, Fax 945-7055,   C-121C

Jethawks (Lancaster Municipal Stadium), 2400 W Ave I, 93536, 661-726-5400
F/A-18

Milestone of Flight Museum, Mail: POB 2585, 93534, 661-942-6555,
B-25C   C-97G   F-102A(TF)

Poncho Barnes Aviation, 4555 W Ave G, 93536, 661-948-4048,
Travel Air Mystery NR-613K

Lemoore - Leemore Naval Air Station, 93245, 559-998-4045,   A-1, A-4, A-7E

Los Alamitos - Naval Air Station, US 405 & 605, 90720, 562-795-2533, UH-1, XFV-1

Los Angeles - California Science Center, 700 State Dr, 90037, Exposition Park,
323-724-3623, 7547, Daily 10-5, Free Adm, Space Shuttle Cargo Bay, www.casciencectr.com

A-12	F-104D	T-38
Bell 47G-5	Gemini 11	Velie Monocoupe 70
Comet Glider	Capsule	Wright Glider
DC-8-52	Mercury MR-2	X-1
F-20	Capsule	

The Cockpit, 7510 Melrose Ave, 90046, 323-782-0617, Mon-Sat 10-6,
Sun 12-5, Aviation Clothing (WWI-Today Military & Civilian),
P-51 Suspended From Ceiling

Marysville - Beale AFB, 9SRW/CCX, 95903-5000, 530-634-2038, Mon-Fri 10-4,
Closed Holidays, Free Adm, BIG RED 1 Reenactment Grp.

A-26	B-25	C-97L(KC)	SR-71A	U-2R

Forgotten Warriors Museum, 530-742-3090, Thur 7-10, 1st Sat Each Month,
Open Memorial / Veterans Day,   H-1H(UH)   H-6(OH)

Mather - Military Hospital, Mather AFB, 95655, 916-364-2177,

F-105G	H-1H(UH)	H-58(OH)

Modesto - CAF Central California Valley Squadron, County Harry Sham
Airport, 209-577-5318, L-5E

Mojave - Mojave Airport, 1 Mi East of City, 93501, 661-824-2433

Convair 880	F-4

Mt View - Moffett Field, NASA Ames Visitor Center, Moffett Field, 94305,
650-604-6274, Wed-Sat 10-2, 1st & 3rd Sun 12-2, Free Adm, Gift Shop,
www.moffettfieldmuseum.org/index.html

F-104	Mercury Space Capsule	U-2
HiMAT	Space Shuttle 1/3 Scale	

U.S. Space Camp, Moffett Federal Airfield, P.O. Box 6, 94035, 800-637-7223,
650-603-8902, Space Camp for Grades 4-12 & Adult, One Week of: Space Training
& Missions From $399-799. Www.spacecampecalifornia.com.

Oakland - CAF Golden Gate Squadron, Oakland Int'l Airport, 94601, Mail: POB 6056, 94603
510-568-7708, www.ghostsquadron-ggw.org, MiG-17   SNJ   T-33A

Museum Department of History, 1000 Oak St, 94607,
510-273-3842, Wed-Sat 10-5, Sun 12-7, Free Adm,   1919 Meteor.

Oakland Western Aerospace Museum, Oakland Int'l Airport, Bldg 621, 8260 Boeing
St, North Field, Across From Hangar 6, Mail: POB 14264, 94614-4264
510-638-7100, Fax 6530, Wed-Sun 10-4, Adm Adult $7, Snrs $6, 6-12 $3, 5 & Under Free
Gift Shop, Library, Short Solent Tour $3, www.westernaerospacemuseum.org

A-3B(KA)(A3D)	AV-8A(TAV)	Glasair	Monocoupe 110
A-4M	Bede BD-5B	Ikarus Aero 3A	PT-13
A-6D(KA)	F-86H	Link Trainer	Short Solent Mk.3
A-7E	Funk Model B	Lockheed 10-A	TBM-3
Arrow Sport F	GAM-72	MiG-15	Wright EX Vin Fiz

Old Sacramento - Discovery Museum, 101 "I" Street, 95814, 916-264-7057,
The Challenger Learning Center

Palm Springs - Palm Springs Air Museum, 745 N Gene Autry Trail, 109 S
Indian Canyon Dr, Palm Springs Regional Airport, 92262-6603, 760-778-6262,
Daily 10-5, Closed TD, CD, Adm Adult $7.50, Snrs/Mil $6, Child 6-12 $3.50,
Child Under 6 Free, Dir: Fritz Frauchiger 778-6262, www.air-museum.org
E-Mail: info@air-museum.org

A-6	F4F	J-3C	SBD-5
A-26C(JD-1)	F	P-40	Spitfire Mk.XIV
AT-6G	F6F-5K	P-47D	T-28
B-17G	F7F-3	P-51D 2ea	T-34
B-25J	F8F	P-63	TBM-3E
C-1A(S-2)	F-16N	PT-17	
F-14	G-21(OA-13)	PT-22	

Palmdale - Palmdale, AFCMD/OL-AD, Plant 42, 661-272-6718, Blackbird Airpark
Fri-Sun 10-1, www.edwards.af.mil/museum/doc_html/blackbird_airpark.html

A-12	D-21	F-86H	F-105D	SR-71A

Paso Robles - Estrella Warbird Museum, CAF Estrella Squadron, 4251 Dry Creek Rd,
From Hwy 101 Go East on Hwy 46, North on Airport Rd, To Dry Creek Rd, 93446,
805-227-0440, Fax 238-9317, Tue-Sat 10-5:30, Free Adm, Mail: POB 570, 93447,
Gift Shop, Curator: Warren Bailey, * = Privately Owned, http://ewarbirds.org

A-4A	F-8G(RF)	L-16A	Titan II
A-6E	F-86F(QF)	Morrissey 2000C	x Allison 250-C18 Engine
A-7C	H-1(UH)	S-2D	x J-47 Engine
AT-11 *	JN-4D *	Stinson V-77	x J-79 Engine
F-104G(TF)	L-5E	T-28B	x T-53 Engine
F-4D	L-17A	T-33A	x TF-30 Engine

Point Mugu - Point Mugu Missile Park, SR 1 & Pacific Ave, 805-989-1110
   F-4   F6F   F-14   Missiles

Port Hueneme - Channel Island ANGB, 146th AW, Mail: POB 4001, 93041-4001,
   Wing Historian: T/Sgt C Washbum,   F-86

Ramona - Classic Rotors, 300 Montecito Rd, Airport Hangar #310, Ramona Airport,
   760-787-9661, 619-427-1330, 949-466-9682, Sat Appt, www.rotor.org

Brantly 305	H-30(YH)	HUP-1	Roton
H-19	H-32	HUP-1(H-25)	Rotorway 133
H-19D	H-37	Ka-26	V-44B
H-21B	HOK	Monte Copter 15	
H-23B(OH)			

Rialto - Klaers Aviation, 1462 N Fitzgerald Ave, 92376-8621, 909-874-9108
Restores P-47's, Has two P-47D's from Brazil, B-25

Ridgecrest - US Naval Museum of Armament and Technology, China Lake Naval Weapons Center
   Mon-Fri 10-4, 760-939-3105, Gift Shop, 760-939-3530, www.chinalakemuseum.org,

A-4F(NT)	F-8L(DF)	H-1(UH)	Sidewinder
A-6E	F-11B	RA-5C	Tomahawk
A-7C	F-4B(RF)	Missiles:	
AV-8A	F-4D(XF)	Polaris	
F/A-18	F-86(QF)	Shrike	

Riverside - P-38 National Assoc, Tony LeVier Hangar Museum (At March AFB),
   Mail: P-38 National Assoc, POB 6453, March ARB, 92518, www.p38assn.org; P-38   P-51

475th Fighter Group Historical Foundation, March AFB, Mail: POB 6463, 92518-0394,
Next to the P-38 National Assoc, www.475th.org, Artifacts

March Field Air Museum, 22550 Van Buren, Off I-215, 92518-6463, 909-697-6600
Fax 697-6605, Mail: POB 6463, Daily 10-4, Mem Day-Labor Day 10-5, Closed CD,TD,ND,ED
Gift Shop, 697-6603, Library 697-6604, Theater, Restoration Facility,
Donations Family $10, Adult $5, Child 6-18 & Military $2, Under 6 Free,
Dir: Sally Ann Maas, www.marchfield.org,

A-7D	C-123K	F-105B	P-39Q
A-9A(YA)	C-131D	F-105D	P-6 Hawk
AN-2 Colt	C-135A(KC)	FB-111A	P-40 Replica
A-26C	C-141B	FO-141	P-59A
B-8M Bensnon	CT-39A	H-1F(UH)	PT-6A
B-17G	F-4C	H-6A(OH)	PT-13
B-25J	F-4C(RF)	H-21B(UH)	PT-19B
B-29A	F-4E	HU-16E	R50-5
B-47E	F-14	L-5	SNJ-4
B-52D(GB)	F-84C	LGM-30 Minuteman II	SR-71A
B-57(EB)	F-84F	MiG-19	T-33A
BT-13A (2ea)	F-86H	MiG-21	T-37B
C-45F(JRB-4)	F-86L	MiG-23	T-38A
C-47A(VC)	F-89J	Nieuport II Rep	T-39A
C-54D	F-100C	O-2B	TG-2
C-97L(KC)	F-101B	OH-6A	U-9A
C-119F	F-102A	OH-58A	

Rosamond - Edwards AFB, NASA Ames-Dryden Visitor Center, POB 273, 93523-0273, 661-258-3954,
   Gift Shop,   SR-71   X-1E   X-15   X-29

Edwards AFB, Air Force Flight Test Center Museum, 95ABW/MU, 405 S Rosamond Blvd,
Bldg 7211, 93524-1850, 661-277-8050, Fax 277-8051, Tue-Sat 9-5, Closed Sun-Mon,
TD, CD, ND, Free Adm, Gift Shop 277-6500, e-mail: museum@po-box1.edwards.af.mil
www.edwards.af.mil/museum/index.html, INC = incomplete, OD = On Display,
OS = Off Station, R = Restoration, S = Storage, AT = Awaiting Transportation,
NS = Non Standard; Jet Engines: J35, J47, J57, J79, J85, YJ93, YF101, F-109;
Rocket Engines: XLR-8, XLR-11, XLR-99, LR-121

A-3D-1	S	C-123K	S	F-94A(YF)	R	NF-11(TT-20) OD
A-7D(Y)	R	C-135A	S	F-100A	INC	P-59B(XP) OD
A-7F(Y)	R	C-140A	S	F-100A	OS/AT	PA-48 R
A-9A(YF)	S	C-141A(NC)R		F-100A(YF)	R	PGM-17A OD
A-10B(Y)	R	CH-3E	OD	F-100A(YF)	S	Rutan 354 S
A-12	OD	CT-39A	OD	F-101B	OD	SR-71 OD
A-37B(NA)	OD	D-21	OD	F-102A(TF)	S	T-28B OD
AQM-34	OD	F-4C(NF)	OD	F-104A	OD	T-33A OD
AT3	R	F-4C(RF)	R	F-104A	OD	T-33A OD
B-26B(T)	R	F-4E(YF)	R	F-104A(NF)	OD	T-38A OD
B-47B	INC	F-8G(RF)	S	F-105D	R	T-46A S
B-52D	OD	F-10B	R	F-106B	R	Titan Missile
B-57B	R	F-16B	R	F-111A(N)	R	U-2D OD
B-58A(N)	INC	F-16B	OD	F-111A	OD	X-4 R
BQM-34A	S	F-20		H-21C	S	X-21A INC
C-7B	S	F-80A(EF)R/OS		H-34C(VH)	S	X-25B OD
C-45J(U)	OD	F-84F	OD	H-34G(SH)	OD	
C-53	R	F-86F	OD	HUP-2	S	
C-119B	S	F-89D	S	MMC-845	S	

Sacramento - McClellan AFB, McClellan Aviation Museum, North Highland
Palm Gate Entrance Off Watt Ave, 95652-5990, 916-643-2111, Mon-Fri 9-3,
Sat 9-4, Sun 12-4. Free Adm, Closed Holidays, Gift Shop, www.sacmuseums.org/mcclellan

A-1E	C-131D(VC)	F-100D	L-2M
A-7D	CH-3E	F-101B	MiG-17PF
A-10A	EC-121D	F-102A	MiG-21F
AT-6G	F-4C	F-104B	T-28B
C-45HJ(UC)	F-80B	F-105D	T-33A
C-53D	F-84F	FB-111A	T-39A
C-54D	F-86F	H-21C(CH)	
C-119G	F-86L	HU-16B	

San Bernardino - Norton AFB, 92409-5000, 909-382-1110, CT-39A, F-105D

San Carlos - Hiller Northern California Aviation Museum, 601 Skyway Rd on Freeway 101,
94070, 650-654-0200, Fax 654-0220, 10-5 Daily, Adm Adult $8, Snrs & Child 8-17 $5,
Under 8 Free, Gift Shop, Library, Theater, Restoration Viewing, www.hiller.org

Avitor Hermes, Jr	H-23A #234	PG-185
Boeing 747 Cockpit	H-23B(OH)	PT-22
Boeing Condor SST	H-23D(OH)	PT-24
Cole Flyer	H-23F(OH)	RC-3 Seabee
Coleopter	H-31(YH)(LZ-5)	Santa Clara Glider
Christen Eagle	H-32(HOE)	Sopwith Camel
Curtiss D	H-44(XH)	Stearman Hammond YS-1
Diamond	Hiller 360(HTE2)H-23A)	Stinson Detroiter
Doman	HOE-1(HJ-1,YH-32) Hornet	T-13
FH-1099 CAMEL	J-10-Jet	Thaden Transporter
FH-1100	"Little Looper" Aerobatics	VZ1 Hiller 1031
Flying Crane	Montgomery "Gull Glider"	Waco 10
Gazda Helicospeeder	Montgomery "Evergreen"	Wright Brothers B
H-12(UH) 360	Montgomery "Santa Clara"	X-18(XC-142)
H-12B(UH)	Nasa Swing Wing	XROE (3ea)
H-12C(UH)-E4	NC5	YO3A
H-12E(UH)-NASA	Nelson Hummingbird	
H-12L(UH)	Pietenpol Aircamper	

San Diego - Miramar - Flying Leatherneck Aviation Museum, Bldg T2002 Anderson Ave,
MCAS Miramar, N Gate, Corfner of Miramar Rd & Rigel Ave, 92709, Mail: POB 45316,
92145-0316, 858-577-6125, Fax 577-4026, Mon-Sat 9-3, Free Adm, Gift Shop 693-1791,
Wed-Sun 10-4, Restoration Facility, www.usmcavhistory.org, S=Storage,
P=Project, PX=at PX, L=On Loan to Pensacola Wings of Gold TV Series,

A-4C	F/A-18A (L)	HOK-1(HH-34D)	R4D-8(C-117)2ea
A-6E	F2H-2 (P)	HRS-3(H-19)	R4Q-2(C-119)
A-4M	F3D-2(EF-10)	HUP-2(H-25)	R5D-2Z(C-54)
AH-1J	F4F-3(FM-2)	HUS(UH-34)(P)	RF-4B (P)
B-25(PBJ)	F4U-5NL	MiG-15	RF-8G(F8U-1P)
Bell 214	F9F-8P	OV-10D	SNJ-5 (S)
CH-53A	FJ-3	OY-1(L-5) (S)	TBM-3E(TBF)

San Diego Aerospace Museum, Inc, 2001 Pan American Plaza, Balboa Park,
92101, 619-234-8291, Daily 10-4:30, 10-5:30 Summer, Closed TD, CD, ND
Adm Adult $8, Child 6-12 $3, Under 5 Free, Theater, Restoration Facility,
Adm $2,Gift Shop 234-8291 Ext 31, www.aerospacemuseum.org
See also El Cajon, CA Restoration Facility,
GF=Gildred Flight Rotunda, EC=East Concourse, SC=South Concourse,
WC=West Concourse, CY=Court Yard, FY=Front Yard, S=Storage,

A-4C	EC	F4B-4	SC	Nieuport 11 (R)	WC
A-6	S	F4F-3A (P)	EC	Nieuport 28	WC
A-7	S	F6F-3	EC	NYP	GF
A-12	FY	F8U	GF	OQ-2	SC
A6M7	EC	Fleet 2	SC	Ornithopter	WC
Albatross D-Va (R)	WC	Fokker DR.I (R)	WC	P-40E	EC
Am Eagle A-1	GF	Fokker Eindecker(R)		P-51D	GF
Apollo Capsule	EC	Ford 5-AT-B P	S	PBY-5A	CY
ASG-21	S	Gemini	EC	PCI-1A	EC
B-5	SC	H-1(AH)	GF	Pitts S-L-S	EC
Bf-109G(Mock-Up)	EC	H-1B(UH)	GF	PT-1	S
Bleriot XI	WC	J-1	SC	PT-22	SC
Bowers Flybaby 1A	GF	J2F-6	EC	Quicksilver	S
Bowlus Albatross	EC	J-3	SC	Rearwin Cloudster	GF
Brunner Bird BK	GF	JN-4D	WC	RV-4	EC
C-3	WC	Jungster VI		Ryan STA	SC
Cayley Glider	WC	Lilienthal Glider	WC	S-4C	WC
Curtiss A-1 Traid	GF	Link Trainer		SBD-5 (P)	EC
Curtiss B-1 Robin	SC	M-1	WC	SPAD VII	WC
Curtiss L. Looper	WC	Mercury Capsule	EC	Spitfire Mk 16	EC
CW-1	WC	Mercury Air Racer	EC	Sundancer I Racer	WC
DH 2		MiG-15	EC	Swallow TP	SC
DH 60-M	SC	MiG-17	CY	Waco YKS-7	SC
Deperdussin C	WC	Montgolfiere	WC	Wee Bee	WC
F-4J	CY	Montgomery	WC	Wright EX Vin Fiz	WC
F-14	S	MS-230	GF	Wright Flyer	WC
F-86	EC	N2S-3	SC	X-13	
				YF2Y-1	FY

12

North Island NAS, C-2, S-3, SH36, SH60, SH2F

San Francisco - Crissy Field Aviation Museums Assoc, Pier One, Ft Mason
Mail: POB 210671, 94121, 415-221-4907, Fax 425-977-9349, Appt Only, DH-4 Project

Pacific Heritage Museum, 608 Commercial, 94111
415-399-1124 Mon-Fri, 10-4, Artifacts of Pacific Flight

San Francisco Int'l Airport, North Terminal By United, Airlines Area, Arrow Sport

The Exploratorium, 3601 Lyon St, 94123, 415-563-7337, Sun-Wed 1-5, Free Adm,
Glider   Spacecraft

San Luis Obispo - O'Sullivan AAF, Camp San Luis Obispo, Cal Rt 1,
Officers Club, 805-541-6168,
H-13(OH)   H-23(OH)   H-47(CH)   U-6
H-19(CH)   H-34(CH)   O-1

San Martin - Wings of History Air Museum, S County Airport, 12777, Murphy Ave, Off Hwy 101
Just North of Gilroy, POB 495, 95046-0495, Sat-Sun 11-4, 408-683-2990, Fax 683-2291,
Airshow Memorial Day, Restoration Facility, Gift Shop, Restaurant, Curator: Hue Brown,
www.wingsofhistory.org

Alexander Primary Glider	Nieuport 11 Rep
American Eagle A-101	Peel Glider Boat
AT-11	Penguin Trainer
Avro 595 (P)	Pietenpohl Air Camper (P)
Beech 23	Rutan Quickie
Bensen B.8M	Security Airster (P)
Bowlus Albatross	Sopwith Pup Rep
Bowlus Baby Albatross	Spad VII (P)
Bowlus Flybaby	Stahltaube 3/4 Scale
Bowlus Super Albatross	Stan Hall Cherokee II
Culver Cadet (P)	Stan Hall Safari
DH 88 Rep	Stinson 10A
EAA Biplane	Stolp 7/8 Scale
Link Trainer	Taylor Titsch
LNE-1	VJ-21
Marske Pioneer II	Waco 10
Mitchell Wing	Wright Flyer Rep
Nelson Glider	

Santa Maria - Santa Maria Museum of Flight, 3015 Airpark Dr, 93455, 805-922-8758
Fax 922-8958, Fri-Sun 10-4, Closed Holidays, Donations Requested, Pres: Dick Weber,
www.smmof.org, E-mail: smmof@thegrid.net

Bowers Fly Baby	F-86	Klemm 35	Stinson Reliant
DH 82a	Fleet II	KR-2	Volmer Jensen Glider
F-4S	Great Lakes 2T-1A	Parker Sailplane	

Santa Monica - **Closed until New Facility Complete in 2004**, Museum of Flying, Exit 405,
2772 Donald Douglas Loop North, 90405, 310-392-8822, FAX 310-450-6956,
Summer Tue-Sun 10-5, Winter Wed-Sun 10-5, Adm Adult $8, Snr $6, Child 3-17 $4,
Under 3 Free, Gift Shop, www.museumofflying.com, email: webmaster@mof.com,

A-4D	F=Flyable	Curtiss Robin	Hurricane Mk.XII F
A6M3 F		DC-3(R4-D)	JN-4D	Stinson SA-10
AD-6		DWC-4	KI-61 (Project)	T-28B F
AT-19(V-77)		Fairey Swordfish	N2S-4 F	Voyager
Beachey		Fleet Finch 2	P-38 F	Waco Cabin
Beech D-17S		Fokker DR.I	P-39Q	Waco Model 10
BD-5J		G4M (Project)	P-51D F	YAK-3UA
Bf-109E F		Gee Bee Z Rep	Rutan Variviggen	

Santa Paula - Aviation Museum of Santa Paula, 824 E Santa Maria St, 93060, 805-525-1101
Contact: Sally Phelps, Appt Only, www.amszp.org, Beech D17S, Fairchild F-24, Howard DGA

Santa Rosa - Pacific Coast Air Museum, Sonoma County Airport, 2330 Airport Blvd, 95403
707-575-7900, Fax 545-2813, Tue/Thur 10-2, Sat/Sun 10-4, $3 Donation, Pres: Don Doherty,
Gift Shop, Restoration Facility, Airshow 3rd Weekend Aug,
3rd Weekend Climb In Museum Aircraft Monthly, www.Pacificcoastairmuseum.org,

A-4E	F-14A	HU-16A & (P)	T-28B
A-6E	F-16N(FC)	IL-14P	T-28C (P)
A-26 (P)	F-84F(P)	L-3 (P)	T-33
BD-5	F-86F(RF)	MiG-15 (P)	T-37
Broussard MH.1512	F-86H	Nanchang CJ-6 2ea	T-38
C-118(DC-6)	F-105F	P-51D	YAK 52
F-4C	F-106	PA-22	
F-8U	H-1H(UH)	PA-23(U-11A)	

Aero Crafters, 2232 Airport Blvd, 95403, 707-527-8480, Contact Steve Penning,
WWII Aircraft Used as Fire Bombers

Shafter - Minter Field Air Museum, RTE 11, Shafter Airport, Mail: POB 445
93263, 661-393-0291, Fax 393-3296, Sat 10-2, Airshow in April,
www.minterfieldairmuseum.com, F-80 Cockpit, Link Trainer

AT-6	L-3	PT-17	T-33
BT-13	P-51 (3ea)	PT-26	T-50

Simi Valley - Regan Library, 40 Presidental Dr, 800-410-8354, Daily 10-5, Adult $5
Over 62 $3, Under 16 Free, www.reganfoundation.org, Boeing 707 Air Force 1

Stockton - Aero Nostalgia Co, WWII Restoration Facility, Stockton Airport,
7030 S C E Dixon St, 95206, 209-983-0235, Mon-Thur 8-4, By Appointment
Only, Misc Restorations In Progress.

B-25	B-34	O3U-6

Tulare - Tulare Mcpl Airport, Mefford Field, 93275, 559-688-0660, B-17, BT-13, F-4

Twentynine - Twentynine Palms Marine Corps Air-Ground Combat Center, Box 788100
92278-8100, 760-830-6000,   A-4

Van Nuys - Main Gate, F-104C

Victorville - George AFB, 92394-5000, 760-269-1110,   F-4C   F-100D

F-86H	F-105D	F-104C	F-105G

Willows - Willows Airport, 95988, 530-934-6489, AN-2

COLORADO

Aurora - Colorado ANG/PA, Buckley ANGB/STOP # 24, 140 TFG, 80011-9599
303-366-5363, PA Officer: Bruce Collins,

DHC-2	F-100A	F-86D	F-86F(RF)	T-6A

Weary Warriors Squadron, B-25H

Cannon - Cannon Airport, F-4

Colorado Springs - Fort Carson, Butts Airfield, Free Adm, OH-6, OH-13, Many Tanks
US Air Force Academy/PA, 80840-5151, 719-472-2025, 472-2555,

B-52D	F-16	F-105D	SV5-J	X-4
F-4C	F-104A	GF-16A	T-38A	Minuteman II

Peterson Air & Space Museum, Peterson AFB, 150 E Ent Ave, Bldg 981, 80914-5000,
PA: 719-556-4615, Summer Tue-Fri 8:30-4:30, Sat 9:30-4:30, Closed Sun, Mon &
Holidays, Free Adm, Gift Shop, Curator 554-4915, www.petemuseum.org; (P = Project

CF-100	F-15A	F-102A	Air-2A Genie
CF-101B	F-86L	F-104C	CIM-10A BOMARC (P)
EB-57E	F-89J	F-106A (P)	Hawk
EC-121T (P)	F-94C	P-40E Replica	Nike Ajax
F-4C	F-101B	P-47N (P)	Nike Hercules
		T-33A	Vela Satellite

Denver - Centennial Airport - P-51D,

The 69th Battalion, POB 24286, 80224, 303-782-3681, Fax 782-3694,
E-mail: robert@carik.com, Pyro/Special Effects Contractor, Flying:
A1-D,   A-37,   O1-A,   O-2A,   OV-1D,   UV-18A,

Denver Int'l Airport, 303-270-1500, JN-4D Hanging in Main Concourse
1930 Alexander Eaglerock Model A-14 Hanging at Opposite Concourse
Link Trainer at United Air Lines

J W Duff Aircraft Salvage, 8131 E. 40th Ave, 80207, 303-399-6010,
Mon-Fri 8-4:30, Over 500 Aircraft Some Complete, Mostly Fuselage & Wings
www.jwduffaircraft.com/index.html

AT-6	L-4	PT-22	U-3A
AT-11	L-5	PT-26	U-6A
C-45	L-16	O-2	U-8
H-12(UH)	L-17	T-6	U-10
H-13(UH)	L-18	T-28	U-21
H-204	L-19	T-34B	UC-64
JR-3	N3N	TG-3A	UC-78

Aviation & Space Center Rockies, Lowry AFB, 7711 E Academy Parkway, Hangar 1
80230-6929, 303-360-5360, Fax: 360-5328, Winter Mon-Sat 10-4, Sun 12-4,
Memorial to Labor Day Mon-Sat 9-5, Sun 12-5, Closed: ED, TD, CD, ND,
Adm Adult $6, Snr & Child 6-12 $4, 5 & Under Free, Director: Steve Draper,
Gift Shop, 360-5325, e-mail: worm@dimensional.com, www.wingsmuseum.org,

A-7D	F-4E	F-101B	Glider 1920
Alexander Eagle Rock	F-84K(RF)	F-104C	H-21C
B-1A	F-86H	F-105D(GF)	KR-1
B-18A	F-100D	F-106A	Space Module
B-52B(GB)	F-100D(GF)	F-111A	"Freedom"
B-57E	F-4E	F4U	T-33A
C-45	F-84K(RF)	Fokker D.VII	U-3A
DC-3	F-86H		

14

Fruita - Western Slop Vietnam War Memorial Park - I-70 Exit, Mail: PO Box 340, 81521, 970-242-0073, www.field-of-dreams.org, UH-1

Grand Junction - CAF - Rocky Mountain Wing, Walker Field 303-244-9100, 970-856-3412, J-3, TBM-3   A-6 (F-11-F) Airport Pedastal

Pueblo - Pueblo Weisbord Aircraft Museum, 31001 Magnuson Ave, 81001, 719-948-9219, Fax 948-2437, Mon-Fri 10-4, Sat 10-2, Sun 1-4, Adm Adult $4, 12 & under Free, Sit In A Cockpit, Last Sat Monthly, Different Aircraft Each Month, Gift Shop, www.pwam.org

A4D-2	C-119	F-80	RA-5C
A-26C	F-6A	F-84	RB-37
B-29A	F8	F-100D	T-26C
B-47E	F9F-8	H-21	T-33A
C-47	F11F-1	H-131A	

Int'l B-24 Memorial Museum, 31001 Magnuson Ave, 81001, 719-543-3605, Mon-Fri 10-4, Sat 10-2, Sun 1-4, Free Adm, Gift Shop, www.pwam.org

Westminster - CAF - Mile High Wing, Front Range Airport, Main Terminal, 80034-0528, Mail: POB 4805, Parker, CO 80134-1462, 303-851-1499, Info 303-841-3004, www.milehighcaf.org, C-60A

CONNECTICUT

Windsor Locks - Air National Guard, Bradley Airport, A-10, F-105, F-106

Hartford - Prop-Liners of America, www.propliners.com/index.html
Convair 240 Restoration

Stratford - National Helicopter Museum, 490 Sherwood Place, Apt C 12, 06497, 203-375-5766, Old Train Station, May-Oct Tue-Thur 1-4, www.libertynet.org/~ahmec, H-1B(UH)

Sikorsky Memorial Airport, 203-576-7498, FG-1D

Windsor Locks - New England Air Museum, Bradley Int'l Airport, 06096, Exit 40(I-91) SR20W,SR75N, Suffield W, 860-623-3305, Fax 627-2820, Daily 10-4, Closed TD, CD, NY Adm Adult $7.50, Snr $6.00, Child 6-11 $4, Under 6 Free, Gift Shop, Theater, Restoration, www.neam.org,

A-3B	F-4A	HU-16E	PT-23A
A-4A	F-4B	HUP-1	R-3(M-B)
A-10A	F-8K LTV	HUP-2(H-25)	R-4B
A-26C	F-104C	J-3	Rearwin Cloudster
A-24B	F-89J	JB-2	Republic Seabee
AD-4N	F-94C	K-225	Rutan Quickie
AEW3	F-100 Cockpit	K-16 V-STOL	Rutan Vari-eze
AT-6	F-100A	Laird Solution	S-39
B-25H	F-105B	LH-34D	S-60
B-29A	F4D-1	Link ANT-18	S-51
B-57A(RB)	F4U-4(XF)	Lockheed 10A	SBD(A-24)
Bell 47D-1	F6F-5K	Lockheed 12	SP-2E
Bensen B-8M	F9F-2	Lockheed 14	SR 71 Engine Only
Blanchard	FJ-1	Marcoux-Bromberg	Stinson Detroiter
Bleriot X1	FM-2	MC200	SUD VI-R
BT-13	Fokker DR.1	Mead Rhone Ranger	T-28C
C-7A	Gee Bee Model E	MiG-15	T-33A
C-50	Gee Bee R-1	Monerai S Sailplane	TV-2
CBY-3	Gee Bee Model A	Mosquito H. Glider	U-6A
CH-54B	Goodyear ZNP	NIK2-J	UH-1B
Chanute Glider	Great Lakes 2T-1A	Nixon Special	Viking Kittyhawk
Corben Jr Ace	H-5H	OH-23G	VS-44A Sikorski
Curtiss Pusher	Hanson-M. Quickie	OH-50C	XF15C-1
D-558-11	Heath Parasol	P-47D	Zephyr
DC-3	HH-43F	P-51D	
Dyndiuk Sport	HH-52A	Pioneer Flightstar	
E-1B	HRP-1	Pratt-Read Line-1	

Delaware

Dover - Air Mobility Command Museum, 1301 Heritage Rd, 19902-8001, 302-677-5938 Fax 677-5940, Tue-Sat 9-4, Free Adm, Gift Shop, Restoration Facility, Curator: Jim Leech www.amcmuseum.org/ email: museum@dover.af.mil

AT-6	C-97(KC)	CG-4A Project	Link Trainer
B-17G	C-119G	F-16	P-51D
BT-13	C-121	F-101B	PT-17
C-5	C-123K	F-106	Sopwith Pup Project
C-7A	C-131D	F-106 Simulator	T-33A
C-45G	C-133	H-1(UH)	
C-47A	C-141A	H-43(HH)	
C-54M	C-141B	H-58(OH)	

New Castle - ANG, Greater Wilmington Airport, 19720, 302-322-3361,   F-86H

D.C.

Anacostia NAS, SE Wahsington D.C. Off Route 295 and Potomac River, T-28

Bolling AFB, 20332-5000, 202-545-6700, 1100th ABG/CC,   F-105D

US Postal Museum, 2 Massachusetts Ave, 20002, 202-357-2991, Mon-Fri 10-5:30, Sat-Sun 10-5,
www.postalmuseum.si.edu/,   DH 4   SR-10F   Weisman Cook

US Soldiers and Airmens Home, 3700 N Capital St, 202-722-3000, F-86, M60 Tank

National Air & Space Museum, Smithsonian Institution, Independence Ave SW, 20560,
202-357-2700 / 1729, Daily 9:45-5:30, Free Adm, Gift Shop, Chairman - Dept of Aeronautics:
Dr Thomas Crouch, www.nasm.si.edu

Gallery Number	Gallery Number	Gallery Number
203 A4D-2N(A-4C)	Fi-103	205 P-51D
205 A6M5	209 Fokker D.VII	9 P-59A(XP)
209 Albatross D.Va	2 Ford 5-AT	6 P-80(XP)
205 B-26B	2 G-21	2 PA-5
205 Bf 109G	4 G-22	206 Pfalz D.XII
7 Bleriot XI	7 Gallaudet Hydro-Kite	208 R3C-2
0 Boeing 247D	208 Gossamer Condor	213 Rockwell HiMAT
5 C-17L	5 H-1	LOB Rutan Voyager
7 Curtiss D	9 Hawker Siddeley Kestrel	203 SBD-6
2 DC-3	5 J-1	209 Spad XIII
2 DC-7 Fuse	7 Lilienthal	205 Spitfire Mk.VII
10 DH 4	208 Lockheed 5B Vega	206 Sopwith Snipe
ESC D-558-2	9 Lockheed 5C Vega	208 T-2(F.IV)
208 DWC-2	208 Lockheed 8 Sirius	10 U-2C
7 Ecker Flying Boat	2 M-2	206 Voisin Model 8
206 Explorer II	205 MC-202	5 Wittman
203 F4B-4	6 Me 262A	0 Wright Kitty Hawk
203 F4F-4(FM-1)	2 Northrop 4A Alpha	7 Wright Military Flyer
ESC F-104A	5 Northrop Gama	208 Wright EX Vin Fiz
2 FC-2	14 Northrop M2-F3	0 X-1
206 FE-8	0 NYP	0 X-15A-1
6 FH-1	4 P-26A	213 X-29

FLORIDA

Arcadia - Municipal Airport, 863-494-7844,   Fr 24, West Hanger

Starfighters, Inc, 15707 Fairchild Dr, 33762, www.starfighters.net
CF-104   CF-104D Both Flown at Airshows

Cocoa Beach - US Air Force Space Museum Cape Canaveral, AF Station, 32925,
321-867-7110, Daily 9-3, Free Adm, 80 Spacecraft, Rockets & Missiles

Astronaut Memorial Planetarium and Observatory, Brevard Community College
1519 Clearlake Rd, 32922, 321-634-3732, 631-7889

Daytona Beach - Embry-Riddle Aeronautical Univ, 32114, 386-226-6175
Aircraft Here Are For Training Purpose Only, Dir: Helen S Riger, APRP

Aerospatial Tampico	Beechcraft Dutchess	C-172Q	Mooney M.18
American General Tiger	C-303	C-303	PA-44
Beechcraft 35	C-172	C-182RG	Piper Cadet

Wright Flyer Replica In Front Of School For Public Viewing.

Miniature Golf, South Atlantic Ave, Beechcraft 18

DeLand - CAF - Florida Wing, PO Box 1944, 32721-1944
www.members.aol.com/CAFFFL/index.html, Beechcraft D-18, L-17B

Naval Air Station Museum, Mon-Sat 9-5, Wed & Thur 1-5, 386-738-4149,
A-6 Intruder

Fernandina Beach - Amelia Island: Island Aerial Tours, 1600 Airport, 32034-0204,
35 Mi S of Jacksonville, 904-261-7890, J-3   Waco Model 10

Ft. Lauderdale - The Discovery Center, 231 SW 2nd Ave, 33301-1892, Space Artifacts

Ft Lauderdale Executive, HU-16 (5 ea)

World Jet Aircraft Int'l Sales & Leasing, 1710 W Cypress Creek Rd,
33309-1806, 954-776-6477, Planes May Be Sold, Check Ahead
B-25   Me-109   TBM
P-51   Nord

Ft. Myers - Ft. Myers Historical Museum, Jackson St, 1 Block S of Martin Luther King
Blvd (SR 82), 33901, 239-332-5955, Tue-Sat 9-4, Adm Adult $6, Snr $5.50, Child 3-12 $3
Under 3 Free,   P-39   Railroad Caboose

Homestead - AFB, 33039-5000, 305-257-8011,   F-4D   F-100D

16

Indian Rocks Beach - Florida Aviation Historical Society, POB 127, 33535, Ford Flivver

Jacksonville - Commanding Officer Naval Reserve Officer Training Corps Jacksonville
  University NROTC, 2800 University Blvd North, 32211-3394, 904-745-7480,
  Daily 8-4:30, JU Pub Affairs: Doris Barletta, By Direction: SL Vencel,
  A-7E (In Front of NROTC Building)

  Jacksonville ANG, Int'l Airport, 904-741-4902, F-106A   T-33A

  MCAS New River, Heros Park, Off Hwy 17 S of City, AH-1W, CH-34, CH-53E, MV-22, UH-1

  Museum of Science and History, 1025 Museum Circle, Southbank, 32207
  904-396-7062, Mon-Fri 10-5, Sat 10-6, Sun 1-6, Adm Adult $5, Child $3, PT-17(N2S)

  Naval Air Station Jacksonville, Aircraft At Main Gate, 904-270-6100
  F/A-18   P-3A   P2V-5   PBY-5A   SH-3B

  Naval Aviation Station Cecil Field, 14 Mi SW of Jacksonville, I-10 Then
  Whitehouse Exit, S on Chaffe Rd to Normandy then R, Passes at Bldg 327 Main Gate,
  Daily 7:30-2pm, 33821, PA: 904-778-6055, HR: 778-5781, Info 778-5627,
  http://cecilfield.com, e-mail:pao@cecilfield.com
  TR=Road To Tower, SS=Sea Strike Wing 1 HQ, CT=At Cecil Tower
  A-4C (TR)   F8U-1 (TR)   S-2A   (TR)
  A-7E (MR)   F/A-18A (TR)   S-3A   (TR)
  A-7E (ST)   F9F-8 (TR)   TBM-3E (SS)

Key West - Naval Air Station Key West, 305-293-3700, A-4E, A-5, F-4, EA-6A

  Conch Republic Trading Company, 725 Duvall St, 33040, 305-292-9002, Fax 292-0270
  1946 Sea-Bee

  HT Chittum & Co Sport Clothing Store, 725 Duval St, 305-292-9002, RC-3

  Key West Int'l Airport, 33040, 305-294-8687, Waco UPF-7   Pitts S-2A

Kissimmee - Flying Tigers Warbird Restoration Museum - Tom Reilly Vintage Aircraft, Inc,
  231 N Hoagland Blvd, Off Hwy 192, 34746, 407-933-1942, 847-7477, Fax 933-7843,
  Mon-Sat 9-5:30, Sun 9-5, Closed CD, Adm Plus Tax Adult $9, Over 60 & Child 7-11 $8
  Under 7 Free, Group Rate: (10 or more) Adult $7, Child $5, Restoration Facility with Tours
  Gift Shop, Warbird Restoration Training Course $995 5 Days,
  E-mail: programs@warbirdmuseum.com; www.warbirdmuseum.com
  A-4 (P)(8ea)   F-100D (D)   HUP-1 (D)   PT-17 (F)
  A-7 LTV(D)   F-101A (D)   J-3 (F)   PT-22 (F)
  A-26 (F)(2ea)   F-101B Simulator KR-21 (F)   S-2 (F)
  AT-6G (F)   F-104A (D)   KR-34 (F)   SNJ-3 (F)
  B-17 (P)(2ea)   F4U-4 (P)   L-2 (F)   SNJ-4 (P)
  B-25J (F)   F9F-7 (D)   MiG-21 MF (D)   SNJ-6 (2ea) (F)
  C-1 (F)   FG1D (P)   OX-5 (F)   Taylor Young (F)
  C-3 (F)   Fouga Magister (F) P-38 (P)(2ea)   TB-25N (P)
  C-47(F)   Fw-190 (P)   P-40E (F)
  DH-100 (F)   Funk (F)   P-1127 Kestrel
  F-4C (D)   H-34 (D)   PA-11 (F)

  Howard Johnson Lodge, Fountain Park Plaza Hotel & Conference Center
  5150 W Space Coast Pkwy, 800-432-0763, Titan I Missile

  Mustang Operations & Preservation Soc, 3951 Merlin Dr, 34741, 407-846-4051,
  www.mustangops.com, email: angela@mustangops.com

  Warbird Adventures, Adjacent to Flying Tigers Warbird Air Museum, 800-386-1593,
  407-870-7366, Web: warbirdadventures.com, e-mail: warbirdadventures.com,
  Warbird Flights

  White 1 Foundation Inc, 822 N Hoagland Blvd, 34741, 407-933-0277,
  www.white1foundation.org, Restoring FW-190F-8

Lakeland - Florida Air Museum, 4175 Medulla Rd, Lakeland - Linder
  Regional Airport, POB 6750, 33807, I-4 Exit 15, Go East on Medulla Rd,
  863-644-0741 & 2431, Mon-Fri 9-5, Sat 10-4, Sun 12-4, Adm Adult $4,
  Child Under 12 $2, Gift Shop, Theater, Dir: Arthur Henderson, www.sun-n-fun.org
  AT-11   Bede BD-5   CW-12W
  Aeronca LB   Beech D-17S   DGA 1-A
  Aerosport Scamp   Bensen B.8M   EAA Acro-Sport
  American Eagle   Boeing A75N1   Ercoupe 415-C
  Anderson Kingfisher   Bowers Fly Baby   F-101F
  Anglin Spacewalker II   Brokaw Bullet   Flying Flea
  Atkinson Eaglet   Butler Blackhawk   Ford Fliver
  Auster Mark 9   C-3   FP-303
  B-17 Ball Turret   Chief Oshkosh   Glassair
  B-17 Fuselage   Cieslak Model 2   GW-44A
  B-29 Nose   Command-Aire   Hawker Tempst Mk II
  Bakeng-Duce   CP-65   Heath Super Parasol
  Barracuda   CP-65 P   HU-16
  Bede BD-4   Cricket MC-10   Jurga-Tepete

17

Kit-Fox Model #1	Pitts Special	Super Lancer Hang Glider
Laird Baby	Q-1 Quickie	Swearingen SX-300
Lazair	Q-200 Quickie	T-33A
Loving's Love	Ranchero	Taylorcraft 1940
Lysander	Rand KR-1	Travelair D4000
Mitchell P-38	Rans S-9	Travelair 2000
Monnet Moni	Revolution Mini 500	UH-1H
Mooney M.18L Mite	Russ Ritter Special	Vangrunsven RV-3
N2S-4	Rutan Vari-eze	V-22 Osprey
Nesmith Cougar	Rutan Variviggen	VJ-24
Nieuport 17-C1	SE5A	VP-1
OQ-19(KD2R-3)	Smyth Sidewinder	Woody Pusher
P-51D	Steen Skybolt	XFV-1 VTO
P-63	Stits Playmate	YF2Y-1
Pietenpol B-4	Sunshine Clipper	

Exploration V, 125 Kentucky Ave, S, 863-687-3869, Small Plane Cockpit

Mary Esther, Hurlburt Air Park, Hulburt Field, 131 Bartley St, Suite 315, 834 ABW/HO, 32544-5000, 850-884-6402, Off Highway 98, www.hurlburt.af.mil/basewide/airpark

A-1E	C-46D	C-130A(AC)	O-2A
A-26A	C-47A(AC)	H-1P(UH)	OV-10
A-37B(OA)	C-119G(AC)	H-3E(HH)	T-28D(AT)
B-25N	C-123K(UC)	O-1E	U-10A

Merritt Island - NASA Kennedy Space Center, 32899, 321-452-2121, Mon-Sun 9-Dusk, Tours 9:45-3:30,Closed CD, Free Complex Adm, Bus Tour & 3-D IMAX Theater: Adult $19, Child 3-11 $15, Gift Shop, Restaurant, www.kennedyspacecenter.com,

| Apollo II | Space Shuttle | Saturn V | Missiles | Launch Vehicles |

Miami - Wings Over Miami Museum, 14710 SW 128th St, Kendall-Tamiami Airport SW of Miami, 33196, 305-233-5197, Thur-Sun 10-5:30, Adm Adult $9.95, Snrs & Child Under 12 & Grps of 110 $5.95, Gift Shop, www.wingsovermiami.com

A-26C	F6F-3	P-38L Fuse
Abernathy Streaker	F7F-3	P-40N(TP)
Stephens Super Akro	F-86F	P-51D
B-17G	Fairey Swordfish Mk.IV	PBY-5A
B-23	Fairchild 24R	Pitts Special S-2-B
B-25	Fouga Magister	PT-17
B-29(P2B-1S) Nose	Hawker Tempest	PT-22
Boeing B-100	J-S	Sopwith Pup
Boeing 707 Simulator	J2F-6	Sopwith 1½ Strutter
Beech D17S	JN-4D	Sopwith Triplane
British Provost	KA-61	Spad VII
Cap 231	C-135(KC)	TBM-3
CJ6A Nanchang (2ea)	L-29	TU-2
Cessna 195RS	Me-108	Weeks Solution
Curtiss Falcon	MiG-15	Weeks Special
DeWoitine D.26	DH 98	YAK-11
DH-82	P2B-1S	YAK-52
F4U-4	P-35A	

George T Baker Aviation School, 3275 NW 42nd Ave, 33142, 305-871-3143 Ext 300
www.universities.com/Schools/G/George_T_Baker_Aviation_School.asp

| A-4 | Boeing 707 | Martin 4-0-4 |
| Beech D18S | F-86 | T-33 |

Opa Locka - Opa Locka Airport, HU-16 (2ea)

Orlando - Church Street Station, 129 W. Church St, 32801, 407-422-2434,
Commander Ragtimes, Fokker D.VII   Fokker DR.1   SE-5A

Helicopter Inc, 240 N Crystal Lake Dr, 32803, 407-894-7428,Owner: Fred Clark,
Curtiss Robin B   Paramount Cabinaair

John Young Museum & Planetarium, 810 E Rollings St, 32803,
305-896-7151, Daily 10-5, Free Adm, Spacecraft

Orlando Int'l Airport, Memorial Park (Near Air Freight Section) B-52D
1 Airport Blvd, 32827-4399, 407-825-2001 Info, 825-2055 Commun.Relation

West Orlando Airport, 305-656-7813, Byrid, Fr Kr 21, Taylorcraft A

Panama City - Vets Memorial Park, 1 Block E of Callaway Plaza, F-101B, F-15C

Gulf Coast Community College, Hwy 98 E, 12 Miles E of Gulf Coast Community College
F-101B, ½ Mile East of Hathaway Bridge, F-15C

Tyndall AFB, 325 TTW/MAM, 32403, 850-283-1113, Aircraft Along I-98 Thru
Base, Inside Building At Flag Park.

B-57B(EB)	F-4C/D	F-100D	F-106A
BQM-34A	F-15D	F-102A	MQM-107
BQM-34F	F-86D	F-102A(TF)	T-33A
CGM-13	F-89J	F-104C	

Pensacola - Pensacola Regional Airport, 3 Miles NE of City, 904-43 5-1746, F11F-1 Blue Angels

Visitors Center, 3 Miles West of City, F9-5 "Blue Angels #1"

National Museum of Naval Aviation, Bldg 3465, 1750 Radford Blvd, Exit 2 (I-10), Mail: Box 33104, 32508, 850-452-3604, 800-327-5002, Daily 9-5, Closed: TD, CD, ND Free Adm, Gift Shop, Dir: Bob Rasmussen, www.naval-air.org, SW = South Wing, WW = West Wing, AD = Antrium Display, OD = Outside Display, IS = Inside Storage, OS = Outside

SW A-1 (TRIAD)	WW F2H-2P	CG HO3S-1G	SW NT-1
IS A-4A(A4D-1)	SW F2H-4	SW HO4S	OD NU-1B
IS A-4E (2ea)	OD F3D-2(F-10B)	SW HO5S-1	OE-1
AD A-4F (3ea)	SW F3F-2	SW HTE-1	WW OS2U-3
SW A-6E	SW F4D-1(F-6A)	IS HTK-1	SW OY-1
SW A-7E	SW F4F-3 (2ea)	SW HTL-4	OD P-3A
OD A3D-1(A3A-1)	WW F4U-4(2ea)	OD HU-16E	WW P-40B
WW A6M-2B	SW F6C-1	WW HUP-3(UH-25C)	WW P-80A
OD AD-5Q(EA-1F)	WW F6F-3	OD HUS-1(UH-34D)	OD P2V-1(XP)
WW AD-6(A-1H)	SW F6F-5	IS Goodyear 195	OD P2V-7
WW AF-2S	SW F7C-1	WW J-3	OD P5M
SW AH-1J	WW F7F-3	WW J2F-6	WW PBY-5
OD AJ-2	SW F7U-3M	WW J4F-1	OD PB2Y-5R
WW AM-1	WW F8F-2	OD JD-1	OD PB4Y-2
AQM-37A	SW F8U-1(F-8A)	SW JN-4	PS-2
Arado AR 196A	OS F8U-1P(RF-8G)	IS JRC	OD RA-5C
SW AV-8C	WW F9C-2	WW JRF-3	OD R4D-5
SW BFC-2	WW F9F-2	WW K-47 CAR	SW RR-5
Bleroit XI	IS F9F-5P	KD-3G	SW S-4C
OD C-1A	SW F9F-6	KD2G-2	OD S2F-3
OD C-46(R5C)	SW FF-1	KDB-1	WW SB2C-5
OD C-47H(R4D-5)	WW FG-1D(F4U)	L-4B	IS SB2U
OD C-117D(R4D-6)	WW FH-1	SW Le Rhone	WW SBD
OD C-118B(R6D-1)	WW FJ-1	IS LNE-1	WW SBD-3
OD C-121K(EC)(WV-2)	SW FJ-2	SW LNS-1	OD SH-3G
OD C-131F(R4Y-2)	IS FJ-3M	IS Meyers OTW	OD SNB-5P
Cessna 180F	SW FJ-4(F-1E)	SW MF-Boat	WW SNC-1
CH-19(HRS-2)	WW FM-2(F4F)2ea	SW N-9H	AD SNJ-5C
OS CH-19E(HRS-3)	SW Fokker D-VII	SW N2C-2	WW SNV-1
OD CH-37C(HR2S-1)	SW GB-2	SW N2S-3	SW Sopwith Camel
OD CH-53A	IS GK-1	N2S-5	SW T-28B
SM Command Module	SW H-1K(HH)	SW N2T-1	AD T-34B
IS D-558-1	IS H-2D(HH)	WW N2Y-1	WW TBM-3E
OD E-1B(WF-2)	OD H-3F(HH)	SW N3N-3	WW TD2C-1
OD E-2B	SW H-13M(TH)	SW NC-4	WW TDD-1
SW F-4N(F4H)	SW H-52A(HH)	WW NC-9-A	WW TDD-2
SW F-11A(F11F-1)	SW H-57C(TH)	N1K1	WW TDR-1
OD F-14A	SW HD-1	WW N1K2-J	SW TS-1
SW F-17(YF)	WW HNS-1	SW Nieuport 28	SW YRON-1
F/A-18(YF-18)	SW HO-49	WW NR-1	WW ZPG Rudder

Veterans Memoria l Park, Bay Front Av e at 9th Ave, Next to Gulf Power Building, Mail: Vietnam Veterans Wall South Foundation POB 17886 32522-7886, 904-433-8200, UH-1M, The Wall South - 58,204 American Names

Pinellas Park - Freedom Lake Park, 9990 46th St N, US 19, F-16

Polk City - Fantasy of Flight, 1400 Broadway Blvd SE, I-4, Exit 21 N to SR 559 E, 33868-1200, 863-984-3500, Fax 984-9506, Daily 9-5, Adm To All Exhibits, Adm Adult 13-59 $24.95, 60+ $21.95, Child 5-12 $13.95, Under 5 Free, Year Pass $59.95, Limited Time Simulator $3.25, Compass Rose Restaurant 8-4, Gift Shop, Owner: Kermit Weeks, Marketing Dir: Debra Johnson Ext 221, www.fantasyofflight.com,

A-1	DH 98	Norde Stampe
A-20	E-1 Standard	NYP
A.V. Roe 504J	F4U-4	P-35A
A6M5	Fi-156	P-39
AN-2	FM-2	P-51C
AT-6D	Ford 5-AT-34-B	P-63
B-17G	FW-44J	SBD
B-24J	Gee Bee Model Z	Short Sunderland Mk.V
B-25	HOE-1	Spitfire Mk.XVI
B-26	J-1 Standard	SV-4C
Ba 349	J2F	TBM
Beech D-17S	JN-4D	Thomas-Morse T4M
Bell 47G	JU-52	Travel Air B-4000
Bristol Bolingbroke	Ki-61	Trautman Road Air #1
BT-15	L-1 (2ea)	Valkyrie Replica
Bu 133	L-4	Week Solution
Bu 181	Lockheed Vega 5A/5C	Wright Flyer Replica
Curtiss Jr CW-1	Morane Saulnier 230	
Curtiss Pusher D	Neuport 17	

Pompano Air Center, 305-943-6050, Dir: Brian Becker, PT-13 Model 75

Sanford - Orlando-Sanford Airport, 407-688-1198, Contact: Maurice A Roundy, starliner@gwi.net
www.starliner.net, L-1649A Project

Vertical Aviation Technology, Inc, Sanford Orlando Airport,
1642 Hanger Rd, 407-322-9488, Fax 330-2647, Owner: Brad Clark
Restores Sikorsky S-55 Helicopters, Kits for "Humming Bird" Helicopter

Shalimar - Air Force Armament Museum, 100 Museum Dr, Building 3201, Eglin] AFB,
32542-5000, 850-882-4063, Daily 9:30-4:30, Closed TD, CD, ND, Theater, Gift Shop

A-10A	F-4C	F-101C	TM-76	* = Inside,
B-17G	F-4C(RF)	F-104D(TF)	UH-1H	
B-25J	F-15A	* F-105D	V-1	
B-47N(RB)	F-16	F-111E	Apollo Module	
B-52G	* F-80-1D	O-2A	BQM-34A	
B-57B	F-84F	* P-47N	BQM-34F	
C-47A(AC)	F-86D	* P-51D-11	IM-99 Bomarc	
C-130(AC)	F-89J	SR-71A	GAM-77/AGM-28	
C-131B	F-100C	T-33A	MIG-21	
			MGM-13A	

St Augustine - St John's County Airport, US Hwy 1 N, 904-824-1995,
Ernie Moser's Aero Sport

St. Petersburg - St Petersburg Historical & Flight One Museum, 335 Second Ave, 33701
727-894-1052, Mon-Sat 10-5, Sun 1-5, except Major Holidays, Adm Adult $5, Snr 62 $4
Child 7-17 $3, Under 6 Free,Gift Shop, www.stpetemuseumofhistory.org,
Benoist Airboat 1914 Replica, Ford Flivver Replica

Starke - Camp Blanding Museums and Memorial Park, Off SR16 Front Gate, Daily 12-4
Free Adm, Gift Shop, 904-xxx-xxxx
A-6A, A-7, Bell 206, C-47, OH-13, UH-1 (2ea), M4 Tank, M60 Tank, Cannons

Tampa - McDill AFB, 56 CSG/CC, 33608-5000, 813-830-1110, B-50J(KB)   F-4E   F-15

Titusville - Air America Foundation, 589 S Wickham Rd, 802-333-9254, www.airamfoundation.org
C-123 2ea

Astronaut Hall of Fame, 6225 Vectorspace Blvd, 32780, 321-269-6100,
www.spacewalkoffame.org, Mercury Space Capsule   Space Shuttle Simulator

U.S. Space Camp, 6225 Vectorspace Blvd, 32780, 800-637-7223, 321-267-3184,
Space Camp for Grades 4-12 & Adult, One Week of: Space Training & Missions, From $300-875

Valiant Air Command Museum, Space Center Executive Airport, 6600 Tico Rd
32780-8009, 321-268-1941, Fax 268-5969, Daily 10-6, Closed TD, CD, ND, Adm Adult $9.00
Mil/Snr/Child $8, 12 & Under Free, Gift Shop, Restoration Facility, www.vacwarbirds.org
F = Flyable, O = Outside, R = Restoration, P = Partial Aircraft, X = Periodic Display

A-6E	F-14A	Me-208 (R)	T-2 (P)
A-7A	F-84F Project	MiG-17 (O)	T-28D (F)(X)
AN-2 (X)	F-86F (P)	OV-1D (O)	T-33A
AT-6(SNJ)(X)	F-101B-115-MC(D)	OV-1 Simulator	TBM-3E (R)
C-45 (X)	F-105D (O)	P-51 3/4 Scale	TM-61A
C-47A (R)	F-106 Simulator	PT-17 (X)	UH-1A (O)
C-123 (X)	F4U-1 1/2 Scale (X)	Rutan Variviggen	UTVA-66 (F)
Epps 1907	FM-1	S2F	2B13 Mult Eng Sim
F-4J (O)	HA 200A (X)	SM8Z (X)	
F-8K	L-4J	Super Sport	
F9F-5 (R)	Link Trainer		

Wauchula - Wauchula Municipal Airport, 33873, 863-773-9300
POB 891, 33873, Adm Adult $2, Child $1, Sat 10-3

Aero Commander	Beechcraft 35	Grand Commander	PA-23
AG-CAT	C-45	HH-3F	UH-1H
Beech D18S	F-86L	Lake Buccaneer	Missiles

Whiting - Naval Air Station, 904-623-7011,

HU-57	SNJ-5C	SNJ-6	T-34C

Zellwood - Bob White Airport, 7011 W Jones Ave, NE Orange County,
From US 436 Turn W on Jones Ave, Go 1 Mi, 407-886-3180, Appt Only
J-3 (3ea)   RV6 Homebuilt   Smith Mini Plane Stearman (8ea)

Jim Kimball Enterprises, POB 849, 32798, Restores Old Aircraft
Builds Replicas, Call 407-889-3451 For Current Project, By Appt Only

GEORGIA

Atlanta - CAF - Dixie Wing, Falcon Field Airport, Bldg #410, Kennesaw, 30144,
404-427-0281, www.dixiewing.org, C-45, F-16, P-63, PT-26, SBD

Delta Air Transport Heritage Museum, (Still in Planning Stages), 1050 Delta Blvd
Bldg B, Hartsfield Atlanta, Int'l Airport, Dept 914, 30354, Mail: POB 20585,
30320-2585, 404-714-2371, Fax 715-2078, Mon-Fri 8-5, www.deltaairlinesmuseu.com
DC-3   L-1011 Ground Trainer   Travel Air S-6000B

Fernbank Science Center, 156 Heaton Park Dr NE, 30307,
404-378-4311, Mon-Fri 9-5, Free Adm, Apollo Space Capsule

Augusta - ATZH-DPM, Bldg 36305, 37th St, 2 Mi Inside Gate 5, Ft Gordon, 30905-5020,
706-791-2818, 780-2818, Mon-Fri 8-4, Sat-Sun 12-5, CLosed ES, TD, CD, ND,
Independencs Day, Free Adm,   USD-4   USD-5

Calhoun - Mercer Air Museum, Mercer Airfield, 411 Belwood Rd, 30701, 706-629-7371,
I-75 exit 312, Daily 8-5, Free Adm, 17 Aircraft from 1944

A-7	F8U-1	MGM-13	T-33A
Bechcraft 35	F-84F	L-17	U-8D
C-47	F-86C	L-21	
DC-3	H-34 2ea	T-29	

Cordele - Exit 32 of I-75 At Hwy 300,   Titan I

Georgia Veterans Memorial State Park & Gen Courtney Hodges Museum, Rte 3,
9 Mi W of City on US 280, Mail: Box 382, 31015, 229-276-2371
Museum Daily 8-4:30, Park Daily 7am-10pm, Free Adm,

B-29	FJ4B	German Tank	Stewart Tank
F-84F	T-33A	Patton Tank	LTV

Douglas - Brooks Aviation, POB 610, 31533, 912-384-7818, DC-3 (Flights Available)

Ft. Benning - Army Ft Benning National Infantry Museum, Baltzell Ave, 31905,
706-687-3297,   CG-4A (Storage)   C-119

Griffin - Alexander Aeroplane Co, Spalding County Airport, 118 Huff Daland Cir,
30223, 770-228-3901, 800-831-2949, DC-3 (2 Hour Flights), T-33

Atlanta Air Salvage, 1146 Uniform Rd, 30224, 770-227-4042, Parts

Curtiss Hawk Factory,   P-36   P-40E   P-40K   P-40N

Low Pass Inc, 127 Airport Rd, 30224, 770-228-5875, F9F-5

Hampton - Army Aviation Heritage Foundation, Clayton County Airport, Tara Field,
506 Speedway Blvd, 30228, 770-897-0444, Fax 897-0066, Appt Only, Pres: Mike Brady
Membership: Skip Powell, email: skippowell@aol.com, www.armyav.org

DH CV-2B	L-19A Project	H-1P(TAH)	U-21G
H-1(UH) Project	L-19D Project	OH-6A	U-8F Project
H-13 Project	H-1G(AH)	OH-23B	YF-17 Cobra
H-23	H-1B(UH)	OV-1B	
L-4B	H-1H(UH)	T-41B	
L-17	H-1M(UH)	T-42A	

Kennesaw - Atlanta FAA ARTC, McCollum Airport, 30144, 770-422-2500,   F-100C

Macon - Macon ANG, Cocran Field, 912-788-3423, F-86L

Warner Robins AFB, Museum of Aviation 78ABW/MU, 1942 Heritage Blvd,
31098-2442 Hwy 41/129 South, 478-926-6870, 926-4242, Mail: POB 2469, 310,
Gift Shop, I-75, Exit 126 East to Hwy 247, South 2 Mi, Daily 9-5,
Closed TD, CD, ND, Free Adm, Curator: Darwin G Edwards, *=Hangar 01,
C=Century of Flight Building, E=Eagle Building, P=Project,
www.museumofaviation.org

A-37A	[C]	C-54G		F-105G		RF-101C	
AC-47		C-60A		F-106A		SR-71A	[C]
AC-130	[E]	C-119B		F-111E	[C]	T-28A	[*]
Aeronca Champ 7AC		C-124C		HH-3E	[C]	T-33A	
AGM-136A	[S]	C-103A		HH-19D	[*]	T-37B	
AIM 4D-G	[S]	C-141C		HH-34J		T-39A	[C]
AIM 9J	[S]	CH-3E		HH-43A	[*]	TG-4A	[E]
AIM-26A	[S]	CH-21B	[*]	HH-43F	[C]	TH-13M	[P]
AIR-2A	[S]	Chanute Glider	[E]	HU-16B	[C]	TM-61A	
AQM-34V	[C]	D-21 Drone		KC-97L		U-2D	[C]
AT-6G	[*]	EC-121K	[E]	L-19A/O-2A	[*]	U-3B	[C]
AT-11		Epp's Monoplane		MGM-13A		U-4B	[C]
B-25J	[C]	F-4C		MGM-107B		U-6A	[C]
B-26C		F-15A	[E]	MiG-17		U-10D	[C]
B-29B-55	[C]	F-80C	[*]	O-1E	[*]	UC-78	[P]
B-52D		F-84E	[E]	O-2A	[*]	UC-123K	
B-66D(WB)		F-84F(RF)		OH-23C		UH-IF	[*]
Bae Mk.53		F-84F	[*]	OH-50C		UH-1P	
Bensen X-25A		F-86H		P-40N		UH-13P	
BQM-34F		F-89J		PT-17D	[E]	VC-140B	[C]
BT-13A	[*]	F-100C		PT-19A	[*]	X-25	
C-7A	[C]	F-101F		PT-22	[C]	YCGM-121B	
C-45G		F-102A		RB-57A		YMC-130H	
C-46A		F-104A		RB-57F			
C-47A		F-105D		RB-69A			

Marietta - Cobb County Youth Museum, POB 78, 30061, 770-427-2563,
Mon-Sat 9-2, Free Adm, Curator: Anita S Barton,   F-84F

21

```
        Dobbins AFB ANG, 14th AF, 94th TAW, 30069-5000, PA: 770-421-5055,
        B-29              F-84F              F-105G              P-40E
        F-4C              F-100D             OV-1
```

Lockheed Plant, Dobbins AFB, Building L 22, F-22 ½ Scale Model

NAS Atlanta, Dobbins AFB, 1000 Halsey Avenue, Marietta, GA 30060-5099
770-919-6392, http://www.nasatlanta.navy.mil/ A-6, A-7E, AT-11, E-2C, T-33

Pooler - Mighty Eighth Air Force Heritage Museum, 175 Bourne Ave, I-95 & US 80
Exit 18, 31322, Mail: POB 1992, Savannah 31402-1992, 800-421-9428, 912-748-8888,
Fax 748-0209; Daily 9-5, Adm Adult $8, Snrs $7, Child 12-6 $5.50, Under 6 Free,
Gift Shop; Canteen, Mission Experience Theater, WWII Flight Simulation,
www.mighty8thmuseum.com; email marketing@mightyeighth,org; O=Outdoors / Rest Inside
```
B-24 Cockpit        Bf-109 Replica      Me-163              PT-17          1/6th B-24
B-47 (O)            F-4 (O)             P-51 Replica        MiG-21 Cockpit
```

Savannah - Savannah ANG, 165 TAG/MA, Savannah Int'l Airport, 31402, 912-964-1941,
```
165th TAG           F-84D               F-86L
```

Savannah State College, 31404, 912-356-2186, PR Office, 356-2191, A-4L

Sparta - Georgia State Military Academy, National Guard Academy Off Hwy 16 South
```
H-54D(CH)           OV-1D
```

Woodstock - Air Acres Museum, 376 Air Acres Way, 30188.
```
J-5 (3ea),       J-35,       L-17,       PT-17,       Luscombe 8E
```

Warbirds of America Sq 17, 455 Air Acres Way, 30188
770-928-9042, All are Projects in Process, except (X = Pending)
```
B-25             Cessna 182              L-2M (2ea) (X)          PT-17
BobCat Kit       Cessna 180              Loehle 5151 Mustang     PT-17 (X)
C-45J(RC) (X)    Grumman AgCat Custom (X) Pietenpol Aerial       Stinson 108-3
```

HAWAII
OAHU
Barbers Point NAS, A-4 (2ea),   A-4E,   F-4C,   P-3

Honolulu - Hickam AFB, 15 ABW PA, 808-449-2490, Tours only Wed 10-11, * = Location
```
B-25J * Scott Circle      F-86E * O'Malley Blvd
RB-26C *Scott Circle      F-102A (2ea)* Bas Op, Vickers & O'Malley
```

Located on O'Malley Blvd, F-4C,   F-15A,   F-86E,   MiG-15

Hawaiian ANG, F-4C,   F-86E,   F-86L,   F-106

Hickman AFB Firefighting Unit, F-4C (2ea)

Pacific Aerospace Museum, Honolulu Int'l Airport, Departure Level - Main Terminal
96819, Mail: Box 7, 808-839-0777, Mon-Sun 9-6, Shuttle Cockpit

Kaneohe - Kaneohe Bay MCAS Marine Base (North Shore) 96744,
```
CH-53D,     F-4S,     F-8J,     P-3,     P2V-5,     S2
```

Waikiki - Fort DeRussy Army Museum, AH-1S

Wheeler AFB, 96854-5000, 808-422-0531, Main Gate, P-40 Mock-Up
```
AH-1S,          OH-23G,          OH-58A,          UH-1H
```

IDAHO
Boise - Boise ANG, Gowen Field, 83707, 208-385-5011, 124th TRG,   F-102A

Driggs - Teton Aviation Center. 675 Airport Rd, Off Hwy 33, Mail: POB 869, 83422
800-472-6382, 208-354-3100, Fax 354-3200, Daily 8-5, Closed TD, CD, Free Adm
Curator: Rich Sugden, www.tetonaviation.com, E-Mail: tetonav@pdt.net,
All Aircraft Flyable, Glider Rides Available & Aviat Husky A-1 Rides
```
A-1 Aviat           L-39                SNJ-5
Blanik Glider       MiG-15              T2-B
HU-16               N3N                 T-28
```

Idaho Falls - Idaho Falls Airport Administration, 83402, 208-529-1221,   F-86

Mountain Home - Mountain Home AFB, 83648-5000, 208-828-2111,
```
F-84F               F-100C              F-111A(RF)
```

Nampa - Warhawk Air Museum, 201 Municipal Dr, Nampa Municipal Airport, 83687,
208-465-6446, Fax 465-6232, April 1-Oct 15, Tue-Fri 10-5, Sun 11-5,
Oct 15-March 31 Tue-Fri 10-4, Sat 10-5, Adm Adult $5, Age 65 & 4-9 $4
3 & Under Free, Gift Shop, Library, Restoration Facility, All Flyable
www.warhawkairmuseum.org, DR-1   P-40E   P-40N
```
P-51C (Project)        P-51D         YAK-3
```

Twin Falls - N W Warbirds Inc, POB 1945, 83303-1945, 208-734-1941,

Twin Falls Airport, Mon-Fri 8-5, Manager: Rob Werner, N3N TBM

CAF - Idaho Squadron, Joslin Field 208-733-5215, Squadron Leader: John H.
Lane Jr, 472 State Hwy 25, Jerome Airport, 83338, 208-324-3650

ILLINOIS

Belleville - Scott AFB, 62225-5000, 618-256-1110, C-45J, T-39A(CT), C-140(VC)

Bloomington - McLean County Historical Society, 200 N Main, 61701,
309-827-0428,   Tilbury Flash Racer

Prairie Aviation Museum, Bloomington-Normal Airport, 2929 E Empire St, 61701,
Mail POB 856, 61702, 309-663-7632, Tue-Sat 11-4, Sun 12-4, Adm Adult $2,
Child 6-11 $1, Under 6 Free, Charles Lindbergh's De Havilland Remains of
Mail Run Crash in the Area, DC-3 Rides $80, www.prairieaviationmuseum.org

A-7A	B-25	DC-3	T-38
AH-1J	Cessna 310B	T-33 (Project)	

Cahokia - Saint Louis University Parks College, 62206, 618-337-7500,
Mon-Fri 8-4:30, Dir of Public Relations: For Any Information

AT-6	Cessna 320	QU 22	T-33	T-39A(CT)
Cessna 310	H-1(AH)	Short Skyvan	T-39	

Cahokia / St. Louis St Louis Downtown-Parks Airport, 618-337-6060, 1 Mi E
of Cahokia. Aerospatiale Tampicos, Cessna's, Mooneys Used As Trainers
For Parks Univ,   U-6A   Parks P-1

Cary - Phoenix Restoration Group, Inc, 209 Cleveland, Unit E, 60013-2978
847-516-0141, Mon-Fri 8-5, Sat Appt, Restoring Weeks Air Museum Aircraft

Chicago - Butch O'Hare Memorial, Terminal 2, O'Hare Int'l Airport, 60607
General info: 773-686-2200, F4F-3

CAF Great Lakes Wing,Gary Regional Airport, 219-977-0834, www.greatlakeswing.org
C-47,   C-49   JU-52

Museum of Science & Industry, 57th St & S Lake Shore Dr,
60637-2093, 773-684-1414, Summer Daily 9:30-5:30, Winter Weekdays 9:30-4,
Sat-Sun 9:30-5:30, Adm Adult $5, Child $4, Free on Thursdays, Gift Shop,
Closed cd, Collection Coordinator: Sue Elduterio, www.msichicago.org

Apollo 8	HH-3 (S-61)	Morane-Saulnier
Boeing B 40B-2 Mail	HH-52A	Spitfire Mk.1A
Boeing 727	JN-4D	Travel Air Mystery S
Brown B-1 Racer	JU-87B-2/Throp	U-505 Sub
Curtiss Pusher	Mercury Aurora 7	Pioneer Zephyr Train
F-104C	New York Central 999 Train	

Danville - Midwest Aviation Museum, Vermillion Co Airport, 22563 N Bowman Ave, 61834,
217-431-2924, 217-1998, Fax 431-8989, Contact Mike VadeBonCoeur, email T6flier@aol.com,

BT-13	FG-1D	P-51F-6
F-86	P-47D	T-6G

Edgewood - Keeler-Adams American Legion Post, Hwy 57, 618-238-4193, 5" Naval Gun

Elliott - Commanche Flyer Foundation, Inc, Gibson City Municipal Airport, RR1,
574 N 1000 E Rd, Box 31, 60936, 217-749-2371, 749-8295
Piper Commanche 1959 World Flying Record, Owner: Schertz Richard 749-2293

Glenview - Von Maur - 1960 Tower Dr, 60023, 847-724-4199, PT-17

Great Lakes - Great Lakes Naval Training Center, Main Entrance at Buckley & Sheridan Rd
A-4

Harvard - Blackstone Aeroplane, Richard C. Hill, 23903 Graf Rd, PO BOX 328
60033, 815-943-7205, Appt Only, Bird Biplane Projects (4ea)

T-50	E-2	J-2	PA-20	PA-22

Joliet - Replica Fighters Assoc, 2409 Cosmic Dr, 60435, 5/8 & 3/4 Scale
Aircraft Thru The US consisting of the Following Squadrons: 999th Sq

DH 98	F8F	Hawker FB.11	P-38	P-51
F4U	Fw 190	Ju 87 Stuka	P-40	Spitfire
F6F	Hawker Tempest	Me-109	P-47	F-86

Kirkland - Kirkland (Harold Bunger) Airport, 4 Mi S of City, 815-522-3367,
Baby Ace   Fleet

Lincoln - Heritage in Flight Museum, Logan County Airport, 1351 Airport Rd,
62656, 217-732-3333, Sat-Sun 8-5, Weekdays By Appt, Free Adm, Donations
Accepted, Housed in WWII German P.O.W. Barracks, www.heritageinflight.org

A-7E	F-4B	H-13T(TH)	L-17
C-45	H-1H(UH)	L-16	T-33A

Marengo - B-17E Restoration Project, Contact Mike & Ken Kellner, 21010 Anthony Rd, 60152
   815-568-9464, B-17E (XC-108) S/N 41-2595

Marengo - Mascoutah Community Unit Museum, 1313 W Main St, 62258,
   815-566-8523, Curator: John D Roy III, 8-3:30, Free Adm, Military, Artifacts

Milford - Lions Club Sign on Route 1, JB-2 Buzz Bomb

Paris - Heartland Antique Auto Museum, 1208 N Main, 61944, 217-463-1834
   Lincoln Page LP3A, PT-22, Engines, Artillery, Antique Autos

Peoria - Peoria ANG, Greater Peoria Airport, 61607, 309-697-6400, F-84F

   Wheels of Time Museum, 11923 N Knoxville Ave, 61601, 309-243-9020, Red Baron Replica

Poplar Grove - Vintage Wings & Wheels Museum, 11619 Route 76, Mail: POB 236
   61065, 815-547-3115, www.poplargroveairmotive.com/Museum, Circa

Rantoul - Octave Chanute Aerospace Museum, Rantoul National Aviation Center, Frank Elliott
   Field, 1011 Pacesetter Dr, 61866-0949, 217-893-1613, Fax: 892-5774, Mon-Sat 10-5,
   Sun 12-5, Closed: ND,ED,TD,CD, Adm Adult $5, Mil & Over 62 $4, 4-12 $3, Under 4 Free,
   Gift Shop, Ntn'l Balloon Races, First Week-end in Aug, www.aeromuseum.org

A-4F	C-47D(VC)	F-86A	ICBM Silo(3Sections)
A-7D	C-97G	F-100C	JN-4D Rep
Aeronca 65LB	C-121K(EC)	F-100D	LGM-30A Minuteman I
AGM-28	C-130A	F-101B	Mong Sport
American Eagle	C-133A	F-104A	O-2A
AT-6A	Cessna 120	F-105B	P-51H
B-25J	Chanute Glider Rep	F-105F	Ryan NYP Rep
B-47E(XB)	F-4C(RF)	F-111A	T-33A
B-52D Cockpit	F-15A	Foker DRI	T-38A(F-5B)
B-58A	F-84F	H-1B(UH)	T-39A(CT)
B-66B	F-84G	HU-16B	Wright Flyer Rep

Rockford - Greater Rockford Airport, Midway Village & Museum, 60 Airport Dr
   61109, 815-965-8635, T-28

   Courtesy Aircraft, Inc, 5233 Falcon Rd, 61109-2991, 815-229-5112
   Sells Replica Aircraft, www.courtesyaircraft.com

Springfield - Air Combat Museum, 835 S Airport Dr, 62707, 217-522-2181,
   Tue-Sat 10-6, Closed Major Holidays, Donations, Curator: Mike George

AeroCommander	Extra 300L	F4U-5	Soko Galeb
AeroStar	F-86F	L-2M	T-34
AT-11	F-4	P-51D	All Aircraft Fly
B-25	F-84F	PT-22	

   Springfield ANG, Capitol Airport, 62707, 217-753-8850, 183rd TFG,
   F-4 F-84

   Army Reserve Center, 62708, 217-785-3600, F-86F, Tank, M9 3" Gun

   Springfiled Airport Terminal, 3 Mi NW of City, 217-788-1060,
   Pietenpohl Air Camper

St Charles - St Charles Airport, 630-377-4500, DC-3

Sugar Grove - Air Classics Museum of Aviation, 43W636 Veterans Memorial Parkway
   Aurora Mncpl Airport, 60554, US 30, 630-466-7000, Tue-Sun 10-3, By Appt
   Adm Adult $5, Snr $4, Child $3, Under 6 Free, www.airclassicsmuseum.org

A-4J(TA)	F-4	H-1H(UH) 2ea
A-7E	F-86F(RF)	T-33
DHC-2(U6-A)	F-105	T-39A

Urbana - Frasca Air Museum, Illinois Airport, Frasca Field, 1402 E Ellini,
   61801, 217-367-8441, Appointment Only

F4F	Luscombers	P-40E	Travelair	Waco

INDIANA

Auburn - Auburn-Cord-Duesenburg Museum, 1600 S Wayne St, Mail POB 271,
   46706-3509, 260-925-1444, Daily 9-6, Adm Adult $5, Snr & Child $3.50,
   Under 6 Free,   Stinson 1911

   Hoosier Warbirds, Inc, 2822 CR 62, SW Side of Airport, Mail: POB 87, 46706
   260-927-0443, Mon-Sat 10-4, Sun 1-4, Adm Donation, Pres Niles Walton,
   www.hoosierwarbirds.org

AT-11 On Loan	J-3	PT-17 On Loan	Stearman
C-45	LNE-1	Smith Mini Plane	T-50 (UC-78)
H-1(AH)	P-51 7/10 Scale	Speedbird	V-77 (Gullwing)

Bippus - Penn Aviation Company, 46713, 260-344-1168, Dave Van Liere, AT-6D

24

Columbus - Atterbury-Bakalar Air Museum, 4742 Ray Boll Blvd, Columbus Mncpl
  Airport, 47203, 812-372-4356, Tue 10-12, Wed-Fri 10-2, Sat 10-4,
  Donations Requested, Curator: Bob Henry, www.atterburybakalarairmuseum.org;
  F-4,   CG-4A Nose Project,   1/8:(B-25, C-47, C-119, CG-4A)

  VFW, F-80, M1 Tank

  CAF Columbus Squadron, Municipal 812-376-2519, Squadron Leader:
  Michael A Bealmer, 2990 S 130 W, 47201-9114, 812-342-3645

  Rhoades Aviation Inc, Columbus Mncpl Airport, 47203, 812-372-1819, Fax 378-2708
  Operations Manger: Jim Davis,   DC-3 (4 ea)

Covington - VFW Post 2395, Liberty St & 12th, T-33A

Crown Point - Crown Point Village, Owner Bill Thornberry, Westfield, IN, 46074, L-17B

Edinburg - Camp Atterbury Museum and Memorial Complex, US 31 2 Mi N of Exit 76 (I-65)
  Jan-March Wed & Sun 1-4, Sat 12-4, RoY Wed & Sun 1-5, Sat 12-5, Gift Shop,
  www.IndianaMilitary.org, email: JimWest@IndianaMilitary.org
  H-1M(UH), Tanks: M4A1 (2ea), M41, M42, M47, M50, M60, Rocket Launcher: M139C, XM33
  Cannon: M5, M115, M1918A3

Elkhart - Northern Indiana Aviation Museum, 12264 County Rd 148, Ligonier, In 46767
  Pres Steve Hay, 574-642-4961, email: wawaseeaircraft@skyenet.com, www.niam.org
  A-4J(TA)   NA-50   T-33A Project

  AM Post 233, 500 Memorial Dr, 46124, 812-526-9001, Historian Peter Long, T-38

Fairmount - American Legion Post 313, 522 E 8th St, IN 26, 46928, 765-948-4431
  F-4C   UH-1A   M60 A1 Tank

Fort Wayne - Mercury, 4021 Air St, 46809, 260-747-1565, Appt Only,
  Owner of Aircraft: Dean Cutshall, F-5A,   F-100F-16,   GNAT

  Lt Paul Baer Terminal Bldg, 2nd Floor, Ft Wayne Int'l Airport, 3421 Air St, Mail:
  POB 9573, 46899, 260-478-7146, Daily 7-7, Free Adm, Smith Aeroplane, Artifacts
  www.fwairport.com/museum.html

  Indiana ANG, 122nd TFW, Baer Field, Ft Wayne Municipal Airport,
  46809-5000, 260-478-3210, F-4   F-86   F-100

  Kloffenstein Furniture, 6314 Lima Rd (Hwy 3), 260-627-2115, 3/4 Scale P-51

  Memorial Coliseum, 4000 Parnell Ave, 260-482-9502,   F-84F

Green Castle - Court House Downtown, Fi 103 Buzz Bomb

Hagerstown - Wilbur Wright Birthplace Museum, 1651N CR 750E, 47346,
  765-332-2495, Apr-Oct Mon-Sat 10-5, Sun 1-5, www.wilburwrightbirthplace.org
  F-84F, Wright Flyer Rep

Hobart - Richard A Boyd, 5253 S Liverpool Rd, 46342, 219-942-8692,   T-33

Indianapolis - CAF Indiana Wing, Squadron Leader: Karl Franzman, 1045 North
  Shore Dr, Martinsville, 46151, 317-342-3257, PT-26

  American Military Heritage Foundation, 1215 S Franklin, Post Air Hangar, Mon-Sat 9-5
  317-897-7000, www.amhf.org
  BT-13A   O-2B "FAC" Cessna   SNJ-5B
  LC-126 Cessna 195   PV-2

  Ropkey Armor Museum, 6424 W 79th St, 46278, 317-632-5446, 8-5, 317-875-0141 After 5,
  Fred N Ropkey III,
  A-4B   O-1   PT-17   T-11
  DH100 MK.IIc   P2V-7   T-2   T-33B

  Paul King Air Museum, 2750 E 62nd St, 46220, 317-259-7979, Artifacts

Lake Village - Lake Village Airport, 1 Mi NW of City, 219-992-3100,
  Owner: Larry Wells, Crown Pt,   Aeronca 65-TAC (L-3)

La Porte - Door Prairie Auto Museum, 2405 Indiana Ave, Mail: POB 1771, 46350
  574-326-1337, Fax: 326-1437, Tue-Sat 10-4:30, Sun 12-4:30, Adm Adult $5, 60+ $4,
  Child 10-18 $3, Under 10 Free, www.dpautomuseum.com/index.htm,
  Pietenpol Air Camper   Sonerai II

Marion - Marion Municipal Airport, Ray Johnson, 317-664-2588, Aeronca Chief

Mentone - Mentone Airport, 2 Mi SW of City 574-353-7330, BT-13, T-50

  Lawrence D Bell Aircraft Museum, S Oak St, Mail: Box 411, 46539, US31 Exit N on
  SR25, 574-353-7296, June 1- Oct 1, Sun 1-5pm, Adult $1, www.bellaircraftmuseum.com,
  OH-13,   UH-1H,   UH-12,   Artifacts from Lawrence Bell

Mitchell - Spring Mill State Park, 812-849-4129, Grissom Gemini Capsule

Muncie - Academy of Model Aeronautics / National Model Aviation Museum,
5151 E Memorial Dr, 47302, 765-289-4236, Mon-Fri 8-4:30, Sat-Sun 10-4,
Closed Sun TD thru ED, Adm Adult $2, Child $1, Gift Shop, www.modelaircraft.org
Displays Model Airplanes

Fishers - 317-773-5298, Indianapolis Metro 404-3, 9913 Willowview Rd, 46038
email: Larry at ljacobi@netzero.net, By Appt: Walt Gdowski, 317-816-1023, AT-6G

Peru - Grissom Air Museum, 1000 W Hoosier Blvd, 46970-3647, US 31,
765-689-8011, Fax 688-2956, Indoor Displays Tue-Sun 10-4, Closed Mid Dec-Mid Feb;
Outdoors Daily 7-Dusk, Closed Holidays, Free Adm, Gift Shop, Curator: John S Marsh,
www.grissomairmuseum.com, e-mail: gamuseum@iquest.net

A-10A	C-47D	F-89 Project	T-41
B-17G	C-97L(KC)	F-100C	T-33A Project
B-25J	C-119G	F-101B	U-3(A)
B-47D	C-135L(EC)	H-1(UH)	YS-11
B-58A(TB)	F-4C	F-105D	
C-1	F-11F	O-2A	

Portland - Museum of the Soldier, 510 East Arch St, Mail: PO Box 518, 47371, 260-726-2967
April-Nov 1st & 3rd Sat & Sun each Month, Adm Adult $2, Student & Snr $1, Under 10 Free
Jeep, M-37 Truck

Richmond - Wayne County Historical Museum, 1150 N, A St, 47374, 765-962-5756, Davis Aircraft 1929

Seymour - Freeman Army Air Field Museum, 1040 A Ave, Freeman Mncpl Airport, Mail: POB 702,
47274, 812-522-2031, US 50 go S on S Airport Rd(1st Ave).
www.indianamilitary.org/FreemanAAF/; Parts from WWII Enemy Aircraft Stored There

South Bend - Jeep Acres - Contact: Charles R Dadlow 29430 SR2, 46624, 574-654-8649, HRP-3

Military Honor Park, South Bend Regional Airport,
P-80(T-33), UH-1, M-60 Tank, M-42 Tank, 155 Howitzer, Mk 14 Torpedo, 3" Guns, 2½ Ton Truck

Terre Haute - Terre Haute ANG, Hulman Regional Airport, 47803, 812-877-5210,
F-4C   F-84F   F-100D

Valparaiso - Indiana Aviation Museum, Porter County Municipal, 4601 Murvihill Rd,
46383, 219-548-3123, Sat 10-4, Sun 1-4, Adm Adult $3, Child Under 13 Free.
Curator: Jim Read, www.indianaaviationmuseum.org

AT-6G	P-51D	T-28B
F4U-5N	T-28B	T-34B
L-2	PT-17	T-37A(AT)

Vincennes - Indiana Military Museum, 4305 Bruceville Rd, 2.8 Miles E of
Holiday Inn, 47591, 812-882-8668, 882-4002, Mail: POB 977, Adm Adult $2,
Child 1-18 $1, Outdoors Daily 8-5, Indoors Daily 12-4,
Winter Sat-Sun 12-5, Weekdays by appointment, Curator: Jim R. Osborne.

C-47 Nose	1/2 Track	M3A1 Tank	M5A1 Tank
H-1(UH)	German PAK 40 Gun	M4A1E8 Tank	M-114

IOWA

Altoona - Sam Wise Youth Camp, Veterans Memorial, 8th St, A-7D

Des Moines - Iowa State Historical Society, 600 E Locust, 50319, 515-281-5111,
Tue-Sat 9-4:30, Sun 12-4:30, Free Adm, Curator: William M Johnson,
Bleriot XI,   Curtiss Pusher   Quickie   Solbrig

Iowa National Guard, Beaver Dr, 50318, 515-252-4236,
A-7   F-84   H-1(AH)   H-1(UH)   6 Tanks   7 Cannons

Ft. Dodge - Ft Dodge IA ANG, 133 TCF/CC, 50501, 515-573-4311, 3611,   F-84F

Greenfield - Iowa Aviation Museum, 2251 Airport Rd, Greenfield Mncpl Airport,
Mail: POB 31, 50849-0031, 641-343-7184, Mon-Fri 10-5, Sat-Sun 1-5, Closed E,
TD, CE, CD, ND, Adm Adult $3, Sr $2.50, Child 5-12 $1.50, Under 4 Free,
www.flyingmuseum.com

A-7	DH 82C Canadian	Mead Primary Glider
AH-1	DH-87A	Northrup Primary Glider
Aetna-Timm #4	Easy Riser Glider	Schweitzer Secondary Glider
Curtiss Robin #6	J-2	Taylorcraft
DH 82C Australian	J-3	

Grimes - Grimes ANG, Des Moines Municipal Airport, 50321, 515-285-7182, F-84F

Grinnell - Grinnell Airport, 641-236-8007, Artifacts

Ida Grove - Cobb Memorial Park, Hwy 59/175, AH-1, RF-84F

Indianola - US National Balloon Museum, 1601 N Jefferson St, Box 149, 50125,
515-961-3714, Summer: Mon-Fri 9-4, Sat 10-4, Sun 1-4, Free Adm,
Helium/Hot Air Balloons, www.nationalballoonclassic.com/museum.htm;

Johnston - Camp Dodge (HQ Iowa National Guard), NW Beaver Dr, Main Gate, A-7D, 2 Tanks

Marshalltown - Central IOWA All Veterans Memorial, American Legion
  Post 46, 1301 S 6th St, Curator: Jeff Heiden, 641-752-0544, F-4C

Ottumwa - Airpower Museum, 22001 Bluegrass Rd, Antique Airfield, Route 2, Box 172,
  52501-8569, 641-938-2773, Mon-Fri 9-5, Sat 10-5, Sun 1-5, www.aaa-apm.org

Aeronca K	Culver LCA Cadet(LFA)	Nesmith Cougar
Aeronca C-2	Culver Cadet PQ-14B	Pietenpohl Sky Scout
Aeronca C-3	DSA-1 Smith Miniplane	PT-22 Ryan Recruit
Aeronca 65CA	Fairchild 22	Rearwind Cloudster
Aeronca LA65	Fairchild 71	Rearwind Skyranger 190F
Aeronca 65TC	Fleet 7	Rearwind Sportster
Aeronca 7AC	Funk Model B	Ritz Ultrlight
Aeronca 11AC	Great Lakes 2T-1A	Rose Parakeet A-1
AmEagle Eaglet	Kinner Sportster	Ryan STA
Anderson Z	L-4	Stinson S Junior
Arrow F Sport	LH-2	Stinson 10
Backstrom Plank	Luscombe 8F	Taylo-Young A
BD-5	Monocoupe 90	VJ-23
Bolkow Bo 208A-1 Jr	Monoprep	VP-1 Evans Volksplane
Brewster B-1	Mooney M-18 Mite	Welch QW-8
CP-40 Porterfield	Morrisey Bravo	

  Indian Hills Community College, 60 Aviation Program Center, 52501, 641-683-5111
  www.ihcc.cc.ia.us

C-45	Cessna 421	Piper Aztec
Cessna 150	F-84	T-39
Cessna 172	H-1H(UH)	
Cessna 310	PA-22	

Sioux City - Mid America Air Museum, Sioux Gateway Airport, 6715 Harbor Dr,
  Mail: POB 2199, 67905-2199, Off I-29 Exit 141 Go West, 712-624-5263, Tue-Sun 9-5
  Closed TD, CD, ND, Easter, Adm Adult $3, Child 6-18 $1, Group Rates Available,
  Gift Shop, Chairman: Maurey Topf, www.midamericaairmuseum.com, e-mail: airmuseum@pionet.net

A-7D	H-1B(UH)	T-18
A-6A	Hawker-Siddeley Argosy	T-33
CallAir Spray Plane	GLider	Ultralight Snoopy's BobCat
F-84F	KR-2	

  Sioux City ANG, Sioux City Mun Airport, 51110, 712-255-3511,

A-7D	F-84F	F-100c
A-7K	F-84F Photo Recon	T-33

St Maries - David Freeman, Nicholas-Beazley Racer NR-1W

KANSAS

Ashland - Pioneer Krier Museum, 430 W 4th Hwy 160, N of Route 160, 67831,
  620-635-2227, Summer Daily 1-5, Winter Daily 1-4, Free Adm,
  Curator: Rosa Lee McGee, Krier Kraft,   DHC 1,   Great Lakes Special

Hutchinson - Kansas Cosmosphere Museum, 1100 N Plum, 67501, 800-397-0330,
  620-662-2305, Mon-Sat 9-9, Sun 12-9, Adm Adult $11, Age 60+ or Child 5-12 $10.50,
  Child 5 & under Free, After 6pm $6, Museum, OMNIMAX, Planetarium: $2.50, Gift Shop,
  Cafe, Astronaut Training Programs: 7th-9th Grade 2 Day ($495 Room-Board-Meal
  Flight Jacket, Tshirt, Model) ($545 Same & Johnson Space Center Trip), 10th-Adult
  10 Hr Astronaut, Training Program ($115 T-Shirt, GrpPhoto), www.cosmo.org

Apollo 13	Lunar Lander	V-2 Flying Bomb	SR-71
Gemini	Lunar Rover	V-1 Rocket	T-38
Mercury 7	F-1 Saturn V Engine	F-104B	

Liberal - Mid-America Air Museum, 2000 W 2nd St, POB 2585, Welch Blvd.
  67905-2585, 620-624-5263, Sat 9-5, Sun 1-5, Closed: TD, CD, ND, Adult $5,
  Snr $4, Child $2 (6-16), 5 Under Free, Exec Dir: Greg Kennedy, Gift Shop,
  Restoration Facility, Air Show In Mid Sept,
  www.liberalairmuseum.com, e-mail:maam@ozsome.com

A-4L	BT-13A	F-8U-2N	HUP-3
A-7E	Bushby Mustang	F-14A	J-2
Aero Commander	C-45	F-80C	J-3C
Aeronca 65C	Cessna 120	F-86H	J-4A
Aeronca 65TC	Cessna 140	F-104C	J-4F
Aeronca K	Cessna 145	F-105	KR-1
Aeronca 7AC/L-16	Cessna 165	F4U-5	Koala II
Aeronaut	Cessna 175	Fairchild 23	L-2
Avid Flyer	Cessna 195	Fairchild 24-C8F	L-3B
AT-19(V-77)	Cessna 195A	Fisher Koala 202	L-5
Avid Flyer	Cessna 310	Fly Baby	L-6
B-25J	Culver V	Funk B-75	L-9
Baby Great Lakes	CW-1 Jr	Globe Swift GC-1B	L-17
Beech 35	D-16	H-1S(AH)	LB-5
Beech 150	DC-3	H-1B(UH)	Leak Avid Flyer
Beech D17S	Dragonfly	H-13	Lockheed 5 Vega 1
Bellanca 190	Ercoupe 415C	Hawker Siddley Gnat	Luscombe 8
Bellanca 260 ?	F-4D	Hot Air Balloon	Luscombe 8A

Miller Fly Rod	PA-24	Rearwin 7000RearwinT-28A	
Moni Motor Glider	Phoenix Glider	Rearwin Skyranger	T-37(XT)
Mooney M.18C Mite	Pietenpol B4A	RLU-1 Breezy	T-38
Mooney M.20B	Pober Pixie P-9	Rutan Vari-Eze	T-50D
N2S3(B75N1)	PT-13	Rutan Quickie	TBM-3
NW Porterfield	PT-17/LN2S-3	S2F-1	U-4(Model 690B)
OH-6	PT-19A	SA 102-5	U-9 Aero 520
OQ-19	PT-22	Shober Willie II	U-11
OV-10	PT-23	Skybolt	Viking Dragonfly
PA-22	PT-26	Stinson 108-3	X-28
PA-23	Rally 3	T-18	

Newton - Blockbuster Video Store, 1411 N Main St, 67114, 620-283-7086, Tail of Aircraft Sticking Out of Front of Building.

Olathe - Old Olathe Naval Air Museum, 1 Navy Park Dr, 913-768-1153
Mail: POB 1942, New Century Air Center, KS 66031,

A-4D	A-7D (2ea)	1930 Bi-Plane

New Century - CAF Heart of America Wing, #3 Aero Plaza, 66031, 913-397-6376, Mail:
15011 West 147th St, Olathe, KS 66062, www.kcghostsquadrom.org

AT-6	L-2 2ea	MiG-17	PT-19 2ea	T-28
BT-13 3ea	L-39	PT-17		
F4F-3				

Topeka - Kansas Museum of History, 6425 SW 6th St, 66615-1099, 785-272-8681, Mon-Sat 9-4:30, Sun 12:30-4:30, Free Adm, Dir: Robert J Keckeisen,

Curtiss Pusher	Experimental Helicopter

Museum of Kansas Army National Guard, Forbes Field, 6700 S Topeka Blvd, 66619, 785-862-1020, Tue-Sat 10-4, Theater, F-16 Model ½ Scale

H-1(AH)	H-1(UH)	H-6(OH)	H-54(CH)	H-58(OH)

Air Guard, 190th ARW, Forbes Field, 66619-5000, B-57, Helicopters, Tanks

Spooky Squadron, Hangar 603, Forbes Field, Mail: 2630 SE Bennett Dr, 66605, 785-862-1234, www.squadron14.com, C-47(AC)   O-2

Combat Air Museum, Forbes Field, Hangar 602 & 604, J St, Mail POB 19142, 66619-0142, 785-862-3303, Fax 862-3304, Mon-Sat 9-4:30, Sun 10-4:30, Closed: ES, TD, CD, ND, Adm Adult $5, Over 55 $4, Child 6-17 & Military $3 Under 6 Free, Ex Dir: Jerry Holley, Curator: Danny J. San Romani, E-mail CAMTopeka@aol.com Hangar 602 = 2; Hangar 604 = 4; Outside Display = O, www.combatairmuseum.org/

A-4J(TA)	2	F-86H	4	H-1M(UH)	4	Nike Ajax	O
AT-6 Harvard Mk IV	2	F-105D		H-1B(UH)	O	O-47B	2
Bf-109 Rep Disa	4	F-101B	4	Honest John	O	RU-8D	4
BT-13 Disa	4	F11F-1	2	Little John	4	S-2A(US)	4
C-47D (2ea)	4	F3D	2	JN-4D	2	SNB-5	4
C-121T(EC)	O	F9F-5 Disa	4	Meyers OTW	2	T-28B	4
C-61K(UC)	4	H-53A(NCH)	4	MiG-15	2	Tartar Navy Missile	
Corporal M2 Missile	O	H-54(CH)	4	MiG-17	4		
F-84F (2 ea)	4,0	H-1H(UH)	2	Nike Tartar	2		

Wichita - Aviation Education Center, 2021 S Eisenhower, 316-833-3595, F-86

Kansas Aviation Museum, 3350 George Washington Blvd, 67210, 316-683-9242, Fax: 683-0573, Dir: Donald Livengood, Tue-Fri 9-4, Sat 1-5, Closed ES, TD, CD, Adm Adult $2, Child 6-12 $1, 6 & Under Free www.kansasaviationmuseum.org, kam3350@juno.com

American Eagle	Funk	Prescott Pusher	Swallow
B-52D	Jayhawk	O-2B	T-33
Beech 73 Mentor	Laird Swallow	Rans Ultralight	T-37
BD-5	Lear 23	Sonerai	TV-2
Cessna 206	Mooney Mite	Stearman Ariel	U-8
Cessna 310	NS-1	Stearman 4D	
F-84F	Poude Ceil		

Kansas & Historical Air, McConnell AFB, 184th TFG, 2801 S Rock Rd, 672221-6225, 316-652-3141, Historic Property Custodian: Jerry L Ferguson, MSTG

F-4D	F-84C	F-100C	F-105F
F-80C	F-86L-LO	F-105D	T-33A-5-LO

CAF Jayhawk Wing, 2558 S Kessler, Westport Airport, 67217, 316-943-5510, www.cafjayhawks.org

AT-11	L-2M	PT-22	PT-26
C-45G	L-3B	PT-23	UC-78

KENTUCKY

Fort Campbell - Don F Pratt Memorial Museum, 42223-5335, 720-798-3215, Mon-Fri 12-4:30, Sat 10-4:30, Sun 12-4:30, Free Adm, Curator: Don Pratt, www.campbell.army.mil/pratt/index.htm

A-10	C-47	C-119	CG-4A	H-1(UH)	H-65(AH)

Fort Knox - Patton Museum of Calvary & Armor, POB 208, 40121,
502-624-3812, Daily 9-5, Free Adm, Registrar: C Lemon,

H-1B(UH)(2ea)	H-1G(AH)	H-13E(OH)	H-23B(OH)	L-19A

Frankfort - Boone National Guard Center, 40601, 502-564-8464,

F-84F	F-101C(RF)

Lexington - Aviation Museum of Kentucky, Blue Grass Airport, Hangar Dr, Off
US 60 Right off Airport Rd, Mail: POB 4118, 40544, 859-231-1219, Gift Shop
Tue-Sat 10-5, Sun 1-5, Adm Adult $3, Seniors $2, Students $1.50, Under 6 Free
www. aviationky.org/

A-4L	H-58A(OH)	LNE-1	Travel Air D4D
Aeronca Model K	Heath Center Wing	Nimbus II Glider	Youngsters Sim
Cessna 150	L-4B	Pulsar Ultralight	
Crosley Moonbeam	L-10 Electra	Sellers Quadraplane	
F-4S	Link Trainer	T-38B(AT)	

Louisville - Bowman Field, 5 Mi SE of City, 502-368-6524, AT-6, DC-3/C-47 Flights

Clark County Airport, FG-1D, FJ-1, P-51, P-51D

Louisville ANG, Standford Field, 40213, 502-364-9400, F-4C(RF), F-101H(RF)

Museum of History & Science, 727 W Main St, 40202, 502-561-6100,
Daily 10-5, Adm Adult $5.00, Child 2-12 $4.00, Curator: Alan Goldstein,
561-6103; 561-6111 Tours,

Bushbee Mustang I,	Apollo XIII,	Gemini Trainer
	Sellers Quadruplane Rep,	

Middlesboro - Lost Squadron, Bell County Airport, POB 776, 40965, 606-248-1149,
Daily 8-5, Gift Shop, Restoration Facility, www.thelostsquadron.com,

E-mail: mrp38@eastky.net, P-38,	F-86	M-60 Tank

LOUISIANA

Alexandria - England AFB, Flying Tiger Heritage Park, 23TFW/PA, 71311-5004,
318-448-2401, 1406 Van Gossen Ave 448-1083 Or 3908 Coliseum Blvd 448-0701,
A Sponsor or Escort & Public Affairs Office Is Required To Visit Museum,

A-7D	A-10	F-84F	F-86E	F-105G

Baton Rouge - USS Kidd & Nautical Center, 305 S River Rd, 70802-6220, 225-342-1942
Daily 9-5, Closed TD, CD, Adm Adult $4, Sr $3, 6-12 $2.50,

A-7E	P-40E	USS KIDD (Camping aboard available groups of 20)

Bossier City - Barksdale AFB, 8th AF Museum, 71110, 318-456-3065, North
Entrance, POB 10, Daily 9:30-4, Closed TD, CD, ND, Gift Shop
www.8afmuseum.net/

B-17G	Sled	Beech 18	F-111(FB)	T-33
B-24J	C-47A		MiG-21	Vulcan B Mk.2
B-29	C-97L(KC)		P-51D	
B-47E	F-84F		SR-71	
B-58A	Rocket			

Many - VFW, 318-256-2143, State Rd 6 Off of US 6.   M4 Sherman Tank

Monroe - Aviation Historical Museum of Louisiana, Kansas Lane, Monroe Regional Airport
(Formerly Selman Field), 318-361-9020, Sat 9-5, Sun 1-5,www.airhistory.org, Artifacts

New Orleans - D Day Museum, 945 Magazine St, 70130, 504-527-6012, Daily 9-5,
Adm Adult $7, Student & 65 $6, Child 5-17 $5, Under 5 Free, wwwDdaymuseum.org

L-5,	Spitfire Mk.VI,	TBM,	Higgins LCVP Boat, M4A3 Tank, M3 Half Track

Friends of Jackson Barracks Military Museum, Jackson Barracks, Bldg 53,
70146-0330, 504-278-8241, Mon-Fri 7:30-4:00, Free Adm,
Curator: Kevin Petty, www.122nd.com, e-mail jbmuseum@cmq.com, R-2800 Engine

A-26	F-15	F-102(YF)	T-33A
AT-11	F-86D	H-23	
F-4C	F-100D	OH-58A	

New Orleans Naval Air Station, Alvin Callender Field, 70143,
504-394-2818, 159th TFG, F-86D   F-100D   F-102A(YF)

Patterson - Wedell-Williams Memorial Aviation Museum, 394 Airport Circle, Off
IA 182 Hwy, Mail: POB 655, 70392, 985-395-7067, Tue-Sat 8:30-5, Adm Adult $2
Curator:Lisa Cotham, http://lsm.crt.state.la.us/wedellex.html

Aero Commander 680	Farley Vincennt-Starflight	Stearman
Beech D17S Replica	P-47 (½ Scale)	Wedell-Williams Racer 44
Bf 109 (½ Scale)	PT-17	

Reserve - American Military Heritage Foundation Museum, St John Baptist
Airport, 355 Airport Rd, 70084, 985-536-1999

A-4	AT-6G (2ea)	H-6(OH)
A-7E	C-45	T-28 (2ea)

Ruston - LA Tech Univ ROTC, Det 305, 318-257-4937, Col: Stamm,

T-33A	ICBM	Minuteman 1

MAINE

Auburn - Starliner Place, Lewiston-Auburn Airport, 2355 Hotel Rd, 04210-8821, 207-783-2680, 782-3912, Fax 753-1153, By Appt Only, Contact: Maurice A Roundy, starliner@gwi.net www.starliner.net, L-1649A (2ea)

Bangor - Bangor ANG, 04401-4393, 207-947-0571, 101st ARW, F-101B(CF)

Maine Air Museum (Maine Aviation Historical Society), Waterville Airport, Next To The Civil Air Patrol Headquarters, 04901, Mail: POB 2641, 04402, 207-941-6757, 800-280-MAHS In State, www.acadia.net/mahs, email: townsend@acadia.net

EAA Balloon	P2V-3	F-89J	Bo-Mark Silo
Luscuming 8A	Stinson 10A	P-3 Possibly	

Brunswick - Naval Air Station Brunswick, 010 Bath Rd, 04011-0010, 207-921-1110, P-3A P2V-5

Owls Head - Owls Head Transportation Museum, Box 277, Knox County Airport Route 73, 04854, 207-594-4418, Fax 594-4410, April-Oct Daily 10-5, Nov-Apr Daily 10-4, Closed CD, ND, Adm Adult $7, Snrs $6, Child 5-12 $5, Family $18, www.ohtm.org, email: ohtm@medcoast.com

Antoinette	Etrich Taube	Nieuport 28
Bellanca	FE8	Penaud Planaphore
Bleriot XI	Fokker C.IVa	S.E.5a
Burgess-Wright F	Fokker DR.I	Sopwith Pup
Cayley Glider	Henri Farman III	Spad XIIIc.1
Chanute Glider	J-1	Stearman A75N/1
Clark Bi Wing	J-3C	Waco UBF-2
Curtiss Pusher D	JN-4D	Wright B Flyer
Damenjoz	Lilienthal Glider	
Deperdussin	Milliken Special	

Presque Isle - Presque Isle Air Museum, 650 Airport Rd, 04769-2088, 207-764-2542 http://welcome.to./piairmuseum, email: piairmuseum@femail.com

MARYLAND

Aberdeen - Aberdeen Proving Ground, 21005-5201, 410-278-3602, 2396, 7472, End of State Route 22, Tue-Fri 12-4:45, Sat-Sun 10-4:45, Closed Holidays, Free Adm, Gift Shop Tue-Sun 12-4, 225 Items of a 25 Acre Tank & Artillery Park, www.ordmusfound.org Some Examples: FZG-76, Rheintocher, V-2, Mk IV Tank

Andrews AFB, 89th Airlift Wing/PA (MAC), 20331-5000, 301-981-9111, www.andrews.af.mil Open House May 22-23, F6F, F-4, F-105D, F-106, H-1B(UH)

Annapolis - US Naval Academy Museum, 118 Maryland Ave, 21402-5034, 410-293-2108, Daily, 9-5, Curator: James W Cheevers, www.nadn.navy.mil/Museum/ A-4A F4F

Baltimore - Baltimore ANG, GL Martin Airfield, 212220-2899, 410-687-6270, F-86H HU-16B XF2Y-1

Baltimore Museum of Industry, 1415 Key Hwy, 21202, 410-727-4808, Martin 162A PBM-1 2/3 Scale

Beltsville - Naval Reserve Center, 2600 Powdermill Rd, 301-394-3966, Missle

Cambridge - Cambridge Airport, 410-228-4571, UC-78CE

College Park - College Park Aviation Museum, 1985 Corporal Frank Scott Dr, 20740, I-495, S on Kenilworth Ave,W on Paint Branch Pkwy, 301-864-6029, Fax 927-6472, Daily 10-5, Closed Holidays, Adm Adult $4, Snr Ctz $3, Child $2, Annual AirFair Sept, www.avialantic.com/collpark.html

Berliner 1924 Helio	DC-3	JN-4D	Wright B Aeroplane
Boyd Airplane C2	Ercoupe 1946	Monocoupe 110	J-2

Ft Meade - National Vigilance Park, East Off of I-95 on Route 32, Left on Colony 7 Rd After Passing Baltimore-Washington Parkway (Rt295), C-130A RU-8D(L-23D)

Quest Masters, Box 131, 20755, Curator: Chris Van Valkenburgh, http://www.geocities.com/quest_masters, email: questmasters@bigfoot.com All Projects in Storage, By Appt Only

B-24J Nose LNE-1 Cockpit	P-61B Nose	UC-45F Cockpit
B-24L Fuse SNJ-5B	TBM-1C (Firewall to Radio compartment)	

Frederick - CAF - Stars & Stripes Wing, 140 W Patrick St, 21702, 301-631-5357, TBM-3E

Hagerstown - Washington County Regional Airport, Rt 12, Box 62, Off Rt 11 & I-81, Dave Rider 301-791-6231, AT-6 DC-3 J-2

Lexington Park - Patuxent Naval Air Test & Evaluation Museum, St Hwy 235 &
Shangri-La Dr, Mail: POB 407, 20670-0407, 301-863-7418, July-Sept Wed-Sat
11-4, Oct-Jun Fri-Sat 11-4, Sun 12-5 (Yearly), Closed ED, TD, CD, Free
Adm, Gift Shop, Ex Dir: Jack Nial, www.paxmuseum.com

A-4M	F4J	H-1J(AH) 2ea	T-39D
A-6E	F4 Cockpit	H-53A(CH)	TH-1L
A-7A	F-6A(F4D-1)	RA-5C	
AV-8B	F-14A 2ea	S-2	
E-2B	F/A-18A	SH-2G	

Middle River - Glenn L Martin Aviation Museum, Martin State Airport, Hangar 5,
Suite 531, Room 115, POB 5024, 21220, 410-682-6122, Mon-Fri 10-2, Sat 1-5,
Closed Holidays, Free Adm, Gift Shop Fri 12-3, Mus Illustrator Rober Hanauer
410-252-4191, www.marylandaviationmuseum.org, * = Storage

A7D	* F9F	* F-101F	* P6M Fuse/Tail
B-57A(RB) 2ea	F-84F(RF)	* F-105G	T-33
F-4	F-100F 2ea	Martin 4-0-4	P&W R2800

Wallops Island - NASA/Goddard Visitor Center, Rte 175, 20771, 301-286-8981
10-4: March-June Thru-Mon, July-August Daily, Sept-Nov Thur-MonDec-Feb Mon-Fri
Free Adm, Tours on Thur at 2pm, 1.5 Hrs long, Gift Shop,
Special Events every Sun, www.wff.nasa.gov/vc; Rockets only

West River (Baltimore)- Due to Open in Spring 1999, USS Forrestal Naval Museum,
P.O. Box 59, 20778, Inner Harbor Area and Ft McHenry, CSX Pier A/B
www.forrestal.org, USS Forrestal Aircraft Carrier

Suitland - Paul E Garber Facility, (Closed to Public), 3904 Old Silver Hill Rd, 20746, 202-357-1552,
www.nasm.si.edu/museum/garber, All Aircraft to Be Sent to Udvar-Hazy Center in Next 7 Years.
Building Number (2, 3, 6, 7, 9, 22) = Storage

Building Number		Building Number		Building Number	
23	A-26(VB)	24	Daedalus 88	07	J7W1
22	A-1H	23	de Bothezat	?	JB-2 Loon
21	Abrams Explorer	20	DO 335	21	JC-1
23	Akerman Tailess	21	Double Eagle II	20	JN-4D
21	American Aerolights	23	DQ-2A/TDD-1	23	JRS-1(S-43)
20	AN-2	24	DQ-14	20	Ju-388L
22	Ar 196A	22	DSI/NASA RPRV	23	K-225
20	Arlington Sisu 1A	09	Eberhart Target	21	Kasperwing 180B
22	B-43 (XB)	20	Erco 415	20	Ki-46
22	B-42A(XB)	23	Extra 260	07	Ki-115
22	B-17D	22	F-4A	20	Laird LCDW 500Fus
0D	B-17G	23	F-101C(RF)	06	Lazair SS EC
0D	B-25J(TB-25M)	24	F-100	07	Lippisch DM-1
0D	B-57B(EB)	22	F-100D	21	M.18C
24	B-58 Escape Capsule	23	F-5L	24	Mahoney Sorceress
22	B6N2	D	F-8G(RF)	24	Martin, JV, K-III
22	B7A1	22	F-105D	07	Maupin-Lanteri
20	Bachem Ba 349	23	F9F-6	22	Me 410A-3
23	Baldwin Red Devil	23	Fa 330	22	Moni Motor Glider
24	BB-1	22	FA-3-101	02	MX7Y-K2
22	Beechcraft D18S	21	Farman Sport	22	N1K2-J
23	Beechcraft 35	10	FE-8	22	Nakajima Kikka
20	Bell 206	20	Fi 156	23	NASA Parasev
24	Bell 30	24	Fowler-Gage	10	Nieuport 28C-1
07	Bell Rocket Belt	07	Fw Ta-152H	24	O-60(XO)
23	Bell ATV VTOL	20	G4M3 Nose	23	O-2
23	Bellanca 14-13	22	Go 229	22	O-47A(RO)
24	Bellanca C.F.	0D	Goodyear K-Car	23	O-1A(L-19)
23	Bensen B-6	22	Goodyear Gondola	06	Olmstead Pusher
24	Bensen B-8M	D	Gossamer Albatross	23	P-39Q
22	Berliner Helicopter	23	H-34D(UH)	23	P-55(XP)
23	Bertelsen Aeromobile	23	H-1H(UH)	22	P-61C
21	Bu 181	20	H-13J(VH)	20	P-63A
07	Burgess-Curtis	23	H-44 (XH)	23	P-84(XP)Fuse
22	BV-155B	22	HA-200B	07	P1Y1-C
07	C-8	07	He 219A	23	PA-12
07	C-64(YC)	20	He 162A	0D	PA-23
0D	C-121	20	Helio No. 1	07	PCA-1A
23	C-35(XC)	20	Henschel 293B	23	Pentecost E III
20	C-2	20	Henschel 117	23	PG-185B
0D	C-130	24	Hiller 1031	21	Phoenix Streak
24	C-35(AC)	07	HJD-1(XHJD)	21	Phoenix Vipper
24	C-97L(KC) Cockpit	?	HMM 163	21	Phoenix 6
07	C6N1-S	23	HOE-1	24	Pitts S-1-S
20	CCW-1	22	HRP-1(XHRP)	20	Princeton Air Scooter
23	Cessna 150L	23	HV-2A	20	PS-2
23	Cessna 180	03	Icarus I	23	PT-19A
22	Convair 240	24	Ikenga 530Z	23	PV-2
22	Crowley Hydro-Air	23	Ilyushin IL-2m3	07	R-8(XR)
22	Curtiss E Boat Fuse	21	J-1	23	R-5(XR)(VS-317)
22	CW 1 Junior	22	J-2A	23	R-4(XR)(VS-316)
23	CW X-100	23	J-29	21	RC-3
23	DH 98 Mk.35	21	J1N1-S	23	Rotorway Scorpion Too

24 RT-14	24 Turner Meteor	22 Waterman Whatsit
21 Rutan Quickie	23 U-2	21 Waterman Aeromobile
23 SG. 38	07 V-173	23 Westland Lysander
23 SNJ-4A(AT-6)	23 V-1(XV)	23 Windecker Eagle I
07 Stanley Nomad	20 Valkyrie Glider	22 XF2Y-1
21 Stearman-Hammond Y	22 VZ-9V	22 XFY-1
21 Stout Skycar	24 VZ-1	07 XR-1
21 T-33	23 VZ-2A	23 Yak-18
20 TBF-1	09 Waco Primary Glider	23 Yokosuka P1Y1c
20 TD2C-1	24 Waco UIC Cabin	23 Zimmerman
23 TG-1A	24 Waco 9	
24 TTD-2 Radioplane Drone		

Airmen Memorial Museum, 5211 Auth Rd, 20746, Take I-95 Exit 7B, Then North on Branch Ave, Right on Auth Rd 3 Blocks, 800-638-0594, Mon-Fri 8-5, www.afsahq.org/AMM/amm-htm/mwelcome.htm, Artifacts

MASSACHUSETTS

Bedford - Hanscom AFB, 01731, 781-861-4441, F-86H ?   P-40N ? May not be there

Boston - Museum of Science Park, 02114-1099, 617-589-0100, Daily 10-5,
Adm Adult $2, Child $.50   Five Spacecraft

Cape Cod - Coast Guard Air Station, Race Point Beach, End of Rte,
HH-60   HU-16E   HU-25

Hq Massachusetts Military Reservation, 02542, 508-968-1000, 7:30-4, T-33

Otis ANG, MASS ANG Museum, 02542-5001, 508-968-4090, 102nd FIW,
Group Tours of 30 or More Only
F-84F   F-86   F-100D   T-33A

Chambridge - New England Escadrille, 26 Cambridge St, 01803-4604, Mail: POB 605,
Kendal Square Station, 617-273-1916, 02142, By Appt Only

Needham - New England Warbird Assoc, 140 Gould St, POB 849, 02194

Stow - Bob Collings Foundation, POB 248, 978-568-8924, www.collingsfoundation.org,
R=Restoration, All Flyable except (NF)

A-4J (R)	Bleriot	H-1E(UH) (R)	TBM
A-26 (R)	C-78(UC)	PT-17	Wright Ex Vin Fizz (NF)
A-36 (R)	F-4D	S-2F	Yak 3UA (R)
B-25J	F4U-1 (R)	T-6	
B-17G	Foker DR-1 Rep	T-33 (R)	
B-24J	Fi-156	T-33	

Westfield - MA ANG, 104 TFG/CC, 01085, 413-568-9151   F-100D

Pioneer Valley Military & Transportation Museum, Inc.

MICHIGAN

Battle Creek - ANGB, 49015-1291, 269-963-1596, A-10(Active),
A-37   F-100F   T-37B   UH-1B   Tank

Belleville - Yankee Air Museum, 2041 A St, Willow Run Airport - East, 48112-0590
I-94 go N on Belleville Rd, W on Tyler Rd, N on 3rd, W on A St.
Mail: POB 590, 48112, 269-483-4030, Fax 483-5076, Tue-Sat 10-4, Sun 12-4,
Jan 1-Mar 1, Thur-Sat 10-4, Sun 12-4, Adm Adult $5, Child 6-12 $3, 60+ $4,
Gift Shop Manager: Dale Worcester, Restoration Facility Viewable
www.yankeeairmuseum.org; e-mail: yankeeairmuseum@provide.net
(:) = Privately Owned Based at Willow Run.

Divisions of the Yankee Air Force are at the following locations:
NE = North-East Division, Sussex Airport, POB 1729, Fairfield, NJ, 07007-1729
SAG = Saginaw Valley, Michigan - Harry Browne Airport, Saginaw, MI
WUR = Wurtsmith, Michigan - Oscoda County Airport, Division - Oscoda, MI
See Aircraft Status Codes Page 1; (L) = Loan from USAF Museum

A-4 Cockpit		B-57A(RB)	(O)(L)	HM-293		(D)
A-6A(EA)	(S)	C-47B(TC)	(F)	L-39C :Bob Lutz		(F)
A-7D Project	(L)	C-60A-5-LO	(P)	Link Trainer		
A-10 Cocpit		CG-4A	(P)	OV-10A(YOV)		(D)
A-W 650-101	(O)	DC-6B(C-118)	(O)	P-38J		
Argosy		F-4C	(L)	P-51D(2ea)J Roush		(F)
AT-6D :Yankee Flyers	(F)	F-4 Cockpit		PB4Y-2G		(O)
AT-6D :Max Holman	(F)	F-84F	(S)(L)	PT-19A :Leslie Day		(F)
AT-6D :Jack Rouch	(F)	F-84F(RF) (3ea)	(O)(L)	SA-300 Starduster Too		(D)
AT-11	(S)	F-86D	(O)	T-28A :Yankee Flyers		(F)
AT-19(V-77)	(F)	F-101B(NF)	(O)(L)	T-28C :Stu Dingman		(F)
B-8M Bensen	(D)	F-102A(TF)	(O)(L)	T-33A (2ea)		(O)
B-17G		F-102 Cockpit		T-33A :Connie Katitta		
B-25D	(F)(P)	F-105B	(D)(L)	TS-11 :Yankee Spark Flyers	(F)	
B-52D	(O)(L)	H-1D(UH)	(O)	Wallis Model 3 1976	(D)	

Blissfield - American Legion Hall, High St & US 223, 517-486-3312, F-105D

Calumet - Calumet AFS, 49913, 906-337-4200, T-33A

Dearborn - Henry Ford Museum, 20900 Oakwood Blvd, POB 1970, 48121-4088,
313-982-6100, Mon-Sat 9-5, Sun 12-5, Closed TD, CD, Adm Adult $14, Snr $13, Child 5-12 $10
Under 5 Free, Gift Shop, www.thehenryford.org/museum/heroes/home.asp

Bleriot XI	Ford 4-AT-15	NYP
Boeing 40B-2	Ford Flivver	PA-18
Curtiss Canuck	Laird LC-D W500	RB-1 Racer
DC-3	Lockheed Autogyro	Stinson SM-1
Fokker F.VIIa	Lockheed Vega	VS-3000A

Detroit - The National Museum of Tuskegee Airmen, 6325 W. Jefferson Ave, 48209
313-297-9360, Wed-Sun 9-5, Artifacts Only, wwwtuskegeeairmen.org

Farmington - Marvin's Marvelous Mechanical Museum, 3100 Orchard Lake Rd, 248-626-5020
100 Model Airplanes suspended on Conveyor Line,

Frankenmuth - Michigan's Own, Inc, Military & Space Museum, 1220 Weiss St, 48734,
989-652-8005, Mar-Dec Mon-Sat 10-5, Sun 12-5, F-86 Rep

Grand Haven - Grand Haven Memorial Airpark, Gate Entrance, 49417, 616-842-4430, F-100

Grand Rapids - CAF West Michigan Wing, Wing Leader: Shirley A. Schouw, 19788 92nd
St, Byron Center, 49315, 616-878-9145, AT-11

Gerald R. Ford Museum, 303 Pearl St, NW, Off US 131 Exit 85B, 49501, 616-451-9263
Mon-Sta 9-4:45, Sun 12-4:45, Closed ND, TD, CD, Adm Adult $2, Snr $1.50, Child
Under 16 Free,   UH-1

Greenville - Fighting Falcon Military Museum of the Flat River Historical Museum,
PO Box 188, 48838, 616-754-3686 or 5296, Contact: Laura Van Syckle, CG-4A Project

Jackson - EAA Chapter 304, Jackson County Airport, 49202, www.eaa304.org, T-33

Michigan Space Center, Jackson Community College, 2111 Emmons Rd, 49203
517-787-4425,   Rockets

Kalamazoo - Kalamazoo Air Zoo, 3101 E. Milham Rd, 49002-1700, 269-382-6555, Fax:
382-1813, June-Aug Mon-Sat 9-6, Wed 9-8, Sun 12-6, Sept-May Mon-Sat 9-5, Sun 12-5,
Closed Holidays, Adm Adult $10, 60 & Above $8, Child 6-15 $5,5 and Under Free,
Annex Adm Adult $3, Child 3-5 $1, Under 3 Free, Dir Marketing: Gerald Pahl,
Simulator F4U Corsair Adult $3, Child 3-5 $1, Ford Trimotor Ride $45,
Gift Shop, Daily Plane Flights, May-Oct, Wed, Sat-Sun, www.airzoo.org

A4D-2(A-4B)Project	F-84F-35RE	HUP-3	PT-22
AD-4NA	F-86A	J-3C-65	PT-23HO
Aeronca 65 CA	F-80 Cockpit	Lear-23	Renegade Spirit
Aeronca O-58B	F-104	Link Trainer	SBD-3 Project
AT-6G	F-106 Cockpit	L-4H	SNJ-5 2ea
Avid Flyer	F4U-4B 1/2 Scale	L-19	Sopwith Camel
B-25J	F6F-5K	LNS-1	SPad VII
B-57B	F7F-3P	MiG-15	SR-71B
Boeing 727-25C	F8F-1D	MiG-21PF Project	SRC-B7
BT-13	F9F-2 Project	Morane-Saulnier 733	Sun Hang Glider
C-4A (5-AT)	F11A-1	N2T-1	T-28 Cockpit
C-47	FG-1D	N3N	T-28B
C-135(KC)	FM-2	OQ-20A	T-33B(TV-2)
CG-4A	Ford Tri-Motor 5-AT	OV-1D	T-34B
Doran Simulator	GH-2	P-38J Rep	Taylor Monoplane
Ercoupe 415C ProjectGuff R/C		P-39Q-20BE(RP)	TG-2(LNS-1)
F-4E	H-1J(AH)	P-40N	TG-4A
F-8J	H-23(UH-12)	P-47D	Waco INF
F-9J(TF)	H-25(UH)	P-51 (Winter Only)	Wright Flyer Rep
F-14A	H-53(CH) Cockpit	P-55-CS(XP)	X-28
F-16 Cockpit	HA-1112-M1L	P-80	
F/A-18	Heath Parasol	PT-13D-BW/N2S	

Lake Orion - Canterbury Village Toy Shop, 2369 Joslyn Ct, 48361, SE-5A Replica

Lansing - Michigan Historical Museum, 717 West Alliegan St, 517-373-3559, 48918
Mon-Fri 9-4, Sat 10-4, Sun 1-5, Free Adm, Gift Shop, Daily Except Mondays.
B-24 Nose Section

Lapeer - Yankee Air Force Mid-Michigan 3rd Division, Lapeer Airport, 1232 Roods
Lake Rd, 48446-8366, 810-664-6966, These Aircraft Are In Storage:
A-6	F-84K	F-84F(RF)	Stinson Model 10A	UH-1D

Ludington - Mason Cnty Airport, E Ave, 49431, 231-843-2049, T-38

Marquette - KI Sawyer AFB, 49843, 906-346-6511, 41 BMW/MAT, B-52D   F-101B (2ea)

33

Mt Clemens - American Legion Post 4, 401 Groesbeck, F-101

Selfridge Military Air Museum, 127WG/MU, 2733 C St, Bldg 1011, Mail: Box 43,
48045, 586-307-5035, Fax 307-6646, April-Oct, Sat-Sun 12-4:30, Closed ED,
$3 Donation, Gift Shop, www.selfridgeairmuseum.org

A-4B	F-4C	F-101C(RF)	O-2A
A-7D	F-16A	F-102A(TF)	P-3B
B-26C(GB)	F-84F	F-106A(NF)	S-2F
B-57A(RB)	F-84F(RF)	FG-1D	SNB-5
C-45B	F-86A	H-1F(AH)	T-33A
C-130A	F-100D	H-1H(UH)	U-3A
C-131D	F-100F	HH-52A	Nike-Ajax & Hercules

Muskegon - Hidden Cove Park, Norton Shores, Mona Lake, BS 96, UH-1

Oscoda - Yankee Air Force Wurtsmith Division, Oscoda-Wurtsmith Airport,
Mail: POB 664, 48750, 989-739-7555, Fax 739-1974, Mid May-Mid Oct Fri-Sun 11-3
Adm Adult 3, Uchild Under 12 $2, Gift Shop, Restoration Facility Viewable, Library
www.wurtsmith-yaf-museum.org, email: YAF@theenchantedforset.com,
(See Aircraft Status Codes Page 1)

Barracuda Homebuilt	(D) L-9B	(S) T-33A-1-LA	(S)
CG-4A	(P) L-19A-CE	(P) T-33A-5-LO	(P)
DC-8-55JT	(O) Link Trainer	(P) Stinson 10A	
H-1D(UH)-BF	(D) Sperry Messenger	(P)	

Plainwell - Plainwell Municipal Airport, 630 10th St, 49080-1005, 269-685-5343, T-38

Saginaw - Yankee Air Force Saginaw Valley Division, Harry Browne Airport,
Airport Number 989-754-2459, 4821 Jones St 48601, Not Available to Public
DC-65 (L-2B) Flyable   L-4 Replica Project

Sterling Heights - Freedom Hill McComb County Park, Metropolitan Parkway Between Schoenherr &
Utica Rds, F-4,   HU-1,   M60A1 Tank   US Navy Torpedo Mk.14

MINNESOTA

Alexandria - Alexandria Airport, Chandler Field, 2 Mi SW of City, 210 Nokomis St
56308, 320-762-1544, 762-2111,   T-33

Blaine - American Wings Air Museum, NW Corner of Anoka County Airport, 8891 Airport Rd NE,
55449, 763-786-4146, Tue & Wed Evenings, Sat 8-5, Mail: POB 49322, 1260 Colorado Ave
St Paul, MN 55112-0901, www.americanwings.org

An-2	H-34D(CH)	O-2	OV-1D
AO-1A	L-2M	OV-1 Cockpit	S2F-1
JOV-1A	L-3B	OV-1B	T-34A
JOV-1C	O-1E	OV-1C	

Airport, L-39, Ryan Navion B;   SE Asia Cammo, C-123 (2ea)

Golden Wings Flying Museum, 8891 Airport Rd, Anoka County Airport, C-6, 55449, 763-786-5004
Greg Herrick's Collection, www.goldenwingsmuseum.com, All Flying Except (R)=Restoration

Aero Car	Ford 4-AT (R)	PT-19	Stinson SM-7A (R)
Aeronca C-3	Hawker Hurricane	PT-23A	Stinson SM-6000-B
Alliance Argo	Interstate S-1-A	PT-26 (2ea)	Stinson SM-1B
Arrow Sport M (R)	Keystone K-84 (R)	Sikorsky S-39-C (R)	Taylor Aerocar
Avro Avian	Krutzer K-5	SM-6000-B	TG-1A
Buhl Sport Airsedan	KR-34C (R)	Spartan C2-60	Travel Air A-6000-A
Call-Air A-4 (R)	Kreutzer K-5	Stearman	Waco CUC-1
Fairchild F-45 (R)	N2S-4(A75L3)	Stinson A Tri-Motor (R)	Waco UKC
FC-2-W2	Paramount Cabinair (R)	Stinson C2-60 (R)	YPT-9
Fleetwings Seabird	PT-6F	Stinson Detroiter (R)	

Brainerd - Crow Wing County Regional Airport, 3 Mi NE of City, 218-829-6873, F9F-6

Chisholm - Minnesota Museum of Mining, 218-254-5543, F-94C

Duluth - Duluth Int'l Airport, 6 Mi NW of City, 218-727-2968, F-4

Lake Superior Squadron 101, 4931 Airport Rd, Hangar S101, Duluth International Airport Duluth,
55811, 218-733-0639, www.cafduluth.org, B-25 Simulator, Link Trainer, PBY-6A, PBY-6ACF

Eden Prairie - Planes of Fame East, Flying Cloud Field, 14771 Pioneer Trail, County Rd 1
952-941-2633, Restoration Only of: P-47   P-51D   T-28

Wings of the North, 9960 Flying Cloud Dr, Suite 204, 55347, 952-746-6100
http://www.wingsofthenorth.org, email: info@wotn.org, AT-6

Fountain - Fillmore County Museum, 55935, 507-268-4449, Limited Hours, Pietenpohl

Minneapolis - Jim Johns, 612-881-1797, 9108 Logan Ave, 55400
AT-6 Harvard   BT-13   L-13   TBM-3

34

Minnesota Air Guard Museum, Temporarily Closed for F-16 Crews, All Aircraft in Airpark
POB 11598, ANG, Minneapolis-St Paul, International Airport, 1 Scanlan Plaza, 55111-0592,
612-713-2523, Sat-Sun 11-4, April 15-Oct 15, Winter 2nd & 3rd Sat 11-4, Gift Shop,
Curator: Gen Alfred C Schwab,Jr, www.mnangmuseum.org

A-12(SR-71)	C-131E	F-94C	L-4
BC-1A(AT-6)	Curtiss Oriole	F-101(Black)	MiG-15
C-45	F-4C(RF)	F-101B	O-47
C-47B	F-4D	F-102A	P-51D
C-97	F-4E(RF)	H-1H(UH)	T-33A
C-130A	F-89H	JN-6H	A-7

Minneapolis/St.Paul Int'l Airport, Wold Chamberlin Field, 6 Mi SW of
City, Gate 12 West side of Main Lobby, 612-726-5032,
Spirit of St Louis Replica,   Waco 125 Gate 15
Link Trainer at North West Air Lines   Curtiss Pusher Gate 12

St Paul - CAF S Minnesota Wing, Wing Leader: Kent Smith, Hangar #3, Fleming Rd
55073, 651-459-7580, www.cafsmw.org,

B-25J	Harvard Mk IV	P-51C
BT-13A	L-5A	PBY-6A

Minnesota Air & Space Museum, Holman Field Airport, POB 75654, 55175
651-291-7925, DC-7   Steco Aerohydro-Plane

Stewartville - Carr Care Center, 211 S Main St, 55976, 320-533-8175, Culver Dart

Winoma - Max Conrad Airfield, Winoma Mncpl Airport, F9F-5, O-1, T-33

Winoma Technical Institute,

C-45	Erocoupe	Luscombe 8	Taylorcraft
Cessna 2ea	Hiller	PA-31	Unident Aztec
Colt	L-19	S-61	

MISSISSIPPI

Bay St Louis - NASA's National Space Technology Laboratories, Visitor Center Bldg,
1200, NSTL, 39529, 228-688-2211

Biloxi - Keesler AFB, 39534-5000, 228-377-1110

F-104C	F-101C(RF)	T-33A
F-105D	T-28	F-100(YF)

Columbus - Columbus AFB, 39701-5000, 662-434-7322   T-37B   T-38A

Jackson - Jackson ANG, Jackson Municipal Airport, Allen C Thompson Field,
39208-0810, 601-968-8321, 173rd TAG, A-26B   F-84F(RF)   F-101C(RF)

Jackson AFB Museum, Hawkins Field, 39201, 601-373-1574, 965-5790

National Agricultural Aviation Museum / Jim Buch Ross Mississippi Ag &
Forestry Museum, 1150 Lakeland Dr, 601-354-6113, www.msaaa.com/naam.htm

CAF - Mississippi Wing, Wing Leader: Robert L Bates, POB 16907,
39236-6907, 601-992-1074,   C-45

Meridian - NAS, T-2A

Petal - M W Hamilton Machine Museum, 39465, 601-583-9117 / 583-8836
Aircraft Restorations - All Aircraft Semi-Restored

B-25J	C-47	F9F	PT-17
BT-13	DC-3	HUB-1	

McLaurin - Armed Forces Museum at Camp Shelby, 12 Mi S of Hattiesburg on Hwy 49
601-558-2757, Mon-Fri 9-4, Sat-Sun 1-5, Free Adm, CH-54

MISSOURI

Branson - Veterans Memorial Museum, 1250 W 76 Country Music Blvd, 65616, 417-336-2300
   Fax: 336-2301, Daily 8-9pm, Adm Adult $10, www.veteransmemorialbranson.com,   P-51

Chillicothe - Chillicothe Municipal Airport, 64601, 660-646-5270, F-105

Kansas City - Airline History Museum Inc, 201 NW Lou Holland Dr, Hangar 9
   64116, 816-421-3401, 513-9484, Mon-Sat 10-4, Sun 11-5, Closed Holidays
   Adm Adult $7, $6 Snrs 65, $3 6-13, Under 6 Free, Gift Shop,
   Restoration Facility, Dir: Ona Gieschen, www.airlinehistorymuseum.com
   L-1049H,   Martin 404   DC-3

Knob Noster - Whiteman AFB, 351 CSG/DEER, 65305, 660-687-1110,
   B-29   B-52D   B-47B   C-97G(KC)   H-1F(UH)

Maryland Heights - Historic Aircraft Restoration Museum, Dauster Flying Field,
Creve Coeur Airport, 3127 Creve Coeur Mill Rd, 63146, 314-434-3368, Fax 878-6453
Sat-Sun 10-4, By Appt, Adm Adult $10, Child 5-12 $3, Under 5 Free,
Rides: SNJ $75, Stearman $50, www.historicaircraftrestorationmuseum.org

Aeronca C-3	JN-4D	Stinson SM.8A
AN-2	KR-31	Timm Collegiate
AT-6(SNJ)	KR-21	Travel Air 4000 (R)
C-2	Monocoupe Clipwing	Waco ARE
Curtiss Air Sedan	Monocoupe 90	Waco ATO
Culver Dart	Mooney Mite	Waco JWM
Curtiss Robin (R)	N3N-3	Waco QCF-2
DH-89	NB-8G	Waco UBA
Driggs Dart	Pietenpohl Air Camper	Waco VKS-6
Fairchild CBA	Piper Vegabond	Zenith Biplane (R)
Flagg	PT-22	
Hisso Standard	Stearman	

St Charles - CAF Missouri Wing, St Charles County Smart Field, Mail: POB 637
636-250-4515

A6M	B-25	P-63
AT-6	L-3B	SNJ

St Joseph - St Joseph ANG, 139 TAG/CC, Rosecrans Memorial Airport 64503,
816-271-1300,   C-97L(KC)

St Louis - McDonnell Douglas Prologue Room, McDonnell Blvd, & Airport Rd,
Lambert St Louis Airport, Box 516, 63166, 314-232-5421, 10 Mi NW, June-August,
Mon-Sat 9-4, Curator: Larry Merritt, Replica Gemini,   Mercury Capsules

McDonnell Planetarium, 5100 Clayton Rd, 63110, 314-535-5810, Daily 9-5,
Adm Adult $1.25, Child $0.75,   PGM-17   Spacecraft

National Personnel Records Center, 9700 Page Ave, 314-538-4261
H-1B(UH)   Bradley Fighting Vehicle   WWII 8" Howitzer

Missouri History Museum, Forest Park, 314-746-4599, Ryan NYP Replica

MO ANG St Louis, Lambert Field, 63145, 314-263-6356, F-4E, F-15A, F-100D

Museum of Transportation, 3015 Barrett Station Rd, Lambert St Louis
Int'l Airport, 63122-3398, 314-965-7998, Daily 9-5,Closed TD, CD, ND, Adm Adult $4
Child 5-12 & Snr 65 $1.50, Under 5 Free, Gift Shop 965-5709, Restoration Facility
www.museumoftransport.org, C-47A(VC)   T-33 Project

St Louis Lambert Int'l Airport, Terminal Entrance C Concourse,
17 Mi W of City, 314-532-2222, Monocoupe

St Louis Aviation Museum, Spirit of St Louis Airport, POB 5867, 63134, 17 Miles
West of City, JS McDonnell Personnel Cart

AT-6	F-101	Meyers
F-2H-2N	Fairchild	Stearman

Sikeston, Sikeston Veterans Park, One Industrial Dr, 63801, 573-471-2498, F-4J, M-60 Tank

Springfield - Air & Military Museum of the Ozarks, CAF Ozark Mountain Squadron,
Springfield Regional, 2305 E Kearney St, North off I-65, 417-864-7997, Fax 882-0188,
May 1-Oct 31, Thur-Sat 1-5; Nov 1-Feb 28, Thur-Sat 1-4, or Appt, Artifacts,
www.ammomuseum.org, AH-1

MONTANA

Dutton - American Legion Freeborn Post 64, 201 Main East, 59433, 406-476-3304, F-104

Great Falls - Great Falls ANG, Great Falls Int'l Airport, 59401-5000, 406-727-4650,
F-86A   F-89J   F-106A   T-33

Lion's Park, 10th Ave, F-102A

Malmstrom AFB & Airpark, 314 Space Wing/MU 2177th St North, 59402-5000, 406-731-2705
June-Aug Mon-Sat 12-3, Apr-May & Sept-Oct Mon-Fri 12-3, Rest of Year Mon,
Wed & Fri 12-3,

B-25M	C-97L(KC)	F-101F	T-33A
B-57B(EB)	F-84F	H-1F(UH)	

Helena - Montana Historical Society's Museum, Helena Municipal Airport,
South Side Corner, 59620, 406-444-, Summer Mon-Sat 9-5, Curator: Larry Sommerrchibald,
DH 60 #179, UH-1

College of Technology, 2300 Poplar(Airport)Rd, 59601, 800-241-4882, www.hct.umontana.edu/
EC-121   F-89   F-102A   H-19(S-65)   T-39

Firefighting Training Center, Helena Municipal Airport, A-7D

Missoula - Museum of Mountain Flying, Missoula Int'l Airport, 713 S 3rd St West, 59801,
406-549-8488, May-Oct Daily 10-5, Thur-Mon Rest of Year, Adm Adult $4, Snr/Mil $2, Student $1
C-45   C-47(DC-3)   J-3   Homebuilts   PT-17   Smokejumper & Parachutes Artifacts

Smokejumper Center,US Dept of Agriculture, US 10W, Aerial Fire Depot
Airport Terminal, Box 6, 59801, 406-329-4900, Memorial Day - July 4th Mon-Fri
8:30-5, July 4th-Labor Day 8:30-5 Daily, Hourly Tours, Curator: Wayne Williams

Beech 58P	Cessna 206	DHC 6
Beech 99	DC-3	Sherpa C203A

NEBRASKA

Bellevue - Strategic Air and Space Museum, Mahoney State Park, 28210 West Park Hwy,
68003, Exit 426, Off I-80, Mail: POB 8343, Omaha, NE, 68108-0343, 800-358-5029,
Daily 9-5, Closed TD, CD, ND, Adm Adult $7, Sr $6, 5-12 $3, Under 5 Free, Gift Shop,
Snack Bar, Curator Carl Janssen, www.strategicairandspace.com

A6M3	B-58A	F-101B	Ki-43
Atlas D	C-47A	F-102A	MiG-21
A-26B	C-54D	F-105	P-40C
B-17G	C-97G(KC)	F-111A(FB)	SR-71A
B-25J (2ea)	C-119G	F6F	T-29A
B-29(BA)	C-124A	H-19B(UH)	T-33A
B-36J	C-133B	H-21B(CH)	T-39A
B-45C(RB)	C-135C(EC)	He-111	U-2C
B-47E	F-84F	HU-16B	Vulcan B-2 Mk.II
B-52B(RB)	F-86F	ICBM,Minuteman I	XF-85
B-57E	F-86H	JN-4	

Fairbury - Engels J T Airport, 68352, 402-729-3248, F-100

Lincoln - Lincoln ANG, Lincoln Municipal Airport, 68524-1897, 402-473-1326, 155th TRG
F-4C(RF)   F-84F(RF)   F-86L   T-33A

Minden - Harold Warp Pioneer Village Foundation, POB 68, 68959-0068, 138 E Hwy 6,
800-445-4447, 308-832-1181, Daily 8-5, Closed CD, Adm Adult $8, Child $3.50,
Under 6 Free, Manager: Marvin Mangers, Gift Shop, Cafe 832-1550, All Indoor Exhibit,
Motel and Campground in Village, Airport .5 Mi North; www.pioneervillage.org

Bensen B-6	Ercoupe 67	P-59	Swallow
Bensen B-7	Hartman	PA-23	Weed Hopper
Cessna	Heath Parasol 5	PCA-2	Wright Flyer
Curtiss	J-2	Sikorsky	
Curtiss JN9	JN-4D	Stinson Detroiter 30	

Omaha - Freedom Park, 2497 Freedom Park Rd, 68110, 402-345-1959, From I-29 Go W
on I-480 Then N on Freedom Park Rd, Apr 15-Oct 31, Daily, 10-5, Adm Adult $4,
Snr $3, Child $2.50, Group Rates, www.freedomparknavy.org

		USS Hazard AM-240 Mine Sweeper
A-4D	H-1(UH)	USS Marlin SST-2 (Submarine)
A-7	SH-3	USS Towers DDG-9 Captains Gig

Offutt AFB, 68113-5000, Hangar 20 E, 402-294-1110, 8 Mi S of Omaha,
B-17G   B-52   C-135(KC)

S Sioux City - Martin Flying Service, W. Hwy 20, 68776, 402-494-3667,   A-7D

NEVADA

Carson City - Yesterday's Flyers Ltd, Carson City Airport, 3 Mi NE of City, 775-882-1551

Bellanca	Curtiss Robin	N3N	Stinson SR-4E
BT-13	Depordussin	Starduster II	T-28
Curtiss Junior	Pfalz D.XIII	Steen Skybolt	

Fallon - Naval Air Station Fallon, 4755 Pasture Rd, 2 Mi NE of City, 89496-5000
775-426-5161, AP = Air Park; CU = Credit Union; MG = Main Gate

A-4	MG	AD-4B	MG	F-16	AP	MiG-23	AP
A-4	AP	E-2C	AP	F-86	AP	RA-5C	CU
A-7	MG	F-4	AP	FA-18	AP	UH-1	MG
A-7E	AP	F-8	AP	MiG-15	AP		
A-6	AP	F-14	AP	MiG-17	AP		

Indian Springs - City Park, West 1 Block Off I-95, Between the 2 exits, F-84F

Jean - Casino, South Side of the Highway, WWI Replica Fighters From Ceiling

Las Vegas - CAF Nevada Wing, Wing Leader: Lois Larson, POB 27476, 89126-1476, AT-19

Lost Birds, 3172 N Rainbow Blvd, Mail: Box 266, 89108, 775-646-6524,
Contact Doug Scroggins, www.LostBirds.com,

B-720B Boeing(Cockpit)	CV-880-22 Convair	KC-97G (Cockpit)
Boeing 737-222 (Cockpit)	DC-3 (Cockpit)	L-1011 (Cockpit)
C-402 Cessna (Fuse)	F-27A Fairchild (Cockpit)	

McCarran Int'l Airport, 5757 Wayne Newton Blvd, 2nd Level Above Baggage Claim,
Near Scenic Airlines, 89119, 775-261-5192, POB 11005, 89111, Open 24 Hrs,
Free Adm, Ford 5AT, Cessna 172,   C-124 next to Comfort Inn South

Military Heritage Command, POB 12543, 89112-0543, 800-347-4385, Dir: Gen D Smith,
P2V-7(SP2H)

Nellis AFB, 157 NFWW, 89191-5000, 775-643-1800,
F-4C	F-86	F-105G
F-5E	F-100D	F-117A

Reno - May ANG Base, Cannon Int'l Airport, 89502, 775-788-4500, RF-101B

Reno-Stead Airport, 4895 Texas Ave, 89506-1237, 775-328-6570,
MiG-15	MiG-17	MiG-19

Nevada Aviation Historical Society, 3035 Slatter Court, 89503, 775-747-3888, F-86D

NEW HAMPSHIRE

Danville - Atlantic Warbirds, 23 Pleasant St, 03819-3221, Mail: POB 715, 01845,
North Andover, MA, 603-382-3493, DC-4 (C-54)

Mason - Dakota Aviation Museum, 492 Old Ashbury Rd, 03048, 603-878-1622

Nashua - FAA Air Traffic Control Center, A-4

Wolfeboro - Wright Museum of American Enterprise, 77 Center St, 03894, 603-569-1212
Army Spotter Plane, 2 Tanks

NEW JERSEY

Fairfield - Yankee Air Force NE Division, Caldwell-Wright (Essex County) Airport
171 Passaic Ave, 07004-3502, Mail: POB 1729, 07007-1729, Not Open to Public
C.51 Pembroke (Storage)	DC-62 (L-2C)(Flyable)	L-13A (Storage)

Farmingdale - Berlin Airlift Historical Society, Mail To: POB 782, 07727
732-818-0034, www.spiritoffreedom.org,   C-54   C-97G

Ft Monmouth, US Army Communications-Electronics Museum, Kaplan Hall Bldg 275,
07703-5103, 732-532-4390, 542-7267, Mon-Fri 12-4, Free Adm,
Curator: Mendy Rosewitz, ANTSC-54 Satellite

Lakehurst - Navy Lakehurst Historical Society, POB 328, 08733, 732-244-8861
www.nlhs.com, Crash Site Tour & Artifacts from Hindenburg

Naval Air E Center,	A-7B	E-2B

Lumberton - Air Victory Museum, 68 Stacy Haines Rd, South Jersey Regional Airport,
08055, 609-267-6268, Fax: 702-1852, Daily 10-4, Nov 1-March 31 Closed Sun
Adm Adult $4, Snrs $3, Child 4-13 $2, Gift Shop, www.airvictorymuseum.org/
A-4B	F-4B	F-104G	H-53D(RH)
A-7A	F-14A	FP-404	
E-2B	F-86L	H-1A(AH)	

Millville - Millville Army Air Field Museum, Municipal Airport, 1 Leddon St,
08332, 856-327-2347, Mon-Fri 10-2, Sat-Sun 10-4, Closed Holidays, Free Adm
Gift Shop, www.p47millville.org
Link Trainer,	A-4

Pomona - Air National Guard - Atlantic City Int'l Airport, F-100F,   F-106B

Rio Grande - Cape May, Naval Air Station Wildwood Foundation, Cape May Airport,
500 Forrestal Rd, 609-886-8787, Spring-Summer: Mon-Fri 8-5, Sat-Sun 9-5,
Fall-Winter: Mon-Fir 8-4, Sat-Sun 9-3, www.usnasw.org
A-4	H-6(OH)	MiG-15	T-33
H-1(AH)	H-52A(HH)	PT-17	T-33 2Seater
H-1(UH)	L-19	T-28	TBM

Rockaway - Picatinny Arsenal Museum, 07801, Rt 15, Pitcatinny Base, Phipps Rd,
973-724-2797, Tue, Wed & Thur 9-3, Outdoor Displays Open Daily, Free Adm,
AGM-22 M3	M31	M51

Sea Girt - National Guard Militia Museum, P.O. Box 277, 08750, 732-974-5966
Gift Shop, Library, Artifacts

Teterboro - Aviation Hall Of Fame & Museum of New Jersey, 400 Fred Wehran Dr,
Teterboro Airport, 07608, 201-288-6344, Fax 288-5666, Tue-Sun 10-4, Adm Adult $5
12& Under $3, Gift Shop, www.njahof.org
H-1 (UH)H-13	Lockheed Bushmaster	Cobra
H-52A(HH)	Martin 202 Airliner	Stinson Voyager

NAPC Trenton,	A-4B

Wrightstown - McGuire AFB Museum, 08562, 609-724-1100, 724-1110, 438 MAW/SEN,
C-118A	F-4	F-84F	P-38L	F-105B

NEW MEXICO

Alamogordo - Holloman AFB, 833 CSG/CD 88330-5000, 505-479-6511,

F-4C	F-84F	F-100D	F-105D
F-80C	F-86E	F-104C	

New Mexico Museum of Space History, 877-333-6589, Mail: POB 5430, 88311,
Gift Shop, Daily 9-5, Adm Adult $2.50, Snrs $2.25, Child 4-12 $2,
Under 4 Free, IMAX Theater, Shuttle Camp $85-450, www.spacefame.org
Little Joe Rocket   Satellites,   Sonic Wind I Rocket Sled,

Albuquerque - New Mexico ANG Complex, Bldg 1055, 87100, 505-678-3114, A-7D, F-100A
At Falcon Rd & Air Guard Rd - F-80, P-51
At 551st Op Sq, Bldg 4279, Frances St & Hercules Way SE - CH-3

Albuquerque Int'l Airport, 4 Mi SE of City, 505-768-3830, Coordinator:
Jane Sprague,   Ingram/Foster Biplane

Anderson/Abruzzo Int'l Balloon Museum, Opens Fall 2005, 6121 Indian School Rd NE,
87110, South End of Fiesta Park, POB 16314, 87191, 505-271-12119, Fax: 271-2358,
Cafe 880-0500, Theater, Gift Shop, www.balloonmuseum.org

CAF Lobo Wing, PO Box 20576, 87154-0576,   PT-26

Kirtland AFB, 58th Special Ops, 87117-5000, Doris St & Aberdeen Ave,
Sgt Ronald Carrillo: 505-853-5856

CH-21B(2ea)	H-1F(UH)	H-13E(OH)	H-43(HH)
	H-5G	H-19F(UH)	HU-16A

At Eileen St & Aberdeen Ave : HH-34(S-58), PBY-5(OA-10), SC-47

National Atomic Museum, 1905 Mountain Rd NW, Mail: POB 5800, MS 1490, 87104,
505-245-2137, Daily 9-5, Closed ED, TD, CD, ND, Adm Adult $4, Over 55 &
Child 7-18 $3, Child Under 6 Free, Gift Shop, www.atomicmuseums.com

A-7C(TA)	B-52B	F-105D	ICBM	SM-2
B-29	CIM-10A	MGM-13A	TM-61C

Angel Fire - Vietnam Veterans National Memorial, NW of Angel Fire on US64,
28 Miles E of Taos on US64, Contact: David Westphall, POB 608, 87710,
505-377-6900, Fax: 377-3223,   UH-1H

Carlsbad - Carlsbad Museum & Art Center, 418 West Fox, 88220, 505-887-0276,
Mon-Sat 10-5, Free Adm, Artifacts

Cavern City Mncpl Airport, 1505 Terminal Dr, 88220, 505-887-9001,   AT-11

Clovis - Cannon AFB, Public Affairs, 27 FW/PA, Cannon Airpark, 88103-5000,
505-784-4131, PA: Michael Pierson, 1Lt, Historian: 784-2460,
www.cannon.af.mil/default.stm,

F-80B	F-86H	F-101A	
F-84C	F-100D	F-111A *	T-33A

City Display, 7th & West Hwy 60 & Hwy 84,   F-111F
www.cannon.af.mil/facts/clovis.htm,

Gallup - Gallup Municipal Airport, Old Hwy 66,   T-38

Hobbs - CAF New Mexico Wing, Flying Museum, POB 1260, Lea County Airport,
505-395-2377, Daily 8-Sunset, Wing Leader: Philip L Ross

BT-14	C-45	Me-108	SNJ-4

National Soaring Foundation, POB 684, 88241, 505-392-6032, http://207.149.139.31/nsf/

Blanik L-13	Grob 103	Schweizer 1-26	Schweizer 2-33

Las Cruces - Las Cruces Int'l Airport, 8960 Zia Blvd, 88000, 505-525-2762,

C-46	F-100F

Southwest Aviation, Las Cruces Int'l A, 88000, 505-524-8047, 7 Mi West of City,

A-26B	C-46	PV-2

White Sands Missile Range Museum & Park, Las Cruces or El Paso Gate, 88002-5047,
505-678-2250, Mon-Fri 8-4, Sat-Sun 10-3, Free Adm, Gift Shop 678-8824,
www.wsmr-history.org C-6A(VC)   H-1M(UH)   V-2 Rocket

Melrose - Melrose Bombing Range, N of Hwy 84, In Town, 505-784-6644,
www.cannon.af.mil/facts/melrose.htm,   F-100

Moriarty - Southwest Soaring Museum, POB 3626, 87035, 505-832-0755, www.swsoaringmuseum.org

B-10	KA-6	SG-1A	TG-4A
KA-4	MSK	TG-1	Zoegling Rep

Portales - Hwy 70 & Ave K, Between 1st & 2nd St, Contact: Robert Meeks, 181 Airport
Rd, 80130, 505-478-2863, www.cannon.af.mil/facts/portales.htm, F-111F

Roswell - Int'l UFO Museum & Research Center, 114 N Main, 88202, 505-625-9495,
Fax 625-1907, Daily 9-5, Free Adm, Gift Shop, Library, www.iufomrc.com

Roswell Goddard Rocket Museum, 100 W Eleventh St, 505-624-6744,
Mon-Sat 9-5, Sun & Holidays 1-5, Free Adm,

UFO Enigma Museum, 6108 S Main, 505-347-2275, Mon-Sat 9:30-5, Sun 12-5, Adult $1,
Child $0.50

Santa Teresa - War Eagles Air Museum, 8012 Airport Rd, 88008, Santa Teresa Airport,
Mail: POB 1225, 88008, 505-589-2000, Tue-Sun 10-4, Adm Adult $5, Sr $4,
Child Under 12 Free, Gift Shop, www.war-eagles-air-museum.com

A-4 Simulator	CW Simulator	Hawker Sea Fury	P-51D(TF)
A7-E	DC-3	J-3	T-28
A-26C	DH 82	L-13A	T-33
AT-6F	F4U-4	Link Trainer	T-38A
AT-19	F-84F	MiG-15 2 Seater	Target Drone
BT-13	F-86 Mk VI	MiG-21PFM	TBM-3E
C-5A Simulator	FJ-2	P-38	TU-2
C-141 Trainer	Fi-156	P-40E	
Cessna 140A	Great Lakes Sport	P-51D	

NEW YORK

Albion - Vintage Aircraft Group, 4906 Pine Hill Rd, 14411, www.vintageaircraftgroup.org
PT-26 Project   T-33 Project

Amherst - Amherst Museum, 3755 Tonawanda Creek Rd, 14228-1599, 716-889-1440, GA-36

Bayport - Bayport Aerodome, Hangar 23, POB 728, 11705, Rte 97 Go West on Church St to Vitamin Dr,
June-Sept Sat-Sun 10-4, Adm Free, www.bayportaerodrome.org

Aeronca C3	DH 82C	PA-20
Aeronca 7AC	Fleet 16B	PT-26
Aeronca 11AC	N2S-3(V)	Stearman
Brunner-Winkle Bird	N3N-3	Tiger Moth
Cessna C-140	Nicholas-Beazley NB-86	

Binghamton - Link Flight Simulation Corp, Colesville Rd, 13904, 607-721-5465, Link Trainer

Binghamton Regional Airport, 13901, 607-763-4471, 763-4456, Link Trainer

Brooklyn - Northeast Aircraft Restoration Facility & Museum, Floyd Bennett Field
718-338-3799, Mon, Thur & Sat 9-1, www.narf.org

A-4	DC-3	SH-3A Coast Guard Helio
C-45 Twin Beech	P2V	HU-16 Albatross Coast Guard
C-54	PBY	Fantasy Island Sea Plane

Buffalo - Amherst Museum, 3755 Towanda Rd, 14228, Aircraft

Buffalo & Erie County Historical Museum, 25 Nottingham Court, 14216,
716-873-9644, Tue-Sat 10-5, Sun 12-5, Adm Adult $1.50, Child $0.75, Family $3,
Senior Citizen $0.90,   J-1

Buffalo & Erie County Naval & Military Park, 1 Naval Park Cove, 14202,
716-847-1773, Daily April 1-Oct 31 10-5, Nov Sat-Sun Only, Adm Adult $6.00,
6-12 $3.50, 5 & Under or Senior Citizen Free, Curator: James W Swinnich,
www.buffalonavalpark.org, npark@ci.buffalo.ny.us

F-101F	P-39Q "Snooks 2nd"	USS Little Rock (CLG-4)
FJ-4B	PTF-17 Boat	USS Croaker SSK-246
M-84 A.P.C.	UH-1H	USS Sullivans (DD-537)
M-41 Tank	X-RON 1	

Buffalo Intl Airport, New Terminal, Bell 47

Calverton - Grumman Memorial Park, I-495 Go W on Rte 25(Edwards Ave)to Rte 25A,
Daily 9-5, Mail: POB 147, 11933, 631-369-9449, Fax 9489, www.grummanpark.org, F-14A

Cheecktowaga - Cal Span Cheecktowaga Airport, 42 Stone Church Rd, 716-632-7500,
A-26   X-22

Coronia - New York Hall Of Science 47-01 111th St, 11368, 718-699-0005,
Dir: Marily Hoyt, Atlas-Mercury   Saturn V Boat Tail   Titan II-Gemini

Elmira - National Soaring Museum, 51 Soaring Hill Dr, 14903-9204, 607-734-3128,
Fax 732-6745, Daily 10-5, Adm Adult $3, Child $2, Curator: Paul Prunier
www.soaringmuseum.org

Albatross	CG-4A	Primary LNE-1	Teasdale
Baby Bowlus	Hutter	Rigid Midget	TG-3A
BG-12BD	Minimoa	SGS 1-19 & 26	Wright Glider #5

Farmingdale - American Airpower Museum, New Highway South of Conklin Ave,
Thur-Sun 10:30-4, Adm Adult $9, Snr $6, Child $4, www.americanairpowermuseum.org

A-1	B-17	C-47	L-39	P-47
AT-6	B-25	F4U-1	P-40	TBM

Garden City - Cradle of Aviation Museum, Lindbergh Ave, Mail: One Davis Ave,
11530, 516-572-4111, Daily 10-5, Adm Adult $7, Child 2-14 $6, Gift Shop
IMAX Theater Adult 8.50, Child 2-14 $6.50, Museum & Theater Adult $14.50 Child 11,
www.cradleofaviation.org

A-6F	F6F-5	TBM-3E
A-10A Cocpit	F9F-7	Veligdans Monerai
Aircraft Eng Co Ace	Fleet 2	Wright EX VinFiz
Bleriot-Queen XI	G-21	XRON-1
Boeing 707 Cockpit	G-63	Spacecraft, Missiles
Breese Penguin	Gyrodyne 2C	Convair/Sperry SAM-N-7
Brunner-Winkle Bird	JN-4	Douglas M-6 Nike Hercules
C-47 Simulator	Lilienthal	Fairchild Petrel
Cassutt B	Merlin Glider	Goddard A-Series Rocket
CG-4	NGT(T-46)	Grumman Missile Rigel
Commonwealth	OV-1B	Grumman Echo Cannister 7
Convertawings A	P-47N	Grumman AWS
Convair 340 Cockpit	Paramotor FX-1	Grumman LM Simulator
Curtiss Robin 50C	Peel Z-1 Glider	Grumman LM L-13, LTA-1
E-2C	QH-50C	Grumman LRV Molab
F-11A	RC-3	Grumman TBM
F-14A & Cockpit	Ryan B-1	Maxson AQM-37A Drone
F-84B	Ryan NYP	Maxson A6M-12C Bullpup
F-84F	S-56	Republic JB-2 Loon
F-105B	S2F & Cockpit	Republic Rocket Terrapin
F-105D Simulator	S4C	Rockwell Command Module
F3F	Sperry AT	Sperry SAM-N-7 Terrier
F4F-3	Sperry M1	Sputnik Satilite

Geneseo - 1941 Aircraft Group, Geneseo Airport, 3489 Big Tree Lane, 14454, Mail: POB 185, 14454
585-243-2100, April 14-Nov 1 Mon, Wed, Fri, 10:30-4, Closed TD, CD, ND, Adm Adult $4,
Child 12 & Under $1, Restoration Facility, www.1941hag.org

AD-4W	Ercoupe 415C YO-55 2ea	L-17	Me-208
AN-2 (2ea)	L-2	L-21B	
C-119G	L-16A	Lancair Simulator	

Ghent - Parker-O' Malley Air Museum, 435 Old Rte 20, SW Side of Columbia County Airport,
POB 216, 12075, 518-392-7200, Curator: James McMahon, www.parkeromalley.org

Fleet 2	Me-108	Star Cavalier
Harvard IV	NE-1	Travel Air 4000
Link Trainer	PT-17	

Hammondsport - Curtiss Museum, 8419 Route 54, 14840, ½ Mile South of Hammondsport,
607-569-2160, Fax 569-2040, May 1-Oct 31, Mon-Sat 9-5, Sun 11-5, Nov 1-April 30,
Mon-Sat 10-4, Sun 12-5, Closed Mon-Wed Jan-Mar,TD,CE,CD,ND, Adm Adult $6, Snr $4.50,
Child 7-18 $3.50, 6 & Under Free, Gift Shop, Theater, Restoration Facility,
Curator: Kirk House, www.linkny.com/~curtiss/

C-46 (Project)	Curtiss June Bug	Link Trainer (Proj)	Silver Dart
Curtiss A-1 Triad	Curtiss Oriole	Mercury S-1 Racer	Target Drone
Curtiss D Pusher	Curtiss Robin	Mercury Chick	OX-5 Engine
Curtiss E Boat	Curtiss Wright Jr	OHM Special Racer	Curtiss Motorcycles
Chanute Glider	JN-4D	P-40 3/4 Scale	

Horseheads - Corning Regional Airport, 6 Mi NW of City, 607-739-5621,
Stuka Ju-87-B 7/8 Scale, By Richard H. Kurzenberger, Horseheads, NY

National Warplane Museum, 17 Aviation Dr, Elmira-Corning
Regional Airport, 14845, Off Route 17, Exit 51, 607-739-8200, Fax: 739-8374, Mon-Fri 10-4
Sat 9-5, Sun 11-5, Closed CD, ND, Adm Adult $7, 65+ $5.50, Child 6-17 $4, Under 6 Free, Exec Dir:
Stephen Low, Gift Shop, Snack Bar, Art Gallery, Theater, Restoration Facility,
Display Hangar, Wings of Eagles Airshow Third Weekend of September
www.wingsofeagles.com,

A-10A	C-45H(SNB)	H-6A(OH)	OV-1C
A-37B	F-14A	L-3B	PBY-6A
AT-6D	F2H-2P	LNE-1(X)(HH-2)	PT-17(N2S-3)
B-57A(RB)	F4-B	MiG 17	PT-19B
B-17G	FH-1	MiG 21	TBM-3E
BTD-1	H-1C(UH)	LNS-1(TG-2)	

Jamestown - Lucille M Wright Air Museum, Chautaqua County Airport, 20 Meadow Lane,
14701, 716-487-0838, Curator: Joseph T Minarovitch

Long Island City - The Cockpit, 595 Broadway, 718-925-5455,   AT-6

Manhattan - The Cockpit, 652 Broadway, 10012, 212-254-4000

Mayville - Dart Airport, POB 211, Route 430, 14757, 716-753-2160,
Mon-Fri 8-5 Appt Only, Summer Weekends, Free Adm, Owner Bob Dart

Curtiss Wright Jr	Heath Parasol	Mead Primary
Ercoupe 415	J-2	Melberg
Fleet 16B	J-3	Schweizer I-19

Moria - American Legion Post 939, Hwy 11 East of Town, T-38

New York City - Intrepid Sea-Air-Space Museum, 1 Intrepid Plaza, Pier 86, 46th &
12th, 10036, 212-245-0072, 2533, MD-LD 10-5, RoY Wed-Sun 10-5, Closed TD, CD, ND,
Adm Adult $10, Snr & Child 12-17 $7.50, 6-11 $5, 2-5 $1, Under 2 Free, Grp Discounts
Wheelchair & Active Military ½ Price, www.intrepidmuseum.org/index2.htm

A-3D	F11F-1	M-42 Duster Tank
A-4B	F3D (TF-10B)	M-60 Patton Tank
A-4D	F3F-2	Neptune Submersible
A-6A	F6F-5 Rep	RA-5C
A-7E	F9F	SB2C-4 Replica
AH-1J	FJ-3	SE5A
AV-8C	Gemini Capsule Rep	S-2PE
Apollo Capsule Rep	H-1A(UH)	S-58D
Boeing 707 Cockpit	H-1M(UH)	Sea Hawk F.1
Curtiss Pusher Rep	H-3S(OH)	SP-2E
Demoiselle Rep	H-21C	SR-71A(A-12 Actually)
E-1B	H-34 (UH)	Supermarine Scimitar F1
F-3B	H-52A(HH)	T-33A
F-3H	HU-16E	TS-2A
F-4N	LEM Grumman	TS-2E
F-14	Lunar Lander Rep	TV-2
F-16	H-13S(OH)	UH-34O
F-80F	H-23(OH) (2 ea)	Voisin Rep
F-84F	Mercury Aurora 7 Capsule	YF-17
USS Intrepid	USS Growler	USS Edson

Westchester County Airport Museum (HPN), 914-997-1612, Artifacts Only

Niagara Falls - Niagara Aerospace Museum, 345 Third St, POB 1181, 14304-8021,
716-278-0060, Daily 10-6, Closed ND, TD, CD, ED, Adm Adult $7, Snrs/Students $6,
Child 5-18 $4, Under 5 Free, Gift Shop, Theater, Restoration Facility,
www.niagaramuseum.org/, e-mail: niagaeromus@juno.com

Bell 47B-3	F-94G	J-2	X-22A
Bell 47H-1	GA-36	JN-4D	
Curtiss Robin	H-1F(AH)	P-39Q	
F-94A	I-23	Pietenpol Air Camper	

Niagara Falls ANG, Int'l Airport, 914 TAG/RMX, 14304-5000, 716-236-2000

F-100D	F-101F	F-101C(RF)	F-4C

Oriskany - Village of Oriskany, 13424, 315-736-3512,   A-4E

Plattsburg - Plattsburg AFB Military Museum, Route 22, 12901, 518-565-5000,
565-5165,   B-47E   F-111

Rhinebeck - Old Rhinebeck Aerodrome (See Top of Next Page)

Riverhead - Raceway Equipment, RD #2, BOX 92K, Horton Ave, 11901, 631-727-6191,
Mon-Fri 8:30-4:30, Sat By Appt, President: Joe Gertler

Aeronca C-3	C-78(UC)	L-19	Taylorcraft BC-12D
Birdwing Imperial	Emigh Trojan	Luscombe 8E	
Bleriot Original	J-3	Nieuport 27	

Talmage Field Aircraft Collection, Friars Head Farm, 36 Sound Ave, 631-727-0124, John Talmage

Aeronca Champ	Curtiss OX5 Engine	Hovercraft
Burnner CK Bird	Curtiss OXX6 Engine	Quick Kolt Seaplane
Continental R670	Fokker D VII Project	Rearwin Cloudster
Curtiss J6-7	Hispano-Suiza	Travel Air 4000

Rome - Griffiss AFB Museum, Mohawk Valley B-52 memorial, 13441-5000,
Contact: Henry P Smith Post 24, 325 Erie Vlvd W, 13440, 315-336-2680,
www.borg.com/~post24/monument.html,   B-52G

Scotia - Empire State Aerosciences Museum, Schenectady County Airport,
250 Rudy Chase Dr, (Route 50), 12302-4114, 518-377-2191, Tue-Sat- 10-4,
Summer Same & Sun 12-4, Adm Adult $5, Child 12-16 $2, Under 12 Free Gift Shop,
Restoration Facility, Research Library, Pres: Rowland Whiteman, www.cana.com/easm,
E-mail: esam@crisny.org , AKAGI Replica Aircraft Carrier,

A-4F (O)	Curtiss Pusher Rep (D)	H-1F(UH) (O)		RAND Kr-2	(S)
A-6E (O)	F-4D II (O)	H-6A(LOH) (O)		RP-1	(D)
A-7E (P)	F-14A (O)	Huntington Chum (D)	Sky Scooter Rep	(D)
A-10 (O)	F-84F (O)	J4 Javelin	(S)	Sonerai II	(D)
AKAGI Rep	F-86D	L-3	(P)	Starlite	(S)
B-26 (P)	F-101F (O)	Lockheed 10	(D)	Stits Skycoupe	(D)
C-47 (P)(O)	F-105G (O)	MiG-17F	(O)	STRAT M-21	(O)
C-123K (O)	Fisher 303 (S)	MiG-21MF	(O)	T-38	
Chanute Hang Glider(D)	GNAT (O)	Mooney Mite	(S)		

Shirley - Brookhaven L.I. Airport, Dwn Dr, 11967, 631-281-5100

Convair 240	Me-109	SNJ-4
Erocoupe F-1 (Fornaire)	Swift GC-1 Globe	

National Aviation & Transportation Center, Dowling College Annex, Brookhaven
Airport, Pitts Special   PT-17   PT-26

Rhinebeck - Old Rhinebeck Aerodrome, 44 Stone Church Rd, Mail: BOX 229, 12572
845-752-3200, Fax: 758-6481, May 15-Oct31, Daily 10-5, Adm Adult $6, Snrs $5
Child 6-10 $2, Under 6 Free, June 15-Oct 15 Sat-Sun Airshows 2pm, Adult $12,
Snrs $10, Child 6-10 $5, Gift Shop, Cafe, Restoration Viewing,
1929 New Standard Biplane Rides 15 Min $40 Per Person, www.oldrhinebeck.org/,
(1)=Pioneer Bldg, (2)=WWI Bldg,(3)=Lindberg Era Bldg, (4)=New Bldg,
(F)=On Field, (EF)=EastSide of Field.

(Aircraft)	(Building)	(Aircraft)	(Building)
Aeromarine 39B	(Pieces)	J-1	(Pieces)
Aeromarine Klemm	(3)	J-2	(F)
Aeronca C-3	(F)	J-3	(EF)
Albatross D-Va	(2)	J-5A	(EF)
Albree Pigeon Fras.	(2)	JN-4D	(F)
American Eagle	(4)	Morane Saulnier A-1	(4)
Ansaldo Ballila SVA-5	(2)	Morane Saulnier MS130	(3)
Avro 504-K	(F)	Morane Saulnier N	(2)
Bleriot XI (3ea)	(1,4,F)	New Standard D-25(4ea)	(F)
Boeing-Stearman	(F)	New Standard D-29(2ea)	(4F)
Breguet 1911	(Pieces)	Nicholas Beasley	(3)
Brunner Bird CK	(3)	Nieuport 2N	(1)
Bucker Jungmann		Nieuport 10/83	(2)
Caudron G.III	(F)	Nieuport 11	(F)
Chanute Glider	(1)	Passett Ornithopter	(1)
Curtiss Fledgling	(F)	Pietenpol Air Camper	(F)
Curtiss Pusher D (2ea)	(F)	Piper Vagabond	(EF)
Curtiss Wright CW-1	(F)	Pitcairn Mailwing	(3)
Davis DIW	(F)	PHSC Scout	
DH-80A		RAF BE.2C (2ea)	(EF)
DH-82 (3ea)	(EF)	RAF FE.8	(2)
Demoiselle (2ea)	(4F)	Rabkaatsentein Glider	(2)
Deperdussin (2ea)	(1)	Ryan NYP	(1)
Dickerson Glider	(3)	Short S-29	(1)
Ercoupe	(EF)	Siemens-Schucker DIII	(2)
Fairchild 24-C8F	(4)	Sopwith Camel	(2)
Fleet Finch 16B	(F)	Sopwith Dolphin	(2)
Fokker Dr.I (3ea)	(2,F)	Spad XIII C1	(4)
Fokker D.VII (2ea)	(F)	Spartan C-3	(3)
Fokker D.VIII	(F)	Stampe SV-4B	(F)
FOkker E.III	(Stored)	Taylor E-2	(Shop)
Great Lakes T21MS	(F)	Thomas-Morse S4.B	(2)
Gyrodyne 2B Chopper	(4)	Thomas Pusher E	(1)
Handriot HD1	(F)	Voisin 8 Bomber	(4)
Heath-Parasol LNA	(3)	Waco 9	
Howard DGA-15P	(EF)	Waco 10	(3)
Luscombe 8A	(EF)	Wright Flyer	(1)
Monocoupe 90	(3)	Wright Glider	(1)
Monocoupe 113	(3)		

Syracuse - Syracuse ANGB, Hancock Field, 13211-7099, 315-458-5500,

F-86H	F-94B	F-102A

Airport Exhibit, I-81, Hancock Int'l Airport, Center Lobby Main Floor, Artifacts, Cafe

Westhampton Beach - Francis Gabreski Airport, 11978-1294, 631-288-4200,   F-102A

Williamsville - Niagara Frontier Aviation & Space Museum, 5583 Main St,
Municipal Bldg, 14221, 716-631-3276, Vice Chairman: Jack Prior

NORTH CAROLINA

Asheboro - North Carolina Aviation Museum, 2109 Pilots View Rd, 27203, Mail: POB 1814,
27204-1814, 336-625-0170, Fax 629-1520, Mon-Sat 10-5, Sun 1-5, Adm Adult $5,
Students $3, Child Under 6 Free, Grp Rates, Gift Shop, Restoration Facility,
Airshow 1st Weekend in June, www.ncairmuseum.com

AT-6G	F-84F	O-2A 2ea	T-34A
B-25J Project	J-3 Flitfire	P-3 Pilatus	TBM-3E
BT-13A	L-4	PT-13D	
C-45H	L-19A	T-28B	

Candler - Enka Junior High School, 475 Enka Lake Rd, 28715, 828-667-5421, F-84F(RF)

Charlotte - Carolinas Aviation Museum,, 4108 Airport Dr, Hangar 4108, Charlotte/Douglas Int'l Airport,
28208-5709, Mail: POB 555, Richfield, 28137, 704-359-8442, Fax 704-359-8442,
Mon-Sat 10-5, Sun 1-5, Adm Adult $3, Snrs $2, Gift Shop, Restoration Facility
www.chacweb.com

A-4	F-84G	HOK-1	T2A
A-7	F-80C	L-5	T-28 Cockpit
An-2	F-101F	Link Trainer	T-28B
Bellanca 14-9L	F-102A(YF)	Mercury Capsule rep	T-33 Cockpit
Bushby Mustang	H-1HA(UH)	OV-1D	T-33A
C-97 Cockpit	H-1HB(UH)	OV-10	T-33B
CG-15A	H-1J(AH)	P-80	Wright Glider
DC-3	H-34C(CH)	Regulasa Missile	M551A Sheridan Tank
F-4	H-50C(QH)	Skycat	
F-86L	HO3S-1	SNJ-5C	

Charlotte ANG, Charlotte/Douglas Municipal Airport, 28208, 145 TAG/CC
704-399-6363, 145th TAG,   F-86L

Cherry Point - Cherry Point Marine Base, Pres Edward Ellis, 252-447-2346, F-4U PBY

Durham - North Carolina Museum of Life & Science, 433 Murray Ave, POB 15190, 27704-
3101, 919-220-5429, Mon-Sat 10-5, Sun 1-5, Adm Adult $3.75, 4-12 $2.75 DC-3 F-11A

Fayetteville - Fort Bragg, 82nd Airborne Division War Memorial Museum, POB 70119,
Ardennes & Gela St, Bldg C-684128307-0119, 910-432-3343, Tue-Sun 10-4:30, Free Adm,
Gift Shop 436-1735, www.bragg.army.mil/18abn/museums.htm

C-7	C-47B	C-123K
C-46F	C-119L	H-1(UH)

Airborne & Special Operations Museum, 100 Bragg Blvd, From I-95, 28301, 910-483-3003,
Fax 485-2024, Tue-Sat 10-5, Sun 12-5, Free Adm, www.asomf.org,

C-47,	CG-4A	H-6 (AH)	H-1(UH)	M551 Tank

John F Kennedy Special Warfare Museum, Ardennes & Marion St, Bldg D-2502, 910-432-1533
Tue-Sun 11:30-4

Pope AFB, Main (Reilly Gate), 28308, 910-394-0001, * Located Off Hwy 23 FW Ramp

A-7D *	A-10A(OA) *	C-119	F-105D *
A-10A *	C-47B	C-123K	P-40

Goldsboro - Seymour Johnson AFB, 4th Wing HQ Wright Brothers Ave, 27531-5000, 919-736-5400,

F-4C	F-15B/E	F-86E	F-105D
F-4E	F-15E	F-86H	

Havelock - Cherry Point Marine Corps Air Station, Hwy 70 & Cuningham Blvd, 28533-5001,
2 Hour Tour 1st & 3rd Thur ea Month at 8:45am, Adm Free, 252-466-5895,   AV-8

Havelock Tourist Center, 202 Tourist Cntr Dr, 28532, 252-444-6402, Mail: POB 368

A-4M	F4B-3	F9F-6P	RF-4B

Hendersonville - Western North Carolina Air Museum, 1340 Gilbert St, 828-698-2482, Mail To:
POB 2343, 28793, (Mar-Oct) Sat 10-6, Sun & Wed 12-6; (Nov-Feb) Sat-Sun & Wed 12-5, Free Adm, Gift Shop,
Pres: Lee Harney, Dir: Jim Granere, e-mail: linda@harney.org, www.wncairmuseum.com (P)=Project

Aeronca C-3	Curtiss Robin 4C-1A E-2	J-5	SNJ-5
Aeronca Champ	Ercoupe 415CD	L-2	Stearman N2S
BC-12D Taylorcraft(P)	Heath Parasol (P)	Nieuport Bebe 11	Stearman N4S
Cessna 120	J-2	PA-12	Wittman Tailwind W-8
Corbin Junior Ace	J-3C	SE-5	

Hickory - Hickory Municipal Airport, 828-328-4078,

A-7B	F-4B	F-105B	FJ3	T-33	LTV

Kill Devil Hills - Wright Brothers National Memorial, US 158(Croaton Hwy)
& E Ocean Bay Blvd, 252-441-7430, Mail: POB 1903, 27948, Mon-Sat 10-4, Sun 1-4
www.nps.gov/wrbr/index.htm, Dec 17, 2003 100th Anniv Flight

Manteo - Wright Brothers National Memorial, POB 457, 27954, Virginia Dare
Trail-By Pass, 252-441-4481, Daily 8-8, Free Adm, Wright Flyer, Glider

Maxton - Gulledge Aviation, Laurin-Maxton Airport, 910-844-3601, Jetliner Salvage

Raleigh - North Carolina Museum of History, 5 E Edenton St, 27601-1011,
919-715-0200, B-8M Bensen Gyrocopter, Rogallo Wing, Wright Flyer Replica

Newbern - Clarendon Blvd, Hwy 17 South, City Park,   F-11A

Southern Pines - CAF - Carolinas Wing, Moore County Airport, http://30seconds.org/caf/,   AT-19

Surf City - Topsail Island Museum, The Assembly Bldg, 720 Channel Blvd,
Mail: POB 2645, 28445, Mid April-Oct Mon, Tue, Fri-Sat, 2-4, Nov-March Appt Only
800-626-2780, 910-328-4722, Gift Shop, Talos Rocket from Operation Bumblebee 1959

NORTH DAKOTA
Bismarck - State Historical Society Museum, Liberty Memorial Blvd, 58501,
701-224-2666, Daily 8-5, Sat 9-4, Sun 1-5, Free Adm,

Casselton - Aero Replicas, Casselton Regional Airport, 58012, 701-347-4680, 2½ Mi S
of City, Mail: POB 64, email: RJM1003@acol.com, Daily 8-5,

Bf-109 Replica	F-4C	Pitts S-1-C

Fargo - CAF - Red River Valley Wing, Hector Int'l, 701-241-1501, Elden C Herrmann,
Curtiss Golden Flyer

Fargo Air Museum, 1609 19th Ave N, Mail: POB 8190, 58109-8190, 701-293-8043, Fax 293-8103
Mon-Sat 9-5, Sun 12-4, Closed E, TD, CD, ND, Adm Adult $6, Snrs/Mil $5, Child 5-12 $4,
Under 5 Free, Gift Shop, Restoration Facility, www.fargoairmuseum.org

A6M2 Model 21 Beech D17	F4U	P-51D	
AT-6	DC-3	LNE-1	PT-19
B-25	F2G-1D	P-40	TBF

```
       Fargo ANG, Hector Field, 58105-5536, 701-237-6030,
       C-45J          F-16A           F-101B              F-104C
       C-47B          F-89J           F-101F              P-51D
       F-4D           F-94C           F-102A


       North Dakota State University, 1301 12 Ave N 58102, 701-237-7130,  F-104

  Grand Forks - Center For Aerospace Sciences, Box 8216, Univ Station, 58202
     701-777-2791, Project Officer: Lt Col Terry Young

       Grand Forks AFB Heritage Center, Building 125, 58205, 701-747-6924, 319BW
       A-26C               B-52G           F-102A       H-19D      Minuteman III
       B-25J               F-101B          H-1F(U)      Transporter Erector

  Minot - Dakota Territory Air Museum, Minot Int'l Airport, Mail: POB 195, 58702-0195
     701-852-8500, May-Oct Mon, Wed, Fri-Sat 10-5, Sun 1-5, Adm Adult $2, Child 6-17 $1
     www.dakotaterritoryairmuseum.com
       A-7                 Ercoupe             T-33
       Arrow Sport         J-2                 TBM
       Arrow Monoplane     J-3                 Veri-ezee
       Breezy              L-29                Volks Plane
       C-47 Cockpit        Monocoupe 110       Waco
       C-47                Pietenpol           Waco UPF-7
       Cessna 195          SR-5A


       Minot AFB, 919 MW/CVS58705, 701-727-4761,
       F-102A              F-106A              H-1F(UH)              T-33A

  Wahpeton - Tri State Aviation, Wahpeton Airport, 701-642-5777,
     Mon-Fri 8-5, Manager: Jerry Beck
       B-25                Howard DGA,         P-51                 TBM
       F4U-4               L-4                 PT-17

  West Fargo - Bonanzaville USA Historical Museum, Civil and Military Aircraft
     W Fargo Fairgrounds I-94 & Hwy 10, 701-282-2822, Oct-May Tue-Fri 9:30-4,
     Sat-Sun 1-5, Bowers Fly Baby          J-1                  VC-47
```

OHIO

  Akron - Goodyear World of Rubber, 1144 E. Market St, 4th Floor, 44316, 330-796-2121
     Daily 8:30-4:30, Free Adm, Curator: Richard Willett   FG-1D Fuse

  Alliance - Alliance High School, 400 Glamorgan St, 44601, 330-821-2100, A-7

       Forest Barber, Airport, 3 Mi N of City, 216-823-1168, Taylorcraft Model A Series 45

  Bryan - Military Heritage Museum, American Legion Post 284, 519 E. Butler St
     43506, 419-636-7354, Curator: JD Bouman, By Appt, Artifacts all Wars

  Carroll - Historical Aircraft Squadron, 3266 Old Columbus Dr, 43112, 641-653-4778
     Wed, Sat 9-5, Gift Shop, Restoration Facility, www.historicalaircraftsquadron.com,
     A-26 Project   BT-13 Project

  Chardon - Curtiss Robert, 15215 Chardon Airport, 44086, 440-298-1417, D-31 New Standard

  Cincinaatti - Blue Ash Airport, B-17E "My Gal Sal" Restoration from Greenland
     Contact: Bob Ready, Exec Aviation, 4393 Glendale Milford Rd, 45242, 513-984-3881,
     www.ultimatesacrifice.com,   E-mail: bob_ready@hotmail.com

       Cinncinnati Municipal Airport Lunken Field, 3 Mi SE of City, 513-321-4132,
       Fax 871-6801, E-mail: dan.dickten@cingen.rec.org, F-86

  Cleveland - Burke Lakefront Airport, Marjorie Rosenaum Plaza, 1501 Marginal Rd, 44100,
     216-781-6411, F-4J   F-4E

       Frederick Crawford Auto-Aviation Museum, 10825 E Blvd, 216-721-5722,
       Mon-Sat 10-5, Sun 12-5, Adm Adult $3, Child $1.50, www.wrhs.org/crawford
       Cessna 182P   DGA-3   Gee Bee R-1 Rep
       Chester Special   DH-4   Great lakes 2T-1A
       Curtiss Bumblebee   F2G-2D   P-51K
       Curtiss MF   Fulton Airphibian   Weddell-Williams Special

       International Women's Air & Space Museum, Inc, Burke Lakefront Airport
       Room 165, 1501 N Marginal Rd, 44114, 216-623-1111, Fax: 623-1113,
       Curator: Joan Hrubec, Free Adm, :www.iwasm.org, Artifacts

       NASA-Lewis Research Center/Visitor Information, 21000 Brookpark Rd,
       MS 8-1, 44135, 216-433-2000, Mon-Fri 9-4, Sat 10-3, Sun 1-5, Free Adm,
       Curator: Jim Francescangeli,   Apollo Skylab III Command Module

  Columbus - CAF - Ohio Valley Wing, 2000 Norton Rd, Bolton Field, 43228,
     www.cafohio.org, L-5(OY-2)

       Center of Science & Industry, 333 W Broad St, 43215, 614-221-2674,
       Mon-Sat 10-5, Sun 1-5:30, Adm Adult $3.50, Child $2,PT-12, Mercury Capsule

Columbus DCSC, 3990 E Broad St, 43213, 614-238-3131, F-100D,   F-105D

Dayton - Carillon Park, 2001 S Patterson Blvd, 45409, 937-293-3412,
Tue-Sat 10-8, Sun 1-8, Free Adm, www.nps.gov/daav/index.htm, Wright Flyer, Six Trains

National Aviation Hall of Fame, 1100 Spaatz St, WPAFB, 45433,Mail: POB 31096,
45437, 937-256-0944, Daily 9-5, Closed: TD, CD, ND, ED, Adm Free, Artifacts

US Air Force Museum, 1100 Spaatz St, Wright-Patterson AFB, From I-75S Exit 61A
To I-70E to Exit 44A to I675S to Exit 15; From I-75 Exit 43 to I-675S to Exit 15
45433-7102, 937-255-3284, Daily 9-5, Closed TD, CD, ND, Free Adm, Annex Hours:
Daily 9:30-3, IMAX Theater 937-253-IMAX, Media Relations: Diana Bachert 255-4704 ext 332,
www.wpafb.af.mil/museum, **Location Codes:** OP = Outdoor Airpark S = Storage
Gallery Codes:

Cold War	= CW	Missiles	= M		Space Flight	= SF
Early Years	= EY	Modern Flight	= MF		Vietnam War	= VW
Inter War Years	= IWY	Presidential	= P		World War I	= WWI
Korean War	= KW	Research & Development	= RD		World War II	= WWII

A-1E Skyraider	KW	Bristol Beaufighter	WWII
A-7D	MF	BT-9B	IWY
A-10A Thunderbolt II	MF	BT-13B Valiant	WWII
A-10(YA)	OP	BT-14	EY
A-17A	IWY	C-6A(VC)	P
A-20G Havoc	WWII	C-7A Caribou	KW
A-24	WWII	C-39A	
A-25A	WWII	C-43(UC) Beech Staggerwing 17	EY
A-26C Invader	KW	C-45H Expeditor	CW
A-36A Apache	WWII	C-46D Commando	WWII
A-37A(YA) Dragonfly	KW	C-47D Skytrain	WWII
A6M2 Zero	WWII	C-54C(VC) Sacred Cow	P
AC-130A	MF	C-60A	OP
ADM-20 Quail	CW	C-82A	OP
Aerojet Aerobee Rocket	SP	C-97L(KC) Stratofreighter	CW, OP
Agena Space Vehicle	SP	C-118(VC) Independence	P
AGM-28B Hound Dog	CW	C-119J Flying Boxcar	SP, OP
AGM-86B (ALCM)	CW	C-121D(EC) Constellation	KW, OP
AGM-129A	CW	C-121E(VC) Columbine III	P
AGM-136A Tacit Rainbow	RD	C-123K Provider	KW
Apollo Capsule	SP	C-124C Globemaster	KW
AQM-34L Firebee	KW	C-125B(YC) Raider	OP
AQM-34N	CW	C-126A(LC)	CW
AQM-91A Compass Arrow	RD	C-130A(AC)	OP
ASV-3 ASSET Lifting Body	SP	C-130A(JC)	OP
AT-6D	MF	C-131D	OP
AT-6G	S	C-133A Cargomaster	CW
AT-6G	EY	C-135E(EC)ARIA	OP
AT-9 Jeep	WWII	C-135A(NKC)	OP
AT-10 Wichita	WWII	C-137C(VC)	P
AT-11 Kansan	WWII	C-140B(VC) Jetstar	P
AT-38B	CW	C-142A(XC) LTV	RD
Avro 504K	WWI	Caproni Ca.36	WWI
B-1B	MF	Caquot Type R Obser Balloon	WWI
B-2 Spirit	MF	CG-4A Hadrian	WWII
B-3	RD	CGM-13B Mace	CW, OP
B-10	IWY	CIM-10A Bomarc	CW, OP
B-17G Flying Fortress	WWII	Convair Atlas Missile	CW
B-18A Bolo	WWII	Curtiss 1911 Model D	EY
B-23	OP	D-21B	CW
B-24D	EY	Dart Aerial Target	CW
B-25B Mitchell	WWII	DH-4B	IWY
B-26G Marauder	WWII	DH 82A Tiger Moth	IWY
B-26K Counter Invader	KW	DH 89B Dominie	WWII
B-29 Fuselage	KW	DH 98 Mosquito	WWII
B-29 Superfortress	WWII	DSP Satellite	SP
B-36J	CW	EF-111A Raven	MF
B-45C Tornado	KW	Ercoupe 415	S
B-47E	MF	Excelsior Gondola	SP
B-47H(RB)	CW	F-4 Phantom cockpit Rep	KW
B-50D(WB) Superfortress	CW, OP	F-4C Phantom II	KW
B-52D Stratofortress	KW	F-4C(RF)Phantom II	MF
B-57B(EB) Canberra	KW	F-4E(YF) Phantom II	RD, OP
B-57D	CW	F-4G Wild Weasel	MF
B-58 Hustler	CW	F-5A Skoshi Tiger	KW
B-66B Destroyer	KW	F-12A(YF)	RD
B-70(XB) Valkyrie	RD	F-15 Streak Eagle	OP
Bf 109G-10	WWII	F-15A Eagle	CW
BGM-109A Griffon	M	F-16 Cockpit Mock-up	CW
Bleriot Monoplane	EY	F-16A	MF
Block IV Satellite	SP	F-22(YF) Raptor	MF
Boeing Bird of Prey	MF	F-80C Shooting Star	KW
Boost Glide Reentry Vehicle	SP	F-80R(XF)	AP
Boeing 707, (Air Force One)		F-82B Twin Mustang	KW
BQM-34	CW	F-84E Thunderjet	KW
BQM-34F	CW	F-84F Thunderstreak	CW

F-84F(YRF)FICON	RD	MiG-19S Farmer	CW
F-84K(RF)	CW	MiG-21PF Fishbed	KW
F-84H(XF)	RD	MiG-23	OP
F-85(XF) Goblin	RD	MiG-29 Fulcrum	CW
F-86A Sabre	KW	Minuteman II Trainer	M
F-86D Sabre	CW	MQM-107	CW
F-86H Sabre	CW	MXY7-KI	AP
F-89J Scorpion	CW	N1K2-J George-21	WWII
F-90(XF)	CW	Nieuport N.28C-1	WWI
F-91(XF) Thunderceptor	RD	NT-33A	RD
F-92A(XF)	RD	O-1G	KW
F-94A Starfire	KW	O-2A Skymaster	KW
F-94C Starfire	CW	O-38F	IWY
F-100(CF) Mk IV	CW	O-46A	IWY
F-100D Super Sabre	MF	O-47B	IWY
F-100F Super Sabre	KW	O-52 Owl	IWY
F-101B Voodoo	CW	OA-1A	IWY
F-101C(RF) Voodoo	CW	OA-10 Catalina	WWII
F-102A Delta Dagger	CW	OA-12 Duck	CW
F-104A		OQ-14	WWII
F-104C Starfighter	CW	OQ-2A Aerial Target	WWII
F-105D Thunderchief	KW	OV-10A Bronco	KW
F-105F Thunderchief	KW	OV2-5	SP
F-106A Delta Dart	CW	P-6E	IWY
F-107A	RD	P-12E	IWY
F-111A	KW	P-26A	IWY
F-111F Aardvark	MF	P-35A	WWII
F-117A Nighthawk	MF	P-36A Hawk	WWII
Fa-330 Sandpiper	WWII	P-38L Ligntning	WWII
Fairchild Model 24-C8F	WWII	P-39Q Airacobra	WWII
Fi 156C-1 Storch	WWII	P-40E Warhawk	WWII
Fokker D.VII	WWI	P-47D Razorback	WWII
Fokker Dr.I	WWI	P-47D-30	WWII
Fw 190D-9	WWII	P-51D Mustang	WWII
Gemini Capsule	SP	P-59B Airacomet	RD
H-3E(CH)	KW	P-61C Black Widow	WWII
H-5A(YH)	KW	P-63E Kingcobra	WWII
H-1P(UH) Iroquois	KW	P-75A	RD
H-13J(UH) Sioux	P	P-80R(XP)	RD
H-19B(UH) Chickasaw	KW	P-81(XP)	RD
H-20(XH) Little Henry	RD	PA-48 Enforcer	RD
H-21B(CH) Workhorse	CW	Packard LePere LUSAC	IWY
H-26(XH)	RD	Panavia Tornado	MF
Halberstadt CL IV	WWI	Peacekeeper RV Bus	M
Hawker Hurricane MkIIa	IWY	PGM-17 Thor	M, OP
HE-111	S	PGM-19 Jupiter	M, OP
HGM-25A Titan I	M, OP	PQ-14B	WWII
HH-43B Huskie	KW	PT-1 Trusty	IWY
HU-16B Albatross	CW	PT-13D Kaydet	IWY
ICBM Hard Mobile Launcher	SP	PT-16(YPT)	RD
J-1	WWI	PT-19A Cornell	IWY
J-1 (Fabric removed)	WWI	PT-22 Recruit	WWII
J-3 Cub	WWII	PT-26	
JN-4D Jenny	WWI	QU-22B	KW
JU-52	OP	R-4B Hoverfly	WWII
Ju-88D-1	WWII	R-6A Hoverfly II	WWII
Kettering Bug Torpedo	WWI	Redstone Booster	SP
L-1A Vigilant	WWII	RK-86F	CW
L-2M Grasshopper	WWII	RQ-1A Predator	MF
L-3B Grasshopper	WWII	RQ-3A Dark Star	RD
L-4 (O-59A)	EY	RQ-3A Global Hawk	MF
L-4A Grasshopper	WWII	S4C Scout	WWI
L-5 Sentinel	WWII	SA-2 Surface-to-Air Missile	KW
L-6 Grasshopper	WWII	SE-5E	IWY
L-17A Navion	CW	SICM	M
LGM-30 Minuteman II	M	SM-62 Snark	RD, OP
LGM-30A Minuteman I	M, OP	SM-65 Atlas	M
LGM-30G Minuteman III	M, OP	SM-68 Titan II	M
LNE-1 (TG-3A)	S	Sopwith F-1 Camel	WWI
Lockheed Satellite	SP	SPAD VII	WWI
LTV A-7D Corsair II	KW	SPAD XIII	WWI
LTV ASAT Missile	SP	SPAD XVI	WWI
Lusac-11	EY	SR-71A	CW
M-1 Messenger	IWY	Stargazer Gondola	SP
Manhigh II Gondola	SP	Supermarine Spitfire Mk XI	WWII
Martin Peacekeeper	M	Supermarine Spitfire MkVc	WWII
MB-2	IWY	SV-5D PRIME Lifting Body	SP
MC-200 Saetta	WWII	T-28A	MF
McCook Field Wind Tunnel	WWI	T-28B Trojan	KW, OP
Me 163B	WWII	T-33A(NY)	AP
Me 262A Schwalbe	WWII	T-33A Shooting Star	CW
Mercury Capsule	SP	T-34A Mentor	CW
MiG-15bis Fagot	KW	T-37B Tweety Bird	CW
MiG-17 Fresco	KW	T-38A Talon	CW

T-39A Sabre Liner	P	X-3 Stiletto	RD
T-41A Mescalero	CW	X-4	RD
T-6	KW	X-5	RD
Tacit Blue (Whale)	RD	X-7A	RD
Teal Ruby Satellite	SP	X-10	RD
TM-61A Matador	CW, OP	X-13 Vertijet	RD
U-2A	CW	X-15A-2	SP
U-3A	CW	X-17	SP
U-4B	P	X-21	RD
U-6A Beaver	CW	X-24A	SP
U-10D Super Courier	KW	X-24B	SP
UC-43 Traveler	WWII	X-25A Gyrocopter	RD
UC-64A Norseman	WWII	X-29A	RD
UC-78B Bobcat	WWII	X-32 Joint Strike Competitor	MF
V-1 Buzz Bomb	WWII	XC-142A	
V-2 with Meilerwagen	WWII	XGAM-63 Rascal	RD
V-6A(XV) Kestrel	RD	YCGM-121B Robotic Vehicle	RD
Wright 1909 Military Flyer	EY	Yokosuka Ohka Trainer	WWII
Wright Brothers 1901 Wind Tunnel	EY	YQM-94A Compass Cope B	RD
Wright Brothers 1911 Wind Tunnel	EY		
X-1B	RD		

Museum of Pioneer Aviation and Wright Brother's Aeroplane Company, PO Box 204
45383, 4th & Ludlow St (Wilkies Bookstore), www.first-to-fly.com
Replica Wright Flyer 1 & 3

Elyria - CAF - Cleveland Wing, Lorain Co Reginal Airport, 44050 Russia Rd, 44035
440-323-8335, SNJ

S Euclid - United States Aviation Museum Assoc, Mail: PO Box 21846 Cleveland, 44121,
Contact: Tony Mazzolini, 4477 Mackall Rd, 44121, 216-381-5270, Fax 318-8801

A-1	B-25	C-45

Fairborn - Wright-Patterson Material Command Headquarters, Route 44, Bldg 262, F-4 2ea

Fremont - Fremont Airport, St Rd 53, 43420, 419-332-8037, Howard DGA-5 In Storage

Groveport - Motts Military Museum, Inc, 5075 S Hamilton Rd, 43125, 614-836-1500
Fax 836-5110, Tue-Sat 9-5, Sun 1-5, Adm Adult $5, Seniors $4, Student $3
www.mottsmilitarymuseum.org, M47 Tank - Arnold Schwarzenegger Drove in the Austrian Army
M42A1 Tank, M151 Jeep, PA 36-7 Higgins Boat, M110A2 Howitzer, 105mm Iraq Cannon

Lockbourne - Rickenbacker ANGB, 43217, Off Rte 317, 614-492-8211, 121st TFW

A-7D 2ea	F-15A	F-100D	T-33A
C-131E(TC)	F-84E	O-2A	
F-4C(RF)	F-84F	P-80C	

Madison - Charles F Reed, 5782 Trask Rd, 44057, 440-298-1314, Appt Only

Aeronca Champ (2 ea)	Luscombe	Smith Miniplane
Bowers Flybaby Biplane	OTK Myers	Stinson 108
Fleet Model 2	Piper J-5	
Fokker Dr.I	PT-22	

Miamisburg - Wright B Flyer Museum, 10550 Springboro Pike, Off Rte 741, Wright Brothers Airport
(Dayton General Airport), 45342, 937-885-2327, Tue,Thur,Sat 9-2:30,
Closed Holidays, www.wright-b-flyer.org, Wright B Flyer Flyable Rides for $150

Mansfield - Mansfield ANG, Mansfield Lahm Airport, 44901-5000, 419-522-9355, F-84F

Newark - Newark AF Museum, 2803 ABG, 43057-5000, PA: 740-522-7779, F-4C, T-33A

Newbury - **(Closing)** Walter A Soplata Aviation Collection, 11721 Hickory Dale Rd,
440-564-5326, Private Collection. Appt Only

A-1E	C-45	F-86I	P-80A
AT-6G	C-82	FG-1D	P-82(XP)
AT-11	DC-7	H-34(SH)	PT-19
B-25J	F2G-1	KC-97	T-2
B-26(VB)	F7U-3	O-52	T-28A
B-36A(YB)	F11F-1	P2V-7	T-33A
B-57	F-84E	P-39	T-50
BT-12(YBT)	F-84F	P-47L	TBM
BT-13A	F-84F(RF)	P-51K	
BT-15	F-86E	P-63	

North Canton - Maps Air Museum, 2260 Int'l Prkwy, 44720, 330-896-6332,
W Side of Akron-Canton Airport Off Rte 241 Mon 9-4 (Spring-Fall), Wed 6pm-9,
Sat 8-4, Adm Adult $4, Seniors $3, Child Under 12 $2, Gift Shop, www.mapsairmuseum.org,
(UR) = Under Restoration   (S) = Storage

A-24B(SBD-5) (S)	F-4	L-17B	P-40N (UR)
B-25	H-1B(UH) (S)	Link Trainer 2ea	P-51
B-26(UR)	H-1S(AH)	MiG-17F (UR)	PT-19
C-47B(UR)	H-58(OH)	O-2A	S-2F
DHC-6	L-2D	P-39Q (2ea)(UR)(S)	T-28S (S)

Norwalk - Firelands Museum of Military History, 4755 SR601, 419-668-8161,
Mail: c/o Richard Rench, 202 Citizens Bank Bldg, 448547,
UH-1H,(Rides Available), AH-1A, Tanks: M-42, M-60; APC Fort T-16, Mark VII Ferrett
(UH-1H 2ea in Storage 961, 20 East Norwalk Airport)

Oberlin - Oberlin FAA, ARTCC, 58357, 440-774-0100,   F-101B

Springfield - OH ANG, Springfield ANG, 183rd TFG,Springfield-Beckley Mncpl, 45502-8783
5 Mi S of Town Off Hwy 68 on Rd 794, 937-327-2100, F-84C   F-84F   F-100D

Swanton - Toledo ANG, Toledo Express Airport, 43558, 419-866-2078, F-84F   F-100D

Toledo - Toledo Suburban Airport, D Keller, 4720 S Arvilla Dr 43623,
419-885-3907,   BT-14

Troy - Waco Aircraft Museum & Aviation Learning Center, 105 S. Market St, 45373, Mail: POB 62
937-335-9226, May-Oct Sat-Sun 1-5, Gift Shop,   www.wacoairmuseum.org, Junkin Brukner
Waco: CG-4A,   ATO,   CTO,   Glider,   UPF-7W,   YMF,

Wapakoneta - Neil Armstrong Air & Space Museum, POB 1978, 45895-0978,
Just West off I-75 Exit 111, 419-738-8811, March-Nov, Mon-Sat 9:30-5, Sun 12-5,
Dec-Feb Reservation, Adult $4, Child 6-12 $1, Under 6 Free, Groups $0.50 ea, $10 per Bus,
www.ohiohistory.org/places/armstron/ and www.artcom.com/museums/vs/mr/45895.htm
Wright Model G Aerobaot, Aeronca 7AC,   F5D-1,   Gemini VIII

OKLAHOMA
Altus - Altus AFB, 73523-5000, 580-482-8100, 443rd MAW, 47th FTW, C-118B, T-34B

Bartlesville - Woolaroc Museum, Frank Phillips Foundation Inc, POB 1647,
74005, 918-336-0308, Tue-Sun 10-5, Adm Adult $2, 16 Under Free, Woolaroc Airplane

Vance AFB, 73705-5000, 580-237-2121, 71st FTW,   F-105D   T-28A   T-33A

Fort Sill - US Army Field Artillery & Fort Sill Museum, 437 Quanah Rd, 73503-5100,
580-422-5123, Daily 8:30-4:30, Closed CD, ND, Free Adm, http://sill-www.army.mil/Museum/
H-1B(OH)   H-23F(OH)   L-4   L-19   T-41B   Missile Park

Lexington - Citizen Potawatomee Territory, Hwy 59 West, H-12

Oklahoma City - CAF Oklahoma Wing, Wing Leader: Vincent S Buraas, 9917 Hefner
Village Place, 73162, 405-728-3335, www.oaklahomawing.org   PT-19

FAA Aeronautical Center, Academy Building, Room 101, 6500 S. Mac Arthur Blvd,
73169, 405-954-4709, POB 25082, AMG-400D, Librarian: Virginia C. Huges,
Aviation: Reference, Electronics, Mathematics, Education, Management.

45th Infantry Division Museum, 2145 NE 36th St, 73111, 405-424-5313,
Tue-Fri 9-5, Sat 10-5, Sun 1-5, Free Adm, www.45thdivisionmuseum.com,
A-7   H-1B(UH)   H-13E(OH)   H-58(OH)   L-17A   L-20
F-86L   H-6A (OH)   H-23C(OH)   L-4B   L-19   T-33A
F-80C

Aerospace Museum, 6000 N Martin King Blvd, 405-685-9546, Curtiss Pusher

Kirkpatrick Center - Air & Space Museum, 2100 NE 52nd, 73111,
800-532-7652, Main 405-427-5461, Hours & Information 405-427-7529, Adm Adult 13-64 $7.50
Snrs & Child 3-12 $6, Under 3 Free, Winter Mon-Fri 9-5, Sat 9-6, Sun 11-6, Gift Shop,
Cafe 425-7529, Omni Dome, Planetarium, Prices start at Adult $7.50 and Child $5.00
www.omniplex.org

American Eaglet	Curtiss Pusher D	Lunar Module	Stinson Voyager
Apollo Capsule	F-104	Mercury Capsule	T-33A
Apollo Module	Fokker DR.1 (2 ea)	Nieuport 11	V-2
Bu.133	Gemini Capsule	Parker Pusher	Wiley Post
Bunker 154	Gulfsteam Peregrine	Star Cavalier	

State Fair Grounds, B-47   B-52D   C-47   Gulfstream SC

Tinker AFB, 73145, 405-734-7321, B-29   B-47(RB)   B-52D
C-47(EB)   C-121K(EC)   C-135(KC)

Tinker ANG, 3000 S, 73125, 405-734-2778, F-105D,   F-86D,   T-33A

Tulsa - CAF - Spirit of Tulsa Squadron, Squadron Leader: Blaine Imel,
5200 S Harvard E5, 74135, 918-492-4156,

Tulsa ANG, Tulsa Int'l Airport, 74115, 918-832-5208, F-100D, F-86D

Tulsa Air & Space Center, Tulsa Int'l Airport, 7130 E Apache, 74115-3708, Hangar 5
918-834-9900, Fax 834-6723, Tue-Fri 10-4, Sat 10-5, Sun 1-5, Adm Adult $4.50, Snrs &
Students $3.50, Child 6-12 $2.50, Under 5 Free, Gift Shop, Library, Closed ES, MD,
July 4, LD, TD, CD, Space Artifacts, www.tulsaairandspacemuseums.com
C-2,   C-3,   F-14A   HK-47   Ranger 2000   T-37

Richard Lioyd Jones Jr Airport, 918-299-5886, Hanging From Main Lobby, JN-4D

Riverside Airport, Contact David Wheaton, B-25 "Martha Jean"

Weatherford - General Thomas P Stafford Museum, Jim Cobb Rd, Stafford Airport, 73096, 580-772-6143, Daily 9-5, www.staffordairandspacemuseum.com

Curtiss D	F-86	Ryan NYP Rep	Wright Flyer Rep
F-16	MiG 21	T-38	

OREGON

Clackmas - Clackmas ANG, 6950 SW Hampton, 97015, 503-557-5368, F-86F(QF), F-86F

Cottage Grove - Cottage Grove State Airport, Wright Tool Co, Owner Jim Younkin, H-1 Hughes Racer Replica

Eugene - Oregon Air and Space Museum, 90377 Boeing Dr, 97402-9536, 541-461-1101, Thur-Sun 12-5, Adm Adult $3, Child 6-11 $1, Under 6 Free, Gift Shop, www.oasm.org

A-6	Fokker DR 1	RLU-1	
A6M2 Rep	L-19	Smith Termite	Yak 50
F-4C	MiG-17	Taylor 21 Buller	
F-86	Nieuport 17		

Klamath Falls - Kinsley Field Oregon ANG, Klamath Falls In't Airport,

F-4	F-15A	F-16A

Hillsboro - Bruce Campbell, 15270 SW Holly Hill Rd, 97123-9074, 503-628-2936 www.leppo.com/~hypatiainc/BC727200.html, Home Built Out of a Boeing 727

Hubbard - Lenair Corp, 29502 S Meridian Rd, 97032-9405, 503-651-2187, www.LenhardtAirpark.com, Restores CG-4A's

McMinnville - Evergreen Aviation Museum, 3850 SE Three Mile Lane, Hwy 18 E of City, 97128, 503-768-5083, 472-0011, 472-9361 Ext 4635, 434-4180, Daily 9-5, June 6-Sept 2 Daily 9-6, Closed TD, CD, ND, Adm Adult $9.50, Vet & 65+ $8.50, Child 6-18 $5.50, Under 6 Free, Groups: Student $4.50, Adult $7.50, Exec Dir: Gary Thompson, www.sprucegoose.org, All Flayable except marked S=Static, R=Restoration

A-26C Storage	DH-4M-1	(S)	J-3C-65		SNJ-4(AT-6)	
A6M3 (R)	DH-100		JN-4	(S)	Spitfire Mk.14	
B-17G	F-89J	(R)	MiG 15 UTI 2ea (S&R)	SR-71		
BD-5B (S)	F-15AF-89J	(S)	OV-1D1		T-28B	
Bf 109G-10	F-102A	(S)	P-38L		T-33A-15-LO	(S)
Bonanza 35	FG-1D		P-40N		T-38A	(S)
C-130 (F)	Ford 5-AT-B		P-51D		TBM-3E	
CW-15-D (R)	Great Lakes Baby		PT-13		TH-55	(S)
CW-A-22	H-1H(UH)		RODA Homebuilt	(S)	Wright Flyer	(S)
D-17A Staggerwing(S)	H-12E(UH) 2ea (S&R)	S-2B		YAK 50		(S)
DC-3A (C-47)	HK-1 Spruce Goose		S-64			

Portland - OR ANG Portland, 142 FIG/MAW, Portland Int'l Airport, 97218-2797 503-288-5611   F-101B

UFO Museum, 1637 Sw Alder St, 97205, 503-227-2975

Medford - Rogue Valley Int'l Airport, 3650 Biddle Rd, 541-776-7222, F-16, KC-97

Tillamook - Tillamook Air Museum, 6030 Hangar Rd, 97141, 503-842-1130, Fax 842-3054, Daily 10-5 Nov-Apr, Closed TD, CD, ND, Adm Adult $9.50, Snrs $8.50 Child 13-17 $5.50, 7-12 $2.00, Under 7 Free, Cafe, Gift Shop, Restoration Center, Theater, Curator: John Matlock, www.tillamookair.com, e-mail: info@tillamookair.com,

A-4B	Boeing 377	H-58(OH)	P2V-7
A-7E	C-47	HUK-1	PBY-5A
A-26	Cessna 180	J2F-6	PT-17
AD-4W	Chris-Teena Coupe	Ki-43	PV-2
Alien Blimp	F-14A	L-17A	Quickie
AM-1	F4F (Project)	L-29 (2each)	SBD-3
AT-6	F4U-7	ME-109(HA-1112)	Sopwith Spad XIII
B-25	F8U Cockpit	Nord 1101	Spitfire Mk.VIII
Beechcraft V35B	FM-2	P-38	T-28 (2each)
Bell Helicopter	GK-1	P-39	TBM-3E
Bellanca 66-75	H-1H(UH) Project	P-47	
Bf-109	H-43B(HH)	P-51	

Tillamook County Pioneer Museum, 2106 Second St, 97141, 503-842-4553, Artifacts

PENNSYLVANIA

Annville - Annville ANG, 17003, 717-948-2200, F-102A(TF)

Beaver Falls - Air Heritage Museum, Inc, Beaver County Airport, 15010, 724-843-2820 Mon-Sat 10-5, Sun 11-6, Free Adm, Restorations in Progress, Gift Shop, http://trfn.clpgh.org/ah/index.html

A-20H	Cessna 401	Nanchang CJ6A	T-28
AT-19	H-1H(UH)	OV-1D	
C-123K	L-21B	P-39N	

Bethel - Golden Age Air Museum, 371 Airport Rd, 19507, 717-933-9566, May-Oct Fri-Sat 10-5
Sun 11-5, RoY by Appt, Adm Adult $5, Child 6-12 $3, Under 6 Free, Gift Shop,
Restoration Facility, Curator: Paul Dougherty Jr, (UR)=Under Restoration,
(AR)=Awaiting Restoration, (F)=Flyable, www.GoldenAgeAir.org

Allison Sport (AR)	E-2 (F)	Pietenpol Air Camper (F)
Bird CK (F)	Great Lakes (F)	Star Cavalier Model B (AR
C-3 (UR)	J-1 (UR)	Star Cavalier Model E (AR)
Cessna AW (AR)	JN4D (UR)	Windstead Special (F)
Cessna 195 (F)	Monocoupe Model 90A (AR)	
Dormoy Bathtub (AR)		
DR.I (UR)		

Eldred - Eldred WWII Museum, 201 Main St, Mail: POB 273, 16731, 814-225-2220, Fax: 225-4407
www.eldredwwiimuseums.org, Artifacts

Greencastle - AR Johns Exper Aircraft, Johns Alvin R, 346 Frank Rd, 17225, 717-597-2256
Homebuilts: Green Demon, Rason Warrior X-3 (5 Seater), Aero Sport, Tornado JV,

Harrisburg - Pennsylvania Historical State Museum, 17108-1026, 717-787-4980
Tue-Sat 9-5, Sun 12-5, Free Adm, J-3C   Jacobs   OX-5

Latrobe - Westmoreland County Museum, 2 Miles SW of City, 15650, 412-539-8100,
AT-19   Stinson Gull-Wing

Lock Haven - Piper Aviation Museum. One Piper Way, 19301, Mail: PO Box J-3,
17745-0052, 570-748-8283, Mon-Sat 10-4, Sun 12-4, Adm Adult $3, Child 6-12 $1,
5 & Under Free, www.pipermuseum.com, PT-1   Link Trainer   Tomahawk Simulator

Middleburg - N of Harrisburg Airport on Hwy 11, W on Hykes, Crossover 81-S on Young 1 Block.
Drone

Philadelphia - Franklin Institute, 20th & Benjaman Franklin Parkway, 19103-1194,
215-448-1200, 9:30-5 Mon, 9:30-9 Tue-Thur, Sun, 9:30-10 Fri, Sat, Adult $8.50,
Child 4-11 $7.50, Omniverse $7 & $6, Planetarium $6 & $5, www.fi.edu/wright
Quickie   PA-38-2   RB-1   T-33   Wright Brothers B

CAF - Delaware Valley Wing, Northeast Philadelphia Airport, L-6

Pittsburg - CAF - Keystone Wing, Wing Leader: Ronald S Gombar, 1647 Rockford Ave,
15226, 412-531-3106, L-5   L-9B

Pittsburgh ANG, Greater Pittsburgh Int'l Airport, 15231, 412-269-8350,
F-51D   F-84F   F-86L   F-102A

Reading - Mid Atlantic Air Museum, Reading Regional Airport, 11 Museum Dr, Bldg #401, RD #9,
Rte 183 North Side of Airport, POB 9381, 19605, 610-372-7333, Daily 9:30-4:00
Closed Major Holidays, Adm Adult $6, Child 6-12 $2, Pres: Russ Strine, www.maam.org/

Aeronca Model K	Heath CNA-40	Pietenpol Aircamper
Am Aerolites Eagle 2ea	HH-52A	PT-13D
Auster MKV J/1	J-2	PT-19
B-25J	KD-1A Kellet	PT-19B
Bede 5B (2 ea)	L-20A	PT-23
Beech G-18S	L-21B	PT-26
Bf-108	Martin 4-0-4	RC-3
BT-13A	N2S3	Reid Flying Submarine
C-3	N3N-3	ROTEC
C-119F	NE-1	Rotorway Exec 152
Cessna 150M	Nord 1002 (2 ea)	Rutan Vari-Eze
Commonwealth 185	Nord 1101 (3 ea)	SNJ-4B
Custer CCW-5	P-61B-1	SP-2H (2 ea)
CV-580 Prop Jet	P-84	T-28D
Elias EC1 Aircoupe	P2V	Taylor Young Model A
Erco 415G	PA-22-125	Troyer VX
F-84B-35-RE	PA-22-150	UC-78
F-86F-25	PA-23-250	UH-34D
H-21B	PA-34-200	Vickers 745D Viscount
Hawker Mk 58A	PA-38-112	

Smethport - Allegheny Arms & Armor Museum, Rte 46, 2 mi N of City, 814-362-2642,
Daily 10-6, Gift Shop, A-6, UH-1 (2ea), Coast Guard Boat, M-42, M-48A1, M-115,

Toughkenamon - Colonial Flying Corps Museum, New Garden Airport, Newark Rd
POB 171, 19374, 610-268-2048, Airshow 2nd Sunday In June, Sat-Sun 12-5, Adm Adult $1
Child Under 12 50¢, Curator: Hayden Shepley,

Barlett M-8	FG-1D	PT-19A
Bergfalke 11	FM-2	PT-19B
C-3	L-2A	PT-26
Cessna 185	Latter	Ryan ST-3KR
DH 82A	Liverpuffin 11	SNJ
DHC.	MPA	

Waterford - Thermal Gliderport Air Museum, 9001 Hamot Rd, 16441, 814-866-1131,
Appointment Only,   Six Gliders

West Chester - American Helicopter Museum, Brandywine Airport, 1220 Americaqn Blvd, 1420 Phoenixville Pike, 19380, 610-644-4430, Thur-Sun 10-5, Adm Adult $6, Snrs $5 Child 3-18 $4, Under 3 Free, Gift Shop, www.helicoptermuseum.org

Air Command Autogyro	H-1L(TH)	PV-2
Bell 30-1A	H-2D(HH)	QH-50C
Bell 47B	H-12D(UH)(H-23)	S-51(R-5)
Bell 47D-1(H-13)	H-21	S-52(HO-55)
Bell 47H-1	HUP-2	S-61(HH-3A)
Bell 47J Cockpit	OH-6A	S-62(HH-52)
Bell Jet Ranger	Parsons Autogyro	TH-55
Benson Autogyro	PCA-1A Autogyro	V-22
Brantley B-2	Princeton Air Cycle	VS-300 Cocpit
Enstrom F 28 A	Rotorway Scorpion	VZ-8P
Eurocpoter Djinn So 1221	Rotorway Scorpion II	XR-4 Cocpit
H-1(AH) Cockpit	RPV Rep	XRG-65

Willow Grove - Willow Grove Naval Air Station, DVHAA Wings of Freedom, 19090-5010, 215-443-6039, Fax 675-4005, Sat 10am or By Appt, Free Adm, e-mail: jbenton@voicenet.com, www.dvhaa.org/

A-4M	F7U-3	Me-262B1-B	YF-2Y
A-10A	F8U-1	P-80C	Z-9 Eastman Rotarcraft Helio
A-37	F9F-2	UH-1V	
C-1A	FJ-4B	UH-34D	
F-14	HUP-2P-3B	UH-53D	

RHODE ISLAND

N Kingstown - **CLOSED** - Quonset Air Museum, Quonset State Airport, 488 Eccleston Ave, I-95N Exit 8, Rte 4S & Quonset Point, Davisville Exit, Mail: POB 1571, 02852, 401-294-9540, Fri-Sun 10-3, Closed TD, CD, ND, Appt Available, Adm Adult $3, Child Under 12 $1, Curator: Howard Weekly, Jr, Gift Shop, Restoration Facility, http://users.ids.net/~qam/qam, email: qam@ids.net,   (P) = Project

A4D-2N(A-4C)(P)	C-1A	H-58A(OH)	Stinson 10A
A-4F	CW XF15C-1	H-21 Project	Stolp Starduster 2
A-4M	F3D-2 Project	L-9B	T-28S
A-6E	F-4A	Me 208 (Nord 1101)	TBM-3E
A-7D	F6F-5 Project	MiG-17f	
Aero Commander 680	H-1S(AH)	Mr D Robert Myer's Racer O-2A	
AH-1S	H-1H(UH)	Pietenpol Aircamper B-4	
American Eaglet	H-1M(UH)H-3H(SH)	Rutan Solitair Glider	
Antonov AN-2TD	H-6A(OH)		

SOUTH CAROLINA

Anderson - Anderson County Airport, 100 S Main St, 29624, Daily 8:30-5, 864-260-4163,   F-105B

Beaufort - Marine Air Station, 843-522-7100,

A-4L	F-4N	FJ-3	F8U-2

Charleston - Charleston AFB, 29404-5000, 843-554-0230,

C-47D(VC)	C-124C	F-106A
C-121C	F-4C	T-33A

The Citadel, 171 Moultrie St, 29409, 843-953-5000, www.citadel.edu/ginfo/tour/jet.html
AH-1,   F-4C,   M4A3 Sherman Tank,   LVT-H-6, Redsotne Missile

Columbia - Ft Jackson Museum, UH-1B

South Carolina State Museum, 301 Gervais St, 29202-3107, 803-737-4978, POB 100107, Daily 10-5, Adm Adult $4, Child, Snr & Military & Student $2, Curator: Ron Shelton, Science Adm: Nat Pemdelton,1929 Clemson Plane, B-25C

McEntire - McEntire ANGB, Memorial Park, 29044-9690, 803-776-5121,

A-7D	F-80H	F-102A	P-51K
F-4	F-86H & L	F-104C	T-33A

Mt Pleasant - Patriots Point Museum, 40 Patriots Point Rd, 29465, 29464, 800-248-3508, 843-884-2727, Apr-Sept Daily 9-6, Oct-Mar 9-5, Closed CD, Adm Adult $11, Snr & Mil $10, Child 6-11 $5, 5 & Under Free, Grp Rates Gift Shop, Snack Bar, www.state.sc.us/patpt

A-4 2ea	F-4J	J-2	USS Laffey
A-6	F-14	H-3	USS Yorktown
A-6B(EA)	F-18	N2S	USS Clamagore
A-7E	F11F-1	S-2E	MARK I Patrol Boat
AD-4N	F4F-3A	SBD	Mercury Capsule Rep
AH-1	F6F	TBM-3E	
B-25D-NC	F8U	UH-34	
E-1B	F9F	UH-1H	
E-2C	F4UF	USCG Ingham	

Myrtle Beach - Myrtle Beach AFB, Air Base Redevelopment A, 1181 Shine Ave, 354 TFW/PA, 29577, 843-238-7211, 238-0681,   F-100D

North Myrtle Beach - Mayday Miniature Golf, 715 Hwy 17N, 29582, 843-280-3535,
Daily 10am-10pm, Adm Adult $6, Child $4.50, www.maydaygolf.com, PV-2, UH-1

Sumter - Shaw AFB, 29152-5000, 803-668-3621, Open House May, PA: Fran Hutchison

B-66C(RB)	F-16A	F-105	O-2A
F-4C(RF)	F-101C(RF)	P-47D Replica	

SOUTH DAKOTA

Great Plains - Great Plains Airport, 57064, 605-368-2841,   A-7D

Huron - Huron Regional Airport, 57350, 605-352-4577,   A-7D

Mitchell - Soukup & Thomas Int'l Balloon & Airship Museum, 700 N Main St, 57301,
605-996-2311, Memorial Day - Labor Day Daily 8-8, May, Sept-Nov Mon-Sat 9-5,
Sun 1-5, Closed January, Feb-April Fri, Sat, Mon 9-5, Sun 1-5, Adm Adult $3,
Sr $2.50, 13-19 $1.50, 6-16 $1, Under 6 Free, Gift Shop, Dir: Becky Pope,
1890's Charles Dolfus Balloon Baskets Shennandoa Gerders/Control Room Doors,
Hindenburg (LZ-129) Dishes
HOT AIR BALLOONS:

Chesty (US Marine Bulldog)	US Aero Star Int'l
Chic-I-Boom (Carmen Miranda)	WWI Observation Balloon Basket
Hilda (13-Story Witch On A Broom)	WWI Paris Basket
Matrioshka Russian Nesting Doll	WWI US Army Gas Balloon
Super Chicken Gondola 1st Non-Stop	"Zanussi" Trans-Atlantic Capsule
Uncle Sam (100 Foot Tall)	

Pierre - SD ANG Pierre, SDNG Museum, Dakota & Chapelle, POB 938, 57501-0938,
605-224-9991,   A-7D

Rapid City - Ellsworth AFB, South Dakota Air & Space Museum, Bldg. 5208, 57706,
605-385-5188, POB 871, Box Elder, 57719-0871, Exit 66 Off I-90, Hours 8:30-6
Daily Mid May-Mid Sept, 8:30-4:30 Winter, Gift Shop: Beverly LeCates, Curator:
Ron Alley, Free Adm, Minuteman Missile Silo Tours,

A-7D	BT-13A	F-101B	T-38
A-26K	C-45	F-102	U-3A
B-2 Replica	C-47A	F-105D	U-8D
B-25J(VB)	C-54	FB-111A	UH-1F
B-29	C-131	H-13-H(OH)	Min. II
B-47	C-135(EC)	L-5	Nike-Ajax
B-52D	F-84F	O-2A	Titan I
B-57B(EB)	F-86H	T-33A	Quail

Sioux Falls - SD ANG Sioux Falls, Industrial & Algonquin, Box 5044, 57117-5044,
605-333-5700,   A-7D   F-102A   T-33A

TENNESSEE

Arnold - Arnold AFS, 37389, 931-454-3000, AEDC/DOPO, F-4C   F-105D

Athens - Swift Museum Foundation, Inc, McMinn County Airport, Hwy 30, Mail: POB 644,
37303, 423-744-9696, Swift Aircraft Displays

Caryville - Campbell County Military Display, I-75 Exit 134 & US 25W on Hwy 116(Old SR 9)
UH-1   M-60A3 Tank

Chattanooga - Chattanooga ANG, 37412, 423-892-1366, F-101B   F-104C

Crossville - Cumberland High School, 660 Stanley St, 38555, 931-484-6194
A-4   T-33A

Johnson City - Radio Controlled Flying Field, Contact: Vic Koening,
502 Steeple Chase Dr, 37601, T-33

Knoxville - Knoxville ANG, McGhee Tyson Airport, 37901, 865-970-3077, 134th ARG,
F-104C

Memphis - Memphis Belle Memorial Association, 125 N Front St, Mud Island, 38103,
Mail:POB 1942, 38101, 901-767-1026, 412-8071, MD-LD Daily 10-5, RoY Tie-Sun 10-5
Adm Charge, 1990 Movie "Memphis Belle" Shown Twice Daily, www.memphisbelle.com
A-7E   B-17 (At Millington Municipal Airport)

Millington - NSA Memphis (NATTC), 38053, 901-873-3033, A-4M   A-5 Outside Officers Club

Nashville - Nashville ANG, Nashville Metropolitan Airport, 37217-0267,
615-361-4600,   F-84F(RF)

Bristol Heritage Collection, 210 Club Parkway, 37221-1900, Mail: POB 210876, 615-646-2473,
383-9090, Mon-Fri 9-5, Wetland Lysander MK111A, Fairey Swordfish, Bristol Beaufort, Bollingbroke

Pigeon Forge - Professor Hacker's Lost Treasure Golf, 3010 Parkway, 37863, 865-453-0307, Beech D18S

Rossville - CAF - Tennessee Volunteer Squadron, Squadron Leader: Gene Johnson, 5917
Blackwell Bartlett, 38134, 901-372-8162,

Sevierville - Tennessee Museum of Aviation, Hanger One, 135 Air Museum Way
Gatlinburg-Pigeon Forge Airport, 37862, Mail POB 37864-5587, 866-286-8738, 865-908-0171
Fax 908-8421, Mon-Sat 10-6, Sun 1-6, Closed TD, CD, Adm 12.95, 65+ 9.95, Child 6-12 6.95
Vets & Military & Child 5 & under Free, Gift Shop, www.tnairmuseum.com Flyable=(F)

AT-6D (F)	MiG 21	T-33-A-N (F)	
F-86	P-47D-40 (2ea)(F)	T-33A	
MiG 17(2ea)	T-28B (F)	TBM-3E (F)	

Tullahoma - Staggerwing Museum Foundation, Inc, POB 550, Tullahoma Airport, 37388,
931-455-1974, Take I-24, Exit 111, Hwy 55 S, Right 130 S, 3/4 Mi. Sat-Sun 1-4
March-Nov, Closed All Holidays, Adm Adult $4, www.staggerwingmuseum.com/Rindex.html

Beech	A17R Staggerwing	Beech F17 Staggerwing	
Beech	B17 Staggerwing	Beech G17 Staggerwing	
Beech	C17 Staggerwing	Travel Air 10D	
Beech	D17 Staggerwing	Travel Air 4000	
Beech	E17 Staggerwing	Travel Air 6000A	

TEXAS

Abilene - CAF - Big Country Squadron, 4886 Newman Rd,Abilene Mun. Airport, Hangar #2,
76601-6720, Mail:POB 6511, 79608, 915-676-1944, Daily 9-5, Squadron Meetings
6:30 PM First Tue Monthly, http://bigcountrysquadron.org, C-94(UC)

Dyess Linear Air Park, Arnold Blvd, Dyess AFB, Mail: 7 WG/CVM 650, 2nd
St 79607-1960, 915-793-2199, Need Free Pass at Visitor's Center, 696-2432, Daily
5:30-10pm, www.dyess.af.mil/airpark/index.htm

A-26C	C-47A	F-86L	T-28A
AGM-28A	C-97L(KL)	F-89H	T-29C
AT-6F	C-123K	F-100C	T-33A
B-17G(DB)	C-130A	F-101B	T-34B
B-47E(EB)	C-135A(KC)	F-104A	T-37B
B-52D	F-4D	F-105D	T-38A
B-57B(EB)	F-84F	HU-16E	T-39A
B-66A(RB)	F-84F(RF)	O-2A	
C-7A(YC)			

Addison - Cavanaugh Flight Museum, 4572 Claire Chennault, Addison Airport, 75001,
972-380-8800, Mon-Sat 9-5, Sun 11-5, Adm Adult $6.00, Child 6-12 $3.00,
Under 6 Free, All Aircraft Flown Regularly, Canteen Area, Gift Shop,
Founder: Jim Cavanaugh, www.cavanaughflightmuseum.com

AT-6D	F4U	Me-109G	PT-19A
B-25(TB)	F9F-2B	MiG-15UTI	PT-22
BT-13(SNV-2)	FM-2	MiG-17	S-2F
Christine Eagle Project	Fokker D.VIIa	MiG-21	Sopwith Camel
DH 82	He-111	N2S	Spitfire Mk.VIII
F-86E	Hawker Hurricane	P-40N	TBM-3E
F-4C	J-3	P-47N	TS-11
F-104A	L-3B	P-51D	
F-105F	L-4J	Pitts S-1-S	

Amarillo - CAF - Dew Line Squadron, 903 S Carolina, Perry Lefors Field, 79103,
806-665-1881, L-5

English Field Air & Space Museum, 2014 English Rd, Mail: POB 31535,
79120-1535, 806-372-6999, Sun-Fri 12-5, Sat 10-5, Winter Sat-Sun 12-5, Free Adm,
Gift Shop, Restoration Facility, Annual Air Show, www.texasaviationmuseum.org

C-71,	F-84F,	OV-1B,	Viking Mars Lander

Arlington - Air Combat, 921 Six Flags Dr #117, 76011-5123, 817-640-1886, Daily
1½ Hour Simulators $39.95: A-4   F-8   F-16   F-111

Austin - Adjutant General's Dept, TAG, Camp Mabry, POB 5218, 78763-5218, F-4C, F-86D

Texas Military Forces Museum, Texas ANG, West 35th St & MoPac Freeway (Loop 1),
Camp Mabry, 512-465-5167, 409-6967, Wed 2-6, Sun 10-4, Closed Holidays,

F-4	F-86	H-1H(UH)	H-1M(UH)	L-4

Bastrop - VFW Post 2527, Rockne Hwy, 78602, 512-321-2610,   F-4

Beaumont - Babe Didrikson Zaharious Memorial Park, Interstate Hwy 10,   RF-101

Beeville - Chase Field Naval Air Station, PA, 512-354-5464,   A-4J(TA)

Courthouse, 105 W Corpus Christi,   A-4

Big Spring - Hangar 25 / McManhon-Wrinkle Industrial Airpark, Webb AFB,
Bldg 1106, 2000 Air Park W, 79720, 915-264-1999, Mon-Fri 9-4, Sat 10-2, Sun 1:30-4
Closed Holidays, Adm Donation, Gift Shop, www.hangar25.org

A-10 Cockpit	B-52 Nose	T-28	T-37
AT-11	Harrier	T-33	T-38

Vietnam Memorial, 7th & Sword St, 7 Blocks E of Hangar 25, F-4E,   UH-1H
www.geocities.com/Cape Canaveral/lab/1083, e-mail: nelda@xraodstx.com,
www.xroadstx.com/users/bscc/,   e-mail: tnewton@xraodstx.com

Brownsville - CAF - Rio Grande Valley Wing, Brownsville/South Padre Is. Int'l Airport, 955
Minnesota, 78523, 956-541-8585, Mon-Sat 9-4, Sun 12-4, Adm Charge,

BT-13 (2ea)	FW-44	L-6	PT-26 (2ea)
C-47 Project	J3C-65	Moth Minor	SNJ
C-54	L-2	PBY-5A Project	Swith Bi-Plane
CM-170R	L-3	PT-17	Train 2-4-2
P.H. 94 S	L-4	PT-19 (2ea)	
Fleet Finch 16B	L-5	PT-22 (2ea)	

Burnet - Highland Lakes Sq CAF (Hill County Squadron), Burnet City Airport
S on US 281, 78611, 512-765-2227, Mail: POB 866, Mon-Fri 10-3, Sat 9-5, Sun 12-5,
Adm Adult $3, Snr $2, Child $1, Gift Shop, www.highlandlakessquadron.com/index.htm

A-7D	L-5	PT-17	T-38
C-47	L-17B	PT-19	
F-100F	PT-13	PT-37	

College Station - George Bush Library Museum, 1000 George Bush Dr, 77845,
979-691-4000, Mon-Sat 9:30-5, Sun 12-5, Closed TD, CD, ND, Adm Adult $7,
Snr 62+ $5,Child 6-17 $2, Under 6 Free, Gift Shop 888-388-2874, 979-862-2874
http://csdl.tamu.edu/bushlib, TBM-3

Conroe - CAF -Big Thicket Squadron, Montgomery County Airport, BT-13A,   YO-55

Corpus Christi - Corpus Christi Museum of Science and History, 1900 N Chaparral,
(Bayfront Arts & Science Park), 78401, 361-883-2862, Tue-Sat 10-5,
Sun 1-5, Closed Holidays, Adm Adult $2, 6-12 $0.50, Sat 10-12 Free Adm

F-4 Cockpit	SNJ (Can Sit In)
N3N	

Int'l Kite Museum, Best Western Sandy Shores Beach Hotel, Quarium
Village, 3200 Surfside, Mail: POB 839, 78403, 361-883-7456, Daily 10-5, Free Adm.

Naval Air Station, PA, 78419, 361-961-2568, PBY-5A, T-28,   TBM-3E

CAF - Third Coast Wing, 921 Ayers St, 78404, 361-882-9556, Gift Shop, www.thirdcoast.org, L-6

USS Lexington Museum, 2914 Shoreline Dr, Mail: POB 23076, 78403-3076,
361-888-4873, Daily 9-5, Adm Adult $9, Child 4-12 $4, Seniors & Military W/ID
$7, Closed CD, Gift Shop, Food Court, On-Going Restoration Projects,
Asst Curator: Margaret Wead, www.usslexington.com

A-4B (2ea)	F-14A	L-4 Storage	T-28B
A-4J(TA) Trainer	F2H-2	N3N-3	T-34B
A-6E	F9F-8T(TF-9J)	PINTA and MARIA	T-6 Storage
A-7B	GH-3	PV-2D	T2C
DGA Storage	H-1S(AH)	SBD-3	TBF-3E
F-4A	KA-3B(A3D)	SNJ-5	USS Lexington

Dallas - Frontiers of Flight Museum, 8008 Cedar Springs Rd, Mail: Love Field Terminal LB-18,
2nd Floor, 75235-2852, 214-350-3600, Fax 351-0101, Mon-Sat 10-5, Sun 1-5, Closed TD, CD, ND,
Adm Adult $2, Child Under 12 $1, Gift Shop 350-1651, Curator: Gen Knox Bishpop,
Airshow 2nd wknd In Sept, e-mail: fofm@iglobal.net, www.flightmuseum.org

BS-1	F-105F	Sopwith Pup	Temple Sportsman
F-4C	Quicksilver MXL-II	T-33	TH-1L

History of Aviation Collection, Univ of Texas at Dallas, Eugene McDermont Library
2901 N Floyd Rd, 75221, Mon-Thur 9-6, 9-5 Fri, Free Adm, Curator: Mike Quinn
James Doolittle Library, Artifacts, Glasflugel BS-1 Sailplane

Del Valle - Del Valle High School 2454 Cardinal Loop, 78614, 512-385-1921, F-4C(RF)

Del Rio - Laughlin AFB, 78843-5000, 830-298-5675, 47OSS/CC

B-57B(EB)	F-84F	T-33A	T-38
C-45J(UC)	T-6	T-34B	U-2C
C-123K	T-28A	T-37A	

Denton - Hangar 10 Antique Airplane Museum, Denton Mncpl Airport, 1945 Matt Wright Ln
76207, 940-565-1945, I-35E, West Oak Exit, R on Airport Rd, Mon-Sat 8:30-3,
Adm Donations, Contact: JR Almand. MW Wright, www.hangar10.org/

LC-126	OH-58	C-60A
Howard DGA	Interstate Cadet	L-17A

Texas Women's Univ Library Blagg H, 76201, 940-898-2665, WASP's Artifacts

World Aeronautical Museum, Jim Holder, 940-464-0080, Tue-Wed

Bear	B-25
L-39	

Ellington - Ellington ANGB,TX 77034-5586, 821-929-2892, 147 FIG/MA,
Curator: Ltc Doug Malloy, F-101F   F-102A   T-33A

El Paso - Air Defense & Artillery Museum, Building 5000, Pleasant Rd,
Near Robert E Lee Rd, Daily 9-4, Artifacts

Fort Bliss - Third Cavalry Regiment Museum, ATZC-DPT-MM, Forrest & Chaffee Rds,
Bldg 2407, 79916-5300, 915-568-1922, Mon-Fri 9-4:30, Free Adm,
S-55,   M-2 Half Track,   M-4AS Sherman Tank,   M-8 Armored Car

US Army Air-Defense Artillery Museum, Blvd 5000, Pleasonton Rd & Robert
E Lee Blvd, 79916-5300, 915-568-5412, Daily 9-4:30, Closed ES, TD, CD, ND,
Free Adm, Bofors 40mm Gun from "Movie 1941", 88mm German Anti-Aircraft Gun, V-2
Missiles: Firebee   Hawk   Nike Ajax   Nike Hercules

Fort Davis - McDonald Observatory, Atop Mt Locke, 16 Miles from Ft Davis on Hwy 118
Mail: WL Moody, Jr Visitors Information Center, POB 1337, 79734-1337,
915-426-3640, Gift Shop, Theater, Daily 9-5, Closed TD, CD, ND, Daily 2pm
Tour (March-Aug 9:30am)Adm Adult $4, Child 6-12 $31, Under 5 Free, Free Solar
Viewing: 11am, 3:30pm, Wed Eve, www.as.utexas.edu/mcdonald/vc/default.html

Fort Worth - American Airlines C.R. Smith Museum, 4601 Hwy 360 & FAA Rd, Next To
American Airlines Flight Academy, Just South of the Dallas/Ft Worth Airport,
76155, 817-967-1560, Tue-Sat 10-6, Sun 12-5, Free Adm, Gift Shop, Theater 967-5922,
www.crsmithmuseum.org, DC-3, Airline Cockpits: 757, 767, F-100

Aviation Heritage Museum, Mail: 306 West 7th St, Suite 311, 76102, 817-551-1967,
www.aviationheritagemuseum.com, B-36 Peacemaker Museum, POB 150943, 76108,
www.b-36peacemakermuseum.org, Restored B-36J Awaiting Building of the New Facility
A-12   B-36J   BT-13   L-450   T-33(Project)

Fort Worth Science and History, 1501 Montgomery St, 76107, 817-255-9300
Sept-Feb Mon-Wed 9-5, Thur-Sat 9-9, Sun 12-9, March-Aug Mon-Sat 9-9, Sun 12-9
Adm Adult $5, Snrs $4, Child 3-12 $3, Under 3 Free, www.fwmuseum.org
Bell 47   Boeing 727 Cockpit   PT-17

NAS Ft Worth Joint Reserve Base, Carswell Field, 76127, 817-782-7815,

A-4J(TA)	F-4E	F-86L	H-34(UH)
A-4M 2ea	F-14A	F-105D	H-58(OH)
C-97L(KC)	F-16N	FA-18	
F-4D	F-80L	H-1(UH)	

Pate Museum of Transportation, 18501 Highway 377 S, 76035, 817-396-4305,
Tue-Sun 9-5 Except Holidays, Free Adm, Curator: Jim Peel, www.pmot.org

A-4	F-8A(F8U-1)	F-100	H-43B(HH)
BQM-34	F9F-6P	F-101B(CF)	T-28
C-119	F-80	F-105	T-33A
C-47	F-84F(RF)	F-86H	UH-34
CH-21B	F-14	H-16B(HU)	
F-4D	F-16	H-23B(OH)(2ea)	

Texas Airplane Factory, Meacham Field, 76106, 817-626-9834, Contact:
George Tischler, Fax 817-626-7354, Fax 609-702-1852, Me-262B-1a (2ea)
Ki-43 (4ea)(Project for Champlin Fighter Museum), 2 are for sale $850,000 ea

Vintage Flying Museum & Texas Air Museum & OV 10 Bronco Assoc, 505 NW 38th St
Hangar 33 S, 76106, S On Main Off US 820, W On 38th St, S Runway of Meacham Airport
Mail: Box 820099, 76182, 817-624-1935, 800-575-0535, Fax 485-4454, Sat 10-5, Sun 12-5
Weekdays by Appt, Adm $4, Gift Shop, www.vintageflyingmuseum.org, wwwov-10bronco.net

American Flea	Convair	Hawker Hunter	OV-10 Replica
AT-6	F-86	Knight Falcon	Piaggio Amphibian
B-17G	Fouga Magister	L-3	Stearman
Beech D18S 3ea	H-1(UH)	L-5	
C-140	H-58(OH) 3ea	L-450	

Fredericksburg - National Museum of the Pacific War, 340 E Main St, POB 777,
78624, 830-997-4379, 7269, Daily 10-5, Adm Adult $5, Child $3, Under 6 Free
Groups $3 ea, Closed CD, www.nationalmuseumofthepacificwar.org

B-25J	LVT4	M7 Priest Tank	N1K-1
D3A-1	MK3 Tank	Japanese Tank Chi-ha	
FM-2	M3 Tank	USS Pinato Conning Tower	
TBM-3E	PT Boat	Japanese Midget Sub Type A	

Fulshear - Covey Trails Airport, 281-531-6540, WF Russel, Houston, Owns: Beech 18R

Galveston - Lone Star Flight Museum, 2002 Terminal Dr, 71554, 409-740-7722, Near
Galveston Airport and Moody Gardens, Off Jones Dr, Curator: TJ Zalar,
Daily 10-5, Closed ED, TD, CD, ND, Adm Adult $6, $4.50 Seniors,
Child 4-13 $2.50 under 4 free, Gift Shop, Theater, Restoration Viewing,
All Aircraft Flyable, Project = P, Non Flyable = N, www.cavanaughflightmuseum.com

A-20G	F-100 (N)	L-5	Spitfire (P)
AT-6A	F3F-2	N3N-3	T-34A
AT-11	F4U-5N	P-38-L5	T-50
B-17G	F6F-5K	P-47	T-28C
B-25	F8F-2	PB4Y-2 (P)	TBM-3E
B-58A(TB) (N)	FM-2	PBY-5A (P)	
Beech D18H4	Harvard Mk.IV	PV-2D (N)	
C-1A Project	Hawker Hurricane	SBD-5(A-24B) (P)	

Graham - CAF - Cactus Squadron, Grahm Mncpl Airport, POB 861, 76450,
   Robert E Richeson Memorial Museum, http://www.wf.net/~jwscott/index.html, SB2C

Grand Prairie - Texas Air Command Museum, 4531 Crane Court, 75052-3516, Mail: P.O. Box
   542071, 75054, 972-642-8282,
   AT-6   F-86F(2ea)   Hawker Hunter   T-33A   UH-1H

Hawkins - RRS Aviation (Restoration Facility), POB 233, 380 N Beaulah,
   75765, 903-769-2904, Pres Bob Schneider,
   Bristol Beaufort   Hawker Hurricane (5ea) PBM   TBM-3
   F9-5   P-40

Houston - CAF - Gulf Coast Wing, 11503 Brantley, Ellington Field, 77089, 281-484-0098
   www.gulfcoastwing.org, A6M Rep, B5N Rep, B-17, BT-13, D3A Rep

   CAF - West Houston Squadron, West Houston Airport, Hangar B-5, 18000 Groeschke Rd
   77084, Hangar: 281-578-1711, www.westhoustonsqdn.org, 3rd Sunday each Month,
   AT-6D   N-3N   SNJ
   BT-13A   P-63   T-28 (2ea)
   C-60A   S-108   T-34

   West Houston Airport Entrance, H-1H(UH) on Groeschke Rd.

   Houston Museum of Natural Science, 5800 Carolina St, 77004, 281-526-4273, Sun-Mon 12-5,
   Tue-Fri 9-5, Sat 9-9, Free Adm, Mercury 6 Spacecraft

   Houston Space Academy, 403 NASA Rd 1, Ste 360, 77598, 281-486-4446,
   Summer Space Camps Ages 6-20, Astronaut Training, Rockets, Simulators

Houston - NASA Lyndon B Johnson Space Center, 2101 NASA Rd 1, 77058,
   281-483-4321, Daily 9-4, Free Adm,   PGM-11A   Spacecraft

   Space Center Houston at LBJ Space Center, 1601 NASA Rd 1, Off I-45, 77058
   281-244-2100, 800-972-0369, Memorial Day-Labor Day 9-7, Labor-Memorial Day
   Mon-Fri 10-5, Sat-Sun 10-7, Adm Adult $16.95, Snrs 15.95, Child 12.95, Closed CD,
   RoY 9-7pm, Shuttle, Gift Shop, www.spacecenter.org

Kerrville - Mooney Aircraft Factory, West Side of Louis Schreiner Field On Hwy 27,
   830-996-6000, Mon-Fri, 1 Hour Tours at 10am.

Kingbury - Pioneer Flight Museums part of Vintage Aviation Historical Foundation,
   190 Pershing Ln, 78638, 830-639-4550, On Farm Road 1104 Off of IH10,
   www.vintageaviation.org, Flyable(F)
   Bleriot XI (F)   Fokker Dr.I (P)   Rearwin 2000C (P)
   Bristol Fighter (P)Rep Luscombe 8A (F)   SE-5a (P) Rep
   Bristol Fighter (P)   Meyers OTW (F)   Thomas-Morse Scout (F)
   Curtiss Canuck(P)   Pietenpol Sky Scout (F)
   Fokker D.VII (P)   Piper J-3 (P)

Kingsville - Naval Air Station, Hwy 77 South of City, 1201 E Caesar Ave, 78363,
   361-516-6200, A4D-2N

Lago Vista - Lago Vista Airpower Museum, Rusty Allen Airport, Flight Line Rd,
   Hangar 9, Lago Vista Airport, 78645, 512-267-7403, Sat-Sun 1-5, From I-35
   Take F.M. 1431, R on Bar-K Ranch Rd, F-4C(RF),   F-100C,   L-4,   PT-13

Lancaster - CAF - Dallas / Ft. Worth Wing, Lancaster Airport, Belt Line Rd, 75146
   972-236-1319, 6 Mi East of I-35E in SE Dallas County, Sat 9-4, Adm $2,
   http://dfwwing.natca.org, BT-15   FG-1D   L-5   R4D   V-77

Laredo - Airport, 3 Mi NE of City, 956-795-2000,
   Aero Commander   C-46   J-3   YS-11
   Beech 35   Convair 340   Rotoway Exec 162F
   Bell 47   Convair 440 (2ea)   T-28
   C-45   DC-3 (3ea)   T-39 Parts

Lubbock - Lubbock State School, 3401 N Univ & Loop 289, 79417, 806-763-7041, T-33A
   Science Center, 2579 S Loop 289, 79423, 806-745-2525,   T-28A

   Silent Wings Museum, 5401 N Martin Luther King Blvd, Rte 3, Box 393, 79403-9710,
   806-775-3126, www.silentwingsmuseum.com
   CG-4A   Culver Cadet   Lyster 1943
   Coffman Glider   L-4   PT-22A

McAllen - McAllen Miller Int'l Airport, Ceiling of Main Lobby, 2 Mi S of City,
   956-682-9101, White Monoplane Rep.

Manchaca - VFW Post 3377, 12921 Lowden Ln, 78652, 512-282-5664, F-4

Marshall - CAF - Lone Star Wing, Gregg County, www.ballistic.com/~dmurphy, PT-17

Midland - Commemorative Air Force Museum, 9600 Wright Dr, Midland Int'l Airport, POB 62000
79711-2000, 915-567-3009, 563-1000 Recording, 567-3047 Fax, Mon-Sat 9-5, Sun &
Holidays 12-5, Closed TD, CD, Adm Adult $7, Child 13-18, 65+ $6, 6-12 $5, 5 & Under Free
Simulator $3, Curator Larry Bowles, Airshow Dates: 800-CAF-SHOW,
www.commemorativeairforce.org,

A-1E	C-45J	F8F-2	P-63A
A-20J	C-54D	FG-1D	PB-1W
A-24B(RA)	C-60	HA-112-MIL	PBY-6A
A-57A(RA)	C-97G(KC)	Harvard Mk.II	PBY-5A
A6M2	C-119C	Harvard Mk.IV	Pliska
AH-G	C-124C	HU-16B	PT-22
AM-1	CG-4A	Kittyhawk IV	PT-19
AT-6B	Cornell II	L-5	PT-17
B-24(LB-30)	D-18S	Lockheed 18-50	R-4
B-25J	DC-3C	Me-108B24	SB2C-5
B-29A	F-4D	Me-109B	SNJ-5
B-47E(RB)	F-89J	Mosquito	TBM-3
B5N Rep	F-84F(RF)	P-39Q	TG-3A
BT-15	F-100	P-47N	
BT-13A	F-102A	P-51C	
C-47D(VC)	F-105D	P-51D	

American Airpower Museum, Midland Int'l Airport, 9600 Wright Dr, 79711,
Mail: PO Box 62000, 79711-2000, Recording 915-563-1000, Direct 915-567-3009
Fax 567-3047, Mon-Sat 9-5, Sun 12-5, Closed TD, CD, Adm Adult $9, Child 13-18 & Snr $8
Child 12-6 $6, Child Under 12 Free, www.airpowermuseum.org,

AT-6	B-25	FG-1D	P-47N
B-17G	DC-3 Cocpit Sim 3ea	P-40N	TBM

CAF - B-29/B-24 Squadron, www.cafb29b24.org, B-24   B-29

CAF - Commando Squadron, C-46

CAF - High Sky Wing, 9600 Wright Dr, Midland Int'l Airport, Mail: POB 61064,
79711-7064, 915-563-5112, C-61(UC)   SNJ-4

CAF - West Texas Wing, Municipal Airport, 915-549-6150,
http://mywebpage.netscape.com/westtexaswing/Home+Page.htm,   SB2C

Odessa - CAF - Desert Squadron, Odessa-Schlemeyer Airport, 915-335-3021, PT-13, T-33A

Pampa - Freedom Museum USA, 600 N. Hobart, VFW Post 1657, 79065, Mail: POB 66,
806-669-6066, Tue-Sat 12-4, Library, Gift Shop, www.freedommuseumusa.org
UH-1F   B-25(PBJ)   M110A2 Howitzer

Paris - Flying Tiger Airport, Hwy 82, 75461, 903-784-3613,
Daily 8-6, Free Adm, A-4D   AT-6   F-86D   SAM

Plainview - Hale County Airport, Hutchinson Air Service Inc, Mail: POB 940, 79073-0940,
806-293-1307, FBO Mike Hutchinson, e-mail: redbaron@texasonline.net, T-33A

Pyote - Pyote Museum and Rattlesnake Bomber Base, 79777, 15 Mi W of Monahans,
On I-20, In Ward County Park (N Hwy 18, 79756, 915-943-5044), Sat 9-6, Sun 2-6,
Artifacts of Former 19th B-17 Base.

Richardson - History of Aviation Collection, 2901 N Floyd Rd, Eugene McDermontt Library,
Special Collections, University of Dallas, 75083, POB 830643, 75083-0643, 972-883-2570,
Fax: 883-4590, Mon-Fri 9-5, Free Adm, www.utdallas.edu/library/special/cataa.html,
(Jimmy Doolittle and China Air Transport) Artifacts

Rio Hondo - Texas Air Museum, Caprock Chapter, 155 N 8th St, 79364, 2 Mi N On FM 400,
Off US84, 956-828-4664, Mail: POB 667, 79364, Contacts:Jim Davis 828-6201,Larry Jordan
829-2509, Mike Delano 828-4334, Mon-Sat 9-4, Adm Adult $4, Child 12-16 $2, 15 & Under Free,
Curator: Malcolm Laing 806-794-0190, e-mail: Mlaing@tnrcc.state.tx.us
Display (D), Flying (F), Project (P), Storage (S)

A-4J(TA)	(S)	Christofferson		L-18	(F)
AD-5	(D)	Convair 240 Nose(D)		L-4	
Aerobat 1-A	(D)	F-105		L-2M	(P)
Aeronca 7AC	(S)	Fi-103/Reiv Rep	(D)	Mystery Ship	(D)
Aeronca 7AC	(F)	Fi-156	(F)	NA Model A	(F)
AN-2 (2ea)	(F)	Fokker D-7		NA Model A	(S)
Arvo 652A	(P)	Fokker DR-1		Northcutt Aircamper	(F)
Avo Anson	(P)	Funk F-23	(F)	P-40	(P)
AT-301(3ea)	(F)	FW-190A-3	(D)	Pietenpohl	
AT-6F	(F)	FW-190F-8	(D)	PT-19	(S)
BC-12D	(P)	FW-190A-8	(P)	Quick Silver MX	(D)
Bleriot		Greenwood Witch	(S)	S-2A	(F)
BT-13	(D)	H-1H(UH)	(D)	Stinson Reliant	
C-46		H-19	(S)	Waco 10	
C-180H	(F)	J-3C65	(F)	Yak-11	(D)

San Angelo - Mathis Field Airport, 8618 Terminal Circle, Suite 101, 76903,
915-659-6409,   UH-1H   CAF Ft Concho Squadron Also There

Goodfellow AFB, 76908-5000, 915-657-3231, 3480 ABG,
B-25N(TB)   F-100A   T-28A

San Antonio - CAF - Yellow Rose Squadron, Squadron Leader: Lynn A Vanderboegh, 8523 Mission Rd,
78214, 210-677-8619, B-25

City Park Between San Antonio and the Coast Off I37, A-4

Museum of Aerospace Medicine(Hangar 9)Museum, (Edward H White II Memorial), Brooks AFB
70th ABG/MU, Inner Circle Rd, 78235-5329, 210-536-2203, Mon-Fri 8-4, Free Adm,
www.brooks.af.mil/ABG/MU/master.html,   F-100D   JN-4

Lackland Static Airplane Display/Lackland AFB,78236-5000, 210-671-3444, 3055,
Mon-Fri 8-4:45, Closed Holidays, Free Adm, Closed ED, TD, CD, ND,
Curator: Enrique Valdez, 671-2211, www.lackland.af.mil/home/Planes/index.htm

A-10A	C-47D	F-84B	P-38L Rep
AT-6D	C-45J(UC)	F-86A	P-47N
B-17G(TB)	C-118	F-100A	P-51H
B-24M Replica	C-119C	F-101B	P-63G(RP)
B-25H	C-121S(EC)	F-101F	SR-71A
B-26C	C-123K	F-104C	T-28A(GT)
B-29A	F-4B	F-104D(TF)	T-29B(VT)
B-52D	F-5B	F-105B(GF)	T-34A
B-587(RB)	F-16	F-105D	T-38A
B-66(WB)	F-82E(EF)	JN-4D	

Int'l Liaison Pilot & Aircraft Assn Museum, 16518 Ledgestone, 78232,
210-490-4572, Pres: Bill Stratton,

AE-1	L-2	L-4	L-6
L-1	L-3	L-5	L-8

Randolph AFB, 78150-5001, 210-652-1110

AT-6D	T-33A	T-37B
T-28A	T-34B	T-38A

San Antonio Museum of Transportation, Hemisfair Plaza, 78209,
210-226-1201, Daily 10-6, Free Adm,   JN-4D

Texas Air Museum, Stinson Chapter, 8406 Cadmus, Stinson Mncpl Airport, 78214
210-977-9855, Fax 927-4447, Adm Adult $4, 55/Mil $3, Child 6-12 $2, Under 12 $1
Gift Shop, www.texasairmuseum.org, AT-6, FW-190A-8, Monoplane

San Marcos CAF - Centex Wing, 1841 Airport Dr, 78666, 512-396-1943,
Appt Only, Meetings At OPS Bldg, 2nd Tue Monthly,
www.realtime.net/centex/index.html

B5N2 Replica	L-5	P-40N
C-78(UC)	P-39Q	PT-17 (8ea)

Schulenburg - Stanzel Model Aircraft Museum, 311 Baumgarten St, 78956,
979-743-6559, Fax 743-2525, Wed 10-5, Thur-Fri 1-5, Sat 11-4, Sun 1:30-4,
Adm Adult $2, Senior $1, Under 12 Free, www.stanzelmuseum.org,
30 Static Model Displays

Slaton - Texas Air Museum, Caprock Chapter, Slaton Airport, Mail: POB 667,
79364, 806-828-4664, Sat 9-4, Adm Adult & Child $2, Gift Shop, Restoration Facility
Contact: Mike De Lano 828-4334, Malcolm Laing 794-0190,

A-7B	F-105D	Rumpler CV 1704	M-16 Halftrack
AT-19	Fw-190A-6	T-2	M-59
BC-12D	HOS4	T-33A	M- 4 HSTractor
CG-15 Waco	L-17	TG-5	
F-4	Me-109f4	M- 2 Halftrack	

Sweetwater - City Park, Mail: Chamber of Commerce, POB 1148, 79556, 915-235-5488
Fax 235-1026,   T-33A   UH-1

Terrell - Terrell Heritage Museum, 207 N Frances St, 972-653-6082, Wed-Thur,
Sat-Sun, Artifacts

Tulia - VFW Post 1798, 300 SE 2nd St, 79088, 806-995-2513, F-86

Waco - CAF - Ranger Wing, Waco Regional Airport, Mail: POB 8060, 76714-8060
www.rangerwing.com/Ranger_Wingx.html, A-26   T-37

Wichita Falls - Sheppard AFB, 76311-5000, 940-851-2511, STTC/XR

B-52D & G	F-15A	F-105D	T-29A
C-130A & E	F-100D(GF)	F-111A	T-33A
C-135	F-101C	GT-29A	T-38A
F-4C & D & E	F-102A	GYA-37A	
F-5E	F-104C	QT-33A	

UTAH

Heber - Herber Valley Aero Museum, 2002 Airport Rd, Russ McDonald Field, 84032
Mail: POB 680405, Park City, UT, 84068, 435-657-1826, Gift Shop
www.hebervalleyaeromuseum.org ,

Boeing Stearman	J-3	MiG-15	P-51	T-28

Ogden - Hill Aerospace Museum, 75th ABW/MU, 7961 Wardleigh Rd, 84056-5842
801-777-6868, Exit #341 & I-15, Mail: POB 612, 84067, Daily 9-4:30,
Closed TD, CD, Adm Free, Gift Shop, Theater, www.hill.af.mil/museum/

A-1E	C-47D(VC)	F-89H	MiG-21F
A-10A	C-54G	F-100A	O-2A
AQM-34L	C-119G	F-101B	OH-6
A-26B	C-123K	F-102A	P-38J
AT-6	C-124C	F-105D	P-40KT-37B
B-1B	C-130B	F-105G	P-51DT-38A
B-17G	C-131D	F-106A	PT-17
B-24D Project	C-140	F-111E	SR-71C
B-25J	CH-3C	H-1(HH)	T-28B
B-26	F-4C(RF)	H-3C(CH)	T-29C
B-29	F-5E	H-13T(TH)	T-33A
B-47E Project	F-15A	H-21B(CH)	T-37B
B-52G	F-18A	H-34J	T-38A
B-57A(RB)	F-80A Mock-Up	H-43B(HH)	T-39
BT-13B	F-84F	JN-4D	U-3A
C-7A	F-84G	L-4	Wright Flyer
C-45H	F-86L	MiG-17	YA-7F

Missiles:

AGM-65	Bomarc A Snark	LGM-30A	SM-2
AGM-86B	Bomarc B Snark	Mark-5	V-1
AIM-04	CIM-10	Mark-6	
AIR-2A	CIM-10B	Mark-7	

Salt Lake - CAF - Utah Wing, Wing Leader: Richard W Meyer, POB 26333, 84126,
801-571-3610,

AT-19	F4U	PT-17

Salt Lake City ANG, Salt Lake City Int'l Airport, 84116, 151st ARG,

F-86A	F-105B

Washington - Southern Utah Air Museum, 400 W Telegraph Rd, 84780
435-656-8292, www.suam.org, Restoration of Nose Sections

Wendover - Historic Wendover Airfield, Inside Operations Bldg, 345 S Airport Apron
84083, Daily 8-6, www.wendoverairbase.com, Artifacts

VERMONT

Burlington - Burlington ANG, Burlington Int'l Airport, 05401, 802-658-0770, 158 TFG

B-57B(EB)	C-131	F-89J	F-102A	T-33A
C-45	F-4D	F-94C	T-29	

Post Mills - Experimental Balloon & Airship Museum, Post Mills Airport, Robinson
Hill Rd, Mail: POB 51, 05058, 802-333-9254, Dir: Brian Boland, Apt Only,
www.myairship.com/ebaa/, Over 60 Balloons and Airships, 24 Other Vehicles.

VIRGINIA

Bealeton - Flying Circus Aerodrome, 15S. Route 17, BOX 99, 22712, 540-439-8661,
Daily 11-Sunset, Adm Adult $9, Child $3, Open Cockpit Rides $25,
Acrobatic Rides $50, Cub Rides $17.50, Airshow Every Sun at 2:30, May Thru Oct,
President: Bex Goppert

Corbin Jr Ace	Fleet Biplane	PT-17		Waco UPF-7
Cub (2 each)	Fokker D.VIII	Stearman A-75 (8 ea)		

Chantilly - Udvar-Hazy Center, 14390 Air and Space Parkway, Washington Dulles Int'l Airport
SE Corner, 20151, 202-357-2700, Mail: National Air & Space Museum, Independence Ave at 6th St SW
Suite 3700, Washington, DC, 20560-0321, 202-357-4487, 135 Spacecraft, www.nasm.si.edu/museum/udvarhazy/
E-Mail: dullescenter@nasm.si.edu, (D) = Displayed, Rest of Collection in Storage
"Double Eagle II" (balloon gondola only)

A-1H (AD-6)	BD-5A/B (D)
A-6E (D)	Beech D18S
American Aerolights Double Eagle	Beech 35 Bonanza
Applebay Zuni II (D)	Bell 47J (VH-13J)
Arado Ar 234B-2 Blitz (Lightning) (D)	Bell Model 30
Arlington 1A Sisu	Bell ATV (Air Test Vehicle)
Arrow Sport A2-60 (D)	Bellanca CF
Avro VZ-9AV Avrocar	Bennett Phoenix Viper 175 Delta Wing (D)
B-17D	Bennett Phoenix Streak Delta Wing (D)
B-25J (TB-25J-20)	Bennett Phoenix 6B Delta Wing (D)
B-26B	Bennett Mariah M-9 Delta Wing (D)
B-29-35-MO (D)	Bennett Phoenix 6 Delta Wing (D)
Bachem Ba 349B-1 Natter (Snake)	Bennett Model 162 Delta Wing (D)
BB-1	Benoist-Korn (D)
	Bensen B-8M Gyrocopter

Bensen B-6 Gyroglider
Berliner 1924 Helicopter No.5
Boeing 727-100
Boeing 307 Stratoliner (D)
Boeing 367-80 (D)
Bowlus BA-100 Baby Albatross (D)
Bowlus-Du Pont Albatross (D)
BT-13A
Bü-133C (D)
Bü-181B
C-121C
C-150L
C-2 Collegian
Caudron G.4 (D)
Cessna 180
Cessna Citation
Concorde (D)
Curtiss E Boat
Curtiss-Wright X-100
CW-1 Junior
Dassault Cargo Fanjet Falcon 20C (D)
DH-98 B/TT Mk.35
DHC.1 (D)
Do-335A-1
Eipper-Formance Cumulus 10 (D)
Erco 415 Ercoupe
Extra 260XP
F-100D
F-105D
F-4S-44 (D)
F-86A (D)
F4U-1D (D)
F6C-4 (D)
F6F-3 (D)
F8F-2
F9C-2
F9F-6
Fa 330A-1 Bachstelze (D)
FA-3-101
Farman Sport
FB-5 Hawk (D)
Felixstowe (NAF) F5L
Fowler-Gage Tractor
Fw 190F-8/R1 (D)
G-21 (D)
G-22(D)
G4M3 (nose section only)
Gates Learjet 23 (D)
Gittens Ikenga 530Z
Goodyear K-Car (airship gondola)
Goodyear (airship gondola)
Grob 102 Standard Astir III
Grunau Baby Iib (D)
H-1H(UH) (D)
H-34D(UH) Choctaw (D)
Halberstadt CL.IV
Hawker Hurricane Mk.IIC (D)
He 162A-2
He 219A-2
Helio No. 1
HM.14 Pou du Ciel (D)
HOE-1
Horten IIIf
Horten IIIh
Horten VI-V2
HV-2A
Ilyushin IL-2 Sturmovik
J-1
J-3 Cub (D)
J1N1-S
JC-24C Windecker Eagle I (D)
JN-4D
Ju 52/3m (CASA 352L)(D)
Junkers 388L-1
Kaman K-225
Ki-43-Iib
Ki-45 (D)
KR-34C (D)
L-5 (D)
Langley Aerodrome A (D)
Lockheed 5C Vega (D)
Loudenslager Laser 200 (D)

M-18C Mite
M6A1 (D)
Mahoney Sorceress
Manta Pterodactyl Fledgling (D)
Martin, J.V., K-III Kitten
Me 410A-3/U1
Me 163B-1a
MIG-15bis (D)
MIG-21F-13 (D)
Monnett Moni (D)
Monocoupe 110 Special(D)
Monocoupe 70
N-1M (D)
N-9H
N1K2-Ja (D)
N2S-5 Kaydet (D)
NAF N3N-3 (D)
Nagler-Rolz NR 54 V2
Nieuport 28 (D)
O-1A (L-19A)
O-2A
O-47A
Ohka 22 (D)
OS2U-3 (D)
P-26A Peashooter (D)
P-38J-10-LO (D)
P-39Q
P-40E Warhawk (D)
P-47D-30-RA (D)
P-51C (D)
PA-12Super Cruiser
PA-18 Super Cub (D)
PA-23 Apache
Pitcairn AC-35
Pitts Special S-1S
Pitts Special S-1C(D)
PV-2
RC-3
RF-8G
Rockwell Shrike Commander 500S (D)
Rotorway Scorpion Too
RP-63A
RT-14
Rutan Quickie
Rutan VariEze (D)
SB2C-5 Helldiver
SGU 2-22 EK (D)
Sharp DR 90 (D)
SNJ-4 (AT-6)
SPAD XVI (D)
Sportwings Valkyrie (D)
SR-71 (D)
Stanley Nomad
Stearman-Hammond Y
Stout Skycar
Su-26M (D)
T-33A
Ta 152H-1
TBF-1C
TG-1A(D)
Travel Air D4D Pepsi Skywriter (D)
U-2
Ultraflight Lazair SS EC
VB-26B
Verville Sport Trainer
VZ-1
VZ-2A
Waco 9
Waco UIC
Waterman Arrowbile
Westland Lysander IIIa
X-35 (D)
XH-44
XO-60
XP-84 (forward fuselage only)
XR-4 (VS-316)
XR-5 (VS-317)
XR-8
XV-1
XV-15 (D)
Yak-18 "Max"

Chesapeake - CAF - Old Dominion Wing, Hampton Roads Executive Airport, Rte 58,
757-421-7161, www.olddominionsquadron.org

| AT-6 | F4U-1 Project | SNJ | T-28 |
| C-60A(L-18) | L-5 Project | Stearman | |

Ft Eustis - US Army Transportation Museum, 300 Washington Blvd, Besson Hall,
23604-5260, 757-878-1115, Daily 9-4:30, Free Adm, Closed Winter, Holidays
www.eustis.army.mil/dptmsec/museum.htm

Bell Rocket Belt	H-13B(OH)	H-37B(CH)	U-1A
CV-7	H-13E	H-54(CH)	U-6A
DeLacker Aerocycle	H-13E(OH)	H-56A(AH)	U-8D
DH 4	H-15A(UH)	H-64(YAH)	VZ-4-DA
GEM	H-19	L-4	VZ-8P1
GEM-2X	H-19C(UH)	L-21	VZ-8P2
GEM X-2	H-21C(CH)	O-1	VZ-4DA
H-1B(UH)	H-23C(OH)	OV-1	X-2
H-6A(OH)	H-25(UH)	RU-8D	
H-13B	H-34C(CH)	TH-55A	

Hampton - Air Power Park, 413 W Mercury Blvd Off Hwy 64 West, 23666,
757-727-1163, Daily 9-4:30, Free Adm,

A-7E	F-101B	(Missiles & Rockets)	
F-4C(RF)	F-105D	Argo-D-4	NIM-14
F-86L	Hawker P.1127	AIM 4	NIM
F-89J50	P-1127	Copral M2	SM-78
F-100D	T-33A-1	MA14/LJ-5B	Polaris A-2

Langley AFB, 23665-5548, 757-764-2018, 1st FW/PA

| B-52D | F-15A(YF) | F-16A | F-86H | F-105D |

Virginia Air and Space Center, 600 Settlers Landing Rd, 23669-4033,
757-727-0900, 800-296-0800, Mon-Wed 10-5, Sun 12-5, Closed CD, Gift Shop, IMAX,
Adm To IMAX & All Exhibits Adult $8, Snr $7.50, Child 4-12 $5.50
www.vasc.org/air-space.html

American AA-1	F4U-1D	F-104C	P-39Q
Apollo 12	F-16A(YF)	F-106B(NF)	Pitts S-1-C
B-24 Nose	F-16 Cockpit	H-1M(UH)	Rutan Vari-eze
F-4E	F-84F	Langley Aerodrome	Schleiche ASW-12

Manassas - CAF - National Capital Squadron, Squadron Leader: Robert C Flint, 5109
Concordia St, Fairfax, 22032, 703-978-4103, www.natlcapsq.org, BT-13, L-5(2)

Newport News - Virginia War Museum, 9285 Warwick Blvd (US 60), Huntington Park,
23607, 757-247-8523, Mon-Sat 9-5, Sun 1-5, Closed TD, CD, Adm Charged,
Curator: John Quarstein, www.warmuseum.org   HH-52A

Norfolk - Naval Air Station,   Eugene Ely Air Park

| A-6 | F-14 | HSL-30 | SH-2F |
| E-2C | H-53 | HT-033 | |

Nauticus Maritime Museum, A-4

Oceana - Naval Air Station, 804-433-3131

A-4F	F2H-3	F4D-1
A-6E	F9F-2	F-8A
AD-1	F-4B	F-14A(009)

Quantico - Marine Corps Air-Ground Museum, Closed Until 2006 at New Facility,
Brown Field, 2014 Anderson Ave, I-95 & US 1, 22134-5002, 703-784-2606 & 5856,
Apr 1-Nov 15, Tue-Sat 10-5, Sun 12-5, Closed ED, Free Adm,
http://users.erols.com/hyattg/usmcguns/usmcvols.htm, (S) = Storage

A-2	F6F-3	HRS-1	PV-1 (S)
B-25D Nose	F9F-2	HTL-4	R4D-6
Balloon Basket	FB-5	JN-4D	SBD-5
DH 4(S)	FG-1D	Link Trainer	SNJ-5
EF-10 (S)	FJ-3 (S)	MiG-12 (S)	T-28C (S)
F-4A (S)	H-1(UH) (S)	MiG-15	Tanks
F4D-1 (S)	H-1J(AH)(S)	N2S-3	TBM-3
F4F-4	H-53A(CH)(S)	OE-2 (S)	Thomas-Morse S.4
F4U-4	HO3S-1	Oka Mod II	YRON-1
F6F-4	H05S-1 (S)	OY-1	

Richmond - Defense General Supply Center, 8100 Jefferson Davis Hwy, 804-279-3861,
F-84F

Science Museum of Virginia, 2500 West Broad St, 804-257-1013,
Barbara & William B Thalhimer Jr Hall of Science,

| A-4 | J-3 | Solar Challenger |
| F-4 | Lear Jet | Wright Glider |

Virginia Aviation Museum, Richmond Int'l Airport, 5701 Huntsman Rd, 23250-2416,
Take Exit 197 South off I-64, 804-236-3622, Mon-Sat 9:30-5, Sun 12-5, Closed TD, CD,
Adm Adult 13-59 $5.50, Snrs $4.50, Child 4-12 $3, Under 4 Free, Group Rates $0.50 Off,
Gift Shop, Theater, Viewable Restoration Facility, www.smv.org

A-7D	Fleet Model	Taylorcraft E-2
Aeronca C-2N	Heath Super Parasol	Travel Air B-2000
Aeronca C-3	J-3 Piper Cub	Vultee V-1
Bellanca Skyrocket	N2S-3	Waco YOK
Bruner Winkle Bird	PietenpohlAir Camper	Wright Brothers 1900
Bucker Jungmeister	Pershing II Missile	Wright Brothers 1901
Curtiss Robin J-1D	Pitcairn PA-5	Wright Brothers 1902
Curtiss A-14	SPAD VII	Wright Brothers 1903
Ercoupe 415-D	SR-71	WB Kite 1899
Fairchild 24G	Standard E-1	XV-6A
Fairchild FC-2W2	Stinson SR-10G	

Sandston ANG, 192 TFG/CC, Byrd Int'l Airport, 23150, 804-272-8884,

A-7D	F-84F	F-105D

The Wright Experience, 10301 Jefferson Davis Highway, 23237, 804-796-4733, Artifacts
Photos, Documentation, Contact: Rick Young, e-mail: ryoung3@richmond.infi.net

Suffolk - Fighter Factory, Tidewater Tech, 240 Municipal Airport Rd, Suffolk Mncpl Airport
23434, 757-539-8440, Fax 539-5331, Mail: Suite 500, 4455 S Blvd, Virginia Beach,
VA 23452, www.tidetech.com/fighterfactory/welcome.html, email dsa@integrityonline18.com
(R) = Restoration   (S) = Storage Virginia Beach Facility

A-26 (R)	Hawker Hurricane II	P-63 (S)	T-28D
AD-4	I-16 (R)	PBY 5-A	T-34TBM
B-25J (R)	L-5	Po-2	V-1
Bf-109E-7 (R)	OS2U	Polikarpov I-15bis	Wright Model B
F4U-1D	P-39 (S)	Spitfire	Yak-55
Fleet 2 (S)	P-40E (R)	Stearman	

Virginia Air National Guard, Camp Pendleton, 23458, 757-437-4600, F-84F

Wallops Island - NASA Visitor Center, Bldg J-17, 23337, 757-824-298, Fax 824-1776
Thur-Mon 10-4, Adm Free, Gift Shop, Rockets, www.wff.nasa.gov/vc/
Beech C23   Rockets: Little John, Nike-Cajun,

WEST VIRGINIA

Charleston - Charles ANG, 25311-5000, 304-357-5100,   P-51D

Clarksburg - Benedum Airport, 304-842-3400, Dave Reese,   AT-6

WASHINGTON

Arlington - Great Planes Air Museum, 19203 59th Dr NE, 98223, 360-403-9352, Fax 403-9382,
A-26 Project   B-17 Project

Eastsound - Heritage Flight Museum, Eastsound Airport, 173 Aeroview lane, Mail: POB 1630
98245, 360-376-7654, Fax 376-5137, www.heritageflight.org, 2nd Hangar in Bellingham Int'l Airport

A6M3	JN-4	L-39	PT-19
F6F	HE-111	P-40C	
F8F	KI-43	P-51D	
F-86F	L-13	PT-13	

Everett - CAF/Evergreen Wing, Snohomish County (Paine Field), Wing Leader: Richard
Scarvie, 2110 S 300th St, Federal Way, 98003, 425-839-8091, L-2

Everett Tour Center, I-5 exit 189, West on Hwy 526 3½ Mi, Gift Shop across from center
at 3003 W Casino Rd, M-F 12-4, Adm Adult $5, Snrs & Child 15 & Under $3, 800-464-1476
Reservations 425-342-8500 Mon-Fri 8:30-2; http://boeing.com/companyoffices/aboutus/tours/

The ME 262 Project, Paine Field (Snohomish County Airport, Bldg 221, (Next to Fire Station)
10727 36th Pl SW, 98204, 425-290-7878, Mon-Fri 9-5, Contact: Jim Byron,
email: me262project@juno.com, www.stormbirds.com, Me-262 (5ea) Reproduction (3 for sale)

Ft. Lewis - Fort Lewis, 98433, 253-967-0015, Exit 120, H-1B(UH), Nike Missile
Ajax Missile   Iraq Vehicle   Tanks Issaquah

Olympia - Olympic Flight Museum, 7637 A Old Highway 99SE, 98501, 360-705-3925,
Gift Hop, www.olywa.net/ofm

A1-E	F4F-3	Hawker Sea Fury	P-63
A6M2	FB-11	L-2	S-E2
AT-6 (2ea)	FG-1D	L-39	Stearman
BAC-167	FM-2	P-51D	TBM-3

Seattle - Boeing Tour Center, POB 3707, m/s OE-44, 98124-2207, 206-342-9330, Fax 342-7787
www.boeing.com/companyoffices/aboutus/tours/; Tours of the Boeing Plant

King County Municipal Airport, Boeing Field,
4 Mi S of City, 206-296-7380,   Boeing 707   P-51D

Pacific Science Center, 200 Second Ave N, 98109, 206-443-2001, Mon-Fri 10-5,
Sat-Sun 10-6, Adm Adult $5, Juniors $4, Child $2, Curator: D Taylor, www.pacsci.org
Gemini XI,   Lunar Orbiter,   Bell 206 Ranger

Seattle Historical Society Museum of History & Industry, 98112, 206-324-1125,
2700 24th Ave, Adm Adult $1.50, Child $0.50, Curator:William Standard,
B-1 Flying Boat

Museum of Flight, 9404 E Marginal Way S, King County Int'l Airport, 98108-4097,
206-764-5720, Daily 10-5, Thur till 9, Adult $9.50, 65 Plus $8.50, Child 5-17 $5,
First Thur of ea Month Free from 5-9pm, Groups 10+ Adults $8.50, 10+ Children $4, Under 5 Free,
Closed TD, CD, Exec Dir: Ralph Bufano, Gift Shop, Cafe, Theater, S=Storage, P=Paine Field,
R=Restoration Facility, www.museumofflight.org

Restoration Facility 2909 100th SW, Hangar C72, Everett, Wa 98204, Tue-Fri 8-5, Sat 9-5,
206-745-5150, Adm Free, I-5 Exit 189, W on Rte 526, Left on Airport Rd to Snohomish County Airport

A-4F	R Durand Mk.V	P-47D-2 (5/8 Scale)
A-6E	R Eipper Cumulus	R P-80C/TV-1
A-12 Blackbird	R Ercoupe 415-C	P P-86A (P)
A-26	F-4C	Pfalz D-XII
AT-6D	F-5A(YF)	PT-13A
Aerocar III	F9F-8	Quickie Q.200
Aeronca C-2	F-14A	QH-50C
Aero Sport Scamp 3	F-18L Mockup	Resurs 500 Capsule
Albatross D Va	F-86	R RF-4D
Alexander Eaglerock	F-104C	S Rotec Rally IIIB
S An-2	Fairchild F-24W	Rotorway Scorpion Two
R AV-8C	Fiat G.91 PAN	R Rutan Quickie
Aviatik D-I	FG-1D	R Rutan Vari-Eze
Bede BD-5B	Fokker D VII	R Rutan Vari Viggen
R Bensen B-8M	Fokker D VIII	Rumpler Taube
R Bf 108	Fokker E III	SE-5A
Boeing 80-A	Fokker DR I	Sopwith F.1
R Boeing 247-D	R FM-2	Sopwith Pup
Boeing 707-100	Gossamer Albatross II	Sopwith 7F.1 Snipe
R Boeing 727-022	R H-1H(UH)	Sopwith Triplane
Boeing 737-130	H-12(UH)	Spad XIII
Boeing 747-121	R H-21B	Spitfire Mk IX
R B-17F (P)	H-32(YH)	P Sorrell Bathtub Parasol
B-29	R H-52(HH)	P SR-71A Cockpit
B-29 Nose	R Heath Parasol	P Stephens Akro
B-47E (P) Boeing Field	R Huber 101-1 Aero	R Stinson 108
R B-52G	Insitu Aerosonde	Stinson SR Float
R BC-12	R J-2	Swallow CAM 3
Bf-109E-3	J-3C-65	T-33 (Project)
Boeing B&W Replica	JN-4D	T-33 Cockpit
R Bowers Flybaby BA-100	S Kolb Ultralight	S Task Silhouette
P Bowlus BA-100	L-3B	R Taylorcraft A
C-1 Curtiss Robin	P L-13B (CL-13B)	P T-18
C-3B Stearman	P L-106 Alcor Glider	Vickers Viscount 724
C-45	Lear Fan 2100	Wickham B
C-137B(VC) #970	R LF-107	Yak-9
S C-140	Lilienthal Glider	R XF8U-1
CA-20	R LNE-1 (PR-G1)	S XF2Y-1
S Cascade Kasperwing 180-B	M-1	Wright Glider
Chanute-Herring	M-21	Missiles:
P CG-2	McAllister Yakima Clipper	AGM-86A
D-21B Drone	MiG-17	GAPA
R da Vinci Uccello	MiG-21 PFM	IM-99 Bomarc
S DC-2	S Monnett Monerai	KD6C-2 Drone
DC-3	P N-62 Sather RPV (DEX-1)	Apollo Module
R DGA-15P	S N1K2	Boeing Upper Stage
R DH 4C Comet	S Nieuport 24	Hibex Nose Section
DH 4M	Nieuport 27	Mercury Capsule Replica
R DH 100	Nieuport 28	R Pterodactyl Ascender
LNE-1	P OMAC-1	R Pterodactyl Ascender II
R Dornier DO.27	P-12	Sputnik

Spokane - Fairchild AFB Heritage Museum, 92-CSG Bldg 3511, 99011, 509-247-2100,
POB 50, Mon, Wed, Sat 10-2, Fri 6-6, Curator: Mrs. Lyla M. Miles,
Director: Col Ruotsala,

B-52D	F-101	F-105	NIKE
C-47D	F-101	T-33A	AJAX
F-86E	F-102	GAM 72	

Stevenson - Columbia George interpretive Center, POB 396, 990 SW Rock Creek Dr
98648, 800-991-2338, www.columbiagorge.org   JN-4

Tacoma - McChord Air Museum, McChord AFB, Bldg 517, 98438-0205, Ext 125 Off I-5,
E on Bridgeport Way, Main Gate to Visitors Center, Mail: POB 4205, 253-982-2485/2419,
Tue-Sun 12-4, Closed: TD, CD, ND, Free Adm, Gift Shop, www.mcchordairmuseum.org

A-10A	C-47C(TC)	F-4C	F-102A
B-18A	C-82A	F-15A	F-106A
B-23A	C-124C	F-86D	SA-10A(PBY)
B-25 Nose	C-141B	F-101F(CF	T-33A Last Built

Glen E Spieth Museum Antiques, 5928 Steilacoom Blvd, 98499, 253-584-3930,
Sat 11-5, By Appt, T-33A   T-33 Fuse   B-17 Parts

Mr Benhouser, AT-11 in Front Yard, 121th Ave

Tillicum - Camp Murray Air National Guard Park, Exit 122, 253-512-8524
F-101B   M-5 Stuart   M-47 Walker Bulldog Tank

Vancouver - Pearson Air Museum, 1115 E 5th St, 98661, 360-694-7026,I-5 Mill Plain Blvd Exit
Go East, Tue-Sun 10-5, Closed TD, CD, ND, Adm Adult $5, Snr $4, Student $3, Child $2,
Gift Shop, Theater, Restoration Facility, Curator: John Donnelly, e-mail: pearson@pacifier.com
www.pearsonairmuseum.org

ADOCK	Formula 1 Racer 3ea	Nieuport Rep	Starduster II
Aeronca C-3B	GAT-1 Link Trainer	Polan Special	Stearman 1942
AN-2	H-1(AH)	PT-17	Student Prince
AT-6(SNJ)	J-3	PT-19B	Taylor Craft
Curtiss Pusher	JN-4D	PT-21/22	Travel Air B-4000
DH 82	L-4	Rearwin Sportster	Waco UPF-7
DC-3	Meyers OTW	Rutan Quickie	Wasol Racer
Fairchild 24	Mini-Cab	Ryan STA	Wright Flyer Rep
Foker Dr.I	Mooney Mite M-18C	Seahawker Biplane	WSA-1

Whidbey Island Naval Air Station, 360-257-2211, KA-6D

Yakima - McAllister Museum of Aviation, 2008 S 16th Ave, McAllister Field,
Yakima Air Terminal, 509-457-4933, Sat 9-5, Free Adm, www.mcallistermuseum.org,
J-3,   Sceptre Twin Tail Pusher

WISCONSIN

Amery - Amery Municipal Airport, 2 Mi S of City, 715-268-8932,
Owner: Bill Geipel, L-29 Czech Delfin (3ea)

Beloit - Beloit Airport, 4046 E County Tk P, 53512, 608-365-1971, T-28

Boscobel - Airport, 5178 Hwy 133 E, 53805, 608-375-5223, AT-6, T-28

Camp Douglas - Wisconsin National Guard Memorial Library & Museum, Camp Williams,
Volks Field, 54618-5001, 800-752-6659, 608-427-1280, Wed-Sat 9-4, Sun 12-4, Free Adm,
www.volksfield.ang.af.mil/doc/aircraft.htm

A-7D	F-4C	F-100C	O-2A
A-10	F-84F	F-102A (2ea)	P-51D
C-97L(KC)	F-86H	F-105B	UH-1

Fond Du Lac - Wisconsin Aviation Museum, N6308 Rolling Meadows Dr, Fond du Lac County Airport
54935, 920-924-9998, Fax 921-3186, www.fdl.net/wami,

Ercoupe	RV-6	Taylor Monoplane
Pietenpol AirCamper	Steen Skybolt	Woodstock Glider

Hardwood Range Target Range, Public Viewing Area, A-4 on Display

Target Planes:	A-6	F-4	T-33	Vigilante
Remnants:	C-135(KC)	USCG Cutter		

Janesville - Black Hawk Airways, Hwy 51 S, 53542, 608-756-1000, Beech D18S(C-45)

Black Hawk Technical School, Aviation Center, P.O. Box 5009
53547, 608-757-7743,   HH-3   T-33

Yankee Air Force Stateline 4th Division, Rock County Airport, POB 10, 53547-0010,
AT-11   F4F   P-40

Pleasant Prairie - Kenosha Military Museum, 11114 120th Ave, 53159, 262-857-3418
Across State Line on I-94 Exit 347 Hwy 165, May-Sept Wed-Sun 9-5, Oct-April
Sat-Sun 12-5, Adm Adult $5, Curator: Mark Sonday, www.kenoshamilitarymuseum.com

A-7C(TA)	Hughes Helicopter	M-7 Stuart Tank
F-4 Cockpit	M-60 Tank	M-38
H-58(OH)	OV-1D (5ea)	M-38A1
H-1(UH) 3ea	T-33A-5-LO	M-41 Walker Bulldog Tank
H-54(CH) (2ea)	M-2 Half Track	M-42 Duster (2ea) Tank M-47
H-6(OH)	M-3 Stuart Tank	Patton (2ea) Tank M-151
HH-3 (3ea)	M-4 Sherman Tank	PBR River Boat Nam
Hiller Helicopter	M-5A Stuart Tank	U-9

Kenosha - Gateway Technical Aviation Center, 4940 88th Ave, 53144, 262-656-6976, F-84F

Madison - Truax Field Museum, Dane County Regional Airport, 4000 Int'l
  Lane, In the New Pax Terminal, 53704, 608-246-3380,
  Corben Super Ace   Cobra   F-16   H-1(UH)

  Wisconsin Veterans Museum, 30 W. Mifflin St, Capitol Square,
  53703-2558, 608-264-6086, Sopwith Pup Rep   P-51

Milwaukee - Milwaukee Aera Tech, 422 E College Ave, 53200, 414-571-4799,
  L-19   H-3 (HH)   T-34

  Milwaukee's General Mitchell Int'l Airport, Gen Billy Mitchell Field, 53207-6156
  414-747-5300, www.mitchellairport.com, B-25J(TB), SBD-3

  Milwaukee ANG, De Havilland Heron   T-33A

  Mitchell Gallery of Flight, 5300 S Howell Ave, Main Terminal Gen Mitchell
  Int'l Airport, 53207-6156, 414-747-4503, Fax 747-4525, Daily 24 Hours,
  www.mitchellgallery.org/, Curtiss Pusher

Monroe - Gen Twining Park, Park Dr, 53566, F-86D

Oshkosh - EAA Air Adventure Museum, Wittman Airfield, 3000 Poberezny Rd,
  POB 3065, 54903-3065, US 41 Exit 44, 920-426-4818, Mon-Sat 8:30-5, Sun 10-5,
  Closed TD, CD, ND, Adm Adult $8.00, Senior Citizen $7.00, Child 8-17 $6.50,
  7 & Under Free, Family $21.00, Group Rates, Gift Shop, Library,
  www.airventuremuseum.org

A-4B(A4D-2)	DSA-1	Hill Hummer
A-1E/AD-5	E-2	HM-360
A-1E/AD-3	EAA Super Acro Sport	HP-10
Acroduster SA-700 H.G.G.	EAA A-1	HP-18-LK-G Sailplane
Aero Sea Hawk	EAA P-8	Hugo VPS HU-GO Craft
Aeronca C-2N	Eipper MX-1 Quicksilver	J-1
Aeronca LC	Ercoupe 415-C	J-2
Aeronca C-3	F-14	J-3
Aeronca K	F-51D	J2F-6
Anderson Greenwood 14	F-80C(GF)	JC-1
B-17G	F-84C	JC24-B
B-25J	F-84F(GF)	JN-2D-1
Baby Ace D Lambert	F-86 Mk V	JN4-D (2ea)
Baker 001 Special	F-86 Mk V/VI	JP-001
Barlow Acapella	F-86H	Kaminskas RK3
Barrage Kite	F-89J	Karp Pusher 107
Bates Tractor	F-100A	Ki-43B
Bede XBD-2	F4U-4	Kiceniuk Icarus V
Bede BD-5 Micro	F8F-2	Knight Twister
Bede BD-4 Stricker	Fairchild 24W-46	Kotula-Lundy Graflite
Bee Honey Bee	Fairchild 24 C8	L-5E-1VW
Bensen B-11 Gyrocopter	Fairchild 24 C8A	LC-DW500
Boeing E75N1	Falck Racer	Learfan LF-2100
Brock Kem 8M Gyroplane	FC-2W2	Lincoln PT-K
Brown-Bushby-Robinson	Fi 156C-2	Lincoln Biplane
Brown Star Lite	Fike Model C	Loving Racer
Brown B-1 Racer	Fokker DR-1	Luscombe Phantom 1
Brugioni Mario Cuby	Fokker DR-1	M-1 Special
Bu 133	Folkerts Gullwing	Mace Model III
Bu 133L	Ford 4-AT-E	Marinac Flying Mercury
Bugatti 100	Ford Flivver 268	MC-12
Burgess Twister Imperial	Funk B	McHolland Acro-Sport
Cessna 150H	GA-22	Meyer Little Toot
CG-2 186V	GA-400-R-2J	MiG-15
Chanute Hang Glider	Glastar 3	MiG-21
Chester Racer	Globe OQ-2A	Midgnet Pou du Ciel
Christen Eagle I 2ea	Globe KD2G-2	Miles M.2.W.
Christen Eagle II	Great Lakes 2-T-1AE	Mitchell Wing A-10
Christen Eagle IF	Grouod Trainer	MJ-5
Collins Aerofoil Boat	Gunderson Trainer	Mong Sport
Corbin D Baby Ace	H-1S(AH)	Monnett Moni Van WYK
Corbin C-1	H-21B	Monnett Sonerai II
Co-Z	H-10	Monnett Monex
CR-4	HA-1112-M1L	Monnett Moni
Curtiss-Wright B-2	Hamilton Glasair	Monocoupe 110 Special
Curtiss/Abbott	Hardly Abelson	Monocoupe 110
Curtiss/Thompson	Harlow PJC-2	Monocoupe 90A
Cvjetkovic CA-61	Haufe Dale Hawk 2	Monocoupe 90AW
DH 98B Mk.35	Hawker Hunter Mk 51	Monocoupe 113
DH DHC-1B2	Heath Parasol	MS 181
DH 100 Mk.35	Heath LNA-40 Super	N2S-2
DH 82A	Heath Feather	Neibauer Lancair 200
DH 89A MK.IV	Heath Super Parasol	Neiuport 24
DC-3	Hegy R.C.H.I.	Nitz Executive
Double Eagle V	Henderschott Monoplane	Oldfield Special BGL
Driggers A 891H	Henderson Highwing	OQ-2A

OQ-19D	Rand KR-1	Stolp SA500L
OTW-145	Rasor 21	Swallow Model 1924
P-5	Riderf A-1	Swenson S1
P-51(XP)	RLU-1 (2ea)	T-18
P-64	Rotorway Scorpion I	T-33 Mk 3
P-6E	Rutan 72 Grizzly	T-33A
P-9	Rutan Solitaire	T-40
P-10	Rutan Vari-eze	Taylor Aerocar
P-38L	Rutan 50-160 Variviggen	Taylorcraft BC
PA-22-150	RV-3 VanGrusven	Tessier Biplane
PA-28-140	RV-4 VanGrunsven	Travel Air E-4000
PA-39	Ryan NX-211	Travel Air 2000
Pedal Plane	Ryan SCW-145y	UFM Solar Riser
Pereira Osprey II	Schemp-Hirth Nimbus II	UHM Easy Riser]
PG-1	Scorpion II 754RW	V-260/USD
Pientenpol B4A Pientenpol	Shafor Ganagobie	Vector 27
Pientenpol P-9	SM-8A	Waco CTO
Piper PT	Smith Miniplane	Waco RNF
Pitts P-6	Smyth Sidewinder	Waco YKS-7
Pitts 1	Sorrell DR-1	Wag-Aero Cuby
Pitts Racer	Spad VII Swanson	Warwick W-4
Pitts S-1	Spartan 7W Executive	WD-A
Pitts S-1 Special	Spinks Akromaster	WE-1
Pitts S-1S Special 2ea	Spitfire Mk.IXE	Welsh Rabbit Model A
Pitts S-2	Starduster SA-300	Whitaker Centerwing
Pitts SC-1	Stinson SR-9C	Wings Avid Flyer
Player Sportplane	Stits SA-2A	Wisman Pusher
Pober Super Ace	Stits SA-3A	Wittman Midwing
Pober Jr Ace	Stits SA-8	Wittman DFA
PQ-14B	Stits DS-1	Wittman Tailwind WO
PT-3	Stits SA-11A	Wittman W
PT-19B/M-62A	Stolp SA300	Wittman WV
Quickie Herron	Stolp V Star	Wright Flyer
Questair 200 Venture		

Basler's Flight Service, Whittman Field, 54901, Restores DC-3's

Stoughton - VFW, W Veterans Rd, 53589, 608-873-9042, T-33

Superior - Richard IRA Bong Heritage Center, 2231 Catlin Ave, 54880, 15 Miles W of Poplar, The Bong P-38 Fund, Inc, POB 326, 54864, 715-364-2623, 392-7151, www.bongheritagecenter.org, P-38

Waukesha - CAF/Wisconsin Wing, N9 W24151 Blu M, 53186, Mail: PO Box 1998, 53110-1998, 262-547-1775, PV-2D

WYOMING

Afton - Cal Air Museum, 1042 S Washington, 83110, 307-886-9881, Callair Airplanes (3ea)

Cheyenne - Francis E Warren AFB Museum, 90 SMW/CV, Bldg 210, 82005-5000, 307-775-2980, Sat-Sun 1-4, Free Adm, www.pawnee.com/fewmuseum/, H-1F(UH)

WY ANG Cheyenne, BOX 2268, Mncpl Airport, 82003-2268, 307-772-6201, CMS: MD Duncan,

F-84F	F-86L	F-86E	T-33A

Greybull - Hawkins & Powers Museum of Flight and Aerial Firefighting, Greybull Airport, 82426, 307-765-4482, On Hwy 14, Firefighter Facility, Mon-Fri 8-5, Sat-Sun 10-7 (Summer), Adm Adult $2.50, Child 6-18 $1, Under 6 Free, Gift Shop, PA: Sue C Anderson

A-26	C-118 2 ea	H-54B(CH)	PB4Y-2
C-45	C-119 2 ea	Hiller 12E	SL-4
C-54	C-130A 2 ea	L-18	
C-82	Fairchild F-27	Monocoupe 1928	
C-97(KC) 2 ea	H-34A	P-2V 2 ea	

Jackson - Golden Wings Flying Museum, Yellowstone Aviation, Inc, POB 6291, 83002-6291, 800-550-4008, 307-739-8175,

Alliance Argo	Hawker Hurricane	PT-19	Stinson 7M-7A
Call-Air A-2	K-84	PT-6F	Stinson SM-1B
Fairchild F-45	KR-34C	PT-23A	Taylor Aerocar
FC-2-W2	Kreutzer K-5	PT-26 (2ea)	TG-1A
Fleetwings Seabird	N2S-4 (A75L3)	SM-6000-B	Travel Air A-6000-A
Ford 4-AT	Paramount Cabinair	Spartan C2-60	Waco CUC-1

ALBERTA   CANADA
Airdrie - Arcot Aviation, Airdrie Airport, RR #2, T4B 2A4, 403-948-2399, Harvard Mk IV

Claresholm - SNJ

Calgary - Aero Space Museum of Calgary, 4629 McCall Way NE, T2E 8A5, 403-250-3752,
Fax 250-8399, Mon-Fri 10-5, Sat-Sun 10-5, Closed ND, CD, Adm Adult $6, 60 & Over $3.50
Child 11-17 $3.50, Child 6-11 $2, Under 6 Free, Family $15, Pres: Ernie Klaffke,
Gift Shop, Restoration Facility, www.asmac.ab.ca/ e-mail: aerospace@lexicom.ab.ca
(C) = Courtyard; (NM) = Naval Museum; (R) = Restoration Project; (S)=Storage

Airspeed AS10 Oxford Mk.II (S)	DH 100	Noorduyn Norseman Mk V (NM)
Avro Anson Mk II(S)	DC-3 (C)	PD-18(HUP-3)
Avro Anson Mk V (C)	F2H-3 (NM)	Quickie II
Avro Lancaster Mk.X (C)	F-86	Rogallo Wing HG
Bagjo BG12 Glider	F-100(CF) Mk.III	S-51 (C)
Barkley Grow T8P-1	F-101B(CF)(C)	S-55 (S)
Barkley Grow T8P-1(S)	F-104(CF) (S)	Sopwith Triplane
Bede BD-5	Fairy Swordfish Mk.IV	Supermarine Seafire Mk.XV (NM)
Beech D-18S Mk.III (C)	Link Trainer	T-33 (S)(2ea)
Bell 47G	Harvard Mk IV	T-50 (R)
Bristol Mk.IV Blenhiem	Hawker Hurricane XIIb	Taylorcraft Auster Mk.VII
C-64 Mk.V	Hawker Sea Fury (NM)	WACO EQC-6
Cessna 188	Mitchell U-2	
DH 98 (R)	Noorduyn Norseman Mk V (S)	

Cold Lake - F-5(CF)F-101(CF), F-104(CF), T-33(CT)

Edmonton - Alberta Aviation Museum Assoc, 1140 Kingsway Ave, T5G 0X4, Bldg 11, 403-453-1078,
Fax: 453-1885, Mon-Fri 10-3, Sat 9-1:30, Adm Donations, Gift Shop, Manager: Pete Bushko,
www.ualberta.ca/EDMONTON/CONTRIB/airmuseum/aammain.html

Argus	Fairchild 24W	Tocan Ultrlight
Avro Anson Mk.II (R)	Harvard	Vickers Viking Mk.IV 7/8 Scale
B-37(RB)	Hawker Hurricane 5/8 Scale	Waco UIC
Beech D18S	Link Trainer Mk.IV (R)	Westland Lysander 2/3 Scale
Cranwell CLA4 (R)	Noorduyn Norseman (R)	
DH98 Mk B35	PT-26	
F-86	Stinson SR-9FM	
F-100(CF)	Stinson 108 (R)	
F-101B(CF) 3ea	T-33	

Venture Memorial Flight Assoc, 14210-24A St, T5Y 1L7, 403-478-8992,

Grand Center - City Diplayed CF-5, CF-104

Harbor Grace - City Displayed DC-3

Leduc - T-33(CT)

Lethbridge - T-33(CT)

Nanton - St Paul (See Next Page)

Wetaskiwin - Reynolds Museum, East of Airport, 4118 57st, T9A 2B6
403-361-1351, Mail: POB 6360, T9A 2G1, Sept 24-May 9, Adm Adult $6.50,
Snr $5.50, Child $3, Under 7 Free,Family $15, RoY Adult $9, Snr $7, Child $5
Family $20, www.cahf.ca/

Aeronca O-58	DH 60	Lincoln Sport
Aeronca C-3	DH 60GM	Link Trainer
Aeronca Chief	DH 60M	Meade Glider
Auster AOP-6	DH 60X	Meyers MAC 145
AT-6 Harvard Mk.4	DH 82C	Miles M11A
Avro Avian CF-CDV	DH 100	N-75
Avro Anson MK II	DHC. 1	Pietenpohl Air Camper
B-25	DC-3	PT-19
BC-12	Fairchild 24-C8E	PT-26
Bellanca Skyrocket	Fairchild 71	RC-3
Beech 18 Expeditor	Fleet 16	Reynolds Sport
Beech D17S	Fleet Fawn II	Reynolds Star
Boeing Stearman	Focke Wulf Weihi	Stinson HW75
Bristol Bolingbroke MK.IV	Funk B.85C	T8P-1
BT-14	H-34	T-33
C-1(EC)	Hawker Hurricane MK.XIII	T-50
C-37	J-2	TBM
C-64	J-5A	Waco UPF-7
C-64 Mk.4	Jacobs Jaycopter	Waco 10 GXE
Curtiss Robin	JN-4	Waco YKS-7
DGA-15P	L-5	Waco YPT-14
	F-101(CF)	Waco ZQC-6
	F-104(CF)	T-134(CT)

Nanton - Nanton Lancaster Society, POB 1051, T0L 1R0, 403-646-2270, Fax 646-2214, May-Oct
Daily 10-5, Free Adm, www.lancastermuseum.ca,

Avro 683 Lancaster 2ea	CF-100	Link Trainer
Avro Anson MkII (P)	DH 82	PT-18
Beech D18	Fleet Fawn Mk II	PT-26
Bristol Blenheim (P)	Fleet 7C	T-20 Crane
BT-14 Yale	Harvard Mk.II	T-33

Stephanville - Harmon Field, F-102

St Albert - T-33(CT)

St Paul - UFO Landing Pad, Hwy 28, NW of City, Mail: Box 887, T0A 3A0, 888-733-8367
780-645-6800, June 22-Aug 31 Mon-Fri 9-6, Sat-Sun 9-5, RoY Mon-Fri 9-5, Artifacts

BRITISH COLUMBIA

Abbotsford - Abbotsford Int'l Airport, F-101(CF)

Lazo - Comox Air Force Museum, Canadian Forces Base, 19 Wing, V0R 2K0
604-339-8162, June-Aug Wed-Sun & Holidays 10-4, Sept-May Sat-Sun 10-4
www.comoxairforcemuseum.ca

C-47	F-101B(CF)(2ea)	P-107(CP)
F-100(CF)	F-104(CF)	S2F(SC)

Kamloops - Kamloops Airport, F-5(CF)

Port Alberum - Sproat Lake, Vancouver Island West of City, Martin Mars Flying Boat 2ea.

Sidney - British Columbia Aviation Museum, 1910 Norseman Rd, V8L 4R1, On Vancouver Island
Next To Victoria Int'l Airport, 604-655-3300, Summer Daily 10-4, Winter Daily 11-3,
Adm Adult $3 Child $2, Gift Shop, www.bcam.net

A-26	Eastman E-2	Pac Aero Tradewind
Avro Anson Mk II	Gibson Twin Plane	Pietenpol
Bell 47D-1	Luscombe 8A Silvaire	RC-3
Bristol Bolingbroke Mk IV	Nieuport 17 7/8	SE.5A
Chanute Glider	Nooruyn Norseman	
DH82C		

Army, Navy and Air Force Assoc, 4th St, F-86 Mk. 6

Langley - Canadian Museum of Flight & Transportation, Hangar #3 - 5333, 216th St,
Langley Airport, V2Y 2N3, 604-532-0035, Fax 532-0056, MidMay-MidOct Daily 10-4:30,
Winter Fri-Sun 10-4, Closed CD, Boxing D, ND, Adm Family $12, Adult $5, Sr/Youth $4
6 & Under Free, Gift Shop, Exec Dir: Sandy Tinsley, Aircraft Mngr: Gogi Goguillot
www.canadianflight.org, E-mail: museum@direct.ca, Flying = F, On Display = D,
Restore to Fly = R, Restore to Static Display = S, Storage = C

Aeronca Chief 11AC		DGA-15P (P)	Piasecki Model 44B (S)
Auster AOP.6		F-11-2 (2ea)	PT-26A
Avro Anson Mk.II	C	F-100(CF) Mk.38	PT-27 (P)RC-3
Avro Anson Mk.V	C	F-104D(CF)	Rutan Quickie
Beechcraft 3 NMT		Fairchild 71	S-55D(H-19) (S)
Bell 47J2	C	Fairchild 82A (P)	S-58D (P)
Bensen B7	C	Fairchild Cornell	Scheibe Bergfalke II (P)
Bensen B8	C	Fleet Finch MkII Rep	SE-5A (P)
Bensen B8M	D	Flight Simulator (S)	Sopwith Camel Replica
Bowers Fly-Baby	C	Grunau Baby IIB (S)	Struchen Helicopter
Bowlus BB-1 (S)		H-21BPH	Supermarine Stranraer (P)
Brantley 305		Handley-Page 52	SV-4C (S)
Bristol Bolingbroke IVT		Harvard Mk IIB	T-18 (P)
C-64 Mk.V (S)		Hawker Hurricane IIB (P)	T-33AN
C-64 Mk.IVW (S)		HM-290	Taylor Monoplane (P)
C-45-3NM		HO3S-1(S-51/H5) (S)	TG-1AFR (2ea)(S)
Cyclo Crane		HUP-3(PD-18)	TG-3ASW (P)
DH 60GM		L-1(O-49)(S)	Vertol 44
DH 82C		Lockheed 18-08	Waco AQC-6
DH 100 Mk3		Mooney M18C Mite	Waco INF (S)
Dagling Primary 1 (S)		Muller Arrow Hang Glider	Westland Lysander MkIII(S)
DC-3		OQ-RP	

MANITOBA

Brandon - Commonwealth Air Training Plan Museum, Inc, Brandon Mncpl Airport, R7A 6N3,
BOX 3, Group 520, RR5, 204-727-2444, Fax 725-2334, N of Trans Canada Hgwy on #10,
Oct-Apr Mon-Fri 9-4:30, May-Sept, Daily 9-4:30, Closed Sat-Sun, Adm Adult $3.50, Child $2,
Preschollers Free, Curator: J Stacy, www.airmuseum.mb.ca, E-mail: hayter@attcanada.net

Anson	DC-3 (CC-129)	Fleet Fort Project	T-134A(CT)
AT-6 Harvard	DH 82	H-136(CH)	T-50
B-25	F-5(CF)	Hurricane	Westland Mk.III
Bristol Bollingbroke	F-86 Mk VI	J-3	X-44(CX)
C-45 (CT-128)	F-100(CF)	P-121(CP)	
Casara Prayer	F-101B(CF)	Stinson	
Cornell	F-104(CF)	T-33(CT)	

Comfort Inn, Route 10 & Trans Canada, Bollingbroke

Brandon Airport, Route 10, T-33

Gimili - 1st Ave Off Center St, T-33

Moncton - F-5(CT)

Moose Jaw - SNJ

Portage La Prarie - Southport, Portage La Prarie Manitoba Airport (CFB), Cresent Rd &
Royal Rd, C-45,   CT-114   CT-134A,   T-33

Fort La Reine Museum, Hwy 26 & Hwy 1A, 204-857-3259, May-MidSept 9-6, July-Aug
Wed-Fri Extended 9-8, Adm Adult $4, Snr $3, Child $2, 5 & Under Free, CT-134A
http://www.rm.portage-la-prairie.mb.ca/museum.htm

Shilo - The Royal Canadian Artillery Museum, CFB, R0K 2A0, 204-765-3000 Ext 3534,
Victoria Day - Thanksgiving Day, Mon-Fri 8-4, Sat-Sun 1-4, Winter Tue-Fri 8-4,
Free Adm, www.artillery.net, E-mail: rcamuseum@artillery.net, Cannons, Rocket

Winnipeg - Ness Ave & Conway, F-5

Western Canada Aviation Museum, Inc, Hangar T2, 958 Ferry Rd, R3H-0Y8,
204-786-5503, Fax 775-4761, Mon-Sat 10-4, Sun & Holidays 1-4, Adult $4.00,
3-17 $2.50, Under 3 Free, Family $8, Closed Boxing Day, Good Fri, CD, ND,
www.wcam.mb.ca/   e-mail: info@wcam.mb.ca

AT-6 Harvard	DH 82C	H-136(CH)
Avro Anson Mk.II	DH 100	HA-1112
Avro Anson Mk.I	DHC.3	Hiller Helicopter
Avro Anson Mk.V	DC-3	JU 52/1M
Beech D18S	DGA-15	Junkers F-13
Beechcraft 23 Musketeer	F-5(CF)	Link Trainers
Bellanca 66-75	F-101B(CF)	Lockheed 10A
Bellanca 31-55	F-100(CF)	Norseman Mk IV
Bellanca 14-19	F-11A	NA-64
Bensen B-7	F-101B(CF) Cockpits	Saunders ST-27
Bristol Bollingbroke	F-104(CF)	Saunders ST-28
Bristol Freighter	F-86 Mk.3	Schweizer 2-22
BT-13	Fairchild Super 71	Stinson SR-8
BT-14	Fairchild 24W46	T-33A 2 ea
C-37	Fairchild 71C	T-50
C-45	FC-2	U-6
CL-84	Fokker F11	Vickers Vedette V
CP-107	Fokker Super Universal	Vickers Viscount
CP-121	Froebe Hellicopter	Waco YKS-6
CT-134	Froebe Ornithopter	
CX-144	Gruneau 2 Glider	

Air Force Heritage Museum, 500 Wing, Memorial Park, Sharpe Blvd, Off Ness,
204-833-2500 ext 5993, Weekly 9-4, Free Adm

B-25	F-101(CF)	Harvard(AT-6)
Beech 23 Musketeer	F-100(CF)	H-136(CH)Kiowa
C-4/6 Canadair	F-101(CF)	S2F(CP-121)
C-47(DC-3)	F-104(CF)	T-33
F-5(CF)	F-86	

Woodland Park, Portage Ave & Woodhaven, T-33

NEW BRUNSWICK

Chatham - Canadian Forces Base, CF-101

Cornwallis - F-101(CF)

Edmunston Airport, Lancaster 10AB

Hillsborough - Preservation Park, Main Rd S of Town, CF-101

Moneton - Centenial Park - CF-100 Mk 5

Moose Bay, Labrador - T-33(CT)

St. John - New Brunswick Museum, 277 Douglas Ave, Market Square, E2K 1E5,
506-643-2300, Mon-Fri 9-9, Sat 10-6, Sun 12-5, Adm Adult $6, Snr $4.75,
Child 4-18 $3.25, 3 & Under Free, Family $13, Wed 6-9 Free,
Dr Wallace Rupert Turnbull Exhibit, TBM

NEWFOUNDLAND

Botwood - In Town, PBY-5A

Gander - North Atlantic Aviation Museum, POB 234, A1V 1W6, May 15- Sept 6
Daily 9-9, Sept 7 - May 14 Mon-Fri 8:30-4:30, 709-256-2923, Faz 256-4477
Adm Adult $3, Senior/Child 6-15 $2, 5 & Under Free, Curator: Duane Taylor,
E-mail: cjtaylor@avalon.nf.ca,

Beech D18S	DC-3 Cockpit	Lockheed Hudson	Quickie 1
CF-101B	Link Trainer	Lockhee Hudson	PBY-5A

Goose Bay - Happy Valley, Labrador Heritage Society Museum, 709-896-5445,
F-101(CF) XL361

Town Hall, Hamilton River Rd, T-33

5 Wing Goose Bay Hq, Forbes Rd, Bldg 512, CF-100

Harbour Grace - DC-3

NORTHWEST TERRITORIES
Hay River - Buffalo Airways, Box 4998, NWT, X0E 0R0, 403-874-3333
C-47(3ea) (Flights To: Yellowknife & Ft Simpson Available)

NOVA SCOTIA
Baddeck - Alexander Grahm Bell National Historic Park, PO BOX 159,
B0E 1B0, HD-4 Hydrofoil Remains, Silver Dart 1909

Bedford - F-101(CF)

Clementsport - HMCS/CFB Cornwallis Military Museum, Bldg 41-3 Cornwallis Park,
Mail: POB 31, B0S 1E0, 902-638-8602, www.cornwallismuseum.ca/Cornwallis.htm
CF-101,   T-33

Greenwood - Greenwood Military Aviation Museum, Canex Bldg, Ward Rd, Mail: POB 786,
B0P 1N0, 902-765-1494, June-Aug Daily 9-5, Sept-May Tue-Sat 10-4, Free Adm, Gift Shop
www.gmam.ednet.ns.ca

CP-140 Arora	C-61	CT-114	T-33
Avro Anson (P)	C-130	KR-34C	
Avro Lancaster Mk X	Ch-113 Labrador	P2V-7	
Bollingbrooke (P)	CP-107 Argus	PBY-5A Canso	

Halifax - Atlantic Canada Aviation Museum Society, 1747 Summer St, B3H 3H6
Exit 6 from Hwy 102, Mail: POB 44006, 1658 Bedford Hwy, Bedford, NS, B4A 3X5
Mid-May to Mid-Sept 9-5, 902-873-3773, Gift Shop, Picnic Area, Wheelchair Acces
http:/acam.ednet.ns.ca, (R=Being Restored), (P=Project) (S=Storage)

Aeronca C-3 (P)	CP-140	Lockheed 1329-8
Bell 47-J-2	Erco 415C Ercoupe	Lockheed Hudson Mk.6 (S)
Bell 206B	F-86 Mk.5	PBY-5A (R)
CL-13	Fi-103(V1)FZG-76 (R)	Pitts Special S1-C
CF-5	Hang Glider Eletroflyer	Scamp 1 Homebuilt
CF-100	Harvard Mk.II	Silver Dart Rep
CF-101B (S)	L-19	T-33(CT) Cockpit
CF-104 (S)	L-Spatz-55	TBM
CP-107 Simulator(S)	Lincoln Sports	
CP-121	Link Trainer	

Halifax Aviation Museum - CF-5,   CF-100 Mk 5,   F-86,   TBM **2ea**

Shearwater - Shearwater Aviation Museum, Canadian Forces Base Shearwater, 12 Wing,
Mail: POB 5000 Stn Main, B0J 3A0, 902-460-1083 & 1011 ext 2139 Chris Noon
May&Sept Tue-Thur 10-5, Sat 12-4, June-Aug Tue-Fri 10-5, Sat-Sun 12-4, Dec-March Closed
Free Adm, Gift Shop, Library & Restoration Facility 460-1011 ext 2165,
www.shearwateraviationmuseum.ns.ca, email: awmuseum@ns.sympatico.ca

AT-6 Mk.II	F2H-3	HO4S-3	TBM-3
CP-121	Fairey Swordfish	S2F-3	
F-116B(CF)(F5B)	Firefly Mk.I	T-133	
F-101(CF)	Harvard 277	T-114(CT)	

ONTARIO
Barrie - RCAF Assoc, 441 Wing, Hwy 90, East of City, T-33A

Borden - CFB Borden Military Museum, L0M 1C0, Dieppe Rd & Waterloo Rd,
705-424-1200, Tue-Fri 9-12 & 1:15-3, Sat-Sun 1:30-4, Closed Day After Holiday Weekend.
AFA = Air Force Annex, Hangar 11, Hangar Rd, Sat & Sun 1-4, Closed Day After Holiday
AP = Air Park

Avro 504	AFA F-100(CF)	AP L-13(CL)		Panzer Tank	
DH 82	AFA F-101(CF)	AP S2F(CS)	AP	Renault Tank	
F-5(CF)	AP F-104(CF)	AP T-33		AFA Sherman Tank	
F-86	AP JN-1	T-114(CT)		AFA Stuart M5AI	

Belleville - Zwicks Centennial Park, Hwy 2 at Bridge, In Town, F-86 RCAF

Bradford - Guild of Automotive Restores Inc, 44 Bridge St, 705-775-0499, A-6 Project

Brockville - Brockville Marina, Blockhouse Island, Hwy 2 West, F-86
  Hwy 2 West of Town, T-134(CT)

Campbellford - Memorial Military Museum, 230 Albert St, K0L 1L0, 705-653-4848,
  Beech 18 Parts   F-100(CF)   PBY Parts   T-50 Project
  F-5(CF)   F-105 Replica   T-33(CT)   T-134(CT)

Cheltenham - The Great War Flying Museum, 13691 McLaughlin Rd, Brampton Airport,
  May-Sept Daily 2-4, or By Appt, www.bramfly.com/museum
  Flyable: Fokker D.VII Rep,   Fokker DR.I,   SE-5A,   SE-5A 7/8

Collingwood - Collingwood Classic Aircraft Foundation, Collingwood Mncpl Airport,
  Mail: Box 143, L9Y 3Z4, 705-445-7545, Thur 9-4, Adm Free,
  www.classicaircraft.ca/homepage.htm, Smith Miniplane, Stinson 105
  Rides in: Aeronca Champ 7AC, DH 82A, Fleet Canuck

Cornwall - RCAFA 424 Wing, Water St, T-33(CT) 2ea

Dunnville - City Library, Chestnut Ave, Off Hwy 3, Harvard
  No 6 RCAF Dunnville Assoc, Dunnville Airport, Hangar 1, Regional Rd 11, 905-701-RCAF
  DH-82,   Harvard

Dundas - T-33(CT)

Ear Falls - Ear Falls Museum, Waterfront off Hwy 105, Beech 18, Mike

Fort Erie - Niagara Parks, Garrison Rd & Central Ave, Royal Canadian Airforce Assoc
  484 Wing, T-33

Goderich - Sky Harbour Gallery, 110 N St, N7A 2T8, 519-524-2686, Fax 524-1922
  www.huroncountymuseum.on.ca/skyh-gen.htm, Artifacts

Grand Bend - Pinery Antique Flea Market, Hwy 21 6 Km S of Town, T-33

Hamilton - Canadian Warplane Heritage, Hamilton Civic (Mt Hope)Airport,
  9280 Airport Rd, L0R 1W0, 800-386-5888, 905-679-4183, Fax 679-4186, 800-365-5888
  Daily 9-5, Thur 9-8, Closed CD, ND, Adm Adult 9, Snr/Student $8, Child $6,
  Family $28, 8 Mi S of Hamilton Off Route 6, Gift Shop, Library, Theater,
  Pres: Phil Nelson, www.warplane.com, e-mail: museum@warplane.com
  AN-2   F-5(CF)   Link Trainer
  AT-6G Harvard 3 ea   F-86   N.A. 64 Yale
  Auster   F-100(CF) Mk.5   PT-26B Cornell
  Avro Lancaster BX683   F-104D(CF)   PT-27 Stearman
  Avro 652 Anson V(2ea)   Fairchild F-24R   S-51
  B-25J   Fairey Firefly Mk.5   Sopwith Pup Replica
  Bollingbroke Nose   Fleet Finch 16B   T-28
  C-45D(UC)   Fleet 21K   T-33A
  CF-104D   Fleet Fort 60K   Westlander Lysander 3
  DH 100   Fleet 7C Fawn II   Widgeon
  DH 82C   Hawker Hurricane
  DHC. 1   Hawker Hunter Mk.IIB
  DC-3   Hurricane Replica

  Hamilton Airforce Assoc, T-33(CT)

  Hamilton Military Museum, York Blvd (Dundurn Park), L8R 3H1, 905-546-4974
  June 15-Labor Day Daily 11-5, Labour Day-June 14 Tue-Sun & Holiday Mondays 1-5
  Closed CD, ND, Military Artifacts

  RCAF Assoc 447 Wing, Unit 350, Mount Hope Airport, 9300 Airport Rd, L0R 1W0, F-100(CF)

Ignace - City Display, Beechcraft D18 on Floats

Kapuskasing - The Kap Air Collection 17 Lang Ave, P5N 1E5, Airport 705-331-2611

Kingston - CFB Kingston, Hwy 2 East, F-5(CF)   H-136(CH)

  Kingston Airport, RCAFA 416 Wing, Regional Rd 1, 613-389-6404, AT-6 Harvard,   CT-134

  Royal Military College, Point Frederick,Hwy 2, East Of Town, 613-541-6000, F-86, CF-100

Kitchener - Spitfire Emporium, 666 Victoria St South, Spitfire Replica

  Kitchener Waterloo Regional Airport, Fountain St (Regional Rd 17), Diamond Katana

Lambeth - Lambeth Legion Hall, Box 701 Lambeth Station, N6P 1R2, 519-652-3412

Lindsay - Lindsay Airport, Hwy 35, West of City, 705-324-8921, F-101B(CF)

London - Airport Hotel, Dundas St East at Airport, Diamond Katana

  London Airport, Crumlin Rd, Diamond Katana

Royal Canadian Regiment Museum, Carriageway Wolseley Hall, N5Y 4T7,
Oxford/Elizabeth Streets, 519-660-5102, 5136

Malton - F-100(CF)

Mount Hope - See Hamilton, AB

North Bay - CFB North Bay, North Bay Airport, F-100(CF)   F-101(CF)

   Lee Park, Memorial Dr by North Bay Marina, Bomarc   F-101(CF)

North Kitchener - Spitfire Emporium, 666 Victoria St, N2H 5G1, 519-745-2661
   Fax 744-1563, www.spitcrazy.com, email: Ray@spitcrazy.com
   Aviation Store with Spitfire MKIX AHV Replica

Oshawa - Oshawa Aeronautical, Military, & Industrial Museum, 1000 Stevenson Rd N, L1J 5P5,
   416-728-6199, Easter-Nov Tue-Sat 12-5, Sun 1-5

A-26	Armored Ambulance	M 24 Tank	Ferret Scout Car
Chevrolet Staff Car 1942	Jeep 1942	Sherman Tank	

   Oshawa Flying Club, Oshawa Airport, Robert Stuart Aero Collection,
   End of Stephenson Rd North,   F-86 Mk.5

Ottawa - Canadian Aviation Museum, Rockcliffe Airport N, K1A 0M8, 800-463-2038,
   613-993-2010, Mail: POB 9724, Station T, Tue-Sun 10-5, Thur 10-9, Adm $6 Adult,
   Senior & Student $4, Child 6-12 $2, Under 6 Free, Family $12, Group Rates
   Curator: AJ Shortt, www.aviation.nmstc.ca/

AEA Silver Dart	DHC. 3	Lockheed 12A
AEG G.IV	DHC. 6	Lockheed Jetstar
AT-6 Harvard Mk.II	DHC. 7	Maurice Farman S.11
AT-6 Harvard Mk.IV	E-2	McDowall Monoplane
AV-8A Harrier	F2H-3	Me 163B (2ea)
Avro 504 (3ea)	F-18(CF)	Mig 15
Avro Anson V	F-100(CF) Mk.5D(2ea)	Northrop Delta Fuse
Avro Lancaster Mk.X	F-101(CF)	P-40
B-24L	F-104(CF)	P-51 Mk.IV
B-25	F-105(CF)	PBY-5A
Bellanca Pacemaker	F-116A(CF)	RAF B.E.2c
Boeing 247D	Fairchild FC-2W-2	Sopwith Camel 2F.1
Boeing M1M-10B	Fairey Swordfish	Sopwith Snipe 7F.1
Bristol Beaufighter	Fleet Model 16B	Sopwith Triplane
Bristol Bolingbroke IVT	G-2 Goose	SPAD SVII
C-47-IV	H-135(CH)	Stearman 4EM
C-64 Mk.VI	Hawker Hind	Stinson SR
CL-13B Mk.6 2ea	Hawker Hurricane XII	Stits SA-3A
CL-28 Mk.2	Hawker Sea Fury F.B.11	Spitfire Mk.IX-LF
CL-84	HO4S-3	T-114(CT)
Curtiss Seagull	HS-2L	Taylorcraft BC-65
DC-3	HTL-6 Bell 47G	Travel Air 2000
DC-4M	HUP-3	V-1
DH 80A	JN-4	Vickers Viscount
DH 98	Junkers W-34f/fi	Westland Lysander III
DHC. 1B2	Lockheed 10A	Wills Wing XC
DHC. 2		

   Canadian War Museum, Museum, 330 Sussex Dr, 613-922 2774, Daily 1-5pm, Closed Monday
   Mid-Sept-Apr, Closes 9pm Tuesdays in summer, H-136(CH), Nieuport 17, Spitfire Mk VII

   Ottawa Int'l Airport, Breadner Blvd & Royal Route (Formerly CFB Uplands), F-101(CF)

Petawawa - CFB Pettawawa Military Museum, 613-687-5511 ext 6238, C-47, L-19A

Peterborough - Riverview Park, Water St, North of Town, F-86 Mk.6

Picton - Along Union St, East of City, T-33, T-134(CT)

Red Lake - Howie Bay Waterfront, Howie St, Norseman

Sarnia - Germaine Park, East St, F-86

Sault Ste Marie - Ontario Bushplane Heritage, 50 Pim St, Station Mall Postal Outlet,
   P6A 3G4, Mail: POB 23050, P6A 6W6, 705-945-6242, Fax 942-8947, Toll-Free 877-287-4752
   June 1-Sept 30 Daily 9-9, Oct1-April30 Daily 10-4, Adm Adult $7.50, Senior $6.75, Student $3.75
   Child $1.50, www.bushplane.com, email: bushplane@soonet.ca,

Aeronca 11AC	DH 83C Fox Moth	Great Lakes 2T-1A	S-2A
Beech D18S (3 ea)	DH 89 Dragon Rapide	Link Trainer	Silver Dart Rep
Bell 47D-1	DHC 2-Mk.I	KR-34	ST-27
Buhl C6 Airsedan	DHC 2-Mk.III (2 ea)	Noorduyn Norseman Mk.I	Stinson SR-9 Reliant
C-3	DHC 3	Noorduyn Norseman Mk.IV	Taylor Model 20
C-64 (CY-AYO)	F-11 Husky	OPAS Buhl	U-6A
C-64 (CF-BFT)	Frasca IFR Simulator	RC-3 Seabee	U-6A Turbo
CL-215			

Smith Falls - Victoria Park, Lombard South, AT-6 Harvard IV

Tillsonburg - Canadian Harvard Aircraft Assoc, Tillsonburg Airport, Mail: POB 774
Woodstock, N4S 8A2, 519-842-9922, By Appt, www.hangarline.com, email: 1sunday@hangerline.com
BT-14 Yale Project   Private Flying Club with:
DH-82 Tigermoth   Harvard MKA
Harvard (4 EA) HWX, MTX, RWN, WPK   Harvard NDB

Toronto - Ontario Science Centre, 770 Don Mills Rd, Sopwith Pup Rep

Toronto Aerospace Museum, Parc Downsview Park, 65 Carl Hall Rd, M3K 2B6, 416-638-6078,
Fax 638-5509, Thur-Sat 10-4, 416-638-6078, Fax: 638-5509, Adult $8, Senior $6,
Child 18-6 $5, Under 6 Free Family $20,www.torontoaerospacemuseum.com,
BD-10   T-114(CT)   Lancaster Project   Zenair Zenith
F-5(CF)   T-134(CT)   Osprey
F-105(CF)Rep   DH-82 Project   Sea Prince
S2F(CF)   Hurricane 5/8 Rep Ultimate 100

Wildwood Park, Derry Rd, NE of Lester B Pearson Int'l Airport, 416-247-7678, F-100(CF)

Trenton - Holiday Inn, Sidney St & Hwy 401 (Glen Miller Interchange) Exit 526, F-5(CF)

RCAF Memorial Museum, Quinte West, 8 Wing, RCAF Rd, K0K 1B0, Mail: POB 1000, Stn Forces, Astra,
K0K3W0, Exit 526 on Hwy 401, 613-965-2140, Fax: 965-2208, Fax: 965-7352, May 1-Oct 1 Daily 10-5,
Oct 1-May 1 Wed-Sun 10-5, Free Adm, www.rcafmuseum.on.ca

Argus 732	DHC 1B (CT-120)	F-104D(CF)	OH-58
Auster AOP Mk6	F-100(CF) MkIV	Handley-Page Halifax	T-33(CT) MkIII
C-47	F-101B(CF) 2ea	Hawker Hunter Mk9	T-114(CT)
Canadair Mk.2	F-86D MkVI	Lancaster	T-133(CT)
CL-41	F-5B(CF)	MiG-21 MF	T-134(CT)

Town Arena, South of Dundas St, F-86

Wellington - Hwy 33 East of Town, On Garage Roof, F4U (1/3 Scale)

Windsor - Canadian Aviation Historical Society Windsor, Windsor Airport
Airport Rd, N8V 1A2, 519-737-9461,
DHC-1   Fleet Fawn   Mosquito Project   Stearman
Jackson Park, Tecumseh Rd East, Lancaster

PRINCE EDWARD ISLAND
Summerside - Heritage Aircraft Society, 173 Victoria Rd, C1N 2G8
Argus 739(CP-107)   F-101(CF)   Tracker 131(CS2F)

QUEBEC
Bagotville Alouette - CFB, F-5(CF), F-86, F-100(CF), F-101(CF)

La Baie - Air Defence Museum, Hwy 170, Mail: POB 5000 Station Bureau-Chief
Alouette, QC, G0V 1A0, 418-677-4000 Ext 8159, Fax 677-4073, Mid-June to
Labour Day Tue-Sun 9-5m Off-Season by Appt, Adm Adult $4, Child & Snr $3,
Under 5 Free, CF-18,   CF-86,   MiG-23,

Knowlton - Brome County Historical Society, POB 690, J0E 1V0
Near Brome, 243-6782, Curator: Marion L Phelps, Fokker D.VII

St Esprit - RB-57
St Hubert - CFB, CF-100
St Jean-sur-Richelieu - Airport, CFB, CF-100   CF-104
College Military Royal, CF-100

SASKATCHEWAN
Assiniboia - Harry & Anne Whereatt, POB 31, S0H 0B0,

Moose Jaw - Western Development Museum, 50 Diefenbaker Dr, 306-693-5989,
Mail: POB 185, S6H 4NB, Gift Shop, www.wdm.ca/mj.html
Aeronca K	Cessna 195	H-10	Stinson 105
Avro Anson	DH 53	Harvard Mk IV	Spitfire Parts
Avro F-100(CF)	DH 60M	Hawker Hurricane	T-33A
B-25	DH 82C	JN-4	T-50
Beech D18D	DH C-1	Jodel D-9	Waco YKS
BT-14 Yale	Fleet Finch	Mead C-III	Zogling Glider
C-64 CF-SAM	Fleet Fort	PT-19	

Regina - C-45
Saskatoon - T-33(CT)

YUKON TERRITORY
Whitehorse - Yukon Transportation Museum, Mile 917 Alaska Hwy, Y1A 5L6, 403-668-4792
Fax: 633-5547, May 22-Spet 5 Dayily 10-7, Adm Adult $3, 60+ $2.50, Child 12+ $2.50,
6-12 $2, Family $7, Ryan NYP, DC-3

CITY DISPLAYED AIRCRAFT

(AP) = Airport; (AM) = American Legion; (VWF) = Verterans of Foreign Wars

State	City	Aircraft
ALABAMA	Atmore	T-33A
	Florala	T-33A
	Mobile	T-33A, F-105
	Monroeville	T-33A
	Montgomery	F-84F
	"	F-86L 3ea
	Ozark	RF-84F
	Selma	T-33A 2ea
	Tuscaloose AP	T-33A
	" I-20/59	A-7, UH-1, M60
ARIZONA	Apache Junction	T-33A
	Chandler	F-86D
	Douglas	RF-101C
Airport	Gila Bend	RF-101C 2ea
	Glendale	F-100D
	Globe(VFW 1704)	F-86D
	Peoria US 60(AL)	F-84F
ARKANSAS	Gravette	T-33A
	Harrison	F-84F
	Helena	T-33A
	Pocahontas	MGM-13B
	Rogers	V-101B
CALIFORNIA	Bakersfield	T-38 (2ea)
	Banning	XGAM-67
	Burbank	F-104D
	Los Gatos	T-33A
	Madera	T-33A
	Porterville	A-4
	Torrance (AP)	T-33
	Tulare AMVet 56	B-17
	West Covina	F-86D
COLORADO	Flagler	T-33A
	"	TGM-13, Mace
	Monte Vista	XQ4
DELAWARE	Dover(AL P-2)	T-33A
FLORIDA	Arcadia	T-33A
	Callaway	F-101
	DeFuniak	T-33A
(Holiday Park)	Ft. Lauderdale	F-86H
	Ft.Walton Bch	CQM-10A
	Homestead	F-4
(I-75N Exit 81)	Lake City	A-7E
	Milton	T-28
	Oelwein	T-33A
	Orlando	B-52
	Panacea	CGM-13B
(Am Leg Post2)	Wauchula	F-84F
(Am Leg Post18)	Wildwood	CGM-13B
GEORGIA	Athens VFW	F-84F
	Cochran	Missile
	Douglas	T-33A
	Griffin	T-33A
	Hawkinsville	MGM-1
	Thomasville	T-33A
	Valdosta	F-86L
	Warner Robins	CGM-13B
	Waynesboro	T-33A
	Willacoochee	T-33A
IDAHO	Burley	T-33A
	Idaho Falls	F-86L
	Lewiston	T-33A
	Malad	T-33A
(Carl Miller Park)	Mountain Home	F-111
	Nampa	F-89B
	Pocatello Airport	F-101
	Sheldon Airport	T-33A
	Twin Falls	T-33A
ILLINOIS	Aurora Airport	F-105D
	Brookfield	F-86L
	Elhert Park, Rte 34(Elm St)	

State	City	Aircraft
	Centralia	T-33A
	Edwardsville	
	RC Stille Twnp Park,	LTV A-7E
	Granite City	F-84F, DC-3
	Highland	T-33A
	Lindenhurst VFW	A-7
	Pekin	F-84F
	Pinckneyville	T-33A
	Quincy	T-33A
	Versailles	T-33A
	Wenona	F-84F
INDIANA	Churubusco	F-86H
	Green Castle	Buzz Bomb
	Hoagland	F-84F
	Huntington	T-33A
	Indianapolis	F-86E
	Monroeville	F-84F
	Montpelier	F-84F
	South Whitley	F-84F
IOWA	Burlington	T-33A
(Vet Memorial)	Cedar Rapids	F-84F, T-33A
	Correctionville	F-84F, A-7D
	Fairfield	F-84F
	Harlan	RF-84F
	Iowa City	F-86L
(Airport)	Sheldon	A-7D, T-33A
	Sigourney	T-33A
KANSAS	Dodge City	B-26C
	Independence	T-33A
	Lynn	F-84L
KENTUCKY	Fulton	T-33A
	Sturgis	F-86D
LOUISIANA	Alexandria	F-80
	Houma	T-33A
(VFW Hwy 6)	Many	M4 Sherman
	Mansfield	T-33A
	Springhill	T-33A
MAINE	Blaine	AGM-28B
	Marshill A.L. Post 118	
	Waterville	F-89J
MARYLAND	Cumberland	T-33A
	Ellicott City	F-86H VFW
	Handcock Nike-Ajax APC	
	Pocomoke City	T-33A
	Rockville	T-33A
MICHIGAN	Breckenridge	T-33A
	Escanaba	F-84F
	Grand Haven	F-100A
	Grayling	T-33A
	Hart	T-33A
	Iron Mountain	T-33A
	Monroe	F-86D, UH-1
	Rosebush	T-33A
	Sebewaing	T-33A
MINNESOTA	Albert Lea	T-33A
	Alexanderia	T-33A
	Buffalo	T-33A
	Duluth	T-38
	Hector	T-33A
	Minnesota Lake	T-33A
	Proctor	F-101F
MISSISSIPPI	Columbia	T-33A
(Hwy 51)	Greneda HS	A-7F
MISSOURI	Caruthersville	T-33A
	LaPlata	F-86H
	Monett	F-4
	Mountain View	T-33A
	Richmond	T-33A

```
                St. Charles    T-33A              Waterford      F-94
                St. Louis      T-33A
                                        S CAROLINA  Greenville    F-86H
MONTANA    Butte         F-86L                      Hartsville    T-33A
           Glasgow       T-33A                      Huron         T-33A
           Great Falls   T-33A                      Lake Norden   T-33A

NEBRASKA   Beatrice      T-33A         TENNESSEE  Athens VFW 5146  F-4
           Creighton     F-84F                    Crossville      T-33A
           David City    RF-84F                   Dayton          T-33A
           Fairbury City T-33A                    Johnson City    T-33A
           Franklin      T-33A                    Knoxville       F-86D
           Kimball       Titan 1                  Nashville       F-86L
NEBRASKA   Mc Cook       F-86H                    Pulaski         T-33A
           Neligh        RF-84F
           S Sioux City  A-7D          TEXAS       Bastrop VFW    F-4
           Valley        RF-84F        (Court House) Beeville     F-80
           York          RF-84F                    Del Rio Commerce T-33A
                                                   Denison         F-86L
NEVADA     Indian Springs  F-84F                   Eagle Pass      T-33A
           Reno Lions Park Jet              VFW    Ellington       F-84G
     Winemucca F-86D, UH-1B, M-3 Tank            Kingsville  NAS A4D
                                        (VFW 3377) Manchaca       F-4
NEW MEXICO Alamogordo    F-80F, XQ-4              Muenster        F-84F
           Artesia Hwy 285 F-84F                  Sherman         F-86L
           Manchester    F-86H-10-NH              Texarkana       T-33A
           Melrose       F-100A
           Truth         T-33A
                                        UTAH        Murray         T-33A
NEW YORK   Baldwinsville  F-102A-80
           Buffalo       F-4J,101F     VIRGINIA   Hampton        CIM-10A
           Central Square F-86H             "                    F-84F
                                            "                    F-86L
           Manchester    F-86H                                   F-89JC
           Monroe        F-86L                                   F-100C
           Tonawanda     F-9                                     F-104C

N CAROLINA Fayetteville  F-94C         WASHINGTON Brewster       YIM-99B
           Goldsboro     F-86H                    Bridgeport     F-86L
           Kings Mountain F-105                                  XGAM-67
(Carolina Beech Rd) Wilmington  T-33A  Oak Harbor City Beach Park EA-6B
                                                   Othello        T-33A
N DAKOTA   Dickenson     T-33A                    Spokane        T-33A
           Grand Forks   F-86L                    Reedsville     T-33A
           Hatton        T-33A                    River Falls    AGM-28A
           Hettinger     F-86H                    Sherwood       T-33A
  Airport  Jamestown     F-86H                    Stoughton      T-33A
           Vela          T-33A         W. VIRGINIA  Milton       F-86L
           Walhalla      F-86H                    Vienna         F-84H
           Wahpeton      A-7D
                                       WISCONSIN  Appleton       F-86L
OHIO       Brooklyn      T-33A                    Argyle         F-86H
           Cincinnati    F-86H                    Brillion       T-33A
           Marietta      T-33A                    Fall River     T-33A
           Wadsworth     T-33A                    Janesville     F9F
                                                  Madison        T-33A
OKLAHOMA   Comanche      T-33A         (Twining Park) Monroe     F-86D
           Hattiesburg   RF-84F, RF-101C (Am. Leg 80) New Richmond P-80
           Hazlehurst    F-86L                    Prentice       T-33A
           Jackson       F-105
(VFW382)   El Reno       A-26          WYOMING    Buffalo        AGM-28A
           Elk City      T-33A                    Milwaukee      B-25
           Midwest       GAM-63                   New Richmond   T-33A
Oklahoma City  AGM-28, B-52F 2ea, WB-47E   I-80   Rock Springs   F-101

OREGON     Nyssa         F-86L         Canada
           Vale          F-86L           Alberta
           Woodburn      T-33A                    Vulcan   Starship Enterprise

PENNSYLVANIA                             Brititsh Columbia
           Beaver Falls  F-86H                    St James       Junkers W34
           Cory          F-94C
           Imperial      F-86L           Ontario
           Mildred       MACE                     Moonbeam       Flying Saucer
           New Kensington T-33A                   Windsor        Flying Saucer
           N Huntington  T-33A
```

RESTAURANTS

The following are restaurants with one or more aircraft in or around them or have been converted into a restaurant.

ARKANSAS **Hot Springs** Granny's Kitchen, 332 Central Ave, 71901, 501-624-6183
Daily 6:30-8pm, Closed January, Home Cooking At Moderate
Prices, Daily Breakfast Special, Daily Lunch Special
Full Lunch and Dinner Menu With 12 Vegetables,
Specialty - Blackberry Cobbler. Hanging From Ceiling Are:

A6M Zero	Ju 87 Stuka	Pitts S-1	Super Chipmunk
DHC. 1	Nieuport 28	PT-19	UC-78
Flybaby Biplane	Nieuport 17	PT-19	
J-3	P-38	RC-3	

CALIFORNIA **Calabasas** Sagebrush Cantina, 3527 Calabasas Rd, 91302, 818-222-6062
Mon-Thur 11am-10pm, Fri-Sat 11am-11pm, Sun 9am-2pm,
Bar: Fri-Sat 9am-1:30am, Sun-Thur 9am-Midnight,
Appetizers Avg $6, Soups and Salads$4-9, BBQ Ribs $15
Mexican Specialties $8-11, Charcaol Broiler $9-17
Bede BD-5J N007JB Ontop Restaurant

Camarillo Camarillow Airport Cafe, Breakfast, Sandwichs

Hawthorne Pizza Hut, 5107 El Segundo Blvd, 90250-4139, 424-676-1100
1 Mile from Northrop Plant, Space & Aviation Artifacts

Los Angeles Proud Bird Restaurant, 11022 Aviation Blvd, 818-670-3093
Leave 405 Freeway on Century Off Ramp, West To Aviation
Blvd, South To 11022 (Just East of LAX South Runway).

F4U	P-38	P-40	P-47	P-51

Sacramento Aces Restaurant, Holiday Inn, 5321 Date Ave, 95841-2597
800-388-9284, www.basshotels.com/h/d/hi/hr/sacne
Breakfast/Lunch/Dinner, Steaks, Seafood, P-51 Replica Above Roof

Santa Ana Nieuport 17 Restaurant, 1615 E 17th , 714-547-9511

San Diego 94th Aero Sqd, 8885 Balboa Ave, 92123, 619-560-6771

San Jose 94th Aero Sqd, 1160 Coleman Ave, 95110, 408-287-6150, Airplane there

Tustin Nieuport 17 Restaurant, 13051 Newport Ave, 92780 714-731-5130

Santa Monica DC-3 Restaurant, 2800 Donald Douglas Loop North, 90405
310-399-2323, Mon & Sun Lunch, Tue-Sat Lunch & Dinner
Specialty - Steaks
Douglas - Sunbeam - Harley Davidson Motorcycle Display

Torrance Doolittle's Raiders, 2780 Skypark, 90505, 428-539-6203
Manager: Keith Sulesky

Van Nuys 94th Aero Sqd, 16320 Raysner Ave, 91406, 818-994-7437

COLORADO **Greeley** State Armory, 6148 8th Ave, 80631, 970-352-7424,
Burgers, Steaks, B-17 Hanging from Ceiling.

CO Springs Solo's Restaurnat, 1665 N Newport Rd (Off Fountain Blvd, One block
East of Powers), CO Springs Mncpl Airport, 719-570-7656, Sun-Thur 11-9
Fri-Sat 11-10, Eat inside a KC-97, Burgers to Steaks
Eat inside a KC-97, Model 8' B-17

CONNECTICUT **Bridgeport** Captains Cove, 1 Bostwick Ave, Restaurant 203-335-7104,
Gostave Whitehead Model 21, 1901 Glider, 203-335-1433,

DELAWARE **New Castle** Air Transport Command Greater Wilmington Airport,
143 N du Pont Hwy(US Hwy 13), 19720, 302-328-3527, C-47

FLORIDA **Clearwater** 94th Aero Sqd, 94 Fairchild Dr, 33520, 727-536-0409

Ft Lauderdale Aviator's Tavern & Grille, Ft Lauderdale Int'l Airport,
Under the Control Tower on the SW Side of the Airport,
1050 Lee Wagner Blvd, 33315, 954-359-0044

95th Bomb Grp, 2500 NW 62nd St, 33309, 954-491-4570

Miami 94th Aero Sqd, 1395 NW 57th Ave, 33126, 305-261-4220

Mayday's, 7501 Pembroke Rd, S Side of North Perry Airport,
33024, 305-989-2210, Manager: Mark Siple,

Miami   Spirit Restaurant, 7250 NW 11th St., 33126, 305-262-9500
Pres Denise Noe, Lunch Specials Daily $4-7, Mon-Fri
Dinner 5pm Mon-Sat $7-11, Happy Hour Mon-Fri & D.J.
Fri/Sat, Steaks - Seafood - Pasta's - Salads - Mexican -
Cuban, Artifacts & 5' Models of Eastern & Pan Am Airlines
DC-3, DC-10, 727, 747, 757,

Orlando   4th Fighter Grp, 4200 E Colonial Dr, 32803, 305-898-4251

Off-The-Wall, Night Club, 4893 S Orange Blossom Tr,
305-851-3962,   Fokker D.VII   Fokker DR.I   SE-5A

Sarasota   306th Bomb Grp, 8301 N Taniani Trail, 33580, 941-355-8591

West Palm Beach   391st Bomb Grp, 3989 Southern Blvd, 33406, 561-683-3919 C-47

GEORGIA   Atlanta   57th Fighter Grp, 3829 Clairmont Rd, 30341, 404-457-7757

Air Superiorty Group, DeKalb-Peachtree Airport, POB 566726, 31156,
AT-6,   C-47,   P-51,   Rides in a N2S-3

IOWA   Cedar Rapids Flyin Weenie, Downtown, PA-22 On Roof

ILLINOIS   Decatur   Decatur Airport Restaurant, R/C Aircraft Hanging From Ceiling,

Moline   Bud's Skyline Inn, 2621 Airport Rd, Rt 6 & 150, 61265,
309-764-9128, Lunch Mon-Sat 11am, Dinner: Ribs, Catfish, Steaks,
Email: skyline@qconline.com, Artifacts, Models

Wheeling   94th Aero Sqdn, 1070 S Milwaukee Ave, 60090, 847-459-3700
P-38 Replica   P-47 Replica   P-51 Replica

INDIANA   Muncie   Vince's Gallery, 5201 N Walnut, Muncie Airport, 47303,
765-284-6364, Mon-Thur 11-10, Fri 11-11, Sat 7-11,
Sun 7-9, Dinners Average: 10.00-12.00, Artifacts

Valparaiso   Strongbow Turkey Inn, 2405 Hwy 30 E, 219-462-5121, 11-10pm

MARYLAND   College Park 94th Aero Sqd, 5240 Calvert Rd, 20740, 301-699-9400

MICHIGAN   Flint   Mister Gibby's Food & Spirits, Mister Gibby's Inn,
Best Western, G 3129 Miller Rd, At I-75 & US 23, 48507,
810-235-8561, 1-800-528-1234, 1/3 Scale Wings of DR.1 in
Cocktail Lounge, Bi-Plane Wings Outside Wall of Building.
Steaks, Seafood and Salad Bar.

Minnesota   Alexandria   Doolittle Restaurant, 4409 Hwy 29 South, 56308, 320-759-0885,
Steaks, Ribs, Pasta, Seafood, Sandwiches, www.doolittlesaircafe.com,
R/C Aircraft, Artifacts, T-33

Coon Rapids   Doolittle Restaurants, 3420 129nd Ave NW, 55448, 612-576-0575
Steaks, Ribs, Pasta, Seafood, Sandwiches, www.doolittlesaircafe.com,
R/C Aircraft, Artifacts,

Eagan   Doolittle Restaurants, 2140 Cliff Rd, 55122, 651-452-6627
Steaks, Ribs, Pasta, Seafood, Sandwiches, www.doolittlesaircafe.com,
R/C Aircraft, Artifacts,

Golden Valley Doolittle Restaurants, 550 Winnetka Ave North, 55427, 612-542-1931
Steaks, Ribs, Pasta, Seafood, Sandwiches, www.doolittlesaircafe.com,
R/C Aircraft, Artifacts,

Plymouth   Doolittle Restaurants, 15555 34th Ave North, 55447, 612-577-1522
Steaks, Ribs, Pasta, Seafood, Sandwiches, www.doolittlesaircafe.com,
R/C Aircraft, Artifacts,

MISSOURI   Berkeley   94th Aero Sqd, 5933 McDonnell Blvd, 63134, 314-731-3300

NEW JERSEY Caldwell   94th Bomb Grp, 195 Passaic Ave, 07006, 973-882-5660

NEW YORK   Buffalo   Inn of the Port, Buffalo Greater Int'l Airport, 716-632-5050,
P-40 Replica

Cheektowaga   Flying Tigers, 100 Amherst Villa Rd, 14225-1432
716-631-3465, Seats 200, Smoking & Handicapped Sections,
P-40: Tail Rudders - Parts of Wing - Propellers
Assistant General Manager: Matthew Rickrode
Appetizers: $2.95-$6.95   Entrees: $10.95-$15.95
Soups & Salads: $2.95   Desserts: $ 1.95-$ 3.95

E Farmingdale 56th Fighter Grp, Republic Airport Gate 1, Route 110
11735, 631-694-8280,   P-47 Replica

NORTH DAKOTA	Grand Forks	John Barley'Corn, 123 Columbia Mall, 701-775-0501, Lunches $5.50 to Dinners $14.00, Hamburger to Lobster EAA Biplane, Hanging From Ceiling In Lounge, 11:30 am -1 am
	Fargo	Doolittle Restaurants, 2112 25 th St South, 58103, 701-478-2200 Steaks, Ribs, Pasta, Seafood, Sandwiches, www.doolittlesaircafe.com, R/C Aircraft, Artifacts,
OHIO	Cleveland	100th Bomb Grp, 20000 Brookpark Rd, 44135, 216-267-1010, P-51
	Columbus	94th Aero Sqd, Port Columbus Int'l Airport 5030 Sawyer Rd, 43219, 419-237-9093
	North Canton	356th Fighter Grp, Akron-Canton Airport, 2787 Mt Pleasant Rd, 44720, 330-494-3500, Lounge Seats 170, Banquet Seats 60, Non-Smoking & Handicapped Sections, Daily : Lunches $4.95-7.95; Dinners $10.95-22.95
OREGON	Milwaukie	Lacey's Bomber Inn, 13515 SE. McLoughlin Blvd, Hwy 99E, 97222, 503-654-6491, B-17G (485790) Breakfast Mon-Sat 6am-1:45, 12:45 Sun, $2.25-6.95 Lunch 11am-5, $3.25-6.50, 25 Selections Dinner 11am-8:30, Till 9 Thr-Sat, $4.95-8.95 12 Selections Daily Specials: Ribs, Seafood, Italian, Steak & Prime Rib, www.thebomber.com and www.glasswing.com/wings/main.htm
PENNSYLVANIA	Reading	Dutch Colony Motor Inn, Antique Airplane Restaurant and Rudder Bar, 4635 Perkiomen Ave, 19606, 610-779-2345 Co-Owner: R.H. Breithaupt, Suspended In Dinning Room 1927 Monocoupe, Left Wing From A Piper Cub From WWII, 1917 Curtiss OX-5 Engine, 1930 Zekely Engine, & Artifacts
	Philadelphia	94th Aero Sqd, N Philadelphia Airport, 2750 Red Lion Rd, 19154, 215-671-9400
	Nashville	101st Airborne Restaurant, 1362-A Murfreesboro Pike, 37217, 717-361-4212, DC-3
Tennesee	Nashville	Sam's Place, 7648 Hwy 70 South, 615-662,7474, Large Models Hanging from Ceiling
TEXAS	Pittsburg	Warrick's Restaurant, 142 Marshall St, 75686, 903-856-7881 Tue-Thur 11-9, Fri-Sat 11-10, 1902 Ezekiel Airship Replica Appetizers, Side Orders, Desserts, Sandwiches, Salads & Soups, Seafood $6-9, Specialty Dishes $7-14, Steaks & Chicken $6-13, Child Menus $3-4
WISCONSIN	Dodgeville	Don Q's INN, Highway 23 N, PO BOX 53533, 608-935-2321, This has a KC-97 in front of the motel.

USS NAVAL SHIP MUSEUMS

ALABAMA
Chickasaw   USS LST 325 Ship Memorial, Inc, LST325 Hook Term, Hardwood Ln,Off Rt 43
251-452-3255, 402-1225, www.lstmemorial.org

Mobile   Battleship Memorial Park, POB 65, 2703 Battleship Parkway, 36601,
251-433-2703, Daily 8-Sunset, Adm Adult $5, Child 6-12 $2.50, Gift Shop,
Located On Battleship Parkway Between Exit #27 & #30, USS Alabama, Uss Drum, YF-17

CALIFORNIA
Alameda Point   USS Hornet Museum, Pier 3, Mail: POB 460, 94501, 510-521-8448, Daily 10-4,
Tue 10-2, Closed TD, CD, ND, Adm Adult $12 ($5 Tue), Mil & 65 $10, Child 5-18 $5,
4 & Under Free, Groups Rates of 15 $2 Off, $1 Off Child, Gift Shop,
www.uss-hornet.org,

A-4A	FJ-2	US2B
F-7U3	H-34	Apollo Lunar Lander BP1102A
F-14A	HUP-1	MQU-004 (Apollo 14)
F8U-1(F-8A)	SBD	
F9F-5P	TBM-3	

Long Beach   SS Queen Mary , Pier J, 1126 Queens Way, POB 8, 90801,
424-435-4747, Mon-Fri 10-6, Sat-Sun 9:30-6, Adm
Overnight Stay on Queen Mary for one person $64 - $94. www.queenmary.com

Naval Ship Visitation Tours, Terminal Island Naval Complex, Pier T
800-262-7838, USS Mobile, Tours change Monthly, Call for current ship.

USS Roncador, 7950 Deering Ave, Canoga Park, 91304

Richmond   Richmond Museum of History, POB 1267, 94802, 510-237-2933,
www.redoakvictory.org, SS Red Oak Victory Ship

San Diego   San Diego Aircraft Carrier Museum, 1355 North Harbor Dr, 92101
619-702-7700, Opens Summer 2003, Admission Charged, www.midway.org,

A-6E	F-4S	F-14	SNJ-7
A-7B	F-9F-8P	S-3A	US-3A
E-2C	F-9J(TF)	SH-2F	

San Francisco   National Maritime Museum , Fisherman's Wharf Pier 32-47 Changes Seasonally,
POB 470310, 94147, 415-775-1943, www.maritime.org/pamphome.htm, Contact: Dave Lerma,
USS Roncador (Submarine SS-301), USS Pamanito (Submarine SS-383)

National Liberty Ship Memorial, Ft Mason Center, Bldg A, 94123, 415-441-3101
www.ssjeremiahobrien.org/   SS Jeremiah O'Brian (Liberty Ship)

San Pedro   US Merchant Marine Veterans of WW2, POB 629, 90733, 424-519-9545, SS Lane Victory Ship

CONNECTICUT
Groton   Submarine Force Museum, X-1

New London   Nautilus Memorial & Submarine Force Library & Museum, New London
Submarine Base, Mail: Box 571, 06349-5000, 800-343-0079, 860-449-3174,
449-3558, Mid-April to Mid Oct Daily 9-5, Tue 1-5, Nov 1-May 14 Daily 9-4,
Closed TueClosed: TD, CD, May 1st Week, Oct 1st Week, Free Adm,
www.ussnautilus.org,   USS Nautilus SSN 571
Bushnells Turtle   SS X-1   Mato-8 (Japanese Midget Sub)
Maiale (Italian Midget Sub)   Seahund (German Midget Sub)

DISTRICT OF
COLUMBIA   The Navy Museum, 805 Kidder Breese St, 20374-5071, 202-433-4882, Mon-Fri 9-4,
Sat-Sun 10-5, Closed: TD, CD, ND, Adm Free, Tours Dahlgren Ave, 8th & Main St,
Dir: Oscar P.Fitzgerald, Gift Shop, www.history.navy.mil

FG-1D	MXY7 Trainer	Posedon Missile	USS Barry
Maiale SSB	Turtle	USS Roncador Tower	
LCVP Higgins	Balao Fairwater		

FLORIDA
Tampa   American Victory Mariners Memorial & Museum Ship, 705 Channelside Dr, 33602,
813-228-8766, www.americanvictory.org, SS American Victory

HAWAII
Honolulu   USS Arizona Memorial BB-39, Shoreline Dr. Pearl Harbor Navy Base off I-99
808-422-0561, 422-2771, 1 Arizona Memorial Place, 96818-3145,
Daily 7:30-5, Closed TD, CD, ND, Free Adm, Theater,
USS Arizona, www.nps.gov/usar/

USS Utah Memorial, www.ussutah.org, Aeronca 65TC,

USS Missouri BB-63, Uss Missouri Memorial Assoc, POB 6339, 96818, 808-423-2263,
Adult $16, Child $8, www.ussmissouri.com, Aeronca 65TC

USS Bowfin Submarine Museum & Park, 11 Arizona Memorial Dr.,

Pearl Harbor, 96818, 808-423-1341, Next to USS Arizona Visitor
Center, Daily 8-5, Adm Charge, Gift Shop, www.bowfin.org
USS Bowfin SS-287, Missile & Rockets

LOUISIANA
  Baton Rouge   Louisiana Naval War Memorial, 305 S River Rd, 70802, 225-342-1942
Daily 9-5, Closed CD, Adm Adult $4, Sr $3, 6-12 $2.50,
USS KIDD (Camping aboard available groups of 20)www.usskidd.com/index.html

MARYLAND
  Baltimore   Baltimore Maritime Museum, Pier 4 Pratt St, Inn Harbor, 21202,
410-396-5528, Mail: 802 S Carolina St, 21231, www.usstorsk.org
USS Torsk,   Lightship "Chesapeak",   USCG "Taney"

Liberty Ship Project, Highland Station, Pier One, 2000 block of South Clinton St,
Mail: Project Liberty Ship, POB 25846 Station, 21224-0546, 410-558-0646
www.liberty-ship.com, email: john.w.brown@usa.net, SS John Brown

USS Constellation, DockPier One, 301 E Pratt, 21202, 410-539-1797,
www.constellation.org,   USS Constellation

MASSACHUSETTS
Boston   USS Constitution Museum, Boston National Historic Park, Charlestown Navy Yard, 02129,
508-242-5601, www.ussconstitution.navy.mil,
USS Constition,   USS Cassin Young,   PT-619,   PT-796

Fall River   Fall River - Battleship Cove, 02721, 508-678-1100, I-95 Exit 5 to Braga Bridge,
July-Labor Day Daily 9-8, Labor Day-June 9-5, Closed TD, CD, ND,
Adm Adult $6, Child $3, Under 5 $0.75, www.battleshipcove.com
USS Cassin Young   USS Fall River   PT-796 Patrol Boat
USS Lionfish   Japanese Suicide Sub   T-28
USS Joseph P Kenndey Jr PT-617 Patrol Boat   UH-1M
USS Massachusetts   PT-617 Patrol Boat   LCM

Quincy   US Naval & Shipbuilding Museum, 739 Washington St, Next to Fore River Bridge Rte 3A
617-479-7900, Voice 7686, Fax 479-8792, Free Adm, April-Sept Daily 10-4,
Oct-March Sat-Sun 10-4, Closed Holidays, Adm Adult $6, Snr & Child 4-12 $4, Under 4 Free
Active Mil with ID Free, Archives James E Fahey, www.uss-salem.org, USS Salem CA 139

MICHIGAN
  Muskegon   USS Silversides SS-236, S Channel Wall, Pere Marquette Park, 134 Bluffton St,
231-755-1230, Fax 755-5883, June-Aug. Daily, 10-5:30, Sept Sat-Sun 10-5:30,
Weekdays 1-5:30, Oct Sat-Sun Only, Adm Adults $5.00, Over 62 $3.50, Child 12-18 $4,
5-11 $3, Under 12 $3.00, Free Overnight Package $15 Per Person Up To 52 People,
www.silversides.org
USS Silversides SS-236,   USCGC,   LST 393

NEBRASKA
  Omaha   Freedom Park, 2497 Freedom Park Rd, 68110, 402-345-1959, From I-29 Go W
on I-480 Then N on Freedom Park Rd, Apr 15-Oct 31, Daily, 10-5, Adm Adult $4,
Snr $3, Child $2.50, Goup Rates,   USS Hazard AM-240 Mine Sweeper
A-4D   H-1(UH)   USS Marlin SST-2 (Submarine)
A-7   SH-3   USS Towers DDG-9 Captains Gig, USS LSM-45 Landing Ship

New Hampshire
  Portsmouth   Portsmouth Maritime Museum, 600 Market St, 03801, 603-436-3680, USS Albacore Sub

NEW JERSEY
  Camden   The Battleship New Jersey BB-62, Home Port Alliance, 2500 Broadway,
08104, 856-966-1652, www.battleshipnewjersey.org, www.bb62museum.org/

  Hackensack   Hackensack - US Naval Museum/Submarine USS Ling, 150 River St, 07601,
Mail: POB 375, 07682, 201-342-3268, Daily 10:15-4, Closed Mon & Thur in
Dec-Jan, Adm Charge, www.njnm.com/NJNM.htm,
USS Ling (SS-297)(Submarine), German Seehund, Japanese Kaiten

  Sea Grit   New Jersey National Guard Militia Museum, Intelligent Whale

NEW YORK
  Albany   USS Slater (DE-766), POB 1926, 12201, 518-431-1943, www.ussslater.org

  Buffalo   Buffalo & Erie County Naval & Servicemen's Park, 1 Naval Park Cove, 14202,
716-847-1773, April 1-Oct 31 10-5, Nov Sat-Sun Only, Adm Adult $6.00,
6-12 $3.50, 5 & Under or Senior Citizen Free, Gift Shop,
www.buffalonavalpark.org,   PTF-17 Boat
USS Croaker SSK-246,   USS Little Rock (CLG-4),   USS Sullivans

  New York City Intrepid Sea-Air-Space Museum, 1 Intrepid Plaza, Pier 86, 46th &
12th, 10036, 212-245-0072, 2533, MD-LD 10-5, RoY Wed-Sun 10-5, Closed TD, CD, ND,
Adm Adult $4.75, Snr $4, Child 7-13 $2.50, Under 6 Free
www.intrepid-museum.com, USS Intrepid,   USS Growler,   USS Edson

NORTH CAROLINA

Kinston   CSS Neuse & Governor Caswell Memorial, 2612 W Vernon Ave (US Bus 70)
Mail: POB 3043, 28502, 252-522-2091, Apr-Oct Mon-Sat 9-5, Sun 1-5
Nov-Mar Tus-Sat 10-4, Sun 1-4, Free Adm,
Hull of Iron Clad Gunboat CSS Neuse 1862
www.ah.dcr.state.nc.us/sections/Hs/neuse/neuse.htm

Wilmington   Wilmington - USS North Carolina Battleship Memorial, POB 417, 28402,
910-762-1829, Daily 8-Sunset, Adm Adult $4, Child $2, www.battleshipnc.com
USS North Carolina OS2U

OHIO

Cleveland   Submarine USS COD, 1089 N. Marginal Dr, Lakefront Between E & 9th St, 44114,
216-566-8770, May-LD Daily 10-5, Adm Charged, www.usscod.org, USS Cod

Newcomerstown National Naval Museum, 132 W Canal St, I-77 Exit 65, 43832, 740-498-4446,
www.ussradford446.org, R/C Helicopter, USS Radford & USS Helena Artifacts

OKLAHOMA

Muskogee   Muskegee - War Memorial Park, POB 253, 74401, 918-682-6294, Mar 15-Oct 15 Mon-Sat
9-5, Sun 1-5, Closed RoY, Adm Charged, www.batfish.org, USS Batfish (Submarine)

OREGON

Astoria   Ft Stevens Historical Military Museum & Trails, Ft. Stevens State
Park, Off US101, 10 Miles West of Astoria, 800-551-6949, 503-861-1671, Adm $3,
www.oregonstateparks.org/park_179.php; 5 Inch 38 Caliber Navy Gun Sites WWII.

Deloria Beech Rd., WWII Japanese I-25 Submarine Siting Plaque

Portland   OMSI Oregon Museum of Science & Industry, Washington Park,
1945 SE Water Ave, 97208, 503-797-4600, Daily 9-5, Adm Adult $2, Child $1,
Store 9585 Sw Washington Sq Rd, 97208, 503-684-5202, www.omsi.edu,
email: Garron.Gest@omsi.edu, USS Blueback Sub

Pennsylvania

Philadelphia   Independence Seaport Museum, 131 N Dlwr Avenue & Chstnt, 19104
215-923-9129, Mail: POB 928, www.phillyseaport.org
USS Becuna   USS Olympia

Pittsburgh   Carnegie Science Center, One Allengeny Ave, 15212-5850, 412-237-3400,
March 1-Jun 14 & Sept 2-Dec 8: Sun-Fri 9-4:30, Sat 10-5:30, June 14-Sept 2
10-5:30, Dec 8-March 1: Sat-Sun 10-4:30, Closed Weekdays, Dec 26-31 10-5,
Martin Luther King Birthday & President's Day 10-4:30, Adm Adult $4, Child
3-18 & Snr $2, www.carnegiesciencecenter.org, 45 Min Tours Every 15 Min,
USS Requin SS-481 Submarine

Rhode Island   USS Saratoga Museum, Coddington Cove, Naval Station Newport,
Next to Quonset Air MuseumPOB 28581, 02908, 401-831-8696,
www.saratogamuseum.org, email: SaveSara@aol.com,
Not at site until 2002, Aircraft Carrier CV-60

SOUTH CAROLINA

Mt Pleasant   Patriots Point Museum, 40 Patriots Point Rd, 29464-4377, Mail: POB 986,
29464, 800-248-3508, 843-884-2727, Apr-Sept Daily 9-6, Oct 1-Mar 31 9-5,
Closed CD, Adm Charged, USS Clamagore SS-343, USCG Ingham, USS Laffey,
www.state.sc.us/patpt, USS Yorktown, MARK I Patrol Boat   UH-1 (2ea)

TEXAS

Corpus Christi USS Lexington Museum, 2914 Shoreline Dr, Mail: POB 23076, 78403-3076,
361-888-4873, Daily 9-5, Adm Adult $7, Child 4-17 $3.75, Seniors & Military W/ID
$5, Closed CD, Gift Shop, Food Court, On-Going Restoration Projects,
Asst Curator: Margaret Wead, www.usslexington.com
USS Lexington,   USS PINTA,   USS MARIA

Galveston   Seawolf Park, Pelican Island, Mail: POB 1575, 77550, 409-744-5738, Daily 9-5, Adm Charged,
www.cavalla.org, USS Cavalla (Submarine), USS Stewart (Destroyer), F-86

Houston   USS Houston Museum, 1-800-231-7799, 8:30-5,

La Porte   USS TEXAS BB-35 Battleship SMS, 3527 Battleground Rd, 77571,
281-479-4414, Closed Mon-Tue, www.usstexasbb35.com

Orange   Southeast Texas War Memorial, 2606 Eddleman Rd, 77632, 409-883-8346,
Tue/Fri 9-2, Sat 9-4, Sun 1-4, Adm Donation, www.ussorleck.org, USS Orleck

VIRGINIA

Newport News   USS Savannah

Norfolk   Battleship Wisconsin Foundation, National Maritime Center, 224 E Main, 23510,
757-233-6464, Memorial Day-Labor Day, Daily 10-6, RoY Tue-Sat 10-5, Sun 12-5
www.battleshipwisconsin.org, www.nauticus.org, USS Wisconsin (BB-64)

WASHINGTON
Bremerton   Puget Sound Naval Shipyard, 130 Washington Ave, 98337, 360-479-7447,
Tue-Sat 10-5, Sun & Holidays 1-5, One Block from Port Orchard Ferry
or Hwy 304 These Ships Change and May Be Gone, Check Ahead. www.psns.navy.mil
USS Camden   (AOE-2)   Others Included:
USS Nimitz   (CVN-68)   Destroyers
USS Sacramento (AOE-1)   Battleships

Bremeerton Historic Ship Assn, 300 Washington Beach Ave, 98337, 360-792-2457
North of Ferry at Waterfront, Mon/Thr/Fri 11-4, Sat-Sun 10-4,
USS Turner Joy (DD-951) Destroyer,

Ft Columbia   Ft Columbia, 6 Inch Guns

Keyport   Naval Undersea Museum, End of Route 308, POB 408, 98345-5000,
360-396-4148, Daily 10-4 Summer, Closed Tue Oct-May, Free Adm
Kaiten Japanese Suicide Mini-Sub   USS Etlah Netlayer
Trieste II Deep Submerge Vehicle   USS Safeguard Salvage Vessel

WISCONSIN
Manitowoc   Wisconsin Maritime Museum, 75 Maritime Dr, 54220-6823, 920-684-0218,
Daily 9-5, Nov-March Daily 9-5, Sun 11-5, Closed NYD, ED, TD, CD
Adm Museum & Sub Adult $7, Child 6-12 $5, Family $20, Child 5 & Under Free,
Museum only Adult $5, Child 6-12 $4, 5 & Under Fee, USS Cobia Submarine
www.wimaritimemuseum.org/

Canada
Alberta
Calgary   Naval Museum of Alberta - 1820-24th St SW, T2T 0G6, 403-242-0002,
Tue-Fri 1-5, Sat-Sun 10-6, Closed: CD, ND, www.navalmuseum.ab.ca/aircraft.html
F2H-3, Hawker FB.11 Sea Fury, Supermarine Seafire Mk XV, T-33

ONTARIO
Hamilton   HMCS Haida Tribal Class Destroyer WWII # G63

INFORMATION NEEDED
Seeking the Facility Name, Address, Phone Number, Hours, Price of Admission, Listing
of All Their Aircraft, Contact Person, if they have a Gift Shop, Cafeteria, Restoration

Hayward,   CA   Vintage Air Museum, (Field Bud Aviation)20301 Skywest Dr, 94544
510-782-9063, (Need Address, Hours, Admission, email, Web, Ect)

Ford Island,   HI   Military Aviation Museum of the Pacific, in Planning Stage, Lexington Blvd,
Proposed aircraft: AH-1,   AT-6,   B-25,   MiG-15,   O-1,   UH-1

Westfield,   MA   Pioneer Vally Military & Transportation Museum, Need Address & Phone # & Aircraf

St Paul,   MN   Motel, Luscombe On Top of Roof, Need Name, Address & Phone #

Jackson,   NJ   Amusement Park - F-104D, Serial Number 57-1320

Yellowknife   NWT   Briston Freighter, DH 83C at City Hall

CANADA, Ontario
Mountain View   RCAF Base, Need Address & Phone #

SASKATCHEWAN
St.Chrysostome   Frontiers Antique & Military Aviation Museum, Need Address, Phone # & Aircraft

The Following is Ship Museum Info Wanted
Seeking the Facility Name, Address, Phone Number, Hours, Price of Admission, Listing
of Any Aircraft, Contact Person, if they have a Gift Shop, Cafeteria, Restoration

Newport News   VA   USS Savannah, Address, Phone #, Web

WORLD WAR II LANDMARKS

The following places have an existing landmark that served a purpose during WWII.

CALIFORNIA
Point Loma Cabrillo National Monument, 1800 National Monument Dr, San Diego, 92106, 619-557-5450, Daily 9-5:15, Adm Charged, Two 16" Gun Mounts & Station used for WWII Costal Defenses.

San Francisco Battery Davis Fort Funston, Pacific Side of City, 16" Gun Bunker.

Fort Point National Historical Site, 3" Gun Observation Posts, South End Under the Golden Gate Bridge,

San Miguel Green Mountain, Channel Island National Park, B-24 Crash Remains
Island Story on VHS "Wreckfinding, Lost But Not Forgotten".

CALIFORNIA
Ventura Battery 2 & Camp Seaside, Emma Wood State Beach, Panama Gun Mounts, West 100 Yards from the Ventura River Mouth.

DELAWARE
Lewes Cape Henlopen State Park, 42 Cape Henlopen Dr, 19958, 302-645-8983 This is where you'll find a 12 Inch Gun & Tower 4A, a WWII observation tower that was used to spot enemy submarines & vessels. These towers helped direct eight 16 inch guns buried in sand along the coast. The guns had a range of 24 miles but were never called upon. At the end of the war a German sub surrendered in the area, which claimed the sinking of 400 vessels along the east coast.

FLORIDA
Clearwater Ft Desoto Museum, Tampa Bay, 12 Inch Motar

Miami Dade Metro Zoo. Here you will find still standing a tall blimp support that was part of the NAS Hangar in Richmond during WWII.

New Smyrna Target Rock, Rings of Port, WWII Gunnery & Bombing Target, Beach 13 Miles S of H-1A Hwy, Along Canaveral National Seashore, Remains of an F6F Target, See Ranger Station on Directions.

HAWAII
Honolulu Historic Battery Randolf, US Army Museum,, Kalia Rd Ft. DeRussy 808-438-2821, Mail: POB 8064, 96830-0064, Tue-Sun 10-4:30, Closed Mon, CD, Nd, Free Adm, Gift Shop 955-9552, AH-1, Japanese Tank, 14" Gun

ILLINOIS
Salem Route 37 North of Salem,   WWI Howitzer

Wheaton Cantigny 1st Divison Museum, 1S151 Winfield Rd, 60187, 630-668-5161 10-5 Tue-Sun Memorial-Labor Day, 10-4 Tue-Sun Remaining Year, Free Adm

M5	M47	T26E4	M1896
M4A3E8	M48	M24	M113A2
M41A3	M60	M1917	Howitzer 75mm
M46	M551	M1902	

INDIANA
Brooksburg City Hall, Main St, Cannon 120 mm

Cromwell North of Rail Road Track,   Patton Tank

Huntington Huntington Memorial Park, W Park & Bartlett St, T-33A,   M4A1 Tank

Michigan City Great Lakes Museum of Military History, 1710 E Hwy 20, Evergreen Plaza 46360, 219-872-2702, May 20-Labor Day Tue-Fri 10-5, Sat 10-4, Sun 10-2: Labor Day-May 20 Tue-Sat 12-4: Closed ES, TD, CD, Military Vehicles

Scottsburg Indiana National Guard Center, Sherman Tank

Sunman Aerican Legion, St Leon Exit, M4A3(75)VVSS Sherman Tank,

Van Buren VFW, I-69, Army Tank

Warsaw City Court House, WWII Tank

MICHIGAN Porcupine Mountain Wilderness State Park, On April 19, 1944 a B-17 crashed inside the wilderness where you can still find remains of small parts along with the marks. To see this stop at the park visitor center near junction of M-107 and South Boundary Rd.

NEBRASKA
Mc Cook   Mc Cook Air Base Historical Box 29 or Box B-337, 69001-0029
308-345-3200, under restoration of the facility. Training base
for B-24 & B-29 Bomb Groups. Remains are the buildings, hangars,
water tower, runways and aprons.

NEW JERSEY
Sandy Hook   The Gunnery, Sandy Hook State Park, Long Branch area,
Formerly Ft Hancock, 6" Shore Battery & Bunker System,
Tour Bunkers Used To Protect NY Harbor, Slide Show Twice,
Twice per Season Only, All Evening Tour

NORTH CAROLINA
Camp Mackall   4 Acres of WWII Jeeps, 10 Miles West of Fort Bragg
Near Addor, NC Just Off US 1, Between Southern Pines and Hoffman
Places where to purchase Military Aircraft, Vehicles:

Camp Lejeune   Camp Lejeune,Visitors Center (Bldg 812)at Main Gate on Holcomb Blvd, Off NC 24,
910-451-2197, www.lejeune.usmc.mil or www.ci.jacksonville.nc.us
M-48 & M-60 Tank Infront of Bldg 407, At Courthose Bay: LVTPX12,
LVTP-4, LVTP-5A1, BMP-76PB (From Desert Storm)

OHIO
Hubbard   World War II Vehicle Museum, 5959 W Liberty St (Rt 304), 44425,
330-534-8125, Fax 534-3695, Mon-Fri 9-12 & 1-5, Adm Adult $5,
Child 10 & Under $3, Tanks: M4A1E8, M4A3, M7B1, M19, LVT(A)4
Half Track 3ea, 8 Inch Howitzer, DUKW, 6 Towed Guns 37mm to 175mm

OREGON
Brookings   Siskiyou National Forest, From Hwy 101 - S Bank Chetco River Rd 6mi
Right on Forest Rd 1205 - At 12.7 mi - Take Wheeler Creek Research
Natural Area (#260) - This is a incendiary bomb site of a Japanese
aircraft launched off of a submarine near Gold Beach.

Tillamook   Municipal Airport, Blimp Hangar, Used for patrol along the west
coast during WWII.

Virginia
Danville   American Armoured Foundation Tank Museum, 3401 US Hwy 29, 24540,
434-836-5323, Fax: 836-532, Mon-Sat 10-5, Closed TD, CD, Adm Adult $10,
Snr & Child Under 12 $8, Gift Shop, Tanks: M5A1, M42A1, M551A1, T54-55
M110A1, M-20, Daimler Dingo

Petersburg   Fort Lee, Army Quartermaster Museum, 1201 22nd St, 23801-1601
804-734-4203, Tue-Fri 10-5, Sat-Sun 11-5, Closed TD, CD, ND, Free Adm
http://www.qmmuseum.lee.army.mil/index.html, Artifacts

Fort Lee, US Army Women's Museum, 2100 Adams Ace, Bldg P-5219, 23801-2100
Tue-Fri 10-5, Sat-Sun 11-4:30, Closed TD, CD, ND, Free Adm, Gift Shop 734-4636

WASHINGTON
Coupeville   Fort Casey State Park, 1280 S Fort Casey Rd, 98239, 360-678-4519
Apr 1-Oct 31 Daily 6:30-Dusk, Oct 16-Mar 31 Daily 8-Dusk, Free Adm,
Manager: John Harris, 2 each 3" WWII Guns, 2 each 6" WWII Guns

Port Townsend Coast Artillery Museum, 200 Battery Way, 98368, 360-385-0373
Daily 12-4, Artifacts from Fort Casey, Fort Flager & Fort Worden

WISCONSIN
Racine   American Legion K Rd, Exit 329 Off I-94, Tank, Cannon

WWII Landmarks

Biplane & Warbird Rides

AZ, Scottsdale - Sun Air Aviation, Inc, 15115 Airport Dr, Scottsdale Airpark, 85260, 480-991-0611, 800-382-5030, Rides In The Following Aircraft:
Pitts Special   T-34   Waco   Helicopter & Balloon

CA, Fullerton - Air Combat USA, 230 N Dale Pl, Mail: POB 2726, 92633-2524, 800-522-7590 Fly Laser Dog Fights in the SIAI Marchetti SF260. $695 Phase I/II, $1295 Full Day Training & 2 Flight Missions & G-1 Jacket.
Flights Offer In The Following Cities:

Batavia	NY	Dallas	TX	Nashville	TN
Nend	OR	Detroit	OH	Phoenix	AZ
Boston	MA	Kansas City	KS	Portland	OR
Chicago	IL	Lancaster	PA	San Jose	CA
Cincinnati	OH	Leesburg	VA	Seattle	WA
Fullerton	CA	Long Island	NY	St. Louis	MO

CO, Aurora - Airpower West, 2850 Kerr Gulch Rd, Mail: 3641 S Yampa St, 80013, 303-674-7864, Fax 670-6529, Airshow Coordinator: Mike Baldwin, apwrwest@rmi.net
Scheduled Airshows Flying: A-1, A-37, AT-6's, Beechcraft D17S & 18S, N2S, OV-1

FL, Kissimmee - Stallion 51 Corp, 804 N Hoagland Blvd, 34741, 407-846-4400, Fax 846-0414, Ride/Fly a TF-51 (Dual Cockpit) Mustang $1,700 Per Hour
www.stallion51.com

Warbird Adventures, Ramp 66, Grand Strand Airport, Adjacent to Flying Tigers Warbird Restoration Museum, 800-386-1593, 407-870-7366, www.warbirdadventures.com, E-mail: programs@warbirdmuseum.com, AT-6/SNJ Rides

Awesome Balloon FLights, Inc, 843-215-7990, 1 Hr Flights, 24 Reservation Notice

St Augustine - North American Top Gun, 270 Estrella Ave, 32095, 800-257-1636, AT-6 Rides $190-550, www.natg.com, AT-6G,   AT-6D/G,   SNJ-4,   SNJ-5,   SNJ-6

GA, Atlanta - Sky Warriors, Inc, 3996 Aviation Circle, Hangar B-3, Fulton County Airport, Brown Field, 30336, 404-699-7000, Fax 699-7200,
T-34A Aerial Laser Combat (75 Minute Flights)

Air Superiorty Group, DeKalb-Peachtree Airport, POB 566726, 31156, Rides in a N2S-3

ID, Driggs - Teton Aviation Center. 675 Airport Rd, Off Hwy 33, Mail: POB 869, 83422 800-472-6382, 208-354-3100, Fax 354-3200, Daily 8-5, Closed TD, CD, Free Adm www.tetonaviation.com, Glider Rides Available & Aviat Husky A-1 Rides

KY, Louisville, Bowman Field, 502-368-6524, AT-6

MO, Maryland Heights - Historic Aircraft Restoration Museum, Dauster Flying Field, Creve Coeur Airport, 3127 Creve Coeur Mill Rd, 63146, 314-434-3368, Fax 878-6453 Sat-Sun 10-4,Rides: SNJ $75, Stearman $50, www.historicaircraftrestorationmuseum.org

NC, Durham - Carolina Barnstormers, Durham Skypark Airport, 4340 Ger St, 27704 Off I-85, E on Redwood, N on E Geer St, 919-680-6642, Owner: Mike Ratty, Rides: Waco YPF-7 Two People for 25 Min. $90, 1 Hr $175; PT-17 One Person 25 Min. $75, 1 Hr $150

NY, Rhinebeck - Old Rhinebeck Aerodrome, 44 Stone Church Rd, Mail: BOX 229, 12572 845-752-3200, Fax: 758-6481, May 15-Oct31, Daily 10-5, www.oldrhinebeck.org/ 1929 New Standard Biplane Rides 15 Min $40 Per Person

OH, Miamisburg - Wright B Flyer Museum, 10550 Springboro Pike, Off Rte 741, Wright Brothers Airport (Dayton General Airport), 45342, 937-885-2327, Tue,Thur,Sat 9-2:30, Closed Holidays, www.wright-b-flyer.org, Wright B Flyer Flyable Rides for $150

VA, Bealeton - Flying Circus Aerodrome, 15S. Route 17, BOX 99, 22712, 540-439-8661, Daily 11-Sunset, Adm Adult $9, Child $3, Open Cockpit Rides $25, Acrobatic Rides $50, Cub Rides $17.50,

WA, Vashon - Olde Thyme Aviation Inc, 21704 141st. Avenue SW, 98070, Rides starting at $107 for 2 people, 2 Travel Airs, 2 Waco UPF-7s, 2 Stearman Kaydets (1944 N2S-4 Navy & 1944 PT-17 Army), and 2 Cabin Waco Biplanes (1936 YKS-6 & 1937 YKS-7), http://www.oldethymeaviation.com/index.html, email: Waco@oldethymeaviation.com,

WI, Oshkosh - EAA Air Adventure Museum, Wittman Airfield, 3000 Poberezny Rd, POB 3065, 54903-3065, US 41 Exit 44, 920-426-4818, Mon-Sat 8:30-5, Sun 11-5, Closed TD, CD, ND,
Ford Tri-Motor Adult $30, Child $20   Travel Air E-4000 Biplane $50
Waco YKS-7 Biplane $40, 2 for $70, 3 for $90   Bell 47 $30 , 2 for $50
Spirit of St Louis Replica $100   New Standard D-25 Biplane $50

Canada - Ontario, Collingwood - Collingwood Classic Aircraft Foundation,
Collingwood Mncpl Airport, Mail: Box 143, L9Y 3Z4, 705-445-7545, Thur 9-4, Adm Free, www.classicaircraft.ca/homepage.htm, Smith Miniplane, Stinson 105
Rides in: Aeronca Champ 7AC, DH 82A, Fleet Canuck

Rides in DC-3's, Contact:

CA, San Clemente, Air Cruise America, 1 Via Pasa, 92673-2750, 949-661-8410
DC-3 (Rides Available)

CA, San Leandro, Otis Spunkmeyer Air, 8433 Earhart Rd, Kaaiser Air Jet Center,
Mail: 14490 Catalina St, 94577, 800-938-1900, 510-649-5900, DC-3 & C-41

FL, Marco Island - South Florida Sea Ventures, Inc, 2 Marco Lake Dr, #6, 33907,
800-835-9323, DC-3 Flights in 1940 Interiors From Naples To Key West,
Ft Meyers to Key West, Naples to Ft Lauderdale, Round Trip $139-169.

GA, Griffin, Alexander Aeroplane Co, 118 Huff Daland Cir, 30223, 770-228-3901,
800-831-2949,

KY, Louisville, Bowman Field, 502-368-6524, DC-3/C-47 Flights

OK, Ames, Bygone Aviation, POB 22, 73718, 580-753-4445, DC-3 Rides Available

YUKON TERRITORY
Whitehorse - Whitehorse Airport, 403-667-8440, DC-3(3ea) Flights To:
Dawson City, Fairbanks, Juneau, Old Crow

Credits

Carry Patrick from Waukegan, IL

Has provided me with endless letters each month with lots of useful
information on museums & aircraft. He saved me Months of work.

I would like to thank all museums who have sent me information on their
facility and for the following people who have provided me with
information for this edition.

Bachle	Carl F.	Jackson	MI
Baldenhofer	Thomas A	Waveland	MS
Barrows	Peter	Versailles	KY
Binder	Jack	Port Allegany	PA
Blanchard	Andrea	Linday	Ontario
Boehme	Mike		
Bowser	James	Crystal Beach	Ontario
Carmony	Wayne H	Manilla	IN
Coryell	Dean	South Elgin	IL
Droza	Raymond J	Chicago	IL
Eschweiler	Ron	Wilmington	DE
Fitzgerald	William J.	Lubbock	TX
Ford	Larry	Goshen	IN
Fraser	Woodie	Venice	FL
Gorges	Charles	Wichita	KS
Hatcher	William	Kinston	NC
Havey	John F	Monroe Twp	NJ
Howard	Tony	Monroe	WA
Jensen	Jerry		
Joseph	Franklin H	Garden City	NY
Krankkala	Don	Palm Harbor	FL
Leunig	Thomas	Wauwatosa	WI
Lindell	Chuck	Colorado Springs	CO
Lundberg	Leonard	Livingston	TX
McKenzie	Dan W	El Cajon	CA
Mosher	Doc	Oshkosh	WI
Omlid (USN RET)	Chuck		
Pytel	Ray	Elkhorn	WI
Russell	Thad J	Valparaiso	IN
Saini	Vik	N Olmstead	OH
Soto	Tulio	Brookshire	TX
Spencer	Leon B	Prattville	AL
Strode	G S	Rolling Hills Estates	CA
Sundstrom	David	Rancho Palos	CA
Tagg	Lawrence V.	Tucson	AZ
Wilburn	Nate D	N Great Falls	MT
Wolentarski	Walter	Old Hickory	TN
Zilinsky	Robert F	Willowbrook	IL

Last I want to thank my wife **Sylverta M Blaugher**
for her help and support in my long hours and months putting
this edition together.

Aircraft Type	State	City Abv.	Museum Abv.	Manufacture	Aircraft Name/ SN, N#, Tail#, Side#, Sq#, Nick Name
A-1	CO	Puebl	FWAM	Martin-Marietta	Pershing 15
A-1	FL	Pensa	USNAM	Curtiss	Triad
A-1	OH	S.Euc	USAM	Curtiss	Triad
A-1 EAA	WI	Oshko	EAAAAM	Curtiss	Triad N6077V
A-1(BTD-1)	NY	Horseheads	NWM	Douglas	Skyraider 04959
A-1A(AD-1)	VA	VBeac	ONAS	Douglas	Skyraider 9102, 500, VA-176
A-1C(AD-3)	WI	Oshko	EAAAAM	Douglas	Skyraider 122811
A-1D	CO	Denver	69thB	Douglas	Skyraider Tail: TT822
A-1D(AD-4N)	CA	Chino		Douglas	Skyraider
A-1D(AD-4N)	CT	Winds	NEAM	Douglas	Skyraider
A-1D(AD-4N)	WA	Eastsound	FHC	Douglas	Skyraider 126924, N2692
A-1D(AD-4N)	VA	Suffolk	FF	Douglas	Skyraider 123827, VA-195
A-1D(AD-4NA)	MI	Kalam	KAHM	Douglas	Skyraider 127888, N92334
A-1D(AD-4W)	NV	Fallon	NASF	Douglas	Skyraider 132261, VA-145, 500, NK
A-1D(AD-4W)	OR	Tillamook	TAM	Douglas	Skyraider
A-1E(AD-5)	CA	Lemoore	LNAS	Douglas	Skyraider
A-1E(AD-5)	CA	Sacra	McCelAFB	Douglas	Skyraider 132463, 552, Twin Seater
A-1E(AD-5)	FL	FtWal	HF	Douglas	Skyraider 52-598, Twin Seater
A-1E(AD-5W)	NY	Geneseo	1941AG	Douglas	Skyraider
A-1E(AD-5)	OH	Dayto	USAFM	Douglas	Skyraider 52-13264, 9, Twin Seater, 52-132649
A-1E(AD-5)	OH	Newbu	WASAC	Douglas	Skyraider 165273, Twin Seater
A-1E(AD-5)	SC	MtPleasant	PPM	Douglas	Skyraider Twin Seater
A-1E(AD-5)	TX	Midla	CAFFM	Douglas	Skyraider Twin Seater
A-1E(AD-5)	TX	RioHo	TAM	Douglas	Skyraider SN BUJ132443, Twin Seater
A-1E(AD-5)	UT	Ogden	HAM	Douglas	Skyraider
A-1E(AD-5)	WA	Olympia	OFM	Douglas	Skyraider Side # 21
A-1E(AD-5)	WI	Oshko	EAAAAM	Douglas	Skyraider 132789, Twin Seater
A-1F(AD-5Q)	AZ	Tucso	PAM	Douglas	Skyraider 135018, VR703, Twin Seater
A-1H(AD-6)				Douglas	Skyraider N39606, 39606, D, VA-145
A-1H(AD-6)	FL	Pensa	USNAM	Douglas	Skyraider 135300, NL405, VA- 25
A-1H(AD-7)	MD	Silve	PEGF	Douglas	Skyraider
A-2	CA	Ridgecrest	CLNWC	Lockheed	Polaris
A-2	VA	Hampt	APM	Lockheed	Polaris
A-2	VA	Quant	MCAGM	Lockheed	Polaris
A-3A(A3D-1)	FL	Pensa	USNAM	Douglas	Skywarrior 135418, 70
A-3B(A3D-2)	CT	Winds	NEAM	Douglas	Skywarrior 142246
A-3B(A3D-2)	NY	NYC	ISASM	Douglas	Skywarrior
A-3D(A3D-1)	AZ	Tucso	PAM	Douglas	Skywarrior 130361
A-3D(A3D-4)	CA	Rosam	EAFB	Douglas	Skywarrior 135434
A-3D(A3D-4)	NY	NYC	ISASM	Douglas	Skywarrior "Whale"
A-3D(KA-3B)	CA	Oakla	OWAM	Douglas	Skywarrior
A-3D(KA-3B)	TX	C Christi	USS Lexi	Douglas	Skywarrior
A-4J(TA)	Al	Birmingham	SMoF	McDonnell-Douglas	Skyhawk SC01
A-4	AZ	Yuma	YUSMAB	McDonnell-Douglas	Skyhawk
A-4	CA	Alame	ANAS	McDonnell-Douglas	Skyhawk
A-4	CA	El Centro	ECNAF	McDonnell-Douglas	Skyhawk Sn 159798
A-4	CA	Lemoore	LNAS	McDonnell-Douglas	Skyhawk
A-4	CA	S.Mon	MoF	McDonnell-Douglas	Skyhawk "Blue Angels", #4
A-4	CA	Twentynine	TPMC	McDonnell-Douglas	Skyhawk 5133
A-4	FL	Kissi	FTWAM	McDonnell-Douglas	Skyhawk
A-4	FL	Orlan	ONTC	McDonnell-Douglas	Skyhawk
A-4	HI	Oahu	BPNAS	McDonnell-Douglas	Skyhawk 152061 (HI Hist Avia Fndt)
A-4	HI	Oahu	BPNAS	McDonnell-Douglas	Skyhawk 153689 (MCBH)
A-4	IL	Great Lakes	GLNTC	McDonnell-Douglas	Skyhawk
A-4	LA	Reser	AMHFM	McDonnell-Douglas	Skyhawk
A-4	NB	Omaha	FP	McDonnell-Douglas	Skyhawk
A-4	NC	Charl	CHAC	McDonnell-Douglas	Skyhawk
A-4	NC	CPoin	CPMB	McDonnell-Douglas	Skyhawk
A-4	NC	Havelock	HI	McDonnell-Douglas	Skyhawk
A-4	NH	Nashu	FAAATCC	McDonnell-Douglas	Skyhawk
A-4	NJ	Millville	MAAFM	McDonnell-Douglas	Skyhawk
A-4	NV	Fallon	NASF	McDonnell-Douglas	Skyhawk 142100, VFC-13, 01
A-4	NV	Fallon	NASF	McDonnell-Douglas	Skyhawk
A-4	NY	Brooklyn	FAAATCC	McDonnell-Douglas	Skyhawk
A-4	SC	Mt Pleasant	PPM	McDonnell-Douglas	Skyhawk 149623, VA 163 USS Oriskany, Nose 353, Tail AH
A-4	TX	Beevi	CrtHouse	McDonnell-Douglas	Skyhawk
A-4B	TX	C Christi	USS Lexi	McDonnell-Douglas	Skyhawk
A-4B	TX	C Christi	USS Lexi	McDonnell-Douglas	Skyhawk
A-4	TX	San A	CityPark	McDonnell-Douglas	Skyhawk
A-4	VA	Norfolk	NMM	McDonnell-Douglas	Skyhawk
A-4 (Tail Only)	TN	Memph	LS	McDonnell-Douglas	Skyhawk
A-4A	CA	Alameda	USSHM	McDonnell-Douglas	Skyhawk 139929
A-4A	CA	Hawth	WMoF	McDonnell-Douglas	Skyhawk
A-4A	CA	Paso Robles	EWM	McDonnell-Douglas	Skyhawk 137826
A-4A	CA	S.Mon	MoF	McDonnell-Douglas	Skyhawk
A-4A	CT	Winds	NEAM	McDonnell-Douglas	Skyhawk 2219 , 36
A-4A	KS	Liber	MAAM	McDonnell-Douglas	Skyhawk
A-4A Cockpit	KS	Topeka	CAM	McDonnell-Douglas	Skyhawk 142168
A-4A	MD	Annap	USNAM	McDonnell-Douglas	Skyhawk
A-4A	NY	NYC	ISASM	McDonnell-Douglas	Skyhawk 2833, AF, 300
A-4A	TX	Kings	CityPark	McDonnell-Douglas	Skyhawk
A-4A	TX	Paris	FTAM	McDonnell-Douglas	Skyhawk
A-4B(TA)(A4D-2)	AZ	Tucso	PAM	McDonnell-Douglas	Skyhawk 14928
A-4B	CA	Bishop	INP	McDonnell-Douglas	Skyhawk 142790, Tail 7L, Side 49
A-4B	CA	Chino	PoF	McDonnell-Douglas	Skyhawk
A-4B	CA	Chino	YAM	McDonnell-Douglas	Skyhawk
A-4B	CA	San Diego	SDAM	McDonnell-Douglas	Skyhawk NP302, VA-212
A-4B	DC	Washi	NA&SM	McDonnell-Douglas	Skyhawk
A-4B	IN	Indianapolis	RAM	McDonnell-Douglas	Skyhawk 142834
A-4B(A4D-2)	MI	Kalamazoo	KAHM	McDonnell-Douglas	Skyhawk 057182, 145011
A-4B	MI	Mt Clemens	SMAM	McDonnell-Douglas	Skyhawk 142761, Side # 01
A-4B	TN	Crossville	CCHS	McDonnell-Douglas	Skyhawk 148572, "Blue Angles"
A-4B	NY	NYC	ISASM	McDonnell-Douglas	Skyhawk
A-4B	OR	Tillamook	TAM	McDonnell-Douglas	Skyhawk
A-4B	WI	Oshko	EAAAAM	McDonnell-Douglas	Skyhawk 685
A-4C	AR	Fayet	AAM	McDonnell-Douglas	Skyhawk 147733
A-4C	AZ	Tucso	PAM	McDonnell-Douglas	Skyhawk N401FS, 148571
A-4C	CA	El Cajon	SDAMGF	McDonnell-Douglas	Skyhawk 201, NM
A-4C	CA	Miramar	FLAM	McDonnell-Douglas	Skyhawk DT, VMA-242, "Advisary"
A-4C	CA	S.Mon	MoF	McDonnell-Douglas	Skyhawk
A-4C	FL	Clear	FMAM	McDonnell-Douglas	Skyhawk
A-4C	FL	Jacks	NASCF	McDonnell-Douglas	Skyhawk 147708, AK 301, VA-106
A-4C	NJ	Lumberton	AVM	McDonnell-Douglas	Skyhawk 145072
A-4C	NY	NYC	ISASM	McDonnell-Douglas	Skyhawk
A-4C	RI	NKing	QAM	McDonnell-Douglas	Skyhawk "Mighty Midget", 147790

Model	State	City	Museum	Manufacturer	Name	Notes
A-4D	IN	Goshen	AM	McDonnell-Douglas	Skyhawk	
A-4D	KS	Olath	NPNAS	McDonnell-Douglas	Skyhawk	
A-4D	NB	Omaha	FP	McDonnell-Douglas	Skyhawk	149618, "USS Enterprise", Side # 601, Tail AE, VA-64
A-4D-2	CO	Puebl	FWAM	McDonnell-Douglas	Skyhawk	147702
A-4E	CA	Chino	YAM	McDonnell-Douglas	Skyhawk	
A-4E(A4D)	FL	Pensa	USNAM	McDonnell-Douglas	Skyhawk	149656, VA-164, Tail "AH", #303
A-4E(A4D)	FL	Pensa	USNAM	McDonnell-Douglas	Skyhawk	"Blue Angels", 150076 154180 1
A-4E	HI	Oahu	BPNAS	McDonnell-Douglas	Skyhawk	151030 (Pacific Aerospace Museum)
A-4F(NT)	CA	Ridgecrest	CLNWC	McDonnell-Douglas	Skyhawk	
A-4F	IL	Ranto		McDonnell-Douglas	Skyhawk	52-0898, Blue Angle #6 "Lucy"
A-4F	NY	Scotia	ESAM	McDonnell-Douglas	Skyhawk	155009
A-4F	RI	NKing	QAM	McDonnell-Douglas	Skyhawk	155027
A-4F	VA	VBeac	ONAS	McDonnell-Douglas	Skyhawk	155176, VF-43
A-4F	WA	Seatt	MoF	McDonnell-Douglas	Skyhawk	"Blue Angels", 154180 4
A-4F(A4D)	FL	Pensa	USNAM	McDonnell-Douglas	Skyhawk	"Blue Angels", 154217 4
A-4F(A4D)	FL	Pensa	USNAM	McDonnell-Douglas	Skyhawk	"Blue Angels", 155033 3
A-4F(A4D)	FL	Pensa	USNAM	McDonnell-Douglas	Skyhawk	"Blue Angels", 154983 2
A-4L	AL	Mobil	BMP	McDonnell-Douglas	Skyhawk	147787
A-4J(TA)	IL	Sugar Grove	ACM	McDonnell-Douglas	Skyhawk	153678
A-4J(TA)	IN	Elkhart	NIAM	McDonnell-Douglas	Skyhawk	153671, VT-7, CTW-1, Nose 716
A-4J(TA)	KS	Topeka	CAM	McDonnell-Douglas	Skyhawk	158716, , Side # 771, Tail A, VT-7(CTW-1)
A-4J(TA)	MD	Lexington	USNTPS	McDonnell-Douglas	Skyhawk	158106, Side # 8, TPS Tail
A-4J(TA)	TX	Beevi	CFAFB	McDonnell-Douglas	Skyhawk	
A-4J(TA)	TX	FWort	NASFWJRB	McDonnell-Douglas	Skyhawk	
A-4J(TA)	TX	RioHo	TAM	McDonnell-Douglas	Skyhawk	154291
A-4L	KS	Liberal	MAAM	McDonnell-Douglas	Skyhawk	
A-4L	KY	Lexington	AMoK	McDonnell-Douglas	Skyhawk	147708
A-4L	SC	Beauf	MAS	McDonnell-Douglas	Skyhawk	147772, EX 01, MALS-31
A-4M	CA	Oakla	OWAM	McDonnell-Douglas	Skyhawk	SI 59
A-4M	ME	Lexin	PNAT&EM	McDonnell-Douglas	Skyhawk	
A-4M	NC	Havelock	HTC	McDonnell-Douglas	Skyhawk	
A-4M	PA	Willo	WGNAS	McDonnell-Douglas	Skyhawk	WA 00
A-4M	RI	NKing	QAM	McDonnell-Douglas	Skyhawk	158148
A-4M	TX	FWort	NASFWJRB	McDonnell-Douglas	Skyhawk	
A-5	FL	KeyWe	NASKW	NA-Rockwell	Vigilante	
A-5	FL	Orlan	MGNTC	NA-Rockwell	Vigilante	
A-5(A3J)	MD	Lexington	PRNAM	NA-Rockwell	Vigilante	156643, Side# 643, NATC Tail
A-5A(A3J)	MD	Lexington	SWD	NA-Rockwell	Vigilante	146697
A-5	TN	Millington	NASM	NA-Rockwell	Vigilante	
A-6	CA	San Diego	SDAM	Grumman	Intruder	
A-6	FL	Delan	DNAS	Grumman	Intruder	
A-6	GA	Marietta	NASA	Grumman	Intruder	
A-6	MI	Lapee	YAFDLA	Grumman	Intruder	
A-6	NV	Fallon	NASF	Grumman	Intruder	155627
A-6	NY	NYC	ISASM	Grumman	Intruder	147867
A-6	PA	Smethport	AAAM	Grumman	Intruder	
A-6	VA	Norfolk	NASN	Grumman	Intruder	
A-6	WA	Oak Harbor	City Park	Grumman	Intruder	
A-6 Simulator	CA	Oakla	OWAM	Grumman	Intruder	
A-6A	AL	Starke	CBM	Grumman	Intruder	155661, VA-35, Nose 507, Tail 07, USS America
A-6A	MD	Lexington	PRNAM	Grumman	Intruder	156997, side# 500, NAWC/AD Tail,
A-6A	MI	Belleville	YAM	Grumman	Intruder	156981, "Flight of the Intruder" Movie
A-6A	NY	NYC	ISASM	Grumman	Intruder	162185
A-6B	SC	Mt Pleasant	PPM	Grumman	Intruder	152599
A-6D(KA-6D)	CA	Oakla	OWAM	Grumman	Intruder	
A-6E	AZ	Tucso	PAM	Grumman	Intruder	155713, NJ 562, VA-128
A-6E	CA	Paso Robles	EWM	Grumman	Intruder	154717
A-6E	CA	Ridgecrest	CLNWC	Grumman	Intruder	
A-6E	CA	Miramar	FLAM	Grumman	Intruder	NAWC
A-6E	CA	S.Mon	MoF	Grumman	Intruder	
A-6E	CA	SRosa	PCAM	Grumman	Intruder	
A-6E	CA	El Cajon	SDAMGF	Grumman	Intruder	
A-6E	CA	San Diego	SDACM	Grumman	Intruder	
A-6E	CO	Grand Junction	CAF-RMW	Grumman	Intruder	VMA-533, #7
A-6E	FL	Pensa	USNAM	Grumman	Intruder	155610
A-6E	FL	Tittusville	VACM	Grumman	Intruder	
A-6E	RI	NKing	QAM	Grumman	Intruder	155629
A-6E	TX	C Christi	USS Lexi	Grumman	Intruder	151579, AC501, VA-75
A-6E	VA	VBeac	ONAS	Grumman	Intruder	151579, AC501, VA-75
A-6E	WA	Seatt	MoF	Grumman	Intruder	158794
A-6E(EA)	WA	Tacoma	City Beach Park	Grumman	Intruder	152907, VA-128, NJ, Side # 800
A-6F	NY	Garde	CoAM	Grumman	Intruder	162184
A-7	AL	Starke	CBM	Vought	Corsair II	157503, Nose 301, Tail NE 01, Lt PS Clark
A-7	AL	Tuscalloose	I-20/59	Vought	Corsair II	400
A-7	AR	Pocahontas	PMA	Vought	Corsair II	153150, 300, Tail NL, VA-22, USS Nmitz
A-7	CA	Alame	ANAS	Vought	Corsair II	400
A-7	CA	San Diego	SDAM	Vought	Corsair II	
A-7	CA	San Diego	SDACM	Vought	Corsair II	
A-7(LTV)	FL	Kissimmee	FTWRM	Vought	Corsair II	
A-7	FL	Orlan	ONTC	Vought	Corsair II	
A-7	FL	Titus	VACM	Vought	Corsair II	
A-7	GA	Calhoun	MAM	Vought	Corsair II	145326, 7B, #9
A-7	IA	Des Moines	ING	Vought	Corsair II	75403
A-7	IA	Greenfield	IAM	Vought	Corsair II	
A-7	MD	Lexin	PNA&EM	Vought	Corsair II	
A-7	NB	Omaha	FP	Vought	Corsair II	
A-7	NC	Charl	CHAC	Vought	Corsair II	
A-7	NC	CPoin	CPMB	Vought	Corsair II	
A-7	ND	Minot	DTAM	Vought	Corsair II	
A-7	NV	Fallon	NASF	Vought	Corsair II	154420, 00
A-7	NV	Fallon	NASF	Vought	Corsair II	
A-7	OH	Alliance	AHS	Vought	Corsair II	153142, VA-86
A-7A	FL	Tittusville	VACM	Vought	Corsair II	
A-7A	IL	Bloom	PAM	Vought	Corsair II	NJ412
A-7B	CA	El Cajon	SDAMGF	Vought	Corsair II	154550
A-7B	NJ	Lumberton	AVM	Vought	Corsair II	
A-7B	NC	Hickory	HRA	Vought	Corsair II	144345, VA-82
A-7B	TX	C Christi	USS Lexi	Vought	Corsair II	154431
A-7B	TX	Slanton	TAMCC	Vought	Corsair II	154431
A-7C	CA	Ridgecrest	CLNWC	Vought	Corsair II	
A-7C	CA	Paso Robles	EWM	Vought	Corsair II	156739
A-7C	WI	Kenos	KMM	Vought	Corsair II	156751, VAQ33, #120
A-7C(TA)	NM	Albuq	NAM	Vought	Corsair II	
A-7D	AZ	Tucso	DMAFB	Vought	Corsair II	
A-7D	AZ	Tucso	PAM	Vought	Corsair II	Sn 70-973, "Big D"
A-7D	AZ	Tucso	TANG	Vought	Corsair II	

89

A- 7D	CA	S.Mon	MoF	Vought	Corsair II		
A- 7D	CA	Riverside	MAFM	Vought	Corsair II	69-6188	
A- 7D	CA	Sacra	McCelAFB	Vought	Corsair II	70-998	
A- 7D	CO	Denve	WOR	Vought	Corsair II		
A- 7D	IA	Altoona	SWYC	Vought	Corsair II	71334, Tail IA AF	
A- 7D	IA	Corre	CityPark	Vought	Corsair II		
A- 7D	IA	Johnston	CD	Vought	Corsair II	75403, Tail IA, AF,	
A- 7D	IA	SBluf	MAAM	Vought	Corsair II		
A- 7D	IA	Sheld	CityPark	Vought	Corsair II		
A- 7D	IA	Sioux	SCANG	Vought	Corsair II		
A- 7D	IL	Ranto	OCAM	Vought	Corsair II	69190	
A- 7D	KS	Olath	NPNAS	Vought	Corsair II		
A- 7E	LA	Alexandria	EAB	Vought	Corsair II	69-234, EL 23TFW	
A- 7D	MD	Middl	GLMAM	Vought	Corsair II		
A- 7D	MI	Mt Clemens	SMAM	Vought	Corsair II	72-0261	
A- 7D	MT	Helena	FFTC	Vought	Corsair II		
A- 7D	NC	Fayet	PAFB	Vought	Corsair II		
A- 7D	ND	Wahpe	CityPark	Vought	Corsair II		
A- 7D	NE	S.Sio	CityPark	Vought	Corsair II		
A- 7D	NE	SSiou	MA	Vought	Corsair II		
A- 7D	NM	Albuquerque	KAFB	Vought	Corsair II	72045	
A- 7D	OH	Dayto	USAFM	Vought	Corsair II	69-6192	
A- 7D	OH	Lockb	RANGB	Vought	Corsair II	73-999	
A- 7D	OH	Lockb	RANGB	Vought	Corsair II	73-1006	
A- 7D	OK	Oklah	45IDM	Vought	Corsair II	72-0240	
A- 7D	RI	NKing	QAM	Vought	Corsair II	75-0408	
A- 7D	SC	McEnt	MEANGB	Vought	Corsair II		
A- 7D	SD	Huron	Airport	Vought	Corsair II		
A- 7D	SD	McEnt	MEANGB	Vought	Corsair II		
A- 7D	SD	Pierr	SDNGM	Vought	Corsair II		
A- 7D	SD	Sioux	SDANGSF	Vought	Corsair II		
A- 7D	SD	Tea	Airport	Vought	Corsair II		
A- 7D	TX	Burnet	HLS-CAF	Vought	Corsair II		
A- 7D	VA	Richm	SMAM	Vought	Corsair II	72-0	
A- 7D	VA	Sands	VAM	Vought	Corsair II	"Death Dealer"	
A- 7D	WI	CDoug	WNGML&M	Vought	Corsair II		
A- 7D(YA)	CA	Rosam	EAFB	Vought	Corsair II	67-14583	
A- 7D-3-CV	MI	Belleville	YAF	Vought	Corsair II	69-6193	
A- 7E	Al	Birmingham	SMoF	Vought	Corsair II		
A- 7E	AZ	Tucso	PAM	Vought	Corsair II	160713	
A- 7E	CA	Lemoore	LNAS	Vought	Corsair II		
A- 7E	CA	Oakla	OWAM	Vought	Corsair II	NJ250	
A- 7E	FL	Colum	CityPark	Vought	Corsair II	158003	
A- 7E	FL	Jacks	NASCF	Vought	Corsair II	158662, AC301, VA- 37	
A- 7E	FL	Jacks	NASCF	Vought	Corsair II	152650, 301, VA- 46	
A- 7E	FL	LakeCity	CityPark	Vought	Corsair II	Thunderbird colors	
A- 7E	FL	Pensa	USNAM	Vought	Corsair II	160714	
A- 7E	GA	Marietta	NASA	Vought	Corsair II	158842	
A- 7E	IL	Sugar Grove	ACM	Vought	Corsair II	158842	
A- 7E	IL	Edwardsville	CityPark	Vought	Corsair II	159303, #401	
A- 7E	IL	Linco	HIFM	Vought	Corsair II		
A- 7E	KS	Liber	MAAM	Vought	Corsair II	20	
A- 7E	LA	Baton Rouge	LNWM	Vought	Corsair II	160724	
A- 7E	MS	Greneda	HS	Vought	Corsair II	160255, NMF-213	
A- 7E	NM	STere	WEAM	Vought	Corsair II		
A- 7E	NV	Fallo	NAS	Vought	Corsair II		
A- 7E	NY	NYC	ISASM	Vought	Corsair II	AE 401	
A- 7E	SC	Mt Pleasant	PPM	Vought	Corsair II	Side 301	
A- 7E	TN	Memph	MBMA	Vought	Corsair II	160869, 401, VA- 27	
A- 7E	VA	Hampt	APM	Vought	Corsair II	157500, AC-300, VA-37	
A- 7E Cockpit	OR	Tillamook	TAM	Vought	Corsair II		
A- 7F	OR	Tillamook	TAM	Vought	Corsair II		
A- 7F(YA)	CA	Rosam	EAFB	Vought	Corsair II	71-344	
A- 7F(YA)	UT	Ogden	HAFBM	Vought	Corsair II		
A- 7K	IA	SBluf	MAAM	Vought	Corsair II		
A- 9A(YA)	CA	Riverside	MFAM	Northrop		71-1368	
A-10	KY	Ft Campbell	DFPMM	Fairchild	Thunderbolt II		
A-10	LA	Alexandria	EAB	Fairchild	Thunderbolt II	23-3667, EL 23TFW	
A-10	CT	Windsor	ANG	Fairchild	Thunderbolt II		
A-10 Cockpit	TX	Big Springs	H25	Fairchild	Thunderbolt II		
A-10	WI	CDoug	WNGML&M	Fairchild	Thunderbolt II		
A-10 Wing	WI	Oshko	EAAAAM	Mitchell	Wing		
A-10(YA)	OH	Dayto	USAFM	Fairchild	Thunderbolt II	71-1370	
A-10A	AZ	Tucso	DMAFB	Fairchild	Thunderbolt II		
A-10A	AZ	Tucso	PAM	Fairchild	Thunderbolt II	75-298	
A-10A	CA	Sacra	McCelAFB	Fairchild	Thunderbolt II	76-540	
A-10A	CT	Winds	NEAM	Fairchild	Thunderbolt II	173	
A-10A	FL	Shali	USAFAM	Fairchild	Thunderbolt II	77-205, NO	
A-10A	IN	Peru	GAFB	Fairchild	Thunderbolt II	77-228	
A-10A	NC	Fayet	PAFB	Fairchild	Thunderbolt II		
A-10A	NY	Garde	CoAM	Fairchild	Thunderbolt II	760535	
A-10A	NY	Horseheads	NWM	Fairchild	Thunderbolt II		
A-10A	NY	Scotia	ESAM	Fairchild	Thunderbolt II	75-263	
A-10A	OH	Dayto	USAFM	Fairchild	Thunderbolt II	78-681, TWF-23	
A-10A	PA	Willow	WGNAS	Fairchild	Thunderbolt II		
A-10A	TX	San A	LAFB	Fairchild	Thunderbolt II	76-547	
A-10A	UT	Ogden	HAFBM	Fairchild	Thunderbolt II		
A-10A	WA	Tacoma	MAFB	Fairchild	Thunderbolt II	270	
A-10A(OA)	NC	Fayet	PAFB	Fairchild	Thunderbolt II		
A-10B(YA)	CA	Rosam	EAFB	Fairchild	Thunderbolt II	73-1664	
A-12	AL	Birmingham	SMoF	Lockheed	Blackbird	60-6937	
A-12	AL	Huntsville	HSRM	Lockheed	Blackbird	60-6930	
A-12	AL	Mobil	BMP	Lockheed	Blackbird	60-6938	
A-12	CA	Los Angeles	CMoS	Lockheed	Blackbird	60-6927	
A-12	CA	Palmd	PAFB	Lockheed	Blackbird	60-6924	
A-12	CA	Rosamond	EAFB	Lockheed	Blackbird	60-6924	
A-12	CA	San Diego	SDAM	Lockheed	Blackbird	60-6933	
A-12	MN	Minneapolis	MAGM	Lockheed	Blackbird	60-6931	
A-12	NY	New York City	ISASM	Lockheed	Blackbird 60-6925	
A-12	OH	Dayton	USAFM	Lockheed	Blackbird	60-6935	
A-12	TX	Ft Worth	SAM	Lockheed	Blackbird	60-6935	
A-12(M-21)	WA	Seatt	MoF	Lockheed	Blackbird	60-6940	
A-17A	OH	Dayto	USAFM	Northrop	Nomad	36-207	
A-20G	OH	Dayto	USAFM	Douglas	Havoc	43-22200	
A-20G	TX	Galve	LSFM	Douglas	Havoc	43-21709, N3WF	

Model	State	City	Code	Manufacturer	Name	Notes
A-20H	PA	Beave	AHM	Douglas	Havoc	
A-20J	TX	Midla	CAFFM	Douglas	Havoc	
A-24	OH	Dayton	USAFM	Douglas	Dauntless	
A-24B(RA)	TX	Midla	CAFFM	Douglas	Dauntless	
A-24B-15-DT(SBD-5)	OH	N Canton	MAM	Douglas	Dauntless	42-54654
A-25A (See SB2C)	OH	Dayton	USAFM			
A-26	AL	Birmingham	SMoF	Douglas	Invader	
A-26	AL	Troy	TMA	Douglas	Invader	
A-26	AR	PineB	CAF-RW	Douglas	Invader	N2268N
A-26	AZ	PBluf	RWCAF	Douglas	Invader	
A-26	BC-C	Sidne	BCAM	Douglas	Invader	
A-26	CA	Marys	BAFB	Douglas	Invader	
A-26(JD-1)	CA	Palm Sprg	PSAM	Douglas	Invader	43-5721, N94257, Target Tug, Tail BP
A-26	CA	SRosa	PCAM	Douglas	Invader	
A-26	CA	Stock	ANC	Douglas	Invader	
A-26	FL	Kissi	FTWAM	Douglas	Invader	
A-26(JD-1)	FL	Pensa	USNAM	Douglas	Invader	44-6928, 77141, UH2, VU-5, Target Tug
A-26	LA	N.Orl	FoJBMM	Douglas	Invader	Sn 44-35937
A-26	MA	Stow	BCF	Douglas	Invader	
A-26	MS	Jacks	ThompANG	Douglas	Invader	
A-26	NB	Bellevue	SACM	Douglas	Invader	
A-26	NM	STere	WEAM	Douglas	Invader	
A-26	NY	Cheec	CSCA	Douglas	Invader	
A-26(VA)	OH	Newbu	WASAC	Douglas	Invader	
A-26	OK	ElRen	VFW	Douglas	Invader	"Sonny"
A-26	ON-C	Bradford	GoAR	Douglas	Invader	
A-26	ON-C	Oshaw	MT	Douglas	Invader	
A-26	ON-C	Oshaw	OAM&IM	Douglas	Invader	
A-26C	OR	McMinnville	EAV	Douglas	Invader	44-35439, N74833
A-26	OR	Tillamook	TAM	Douglas	Invader	44-35439, N3222T
A-26	TX	SMarc	CTWCAF	Douglas	Invader	
A-26	TX	Waco	WRA	Douglas	Invader	N240P
A-26B	VA	Suffolk	FF	Douglas	Invader	Project,
A-26	WY	Greyb	H&PA	Douglas	Invader	
A-26A	FL	FtWal	HF	Douglas	Invader	64-666
A-26A	SC	Flore	FA&MM	Douglas	Invader	
A-26B	CA	Rosam	EAFB	Douoglas	Invader	44-34165
A-26B(VB)	MD	Silve	PEGF	Douglas	Invader	
A-26B	MS	Jacks	JANG	Douglas	Invader	
A-26B(VA)	NE	Ashland	SACM	Douglas	Invader	44-34665
A-26B	NM	Las Cruces	SA	Douglas	Invader	
A-26B	NY	Horseheads	NWM	Douglas	Invader	41-39516, N237Y, VA ANG
A-26B	OH	Carroll	HAS	Douglas	Invader	44-34104, N99420
A-26B	OK	Fredi	AAM	Douglas	Invader	
A-26B	TX	Midla	CAFFM	Douglas	Invader	
A-26B	UT	Ogden	HAFBM	Douglas	Invader	
A-26C	AR	Mesa	CAFAW	Douglas	Invader	
A-26C	AZ	Grand	PoFGCVA	Douglas	Invader	39359
A-26C	AZ	Tucso	PAM	Douglas	Invader	43-22494
A-26C	AZ	Tucso	PAM	Douglas	Invader	44-35372, N8028E, "Grim Reaper"
A-26C	CA	Atwater	CAM	Douglas	Invader	43-5648
A-26C(RA)	CA	Chino	PoF	Douglas	Invader	44-35323
A-26C	CA	Riverside	MFAM	Douglas	Invader	44-35224, "Midnight Endeavors", BC-224
A-26C	CO	Puebl	FWAM	Douglas	Invader	44-35892
A-26C	CT	Winds	NEAM	Douglas	Invader	
A-26C	FL	Miami	WOM	Douglas	Invader	N3941
A-26C(TB)	GA	Warner Robin	MoF	Douglas	Invader	44-35732, BC-732
A-26C(RB)	HI	Oahu	HAFB	Douglas	Invader	44-35596/BC-596
A-26C	KS	Dodge	CityPark	Douglas	Invader	
A-26C(GA)	MI	Mt Clemens	SMAM	Douglas	Invader	43-5884 (43-5986)
A-26C	ND	Grand	GFAFB	Douglas	Invader	
A-26C	OH	Dayto	USAFM	Douglas	Invader	44-35733, "Dream Girl"
A-26C	OH	Dayto	USAFM	Douglas	Invader	44-35439
A-26C	TX	Abile	DLAP	Douglas	Invader	44-35913
A-26C	TX	San Antonio	LAFB	Douglas	Invader	44-35918
A-26C	WA	Seattle	MoF	Douglas	Invader	
A-26K	AZ	Tucso	PAM	Douglas	Invader	64-17653 / 41-39378
A-26KD	CA	Fairf	TAFB	Douglas	Invader	
A-26K	SD	Ellsworth	A&SM	Douglas	Invader	
A-26K	SD	Rapid	SDA&SM	Douglas	Invader	44-35896, 64-17640
A-36A	OH	Dayto	USAFM	North American	Apache	42-83665
A-37	CO	Denver	69thB	Cessna	Dragonfly	
A-37	FL	Clear	FMAM	Cessna	Dragonfly	
A-37A	GA	Warner Robin	MoF	Cessna	Dragonfly	67-14525
A-37A	PA	Willow	WGNAS	Cessna	Dragonfly	
A-37A(GY)	TX	Wichi	SAFB	Cessna	Dragonfly	
A-37A(YA)	OH	Dayto	USAFM	Cessna	Dragonfly	62-5951
A-37B(NA)	CA	Rosam	EAFB	Cessna	Dragonfly	
A-37B	NY	Horseheads	NWM	Cessna	Dragonfly	71-0826
A.E.G.GIV	ON-C	Ottaw	CAM	Allquemeine/Elektrizitat/Gesellschaft		574/18
A.W.650-101	MI	Belleville	YAF	Armstrong-Whitworth	Argosy	6651, N896U, "City of Leamington Spa"
A6M	MO	StCha	CAF-MW	Maxson	Bullpup	
A6M-2B	FL	Pensa	USNAM	Mitsubishi	Zero	5450
A6M2	ND	Fargo	FAM	Mitsubishi	Zero	
A6M2	OH	Dayto	USAFM	Mitsubishi	Zero	51553
A6M2	TX	Breck	CAF-DP	Mitsubishi	Zero	5356, N58245
A6M2	WA	Olympia	OFM	Mitsubishi	Zero	9403
A6M3	CA	Camarillo	CAF-SCW	Mitsubishi	Zero	Sn 58245, "E111-142"
A6M3	CA	Camarillo	CAF-SCW	Mitsubishi	Zero	On loan
A6M3	CA	S.Mon	MoF	Mitsubishi	Zero	N58245
A6M3	ID		T&S	Mitsubishi	Zero	3318 Model 32
A6M3	ID		T&S	Mitsubishi	Zero	3685 Model 22
A6M3	OR	Mc Minnville	TNSAM	Mitsubishi	Zero	3318
A6M3	WA	Eastsound	FHC	Mitsubishi	Zero	3852, N3852
A6M5	CA	Chino	PoFAM	Mitsubishi	Zero	5357, N46770
A6M5	CA	Chino	PoFAM	Mitsubishi	Zero	4400
A6M5	CA	S.Mon	MoF	Mitsubishi	Zero	N58245
A6M5	DC	Washi	NA&SM	Mitsubishi	Zero	4340
A6M5	FL	Miami	WOM	Mitsubishi	Zero	4043
A6M5	FL	World Jet	RDW	Mitsubishi	Zero	5350
A6M5	WA	Eastsound	FHC	Mitsubishi	Zero	1303, N1303
A6M5	WA	Eastsound	FHC	Mitsubishi	Zero	4400, N652Z
A6M7	CA	San Diego	SDAM	Mitsubishi	Zero	23186
Air Command Autogyro	PA	WChester	AHM	Air Command	Autogyro	
Abernathy Streaker	FL	Polk	FoF	Abernathy	Streaker	
Abrams Explorer	MD	Silve	PEGF	Abrams	Explorer	

Acro Sport P-8 EAA	WI	Oshko	EAAAAM	Acro	Sport	N9PH
Acro Sport P-8 EAA	WI	Oshko	EAAAAM	Acro	Sport	N1AC
Acro Sport S1	WI	Oshko	EAAAAM	Acro	Sport	N15HS
Acro Sport Super	WI	Oshko	EAAAAM	Acro	Super Sport	N76BM
ADM-20C	AZ	Tucso	PAM	McDonnell	Quail	
ADM-20C	CA	Sacra	SWAM	McDonnell	Quail	
ADM-20C	OH	Dayton	USAFM	McDonnell	Quail	
ADM-20C	SD	Rapid City	SDA&SM	McDonnell	Quail	
ADOCK	WA	Vancouver	PAM		Bi-plane	
Addventura	AR	Little Rock	AEC	Arnet Peryra	Ultrlight	
AEC Ace	NY	Garde	CoAM	Aircraft Eng Co	Ace 1	1
Aero Vodochody L-39C	AL	Birmingham	SMoF	Aero	Albatros	931332, N4679B
Aero Vodochody L-39C	MI	Belleville	YAM	Aero	Albatros	931332, N4679B
Aero Commander	TX	Laredo	Airport	Rockwell	Commander	
Aero Commander 500U	IL	Springfield	ACM	Aero	Commander	
Aero Commander 520	KS	Liber	MAAM	Aero	Commander	
Aero Commander 520	OK	Fredi	AAM	Aero	Commander	
Aero Commander 680	AL	Birmingham	SMoF	Aero	Commander	
Aero Commander 680	LA	Patte	WWMAM	Aero	Commander	
Aero Commander 680	RI	NKing	QAM	Aero	Commander	N2100M
Aero Commander 690B	KS	Liber	MAAM	Aero	Commander	
Aero Commander 690B	OK	Fredi	AAM	Aero	Commander	
See Also (U-4)(U-9)						
Aero Sport	FL	St. A	EM	Aero	Sport	
Aero Sport Champ	FL	Lakel	SFAF	Aero	Sport Champ	N25130
Aero Sport-3	WA	Seatt	MoF	Aero	Sport	12, N23JF
Aero Star	IL	Springfield	ACM	Aero	Starr	
Aerobat Corp 1-A	TX	RioHo	TAM	Aerobat		NX17638
Aerocar	MN	Blaine	GWFM	Taylor	Aerocar	
Aerocar	WA	Seatt	MoF	Taylor	Aerocar	1, N100D
Aerocar Model	ID	Athol	NAM	Taylor	Aerocar	
Aerojet Aerobee	OH	Dayton	USAFM	Aerojet	Aerobee Rocket	
Aerojet V-260	WI	Oshko	EAAAAM	Aerojet-General	Aerojet	V-260
Aeromarine 39B	NY	Rhine	ORA	Aeromarine		Navy Two Seater Biplane
Aeromarine AKL-26A	NY	Rhine	ORA	Aeromarine-Klemm		AKL-26A
Aeronaut	KS	Liberal	MAAM	Aeronaut	Experimental	
Aeronca 7AC	GA	Warner Robin	MoF	Aeronca	Champ	
Aeronca 7AC	IA	Ottumwa	MAAM	Aeronca	Champ	7AC-6740, N3144E
Aeronca 7AC	KS	Liber	MAAM	Aeronca	Champ	
Aeronca 7AC	NY	Bayport	BA	Aeronca	Champ	
Aeronca 7AC	NY	River	TFAC	Aeronca	Champ	
Aeronca 7AC	OH	Madis	CFR	Aeronca	Champ	
Aeronca 7AC	OH	Wapak	NAA&SM	Aeronca	Champ	
Aeronca 7AC	OK	Fredi	AAM	Aeronca	Champ	
Aeronca 7AC	ON-C	Collingwood	CCAF	Aeronca	Champ	
Aeronca 7AC	TX	RioHo	TAM	Aeronca	Champ	SN7AC2118, N83451
Aeronca 11AC	AL	Birmingham	SMoF	Aeronca	Chief	
Aeronca 11AC	BC-C	Langley	CMoF&T	Aeronca	Chief	1261, N9622E, CF-HGN
Aeronca 11AC	IA	Ottumwa	AM	Aeronca	Chief	11AC-956, N9318E
Aeronca 11AC	IN	Mario	MMA	Aeronca	Chief	
Aeronca 11AC	IN	Mario	MMA	Aeronca	Chief	C-FNGV
Aeronca 11AC	NY	Bayport	BA	Aeronca	Chief	
Aeronca 65C	HI	Honolulu	PHNB	Aeronca	Super Chief	Airborne During 12/07/41 Attack
Aeronca 65C	IN	LVill	LVA	Aeronca	Super Chief	Aeronca 65C
Aeronca 65C	KS	Liber	MAAM	Aeronca	Super Chief	Aeronca 65C
Aeronca 65C	MI	Kalam	KAHM	Aeronca	Super Chief	12231
Aeronca 65C	OK	Fredi	AAM	Aeronca	Super Chief	Aeronca 65C
Aeronca 65CA	IA	Ottumwa	AM	Aeronca	Super Chief	N29427
Aeronca 65LA	IA	Ottumwa	AM	Aeronca	Chief	L-750, N24276
Aeronca 65LB	IL	Rantoul	OCAM	Aeronca	Chief	
Aeronca 65TC	HI	Oahu	USSMO	Aeronca	Super Chief	Aeronca 65TC
Aeronca 7DC	NC	Hende	WNCAM	Aeronca	Champ	N4537E
Aeronca C-2	IA	Ottumwa	APM	Aeronca	Robin	301-44
Aeronca C-2	MD	Silve	PEGF	Aeronca	Robin	
Aeronca C-2	ON-C	Ottaw	CAM	Aeronca	Robin	N525
Aeronca C-2	WA	Seatt	MoF	Aeronca	Robin	301-23, N30RC
Aeronca C-2N	VA	Sands	VAM	Aeronca	Robin	Sn 151,N11417
Aeronca C-2N	WI	Oshko	EAAAAM	Aeronca	Robin	NC13089
Aeronca C-3	CA	Hayward	VAM	Aeronca	Duplex	
Aeronca C-3	CA	San Diego	SDAM	Aeronca	Duplex	N13094
Aeronca C-3	FL	Kissi	FTWAM	Aeronca	Duplex	
Aeronca C-3	FL	Lakel	SFAF	Aeronca	Duplex	N17449
Aeronca C-3	IA	Ottumwa	APM	Aeronca	Duplex	A-405, NC14098
Aeronca C-3	MN	Blaine	GWFM	Aeronca	Duplex	
Aeronca C-3	NC	Hende	WNCAM	Aeronca	Duplex	NC11923
Aeronca C-3	NY	Bayport	BA	Aeronca	Duplex	
Aeronca C-3	NY	Rhine	ORA	Aeronca	Duplex	
Aeronca C-3	NY	River	RE	Aeronca	Duplex	
Aeronca C-3	PA	Bethel	GAAM	Aeronca	Master	
Aeronca C-3	PA	Readi	MAAM	Aeronca	Master	
Aeronca C-3	PA	Tough	CFCM	Aeronca	Duplex	
Aeronca C-3	VA	Sands	VAM	Aeronca	Duplex	Sn 426, NC14640
Aeronca C-3B	WA	Vancouver	PAM	Aeronca	Duplex	Flying Bathtub
Aeronca C-3	WI	Oshko	EAAAAM	Aeronca	Duplex	NC16291
Aeronca C-3 (Fuse)	NS	Halifax	ACAM	Aeronca	Duplex	
Aeronca K	AL	Birmingham	SMoF	Aeronca	Scout	
Aeronca K	IA	Ottumwa	APM	Aeronca	Scout	K-147, NC18872, Model 8135
Aeronca K	KS	Liber	MAAM	Aeronca	Scout	
Aeronca K	KY	Lexington	AMoK	Aeronca	Scout	K165, NC18896
Aeronca K	OK	Fredi	AAM	Aeronca	Scout	
Aeronca K	PA	Readi	MAAM	Aeronca	Scout	
Aeronca K	SK-C	MJaw	WDM	Aeronca	Scout	
Aeronca K	WI	Oshko	EAAAAM	Aeronca	Scout	NC19732
Aeronca LC	IA	Ottumwa	APM	Aeronca	LC	90 Hp Warner Junior
Aeronca LC	WI	Oshko	EAAAAM	Aeronca	LC	NC17484, 90 Hp Warner Junior
Aeronca Sedan Floats	AL	Birmingham	SMoF	Aeronca	Sedan	On Floats
Aerospatial SA 341	CA	Ramona	CR	Aerospatial	Gazelle	
Aerospatial Tampico	FL	Dayto	ERAU	Aerospatial	Tampico	
Aerosport Quail	AZ	Tucso	PAM	Aerosport	Quail	54716941, Q547169410
Aerosport Scamp	FL	Lakeland	SNFAM	Aerosport	Scamp	
Aetna-Timm #4	IA	Greenfield	IAM			
AEW.3	CT	Winds	NEAM	Fairey-Gannet	Gannet	AS.1-4 1949 Anti-Sub
AF-2S(G-82)	AZ	Mesa	CAF-AW	Grumman	Guardian	N9993Z
AF-2S(G-82)	WA	Seattle	MoF	Grumman	Guardian	
AF-2S(G-82)	AZ	Tucso	PAM	Grumman	Guardian	129233, N9995Z
AF-2S(G-82)	FL	Pensa	USNAM	Grumman	Guardian	123100, SK30, VS-25

AG Tiger	FL	Dayto	ERAU	American-General	Tiger	
Agena Space Vehicle	OH	Dayton	USAFM	Agena	Space Vehicle	
Aichi D3A Val	TX	Frede	NMofPW	Aichi	Val	
Aichi D3A2 Val	CA	Chino	PoFAM	Aichi	Val	
Alien Blimp	OR	Tillamook	TAM		Blimp	
AIM-4	AZ	Tucso	PAM	Hughes	Falcon	AF3660021263
AIM-4	UT	Ogden	HAM	Hughes	Falcon	
AIM-4	VA	Hampton	HAP	Hughes	Falcon	
AIM-4D	GA	Warner Robin	MoF	Hughes	Falcon	
AIM-4E	GA	Warner Robin	MoF	Hughes	Falcon	
AIM-4F	GA	Warner Robin	MoF	Hughes	Falcon	
AIM-4G	GA	Warner Robin	MoF	Hughes	Falcon	
AIM-9J	CA	Ridgecrest	CLNWC	Ford	Sidewinder	
AIM-9J	GA	Warner Robin	MoF	Ford	Sidewinder	
AIM-26A	GA	Warner Robin	MoF		Super Falcon	
AIR-2A	GA	Warner Robin	MoF	McDonnell/Douglas	Genie	
AIR-2A	UT	Ogden	HAM	McDonnell/Douglas	Genie	
AIR-21	AZ	Tucson	PAM	Douglas	Genie	Sn TE-04813
AJ-2	FL	Pensa	USNAM	North American	Savage	130418
Akerman Tailless	MD	Silve	PEGF	Akerman	Tailless	
Albatros D.Va	AZ	Mesa	CFM	Albatros	Scout	
Albatros D.Va	WA	Seattle	MoF	Albatros	Scout	NX36DV
Albatros D.Va Rep	CA	San Diego	SDAM	Albatros	Scout	AA, 106, N3767A
Albatros D.Va	DC	Washi	NA&SM	Albatros	Scout	
Albatros D.Va	NY	Rhine	ORA	Albatros	Scout	
Albatros D.Va	OH	Dayton	USAFM	Albatros	Scout	
Albatros D.VII	AL	Gunte	LGARFM	Albatros	Scout	
Alexander Primary Glider	CA	Santa Martin	WoHAM	Alexander	Primary Glider	Year 1930, NC205Y
Alexander Eagle Rock A-14	CO	Denve	DIA	Alexander	Eagle Rock	NC205Y
Alexander Eagle Rock	CO	Denve	DIA	Alexander	Eagle Rock	469, N4648, Combo Wing
Alliance Argo	MN	Blaine	GWFM	Alliance	Argo	
Alliance Argo	WY	Jackson	GWFM	Alliance	Argo	
Allison Sport	PA	Bethel	GAAM	Allison	Sport	
AM-1	FL	Pensa	USNAM	Martin	Mauler	122397
AM-1	OR	Tillamook	TAM	Martin	Mauler	N7163M 22275
AM-1	TX	Midla	CAF-Hq	Martin	Mauler	N5586A
American AA 1	VA	Hampton	VA&SM	Grumman-American	Yankee	N501NA
American Aerolights	IL	Rantoul	OCAM	AmEagle	American Aerolights	
American Aerolights	MD	Silve	PEGF	AmEagle	American Aerolights	
American Aerolights	PA	Readi	MAAM	AmEagle	American Aerolights430R, "Double Eagle"	
American BAT	TX	Frede	NMofPW		American Bat	
American Eagle A-101	AZ	Tucson	PAM	American	American Eagle	Sn 538
American Eaglet	CA	Santa Martin	WoHAM	AmEagle	American Eaglet	
American Eaglet	FL	Lakel	SFAF	AmEagle	American Eaglet	
American Eaglet	NY	Rhine	ORA	AmEagle	American Eaglet	N5AQ
American Eaglet	OK	Oklah	KCASM	AmEagle	American Eaglet	
American Eaglet	RI	NKing	QAM	AmEagle	American Eaglet	NC596Y
American Eaglet A 1	CA	San Diego	SDAM	AmEagle	American Eaglet	N4289
American Eaglet B-31	IA	Ottumwa	APM	AmEagle	American Eaglet	1111, N17007
AN-2	AZ	Grand	GCNPA	Antonov	Colt	
AN-2	CA	Chino	PoFAM	Antonov	Colt	
AN-2	CA	Riverside	MAFM	Antonov	Colt	ANATDSR-IR-16550, N22AN
AN-2	FL	Titusville	VACM	Antonov	Colt	
AN-2	MN	Blaine	AWAM	Antonov		
AN-2	MO	Maryland Hts	HARM	Antonov		
AN-2	NC	Charl	CHAC	Antonov	Colt	
AN-2	NY	Geneseo	1941AG	Antonov	Colt	
AN-2	NC	CPoin	CPMB	Antonov	Colt	
AN-2	ON-C	Hamilton	CWHM	Antonov	Colt	
AN-2D	RI	NKing	QAM	Antonov	Colt	1G6219
AN-2	TX	RioHo	TAM	Antonov	Colt	SN1G17602, N7083D
AN-2	TX	RioHo	TAM	Antonov	Colt	SN1G17344, N7083E
AN-2	WA	Seattle	MoF	Antonov	Colt	1G17527, N615L
AN-2	WA	Vancouver	PAM	Antonov	Colt	
Anderson Greenwood 14	WI	Oshko	EAAAAM	Anderson-Greenwood		N314AG
Anderson Z	IA	Ottumwa	APM	Anderson		2A, N12041
Antoinette	ME	Owls Head	OHTM	Antoinette		
Anglin Spacewalker II	FL	Lakel	SFAF	Anglin	Spacewalker II	N168CM
Anzani Longester Rep	OR	Eugen	OAM	Anzani	Longester	
Apollo	AR	Little Rock	AEC	North American	Command Module	
Apollo	AZ	Flags	MC	North American	Command Module	
Apollo	CA	Chino	PoFAM	North American	Command Module	
Apollo	CA	San Diego	SDAM	North American	Command Module	
Apollo	FL	Shali	USAFAM	North American	Command Module	
Apollo	GA	Atlan	FSC	North American	Command Module	
Apollo	NY	NYC	ISASM	North American	Command Module	
Apollo	OH	Dayton	USAFM	North American	Command Module	
Apollo	OK	Oklah	KCASM	North American	Command Module	
Apollo	WA	Seatt	MoF	North American	Command Module	
Apollo	WA	Vanco	PAM	North American	Command Module	
Apollo 8	IL	Chica	MoS&I	North American	Command Module	First Moon Orbit
Apollo 8	KY	Louis	MoH&S	North American	Command Module	First Moon Orbit
Apollo 12	VA	Hampt	VA&SC	North American	Command Module	Last Apollo
Apollo 13	KS	Hutch	KC&SC	North American	Command Module	
Apollo 14 BP1102A	CA	Alameda	USSHM	North American	Command Module	Training
Apollo 14 MQF004	CA	Alameda	USSHM	North American	Mobile Quarantine	Facility
Apollo Skylab III	OH	Cleve	NASALRC	North American	Skylab III	
Applebay Zuni II	MD	Silve	PEGF	Applebay	Zuni	
AQM-34	AZ	Tucso	PAM	Teledyne-Ryan	Compass Dawn	69-6108
AQM-34	CA	Rosamond	EAFB	Ryan	Firebee	
AQM-34	CA	San Diego	SDAM	Ryan	Firebee	
AQM-34L	AZ	Tucso	PAM	Teledyne-Ryan	Compass Bin	69-432
AQM-34L	OH	Dayton	USAFM	Teledyne-Ryan	Compass Bin	
AQM-34L	UT	Ogden	HAFBM	Teledyne-Ryan	Compass Bin	Firebee
AQM-34N	OH	Dayton	USAFM	Teledyne-Ryan	Compass Bin	
AQM-34V	GA	Warner Robin	MoF	Teledyne-Ryan	Compass Bin	74-2147
AQM-37A	CA	Chino	YAM	Maxson	Drone	
AQM-37A	FL	Pensa	USNAM	Maxson	Drone	
AQM-37A	NY	Garde	CoAM	Maxson	Drone	
AQM-91A	OH	Dayton	USAFM	Ryan	Drone	
AQM-91A	SC	FLore	FA&MM	Ryan	Drone	
Arado Ar.196A	FL	Pensa	USNAM	Arado	Ar.196A	
Arado Ar.196A	MD	Silve	PEGF	Arado	Ar.196A	
Arado Ar.234B-2	MD	Silve	PEGF	Arado	Blitz(Lightning)	
Argo D-4	VA	Hampt	APM	Argo	Javelin Launcher	4 Stage Launch Vehicle
Arlington Sisu 1A	MD	Silve	PEGF	Arlington	Sisu	

Arrow Sport	CA	San F	SFIA	Arrow	Sport	
Arrow Sport	MD	Silve	PEGF	Arrow	Sport	
Arrow Sport	MN	Blaine	GWFM	Arrow	Sport	
Arrow Sport	ND	Minot	DTAM	Arrow	Sport	
Arrow Sport	ND	Minot	DTAM	Arrow	Sport	
Arrow Sport F	CA	Oakla	OWAM	Arrow	Sport	
Arrow Sport F	IA	Ottumwa	APM	Arrow	Sport	18, N18000
Arrow Monoplane	ND	Minot	DTAM	Arrow	Monoplane	
AS.10 MKII	AB-C	Calga	AMoC	Airspeed	Oxford	Pilot,Radio,Navigator Trainer
AS.65	ON-C	Ottaw	CAM	Airspeed	Consul	
ASG-21	CA	San Diego	SDAM	Albatross	Sails HG	Hang Glider 1976
ASV-3	OH	Dayton	USAFM	ASSET	Lifting Body	
AT- 6 (AT-16)	AB-C	Nanton	NLSAM	North American	Harvard	
AT- 6	AB-C	Claresholm	CFB	North American	Harvard	
AT- 6	AB-C	Edmonton	AAM	North American	Harvard	
AT- 6	AZ	Mesa	CAFM	North American	Texan	
AT- 6	AZ	Phoenix	DVA	North American	Texan	
AT- 6	AZ	PBluf	RWCAF	North American	Texan	
AT- 6	AZ	Tempe	AHSM	North American	Texan	
AT- 6	CA	Atwater	CAM	North American	Texan	Side # TA-684
AT- 6	CA	Shafter	MFAM	North American	Texan	"Miss T-N-T"
AT- 6	CA	Shafter	MFAM	North American	Texan	"Warlock"
AT- 6	CO	Denve	JWDAS	North American	Texan	
AT- 6	CT	Winds	NEAM	North American	Texan	
AT- 6	FL	Titusville	VACM	North American	Texan	
AT- 6	GA	Atlanta	ASG	North American	Texan	
AT- 6	GA	Marietta	NASA	North American	Texan	
AT- 6	IL	Aurora	RH	North American	Texan	
AT- 6	IL	Cahok	PCUSL	North American	Texan	
AT- 6	IN	Ft. W	FWAS	North American	Texan	
AT- 6	KS	New Century	CAF-HoAW	North American	Texan	49-3349
AT- 6	KY	Louis	BF	North American	Texan	
AT- 6	MA	Stow	BCF	North American	Texan	
AT- 6	MB-C	Brand	CATPM	North American	Harvard	2557
AT- 6	MB-C	Winni	WCAM	North American	Harvard	20301
AT- 6	MB-C	Winni	WCAM	North American	Harvard	
AT- 6	MB-C	Winni	WCAM	North American	Harvard	
AT- 6	MD	Hager	HRegAirP	North American	Texan	
AT- 6	MI	Kalam	KAHM	North American	Texan	49-3509, 112493
AT- 6	MN	Minne	JJ	North American	Texan	
AT- 6	MO	SChar	CAF-MW	North American	Texan	N9627C
AT- 6	MO	SLoui	SLAM	North American	Texan	
AT- 6	MO	StCha	CAFMW	North American	Texan	
AT- 6	ND	Fargo	FAM	North American	Texan	
AT- 6	ND	Fargo	WEAM	North American	Texan	
AT- 6	NM	STere	WEAM	North American	Texan	
AT- 6	NY	Farmingdale	AAM	North American	Texan	
AT- 6	ON-C	Dunnville	CL	North American	Harvard	2766
AT- 6	ON-C	Kingtons	CFBK	North American	Harvard	AJ-693
AT- 6	ON-C	Smith Falls	WCAM	North American	Harvard	Xx443
AT- 6	ON-C	Tillsonburg	CHAA	North American	Harvard	HWX
AT- 6	ON-C	Tillsonburg	CHAA	North American	Harvard	MTX
AT- 6	ON-C	Tillsonburg	CHAA	North American	Harvard	RWN
AT- 6	ON-C	Tillsonburg	CHAA	North American	Harvard	WPK
AT- 6	ON-C	Tillsonburg	CHAA	North American	Harvard	MKA
AT- 6	ON-C	Tillsonburg	CHAA	North American	Harvard	NDB
AT- 6	OR	Tillamook	TAM	North American	Texan	
AT- 6	TX	Breck	BAM	North American	Texan	
AT- 6	TX	C Christi	USS Lexi	North American	Texan	
AT- 6	TX	Dalla	CFM	North American	Texan	
AT- 6	TX	D Rio	LAFB	North American	Texan	
AT- 6	TX	FtWorth	VFM	North American	Texan	
AT- 6	TX	Galve	LSFM	North American	Texan	77-4601, N78RN
AT- 6	TX	Grand Prairie	TACM	North American	Texan	
AT- 6	TX	Houst	CAF-GCW	North American	Texan	N4447
AT- 6	TX	Houst	CAF-GCW	North American	Texan	N15797
AT- 6	TX	Houst	CAF-GCW	North American	Texan	N11171
AT- 6	TX	Houst	CAF-GCW	North American	Texan	N15799
AT- 6	TX	Houst	CAF-GCW	North American	Texan	N9097
AT- 6	TX	Houst	CAF-GCW	North American	Texan	N3725G
AT- 6	TX	Houst	CAF-WHS	North American	Texan	"Ace In The Hole", N97902
AT- 6	TX	Paris	FTAM	North American	Texan	
AT- 6	TX	S Antonio	TAM	North American	Texan	
AT- 6	TX	SMarc	CAF-WF	North American	Texan	N2047
AT- 6	UT	Ogden	HAFBM	North American	Texan	
AT- 6	WA	Olympia	OFM	North American	Texan	Side # 6N6
AT- 6	WA	Vanco	PAM	North American	Texan	"Scrap Iron IV", 486
AT- 6	WI	Bosco	BA	North American	Texan	
AT- 6	WV	Bride	BA	North American	Texan	
AT- 6 (BC-1A)	MN	Minne	MAGM	North American	Texan	40-2122, 798
AT- 6 (P-64)	TX	Galve	LSFM	North American	Texan	
AT- 6 (SNJ)	WA	Seattle	MoF	North American	Texan	
AT- 6 (SNJ)	AZ	PBluf	RWCAF	North American	Texan	
AT- 6 (SNJ)	CA	El Cajon	CAFFFM	North American	Texan	N7300C
AT- 6 (SNJ)	CA	Oakland	CAF-GGW	North American	Harvard	51697
AT- 6 (SNJ)	CA	Palm Sprg	PSAM	North American	Harvard	49-3367A, N4995C, Side # 16, Tail 22P
AT- 6 (SNJ)	ID	Driggs	TAC	North American	Texan	Side # 69
AT- 6 (SNJ)	MO	Maryland Hts	HARM	North American	Texan	
AT- 6 (SNJ)	PA	Tough	CFCM	North American	Texan	
AT- 6 (SNJ)	TX	C Christi	CCMOS&H	North American	Texan	
AT- 6 (SNJ)	TX	C Christi	USS Lexi	North American	Texan	
AT- 6 (SNJ)	VA	Chesapeake	CAFODW	North American	Texan	
AT- 6 (SNJ-3)	FL	Kissi	FTWAM	North American	Texan	
AT- 6 (SNJ-4)	CA	Camarillo	CAF-SCW	North American	Texan	N6411D
AT- 6 (SNJ-4)	CA	Riversideside	MFAM	North American	Texan	51360, N6411
AT- 6 (SNJ-4)	FL	Kissi	FTWAM	North American	Texan	
AT- 6 (SNJ-4)	FL	St Augustine	NATG	North American	Texan	N55A
AT- 6 (SNJ-4)	IN	Elkhart	NIAM	North American	Texan	
AT- 6 (SNJ-4)	NM	Hobbs	CAF-RB	North American	Texan	N7024C
AT- 6 (SNJ-4)	OH	Elyri	CAF-CW	North American	Texan	N224X
AT- 6 (SNJ-4)	OR	Mc Minnville	EABC	North American	Texan	88-13466, N33CC
AT- 6 (SNJ-4)	VA	Suffolk	FF	North American	Texan	
AT- 6 (SNJ-5)	AZ	Mesa	CAF-AW	North American	Texan	N3246G
AT- 6 (SNJ-5)	CA	Como	CAF-IES	North American	Texan	N96281
AT- 6 (SNJ-5)	CA	Oklan	CAF-GGS	North American	Texan	N3195G
AT- 6 (SNJ-5)	CA	Camarillo	CAF-SCW	North American	Texan	N89014, Side Number 290
AT- 6 (SNJ-5)	CA	Chino	PoFAM	North American	Texan	39

Model	State	City	Code	Manufacturer	Type	Notes
AT-6 (SNJ-5)	CA	Chino	YACM	North American	Texan	
AT-6 (SNJ-5)	CA	Miramar	FLAM	North American	Texan	WD, VMT-2
AT-6 (SNJ-5)	CA	S. Mon	MoF	North American	Texan	90952, N3204G, "Big Thunder"
AT-6 (SNJ-5)	FL	St Augustine	NATG	North American	Texan	
AT-6 (SNJ-5)	MI	Kalamazoo	KAHM	North American	Texan	N1617F
AT-6 (SNJ-5)	NC	Hendersonville	WNCAM	North American	Texan	
AT-6 (SNJ-5)	TX	C Christi	USS Lexi	North American	Texan	
AT-6 (SNJ-5)	TX	Midla	CAFFM	North American	Texan	
AT-6 (SNJ-5)	VA	Quant	MCAGM	North American	Texan	84962
AT-6 (SNJ-5B)	IN	Indianapolis	AMHF	North American	Texan	43963
AT-6 (SNJ-5B)	MD	Ft Meade	QM	North American	Texan	
AT-6G(SNJ-6)	FL	Kissi	FTWAM	North American	Texan	
AT-6 (SNJ-7)	CA	San Diego	SDACM	North American	Texan	
AT-6 Mk IV	KS	Topek	CAM	North American	Harvard	N-294CH, 29, CCF-4-85
AT-6A(SNJ-4A)	MD	Silve	PEGF	North American	Texan	
AT-6A	CO	Auror	BANGB	North American	Texan	
AT-6A	MN	Eden Prairie	WotN	North American	Texan	N77TX, #42
AT-6B	AZ	Tucso	PAM	North American	Texan	41-17246
AT-6B(T-6)	IL	Ranto	OCAM	North American	Texan	42-805, TA-805
AT-6B	TX	Midla	CAFFM	North American	Texan	
AT-6B(SNJ-4B)	PA	Readi	MAAM	North American	Texan	88-12281, N24554
AT-6C	AB-C	Wetas	RM	North American	Harvard Mk.II	
AT-6C	NY	Geneseo	1941AG	North American	Harvard Mk.II	
AT-6C	NS-C	Shear	CFBS	North American	Harvard Mk.II	
AT-6C	AB-C	Nanton	NLSAM	North American	Harvard Mk.II	
AT-6C	ON-C	Ottaw	CAM	North American	Harvard Mk.II	66-2265
AT-6C	TX	Midla	NAM	North American	Texan	
AT-6C(SNJ-5C)	FL	Pensa	USNAM	North American	Texan	51849
AT-6C(SNJ-5C)	NC	Charl	CHAC	North American	Texan	
AT-6C(SNJ-5C)	NC	CPoin	CPMB	North American	Texan	
AT-6D	AK	Ancho	KANGB	North American	Texan	
AT-6D	DE	Dover	DAFB	North American	Texan	41-33070, Side U238,
AT-6D/G	FL	St Augustine	NATG	North American	Texan	N1364N
AT-6D	FL	Polk	FoF	North American	Texan	
AT-6D	IN	Bippu	PAC	North American	Texan	
AT-6D-NT	MI	Belleville	YAF	North American	Texan	42-85377, N555Q
AT-6D	MI	Detro	WR	North American	Texan	
AT-6D	NY	eads	NWM	North American	Texan	41-16667
AT-6D	NY	longI	TC	North American	Texan	
AT-6D(SNJ-5)	TN	Sevierville	TMoA	North American	Texan	49-2977, N29963 Flyable
AT-6D	TX	San A	LAFB	North American	Texan	
AT-6D	TX	San A	RAFB	North American	Texan	
AT-6D	WI	Oshko	EAAAAM	North American	Texan	42-44629
AT-6D(T-6)	OH	Dayto	USAFM	North American	Texan	42-84216
AT-6D-NT	MI	Belleville	YAF	North American	Texan	42-84678, N7095C, 26, "Turtle Bay"
AT-6D-NT	MI	Belleville	YAF	North American	Texan	44-81346, N6637C
AT-6F	AB-C	Calga	NAM	North American	Harvard Mk.IV	
AT-6F Mk IIB	BC-C	Langley	CMoF&T	North American	Harvard Mk.IV	
AT-6F	NY	Ghent	POMAM	North American	Harvard Mk.IV	
AT-6F	ID	Zellw	BWA	North American	Texan	
AT-6F	KS	Liber	MAAM	North American	Texan	
AT-6F	OK	Fredi	AAM	North American	Texan	
AT-6F	MN	StPau	CAF-SMW	North American	Harvard Mk IV	N13595
AT-6F	ON-C	Hamilton	CWH	North American	Harvard Mk.IV	20431, CF-UZW
AT-6F	ON-C	Hamilton	CWH	North American	Harvard Mk.IV	3372
AT-6F	ON-C	Hamilton	CWH	North American	Harvard Mk.IV	20213, RAF, CF-UUU
AT-6F	ON-C	Ottaw	CAM	North American	Harvard Mk.IV	20387
AT-6F	ON-C	Ottaw	CAM	North American	Harvard Mk.II	81-4107
AT-6F	SK-C	MJaw	WDM	North American	Harvard Mk.IV	20456
AT-6F	NS-C	Halifax	ACAM	North American	Harvard Mk.VI	
AT-6F	TX	Galve	LSFM	North American	Texan	20247 NX 1811B
AT-6F	TX	Midla	CAFFM	North American	Texan	
AT-6F	TX	RioHo	TAM	North American	Texan	SN112501, N9806C
AT-6F(T-6)	TX	Abile	DLAP	North American	Texan	44-81819
AT-6F(T-6)	TX	Slanton	TAM	North American	Texan	
AT-6G	AL	Birmingham	SMoF	North American	Texan	
AT-6G	AR	Fayet	AAM	North American	Texan	N6FD
AT-6G	AZ	Grand Canyon	PoFGCVA	North American	Texan	
AT-6G(T-6)	AZ	Grand Canyon	PoFGCVA	North American	Texan	
AT-6G	CA	Sacra	McCelAFB	North American	Texan	51-5124
AT-6G (SNJ-5)	FL	Kissi	FTWAM	North American	Texan	
AT-6G	FL	St Augustine	NATG	North American	Texan	N49NA
AT-6G (SNJ-6)	FL	St Augustine	NATG	North American	Texan	N1044C
AT-6G	GA	Warner Robin	MoF	North American	Texan	
AT-6G	IN	Fishers	WG	North American	Texan	49-3254
AT-6G	IN	Hunti	WoF	North American	Texan	53- 4568, N153NA, 13, TA-568, "Lackland"
AT-6G	IN	Valparaiso	IAM	North American	Texan	51-14726
AT-6G	NC	Asheboro	PFAC	North American	Texan	
AT-6G	NJ	Trent	MGAFB	North American	Texan	
AT-6G	OH	Newbu	WASAC	North American	Texan	
AT-6G	ON-C	Hamilton	CWH	North American	Harvard	
AT-6G(SNJ-5)	MI	Kalam	KAHM	North American	Texan	91005, N333SU, 1
AT-6G(T-6)	AL	Birmi	Southe	North American	Texan	TA-963
AT-6G(T-6)	GA	Warner Robin	MoF	North American	Texan	49-3217, TA 217
AT-6G(T-6)	LA	Reser	AMHFM	North American	Texan	
AT-6G(T-6)	MI	Ypsil	YAF	North American	Texan	
AT-6G(T-6)	OH	Dayto	USAFM	North American	Texan	49-3368
AT-6G(T-6)	OH	Dayto	USAFM	North American	Texan	50-1279
AT-6H	WA	Olympia	MAHSM	North American	Texan	Side # 25, Tail ZE
AT-9	OH	Dayto	USAFM	Curtiss-Wright	Fledgling Jeep	41-12150
AT-9A	AZ	Tucso	PAM	Curtiss-Wright	Fledgling Jeep	42-56882
AT-10	OH	Dayto	USAFM	Beech		42-35143
AT-10	OH	Dayto	USAFM	Beech		42-35180
AT-11(Beech D18S)	AZ	Tucso	PAM	Beech	Kansan	41-9577, N6953C
AT-11(Beech D18S)	CA	Fairf	TAFB	Beech	Kansan	
AT-11(Beech D18S)	CA	Paso Robles	EWM	Beech	Kansan	
AT-11(Beech D18S)	CA	Sacra	SWAM	Beech	Kansan	
AT-11(Beech D18S)	CA	Santa Martin	WoHAM	Beech	Kansan	
AT-11(Beech D18S)	CO	Denve	JWDAS	Beech	Kansan	9639, 619
AT-11(Beech D18S)	FL	Clear	FMAM	Beech	Kansan	
AT-11(Beech D18S)	FL	Lakeland	SNF	Beech	Kansan	
AT-11(Beech D18S)	FL	Polk	FoF	Beech	Kansan	
AT-11(Beech D18S)	GA	Warner Robin	MoF	Beech	Kansan	41-27391
AT-11(Beech D18S)	IL	Springfield	ACM	Beech	Kansan	
AT-11(Beech D18S)	IN	Auburn	HW	Beech	Kansan	On Loan from
AT-11-BH(Beech D18S)	MI	Belleville	YAF	Beech	Kansan	43-10404, N7340C

Model	Loc	City	Code	Manufacturer	Type	Serial/Reg
AT-11(Beech D18S)	MI	GRapi	CAF-WMW	Beech	Kansan	N320A
AT-11(Beech D18S)	OH	Dayto	USAFM	Beech	Kansan	41-27561
AT-11(Beech D18S)	OH	Newbu	WASAC	Beech	Kansan	41-27332
AT-11(Beech D18S)	TX	Big Springs	H25	Beech	Kansan	
AT-11(Beech D18S)	TX	Galve	LSFM	Beech	Kansan	42-37240, N81Y
AT-11(Beech D18S)	WI	Janes	YAFS	Beech	Kansan	
AT-11(Beech D18S)	WI	Janesville	YAFS4D	Beech	Kansan	
AT-12A/2PA	CA	Chino	PoFAM	Sikorsky	Guardian	
AT-19	AK	Ancho	AAHM	Stinson	Gullwing	
AT-19-VW(V-77)	MI	Belleville	YAM	Stinson	Reliant	43-44165, N15JH
AT-19	NC	Morga	CWCAF	Stinson	Gullwing	
AT-19	NC	S.Pin	CAF-CW	Stinson	Gullwing	1335, V77-333, N60634
AT-19	NM	STere	WEAM	Stinson	Gullwing	
AT-19	NV	Las Vegas	CAFNW	Stinson	Gullwing	
AT-19	OK	Fredi	AAM	Stinson	Gullwing	
AT-19	PA	Beave	AHM	Stinson	Gullwing	
AT-19	TX	Slanton	TAMCC	Stinson	Gullwing	477
AT-19	UT	SLake	CAF-UW	Stinson	Gullwing	N67227
AT-19(V-77)	AK	Fairb	APAM	Stinson	Reliant	"Peter Pan", NC60924
AT-19(V-77)	CA	S.Mon	MoF	Stinson	Reliant	
AT-19(V-77)	TX	Lancaster	CAF-DFW	Stinson	Reliant	
AT-301	TX	RioHo	TAM	Air Tractor	Air Tractor	SN301-0051, N43925
AT-301	TX	RioHo	TAM	Air Tractor	Air Tractor	SN301-0053, N43935
AT-301	TX	RioHo	TAM	Air Tractor	Air Tractor	SN301-0062, N44026
Atkinson Eaglet	FL	Lakel	SFAF	Atkinson	Eaglet	N5AQ
Atlas Mercury	NY	Coron	NYHoS	Atlas	Mercury	
Auster	AB-C	Wetas	RM	Auster		
Auster AOP Mk6	BC-C	Langley	CMoF&T	Auster		16685, N2863
Auster AOP Mk6	ON-C	Trenton	RCAFMM	Auster		VF-582, C-FLWK
Auster AOP.9 Mk.IX	FL	Lakel	SFAF	Auster		N408XN
Auster MK.V1-J	PA	Readi	MAAM	Auster		
Auster	ON-C	Hamilton	CWH	Auster		16652
Auster Mk.VI	ON-C	Ottaw	CAM	Auster		16652
AV-2	TX	Amari	EFA&SM		Balloon Launch	
AV-8	AZ	Yuma	YUSMAB	McDonnell	Harrier	
AV-8	NC	Havel	CPMCAS	McDonnell	Harrier	
AV-8	TX	Big Springs	H25	McDonnell	Harrier	
AV-8A	CA	El Cajon	FFM	McDonnell	Harrier	
AV-8A	CA	Ridgecrest	CLNWC	McDonnell	Harrier	
AV-8A	ONT-C	Ottawa	CAM	McDonnell	Harrier	
AV-8B	AL	Huntsville	AC	McDonnell-Douglas	Harrier	
AV-8B	MD	Lexington	PRNAM	McDonnell-Douglas	Harrier	161396, Side # 623, SD Tail
AV-8C	AZ	Tucso	PAM	McDonnell-Douglas	Harrier	159241
AV-8C	CA	Oakla	OWAM	McDonnell-Douglas	Harrier	
AV-8C	FL	Pensa	USNAM	McDonnell-Douglas	Harrier	158975, WF
AV-8C	NY	NYC	ISASM	McDonnell-Douglas	Harrier	
Avian Falcon II	AZ	Tucson	PAM	Avian	Falcon II	Man Sn 12, N4369Z, N3AV
Aviat A-1	ID	Driggs	TAC	Aviat	Huskey	
Aviatik D.II	AZ	Mesa	CFM	Aviatik	Berg Scout	101,40
Aviatik D.II	WA	Seattle	MoF	Aviatik	Berg Scout	101,40
Avid Flyer	KS	Liber	MAAM	Wings An Things	Avid Flyer	
Avid Flyer	MI	Kalamazoo	KAHM	Wings An Things	Avid Flyer	
Avid Flyer	WI	Oshko	EAAAAM	Wings An Things	Avid Flyer	N4636J
Avitor Hermes, Jr.	CA	SCarl	HAM	Avitor	Hermes Jr.	
Avro 504 (3 ea)	ON-C	Ottaw	CAM	Avro	Gosport	D-8971
Avro 504J/K	FL	Polk	FoF	Avro	Gosport	
Avro 504K	MB-C	Winni	WCAM	Avro	Gosport	
Avro 504K	NY	Rhine	ORA	Avro	Gosport	
Avro 504K	OH	Dayton	USAFM	Avro	Gosport	
Avro 504K Replica	MB-C	Winni	WCAM	Avro	Gosport	
Avro 581	AB-C	Wetas	RM	Avro	Avian	
Avro 581	MN	Blaine	GWFM	Avro	Avian	
Avro 595	CA	Santa Martin	WoHAM	Avro	Avian	Cirrus Engine
Avro 616 Mk.IV M	ON-C	Ottaw	CAM	Avro	Avian	
Avro 652	AB-C	Nanton	NLSAM	Avro	Anson	
Avro 652	SK-C	MJaw	WDM	Avro	Anson	
Avro 652	MB-C	Brandon	CATPM	Avro	Anson	
Avro 652 Mk.I	MB-C	Winni	WCAM	Avro	Anson	
Avro 652 Mk.II	AB-C	Calga	AMoC	Avro	Anson	
Avro 652 Mk.II	AB-C	Wetas	RM	Avro	Anson	
Avro 652 Mk.II	BC-C	Langley	CMoF&T	Avro	Anson	7139
Avro 652 Mk.II	MB-C	Winni	WCAM	Avro	Anson	
Avro 652 Mk.II	NS-C	Greenwood	GMAM	Avro	Anson	
Avro 652 Mk.V	BC-C	Langley	CMoF&T	Avro	Anson	12032
Avro 652 Mk.V	MB-C	Winni	WCAM	Avro	Anson	
Avro 652 Mk.V	ON-C	Ottaw	CAM	Avro	Anson	12518
Avro 652 Mk.VI	ON-C	Hamilton	CWH	Avro	Anson	
Avro 652A Mk.VI	TX	RioHo	TAM	Avro	Anson	SN266324
Avro 683 Mk.X	AB-C	Calga	AMoC	Avro	Lancaster	FM136, BX
Avro 683 Mk.X	AB-C	Nanto	TBGLTD	Avro	Lancaster	FM159
Avro 683 Mk.X	AB-C	Nanto	NLS	Avro	Lancaster	
Avro 683 Mk.X	NB-C	Edmunston	EA	Avro	Lancaster	KB882
Avro 683 Mk.X	NS-C	Greenwood	GMAM	Avro	Lancaster	KB829
Avro 683 Mk.X	ON-C	Hamilton	CWH	Avro	Lancaster	BX
Avro 683 Mk.X	ON-C	Ottaw	CAM	Avro	Lancaster	BX
Avro 683 Mk.X	ON-C	Toronto	TAM	Avro	Lancaster	
Avro 683 Mk.X	ON-C	Trenton	JP	Avro	Lancaster	
Avro 683 Mk.X	ON-C	Windsor	CAM	Avro	Lancaster	FM212
Avro Anson Mk.II	AB-C	Edmonton	AAM	Avro	Anson	
B 1	CA	Chino	YACM	Mahoney-Ryan		141, NC6956
B-1	WA	Seatt	SHSM	Boeing	Flying Boat	I-13, M-92, Model 6, "U.S. Mail"
B-1A	CO	Denver	WoR	Boeing	Stealth	
B-1A	OH	Dayto	USAFM	Rockwell	Lancer	76-174
B-1B	OH	Dayto	USAFM	Rockwell	Lancer	84-0051
B-2	PA	WChes	AHM	Brantly-Hynes	Model 305	
B-2	OH	Dayton	USAFM	Boeing	Spirit	
B-3	OH	Dayton	USAFM	Northrop	Bomber	
B-5	CA	San Diego	SDAM	Ryan	Brougham	NC9236
B-10	AK	Fairb	APAM	Mitchell	Wing	
B-10	AZ	Tucson	PAM	Mitchell	Wing	Sn 285, N4232A
B-10	NM	Moriarty	SSM	Mitchell	Wing	
B-10	OH	Dayto	USAFM	Martin	Bomber	
B-17	CO	Greel	SA	Boeing	Flying Fortress	
B-17 Ball Turret	FL	Lakeland	SNF	Boeing	Flying Fortress	
B-17 Fuselage	FL	Lakeland	SNF	Boeing	Flying Fortress	
B-17	WA	Arlington	GPAM	Boeing	Flying Fortress	

Model	State	City	Org	Manufacturer	Name	Serial/Notes
B-17D	MD	Silve	PEGF	Boeing	Flying Fortress	40-3097, "Swoose"
B-17E	OH	Cincinatti	BR	Boeing	Flying Fortress	41-9032, 2504, "My Gal Sal"
B-17E	IL	Marengo	MK	Boeing	Flying Fortress	41-2595, 2406, "Desert Rat"
B-17E	WA	Eastsound	FHC	Boeing	Flying Fortress	41-9210, N8WJ, 2682
B-17F	IA	Offutt	OAPB	Boeing	Flying Fortress	42-30230, "Homesick Angel", Blk H/W Sq/Yel L
B-17F	TN	Memph	MBMA	Boeing	Flying Fortress	41-24485, 3170,"Memphis Belle"
B-17F	WA	Seatt	MoF	Boeing	Flying Fortress	42-29782, N17W , 4896, "Boeing Bee"
B-17G	OR	McMinnville	EAEC	Boeing	Flying Fortress	44-83785, N207EV , K32426, "Shady Lady"
B-17G	AZ	Mesa	CAF-AW	Boeing	Flying Fortress	44-83514, N9323Z, U, 32155, "Sentimental Journey"
B-17G(PB-1G)	AZ	Tusco	390thMM	Boeing	Flying Fortress	44-85828, N9323R ,JDIH "I'll Be Around"
B-17G	CA	Atwater	CAM	Boeing	Flying Fortress	43-38635, N3702G, A-N, 9613, "Virgin's Delight",
B-17G	CA	Chino	PoFAM	Boeing	Flying Fortress	44-83684, N3713G, 32325, "Picadilly Lilly"
B-17G-105VE	CA	Palm Sprg	PoF	Boeing	Flying Fortress	44-85778, N3509G, 8687, "Miss Angela"
B-17G	CA	Riverside	MFAM	Boeing	Flying Fortress	44-6393, 22616, 230092, "Starduster II", "Return to Glory"
B-17G	CA	Tular	VMVETS56	Boeing	Flying Fortress	44-85738, K,8647, "Reston's Pride"
B-17G	DC	Dulle	AP	Boeing	Flying Fortress	44-83814
B-17G	DE	Dover	DAFB	Boeing	Flying Fortress	44-83624, 381BG, 32265, "Sleepy Time Gal"
B-17G	FL	Kissi	FTWAM	Boeing	Flying Fortress	44-85734, N5111N, 8643, "Outhouse Mouse"
B-17G	FL	Miami	WOM	Boeing	Flying Fortress	44-83525, N83525, 32166, "Suzy Q",
B-17G	FL	Polk	FoF	Boeing	Flying Fortress	44-83542, N9324Z, 32183
B-17G	FL	Shali	USAFAM	Boeing	Flying Fortress	44-83863, 32504
B-17G	IN	Peru	GAFB	Boeing	Flying Fortress	44-83690,XK-D,305BG 32331/231255, "Miss Liberty Bell"
B-17G	LA	Bossi	BAFB	Boeing	Flying Fortress	44-83884 , 32525 / 333284, "Yankee Doodle II",
B-17G	MA	Stow	BCF	Boeing	Flying Fortress	44-83575, N93012, OR-R, Resembles Scraped 42-31909, "909"
B-17G-110-VE	MI	Belleville	YAF	Boeing	Flying Fortress	44-85829, N3193G, "Yankee Lady", Side GD, Tail L Y
B-17G	NE	Ashland	SACM	Boeing	Flying Fortress	44-83559, EP-B, 32200 / 23474, "King Bee"
B-17G	NY	Farmingdale	AAM	Boeing	Flying Fortress	44-83563, N95637, KE, 32204 / 297400, "Fuddy Duddy"
B-17G-35-BO	OH	Dayto	USAFM	Boeing	Flying Fortress	42-32076, 7190, 91, "Shoo Shoo Baby"
B-17G	OR	Milwa	BG	Boeing	Flying Fortress	44-85790, "Lacey Lady"
B-17G	OR	Mc Minnville	EAEC	Boeing	Flying Fortress	44-83785
B-17G(DB)	TX	Abile	DLAP	Boeing	Flying Fortress	44-85599, 8508, 238133
B-17G	TX	FWort	BCVintag	Boeing	Flying Fortress	44- 8543, N3701G, 7943, 44- 8543A, "Chuckie",
B-17G	TX	Galve	LSFM	Boeing	Flying Fortress	44-85718, N900RW, BN-U ,8627, 238050, "Thunder Bird"
B-17G	TX	Houst	CAF-GCW	Boeing	Flying Fortress	44-83872, N7227C, 32513, "Texas Raiders"
B-17G	TX	San A	LAFB	Boeing	Flying Fortress	44-83512, HT, 32153, "Heavens Above"
B-17G	UT	Ogden	HAFBM	Boeing	Flying Fortress	44-83663, 32304, "Short Bier"
B-17G-VE	WI	Oshko	EAAAAM	Boeing	Flying Fortress	44-85740, N5017N, FU-D, 8649, "Aluminum Overcast"
B-17 Parts	CO	Denve	JWDAS	Boeing	Flying Fortress	
B-17G (Parts)	CA	Wells	Ocotillo	Boeing	Flying Fortress	44-83722, 32363
B-17G (Parts)	FL	Kissi	FTWAM	Boeing	Flying Fortress	44-85813
B-18A	CA	Atwater	CAM	Douglas	Bolo	37-029, Tail # BI
B-18A	CO	Denve	WOR	Douglas	Bolo	
B-18A	OH	Dayto	USAFM	Douglas	Bolo	37-469
B-18A	WA	Tacoma	MAFB	Douglas	Bolo	37-505, N18AC
B-18B	AZ	Tucso	PAM	Douglas	Bolo	38-593, N66267
B-23	CA	Atwater	CAM	Douglas	Dragon	39-45, Tail # 112MD
B-23	FL	Miami	WOM	Douglas	Dragon	N4000B
B-23	OH	Dayto	USAFM	Douglas	Dragon	39-37
B-23	WA	Tacoma	MAFB	Douglas	Dragon	1089R
B-23(UC-67)	AZ	Tucso	PAM	Douglas	Dragon	39-51, N534J
B-24 *One Tail version See PB4Y*						
B-24M-5-CO		Atwater	CAM	Consolidated	Liberator	44-41916, RE,Tail B, "Shady Lady"
B-24(LB-30)	TX	Midla	CAF-B29	Consolidated	Liberator	AM927, N24927, "Diamond Lil"
B-24J Nose	MD	Ft Meade	QM	Consolidated	Liberator	44-40332
B-24L Fuse	MD	Ft Meade	QM	Consolidated	Liberator	44-50022
B-24	TX	San Antonio	LAFB	Consolidated	Liberator	
B-24 Cockpit	GA	Savan	MEHM	Consolidated	Liberator	
B-24 Nose	VA	Hampt	VA&SC	Consolidated	Liberator	"Old Bessie"
B-24 Nose Turret	MI	Lansi	MHM	Consolidated	Liberator	
B-24D-160-CO	OH	Dayto	USAFM	Consolidated	Liberator	42-72843, "Strawberry Bitch"
B-24D	UT	Ogden	HAFB	Consolidated	Liberator	40-2367, N58246, Project
B-24J-90-CF	AZ	Tucso	PAM	Consolidated	Liberator	44-44175, N7866, "Bungay Buckaroo"
B-24J-95-CF	FL	Polk City	FoF	Consolidated	Liberator	44-44272, N94459, 250551,"Joe"
B-24J-25-FO	LA	Bossi	BAFB	Consolidated	Liberator	44-48781, "Laden Maiden"
B-24J	MA	Stow	BCF	Consolidated	Liberator	44-44052, N224J, JHK191, "All American"
B-24L-20-FO	ON-C	Ottaw	CAM	Consolidated	Liberator	44-50154, 11130
B-25	AB-C	Westaskiwin	RM	North American	Mitchell	44-86726
B-25	AL	Troy	TMA	North American	Mitchell	
B-25	AZ	Mesa	CAF-AW	North American	Mitchell	Sn 43-35972N9552Z
B-25	CA	Fierbaugh	HEM	North American	Mitchell	Sn 44-30748, "Heavenly Body"
B-25	CA	Marysville	BAFB	North American	Mitchell	Sn 43-28222
B-25	CA	Rialt	KA	North American	Mitchell	Sn 44-29199, N9117Z, "In The Mood"
B-25	CA	Stock	ANC	North American	Mitchell	
B-25	FL	FtLau	WJAIS&L	North American	Mitchell	Sn 44-28938, N7946C, "Dream Lover"
B-25	FL	Miami	WOM	North American	Mitchell	Sn 43-28059, N1943J
B-25	GA	Woodstock	NGWS	North American	Mitchell	
B-25				North American	Mitchell	Sn 44-86725, N25NA
B-25	MO	SChar	CAF-MW	North American	Mitchell	Sn 44-31385, N3481G, "Show Me"
B-25	MB-C	Brandon	CATPM	North American	Mitchell	
B-25	MB-C	Winnipeg	AFHM	North American	Mitchell	5203
B-25	NC	Charl	CHAC	North American	Mitchell	
B-25	ND	Fargo	FAM	North American	Mitchell	
B-25	ND	Wahpe	TSA	North American	Mitchell	
B-25	OH	N Canton	MAM	North American	Mitchell	44-30324
B-25	OH	S.Euc	USAM	North American	Mitchell	Sn 44-30010, N9641C
B-25	OK	Tulsa	RA	North American	Mitchell	"Martha Jean"
B-25	ON-C	Ottaw	CAM	North American	Mitchell	Sn 44-86699
B-25	OR	Tillamook	TAM	North American	Mitchell	Sn 44-30456, N43BA, "Silver Lady"
B-25D-NC	SC	Mt Pl	PPM	North American	Mitchell	Sn 41-29784, "Furtile Turtle"
B-25	SK-C	MJaw	WDM	North American	Mitchell	
B-25	TX	Breck	BAM	North American	Mitchell	
B-25	TX	Dalla	CFM	North American	Mitchell	44-28925, N7687C, 380BS, 310BG, "How Boot That"
B-25	TX	FtWor	CAF-JH	North American	Mitchell	Sn 44-86758, N9643C
B-25	TX	Galve	LSFM	North American	Mitchell	44-86734, N333RW, "Special Delivery"
B-25	WA	Bellevue	AM	North American	Mitchell	44-30254, N41123
B-25	WI	Milwaukee	GMF	North American	Mitchell	Sn 44-30444
B-25	WY	Milwa	CityPark	North American	Mitchell	
B-25 Nose	WA	Tacoma	MAFB	North American	Mitchell	
B-25 Simulator	MN	Duluth	CAF-LSS	Curtiss Dehmel	Simulator	
B-25A	CA	Atwater	CAM	North American	Mitchell	Sn 44-86891, "Lazy Daisy Mae"
B-25C	CA	Lanca	MoFM	North American	Mitchell	Sn 41-13251
B-25C	SC	Colum	SCSM	North American	Mitchell	Sn 41-13285
B-25C(PBJ-1C)	CA	Miramar	FLAM	North American	Mitchell	44-46727
B-25C(PBJ-1C)	TX	Pampa	PAAF	North American	Mitchell	43-3308
B-25D-35-NC	MI	Belleville	YAF	North American	Mitchell	43- 3634, NX3774, "Yankee Warrior"
B-25D	OH	Dayto	USAFM	North American	Mitchell	43- 3374

B-25D(PBJ-1) Nose	VA	Quant	MCAGM	North American	Mitchell	43-3308
B-25G	ND	Grand	GFAFB	North American	Mitchell	44-28834
B-25H	AL	Mobil	BMP	North American	Mitchell	44-31004, NC44310004
B-25H	CT	Winds	NEAM	North American	Mitchell	Sn 43-4999, "Dog Daze"
B-25H	TX	San A	LAFB	North American	Mitchell	Sn 44-29835J, 35103
B-25J	AL	Montg	MAFB	North American	Mitchell	Sn 44-30649
B-25J	AZ	Tucso	PAM	North American	Mitchell	43-27712
B-25J	CA	Camarillo	CAF-SCW	North American	Mitchell	Sn 44-30988, N5865V, "Big Ole Brew"
B-25J	CA	Chino	PoFAM	North American	Mitchell	44-30423, N3675G
B-25J	CA	Chino	YAM	North American	Mitchell	44-86791, N6116X
B-25J	CA	Palm Sprg	PSAM	North American	Mitchell	44-86747, N8163H, A
B-25J	CA	Riverside	MFAM	North American	Mitchell	Sn 44-31032, "Problem Child"
B-25J	DC	Dulle	DA	North American	Mitchell	Sn 44-29887
B-25J	FL	Kissimmee	FTWAM	North American	Mitchell	
B-25J	FL	Shali	USAFAM	North American	Mitchell	Sn 44-30854, "Doolittle Raider"
B-25J	GA	Warner Robin	MoF	North American	Mitchell	44-86872, N2888G
B-25J	HI	Hickm	HAFB	North American	Mitchell	Sn 44-31504
B-25J	IL	Springfield	ACM	North American	Mitchell	896, "Access Nightmare"
B-25J	IN	Peru	GAFB	North American	Mitchell	44-86843, "Pasionate Paulette"
B-25J	KS	Liber	MAAM	North American	Mitchell	Sn 44-30535, N9462Z, "Iron Laiden Maiden"
B-25J	MA	Stow	BCF	North American	Mitchell	Sn 44-28932, N3478G, "Hoosier Honey"
B-25J	MI	Kalam	KAHM	North American	Mitchell	Sn 43-4899
B-25	MN	StPau	CAF-SMW	North American	Mitchell	Sn 44-29869, N27493, "Miss Mitchell"
B-25J	MS	Petal	MWHMM	North American	Mitchell	
B-25J	NC	Asheboro	PFAC	North American	Mitchell	
B-25J	ND	Grand	GFAFB	North American	Mitchell	Sn 44-28834
B-25J	OH	Newbu	WASAC	North American	Mitchell	44-31121
B-25J	OK	Fredi	AAM	North American	Mitchell	
B-25J	ON-C	Hamilton	CWH	North American	Mitchell	Sn 45-8883, C-GCWM, "Hot Gen"
B-25J	TX	Frede	NMofPW	North American	Mitchelle	
B-25J	TX	Midla	CAFFM	North American	Mitchell	Sn 43-27868, N25YR, "Yellow Rose"
B-25J	UT	Ogden	HAFBM	North American	Mitchell	
B-25J	VA	Suffolk	FF	North American	Mitchell	
B-25J	WI	Oshko	EAAAM	North American	Mitchell	Sn 43-4432, N10V, "City of Burlington"
B-25J(TB)-NC	NE	Ashland	SACM	North American	Mitchell	44-28738
B-25J(TB)-NC	NE	Ashland	SACM	North American	Mitchell	44-30363, Desert Boom
B-25J(VB)	SD	Rapid	SDA&SM	North American	Mitchell	43-4030
B-25J-10-NA	PA	Readi	MAAM	North American	Mitchell	Sn 44-29939, N9456Z, 9D, Model 108, "Briefing Time"
B-25M	MT	Great	MAFB	North American	Mitchell	Sn 44-50493
B-25N	FL	FtWal	HF	North American	Mitchell	
B-25N	IL	Ranto	OCAM	North American	Mitchell	Sn 44-30653, "Whiskey Pete"
B-25N	Ny	Farmingdale	AAM	North American	Mitchell	
B-25N(TB)	FL	Kissi	FTWAM	North American	Mitchell	44-30077
B-25N(TB)	TX	San A	GAFB	North American	Mitchell	44-28875
B-26	FL	Polk	FoF	Martin	Marauder	40-1464 N 4297J
B-26	NY	Scotia	ESAM	Martin	Marauder	40-1459
B-26	OH	N Canton	MAM	Martin	Marauderr	40-1501, "Million Dollar Valley"
B-26B	DC	Washi	NA&SM	Martin	Marauder	41-31773, "Flak Bait"
B-26G-MO	OH	Dayto	USAFM	Martin	Marauder	43-34581, "Shootin In"
B-26K	OH	Dayton	USAFM	Martin	Counter Invader	
B-29	CA	Fairf	TAFB	Boeing	Super Fortress	42-65281, R, "Miss America 62"
B-29	CA	Inyokern	USAM	Boeing	Super Fortress	44-69972, "Doc"
B-29	CA	Inyokern	USAM	Boeing	Super Fortress	44-70102, "Here'S Hopin"
B-29	CO	Puebl	FWAM	Boeing	Super Fortress	44-62022, "Peachy"
B-29	FL	Polk City	WAM	Boeing	Super Fortress	44-70049, Nose at Borrego Springs, CA
B-29	FL	Polk City	WAM	Boeing	Super Fortress	44-84084, at Borrego Springs, CA
B-29 Nose	FL	Lakeland	SNF	Boeing	Super Fortress	Nose
B-29	GA	Cordele	GVMSP	Boeing	Super Fortress	42-93967
B-29	GA	Marie	DAFB	Boeing	Super Fortress	44-70113, "Sweet Loise"
B-29	LA	Bossi	BAFB	Boeing	Super Fortress	44-87627
B-29	MD	Silve	PEGF	Boeing	Super Fortress	44-86292, "Enola Gay"
B-29	MO	White	WAFB	Boeing	Super Fortress	44-61671, 89, 509BW, "The Geat Artist"
B-29	NM	Albuq	NAM	Boeing	Super Fortress	45-21748, "Duke of Albuquerque"
B-29	OH	Dayto	USAFM	Boeing	Super Fortress	44-27297, "Bockscar"
B-29 Cockpit	OH	Dayto	USAFM	Boeing	Super Fortress	42-24791, Forward Half only, "Big Time Operator"
B-29 Cockpit & Bomb Bay	OH	Dayto	USAFM	Boeing	Super Fortress	44-62139, "Command Decision"
B-29	OK	Tinke	TAFB	Boeing	Super Fortress	44-27343, "Tinker Heritage"
B-29	SD	Rapid	SDA&SM	Boeing	Super Fortress	44-87779, "Eagle II"
B-29	TX	San A	KAFB	Boeing	Super Fortress	
B-29	UT	Ogden	HAFBM	Boeing	Super Fortress	44-86408, "Haggerty's Hag"
B-29	WA	Seatt	MoF	Boeing	Super Fortress	44-69729, "T-Squre 54"
B-29(P2B-1S) Nose	FL	Miami	WOM	Boeing	Super Fortress	45-21787, N91329, Nose Section Only, "Fertile Myrtle"
B-29(TB)	AZ	Tucso	PAM	Boeing	Super Fortress	44-70016, "Sentimental Journey"
B-29-60-BA	NE	Ashland	SACM	Boeing	Super Fortress	44-84076, "Man O" War"
B-29A(B-50)	CA	Atwater	CAM	Boeing	Super Fortress	44-61535, "Raz'n Hell" 49-351, 46-010
B-29A	CA	Riverside	MFAM	Boeing	Superfortress	44-61669, E, "Flag Ship 500"
B-29A	CT	Winds	NEAM	Boeing	Super Fortress	44-61975, "Jack'S Hack"
B-29A	TX	Midla	CAF-B29	Boeing	Super Fortress	44-62070, N5298, "FiFi"
B-29A	TX	San A	KAFB	Boeing	Super Fortress	45-22220
B-29B-55	GA	Warner Robin	MoF	Boeing	Super Fortress	44-87627
B-36A(YB)	OH	Newbu	WASAC	Convair	Peacemaker	42-13571
B-36J	OH	Dayto	USAFM	Convair	Peacemaker	52- 2220
B-36J-111-10	TX	FWort	AHM	Convair	Peacemaker	52-2827A
B-36H(RB)	CA	Atwater	CAM	Convair	Peace Maker	51-13730, Circle W
B-36J-65-CF	NE	Ashland	SACM	Convair	Peacemaker	52-2817
B-37(RB)	AB-C	Edmonton	AAM	Lockheed	Ventura	5324
B-37(RB)	AB-C	Edmonton	VMFA	Lockheed	Ventura	2195, CF-FAV, CAF447
B-37(RB)	CO	Puebl	FWAM	Lockheed	Ventura	342-17
B-37(RB)	QU-C	St Esprit	Airport	Lockheed	Ventura	CF-SEQ
B-377SG	AZ	Tucso	PAM	Aer0 Spacelines	Super Guppy 201	52-2693, N940NS
B-42A(XB)	MD	Silve	PEGF	Douglas	Mixmaster	
B-43(XB)	MD	Silve	PEGF	Douglas	Jetmaster	
B-45A	AZ	Tucso	PAM	North American	Tornado	47-63
B-45A	CA	Atwater	CAM	North American	Tornado	47-008, Tail B
B-45C	OH	Dayto	USAFM	North American	Tornado	48-10
B-45C(RB)	NE	Ashland	SACM	North American	Tornado	48-17
B-47	OK	Oklah	SFG	Boeing	Stratojet	012387
B-47	SD	Rapid	SDA&SM	Boeing	Stratojet	
B-47A Nose	AZ	Tucso	PAM	Boeing	Stratojet	49-1901, 450002
B-47B	CA	Rosam	EAFB	Boeing	Stratojet	51-2075
B-47B	MO	Knob	WAFB	Boeing	Stratojet	
B-47B(WB)	GA	Pooler	M8thAFM	Boeing	Stratojet	
B-47D	IN	Peru	GAFB	Boeing	Stratojet	51-2315
B-47E	AR	Littl	LRAFB	Boeing	Stratojet	52-595384th BW
B-47E	CA	Atwater	CAM	Boeing	Stratojet	52-0166, 0166, "Spirit"
B-47E Nose	CA	Riverside	MFAM	Boeing	Stratojet	Used in movie "Strategic Air Command"

Model	State	City	Museum	Mfr	Type	Serial/Notes
B-47E	CA	Riverside	MFAM	Boeing	Stratojet	53-2275, "Betty Boop"
B-47E	CO	Puebl	FWAM	Boeing	Stratojet	532104
B-47E	UT	Ogden	HAFB	Boeing	Stratojet	51-2360
B-47E	LA	Bossi	BAFB	Boeing	Stratojet	
B-47E	NY	Platt	PAFB	Boeing	Stratojet	
B-47E	OH	Dayto	USAFM	Boeing	Stratojet	53-2280
B-47E	OK	Altus	City	Boeing	Stratojet	
B-47E(WB)	WA	Seatt	MoF	Boeing	Stratojet	51-7066
B-47E(EB)	AZ	Tucso	PAM	Boeing	Stratojet	53-2135, 44481
B-47E(XB)	IL	Ranto	OCAM	Boeing	Stratojet	46-0066
B-47E(EB)	OK	Tinke	TAFB	Boeing	Stratojet	
B-47E(EB)	TX	Abile	DLAP	Boeing	Stratojet	52-4120
B-47E(RB)	TX	Midla	CAFFM	Boeing	Stratojet	
B-47E(WB)	OK	Oklah	CityPark	Boeing	Stratojet	
B-47E-35-DT	NE	Ashland	SACM	Boeing	Stratojet	52-1412
B-47H(RB)	OH	Dayton	USAFM	Boeing	Stratojet	53-4299
B-47N(RB)	FL	Shali	USAFAM	Boeing	Stratojet	
B-50(WB)	CA	Atwater	CAM	Boeing	Superfortress	
B-50A Fuse	CA	Chino	PoFAM	Boeing	Superfortress	
B-50D(WB)	OH	Dayto	USAFM	Boeing	Superfortress	49-310
B-50J(KB)	AZ	Tucso	PAM	Boeing	Superfortress	49-372
B-50J(KB)	FL	Tampa	MAFB	Boeing	Superfortress	49-389, Side 48-114A, Tail 0-80114
B-52 Gunner Trainer	CA	Riversideside	MAM	Boeing	Stratofortress	Gunner Trainer
B-52	NE	Offut	OAFB	Boeing	Stratofortress	
B-52	OK	Oklah	SFG	Boeing	Stratofortress	70038
B-52 Nose	TX	Big Springs	H25	Boeing	Stratofortress	
B-52A(NB)	AZ	Tucso	PAM	Boeing	Stratofortress	52-3
B-52B	NM	Albuq	NAM	Boeing	Stratofortress	
B-52B(GB)	CO	Denve	WOR	Boeing	Stratofortress	
B-52B(RB)-15-BO	NE	Ashland	SACM	Boeing	Stratofortress	52-8711
B-52C Cockpit	IL	Ranto	OCAM	Boeing	Stratofortress	
B-52D	AL	Montg	MAFB	Boeing	Stratofortress	
B-52D	AZ	Tucso	DMAFB	Boeing	Stratofortress	
B-52D	AZ	Tucso	PAM	Boeing	Stratofortress	55-67
B-52D	CA	Atwater	CAM	Boeing	Stratofortress	56-0612
B-52D	CA	Fairf	TAFB	Boeing	Stratofortress	
B-52D	CA	Rosam	EAFB	Boeing	Stratofortress	56-585
B-52D	CO	CSpri	USAFA	Boeing	Stratofortress	"Diamond Lil"
B-52D	FL	Orlan	OIAMP	Boeing	Stratofortress	
B-52D	GA	Warner Robin	MoF	Boeing	Stratofortress	55-85
B-52D-25-BW	MI	Belleville	YAF	Boeing	Stratofortress	55-677, N464024, "Clyde"
B-52D	MI	Marqu	KISAFB	Boeing	Stratofortress	
B-52D	MI	Ypsil	YAF	Boeing	Stratofortress	
B-52D	OH	Dayto	USAFM	Boeing	Stratofortress	56-665
B-52D	OK	Tinke	TAFB	Boeing	Stratofortress	
B-52D	SD	Rapid	SDA&SM	Boeing	Stratofortress	56-0657
B-52D	TX	Abile	DLAP	Boeing	Stratofortress	56-685
B-52D	TX	FWort	SAM	Boeing	Stratofortress	
B-52D	TX	San A	KAFB	Boeing	Stratofortress	
B-52D	TX	San A	LAFB	Boeing	Stratofortress	55-68
B-52D	TX	Wichi	SAFB	Boeing	Stratofortress	
B-52D	VA	Hampt	LAFB	Boeing	Stratofortress	
B-52D	WA	Spoka	FAFBHM	Boeing	Stratofortress	
B-52D(GB)	CA	Riverside	MFAM	Boeing	Stratofortress	55-0679
B-52D-40BW	MO	White	WAFB	Boeing	Stratofortress	56-683, 683, 509BG, "Necessary Evil"
B-52F (2 ea)	OK	Oklah	CityPark	Boeing	Stratofortress	
B-52G	AZ	Tucso	PAM	Boeing	Stratofortress	58-183
B-52G	FL	Shali	USAFAM	Boeing	Stratofortress	80185
B-52G	ND	Grand	GFAFB	Boeing	Stratofortress	
B-52G	NY	Rome	MVBM	Boeing	Stratofortress	58-0225
B-52G	TX	Wichi	SAFB	Boeing	Stratofortress	
B-52G	UT	Ogden	HAFBM	Boeing	Stratofortress	
B-52G	WA	Everett	MoF	Boeing	Stratofortress	59-2584, 17066
B-52G Nose	CA	S.Mon	MoF	Boeing	Stratofortress	
B-52G-105-BW	NY	Rome	GAFBM	Boeing	Stratofortress	80225, "Mohawk Valley"
B-52N	AL	Mobil	BMP	Boeing	Stratofortress	55071, "Calamity Jane"
B-57	AZ	Mesa	CAFM	Martin	Canberra	
B-57	KS	Topek	FF	Martin	Canberra	
B-57	MI	Kalam	KAHM	Martin	Canberra	52-1584
B-57	OH	Newbu	WASAC	Martin	Canberra	
B-57A(RB)	UT	Ogden	HAFBM	Martin	Canberra	
B-57A(RB)	CT	Winds	NEAM	Martin	Canberra	52-1488
B-57A(RB)	GA	Warner Robin	MoF	Martin	Canberra	52-1475A
B-57A(RB)	MD	Middl	GLMAM	Martin	Canberra	
B-57A(RB)-MA	MI	Belleville	YAF	Martin	Canberra	52-1426
B-57A(RB)	MI	Mt Clemens	SMAM	Martin	Canberra	52-1485
B-57A(RB)	NY	Horseheads	NWM	Martin	Canberra	52-1459
B-57A(RB)	SC	Flore	FA&MM	Martin	Canberra	
B-57A(RB)	TX	Midla	CAFFM	Martin	Canberra	
B-57A(RB)	TX	San A	LAFB	Martin	Canberra	52-1482
B-57B	CA	Rosam	EAFB	Martin	Canberra	52-1576
B-57B	FL	Shali	USAFAM	Martin	Canberra	52-1516
B-57B(EB)	CA	Riverside	MFAM	Martin	Canberra	52-1519
B-57B(EB)	DC	Dulle	DA	Martin	Canberra	
B-57B(EB)	FL	Panam	TAFB	Martin	Canberra	
B-57B(EB)	MT	Great	MAFB	Martin	Canberra	52-1505
B-57B(EB)	OH	Dayto	USAFM	Martin	Canberra	52-1499
B-57B(EB)	SD	Rapid	SDA&SM	Martin	Canberra	
B-57B(EB)	TX	D Rio	LAFB	Martin	Canberra	
B-57B(EB)	VT	Nurli	BANG	Martin	Canberra	
B-57C(EB)	AR	Littl	LRAFB	Martin	Canberra	53-521
B-57C(EB)	TX	Abile	DLAP	Martin	Canberra	52-1504
B-57D	OH	Dayton	USAFM	Martin	Canberra	
B-57D(RB)	AZ	Tucso	PAM	Martin	Canberra	53-3982
B-57E(EB)	AZ	Tucso	PAM	Martin	Canberra	55-4274
B-57E(EB)	CA	Atwater	CAM	Martin	Canberra	54-00253
B-57E(EB)	CO	CSpri	EJPSCM	Martin	Canberra	55-4279
B-57E(EB)	CO	Denve	WOR	Martin	Canberra	
B-57E(EB)	NE	Ashland	SACM	Martin	Canberra	55-4244, MA
B-57F(WB)	AZ	Tucso	PAM	Martin	Night Intruder	63-13501, N925NA
B-57F(WB)	GA	Warner Robin	MoF	Martin	Canberra	63-13293A
B-58A	AZ	Tucso	PAM	Convair	Hustler	61-2080
B-58A	IL	Ranto	OCAM	Convair	Hustler	55-0666, "Greased Lightning"
B-58A Escape Capsule	MD	Silver Hill	PEGF	Convair	Hustler	
B-58A	OH	Dayto	USAFM	Convair	Hustler	59-2458
B-58A	TX	San A	LAFB	Convair	Hustler	92437

Model	State	City	Code	Manufacturer	Name	Serial/Reg	Notes
B-58A(N)	CA	Rosam	EAFB	Convair	Hustler	55-665, "Snoopy"	
B-58A(TB)	IN	Peru	GAFB	Convair	Hustler	55-663	
B-58A(TB)	TX	FWort	SAM	Convair	Hustler		
B-58A(TB)	TX	Galve	LSFM	Convair	Hustler	55-668	
B-58A-CF	NE	Ashland	SACM	Convair	Hustler	61-2059	
B-66(RB)	TX	Abile	DLAP	Douglas	Destroyer	53-0466	
B-66(RF)	TX	Austi	BAFMlark	Douglas	Destroyer		
B-66(WB)	SC	Flore	FA&MM	Douglas	Destroyer		
B-66A(RB)	SC	Sumte	SAFB	Douglas	Destroyer		
B-66B(RB)	OH	Dayto	USAFM	Douglas	Destroyer	53-475	
B-66D	IL	Ranto	OCAM	Douglas	Destroyer	30412, BB	
B-66D(WB)	AZ	Tucso	PAM	Douglas	Destroyer	55-395	
B-66D(WB)	GA	Warner Robin	MoF	Douglas	Destroyer	55-392, RB	
B-66D(WB)	TX	San A	LAFB	Douglas	Destroyer	55-390	
B-69A(RB)	GA	Warner Robin	MoF		Neptune]	54-4037	
B-70(XB)	OH	Dayto	USAFM	North American	Valkyrie	62-1	
B.2 Mk.II	LA	Bossi	BAFB	Avro	Vulcan	Model 698	
B.2 Mk.II	NB	Belle	SAC	Avro	Vulcan	Model 698	
B.2 Mk.II	CA	Atwater	CAM	Avro	Vulcan		
B.E.2c	ON-C	Ottaw	CAM	Royal Aircraft	B.E.2c	4112	
B.H. 305	BC-C	Langley	CMoF&T	Brantley-Haynes	Model 305	B-2B only 5 Seater Helicopter	
B290	WI	Oshko	EAAAAM	Bauman	Brigadier	N90616	
B6N2	MD	Silve	PEGF	Nakajima	Jill (Tenzan)	Jill	
B7A1	MD	Silve	PEGF	Aichi	Grace (Ryusei)		
BAC-167	WA	Olympia	OFM	Bachem	Strikemaster		
Ba 349	CA	Chino	PoFAM	Bachem	Natter		
Ba 349	MD	Silve	PEGF	Bachem	Natter		
Backstrom EPB-1C Plank	WI	Oshko	EAAAAM	Cleave	Plank	N19C	
BAe Mk 53	GA	Warner Robin	MoF	British	Lightning		
Baby Great Lakes	KS	Liberal	MAAM	Baby	Great Lakes Bi		
Baby Great Lakes	OR	McMinnville	EAM	Baby	Great Lakes Bi	6907M-187, N44ET	
Backstrom Plank	IA	Ottumwa	APM	Backstrom	Plank	1, N20WB	
Bagjo BG12	AB-C	Calga	AMoC	Bagjo	Glider		
Baker 001 Special	WI	Oshko	EAAAAM	Baker	Special	N3203	
Baking Duce Homebuilt	FL	Lakel	SFAF	Baking	Duce		
Baking Duce II (F.M.1)	AK	Fairb	APAM	Baking	Duce II	N75FD	
Baldwin Red Devil	MD	Silve	PEGF	Baldwin	Red Devil		
Ballistic Silo	IL	Ranto	OCAM		Ballistic Silo		
Balloon Basket	CT	Winds	NEAM		Balloon Basket		
Balloon Basket	VA	Quantico	MCAGM	Blanchard	Balloon Basket	Year 1919	
Balloon Capsule	SD	Mitch	S&TIB&AM		Balloon Capsule	"Zanussi"	
Balloon D	TX	FWort	BCVintag				
Balloon EAA	ME	Bangor	MAM				
Balloon Gondola	SD	Mitch	S&TIB&AM		Balloon Gondola	"Super Chicken"	
Balloon Helium	IA	India	USNBM		Balloon Helium		
Balloon Hot Air	IA	India	USNBM		Balloon Hot Air		
Balloon Hot Air	SD	Mitch	S&TIB&AM		Balloon Hot Air	"Hilda"	
Balloon Hot Air	SD	Mitch	S&TIB&AM		Balloon Hot Air	"Chic I Boom"	
Balloon Hot Air	SD	Mitch	S&TIB&AM		Balloon Hot Air	"Chesty"	
Balloon Hot Air	SD	Mitch	S&TIB&AM		Balloon Hot Air	"Matrioshk"	
Balloon Hot Air	SD	Mitch	S&TIB&AM		Balloon Hot Air	"Uncle Sam"	
Balloon Hot Air	SD	Mitch	S&TIB&AM		Balloon Hot Air	"Aero Star"	
Balloon Montgolfiere	CA	San Diego	SDAM	Montgolfiere	Balloon		
Balloon WWI Gas	SD	Mitch	S&TIB&AM		Balloon Gas		
Balloon Works Firefly 7	AZ	Tucson	PAM	Balloon Works	Firefly 7	N4065D	
Barlow Acapella	WI	Oshko	EAAAAM	Barlow	Acapella	N455CB	
Baracuda	MI	Oscoda	YAF	Baracuda	Homebuilt	N29M	
Barrage Kite	WI	Oshko	EAAAAM		Barrage Kite		
Bates Tractor	WI	Oshko	EAAAAM	Bates	Tractor		
BB-1	MD	Silve	PEGF	Nelson	Dragonfly		
BC-12D	AZ	Tucso	PAM	Taylorcraft	T-Craft		
BC-12D	TX	Slato	TAMCC	Taylorcraft	T-Craft	N43584	
BD-10	ON-C	Toronto	TAM				
Beachy Little Looper	CA	S.Mon	MoF	Betchy	Little Looper		
Bede BD-4	AL	Birmingham	SMoF	Bede	Micro		
Bede BD-4	AZ	Tucson	PAM	Bede	Micro		
Bede BD-4	FL	Lakel	SFAF	Bede	Micro	N8826	
Bede BD-4	IA	Ottumwa	APM	Bede	Micro		
Bede BD-4	WI	Oshko	EAAAAM	Bede	Micro	N200SS	
Bede BD-5	AB-C	Calga	AMoC	Bede	Micro		
Bede BD-5	AZ	Tucso	PAM	Bede	Micro		
Bede BD-5	CA	Santa Rosa	PCAM	Bede	Micro		
Bede BD-5	KS	Wichita	KAM	Bede	Micro		
Bede BD-5	WI	Oshko	EAAAAM	Bede	Micro	N500BD	
Bede BD-5B	AL	Birmingham	SMoF	Bede	Micro		
Bede BD-5B	CA	Oakla	OWAM	Bede	Micro		
Bede BD-5B	FL	Lakel	SFAF	Bede	Micro	N51GB	
Bede BD-5B	MD	Silve	PEGF	Bede	Micro		
Bede BD-5B	OR	McMinnville	EAV	Bede	Micro	2392, N110CJ	
Bede BD-5B	PA	Readi	MAAM	Bede	Micro	N5BE	
Bede BD-5	AZ	Tucso	PAM	Bede	Micro	N505MR	
Bede BD-5J	CA	Calab	SC	Bede	Micro		
Bede BD-5J	CA	S.Mon	MoF	Bede	Micro	N64DS	
Bede BD-5V	AZ	Grand	PoFGCVA	Bede	Micro	N327BD	
Bede XBD-2	WI	Oshko	EAAAAM	Bede	Micro		
Bee Honey Bee	WI	Oshko	EAAAAM	Bee	Honey Bee	N90859	
Beech A17R	TN	Tulla	SMF	Beech	Staggerwing'		
Beech B17S	TN	Tulla	SMF	Beech	Staggerwing		
Beech C17L	DC	Washi	NA&SM	Beech	Staggerwing		
Beech C17S	TN	Tulla	SMF	Beech	Staggerwing		
Beech D17A	OR	Mc Minnville	EAEC	Beech	Staggerwing		
Beech D17S	CA	Santa Monica	MoF	Beech	Staggerwing		
Beech D17S	CA	Santa Paula	SPAA	Beech	Staggerwing		
Beech D17S	FL	Miami	WOM	Beech	Staggerwing	N67735	
Beech D17S	ID	Zellw	BWA	Beech	Staggerwing		
Beech D17S	KS	Liber	MAAM	Beech	Staggerwing		
Beech D17S	LA	Patte	WWMAM	Beech	Staggerwing		
Beech D17S	NC	Fargo	FAM	Beech	Staggerwing		
Beech D17S	TN	Tulla	SMF	Beech	Staggerwing		
Beech D17S(AT-11)	FL	Lakel	SFAF	Beech	Staggerwing	43-1452, N65860	
Beech D18D	BC-C	Langley	CMoF&T	Beech	Twin Beech	2307	
Beech D18D	RK-C	MJaw	WDM	Beech	Twin Beech		
Beech D18H-4D	TX	Ralve	LSFM	Beech	Twin Beech	670, N954	
Beech D18R	TX	Fulsh	CTA	Beech	Twin Beech		
Beech D18S *See AT-11*				Beech	Kansan		
Beech D18S See Also (C-45)				Beech	Twin Beech		

Beech D18S	AB-C	Edmonton	AAM	Beech	Twin Beech	2366, CA-245
Beech D18S	AB-C	Nanton	NLSAM	Beech	Twin Beech	
Beech D18S	AB-C	Wetas	RM	Beech	Twin Beech	
Beech D18S	AZ	Tucso	PAM	Beech	Twin Beech	N55681
Beech D18S	CO	Denve	WOR	Beech	Twin Beech	
Beech D18S	FL	Deland	FW-CAF	Beech	Twin Beech	
Beech D18S	IN	Ft. W	BAI	Beech	Twin Beech	
Beech D18S	LA	Bossier City	BAFB	Beech	Twin Beech	
Beech D18S	MB-C	Winni	WCAM	Beech	Twin Beech	
Beech D18S	MD	Silve	PEGF	Beech	Twin Beech	
Beech D18S	NF-C	Gander	NAAM	Beech	Twin Beech	
Beech D18S	OK	Fredi	AAM	Beech	Twin Beech	
Beech D18S	ON-C	Campbellford	MMM	Beech	Twin Beech	
Beech D18S	ON-C	Ear FAlls	EFM	Beech	Twin Beech	
Beech D18S	ON-C	Ignace	City	Beech	Twin Beech	
Beech D18S	ON-C	Sault Ste Marie	CBHC	Beech	Twin Beech	CF-MGY
Beech D18S	ON-C	Sault Ste Marie	CBHC	Beech	Twin Beech	CF-UWE
Beech D18S	ON-C	Sault Ste Marie	CBHC	Beech	Twin Beech	Cockpit Only
Beech D18S	TN	Gatlinburg	PHLTG	Beech	Twin Beech	
Beech D18S	TX	Ft Worth	VFM	Beech	Twin Beech	
Beech D18S	TX	Midla	CAFFM	Beech	Twin Beech	
Beech D18S	WA	Seatt	MoF	Beech	Twin Beech	
Beech D18S	WI	Janesville	BHA	Beech	Twin Beech	
Beech D18S(AT-7)	AZ	Tucso	PAM	Beech	Twin Beech	Sn 42-2438, N8073H, Navigation Trainer
Beech E17S	TN	Tulla	SMF	Beech	Staggerwing	
Beech F17S	TN	Tulla	SMF	Beech	Staggerwing	
Beech G17S	TN	Tulla	SMF	Beech	Staggerwing	
Beech 23 (See C-45)						
Beech 73	KS	Wichita	KAM	Beech	Mentor	Jet
Beechcraft 35	FL	Dayto	ERAU	Beechcraft	Bonanza	
Beechcraft 35	GA	Calho	Mercer A	Beechcraft	Bonanza	
Beechcraft 35	KS	Liber	MAAM	Beechcraft	Bonanza	
Beechcraft 35	MD	Silve	PEGF	Beechcraft	Bonanza	"Waikiki Beach"
Beechcraft 35	OK	Fredi	AAM	Beechcraft	Bonanza	
Beechcraft 35	OR	McMinnville	EAV	Beechcraft	Bonanza	D-1111, N3870N
Beechcraft 35	TX	Laredo	AAM	Beechcraft	Bonanza	
Beechcraft 35(N)	AZ	Tucso	PAM	Beechcraft	Bonanza	N9493Y
Beechcraft 36 (See QU-22B)						
Beechcraft 50(L-23)	IN	Mento	LB	Beechcraft	Seminole	Twin Bonanza Model 50
Beechcraft 50(L-23)	OK	Fredi	AAM	Beechcraft	Seminole	Twin Bonanza Model 50
Beechcraft 50(L-23D)(U-8D)	AZ	Tucso	PAM	Beechcraft	Seminole	Twin Bonanza Model 50, 56- 3701
Beechcraft 50(RU-8D)	GA	Calho	Mercer A	Beechcraft	Seminole	Twin Bonanza Model 50
Beechcraft 50(RU-8D)	KS	Wichita	KAM	Beechcraft	Seminole	Twin Bonanza Model 50,
Beechcraft 50(RU-8D)	KS	Topek	CAM	Beechcraft	Seminole	Twin Bonanza Model 50, "Lonely Ringer"
Beechcraft 50(RU-8D)	MD	Ft Mead	NVP	Beechcraft	Seminole	Twin Bonanza Model 50,
Beechcraft 50(RU-8D)	VA	FtEus	USATM	Beechcraft	Seminole	Twin Bonanza Model 50
Beechcraft 50(U-8A)	AL	Ozark	USAAM	Beechcraft	Seminole	Twin Bonanza Model 50
Beechcraft 50(U-8A)	AL	Ozark	USAAM	Beechcraft	Seminole	Twin Bonanza Model 50, 52- 1700
Beechcraft 50(U-8D-5J)	SD	Rapid	SDA&SM	Beechcraft	Seminole	Twin Bonanza Model 50
Beechcraft 50(U-8F)	GA	Hampton	AAHF	Beechcraft	Seminole	Twin Bonanza Model 50
Beechcraft 55(T-42)	AL	Ozark	USAAM	Beechcraft	Baron	65-12685
Beechcraft 55(T-42)	IN	Valparaiso	IAM	Beechcraft	Baron	
Beechcraft 55(T-42A)	GA	Hampton	AAHF	Beechcraft	Baron	
Beechcraft 58P	MT	Misso	AFDSC	Beechcraft	Baron	
Beechcraft 99	MT	Misso	AFDSC	Beechcraft	Airliner	
Beechcraft Dutches	FL	Dayto	ERAU	Beechcraft	Dutches	
Beagle B.206	AL	Birmingham	SmoF	Beagle	B.206	
Bell 204	CO	Denve	JWDAS	Bell	Model 204	
Bell 205A	BC-C	Langley	CMoF&T	Bell	Iroquois (Huey)	
Bell 206	FL	Starke	ACAM	Bell	Long Ranger	
Bell 206B	NS	Halifax	ACAM	Bell	Long Ranger	
Bell 206L	MD	Silve	PEFG	Bell	Long Ranger	
Bell 214	CA	Miramar	FLAM	Bell	Huey Super	
Bell 260	MD	Silve	PEGF	Bell	Model 260	Bell 206 Jet Ranger
Bell 260	PA	WChester	AHM	Bell	Model 260	Bell 206 Jet Ranger
Bell 47B-3	NY	Niagara Falls	NIA	Bell	Ranger	
Bell 47	WA	Seatt	PSC	Bell	Ranger	
Bell 47B	PA	WChes	AHM	Bell	Sioux	NC5H
Bell 47D (H-13)	AB-C	Calga	AMoC	Bell	Sioux	
Bell 47D (H-13)	ON-C	Sault Ste Marie	CBHC	Bell	Sioux	Sn 665-8
Bell 47D-1(H-13)	BC-C	Sidne	BCAM	Bell	Sioux	CD-FZX
Bell 47D-1(H-13)	CA	Chino	YACM	Bell	Sioux	51-4175, N55230
Bell 47D-1(H-13)	CT	Winds	NEAM	Bell	Sioux	LV AEF
Bell 47D-1(H-13)	ON-C	Sault Ste Marie	CBHC	Bell	Sioux	Replica CF-ODM
Bell 47D-1(H-13)	PA	WChes	AHM	Bell	Sioux	
Bell 47D-1(H-13)	TX	Ft Worth	FWSH	Bell	Sioux	
Bell 47D-5(H-13)	NY	Niagara Falls	NAM	Bell	Sioux	
Bell 47G (HTL-6)	ON-C	Ottaw	CAM	Bell	Sioux	1387
Bell 47G-5(HTL-5)	CA	LAnge	CMoS&I	Bell	Sioux	
Bell 47G	TX	Laredo	Airport	Bell	Sioux	
Bell 47H-1	NY	Niagra Falls	NAM	Bell	Ranger	
Bell 47H-1	PA	WChester	AHM	Bell	Ranger	
Bell 47J	PA	WChes	AHM	Bell	Ranger	
Bell 47J-2	BC-C	Langley	CMoF&T	Bell	Ranger	
Bell 47J-2(H-13)	NS	Halifax	ACAM	Bell	Sioux	
Bell ATV VTOL	MD	Silve	PEGF	Bell	VTOL	
Bell Boeing Tiltrotor RPV	PA	WChester	AHM	Bell	RPV	
Bell Model 30	MD	Silve	PEGF	Bell	Model 30	
Bell Model 30	PA	WChes	AHM	Bell	Model 30	NX41867
Bell Rocket Belt	MD	Silve	PEGF	Bell	Rocket Belt	
Bell Rocket Belt	VA	FtEus	USATM	Bell	Rocket Belt	
Bellanca	NV	Carso	YF	Bellanca		
Bellanca 14-9	FL	Lakeland	SNF	Bellanca		
Bellanca 14-9L	NC	Charlotte	CAM	Bellanca	Crusair	N1KQ
Bellanca 14-13-2	AZ	Tucso	PAM	Bellanca	Crusair	Sn 1551, XB-FOU
Bellanca 14-13-2	AZ	Tucso	PAM	Bellanca	Crusair	Sn 1073, N46LW
Bellanca 14-13-3	KS	Liber	MAAM	Bellanca	Crusair	
Bellanca 14-13-3	MD	Silve	PEGF	Bellanca	Crusair	
Bellanca 14-13-3	OK	Fredi	AAM	Bellanca	Crusair	
Bellanca 14-19C (260)	KS	Liber	MAAM	Bellanca	Cruisemaster	
Bellanca 14-19C (260)	OK	Fredi	AAM	Bellanca	Cruisemaster	
Bellanca 190	KS	Liber	MAAM	Bellanca	Cruisemaster	
Bellanca 31-55A	BC-C	Langley	CMoF&T	Bellanca	Skyrocket	
Bellanca CH-400(1-87)	VA	Sands	VAM	Bellanca	Skyrocket	Sn 187, NX237, "Columbia"
Bellanca 66-75 BTW	MB-C	Winni	WCAM	Bellanca	Aircruiser	
Bellanca 66-75 BTW	OR	Tillamook	TAM	Bellanca	Aircrusier	

Name	State	City	Museum	Manufacturer	Model	Notes
Bellanca C.F.	MD	Silve	PEGF	Bellanca		
Bellanca CH.300	AK	Ancho	AAHM	Bellanca		
Bellanca Pacemaker	ON-C	Ottaw	CAM	Bellanca	Pacemaker	
Bellanca Replica	ME	OwlsH	OHTM	Bellanca		
Bennett Matiah M-9	MD	Silve	PEGF	Bennett	Matiah M-9	
Bennett Model 162	MD	Silve	PEGF	Bennett	Model 162	
Bennett Phonix 6	MD	Silve	PEGF	Bennett	Phonex 6	
Bennett Phonix 6B	MD	Silve	PEGF	Bennett	Phonex 6B	
Bennett Phonix Viper	MD	Silve	PEGF	Bennett	Phonix Viper	
Bennett Streak 130	MD	Silve	PEGF	Bennett	Streak 130	
Bennett (See also Rogallo)						
Benoist Air Boat 1914	FL	Largo	HPPCHM	Benoist	Air Boat	
Benoist-Korn	MD	Silve	PEGF	Benoist-Korn		
Bensen B- 6	MD	Silve	PEGF	Bensen	Gyro-Glider	
Bensen B- 6	NE	Minde	HWPV	Bensen	Gyro-Glider	
Bensen B- 7	BC-C	Langley	CMoF&T	Bensen	Gyro-Glider	
Bensen B- 7	NE	Minde	HWPV	Bensen	Gyro-Glider	
Bensen B- 7M	MB-C	Winni	WCAM	Bensen	Gyro-Copter	
Bensen B- 8M	AL	Birmingham	SMoF	Bensen	Gyro-Copter	
Bensen B- 8M	BC-C	Langley	CMoF&T	Bensen	Gyro-Copter	
Bensen B- 8M	CA	Riverside	MAFM	Bensen	Gyro-Copter	
Bensen B- 8M	CT	Winds	NEAM	Bensen	Gyro-Copter	
Bensen B- 8M	MD	Silve	PEGF	Bensen	Gyro-Copter	
Bensen B- 8M	MI	Belleville	YAF	Bensen	Gyro-Copter	N64808, "Gilber Habicht"
Bensen B- 8M	OH	Dayto	USAFM	Bensen	Gyro-Copter	Model X-25A
Bensen B- 8M	OR	Eugen	OAM	Bensen	Gyro-Copter	
Bensen B- 8M	WA	Seatt	MoF	Bensen	Gyro-Copter	1, N8533E
Bensen B-11	CA	Chino	PoFAM	Bensen	Gyro-Copter	
Bensen B-11	WI	Oshko	EAAAAM	Bensen	Gyro-Copter	N63U
Bensen B-8M	NC	Ralei	NCMoH	Bensen	Gyro-Copter	
Bensen Gyro-Copter	FL	Lakel	SFAF	Bensen	Gyro-Copter	
Bensen Sport Autogyro	PA	Wchester	AHM	Bensen	Gyro-Copter	
Bergfalke 11 Glider	PA	Tough	CFCM	Bergfalke	Glider	
Berliner Helicopter	MD	College Park	CPAM	Berliner	Helicopter	
Berliner Helicopter	MD	Silve	PEGF	Berliner	Helicopter	
Bertelson Aeromobile Hover	MD	Silve	PEGF	Bertelson	Aeromobile Hover	
Bf 109	GA	Savan	MEHM	Messerschmitt	Gustav	
Bf 109	MD	Silve	PEGF	Messerschmitt	Gustav	
Bf 109	ON-C	Ottaw	CAM	Messerschmitt	Gustav	471-39
Bf 109	OR	Tillamook	TAM	Messerschmitt	Gustav	
Bf 109 (1/2 Scale)	LA	Patte	WWMAM	Messerschmitt	Gustav	
Bf 109E	CA	S.Mon	MoF	Messerschmitt	Gustav	
Bf 109E-7	VA	Suffolk	FF	Messerschmitt	Gustav	Out of Country Until 2003, "Black 9"
Bf 109G	DC	Washi	NA&SM	Messerschmitt	Gustav	
Bf 109G-5	OH	Dayto	USAFM	Messerschmitt	GUSTOV	C.4K- 64
Bf 109G	TX	Dalla	CFM	Messerschmitt	GUSTOV	N48157, 14
Bf 109G-10/U4	AZ	Grand	PoFGCVA	Messerschmitt	Gustav	13
Bf 109G-10	OR	Mc Minnvile	EAEC	Messerschmitt	Gustav	610937, N109EV
Bf 109G-14(Mock Up)	CA	San Diego	SDAM	Messerschmitt	Gustav	
BFC-2(F11C)	FL	Pensa	USNAM		Goshawk	9332 2-B-13
BG-12BD	NY	Elmir	NSM	Brieglab	Sailplane	162, N12RK
BGM 109A	OH	Dayton	USAFM	General Dynamics	Cruise Missle	
BGM 109G	AZ	Tucson	PAM	General Dynamics	Cruise Missle	Sn 12436C0001
Biplane	IN	India	CMoI		Biplane	"Lil Chil"
Biplane	KS	Topek	KSHS		Biplane	
Biplane	TX	C Christi	USS Lexi		Biplane	
Bird Biplane	IL	Harva	BA	Bird	Biplane	
Bird CK	PA	Bethel	GAAM	Bird	CK	
Birdwing Imperial	NY	River	RE	Birdwing	Imperial	1930
Blanik	ID	Driggs	TAC	Blanik	Glider	
Blanik L-13	NM	Hobbs	NSF	Blanik	Glider	
Blaty	CA	Chino	PoFAM	Blaty	Orion Hang Glider	
Bleriot X	NY	Rhine	ORA	Bleriot		
Bleriot XI	CA	San Diego	SDAM	Bleriot		
Bleriot XI	CT	Winds	NEAM	Bleriot		
Bleriot XI	DC	Washi	NA&SM	Bleriot		"Domenjoz"
Bleriot XI	FL	Pensa	USNAM	Bleriot		
Bleriot XI	IA	Des M	ISHD	Bleriot		
Bleriot XI	MA	Stow	BCF	Bleriot		
Bleriot XI	ME	OwlsH	OHTM	Bleriot		
Bleriot XI	MI	Dearb	HFM	Bleriot		1, "Boneshaker"
Bleriot XI	NY	Garde	CoAM	Bleriot		153
Bleriot XI	NY	River	RE	Bleriot		Original
Bleriot XI	OH	Dayto	USAFM	Bleriot		1909
Bleriot XI	ON-C	Ottaw	CAM	Bleriot		
Bleriot XI	TX	Kingbury	VAHF	Bleriot		
Blimp (2ea)	OR	Tillamook	TAM			
Block IV Satellite	OH	Dayton	USAFM	Block	IV Satellite	
BobCat	GA	Woodstock	NGWS		BobCat Kit	
Boeing 100	WA	Seattle	MoF	Boeing	Boeing 247D	1143, N872H
Boeing 247D(C-73)	DC	Washi	NA&SM	Boeing	Boeing 247D	1930 - 10 Passenger
Boeing 247D(C-73)	ON-C	Ottaw	CAM	Boeing	Boeing 247D	1930 - 10 Passenger
Boeing 247D(C-73)	WA	Everett	MoF	Boeing	Boeing 247D	1729, NC13347, "Cpt George Juneau"
Boeing 367-80	VA	Sterling	UHC	Boeing	Boeing 367	
Boeing 367-80	WA	Seatt	MoF	Boeing	Boeing 367	
Boeing 377(C-97)	OR	Tillamook	TAM	Boeing	Mini Guppy	
Boeing 40B-2	MI	Dearb	HFM	Boeing	Boeing 40B	NC285
Boeing 40B-2 (727-100)	IL	Chica	MoS&I	Boeing	Boeing 40B	7017, "United Airlines"
Boeing 707 Cockpit	NY	NYC	ISASM	Boeing	Boeing 707	
Boeing 707 Cockpit	TX	Ft Worth	FWSH	Boeing	Boeing 707	
Boeing 707 Simulator	FL	Miami	WOM	Boeing	Boeing 707	
Boeing 707-131B	AZ	Tucso	PAM	Boeing	Boeing 707	Sn 99-18390, N751TW
Boeing 707 Air Force 1	CA	Simi VAlley	RL	Boeing	Boeing 707	Air Force One, 27000
Boeing 720	NV	Las Vegas	LBAHSM	Boeing	Boeing 720	"Kay O'II", Cockpit Only
Boeing 727	IL	Chicago	MoS&I	Boeing	Boeing 727	
Boeing 727-22	WA	Seattle	MoF	Boeing	Boeing 727	18293, N7001U
Boeing 727-25C	MI	Kalamazoo	KAHM	Boeing	Boeing 727	19301, N119FE
Boeing 727	OR	Hillsboro	BC	Boeing	Boeing 727	Home
Boeing 727-100	WA	Everett	MoF	Boeing	Boeing 727	N7001U, 1st Built
Boeing 737-130	WA	Seattle	MoF	Boeing	Boeing 727	19437, 515
Boeing 737-200	WA	Seatt	MoF	Boeing	Boeing 737	
Boeing 747 Cockpit	CA	San Carlos	HAM	Boeing	Boeing 747	
Boeing 747-121	WA	Seatt	MoF	Boeing	Boeing 747	20235, N747001
Boeing 80A-1	WA	Seatt	MoF	Boeing	Tri-Motor	1082, NC224M
Boeing B&W Replica	WA	Seatt	MoF	Boeing	B&W	N1916
Boeing B-100	FL	Polk	FoF	Boeing	B-100	

Name	State	City	Museum	Manufacturer	Model	Notes
Boeing Bird of Prey	OH	Dayton	USAFM	Boeing	Bird of Prey	
Boeing Condor	CA	San Carlos	HAM	Boeing	Condor	
Boeing E75N1	WI	Oshkosh	EAAAAM	Boeing		
Boeing Inertial Upper Stage	WA	Seattle	MoF	Boeing	Upper Stage	
Boeing Lunar Rover	WA	Seattle	MoF	Boeing	Lunar Rover	
Boeing MIM-10B	ON-C	Ottaw	CAM	Boeing	Super Bomarc	60446
Boeing SST	CA	San Carlos	HAM	Boeing	SST	
Boeing SST	FL	CapeC		Boeing	SST	
Bolkow Bo 208A-1 Jr	IA	Ottumwa	APM	Bolkow		525, N208JR
Boost Glide Reentry Vehicle	OH	Dayton	USAFM		Reentry Vehicle	
Bowers 1-A	CA	S.Mon	MoF	Bowers	Fly Baby	
Bowers Fly Baby	FL	Lakel	SFAF	Bowers	Fly Baby	
Bowers Flybaby 1-A	AZ	Tucso	PAM	Bowers	Flybaby	N49992
Bowers Flybaby 1-A	BC-C	Langley	CMoF&T	Bowers	Flybaby	
Bowers Flybaby 1-A	CA	Santa Martin	WoHAM	Bowers	Flybaby	
Bowers Flybaby 1-A	CA	S.Mar	SMMoF	Bowers	Flybaby	
Bowers Flybaby 1-A	CA	San Diego	SDAM	Bowers	Flybaby	
Bowers Flybaby 1-A	ND	WFarg	Bonanzav	Bowers	Flybaby	
Bowers Flybaby 1-A	OH	Madis	CFR	Bowers	Flybaby	
Bowers Flybaby 1-A	WA	Seatt	MoF	Bowers	Flybaby	68-15, N4339
Bowlus Albatross	CA	Santa Martin	WoHAM	Bowlus	Falcon	
Bowlus Albatross	NY	Elmir	NSM	Bowlus	Falcon	N6219Y, 25
Bowlus Albatross	VA	Hampt	APM	Bowlus	Falcon	
Bowlus Albatross I	MD	Silve	PEGF	Bowlus	Falcon	
Bowlus Albatross SP-1	CA	San Diego	SDAM	Bowlus	Falcon	
Bowlus B8-1	BC-C	Langley	CMoF&T	Bowlus	Bumblebee	N34922
Bowlus Baby Ace	CA	Santa Martin	WoHAM	Bowlus	Baby Ace	
Bowlus Baby Ace	NM	Kirkl	KA	Bowlus	Baby Ace	
Bowlus Baby Ace	NY	Elmir	NSM	Bowlus	Baby Ace	
Bowlus Baby Ace	NY	Elmir	NSM	Bowlus-Lambert SL	Baby Ace	
Bowlus Baby Albatross	MD	Silve	PEGF	Bowlus	Falcon	
Bowlus Baby Albatross	WA	Everett	MoF	Bowlus		N25605
Bowlus Super Albatross	CA	M.Maria	WoHAM	Bowlus	Super Albatross	
Boyd C2	MD	Colle	CPA	Boyd		
BQM-34	OH	Dayton	USAFM	Ryan	Firebee Drone	
BQM-34A	CA	Rosamond	EAFB	Ryan	Firebee	
BQM-34A	FL	Panam	TAFB	Ryan	Firebee	
BQM-34A	FL	Shali	USAFAM	Ryan	Firebee	
BQM-34F	CA	San Diego	SDAM	Ryan	Firebee Drone	
BQM-34F	FL	Panam	TAFB	Ryan	Firebee	
BQM-34F	FL	Shali	USAFAM	Ryan	Firebee	
BQM-34F	GA	Warner Robin	MoF	Ryan	Firebee	71-1812
BQM-34F	OH	Dayton	USAFM	Ryan	Firebee Drone	
BQM-34S	CA	San Diego	SDAM	Ryan	Firebee Drone	
BQM-126A	CA	Chino	YAM	Beechcraft	Target Drone	
Brantly 305	CA	Ramona	CR	Brantly	305	
Breese Penquin	NY	Garde	CoAM	Breese	Penquin	33622
Breguet G-3	NY	Rhine	ORA	Breguet		1911, 3 Seater Biplane
Brewster B-1	IA	Ottumwa	APM	Brewster		Sn 1, NC-20699
Bristol Beaufighter	ON-C	Ottaw	CAM	Bristol	Beaufighter	RD 867
Bristol Beaufighter Mk.Ic	OH	Dayto	USAFM	Bristol	Beaufighter	A19-43
Bristol Beaufighter	TX	Kingbury	VAHF	Bristol	Beaufighter	
Bristol Beaufighter	TX	Kingbury	VAHF	Bristol	Beaufighter	Project
Bristol Beufort Mk.I	TX	Hawki	RRSA	Bristol	Beaufort	Torpedo-Bomber 1939
Bristol Blenheim Mk.IV	AB-C	Nanton	NLSAM	Bristol	Blenheim	
Bristol Bolingbroke Mk IV	AB-C	Wetas	RM	Bristol	Bolingbroke	Model 149
Bristol Bolingbroke	BC-C	Sidne	BCAM	Bristol	Bolingbroke	Model 149
Bristol Bolingbroke	BC-C	Langley	CMoF&T	Bristol	Bolingbroke	Model 149
Bristol Bolingbroke	MB-C	Brand	CI	Bristol	Bolingbroke	Model 149
Bristol Bolingbroke	MB-C	Brand	CATPM	Bristol	Bolingbroke	9944
Bristol Bolingbroke	MB-C	Winni	WCAM	Bristol	Bolingbroke	Model 149
Bristol Bolingbroke Mk.IVT	ON-C	Ottaw	CAM	Bristol	Bolingbroke	Model 149, 9892
Bristol Bolingbroke Mk.IVW	ON-C	Hamilton	CWH	Bristol	Bolingbroke	Model 149, 903
Bristol Bolingbroke	NS-C	Greenwood	GMAM	Bristol	Bolingbroke	Model 149
Bristol F.2B	AL	Gunte	LGARFM	Bristol	Brisfit	
Bristol F.2B Rep	AZ	Grand	PoFGCVA	Bristol	Brisfit	PWZ
Bristol Type 170 Mk.31	MB-C	Winni	WCAM	Bristol	Freighter/Wayfarer	
Brock Keb 8BM Gyroplane	WI	Oshko	EAAAAM	Brock	Gyro-Plane	N2303
Broussard MH.1512	CA	SRosa	PCAM	Broussard	MH.1512	
Brown B-1	IL	Chica	MoS&I	Brown	B-1 Racer	
Brown B-1	WI	Oshko	EAAAAM	Brown	B-1 Racer	NR 83Y
Brown-Bushby-Robinson	WI	Oshkosh	EAAAAM	Brown-Bushby-Robinson	Suzie Jane 19	
Brown Star Lite	WI	Oshkosh	EAAAAM	Brown	Star Lite	N81197
Brugioni Mario	WI	Oshkosh	EAAAAM	Brugioni Mario	Cuby	
Brunner-Winkle Bird	NY	Bayport	BA	Brunner-Winkle	Bird	
Brunner-Winkle Bird	NY	Garde	CoAM	Brunner-Winkle	Bird	NC78K
Brunner-Winkle Bird	PA	Bethel	GAAM	Brunner-Winkle	Bird	NC726N
Brunner-Winkle Bird BK	VA	Sands	VAM	Brunner-Winkle	Bird	20250-96, N831W
Brunner-Winkle Bird BK	CA	San Diego	SDAM	Brunner-Winkle	Bird	N731Y
Brunner-Winkle Bird CK	NY	Rhine	ORA	Brunner-Winkle	Bird	
Brunner-Winkle Bird CK	NY	River	TFAC	Brunner-Winkle	Bird	
BT-9B	OH	Dayton	USAFM			
BT-12(YB)	OH	Newbu	WASAC	Fleetwings	Model 23	
BT-13	AZ	PBluf	RWCAF	Vultee	Valiant	
BT-13	CA	Atwater	CAM	Vultee	Valiant	42-16978, Side # E-205
BT-13	CA	Shafter	MFAM	Vultee	Valiant	
BT-13	CA	Fairf	TAFB	Vultee	Valiant	
BT-13	CT	Winds	NEAM	Vultee	Valiant	
BT-13	DE	Dover	DAFB	Vultee	Valiant	K-11
BT-13	IL	Danville	MAM	Vultee	Valiant	
BT-13A	IN	Indianapolis	AMHF	Vultee	Valiant	"Vibrator"
BT-13	IN	Mento	LB	Vultee	Valiant	
BT-13	KS	New Century	CAF-HoAW	Vultee	Valiant	41-21216, N56665, "Good Vibrations"
BT-13	KS	New Century	CAF-HoAW	Vultee	Valiant	N2808
BT-13	KS	Topek	CAM	Vultee	Valiant	
BT-13	MN	Minne	JJ	Vultee	Valiant	
BT-13	MS	Petal	MWHMM	Vultee	Valiant	
BT-13	NM	STere	WEAM	Vultee	Valiant	
BT-13	NV	Carso	YF	Vultee	Valiant	
BT-13	NY	Geneseo	1941AG	Vultee	Valiant	
BT-13	TX	Brown	RGVW-CAF	Vultee	Valiant	
BT-13	TX	Brown	RGVW-CAF	Vultee	Valiant	
BT-13	OH	Carroll	HAS	Vultee	Valiant	
BT-13	TX	Houst	CAF-GCW	Vultee	Valiant	N67208
BT-13	TX	RioHo	TAM	Vultee	Valiant	
BT-13 (SNV-1)	MI	Kalam	KAHM	Vultee	Valiant	11676

Model	State	City	Code	Manufacturer	Type	Notes
BT-13 (SNV-1 VU)	MI	Ypsil	YAF	Vultee	Valiant	
BT-13 (SNV-2)	TX	Dalla	CFM	Vultee	Valiant	13
BT-13	TX	RioHo	CAF-NCS	Vultee	Valiant	
BT-13A	AZ	Tucso	PAM	Vultee	Valiant	42-42353
BT-13A	CA	Riverside	MFAM	Vultee	Valiant	41-1414, Side BI-211
BT-13A	CA	Riverside	MFAM	Vultee	Valiant	41-1306, 21487
BT-13A	GA	Warner Robin	MoF	Vultee	Valiant	42-90018
BT-13A	KS	Liber	MAAM	Vultee	Valiant	
BT-13A	KS	New Century	CAF-HoAW	Vultee	Valiant	N57486
BT-13A	MB-C	Winni	WCAM	Vultee	Valiant	
BT-13A	MN	StPau	CAF-SMW	Vultee	Valiant	N52411
BT-13A	NC	Asheboro	PFAC	Vultee	Valiant	
BT-13A	OH	Newbu	WASAC	Vultee	Valiant	44- 9642
BT-13A	OK	Fredi	AAM	Vultee	Valiant	
BT-13A	SD	Rapid	SDA&SM	Vultee	Valiant	41-22204
BT-13A	TX	Houst	CAF-GCW	Vultee	Valiant	N56336
BT-13A	TX	Houst	CAF-WHS	Vultee	Valiant	N27003
BT-13A	TX	Midla	CAFFM	Vultee	Valiant	
BT-13A(SNV-1)	PA	Readi	MAAM	Vultee	Valiant	41-22441, N60277, 42
BT-13B	AL	Birmingham	SMoF	Vultee	Valiant	
BT-13B	CA	Chino	YACM	Vultee	Valiant	79-326, N4425V
BT-13B	OH	Dayto	USAFM	Vultee	Valiant	42-17800
BT-14 (NA-64)	AB-C	Nanton	NLSAM	North American	Yale	
BT-14 (NA-64)	AB-C	Wetas	RM	North American	Yale	
BT-14 (NA-64)	AZ	Tucso	PAM	North American	Yale	3397, N4735G
BT-14 (NA-64)	MB-C	Winni	WCAM	North American	Yale	
BT-14 (NA-64)	OH	Dayto	USAFM	North American	Yale	38-224
BT-14 (NA-64)	OH	Toled	TSA	North American	Yale	
BT-14 (NA-64)	ON-C	Dunnville	RCAFDA	North American	Yale	
BT-14 (NA-64)	ON-C	Hamilton	CWH	North American	Yale	CF-CWZ, 3350
BT-14 (NA-64)	ON-C	Tillsonburg	CHAA	North American	Yale	3399
BT-14 (NA-64)	SK-C	MJaw	WDM	North American	Yale	
BT-14 (NA-64)	TX	Midla	CAF-Hq	North American	Yale	N4574Y
BT-15	OH	Newbu	WASAC	Vultee	Valiant	42-41597
BT-15	TX	Midla	CAFFM	Vultee	Valiant	
Bu.133	FL	Polk	FoF	Bucker	Jungmeister	
Bu.133	ID	Athol	NAM	Bucker	Jungmeister	
Bu.133	MD	Silve	PEGF	Bucker	Jungmeister	
Bu.133	OK	Oklah	A&SM	Bucker	Jungmeister	
Bu.133	OK	Oklah	KCASM	Bucker	Jungmeister	
Bu.133-C	VA	Sands	VAM	Bucker	Jungmeister	Sn 251N133BU
Bu.133	WI	Oshko	EAAAAM	Bucker	Jungmeister	N515
Bu.133L	WI	Oshko	EAAAAM	Bucker	Jungmeister	N258H
Bu.181	MD	Silve	PEGF	Bucker	Bestmann	
Bugatti 100	WI	Oshkosh	EAAAAM	Bugatti	100	
Buhl Sport	MN	Blaine	GWFM	Buhl	Airsedan	
Buhl Sport	ON-C	Sault Ste Marie	CBHC	Buhl	Airsedan	CF-OAT
Buhl Sport	ON-C	Sault Ste Marie	CBHC	Buhl	Airsedan	CF-OAR Wreckage
Buhl Sport	WY	Jackson	GWFM	Buhl	Airsedan	
Bunce-Curtiss Pusher	CT	Winds	NEAM	Bunce-Curtiss	Pusher	
Bunker 154	OK	Oklah	KCASM	Bunker	Model 154	
Burgess-Curtis SC	MD	Silve	PEGF	Burgess-Curtiss	SC	
Burgess-Dunne Rep	ON-C	Trenton	RCAFMM	Burgess-Dunne		
Burgess Twister	WI	Oshkosh	EAAAAM	Burgess-Knight	Twister Imperial	
Burgess-Wright B	ME	OwlsH	OHTM	Burgess-Wright	Flyer	
Bushby Mustang I	KY	Louis	MoH&S	Bushby	Mustang I	
Bushby Mustang II	AL	Birmi	SMoF	Bushby	Mustang II	
Bushby Mustang II(MM-2)	AZ	Tucso	PAM	Bushby	Mustang Mk.2	Man Sn 581, N53RM
Bushby Mustang II	KS	Liber	MAAM	Bushby	Mustang II	
Butler Blackhawk	FL	Lakel	SFAF	Butler	Blackhawk	
BV 155B	MD	Silve	PEGF	Blohm & Voss	Model 155B	
C- 1	FL	Kissi	FTWAM	Grumman	Trader	
C- 1A	FL	Pensa	USNAM	Grumman	Trader	136754, 754, "Bicentenial"
C- 1A	PA	Willo	WGNAS	Grumman	Trader	62
C- 1A	CA	Palm Sprgs	PoFAM	Grumman	Cod	
C- 1A	RI	NKing	QAM	Grumman	Cod	136792
C- 1A	SC	Flore	FA&MM	Grumman	Cod	
C- 1A	TX	Galve	LSFM	Grumman	Cod	N 81193 146052
C- 2	CA	San Diego	NINAS			Tail RW, Nose 30, Side VRC 30
C- 2	OK	Tulsa	TA&SC		Spartan	
C- 3	OK	Tulsa	TA&SC		Spartan	
C- 5A	DE	Dover	DAFB	Lockheed	Galaxy	
C- 5A	NS-C	Halifax	ACAM	Lockheed	Galaxy	
C- 5A Simulator	NM	STere	WEAM	Lockheed	Galaxy	
C- 6A(VC)	IA	Sioux City	MAAM	Beechcraft	King Air	
C- 6A(VC)	NM	Las Cruces	WSMP	Beechcraft	King Air	
C- 6A(VC)	OH	Dayto	USAFM	Beechcraft	King Air	66-0943
C- 7	NC	Fayet	FBADM	de Havilland	Caribou	
C- 7(CV-7)	VA	FtEus	USATM	de Havilland	Caribou	
C- 7A	CT	Winds	NEAM	de Havilland	Caribou	62-4188
C- 7A	DE	Dover	DAFB	de Havilland	Caribou	
C- 7A(CV2B)	GA	Hampton	AAHF	de Havilland	Caribou	
C- 7A	GA	Warner Robin	MoF	de Havilland	Caribou	63-9756, 756, "Dixie Pub"
C- 7A	OH	Dayto	USAFM	de Havilland	Caribou	62-4193
C- 7A	TX	Abile	DLAP	de Havilland	Caribou	58-82
C- 7A	TX	Amarillo	EFA&SM	de Havilland	Caribou	63-9719
C- 7A	UT	Ogden	HAFBM	de Havilland	Caribou	
C- 7B	CA	Rosam	EAFB	de Havilland	Caribou	63-9765
C- 7B	DE	Dover	DAFB	de Havilland	Caribou	KA-760
C- 12	FL	Lakeland	SNFAM	Curtiss/Wright	Sport Trainer	
C- 14(YC)	AZ	Tucso	PAM	Boeing		72- 1873
C- 15(YC)	AZ	Tucso	PAM	McDonnell		72- 1875
C- 21B(CH)	AK	Palme	MOAT&I			
C- 35 (XC)	MD	Silve	PEGF	Lockheed	Electra	
C- 36(UC)	AZ	Tucso	PAM	Lockheed	Lockheed 10	43-56638, N4963C
C- 37	AB-C	Wetas	RM	Airmaster		
C- 37	MB-C	Winni	WCAM	Airmaster		
C- 39A	OH	Dayto	USAFM	Douglas		38-515
C- 40	CA	Chino	YAM	Lockheed		
C- 41	CA	SLean	OSA	Douglas		2053, NC41HQ, "General Hap Arnold"
C- 43(UC)	CA	Chino	YACM	Beech	Traveler	4890, N51746
C- 43(UC)	OH	Dayto	USAFM	Beech	Traveler	44-76068
C- 45	AR	Mesa	CAFAW	Beech	Twin Beech	
C- 45	WA	Seattle	MoF	Beech	Twin Beech	51-11696, N115ME
C- 45	AZ	Mesa	CAF-AW	Beech	Twin Beech	N145AZ
C- 45	AZ	PBluf	RWCAF	Beech	Twin Beech	

Type	State	City	Code	Mfr	Model	Serial/Notes
C-45	CA	Fairf	TAFB	Beech	Twin Beech	
C-45	GA	Atlan	CAF-DW	Beech	Twin Beech	N70GA
C-45	IL	Linco	HIFM	Beech	Twin Beech	
C-45	KS	Liber	MAAM	Beech	Twin Beech	
C-45	LA	Reser	AMHFM	Beech	Twin Beech	
C-45	MI	Selfridge	PAM	Beech	Twin Beech	42-37511
C-45	MN	Minne	MAGM	Beech	Twin Beech	51-338
C-45	MN	Winoma	WTI	Beech	Twin Beech	N3785
C-45	MO	Missoula	MMF	Beech	Twin Beech	
C-45	MS	Canto	CAF-MW	Beech	Twin Beech	N4207
C-45	NM	Hobbs	CAF-NMW	Beech	Twin Beech	N79AG
C-45	NC	Asheboro	PFAC	Beech	Twin Beech	
C-45	NY	Brooklyn	PFAC	Beech	Twin Beech	90536
C-45(SNB-5)	OH	N Canton	MAM	Beech	Twin Beech	67103, N200KU
C-45	OH	Newbu	WASAC	Beech	Twin Beech	N99662
C-45	OH	S.Euc	USAM	Beech	Twin Beech	
C-45	OK	Enid	CAF-CSW	Beech	Twin Beech	N40074
C-45(CT-134)	CA	Santa Martin	WoHAM	Beech	Musketeer	Model 23
C-45(CT-134)	AB-C	Wetaskawin	CFB	Beech	Musketeer	134232
C-45(CT-134)	MB-C	Brandon	CATPM	Beech	Musketeer	
C-45(CT-134)	MB-C	Portage	S	Beech	Musketeer	134201
C-45(CT-134)	MB-C	Portage	S	Beech	Musketeer	134238
C-45(CT-134)	MB-C	Winni	WRCFB	Beech	Musketeer	134228
C-45(CT-134)	ON-C	Campbellford	CFB	Beech	Musketeer	134219
C-45(CT-134)	ON-C	Picton	CFB	Beech	Musketeer	134211
C-45(CT-134)	ON-C	Toronto	TAM	Beech	Musketeer	
C-45(CT-134)	ON-C	Trenton	RCAFMM	Beech	Musketeer	23
C-45(CT-134A)	ON-C	Brockville	Park	Beech	Musketeer	
C-45(CT-134A)	ON-C	Campbellford	MMM	Beech	Musketeer	
C-45(CT-134A)	ON-C	Prairie LP	PA	Beech	Musketeer	11400
C-45(CT-134A)	ON-C	Prairie LP	FLPRM	Beech	Musketeer	
C-45(CT-134A)	SK-C	Regina		Beech	Musketeer	A141
C-45	SD	Rapid	SDA&SM	Beech	Twin Beech	
C-45	TX	Ladero	Airport	Beech	Twin Beech	
C-45	WY	Greyb	H&PA	Beech	Expediter	
C-45 (2 EA)	CO	Denve	JWDAS	Beech	Twin Beech	
C-45 (JRB Mk.III)	AB-C	Calga	AMoC	Beech	Expediter	Twin Beech
C-45 (D-18 / CT-128)	MB-C	Brandon	CATPM	Beech	Expediter	
C-45 (JRB Mk.III)	MB-C	Portage	S	Beech	Expediter	1560
C-45 (JRB Mk.III)	MB-C	Winni	WCAM	Beech	Expediter	1528
C-45 (JRB Mk.III)	VT	Burli	BANG	Beech	Expediter	
C-45 (SNB) Trainer	AR	Walnut Ridge	WRAFSM	Beech	Kansan	
C-45 (SNB)	CA	Chino	PoFAM	Beech	Kansan	BG-33
C-45 (SNB)	KS	Topek	CAM	Beech	Kansan	
C-45H(SNB)	NY	Horseheads	NWM	Beech	Kansan	52-01539
C-45 (SNB-5)	AZ	Tucso	PAM	Beech	Kansan	N40090, 39213
C-45 (UC)	AK	Fairb	APAM	Beech	Twin Beech	N9199Z
C-45A	CA	Atwater	CAM	Beech	Twin Beech	51-1897
C-45F(JRB-4)	CA	Riverside	MFAM	Beech	Expediter	44588, 52-10588A
C-45F(UC)	AK	Ancho	AAHM	Beech	Twin Beech	
C-45F(UC) Cockpit	MD	Ft Meade	QM	Beech	Twin Beech	
C-45G	DE	Dover	DAFB	Beech	Twin Beech	
C-45H	AK	Ancho	AAHM	Beech	Twin Beech	
C-45H	AL	Ozark	USAAM	Beech	Expediter	51-11638
C-45H	FL	Titusville	VACM	Beech	Twin Beech	
C-45H	GA	Warner Robin	MoF	Beech	Expediter	51-11653, N141ZA
C-45H	IL	Belle	SAFB	Beech	Twin Beech	
C-45H	OH	Dayto	USAFM	Beech	Twin Beech	52-10893
C-45H	UT	Ogden	HAFBM	Beech	Twin Beech	
C-45J	IL	Belle	SAFB	Beech	Twin Beech	
C-45J	ND	Fargo	FANG	Beech	Twin Beech	
C-45J	TX	Midla	CAFFM	Beech	Twin Beech	
C-45J(UC)	TX	San A	LAFB	Beech	Twin Beech	29639, #637
C-45J(RC)(SNB-5P)	FL	Pensa	USNAM	Beech	Kansan	9771, 4P, NATTU, PNCL
C-45J(RC)	GA	Woodstock	NGWS	Beech	Twin Beech	
C-45J(UC)	AL	Ozark	USAAM	Beech	Expediter	43-9767
C-45J(UC)	CA	Sacra	McCelAFB	Beech	Twin Beech	51-291
C-45J(UC)	ON-C	Hamilton	CWH	Beech	Twin Beech	
C-45J(UC)	TX	D Rio	LAFB	Beech	Twin Beech	
C-45J(UC)(SNB-2)	CA	Rosam	EAFB	Beech	Twin Beech	67161
C-45J(UC)(SNB-2C)	AZ	Tucso	PAM	Beechcraft	Expeditor	43-50222, N1082
C-45J(UC)(SNB-5)	AZ	Tucso	PAM	Beechcraft	Expeditor	Sn 39123, N75018, 29585
C-46	CA	Chino	YAM	Curtiss	Commando	43-47218
C-46	NM	Las Cruces	LCIA	Curtiss	Commando	
C-46	NM	Las Cruces	SA	Curtiss	Commando	
C-46(EC)(R5C)	FL	Pensa	USNAM	Curtiss	Commando	398, N611Z, 39611, 14, 398CK
C-46(EC)(R5D-2Z)	CA	Miramar	FLAM	Curtiss	Commando	MARS-37
C-46A	GA	Warner Robin	MoF	Curtiss	Commando	42-10119, 198S, 42-101198
C-46D	AZ	Tucso	PAM	Curtiss	Commando	44-77635
C-46D	AZ	Tucso	PAM	Curtiss	Commando	44-78019, N32229
C-46D	CA	Atwater	CAM	Curtiss	Commando	44-77575
C-46D	FL	FtWal	HF	Curtiss	Commando	44-424
C-46D	OH	Dayto	USAFM	Curtiss	Commando	44-78018
C-46F	CA	Camarillo	CAF-SCW	Curtiss	Commando	78774, N53594, "China Doll"
C-46F(NC)	NC	Fayet	FBADM	Curtiss	Commando	44-78573
C-47 *See C-53*				Douglas	Sky Train	
C-47 *See R4D*				Douglas	Sky Train	
C-47	AA	Starke	CBM	Douglas	Sky Train	12436, nose Z7
C-47	AZ	Tucso	PAM	Douglas	Sky Train	41-7723, 4201
C-47	DE	New Castle	ATC	Douglas	Sky Train	"Kilroy Was Here"
C-47	FL	Clear	FMAM	Douglas	Sky Train	
C-47	FL	Kissimmee	FTWRM	Douglas	Sky Train	
C-47	FL	Polk	FoF	Douglas	Sky Train	
C-47	FL	Stark	CB-FANTC	Douglas	Sky Train	
C-47	FL	Titus	VACM	Douglas	Sky Train	2100591, S U 5, "Tico Belle"
C-47	FL	WPalm	391FG	Douglas	Sky Train	
C-47	GA	Atlanta	ASG	Douglas	Sky Train	
C-47	GA	Calho	MAM	Douglas	Sky Train	45-928, N54599
C-47(R4D-6R)	IL	Chica	CAF-GLW	Douglas	Sky Train	99854, N227GB
C-47(AC)	KS	Topeka	SS	Douglas	Sky Train	45-1120, N2805J, "Spooky"
C-47	KY	FKnox	FC	Douglas	Sky Train	
C-47	MB-C	Winnipeg	WRCAFB	Douglas	Sky Train	
C-47	MI	Kalam	KAHM	Douglas	Sky Train	42-93168
C-47	ND	Minot	DTAM	Douglas	Sky Train	
C-47 Cockit	ND	Minot	DTAM	Douglas	Sky Train	
C-47(SC)	NM	Albuquerque	KAFB	Douglas	Sky Train	035732

105

C- 47(SC)	NM	Albuq	KAFB	Douglas	Sky Train	035732
C- 47	NY	Brooklyn	Bonanzav	Douglas	Sky Train	
C- 47	OK	Oklah	SFG	Douglas	Sky Train	892953, , "U7", T
C- 47	OH	N Canton	MAM	Douglas	Sky Train	45-0928, N54599, "Raptured Duck"
C- 47	ON-C	Ottaw	CAM	Douglas	Sky Train	
C- 47	ON-C	Petawawa	CFBPMM	Douglas	Sky Train	
C- 47	ON-C	Trenton	RCAFMM	Douglas	Sky Train	
C- 47	OR	Tillamook	TAM	Douglas	Sky Train	43-15512, N62376
C- 47	TX	Burnet	HLSCAF	Douglas	Sky Train	
C- 47	TX	FWort	PMoT	Douglas	Sky Train	
C- 47	TX	Houston	1940ATM	Douglas	Sky Train	
C- 47	VA	Peter	FL	Douglas	Sky Train	
C- 47 (R4D)	CO	Puebl	FWAM	Douglas	Sky Train	17217
C- 47 Simulator	NY	Garde	CoAM	Douglas	Sky Train	
C- 47(UH)	MS	Petal	MWHMM	Douglas	Sky Train	
C- 47(VC)	CA	Riverside	MFAM	Douglas	Sky Train	43-15579, "Golden Bear"
C- 47(VC)	ND	WFarg	Bonanzav	Douglas	Sky Train	
C- 47A	AK	Ancho	KANGB	Douglas	Sky Train	
C- 47A	AK	Palme	MOAT&I	Douglas	Sky Train	
C- 47A	CA	Atwater	CAM	Douglas	Sky Train	43-15977, Tail N, Side L7
C- 47A	DE	Dover	DAFB	Douglas	Sky Train	292841, Q9, R, "Turf & Sport Special"
C- 47A	LA	Bossi	BAFB	Douglas	Sky Train	"Hi Honey"
C- 47A	NY	Scotia	ESAM	Douglas	Sky Train	43-12061
C- 47A	SD	Rapid	SDA&SM	Douglas	Sky Train	N226GB
C- 47A	TX	Abile	DLAP	Douglas	Sky Train	41- 8808
C- 47A RAF	NWTC	HayRi	BA	Douglas	Dakota	12327, C- GWZS
C- 47A RAF	NWTC	HayRi	BA	Douglas	Dakota	13155, C- FLFR
C- 47A RAF	NWTC	HayRi	BA	Douglas	Dakota	13333, C- GPNR
C- 47A(AC)	FL	FtWal	HF	Douglas	Sky Train	42-510, AH
C- 47A(AC)	FL	Shali	USAFAM	Douglas	Sky Train	43-10, O
C- 47A(R4D-6)	GA	Warner Robin	MoF	Douglas	Sky Train	43-48957, 15090 EL, "Saylor's Trailer"
C- 47A(VC)	MO	SLoui	NMoT	Douglas	Sky Train	43-15635
C- 47A(VC)	ND	WFarg	Bonanzav	Douglas	Sky Train	42-93800
C- 47A-30-DK	NE	Ashland	SACM	Douglas	Sky Train	43-48098
C- 47B	AL	Montg	GAFB	Douglas	Sky Train	
C- 47B	MN	Minne	MAGM	Douglas	Sky Train	44-7462
C- 47B	NC	Fayet	FBADM	Douglas	Sky Train	
C- 47B	NC	Fayet	PAFB	Douglas	Sky Train	
C- 47B	ND	Fargo	FANG	Douglas	Sky Train	
C- 47B(TC)	WA	Tacoma	MAFB	Douglas	Sky Train	
C- 47D	AZ	Tucso	PAM	Douglas	Sky Train	Sn 41-7723
C- 47D	IL	Ranto	OCAM	Douglas	Sky Train	43-49336
C- 47D	IN	Peru	GAFB	Douglas	Sky Train	43-49270
C- 47D	KS	Topek	CAM	Douglas	Sky Train	45-1074, 476582, 17077 / 34344, "Kilroy", J8
C- 47D	MI	Belleville	YAF	Douglas	Sky Train	44-76716, N33048, "Yankee Doodle Dandy"
C- 47D	MI	Ypsil	YAF	Douglas	Sky Train	
C- 47D	OH	Dayto	USAFM	Douglas	Sky Train	43-49507
C- 47D	TX	San A	LAFB	Douglas	Sky Train	44-76671
C- 47D	WA	Spoka	FAFBHM	Douglas	Sky Train	
C- 47D(VC)	AL	Mobil	BMP	Douglas	Sky Train	40-76326
C- 47D(VC)	SC	Charl	CAFB	Douglas	Sky Train	
C- 47D(VC)	TX	Midla	CAFFM	Douglas	Sky Train	
C- 47D(VC)	UT	Ogden	HAFBM	Douglas	Sky Train	43-49281
C- 47H	AL	Ozark	USAAM	Douglas	Gooney Bird	41-12436
C- 47H(R4D-5)	FL	Pensa	USNAM	Douglas	Sky Train	12418, 18
C- 47J	GA	Warner Robin	MoF	Douglas	Skytrain	43-49442, N50811
C- 49	IL	Chica	CAF-GLW			N17332
C- 50	CT	Winds	NEAM	Douglas	Sky Train	
C- 53	CA	Rosam	EAFB	Douglas	Skytrooper	
C- 53D	CA	Sacra	McCelAFB	Douglas	Skytrooper	42-68835
C- 54	CA	Riverside	WFAM	Douglas	Skymaster	42-72636
C- 54	NJ	Farmi	BAHF	Douglas	Skymaster	"Spirit of Freedom"
C- 54	NY	Brooklyn	BAHF	Douglas	Skymaster	
C- 54	SD	Rapid	SDA&SM	Douglas	Skymaster	42-72592
C- 54	TX	Brown	RGVW-CAF	Douglas	Skymaster	
C- 54	WA	Seattle	MoF	Douglas	Skymaster	
C- 54	WY	Greyb	H&PA	Douglas	Skymaster	
C- 54B(R5D-2)	MA	NAndo	AW	Douglas	Skymaster	N44914, 56498, "Air Transport Command"
C- 54C(VC)	OH	Dayto	USAFM	Douglas	Skymaster	42-10745, 1, 42-107451, "Sacred Cow"
C- 54D(DC-4)	AZ	Tucso	PAM	Douglas	Skymaster	42-72488
C- 54D	CA	Riverside	MAFB	Douglas	Skymaster	42-72636, 56514, N67062
C- 54D	CA	Sacra	McCelAFB	Douglas	Skymaster	42-72449
C- 54D	TX	Midla	CAFFM	Douglas	Skymaster	
C- 54D-1-DL	NE	Ashland	SACM	Douglas	Skymaster	42-72724
C- 54E	CA	Atwater	CAM	Douglas	Skymaster	1373
C- 54G	GA	Warner Robin	MoF	Douglas	Skymaster	45-579, A
C- 54G	UT	Ogden	HAM	Douglas	Skymaster	45-502
C- 54M	DE	Dover	DAFB	Douglas	Skymaster	
C- 54Q	CA	Fairf	TAFB	Douglas	Skymaster	
C- 56 (L.18)	CA	Atwater	CAM	Lockheed	Lodestar	
C- 56 (L.18)	CA	Fairf	TAFB	Lockheed	Lodestar	
C- 60 (L.18)	BC-C	Langley	CMoF&T	Lockheed	Lodestar	
C- 60 (L.18)	CA	Chino	PoFAM	Lockheed	Lodestar	
C- 60 (L.18)	CA	SAnto	CAF-AW	Lockheed	Lodestar	N6371C
C- 60 (L.18)	VA	Chesa	CAF-ODS	Lockheed	Lodestar	N30N
C- 60A(L.18)(PV1)(R50)	CO	Westminster	CAF	Lockheed	Lodestar	43-16438
C- 60A(L.18)	GA	Warner Robin	MoF	Lockheed	Lodestar	42-55918, N18198
C- 60A(L.18)	OH	Dayto	USAFM	Lockheed	Lodestar	43-16445, Military Version L.18
C- 60A(L.18)	VA	Chesapeake	CAFODW	Lockheed	Lodestar	
C- 60A-5-LO(L.18-56)	MI	Belleville	YAF	Lockheed	Lodestar	42-56081, N117G
C- 60C(L.18C)	CA	Atwater	CAM	Lockheed	Lodestar	
C- 61(UC)(FC-24)	AK	Ancho	AAHM	Fairchild	Argus	
C- 61(UC)(FC-24)	KS	Liber	MAAM	Fairchild	Argus	
C- 61(UC)(FC-24)	PA	Reading	MAAM	Fairchild	Argus	NC19133
C- 61(UC)(FC-24)	VA	Sands	VAM	Fairchild	Argus	Sn 2983, Model G, N19123
C- 61(UC)(FC-24)	WA	Seatt	MoF	Fairchild	Argus	
C- 61(UC)(FC-24)	AB-C	Edmonton	AAM	Fairchild	Argus	
C- 61(UC)(FC-24)	ON-C	Greenwood	GMAM	Fairchild	Argus	
C- 61B(UC)(FC-24J)	AK	Fairb	APAM	Fairchild	Argus	NC20617, "Pollack Flying Service"
C- 61F(UC)(FC-24R)	ON-C	Hamilton	CWH	Fairchild	Argus	C-FGZL, 4809
C- 61G(UC)(FC-24H)	OK	Fredi	AAM	Fairchild	Argus	
C- 61G(UC)(FC-24W)	AL	Birmi	Southe	Fairchild	Argus	
C- 61G(UC)(FC-24W)	OK	Fredi	AAM	Fairchild	Argus	
C- 61G(UC)(FC-24W-46)	MB-C	Winni	WCAM	Fairchild	Argus	
C- 61G(UC)(FC-24W-46)	WI	Oshko	EAAAAM	Fairchild	Argus	N81318
C- 61G(UC)(FC-2W) Frame	AK	Ancho	AAHM	Fairchild	Argus	

Model	State	City	Code	Manufacturer	Type	Serial/Reg
C- 61J(UC)(FC-24 C8)	WI	Oshko	EAAAAM	Fairchild	Argus	N13191
C- 61J(UC)(FC-24C-8A)	WI	Oshko	EAAAAM	Fairchild	Argus	N957V
C- 61K(UC)	KS	Topek	CAM	Fairchild	Argus	N-18395
C- 64	AB-C	Edmonton	AAM	Noorduyn	Norseman	
C- 64	ON-C	Red Lake	HB	Noorduyn	Norseman	
C- 64A Mk.I	ON-C	Sault Se Marie	CBHC	Noorduyn	Norseman	CF-AYO
C- 64	AK	Ancho	AAHM	Noorduyn-CCF	Norseman	N725M
C- 64	BC-C	Sidne	BCAM	Noorduyn-CCF	Norseman	"Thunder Chicken"
C- 64A Mk.IV	ON-C	Sault Ste Marie	CBHC	Noorduyn-CCF	Norseman	Sn 17, CF-BFT
C- 64	SK-C	MJaw	WDM	Noorduyn-CCF	Norseman	
C- 64(UC)	CO	Denve	JWDAS	Noorduyn	Norseman	
C- 64(YC)	MD	Silve	PEGF	Noorduyn	Norseman	
C- 64(YC) Mk.IV	MD	Silve	PEGF	Noorduyn	Norseman	
C- 64A Mk.IV	AB-C	Wetas	RM	Noorduyn-CCF	Norseman	
C- 64A Mk.IV	MB-C	Winnipeg	WCAM	Noorduyn-CCF	Norseman	
C- 64A Mk.IVW	BC-C	Langley	CMoF&T	Noorduyn-CCF	Norseman	
C- 64A Mk.V	AB-C	Calga	AMoC	Noorduyn-CCF	Norseman	
C- 64A Mk.V	BC-C	Langley	CMoF&T	Noorduyn-CCF	Norseman	
C- 64A Mk.VI	AK	Fairb	APAM	Noorduyn-CCF	Norseman	N55555, "Alaska Airways"
C- 64A Mk.VI	ON-C	Ottaw	CAM	Noorduyn-CCF	Norseman	
C- 64A(UC)	OH	Dayto	USAFM	Noorduyn	Norseman	44-70296
C- 78(UC) See Also AT-17	AZ	Tucso	PAM	Cessna	Bobcat	42-39162, N66794,
C- 78(UC)	CA	Atwater	CAM	Cessna	Bobcat	
C- 78(UC)	CA	Fairf	TAFB	Cessna	Bobcat	
C- 78(UC)	CO	Denve	JWDAS	Cessna	Bobcat	3806 806
C- 78(UC)	MD	Cambr	CA	Cessna	Bobcat	
C- 78(UC)	NY	River	RE	Cessna	Bobcat	
C- 78(UC)	PA	Readi	MAAM	Cessna	Bobcat	N 41793
C- 78(UC)	TX	Midla	CAF-Hq	Cessna	Bobcat	N 44795
C- 78(UC)	TX	SMarc	CTWCAF	Cessna	Bobcat	
C- 78B(UC)	AZ	Tucso	PAM	Cessna	Bobcat	42-71830
C- 78B(UC)	CA	El Cajon	CAFFFM	Cessna	Bobcat	332578
C- 78B(UC)	GA	Warner Robin	MoF	Cessna	Bobcat	42-71714
C- 78B(UC)	OH	Dayto	USAFM	Cessna	Bobcat	42-71626
C- 82	OH	Newbu	WASAC	Fairchild	Packet	44-22991
C- 82	WA	Tacoma	MAFB	Fairchild	Packet	
C- 82	WY	Greyb	H&PA	Fairchild	Packet	
C- 82A	AZ	Tucso	PAM	Fairchild	Packet	44-23006, N6997C
C- 82A	OH	Dayto	USAFM	Fairchild	Packet	48-581
C- 97(KC)	OH	Newbu	WASAC	Boeing	Stratocruiser	235
C- 97(KC)	WI	Dodge	Restaura	Boeing	Stratocruiser	
C- 97(KC)	WY	Greyb	H&PA	Boeing	Stratocruiser	
C- 97G	AZ	Tucso	PAM	Boeing	Stratocruiser	Sn 52-2626, HB-ILY
C- 97G	CA	Lanca	MoFM	Boeing	Stratocruiser	
C- 97G	IL	Ranto	OCAM	Boeing	Stratocruiser	52-0898
C- 97G(KC)	AZ	Tucso	PAM	Boeing	Stratocruiser	53-151
C- 97G(KC)	MO	White	WAFB	Boeing	Stratotanker	0-30327
C- 97G(KC)	NJ	Farmi	BAHF	Boeing	Stratocruiser	52- 2718, N117GA, "Deliverance"
C- 97G(KC)	NV	Las Vegas	LBAHSM	Boeing	Stratocruiser	53-0317, N971HP, #377, Cockpit
C- 97G(KC)	OR	Medford	RVIA	Boeing	Stratocruiser	20895
C- 97G(KC)	TX	Midla	CAFFM	Boeing	Stratocruiser	
C- 97G(KC)-BN	NE	Ashland	SACM	Boeing	Stratocruiser	53-198
C- 97K(KC)	SC	Flore	FA&MM	Boeing	Stratocruiser	
C- 97L(KC)	CA	Atwater	CAM	Boeing	Stratocruiser	0-0354,
C- 97L(KC)	CA	Marys	BAFB	Boeing	Stratocruiser	
C- 97L(KC)	CA	Riverside	MFAM	Boeing	Stratotanker	53-0363
C- 97L(KC)	GA	Warner Robin	MoF	Boeing	Stratocruiser	53-298
C- 97L(KC)	IN	Peru	GAFB	Boeing	Stratocruiser	52-2297
C- 97L(KC)	LA	Bossi	BAFB	Boeing	Stratocruiser	0240
C- 97L(KC)	MD	Silve	PEGF	Boeing	Stratocruiser	
C- 97L(KC)	MO	StJos	SJANG	Boeing	Stratocruiser	
C- 97L(KC)	MT	Great	MAFB	Boeing	Stratocruiser	53-0360
C- 97L(KC)	NH	Ports	PAFB	Boeing	Stratocruiser	
C- 97L(KC)	OH	Dayto	USAFM	Boeing	Stratocruiser	52-2630
C- 97L(KC)	TX	Abile	DLAP	Boeing	Stratocruiser	53-282
C- 97L(KC)	TX	FWort	NASFWJRB	Boeing	Stratocruiser	
C- 97L(KC)	TX	FWort	SAM	Boeing	Stratocruiser	
C- 97L(KC)	WI	CDoug	WNGML&M	Boeing	Stratocruiser	905
C- 99	TX	San A	KAFB	Convair		
C-103A	AZ	Tucso	DMAFB			
C-117D *See R4D*						
C-118	WY	Greyb	H&PA	Douglas	Liftmaster	
C-118(VC)	OH	Dayto	USAFM	Douglas	Liftmaster	46-505
C-118(YO)	CA	Fairf	TAFB	Douglas	Liftmaster	
C-118A	NJ	Trent	MGAFB	Douglas	Liftmaster	
C-118A	TX	San A	LAFB	Douglas	Liftmaster	51-17640
C-118A(VC)(DC-6)	AZ	Tucso	PAM	Douglas	Liftmaster	53-3240, 33240, "Air Force One"
C-118B	OK	Altus	AAFB	Douglas	Liftmaster	
C-118B(R6D-1)	FL	Pensa	USNAM	Douglas	Liftmaster	128424, 424
C-119	CO	Puebl	FWAM	Fairchild	Flying Boxcar	131688
C-119	GA	FtBen	IM	Fairchild	Flying Boxcar	
C-119	KY	FKnox	FC	Fairchild	Flying Boxcar	
C-119	NV	Battl	BMAM	Fairchild	Flying Boxcar	N5216R, 137
C-119F	PA	Readi	MAAM	Fairchild	Flying Boxcar	N175ML, VMR-52
C-119	TX	FWort	PMoT	Fairchild	Flying Boxcar	0-12675
C-119	WI	Milwa	MANG	Fairchild	Flying Boxcar	
C-119	WY	Greyb	H&PA	Fairchild	Flying Boxcar	
C-119(R4Q-2)	CA	Miramar	FLAM	Fairchild	Flying Boxcar	708, VMR-352
C-119B	CA	Rosam	EAFB	Fairchild	Flying Boxcar	48-352
C-119B	GA	Warner Robin	MoF	Fairchild	Flying Boxcar	51-2566
C-119C	AZ	Tucso	PAM	Fairchild	Flying Boxcar	49-0157
C-119C	AZ	Tucso	PAM	Fairchild	Flying Boxcar	49-132, N13743
C-119C	CA	Atwater	CAM	Fairchild	Flying Boxcar	49-199, N13744
C-119C	TX	Midla	CAFFM	Fairchild	Flying Boxcar	
C-119C	TX	San A	LAFB	Fairchild	Flying Boxcar	51- 2567
C-119F	NY	Geneseo	1941AG	Fairchild	Flying Boxcar	10678
C-119G	CA	Fairf	TAFB	Fairchild	Flying Boxcar	134
C-119G	CA	Riverside	MFAM	Fairchild	Flying Boxcar	RCAF 22122, 452 TCW
C-119G	CA	Sacra	McCelAFB	Fairchild	Flying Boxcar	52-114
C-119G	DE	Dover	DAFB	Fairchild	Flying Boxcar	
C-119G	FL	FtWal	HF	Fairchild	Flying Boxcar	33144
C-119G	IN	Peru	GAFB	Fairchild	Flying Boxcar	52- 5850, "Hash-2-Zero"
C-119G-FA	NE	Ashland	SACM	Fairchild	Flying Boxcar	51-8024
C-119G	UT	Ogden	HAFBM	Fairchild	Flying Boxcar	
C-119J	AR	Littl	LRAFB	Fairchild	Flying Boxcar	53-8084, 314th TAW
C-119J	OH	Dayto	USAFM	Fairchild	Flying Boxcar	51-8037

Type	State	City	Code	Manufacturer	Name	Notes
C-119L	NC	Fayet	FBADM	Fairchild	Flying Boxcar	
C-121 (EC)(L-1049)	TX	San Antonio	LAFB	Lockheed	Constellation	54115
C-121 (L-0749)	DE	Dover	DAFB	Lockheed	Constellation	
C-121 (L-0749)	MA	Stow	BCF	Lockheed	Constellation	
C-121 (L-0749)	MO	River	SACI	Lockheed	Constellation	"TWA"
C-121 (L-0749)	MT	Helena	CoT	Lockheed	Constellation	52-3417
C-121A(L-0749)	AZ	Tucso	PAM	Lockheed	Constellation	48-614, USAF Constellation
C-121A(L-0749A)	AZ	Scott	CG	Lockheed	Constellation	48-609, 2601, USAF Constellation MATS
C-121A(VC)(L-0749)	AL	Ozark	USAAM	Lockheed	Constellation	48-613, USAF Constellation
C-121A(VC)(L-0749)	AZ	Grand	PoFGCVA	Lockheed	Constellation	48-613, N422NA, Constellation, "Bataan"
C-121C(L-0749)	CA	Lanca	CHS	Lockheed	Constellation	54-156, N73544, USAF Constellation
C-121C(L-0749)	SC	Charl	CAFB	Lockheed	Constellation	USAF Constellation
C-121D(EC)(L-1049)	OH	Dayto	USAFM	Lockheed	Warning Star	53-555, USAF Super Constellation
C-121E(VC)(L-0749)	OH	Dayto	USAFM	Lockheed	Constellation	53-7885
C-121G(L-0749)	DE	Dover	DAFBHC	Lockheed	Constellation	
C-121K(EC)	FL	Pensa	USNAM	Lockheed	Warning Star	143221, VT 86
C-121K(EC)(L-1049)	GA	Warner Robin	MoF	Lockheed	Warning Star	141297, USAF Super Constellation
C-121T(EC)(L-1049)	AZ	Tucso	PAM	Lockheed	Warning Star	53-554, USAF Constellation
C-123B	AZ	Tucso	PAM	Fairchild	Provider	55-4505
C-123J	AK	Ancho	KANGB	Fairchild	Provider	
C-123J	AK	Palme	MOAT&I	Fairchild	Provider	N98
C-123K	AZ	Phoenix	DVA	Fairchild	Provider	
C-123K	AZ	Tucso	PAM	Fairchild	Provider	54-580, N3142D, 731TAS, "War Wagon"
C-123K	AZ	Tucso	PAM	Fairchild	Provider	Sn 54-0659, N2129J
C-123K	CA	Atwater	CAM	Fairchild	Provider	54-512, Tail WX
C-123K	CA	Riverside	MFAM	Fairchild	Provider	54-612, "The Chief"
C-123K	CA	Rosam	EAFB	Fairchild	Provider	54-683
C-123K	DE	Dover	DAFB	Fairchild	Provider	WM
C-123K	FL	Titusville	AAF	Fairchild	Provider	54-674
C-123K	FL	Titusville	AAF	Fairchild	Provider	54-603
C-123K(UC)	FL	FtWal	HF	Fairchild	Provider	55-4533
C-123K(UC)	NY	Farmingdale	AAM	Fairchild	Provider	55-4533
C-123K	MN	Aonka	Airport	Fairchild	Provider	N681DG
C-123K	MN	Aonka	SEAC	Fairchild	Provider	54603, NX-4254H, #603, "Cat House", Air America"
C-123K	MN	Minneapolis	MAGM	Fairchild	Provider	
C-123K	NC	Fayet	FBADM	Fairchild	Provider	
C-123K	NC	Fayet	PAFB	Fairchild	Provider	
C-123K	NJ	Trent	MGAFB	Fairchild	Provider	
C-123K	OH	Dayto	USAFM	Fairchild	Provider	56-4362
C-123K	PA	Beave	AHM	Fairchild	Provider	"Thunder Pig"
C-123K	TX	Abile	DLAP	Fairchild	Provider	54-604 A
C-123K	TX	D Rio	LAFB	Fairchild	Provider	
C-123K	TX	San A	LAFB	Fairchild	Provider	54-668
C-123K	UT	Ogden	HAFBM	Fairchild	Provider	
C-123K(UC)	GA	Warner Robin	MoF	Fairchild	Provider	54-633
C-124	NV	L.Veg	LB	Douglas	Globemaster	
C-124	NV	L.Veg	MIA	Douglas	Globemaster	
C-124	NV	LasVe	MIAHM	Douglas	Globemaster	
C-124A	NE	Ashland	SACM	Douglas	Globemaster	49-258
C-124C	AZ	Tucso	PAM	Douglas	Globemaster	52-1004
C-124C	CA	Fairf	TAFB	Douglas	Globemaster	
C-124C	GA	Warner Robin	MoF	Douglas	Globemaster	51-89
C-124A	OH	Dayto	USAFM	Douglas	Globemaster	51-0135
C-124C	SC	Charl	CAFB	Douglas	Globemaster	
C-124C	TX	Midla	CAFFM	Douglas	Globemaster	
C-124C	UT	Ogden	HAFBM	Douglas	Globemaster	
C-124C	WA	Tacoma	MAFB	Douglas	Globemaster	20994, MATS
C-125A(YC)	AZ	Tucso	PAM	Northrop	Raider	48-0636N 2573B
C-125B(YC)	OH	Dayto	USAFM	Northrop	Raider	48-0626N 2566B
C-126A(LC)	CA	Fairf	TAFB	Cessna	Businessliner	Model 195
C-126A(LC)	IN	Indianapolis	AMHF	Cessna	Businessliner	
C-126A(LC)	OH	Dayto	USAFM	Cessna	Businessliner	49-1949, Model 195
C-126A(LC)	TX	Denton	H10FM	Cessna	Businessliner	
C-130	AR	Littl	LRAFB	Lockheed	Hercules	
C-130 Fuse Only 2ea	LA	Alexandria	EAP	Lockheed	Hercules	
C-130	GA	Colum	FB	Lockheed	Hercules	
C-130	MN	Minne	MAGM	Lockheed	Hercules	70485
C-130	NS-C	Greenwood	GMAM	Lockheed	Hercules	70485
C-130	OR	Mc Minnville	EAEC	Lockheed	Hercules	
C-130A	AZ	Tucso	PAM	Lockheed	Hercules	57-457
C-130A	DC	Dulle	DA	Lockheed	Hercules	
C-130A	IL	Ranto	OCAM	Lockheed	Hercules	55-0037, MA ANG
C-130A	MD	Ft Meade	NVP	Lockheed	Hercules	60528, 60528
C-130A	MI	Mt Clemens	SMAM	Lockheed	Hercules	57-0514
C-130A	TX	Abile	DLAP	Lockheed	Hercules	55-23
C-130A	TX	Wichi	SAFB	Lockheed	Hercules	
C-130A	WY	Greyb	H&PA	Lockheed	Hercules	
C-130A(AC)	FL	Shali	USAFAM	Lockheed	Spectre Gunship	
C-130A(AC)	OH	Dayto	USAFM	Lockheed	Spectre Gunship	54-1626
C-130A(JC)	OH	Dayto	USAFM	Lockheed	Hercules	54-1630
C-130A(YMC)	GA	Warner Robin	MoF	Lockheed	Hercules	55-14
C-130B	UT	Ogden	HAFBM	Lockheed	Hercules	
C-130D	AZ	Tucso	PAM	Lockheed	Hercules	57-493
C-130E	TX	Wichi	SAFB	Lockheed	Hercules	
C-130H(YMC)	GA	Warner Robin	MoF	Lockheed	Hercules	74-1686
C-131	CA	Fairf	TAFB	Convair	Samaritan	Model 340
C-131	MN	Minne	MAGM	Convair	Samaritan	54-757, Model 340
C-131D	SD	Rapid	SDA&SM	Convair	Samaritan	55-0292, Model 340
C-131(VC)	CA	Sacra	McCelAFB	Convair	Samaritan	54- 2822 Model 340
C-131A(HC)	AR	Littl	LRAFB	Convair	Samaritan	Model 340
C-131A(HC)	VT	Burli	BANG	Convair	Samaritan	
C-131A(T-29A)	CA	Chino	PoFAM	Convair	Samaritan	Model 240
C-131A(T-29A)	MD	Silve	PEGF	Convair	Samaritan	"Caroline" Model 240
C-131A(T-29A) Nose	TX	RioHo	TAM	Convair	Samaritan	Model 240
C-131A(VC)(T-29A)	AZ	Tusco	HA	Convair	Samaritan	Allison Model 580
C-131B	CA	Chino	PoFAM	Convair	Samaritan	Model 340
C-131D	DE	Dover	DAFB	Convair	Samaritan	Model 340
C-131B	FL	Shali	USAFAM	Convair	Samaritan	Model 340
C-131D	CA	Camarillo	CAF-SCW	Convair	Samaritan	131CW, "samaritan"
C-131D	CA	Riverside	MFAM	Convair	Samaritan	54-2808
C-131D	MI	Mt Clemens	SMAM	Convair	Samaritan	52-0293, Model 340
C-131D	OH	Dayto	USAFM	Convair	Samaritan	55- 301 Model 340
C-131D	UT	Ogden	HAFBM	Convair	Samaritan	Model 340
C-131E	OH	Lockb	RANGB	Convair	Samaritan	55- 4751
C-131F(R4Y-1)	AZ	Tucson	PAM	Convair	Samaritan	141017
C-131F(R4Y-1)	AZ	Tucson	PAM	Convair	Samaritan	141025

Type	State	City	Museum	Manufacturer	Name	Serial/Notes
C-131F(R4Y-2)	FL	Pensa	USNAM	Convair	Samaritan	141015 615 Model 340
C-133A	IL	Ranto	OCAM	Douglas	Cargomaster	
C-133A	OH	Dayto	USAFM	Douglas	Cargomaster	56- 2008
C-133B	AZ	Tucso	PAM	Douglas	Cargomaster	59- 527
C-133B-DL	NE	Ashland	SACM	Douglas	Cargomaster	59- 536
C-135C(EC)-BN	NE	Ashland	SACM	Boeing	Startotanker	63-8049
C-135 (EC)	OH	Dayton	USAFM	Boeing	Stratotanker	
C-135 (EC)	SD	Rapid	SDA&SM	Boeing	Stratotanker	61-0262
C-135(EC)	TX	Wichi	SAFB	Boeing	Looking Glass	
C-135J(EC)	AZ	Tucso	PAM	Boeing	Stratotanker	63-8057
C-135L(EC)	IN	Peru	GAFB	Boeing	Stratotanker	61-269, "Excalliber"
C-135(KC)	FL	Miami	WOM	Boeing	Stratotanker	
C-135(KC)	IL	Belle	SAFB	Boeing	Stratotanker	
C-135(KC)	LA	Bossi	BAFB	Boeing	Stratotanker	
C-135(KC)	NE	Offut	OAFB	Boeing	Stratotanker	
C-135(KC)	OK	Oklah	TAFB	Boeing	Stratotanker	
C-135A	CA	Rosam	EAFB	Boeing	Stratotanker	
C-135A(KC)	CA	Atwater	CAM	Boeing	Stratotanker	55-3139
C-135A(KC)	CA	Riverside	MFAM	Boeing	Stratotanker	55-3130, "Old Grandad"
C-135A(KC)	TX	Abile	DLAP	Boeing	Stratotanker	56-3639
C-135A(NKC)	OH	Dayto	USAFM	Boeing	Stratotanker	55-3123
C-137B(VC)	AZ	Tucson	PAM	Boeing	Air Force One	58-6971, "Freedom One"
C-137B(VC)	OH	Dayton	USAFM	Boeing	Air Force One	
C-137B(VC)	WA	Seatt	MoF	Boeing	Air Force One	58-6970, 1958
C-140	IL	Belle	SAFB	Lockheed	Jetstar	
C-140(1329-8)	NS	Bedford	ACAM	Lockheed	Jetstar	
C-140	NS-C	Halifax	ACAM	Lockheed	Jetstar	
C-140	ON-C	Ottaw	CAM	Lockheed	Jetstar	
C-140	UT	Ogden	HAFBM	Lockheed	Jetstar	
C-140	WA	Seatt	MoF	Lockheed	Jetstar	
C-140(VC)	GA	Warner Robin	MoF	Lockheed	Jetstar	61-2488
C-140(VC)	IL	Belle	SAFB	Lockheed	Jetstar	
C-140A	CA	Fairf	TAFB	Lockheed	Jetstar	
C-140A	CA	Rosam	EAFB	Lockheed	Jetstar	59-5962
C-140B(VC)	AZ	Tucso	PAM	Lockheed	Jetstar	61-2489
C-140B(VC)	OH	Dayto	USAFM	Lockheed	Jetstar	61-2492
C-141	IL	Belle	SAFB	Lockheed	Starlifter	
C-141	CA	Riverside	MFAM	Lockheed	Starlifter	65-0257
C-141B(NC)	CA	Rosam	EAFB	Lockheed	Starlifter	65-0257
C-141A	DE	Dover	DAFB	Lockheed	Starlifter	
C-141B	DE	Dover	DAFB	Lockheed	Starlifter	
C-141B	GA	Warner Robin	MoF	Lockheed	Starlifter	66-0180A
C-142(XC)(X-18)	CA	Redwo	HAM		VSTOL	
C-142A(XC)	OH	Dayto	USAFM		VSTOL	65-5924
C-144(CX)	MB-C	Winnipeg	CFB			144612
C6N1-S	MD	Silve	PEGF	Nakajima	Myrt (Saiun)	
CA-61 Mini-Ace	WI	Oshko	EAAAAM	Cvjetkovic	Mini-Ace	N94283
Callair	MN	Blaine	GWFM	Callair	Callair	
Callair	WY	Afton	CAM	Callair	Callair	
CallAir A-2	WY	Jackson	GWFM	CallAir	A-2	
CAM 3	WA	Seatt	MoF	Swallow-Stearman		
Canard Quickie	PA	Phila	FI	Canard	Quickie	
Cangley Aerodome	VA	Hampt	VA&SC	Cangley	Aerodome	
Cap 231	FL	Polk	FoF	Cap	Cap	
Caproni CA 20	WA	Seattle	MoF	Caproni		1
Caproni 36	OH	Dayto	USAFM	Caproni		Model 36 2378
Caquot Type R Balloon	OH	Dayton	USAFM	Caquot	Observation	
Caravelle VI-R	CT	Winds	NEAM	Caravelle	Sud	
CASA Saeta	IN	Auburn	HW		Trainer	
Casade 180B	MD	Silve	PEGF	Casade	Kasperwing	
Casade 180B	WA	Seattle	MoF	Casade	Kasperwing	
Cassutt B Special	NY	Garde	CoAM	Cassutt	B Special	
Caudron 276	AL	Gunte	LGARFM	Caudron	Model 276	
Caudron G.III	NY	Rhine	ORA	Caudron		France Biplane
Caudron G.IV	MD	Silve	PEGF	Caudron		France 2 Engine Bomber WWI
Cavalier	NY	Ghent	POMAM	Star	Cavalier	
Cavalier	OK	Oklah	KCASM	Star	Cavalier	
Cavalier Model B	PA	Bethel	GAAM	Star	Cavalier	
Cavalier Model E	PA	Bethel	GAAM	Star	Cavalier	
Cayley Glider	CA	San Diego	SDAM	Cayley	Glider	
Cayley Glider	ME	Owls Head	OHTM	Cayley	Glider	
CBY-3 Burnelli	CT	Winds	NEAM	Burnelli		
CCW-1	MD	Silve	PEGF	Custer	Channel Wing	
CCW-5	PA	Readi	MAAM	Custer	Channel Wing	Sn 1, N5855V
Cessna	MN	Winoma	WTI	Cessna		N6766S
Cessna	MN	Winoma	WTI	Cessna		N15153
Cessna	MO	SLoui	SLDPA	Cessna		
Cessna 120	AZ	Tucso	PAM	Cessna	Model 120	NC4191N
Cessna 120	IA	SBluf	MAAM	Cessna	Model 120	
Cessna 120	IL	Rantoul	OCAM	Cessna	Model 120	NC2660N
Cessna 120	KS	Liber	MAAM	Cessna	Model 120	
Cessna 120	NC	Hendersonville	WNCAM	Cessna	Model 120	
Cessna 120	OK	Fredi	AAM	Cessna	Model 120	
Cessna 140	KS	Liber	MAAM	Cessna	Model 140	
Cessna 140	NY	Bayport	BA	Cessna	Model 140	
Cessna 140A	NM	STere	WEAM	Cessna	Model 140A	
Cessna 145	KS	Liber	MAAM	Cessna	Airmaster	NC32450
Cessna 150H	KY	Lexington	AMoK	Cessna	Commuter	N6598S
Cessna 150H	WI	Oshko	EAAAAM	Cessna	Commuter	N23107
Cessna 150L	WI	Oshko	EAAAAM	Cessna	Commuter	N5799G
Cessna 150L	AZ	Tucso	PAM	Cessna	Commuter	N18588
Cessna 150L	MD	Silve	PEGF	Cessna	Commuter	
Cessna 150M	PA	Readi	MAAM	Cessna	Commuter	N714GR
Cessna 165	KS	Liber	MAAM	Cessna	Airmaster	
Cessna 172	FL	Dayto	ERAU	Cessna	Skylane	
Cessna 172	NV	LasVe	MIAHM	Cessna	Skylane	N9712B, "Hacienda"
Cessna 172Q	FL	Dayto	ERAU	Cessna	Skylane	
Cessna 175(T-41B)	OK	Fredi	AAM	Cessna	Mescalero	67-15140
Cessna 175(T-41B)	KS	Liber	MAAM	Cessna	Mescalero	
Cessna 175(T-41B)	FL	Clear	FMAM	Cessna	Mescalero	
Cessna 175(T-41B)	OK	FtSil	USAFAM	Cessna	Mescalero	
Cessna 180	CA	Hayward	VAM	Cessna	Model 180	
Cessna 180	GA	Woodstock	NGWS	Cessna	Model 180	
Cessna 180	MD	Silve	PEGF	Cessna	Model 180	
Cessna 180	OR	Tillamook	TAM	Cessna	Model 180	"Spirit of Columbus"
Cessna 180F	FL	Pensa	USNAM	Cessna	Model 180F	N 2146Z, 18051246

Cessna 180H	TX	RioHo	TAM	Cessna	Model 180H	N180PK, SN 1805218
Cessna 182RG	FL	Dayto	ERAU	Cessna	Model 182RG	
Cessna 182	GA	Woodstock	NGWS	Cessna	Model 182	
Cessna 182P	OH	Cleveland	FCAAM	Cessna	Model 182P	N20920
Cessna 185	PA	Tough	CFCM	Cessna	Model 185	
Cessna 195A	KS	Liber	MAAM	Cessna	Businessliner	
Cessna 195A	ND	Minot	DTAM	Cessna	Businessliner	
Cessna 195A	OK	Fredi	AAM	Cessna	Businessliner	
Cessna 195A	PA	Bethel	GAAM	Cessna	Businessliner	N195PD
Cessna 206	KS	Wichita	KAM	Cessna	Model 206	
Cessna 206	MI	Belle	AFDSC	Cessna	Model 206	
Cessna 303	FL	Dayto	ERAU	Cessna	Model 303	
Cessna 310 (U-3)	AZ	Tucso	PAM	Cessna	Blue Canoe	N182Z, U-3, L-27
Cessna 310 (U-3)	KS	Liber	MAAM	Cessna	Blue Canoe	U-3, L-27
Cessna 310 (U-3)	KS	Wichita	KAM	Cessna	Blue Canoe	U-3, L-27
Cessna 310 (U-3)	MO	SLoui	SLUPC	Cessna	Blue Canoe	U-3, L-27
Cessna 310 (U-3)	OK	Fredi	AAM	Cessna	Blue Canoe	U-3, L-27
Cessna 310B(U-3)	IL	Bloom	PAM	Cessna	Blue Canoe	U-3, L-27
Cessna 320	MO	SLoui	SLUPC	Cessna	Skynight	
Cessna 401	PA	Beaver Falls	AHM	Cessna		
Cessna C-402	NV	Las Vegas	LBAHSM	Cessna		N59SA, Fuse Only, "Scenic Airlines"
Cessna AW	CA	Chino	YACM	Cessna	Model AW 167	N8782
Cessna AW	PA	Bethel	GAAM	Cessna	Model AW 167	
CF-CPY	YT-C	WHors	WA			
CG-15A	NC	Charl	CHAC	Waco	Cargo Glider	
CG-15A	TX	Slato	TAMCC	Waco	Cargo Glider	
CG-2	WI	Oshko	EAAAAM	Cessna	Primary Glider 1	86, V
CG-2A	WA	Seatt	MoF	Cessna	Primary Glider	50, N178V
CG-4	NY	Garde	CoAM	Waco	Hadrian	15574
CG-4A	AZ	Tucso	PAM	Waco	Hadrian	45-14647
CG-4A	CA	Atwater	CAM	Waco	Hadrian	
CG-4A	CA	Chino	YACM	Waco	Hadrian	45-13696
CG-4A	CT	Washi	TFC	Waco	Hadrian	
CG-4A	DE	Dover	DAFB	Waco	Hadrian	
CG-4A	GA	Ft Benning	AFBNIM	Waco	Hadrian	
CG-4A Nose	IN	Columbus	ABAM	Waco	Hadrian	
CG-4A	MI	Belleville	YAF	Waco	Hadrian	43-40833
CG-4A	MI	Greenville	FFMM	Waco	Hadrian	
CG-4A	MI	Kalam	KAHM	Waco	Hadrian	45-15965
CG-4A	MI	Oscoda	YAF	Waco	Hadrian	
CG-4A	NC	Fayetteville	A&SOM	Waco	Hadrian	
CG-4A	NJ	Fairf	YAFDCWA	Waco	Hadrian	
CG-4A	NY	Elmir	NSM	Waco	Hadrian	
CG-4A	OH	Dayto	USAFM	Waco	Hadrian	45-27948
CG-4A	OR	Hubbard	LC	Waco	Hadrian	
CG-4A	TX	Midla	CAFFM	Waco	Hadrian	
CG-4A	TX	Lubbock	SWM	Waco	Hadrian	
Ch-113	NS-C	Greenwood	GMAM			
CH-135	ONT - C	Ottawa	CAM	Bell		
CH-136	ON-C	Kingston	CFBK			
CH-136	ON-C	Ottawa	CWM			
CH-136	ON-C	Trenton	RCAFMM			
CH-300	ON-C	Ottaw	CAM	Zenair	Tri-Zenith	
Chanute Glider	BC-C	Sidne	BCAM	Chanute	Glider	
Chanute Glider	CA	Chino	PoFAM	Chanute	Glider	
Chanute Glider	CT	Winds	NEAM	Chanute	Glider	
Chanute Glider	GA	Warner Robin	MoF	Chanute	Glider	
Chanute Glider	ME	Owls Head	OHTM	Chanute	Glider	
Chanute Glider	NY	Hammo	CM	Chanute	Glider	
Chanute Glider	NY	Rhine	ORA	Chanute	Glider	
Chanute Glider	WA	Seattle	MoF	Chanute	Glider	
Chanute Glider	WI	Oshko	EAAAAM	Chanute	Glider	
Chester Special	OH	Cleveland	FCAAM	Chester	Special Racer	NX-93-Y-Goon
Chester Special	WI	Oshko	EAAAAM	Chester	Special Racer	N12930, "Jeep"
Chief Oshkosh						
Chris-Tena	OR	Tillamook	TAM		Mini-Coupe	
Christen] Eagle	CA	San Carlos	HAM	Christen Industries	Eagle	
Christen Eagle	TX	Dalla	CFM	Christen Industries	Eagle	
Christen Eagle1	WI	Oshkosh	EAAAAM	Christen Industries	Eagle	
Christen Eagle1	WI	Oshkosh	EAAAAM	Christen Industries	Eagle	
Christen Eagle II	WI	Oshkosh	EAAAAM	Christen Industries	Eagle	
Christen Eagle 1F	WI	Oshkosh	EAAAAM	Christen Industries	Eagle	
Cieslak Model 2	FL	Lakel	SFAF	Cieslak		
Circa 1920	WI	Poplar Grove	VW&W	Circa		
CJ6A	FL	Miami	WOM			
CL-13	ON-C	Oshwa	OAM&IM	Canadair	Sabre	
CL-13	MB-C	Winnipeg	WRCAFB	Canadair	Sabre	
CL-13	ON-C	CFB Borden	BHT	Canadair	Sabre	
CL-13	NS	Halifax	ACAM	Canadair	Sabre	
CL-13 Sabre Mk.6	NJ	Lumberton	AVM	Canadair	Sabre Mk.6	31186
CL-13B Mk.6	ON-C	Ottawa	CAM	Canadair	Sabre	23455
CL-13B Mk.6	ON-C	Ottaw	CAM	Canadair	Sabre	23651
CL-13B Mk.6	WA	Seattle	MoF	Canadair	Sabre	23363, N8686F
CL-28(CP-107)	ON-C	Ottaw	CAM	Canadair	Argus Mk.1	10742
CL-28(CP-107)	ON-C	MtVie	MVRCAF	Canadair	Argus Mk.1	
CL-20(CP-107)	ON-C	Trenton	RCAFMM	Canadair	Argus Mk.1	10732
CL-28(CP-107)	PE-C	Summe	PEIHAS	Canadair	Argus Mk.1	20739
CL-28(CP-107) Mk I	NS	Greenwood	GMAM	Canadair	Argus	10717, 732
CL-28(CP-107)	NS	Halifax	ACAM	Canadair	Argus	
CL-84	MB-C	Winni	WCAM	Canadair	Dynavert	
CL-84	ON-C	Ottaw	CAM	Canadair	Dynavert	CX8402, Twin Engine 1970
CL-215	ON-C	Sault Ste Marie	CBHC	Canadair	Water Bomber	F-ZBBT
CL-475	AL	Ozark	USAAM	Lockheed	Rigid Rotor	56-4320, N6940C
Clark Bi Wing	ME	Owls Head	OHTM	Clark	Bi Wing	
Clemson Plane	SC	Colum	SCSM	Clemson		
CM-170R	TX	Brownsville	BIA	Fouga	Magister	N405DM, pVM 3362
CM-170	WA	Everett	MoF	Fouga	Magister	N505DM
CMQ-10A	CO	Puebl	FWAM	Boeing	Bomarc	56-4029
CNA-40	PA	Readi	MAAM	Health	Midwing	
Coffman Glider	TX	Lubbock	SWM	Coffman	Glider	
Cole Flyer	CA	Redwo	HAM	Cole	Flyer	
Coleopter	CA	Redwo	HAM	Cole	Coleopter	
Collins Aerofoil Boat	WI	Oshkosh	EAAAAM	Collins	Aerofoil	
Colt	MN	Winoma	WTI		Colt	N1985AP
Comet Glider	CA	LAnge	CMoS&I	Comet	Glider	
Command-Aire 5-C-3	AR	Little Rock	AEC	Command-Aire		

Command-Aire	FL	Lakel	SFAF	Command-Aire		N345JA, "Little Rocket"
Commonwealth	NY	Garde	CoAM	Commonwealth	Skyranger	N92972
Commonwealth 185	PA	Readi	MAAM	Commonwealth		N93248
Continental R670	NY	River	TFAC	Continental		
Convair 240	CT	Hartford	PLoA	Convair	Convair 240	see also C-131
Convair 240 (T-29)	CA	Tulare	AD	Convair	Convair 240	
Convair 240	MD	Silve	PEGF	Convair	Convair 240	
Convair 340	TX	Ladero	Airport	Convair	Convair 340	
Convair 440 (2ea)	TX	Ladero	Airport	Convair	Convair 440	
Convair 880	NV	Las Vegas	LB	Convair	Golden Arrow	Sn 23, N817TW, Model 22
Convair Airliner	CO	Erie	BJStra	Convair		
Convair Airliner	TX	Ft Worth	VFM	Convair		
Corben Super Ace	WI	Madison	MTFMDCRA	Corben	Super Ace	
Corbin Jr. Ace	NC	Hende	WNCAM	Corbin	Baby Ace	N28LW
Corbin C-1	WI	Oshko	EAAAAM	Ace	Baby Ace	N9050C, "Box Full"
Corbin D	WI	Oshko	EAAAAM	Corbin	Baby Ace	N9017C, "Box Full"
Corbin Jr. Ace	CT	Winds	NEAM	Corbin	Jr. Ace	
Corbin Jr. Ace	TX	Bealt	FCA	Corbin	Jr. Ace	
Corbin Jr. Ace	VA	Bealt	FCA	Corbin	Jr. Ace	
Covertawings A	NY	Garde	CoAM	Convertawings		N63N
Co-Z Corp	WI	Oshkosh	EAAAAM	Co-Z Development Corp	Co-Z	
CP-40	IA	Ottumwa	APM	Porterfield		529, NC18743
CP-65	FL	Lakeland	SNFAM	Porterfield	Collegiate	
CP-107	NS-C	Greenwood	GMAM			
CQM-10A	FL	FtWal	CityPark			
CR-4	VA	Marti		Crosby		
Cranwell CLA4	AB-C	Edmonton	AAM	Cranwell		
Cricket MC-10	FL	Lakeland	SNF	Cricket	MC-10	
Cricket NC-2	CA	Chino	PoFAM	Cricket	Kid Display	
Crosley	KY	Lexington	AVoK	Crosley	Moonbeam	#4, NX147N
Crosley CR-4	WI	Oshkosh	EAAAAM	Crosley	CR-4	
Crowley Hydro-Air	MD	Silve	PEGF	Crowley	Hydro-Air	
CT-114	ON-C	Ottawa	CAM		Tutor	
CT-114	ON-C	Toronto	TAM		Tutor	
CT-114	ON-C	Trenton	RCAFMM		Tutor	
CT-114	NS-C	Greenwood	GMAM		Tutor	
Culver Cadet	CA	Santa Martin	WoHAM	Culver	Cadet	
Culver Cadet	FL	Lakel	SFAF	Culver	Cadet	
Culver Cadet LCA	IA	Ottumwa	APM	Culver	Cadet	443, N-41725
Culver Cadet See PQ-14				Culver	Cadet	
Culver Dart	MN	Stewa	CCC	Culver	Dart	
Culver Dart	MO	HARM	CCC	Culver	Dart	
Culver V	KS	Liber	MAAM	Culver	Cadet	
Culver V	OK	Fredi	AAM	Culver	Cadet	
Cumulus Glider	AL	Birmingham	SmoF	Cumulus	Glider	
Curtiss	NE	Minde	HWPV	Curtiss		
Curtiss A-1	CA	San Diego	SDAM	Curtiss	Triad	
Curtiss Canuck	MI	Dearb	HFM	Curtiss	Canuck	1918
Curtiss Canuck	TX	Kingbury	VAHF	Curtiss	Canuck	1918
Curtiss E Boat	MD	Silve	PEGF	Curtiss		
Curtiss E-8.75	WI	Oshko	EAAAAM	Curtiss	Pusher	N24034, "Sweetheart"
Curtiss Golden Flyer	ND	Fargo	HIA	Curtiss	Flyer	
Curtiss H	NY	River	TFAC	Curtiss	America	OX-5 Engine
Curtiss J6-7	NY	River	TFAC	Curtiss		
Curtiss June Bug Rep	NY	Hammo	CM	Curtiss	June Bug	1908
Curtiss Junior	AR	Fayet	AAM	Curtiss	Junior	1930's
Curtiss Junior	NV	Carso	YF	Curtiss	Junior	1930's
Curtiss Little Looper	CA	San Diego	SDAM	Curtiss	Little Looper	N5599N
Curtiss MF	OH	Cleve	FCAAM	Curtiss	Seagull	1918
Curtiss MF	ON-C	Ottaw	CAM	Curtiss	Seagull	1918
Curtiss Monoplane 1912	AL	Birmi	Southe	Curtiss		
Curtiss N-9	NE	Minde	HWPV	Curtiss		
Curtiss N-9	NY	River	TFAC	Curtiss		Oxx-6 Engine
Curtiss N2C	NY	Rhine	ORA	Curtiss	Fledgling	
Curtiss NC-4	FL	Pensa	USNAM	Curtiss		A 2294 4
Curtiss O-1(F8C)	FL	Miami	WOM	Curtiss	Falcon	
Curtiss Oriole	MN	Minne	MAGM	Curtiss	Oriole	
Curtiss Oriole	NY	Hammo	CM	Curtiss	Oriole	
Curtiss Pusher D	CA	SCarl	HAM	Curtiss	Curtiss Pusher D	
Curtiss Pusher D	DC	Washi	NA&SM	Curtiss	Curtiss Pusher D	
Curtiss Pusher D	IA	Des M	ISHD	Curtiss	Curtiss Pusher D	
Curtiss Pusher D	IL	Chica	MoS&I	Curtiss	Curtiss Pusher D	
Curtiss Pusher D	KS	Topek	KSHS	Curtiss	Curtiss Pusher D	
Curtiss Pusher D	ME	OwlsH	OHTM	Curtiss	Curtiss Pusher D	
Curtiss Pusher D	NY	Hammo	CM	Curtiss	Curtiss Pusher D	
Curtiss Pusher D	NY	NYC	ISASM	Curtiss	Curtiss Pusher D	
Curtiss Pusher D	NY	Rhine	ORA	Curtiss	Curtiss Pusher D	
Curtiss Pusher D	OH	Dayto	USAFM	Curtiss	Curtiss Pusher D	
Curtiss Pusher D	OK	Oklah	AM	Curtiss	Curtiss Pusher D	
Curtiss Pusher D	OK	Oklah	KCASM	Curtiss	Curtiss Pusher D	
Curtiss Pusher D	OK	Weatherford	GTSM	Curtiss	Curtiss Pusher D	
Curtiss Pusher D	SC	MtPleasant	PN&MM	Curtiss	Curtiss Pusher D	
Curtiss Pusher D	WA	Vancouver	PAM	Curtiss	Curtiss Pusher D	
Curtiss Pusher D	WI	Milwa	MGoF	Curtiss	Curtiss Pusher D	
Curtiss Pusher D	WI	Oshko	EAAAAM	Curtiss	Curtiss Pusher D	N 37864
Curtiss Pusher D-5	AL	Birmingham	SMoF	Curtiss	Curtiss Pusher D	
Curtiss Robin	AK	Ancho	AAHM	Curtiss	Robin	
Curtiss Robin	AZ	Grand Canyon	PoFGCVA	Curtiss	Robin	
Curtiss Robin	CA	S.Mon	MoF	Curtiss	Robin	N778M, Model 50
Curtiss Robin	IA	Greenfield	IAM	Curtiss	Robin 6	
Curtiss Robin	ID	Athol	NAM	Curtiss	Robin	
Curtiss Robin	MO	Maryland Hts	HARM	Curtiss	Robin	
Curtiss Robin	NV	Niagra Falls	NAM	Curtiss	Robin	
Curtiss Robin	NV	Carso	YF	Curtiss	Robin	
Curtiss Robin	NY	Hammo	CM	Curtiss	Robin	
Curtiss Robin J-1D	VA	Sands	VAM	Curtiss	Robin	Sn 733, "Ole Miss", NC532N
Curtiss Robin 4C-1A	NC	Hende	WNCAM	Curtiss	Robin	NC563N
Curtiss Robin B	FL	Delan	OHA	Curtiss	Robin	
Curtiss Robin B1	CA	San Diego	SDAM	Curtiss	Robin	N9265
Curtiss Robin B2	WI	Oshko	EAAAAM	Curtiss	Robin	N50H
Curtiss Robin C1	CA	Chino	YACM	Curtiss	Robin	538, N384K
Curtiss Robin C1	WA	Seatt	MoF	Curtiss	Robin	628, N979K
Curtiss Robin J1	NY	Niagara Falls	NAM	Curtiss	Robin	
Curtiss Robin 50C	NY	Garden	CoAM	Curtiss	Robin	
CV-580	PA	Readi	MAAM	Convair	Prop Jet	
CW A-14D	VA	Sandston	VAM	Curtiss-Wright	Speedwing	2009, N12329

111

Model	State	City	Code	Manufacturer	Type	Notes
CW A-22	OR	McMinnville	EAM	Curtiss	Falcon	A22-1, N500G
CW X-100	MD	Silve	PEGF	Curtiss-Wright	Robin	
CW-1	CA	San Diego	SDAM	Curtiss-Wright	Junior •	NC11850
CW-1	KS	Liber	MAAM	Curtiss-Wright	Junior	
CW-1	MD	Silve	PEGF	Curtiss-Wright	Junior	
CW-1	NY	Mayvi	DA	Curtiss-Wright	Junior	
CW-1	NY	Rhine	ORA	Curtiss-Wright	Junior	
CW-1	OK	Fredi	AAM	Curtiss-Wright	Junior	
CW-12W	FL	Lakel	SFAF	Curtiss-Wright	Sport Trainer	N412W
CW-15	MO	Maryland Hts	Harm	Curtiss	Air Sedan	
CW 15-C	AZ	Tucson	PAM	Curtiss-Wright	Sedan	Man Sn 15C-2211. NC12302
CW D-15D	OR	McMinnville	EAM	Curtiss-Wright	Sedan	15-D-2214, N12314
Clyclo Crane	BC-C	Langley	CmoF&T			N240AL
D-21	AZ	Tucso	PAM	Lockheed	Mini Blackbird	Drone, 3, Carried By Blackbird
D-21	CA	Palmd	PAFB	Lockheed	Mini Blackbird	Drone
D-21	CA	Rosamond	EAFB	Lockheed	Mini Blackbird	Drone
D-21	GA	Warner Robin	MoF	Lockheed	Mini Blackbird	Drone
D-21	OH	Dayton	USAFM	Lockheed	Mini Blackbird	Drone
D-21B	WA	Seatt	MoF	Lockheed	Mini Blackbird	90-0510Drone
D-25	NY	Rhine	ORA	New Standard		
D-25	OH	Chard	CA	New Standard		
D-558-1(H-76)	FL	Pensa	USNAM	Douglas	Skystreak	37970
D-558-2	CA	Chino	PoFAM	Douglas	Skyrocket	
D-558-2	CA	Lancaster	AVC	Douglas	Skyrocket	#3 Bu 37975
D-558-2	CT	Winds	NEAM	Douglas	Skyrocket	
D-588-2	DC	Washi	NA&SM	Douglas	Skyrocket	
D-9	SK-C	MJaw	WDM	Jodel		
D.H. 1	OR	McMinnville	EAEC	de Havilland		
D.H. 1A5	AL	Ozark	USAAM	Del Mar	Whirlymite	2
D.H. 2	CA	San Diego	SDAM	de Havilland	1915 Pusher	N32DH
D.H. 2	ID	Athol	NAM	de Havilland	1915 Pusher	
D.H. 4	DC	Washi	NA&SM	de Havilland	1915 Pusher	
D.H. 4	DC	Washi	USPM	de Havilland	1915 Pusher	
D.H. 4B	OH	Cleve	FCAAM	de Havilland	1915 Pusher	
D.H. 4 Rep	VA	Quant	MCAGM	de Havilland	1915 Pusher	
D.H. 4C	WA	Everett	MoF	de Havilland	Comet	6424, N888WA, N6424
D.H. 4M-1	OR	Mc Minnville	EAEC	de Havilland	ET-4, N3258	
D.H. 4M	WA	Seatt	MoF	de Havilland	1915 Pusher	
D.H. 5	AL	Gunte	LGARFM	de Havilland	1915 Pusher	
D.H. 53	SK-C	MJaw	WDM	de Havilland	Hummingbird	
D.H. 60	AB-C	Wetas	RM	de Havilland	Moth	
D.H. 60	MT	Helen	MHSM	de Havilland	Moth 179	N617Y
D.H. 60	ON-C	Ottaw	CAM	de Havilland	Moth	
D.H. 60GM	AB-C	Wetas	RM	de Havilland	Cirrus Moth	
D.H. 60GM	BC-C	Langley	CMoF&T	de Havilland	Cirrus Moth	
D.H. 60GM	CA	San Diego	SDAM	de Havilland	Cirrus Moth	N 917M
D.H. 60M	BC-C	Langley	CMoF&T	de Havilland	Moth Trainer	
D.H. 60M	SK-C	MJaw	WDM	de Havilland	Moth Trainer	
D.H. 61	TX	Brown	RGVW-CAF	de Havilland	Super Moth	
D.H. 80A	NY	Rhine	ORA	de Havilland	Puss Moth	
D.H. 80A	ON-C	Ottaw	CAM	de Havilland	Puss Moth	
D.H. 82	CA	Santa Maria	SMMoF	de Havilland	Tiger Moth	
D.H. 82	NM	STere	WEAM	de Havilland	Tiger Moth	
D.H. 82	NY	Bayport	BA	de Havilland	Tiger Moth	
D.H. 82	OH	Dayton	USAFM	de Havilland	Tiger Moth	
D.H. 82	ON-C	Dunnville	RCAFDA	de Havilland	Tiger Moth	
D.H. 82	ON-C	Tillsonburg	CHAA	de Havilland	Tiger Moth	5030
D.H. 82	TX	Dalla	CFM	de Havilland	Tiger Moth	R5130
D.H. 82	WA	Vanco	PAM	de Havilland	Tiger Moth	
D.H. 82A	IA	Greenfield	IAM	de Havilland	Tiger Moth	Australian
D.H. 82A	ON-C	Collingwood	CCAF	de Havilland	Tiger Moth	86508, C-GSTP
D.H. 82A	WI	Oshko	EAAAAM	de Havilland	Tiger Moth	N16645, CF-IVO
D.H. 82A	PA	Toughkenamon	CFCM	de Havilland	Tiger Moth	N4808
D.H. 82C	AB-C	Calga	AMoC	de Havilland	Tiger Moth	
D.H. 82C	AB-C	Nanton	NLSAM	de Havilland	Tiger Moth	
D.H. 82C	AB-C	Wetas	RM	de Havilland	Tiger Moth	
D.H. 82C	BC-C	Langley	CMoF&T	de Havilland	Tiger Moth	
D.H. 82C	CA	Hawth	WMoF	de Havilland	Tiger Moth	
D.H. 82C	IA	Greenfield	IAM	de Havilland	Tiger Moth	Canadian
D.H. 82C	MB-C	Brand	CATPM	de Havilland	Tiger Moth	
D.H. 82C	MB-C	Winni	WCAM	de Havilland	Tiger Moth	
D.H. 82C	ME	OwlsH	OHTM	de Havilland	Tiger Moth	
D.H. 82C	ON-C	Hamilton	CWH	de Havilland	Tiger Moth	C-GCWT, 8922
D.H. 82C	ON-C	Ottaw	CAM	de Havilland	Tiger Moth	4861
D.H. 82C	SK-C	MJaw	WDM	de Havilland	Tiger Moth	
D.H. 83C	ON-C	S Ste Marie	CBHC	de Havilland	Fox Moth	CF-BNO Replica
D.H. 88 Rep	CA	Santa Martin	WoHAM	de Havilland	Comet	
D.H. 89	CA	Hayward	VAM	de Havilland	Dragon Rapide	
D.H. 89	MO	Maryland Hts	HARM	de Havilland	Dragon Rapide	
D.H. 89	ON-C	S Ste Marie	CBHC	de Havilland	Dragon Rapide	Sn 697, C-FAYE
D.H. 89A Mk.IV	WI	Oshko	EAAAAM	de Havilland	Dragon Rapide	N683DH
D.H. 89B	OH	Dayto	USAFM	de Havilland	Dragon Rapide	NR695
D.H. 94	TX	Brown	CAF-RVGW	de Havilland	Minor Moth	N940H
D.H. 94	TX	Brown	CAFRGVW	de Havilland	Moth Minor	
D.H. 98	AB-C	Calga	AMoC	de Havilland	Mosquito	
D.H. 98 Mk B35	AB-C	Edmonton	AAM	de Havilland	Mosquito	CF-HMQ, VP-189
D.H. 98	BC-C	Langley	CMoF&T	de Havilland	Mosquito	
D.H. 98	FL	Polk	FoF	de Havilland	Mosuqito	
D.H. 98	OH	Dayto	USAFM	de Havilland	Mosquito	RS709
D.H. 98	ON-C	Ottaw	CAM	de Havilland	Mosquito	KB336
D.H. 98	ON-C	Windsor	CAHS	de Havilland	Mosquito	KB336
D.H. 98	TX	Midla	CAFFM	de Havilland	Mosquito	
D.H. 98 Mk.35	MD	Silve	PEGF	de Havilland	Mosquito	
D.H. 98 Mk.35	WI	Oshkosh	EAAAAM	de Havilland	Mosquito	
D.H. U-6	CA	SanLu	CSLO	de Havilland	Beaver	
D.H. U-6	MB-C	Winni	WCAM	de Havilland	Beaver	
D.H. U-6A	CA	Atwater	CAM	de Havilland	Beaver	
D.H. U-6A	CA	Rosam	EAFB	de Havilland	Beaver	53-2781
D.H. U-6A	CO	Denve	JWDAS	de Havilland	Beaver	
D.H. U-6A	CT	Winds	NEAM	de Havilland	Beaver	
D.H. U-6A	IL	Sugar Grove	ACM	de Havilland	Beaver	153678
D.H. U-6A	MO	SLoui	SLDPA	de Havilland	Beaver	
D.H. U-6A	ON-C	Ottaw	CAM	de Havilland	Beaver	
D.H. U-6A	ON-C	Sault Ste Marie	CBHC	Jodel	Beaver	
D.H. U-6A	VA	FtEus	USATM	de Havilland	Beaver	
D.H. U-6A	GA	Warner Robin	MoF	de Hallivand	Beaver	26087

Model		City		Manufacturer	Name	Notes
D.H. U-6A	OH	Dayto	USAFM	de Hallivand	Beaver	51-16501
D.H. U-6A(L-20A)	AZ	Tucso	PAM	de Havilland	Beaver	55-4595, N43906
D.H. U-6A(YU)	AL	Ozark	USAAM	de Havilland	Beaver	51-6263
D.H U-6A6D(L-20A)	GA	Warner Robin	MoF	de Havilland	Beaver	52-6087, N30AR
D.H U-6A(L-20A)	OK	Oklah	45IDM	de Havilland	Beaver	56-0367
D.H U-6A(L-20A)	CA	Atwater	CAM	de Havilland	Beaver	
D.H U-6A(L-20A)	FL	Clear	FMAM	de Havilland	Beaver	
D.H U-6A(L-20A)	PA	Readi	MAAM	De Havilland	Beaver	52- 6112, N4957
D.H.100	AB-C	Calga	AMoC	de Havilland	Vampire	
D.H.100	BC-C	Langley	CMoF&T	de Havilland	Vampire	N68600
D.H.100	FL	Kissi	FTWAM	de Havilland	Vampire	
D.H.100	MB-C	Winni	WCAM	de Havilland	Vampire	
D.H.100	ON-C	Hamilton	CWH	de Havilland	Vampire	
D.H.100	OR	Mc Minnville	EABC	de Havilland	Vampire	IB-1686, N174LA
D.H.100	WA	Seatt	MoF	de Havilland	Vampire	FLDH1367, N25776
D.H.100 Mk 35	WI	Oshko	EAAAAM	de Havilland	Vampire	N11926
D.H.100 Mk III	AZ	Grand	PoFGCVA	de Havilland	Vampire	17018
D.H.100 Mk VI	CA	Chino	PoFAM	de Havilland	Vampire	18
D.H.100 Mk. VI	ON-C	Ottaw	CAM	de Havilland	Vampire	17074, AAP
D.H.100 Mk.IIc	IN	India	IMoMH	de Havilland	Vampire	
D.H.C.-1	AB-C	Wetas	RM	de Havilland	Chipmunk	
D.H.C.-1	AZ	Tucso	PAM	de Havilland	Chipmunk	N48273
D.H.C.-1	KS	Ashla	HKAM	de Havilland	Chipmunk	
D.H.C.-1	ON-C	Hamilton	CWH	de Havilland	Chipmunk	B-2-S5, 035
D.H.C.-1	ON-C	Windsor	CAHS	de Havilland	Chipmunk	
D.H.C.-1	PA	Tough	CFCM	de Havilland	Chipmunk	
D.H.C.-1	SK-C	MJaw	WDM	de Havilland	Chipmunk	
D.H.C.-1A	MD	Silve	PEGF	de Havilland	Chipmunk	
D.H.C.-1B2	ON-C	Ottaw	CAM	de Havilland	Chipmunk	18070
D.H.C.-1B-2	ON-C	Trenton	RCAFMM	de Havilland	Chipmunk	
D.H.C.-1B2	WI	Oshko	EAAAAM	de Havilland	Chipmunk	N 1114V
D.H.C - 2 Mk.I	ON-C	Sault Ste Marie	CBHC	de Havilland	Beaver	Sn 2, CF-OBS
D.H.C - 2 Mk.II	ON-C	Sault Ste Marie	CBHC	de Havilland	Beaver	Sn 1650TB28, C-FOEK
D.H.C - 2 Mk.II	ON-C	Sault Ste Marie	CBHC	de Havilland	Beaver	Sn 1525TB1, C-FPSM
D.H.C.-3	MB-C	Winni	WCAM	de Havilland	Otter	9408
D.H.C.-3	ON-C	Ottaw	CAM	de Havilland	Otter	9408
D.H.C.-3	ON-C	Sault Ste Marie	CBHC	de Havilland	Otter	Sn 369, C-FODU
D.H.C.-3(U-1)NU-1B	FL	Pensa	USNAM	de Havilland	Otter	3824, 144672, F 699
D.H.C.-3(U-1A)	AL	Ozark	USAAM	de Havilland	Otter	
D.H.C.-3(U-1A)	VA	FtEus	USATM	de Havilland	Otter	57-6135
D.H.C.-5	ON-C	MtVie	MVRCAF	de Havilland	Buffalo	
D.H.C.-6	MT	Misso	AFDSC	de Havilland	Twin Otter	
D.H.C.-6	OH	N Canton	MAM	de Havilland	Twin Otter	
D.H.C.-6	ON-C	Ottaw	CAM	de Havilland	Twin Otter	
D.H.C.-6-300	CA	Carls	CAJM	de Havilland	Twin Otter	
DA-1W	IN	Richmond	WCHM	Davis		
DA-1W	NY	Rhine	ORA	Davis		
Daedalus 88	MD	Silver Hill	PEGF	Daedalus		
Dagling Primary 1	BC-C	Langley	CMoF&T	Dagling	Primary Glider	
Dart	OH	Dayton	USAFM	Dart	Aerial Target	
D.A.S.H.	SC	MtPleasant	PPM	Drone Anti Sub Helio		
DC-2	WA	Seattle	MoF	Douglas	Dakota	1368, N1934D
DC-3 *See C-47*				Douglas	Dakota	
DC-3	AB-C	Calga	AMoC	Douglas	Dakota	
DC-3	AB-C	Harbor Grace	City	Douglas	Dakota	
DC-3	AL	Troy	TMA	Douglas	Dakota	
DC-3	BC-C	Langley	CMoF&T	Douglas	Dakota	
DC-3	CA	Ames	BA	Douglas	Dakota	
DC-3	CA	Chino	YAM	Douglas	Dakota	
DC-3	CA	SClem	ACA	Douglas	Dakota	11693, N7500A
DC-3	CA	SLean	OSA	Douglas	Dakota	N97H, 33613
DC-3	CO	Denver	WOtR	Douglas	Dakota	
DC-3	CT	Winds	NEAM	Douglas	Dakota	"Taino Air"
DC-3	DC	Washi	NA&SM	Douglas	Dakota	
DC-3 (2ea)	FL	Marci	SFSV	Douglas	Dakota	NC28341, Ship 41
DC-3	GA	Atlanta	DATHM	Douglas	Dakota	
DC-3	GA	Calhoun	MAM	Douglas	Dakota	
DC-3A	GA	Dougl	BA	Douglas	Dakota	42-92606, N99FS
DC-3	GA	Griff	AAC	Douglas	Dakota	2239, N28AA
DC-3	IL	Bloom	PAM	Douglas	Dakota	N763A, "Ozark Airlines"
DC-3	IL	Grant	CityPark	Douglas	Dakota	
DC-3	IL	St. C	SCA	Douglas	Dakota	
DC-3	KS	Liber	MAAM	Douglas	Dakota	
DC-3	KY	Louis	BF	Douglas	Dakota	
DC-3(CC-129)	MB-C	Brandon	CATPM	Douglas	Dakota	
DC-3	MB-C	Winni	WCAM	Douglas	Dakota	12949
DC-3	MD	Hager	HRegAirP	Douglas	Dakota	
DC-3	MN	Minneapolis	MAG	Douglas	Dakota	
DC-3	MI	Dearb	HFM	Douglas	Dakota	Northwest Airlines
DC-3-362	MO	Kansas City	AHM	Douglas	Dakota	SN3294, NC1945
DC-3	MO	Missoula	MMF	Douglas	Dakota	
DC-3	MS	Petal	MWHMM	Douglas	Dakota	
DC-3	MT	Misso	AFDSC	Douglas	Dakota	
DC-3	NC	Charlotte	CAM	Douglas	Dakota	53-R1830 , 4900, "Piedmont Airlines"
DC-3	ND	Fargo	FAM	Douglas	Dakota	0-93800
DC-3	NF-C	Harbour Grace		Douglas	Dakota	6179
DC-3	NM	STere	WEAM	Douglas	Dakota	
DC-3	NV	Las Vegas	LBAHSM	Douglas	Dakota	3252, N19968, Cockpit Only, "Trans-Texas Airways"
DC-3	OK	Fredi	AAM	Douglas	Dakota	
DC-3	ON-C	Hamilton	CWH	Douglas	Dakota	C-GDAK, KN456, Z
DC-3	ON-C	Ottaw	CAM	Douglas	Dakota	
DC-3	OR	Mc Minnville	EAEC	Douglas	Dakota	1910, N16070, "United Airlines"
DC-3	TX	Brown	RGVW-CAF	Douglas	Dakota	
DC-3	TX	FWort	AACRS	Douglas	Dakota	
DC-3 (3ea)	TX	Ladero	Airport	Douglas	Dakota	
DC-3	WA	Seattle	MoF	Douglas	Dakota	2245, N138D, NC91008, "Alaska Airlines"
DC-3	WA	Vancouver	PAM	Douglas	Dakota	
DC-3	WI	Oshko	BFBO	Douglas	Dakota	
DC-3	WI	Oshko	EAAAAM	Douglas	Dakota	N7772
DC-3	YK-C	White Horse	YTM	Douglas	Dakota	20833 C- GZOF, 4665, CF- CUG 9891, 13070 CF- IMA
DC-3	YK-C	White Horse	WA	Douglas	Dakota	CF-CPY
DC-3 Cockpit	CA	Chino	PoFAM	Douglas	Dakota	
DC-3 Cockpit	MD	Silve	PEGF	Douglas	Dakota	
DC-3 Cockpit	NF-C	Gander	NAAM	Douglas	Dakota	
DC-3 Fuselage	FL	Polk	FoF	Douglas	Dakota	
DC-3 Parts	CO	Denve	JWDAS	Douglas	Dakota	

Model	State	City	Code	Manufacturer	Type	Notes
DC-3(R4D-1)	CA	S.Mon	MoF	Douglas	Dayliner	"Chas S Jones"
DC-3C	IN	Columbus	RA	Douglas	Dakota	19366, N141JR, 41, CFFCUC
DC-3C	IN	Columbus	RA	Douglas	Dakota	20550, N139JR, 40, Parts Missing, "Miss Daisy"
DC-3C	IN	Columbus	RA	Douglas	Dakota	26815, N140JR, 40
DC-3C(C-47A)	IN	Columbus	RA	Douglas	Dakota	32845, N142JR, 42-100903
DC-3C	TX	Midla	CAFFM	Douglas	Dakota	
DC-4M	ON-C	Ottaw	CAM	Canadair	North Star	17515
DC-6(C-118)	CA	SRosa	PCAM	Cessna		
DC-6	NE	Minde	HWPV	Cessna		1929
DC-6B	MI	Belleville	YAF	Douglas		44913, N4913R, "Yankee Volunteer"
DC-7	DC	Washi	NA&SM	Douglas		
DC-7	MN	St Paul	MA&SM	Douglas		Looking for a Museum
DC-7	OH	Newbu	WASAC	Douglas		44924
DC-7B	AZ	Tucso	PAM	Douglas		N 51701
DC-8-52	CA	LAnge	CMoS&I	McDonnell-Douglas	Jet Trader	
DC-8-55	MI	Oscoda	YAM	McDonnell-Douglas	Jet Trader	45856, N6161C
DC-65	MI	Saginaw	YAF	Taylorcraft	Tandem	L-4874, N48102, "Yankee Hopper"
DC-65	NJ	Fairfield	YAF	Taylorcraft	Tandem	L-5041, N9666N
DeLackner	VA	FtEus	USATM	DeLackner	Aerocycle	
Damenjoz	ME	OwlsH	OHTM	Demenjos	Old Orchard Beach	
Deperdussin	ME	OwlsH	OHTM	Deperdussin		
Deperdussin	NV	Carso	YF	Deperdussin		
Deperdussin	NY	Rhine	ORA	Deperdussin		
Deperdussin Model C	CA	San Diego	SDAM	Deperdussin		
Dewoitine D.26	FL	Polk	FoF	Dewoitine		
DG-1	FL	Lakeland	SNFAM		DG-1	
DGA	CA	Santa Paula	SPAA	Howard	Nightingale	
DGA	ND	Wahpe	TSA	Howard	DGA	
DGA	TX	C Christi	USS Lexi	Howard		
DGA	TX	Denton	H10FM	Howard		
DGA	WA	Seatt	MoF	Howard	Nightingale	559, N52947
DGA 3	OH	Cleveland	FCAAM	Howard	Racer	"Pete"
DGA 5	CA	Chino	PoFAM	Howard	Racer	"Ike"
DGA 5	OH	Fresno		Howard	Racer	"Ike"
DGA 6	AR	Fayet	AAM	Howard	Racer	NR273Y, "Mister Mulligan"
DGA 1-A	FL	Lakel	SFAF	DGA	Sportfire	N37835
DGA 11	AR	Fayet	AAM	Howard		NC18207
DGA 15	BC-C	Langley	CMoF&T	Howard	Nightingale	
DGA 18K	AR	Fayet	AAM	Howard	Nightingale	N39668
DGA-15	MB-C	Winni	WCAM	Howard	DGA	
DGA-15P	CA	S.Mon	MoF	Howard	Nightingale	
Diamond 1910	CA	San Carlos	HAM	Diamond	Bi Plane	
Diamond Katana	ON-C	Kitchener	KWRA	Diamond	Katana	
Diamond Katana	ON-C	London	AH	Diamond	Katana	
Diamond Katana	ON-C	London	LA	Diamond	Katana	
Dickerson	NY	Rhine	ORA	Diskerson	Primary Glider	
Do 27	WA	Everett	MoF	Dornier		
Do 335	MD	Silve	PEGF	Dornier	Pfeil	
Doman	CA	Redwo	HAM	Doman	Doman	
Dormoy Bathtub	PA	Bethel	GAAM	Dormoy	Bathtub	
Double Eagle II	MD	Silve	PEGF	Anderson	Double Eagle	
Double Eagle V	WI	Oshko	EAAAAM	Anderson	Double Eagle V	
DQ-14	MD	Silve	PEGF	Radioplane		
DQ-2A/TDD-1	MD	Silve	PEGF	Radioplane		
Driggers A 891H	WI	Oshko	EAAAAM	Driggers		"Sunshine Girl III"
Drone (Jet)	PA	Middl	CityPark			
DSI/NASA RPRV	MD	Silve	PEGF			
DSP Satellite	OH	Dayton	USAFM		Satellite	
Dumont Demoiselle	NV	Carso	YF	Dumont	Demoiselle	
Dumont Demoiselle	NY	NYC	ISASM	Dumont	Demoiselle	
Durand Mk.V	WA	Seatt	MoF	Durand		5, N444JF
DWC	AK	Palme	MOAT&I	Douglas	World Cruiser	"Seattle"
DWC	DC	Washi	NA&SM	Douglas	World Cruiser	"Chicago"
DWC-4	CA	S.Mon	MoF	Douglas	World Cruiser	"New Orleans"
Dyndivic Sport	CT	Winds	NEAM	Dyndivic	Sport	
E-1	VA	Sands	VAM	Standard		
E-1	WI	Oshko	EAAAAM	Standard		N3783C
E-1B	PA	Willo	WGNAS	Grumman	Tracer	146034
E-1B	SC	MtPleasant	PPM	Grumman	Tracer	147225
E-2	BC-C	Sidne	BCAM	Eastman	Sea Rover	Float Plane
E-2	IL	Harva	BA	Taylor	Cub	
E-2	NC	Hende	WNCAM	Taylor	Cub	NC12644
E-2	NJ	Lumberton	AVM	Taylor	Cub	
E-2	NY	Niagra Falls	NAM	Taylor	Cub	
E-2	ON-C	Ottaw	CAM	Taylor	Cub	NC13146
E-2	PA	Bethel	GAAM	Taylor	Cub	
E-2	VA	Sandston	VAM	Taylorcraft	Cub	Sn 33, N15045
E-2	WI	Oshko	EAAAAM	Taylor	Cub	N15045
E-2A	CA	Chino	YAM	Grumman	Hawkeye	
E-2B	FL	Pensa	USNAM	Grumman	Hawkeye	150540
E-2B	ME	Lexin	PNAT&EM	Grumman	Hawkeye	
E-2C	CA	San Diego	SDACM	Grumman	Hawkeye	
E-2C	GA	Marietta	NASA	Grumman	Hawkeye	AA, 600, VAW-125
E-2C	NV	Fallon	NASF	Grumman	Hawkeye	949603, NSAW
E-2C	VA	Norfo	NNAS	Grumman	Hawkeye	AA, 600, VAW-125
EAA Acro-Sport	FL	Lakeland	SNF	EAA	Acro-Sport	
EAA Biplane	ND	Grand	JBC	EAA	Biplane	
EAA P-9 Pober Pixie	OK	Fredi	AAM	EAA	Pober Pixie	
Eagle Eye	AR	Little Rock	AEC	Bell	UASV	
Eastern Rotorcraft Z-9	PA	Willow	WGNAS	Eastern	Rotorcraft	
Easy Riser	AZ	Tucso	PAM	Easy Riser		
Easy Riser	CA	Chino	PoFAM	Easy Riser	Hang Glider	
Easy Riser	IA	Greenfield	IAM		Glider	
Eberhart Target Glider	MD	Silve	PEGF	Eberhart	Drone	
EC1 Aircoupe	PA	Readi	MAAM	Elias	Aircoupe	
Ecker Flying Boat	DC	Washi	NA&SM	Ecker	Flying Boat	
Eipper Cumulus	WA	Seatt	MoF	Eipper	Cumlus	
Eipper Cumulus 10	MD	Silve	PEGF	Eipper	Cumlus	
Eipper MX-1	WI	Oshko	EAAAAM	Eipper	Quicksilver	
Eipper MXL-II	TX	Dallas	FoF	Eipper	Quicksilver	N87MX
EJ-4(F-1E)	FL	Pensa	USNAM	North American	Fury	N139486, 139486, NM 208, VA-192
Elemdord A-1	WI	Oshko	EAAAAM	Elemdorf	Jackrabbit	NX264Y
Emigh Trojan	NY	River	RE	Emigh	Trojan	1951
Enstrom F28A	PA	Wchester	AHM	Enstrom		
Epp's Monoplane	FL	Tittusville	VACM	Epp	Monoplane	
Epp's Monoplane	GA	Warner Robin	MoF	Epp	Monoplane	

114

Ercoupe 67	NE	Minde	HWPV	Erco	Ercoupe	
Ercoupe 415 F-1	AL	Birmi	Southe	Forney	Ercoupe	
Ercoupe 415	MD	College Park	CPAM	Erco	Ercoupe	NC93942
Ercoupe 415	MD	Silve	PEGF	Erco	Ercoupe	
Ercoupe 415	ND	Minot	DTAM	Erco	Ercoupe	
Ercoupe 415	MN	Winoma	WTI	Erco	Ercoupe	N3920H
Ercoupe 415	NY	Mayvi	DA	Erco	Ercoupe	
Ercoupe 415	OH	Dayto	USAFM	Erco	Ercoupe	86
Ercoupe 415	WI	Fond du Lac	WAM	Erco	Ercoupe	
Ercoupe 415C	AZ	Tucson	PAM	Erco	Ercoupe	Sn 1188, N78X / N93865
Ercoupe 415C	KS	Liber	MAAM	Erco	Ercoupe	
Ercoupe 415C	MI	Kalam	KAHM	Erco	Ercoupe	1251
Ercoupe 415C	NY	Geneseo	1941AG	Erco	Ercoupe	
Ercoupe 415CD	NC	Hendersonville	WNCAM	Erco	Ercoupe	
Ercoupe 415C	NS	Halifax	ACAM	Erco	Ercoupe	
Ercoupe 415C	OK	Fredi	AAM	Erco	Ercoupe	
Ercoupe 415C	WA	Seatt	MoF	Erco	Ercoupe	3569, N2944H
Ercoupe 415C	WI	Oshko	EAAAAM	Erco	Ercoupe	NC28961
Ercoupe 415D	CA	Chino	YACM	Erco	Ercoupe	4218, N3593H
Ercoupe 415D	CA	Sands	VAM	Erco	Ercoupe	Sn 1766
Ercoupe 415G	PA	Readi	MAAM	Erco	Ercoupe	
Ercoupe 415G	WI	Oshko	EAAAAM	Erco	Ercoupe	N94898
Etrich Taube	ME	OwlsH	OHTM	Etrich	Taube	
Eurocopter Djinn SO.1221	PA	Wchester	AHM	Eurocopter		
Excelsior Gondola	OH	Dayton	Usafm	Excelsior	Gondola	
Experimental	KS	Topek	KSHS		Helicopter	
Explorer II	DC	Washi	NA&SM	Explorer	Gondola	
Extra 260	MD	Silve	PEGF	Extra		
Extra 300L	IL	Springfield	ACM	Extra		
Ezekiel Airship Rep	TX	Pitts	Restrant	Ezekiel	Airship	
F- 4	AL	Birmi	Southe	McDonnell	Phantom II	
F- 4	AR	FSmit	EANG	McDonnell	Phantom II	
F- 4F	AZ	Mesa	CFM	McDonnell	Phantom II	3016, VF-21, Tail NE, 2118367 SH, VMFAT-101
F- 4	CA	Fresn	FANG	McDonnell	Phantom II	
F- 4	CA	Mojav	MA	McDonnell	Phantom II	
F- 4 Cockpit	CA	Riverside	MFAM	McDonnell	Phantom II	
F- 4	CO	Cannon	CA	McDonnell	Phantom II	
F- 4	FL	KeyWe	NASKW	McDonnell	Phantom II	
F- 4	GA	Pooler	M8AFHM	McDonnell	Phantom II	64-815
F- 4	HI	Kaneohe	MB	McDonnell	Phantom II	
F- 4	IL	Sprin	SMAM	McDonnell	Phantom II	SI 468
F- 4	IN	Columbus	ABAM	McDonnell	Phantom II	64844 BA
F- 4C	IN	Fairmount	ALP313	McDonnell	Phantom II	63-7623
F- 4	IN	FtWay	IANG	McDonnell	Phantom II	
F- 4	MD	Andrews	APG	McDonnell	Phantom II	AF66661
F- 4	MD	Lexin	PNA&EM	McDonnell	Phantom II	
F- 4	MD	Middl	GLMAM	McDonnell	Phantom II	
F- 4	MI	Sterling Hts	FHCMP	McDonnell	Phantom II	66-8755
F- 4	MN	Dulut	DIA	McDonnell	Phantom II	
F- 4	NC	CPoin	CPMB	McDonnell	Phantom II	
F- 4	NJ	Wrightstown	McGAFB	McDonnell	Phantom II	67-0270
F- 4	NV	Fallon	NASF	McDonnell	Phantom II	
F- 4	NV	Fallon	NASF	McDonnell	Phantom II	
F- 4Cockppit	OH	Daton	USAFM	McDonnell	Phantom II	
F- 4	OH	N Canton	MAPS	McDonnell	Phantom II	
F- 4	OR	Klamath Falls	OANG	McDonnell	Phantom II	37479
F- 4	SC	McEnt	MEANGB	McDonnell	Phantom II	
F- 4	TN	Athen	VFW 5146	McDonnell	Phantom II	
F- 4	TX	Bastr	VFW 2527	McDonnell	Phantom II	
F- 4	TX	C Christi	USS Lexi	McDonnell	Phantom II	DC 3 VMFA-122
F- 4	TX	Dalla	DNAS	McDonnell	Phantom II	
F- 4	TX	Manch	VFW 3377	McDonnell	Phantom II	
F- 4	TX	Slato	TAMCC	McDonnell	Phantom II	
F- 4	WA	Seattle	MoF	McDonnell	Phantom II	45-3016, 64-0776, NE 211, VF-21, "NAVY" Rear Fuse
F- 4	WA	Tacoma	MAFB	McDonnell	Phantom II	
F- 4	WI	Milwa	MANG	McDonnell	Phantom II	
F- 4 Cockpit	ME	Lexin	PNAT&EM	McDonnell	Phantom II	
F- 4 Cockpit	TX	C Christi	CCMOS&H	McDonnell	Phantom II	
F- 4 Cockpit	WI	Kenos	KMM	McDonnell	Phantom II	
F- 4(AF)	MI	Kalam	KAHM	McDonnell	Phantom II	74-0658
F- 4A	CO	Puebl	FWAM	McDonnell	Phantom II	
F- 4A	CT	Winds	NEAM	McDonnell	Phantom II	
F- 4A	FL	Clear	FMAM	McDonnell	Phantom II	
F- 4A	FL	Kissimmee	FTWAM	McDonnell	Phantom II	
F- 4A	MD	Silve	PEGF	McDonnell	Phantom II	"Sageburner"
F- 4A	NJ	Lumberton	AVM	McDonnell	Phantom II	148273
F- 4A	RI	NKing	QAM	McDonnell	Phantom II	
F- 4A	TX	C Christi	USS Lexi	McDonnell	Phantom II	
F- 4A	VA	Quantico	MCAGM	McDonnell	Phantom II	143388
F- 4B	CT	Winds	NEAM	McDonnell	Phantom II	148407
F- 4B	IL	Sugar Grove	ACM	McDonnell	Phantom II	
F- 4B	IL	Linco	HIFM	McDonnell	Phantom II	148400
F- 4B	NC	Hickory	HRA	McDonnell	Phantom II	
F- 4B	NY	Horseheads	NWM	McDonnell	Phantom II	152256, VF-21, NE2219
F- 4B	TX	San A	LAFB	McDonnell	Phantom II	149421
F- 4B	VA	VBeac	ONAS	McDonnell	Phantom II	7920, VF- 84
F- 4B(RF)	CA	Ridgecrest	CLNWC	McDonnell	Phantom II	
F- 4B(RF)	CA	Miramar	FLAM	McDonnell	Phantom II	RF, VMFP-3
F- 4B(RF)	NC	Havelock	HTC	McDonnell	Phantom II	
F- 4C	AK	Ancho	EAFB	McDonnell	Phantom II	
F- 4C	AL	Huntsville	AC	McDonnell	Phantom II	
F- 4C	AL	Mobile	BMP	McDonnell	Phantom II	637487
F- 4C	AL	Montg	MAFB	McDonnell	Phantom II	
F- 4C	AZ	Tucso	PAM	McDonnell	Phantom II	64-673
F- 4C	CA	Victorville	GAFB	McDonnell	Phantom II	
F- 4C	CA	Chino	YAM	McDonnell	Phantom II	
F- 4C	CA	Fairf	TAFB	McDonnell	Phantom II	
F- 4C	CA	San Luis	CSLO	McDonnell	Phantom II	64-0827
F- 4C	CA	Riverside	MFAM	McDonnell	Phantom II	63-7693
F- 4C	CA	Rosam	EAFB	McDonnell	Phantom II	63-7407
F- 4C	CA	Sacra	McCelAFB	McDonnell	Phantom II	64-705, MI40706
F- 4C	CA	Sacra	SWAM	McDonnell	Phantom II	
F- 4C	CA	SRosa	PCAM	McDonnell	Phantom II	
F- 4C	CO	CSpri	EJPSCM	McDonnell	Phantom II	64-0799
F- 4C	CO	CSpri	USAFA	McDonnell	Phantom II	
F- 4C	CO	Denve	WOR	McDonnell	Phantom II	

F- 4C	FL	Panam	TAFB	McDonnell	Phantom II	
F- 4C	FL	Shali	USAFAM	McDonnell	Phantom II	40-813, XC
F- 4C	GA	Marie	DAFB	McDonnell	Phantom II	
F- 4C	GA	Warner Robin	MoF	McDonnell	Phantom II	63-7465
F- 4C	HI	Oahu	HAFB	McDonnell	Phantom II	63-15796
F- 4C	HI	Oahu	HANG	McDonnell	Phantom II	40792, Blue
F- 4C	HI	Oahu	HAFBFU	McDonnell	Phantom II	64-00793
F- 4C	HI	Oahu	HAFBFU	McDonnell	Phantom II	66-07540
F- 4C	HI	Oahu	BPNAS	McDonnell	Phantom II	1522291
F- 4C	IA	Marsh	CIAVM AM	McDonnell	Phantom II	
F- 4C	IN	Peru	GAFB	McDonnell	Phantom II	64-783
F- 4C	IN	Terre Haute	THANG	McDonnell	Phantom II	63-565
F- 4C	LA	N.Orl	FoJBMM	McDonnell	Phantom II	
F- 4C-19-MC	MI	Belleville	YAF	McDonnell	Phantom II	63-7555
F- 4C	MI	Mt Clemens	SMAM	McDonnell	Phantom II	63-7534
F- 4C	NC	Golds	SJAFB	McDonnell	Phantom II	64-770 "Jeannie"
F- 4C	ND	Castl	CA	McDonnell	Phantom II	
F- 4C	NM	Alamo	HAFB	McDonnell	Phantom II	
F- 4C	NV	LasVe	NAFB	McDonnell	Phantom II	
F- 4C	NY	Niaga	NFANG	McDonnell	Phantom II	
F- 4C	OH	Newar	NAFM	McDonnell	Phantom II	
F- 4C	OH	Daton	USAFM	McDonnell	Phantom II	
F- 4C	SC	Charl	CAFB	McDonnell	Phantom II	
F- 4C	SC	Citid	CC	McDonnell	Phantom II	
F- 4C	TN	Arnol	AAFS	McDonnell	Phantom II	
F- 4C	TX	Austi	AGDTAG	McDonnell	Phantom II	
F- 4C	TX	Austi	BAFB	McDonnell	Phantom II	
F- 4C	TX	Dalla	CFM	McDonnell	Phantom II	
F- 4C	TX	Dalla	FoF	McDonnell	Phantom II	64-0777, Tail AT, AF-477 Sq, Red Star
F- 4C	TX	Wichi	SAFB	McDonnell	Phantom II	
F- 4C	WA	Seatt	MoF	McDonnell	Phantom II	
F- 4C	WI	CDoug	WNGML&M	McDonnell	Phantom II	
F- 4C(RF)	AR	Littl	LRAFB	MCDonnell	Phantom II	64-0748, 389TFS/366TFW
F- 4C(RF)	CA	Riverside	MFAM	McDonnell	Phantom II	63-7746
F- 4C(RF) Cockpit	CA	Riverside	MFAM	McDonnell	Phantom II	Weapons System Trainer
F- 4C(NF)	CA	Rosam	EAFB	McDonnell	Phantom II	64-1004
F- 4C(RF)	FL	Shali	USAFAM	McDonnell	Phantom II	67-452 ET
F- 4C(RF)	IL	Ranto	OCAM	McDonnell	Phantom II	62-12201
F- 4C(RF)	KY	Louisville	LANGS	McDonnell	Phantom II	64-081
F- 4C(RF)	MN	Minne	MAGM	McDonnell	Phantom II	64-61
F- 4C(RF)	MN	Minne	MAGM	McDonnell	Phantom II	64-665
F- 4C(RF)	NE	Lincoln	LANGB	McDonnell	Phantom II	64-0998, Tail Nebraska AF 64-998
F- 4C(RF)	OH	Dayto	USAFM	McDonnell	Phantom II	64-1047
F- 4C(RF)	OH	Lockb	RANGB	McDonnell	Phantom II	65-903
F- 4C(RF)	SC	Sumte	SAFB	McDonnell	Phantom II	
F- 4C(RF)	TX	LV	LVAM	McDonnell	Phantom II	
F- 4C(RF)	TX	San A	KAFB	McDonnell	Phantom II	
F- 4C(RF)	UT	Ogden	HAFBM	McDonnell	Phantom II	
F- 4C(RF)	VA	Hampt	APM	McDonnell	Phantom II	69-0372, ZZ
F- 4D	FL	Homes	HAFB	McDonnell	Phantom II	
F- 4D	KS	Liber	MAAM	McDonnell	Phantom II	
F- 4D	KS	Topek	CAM	McDonnell	Phantom II	268
F- 4D	KS	Wichi	K&HAP	McDonnell	Phantom II	66-0271
F- 4D	MA	Stow	BCF	McDonnell	Phantom II	
F- 4D	MN	Minne	MAGM	McDonnell	Phantom II	
F- 4D	ND	Fargo	FANG	McDonnell	Phantom II	
F- 4D	NY	Scotia	ESAM	McDonnell	Phantom II	65-626
F- 4D	OH	Enon	VFW	McDonnell	Phantom II	67-5550
F- 4D	OH	Fairborn	WPMCH	McDonnell	Phantom II	66-7554, "City of Fairborn", Tail: DO AF 66554
F- 4D	OH	Fairborn	WPMCH	McDonnell	Phantom II	66-7626, "City of Dayton, Tail: DO AF 66626
F- 4D	TX	Abile	DLAP	McDonnell	Phantom II	65-0796
F- 4D	TX	FWort	NASFWJRB	McDonnell	Phantom II	
F- 4D	TX	Wichi	SAFB	McDonnell	Phantom II	
F- 4D	VT	Burli	BANG	McDonnell	Phantom II	
F- 4D-1	AZ	Tucso	PAM	McDonnell	Phantom II	134748
F- 4D-1	VA	VBeac	ONAS	McDonnell	Phantom II	134950, 101, VF-41
F- 4D-1 Fuse	TN	Memph	LS	McDonnell	Phantom II	
F- 4D(XF)	CA	Ridgecrest	CLNWC	McDonnell	Phantom II	
F- 4E	AZ	Tucso	PAM	McDonnell	Phantom II	66-329
F- 4E	CA	Riverside	MFAM	McDonnell	Phantom II	68-0382
F- 4E	FL	Tampa	MAFB	McDonnell	Phantom II	
F- 4E	MO	SLoui	MOANGSLL	McDonnell	Phantom II	
F- 4E	NC	Golds	SJAFB	McDonnell	Phantom II	74-649
F- 4E	OH	Cleveland	BLA	McDonnell	Phantom II	Thunder Birds #1
F- 4E	TX	FWort	NASFWJRB	McDonnell	Phantom II	
F- 4E	TX	Wichi	SAFB	McDonnell	Phantom II	
F- 4E	VA	Hampt	VA&SC	McDonnell	Phantom II	67-392, JJ
F- 4E(NF)	MO	Monet	CityPark	McDonnell	Phantom II	
F- 4E(NF)	NV	Battl	BMAM	McDonnell	Phantom II	66-286, ED
F- 4E(RF)	MN	Minne	MAGM	McDonnell	Phantom II	
F- 4E(YF)	CA	Rosam	EAFB	McDonnell	Phantom II	
F- 4E(YF)	OH	Dayto	USAFM	McDonnell	Phantom II	62-12200
F- 4F	IL	Urban	RFIA	McDonnell	Phantom II	
F- 4F	MD	Annap	USNAM	McDonnell	Phantom II	
F- 4F	OR	Tillamook	TAM	McDonnell	Phantom II	
F- 4G	OH	Dayto	USAFM	McDonnell	Phantom II	64-829
F- 4J	CA	Chino	YAM	McDonnell	Phantom II	
F- 4J	FL	Tittusville	VACM	McDonnell	Phantom II	
F- 4J	MD	Lexington	PRNAM	McDonnell	Phantom II	153071, Side # 100, SD Tail
F- 4J	MO	Sikeston	SVP	McDonnell	Phantom II	153839, Tail NG (Black Eagle), Side 102, "USS Enterprise
F- 4J	NY	NYC	ISASM	McDonnell	Phantom II	
F- 4J	OH	Cleveland	BLA	McDonnell	Phantom II	153812, Blue Angels #1
F- 4J	SC	Mt Pleasant	PPM	McDonnell	Phantom II	153077, VMFA 333, USS America, Nose 202
F- 4J(YF)	AZ	Tucso	PAM	McDonnell	Phantom II	151497
F- 4N	AL	Birmingham	SMoF	McDonnell	Phantom II	152996
F- 4N	AZ	Phoen	LAFB	McDonnell	Phantom II	
F- 4N	AZ	Tucso	DMAFB	McDonnell	Phantom II	
F- 4N	NY	NYC	ISASM	McDonnell	Phantom II	
F- 4N	SC	Beauf	MAS	McDonnell	Phantom II	152270, DW 2270, VMFA-251
F- 4N(F4H)	FL	Pensa	USNAM	McDonnell	Phantom II	153915, NK 101, VF-154
F- 4S Cockpit	CA	Paso Robles	EWM	McDonnell	Phantom II	155861
F- 4S	CA	San Diego	SDAM	McDonnell	Phantom II	
F- 4S	CA	San Diego	SDACM	McDonnell	Phantom II	
F- 4S	CA	Santa Maria	SMMoF	McDonnell	Phantom II	55014
F- 4S	DC	Dulle	DA	McDonnell	Phantom II	
F- 4S	HI	Kaneohe	KBMCAS	McDonnell	Phantom II	153689, VMFA-212

Type	State	City	Museum	Manufacturer	Name	Notes
F- 4S	KY	Lexington	AMoK	McDonnell	Phantom II	153904, VFMA-321
F- 5(CF)	MB-C	Brandon	CATPM	Northrop	Freedom Fighter	
F- 5(CF)	NS-C	Halifax	HAM	Northrop	Freedom Fighter	116748, 434 Bluenose Squadron
F- 5(CF)	AB-C	Cold Lake	CFB	Northrop	Freedom Fighter	116736
F- 5(CF)	AB-C	Grand Center	City	Northrop	Freedom Fighter	
F- 5(CF)	BC-C	Kamloops	CFB	Northrop	Freedom Fighter	116740
F- 5(CF)	ON-C	Bagotville	CFB-3WB	Northrop	Freedom Fighter	116733
F- 5(CF)	ON-C	Borden	TAM	Northrop	Freedom Fighter	116769
F- 5(CF)	ON-C	Kingston	CFBK	Northrop	Freedom Fighter	
F- 5(CF)	ON-C	Toronto	TAM	Northrop	Freedom Fighter	
F- 5(CF)	ON-C	Trenton	HI	Northrop	Freedom Fighter	
F- 5(CF)	ON-C	Trenton	RCAFMM	Northrop	Freedom Fighter	116721
F- 5L	MD	Silve	PEGF	FelixStow	America Flying Boat	
F- 5A	CA	Hawth	WMoF	Northrop	Freedom Fighter	
F- 5A	IN	Ft Wayne	Mercury	Northrop	Freedom Fighter	
F- 5A(YF)	OH	Dayto	USAFM	Northrop	Freedom Fighter	59-4989
F- 5A	ON-C	Hamilton	CWH	Northrop	Freedom Fighter	116757
F- 5A(YF)	WA	Seatt	MoF	Northrop	Freedom Fighter	59-4987
F- 5B	TX	San A	LAFB	Northrop	Freedom Fighter	C8123
F- 5E	NV	LasVe	NAFB	Northrop	Freedom Fighter	
F- 5E	TX	Wichi	SAFB	Northrop	Freedom Fighter	
F- 10(EF)	VA	Quantico	MCAGM		Skyknight	124618
F- 11	MB-C	Winni	WCAM	Fairchild	Husky	
F- 11	ON-C	Sault Ste Marie	CBHC	Fairchild	Husky	Sn 12, CF-EIR
F- 11-2	BC-C	Langley	CMoF&T	Fairchild	Husky	
F- 11A	CO	Puebl	FWAM	Grumman	Tiger	
F- 11A	NC	Durha	NCMoLS	Grumman	Tiger	
F- 11A	NC	Newbe	CityPark	Grumman	Tiger	
F- 11A (F9F-9)	NY	Garde	CoAM	Grumman	Tiger	141832
F- 11A(F11F-1)	FL	Pensa	USNAM	Grumman	Tiger	141828, AD201, VF- 21
F- 11B	CA	Ridecrest	CLNWC	Grumman	Tiger	
F- 14	AL	Huntsville	AC	Grumman	Tomcat	
F- 14	CA	Imperial	PM	Grumman	Tomcat	159620, Side # 100, Tail NJ
F- 14	CA	Riverside	MFAM	Grumman	Tomcat	157990, VF-1, Tail NE, Nose 100
F- 14	CA	San Diego	SDACM	Grumman	Tomcat	
F- 14	KS	Liber	MAAM	Grumman	Tomcat	
F- 14	NV	Fallon	NASF	Grumman	Tomcat	
F- 14	NY	NYC	ISASM	Grumman	Tomcat	
F- 14	PA	Willow Grove	WGNAS	Grumman	Tomcat	
F- 14	VA	Norfolk	NASN	Grumman	Tomcat	
F- 14	WA	Tillamook	TAM	Grumman	Tomcat	
F- 14	WI	Oshkosh	EAAAM	Grumman	Tomcat	
F- 14A	AZ	Tucso	PAM	Grumman	Tomcat	160684, VF-124
F- 14A	CA	Alameda Pt	USSHM	Grumman	Tomcat	
F- 14A	CA	Camarillo	YAM	Grumman	Tomcat	16100, VX-9
F- 14A	CA	Chino	PoF	Grumman	Tomcat	160686
F- 14A	CA	Chino	YAM	Grumman	Tomcat	
F- 14A	CA	Hawth	WMoF	Grumman	Tomcat	
F- 14A	CA	PalmS	PSAM	Grumman	Tomcat	160898, Side # 101, Tail AJ 41
F- 14A	CA	S.Mon	MoF	Grumman	Tomcat	
F- 14A	CA	El Cajon	SDAMGF	Grumman	Tomcat	VF-24
F- 14A	CA	SRosa	PCAM	Grumman	Tomcat	
F- 14A	FL	Pensa	USNAM	Grumman	Tomcat	157984, NK201, VF- 21
F- 14A	FL	Tittusville	VAC	Grumman	Tomcat	VF-41 Black Aces, "Tico Bell"
F- 14A	OK	Tulsa	TA&SC	Grumman	Tomcat	
F- 14A	MD	Lexington	NASPR	Grumman	Tomcat	162595, Side # 221, SD Tail
F- 14A	MD	Lexington	PRNAM	Grumman	Tomcat	161623, Side # 220
F- 14A	MI	Kalam	KAHM	Grumman	Tomcat	160395
F- 14A	NJ	Lumberton	AVM	Grumman	Tomcat	
F- 14A	NY	Horseheads	NWM	Grumman	Tomcat	161605, VF-32, Tail AC, Side 100
F- 14A	NY	Calverton	GMP	Grumman	Tomcat	
F- 14A	NY	Garde	CoAM	Grumman	Tomcat	157982
F- 14A	TX	C Christi	USS Lexi	Grumman	Tomcat	
F- 14A	TX	FWort	NASFWJRB	Grumman	Tomcat	
F- 14A	WA	Seattle	MoF	Grumman	Tomcat	160382
F- 14A	VA	VBeac	ONAS	Grumman	Tomcat	157988, 9, VF-103
F- 14B	NY	NYC	ISASM	Grumman	Super Tomcat	
F- 15	FL	Tampa	MAFB	McDonnell-Douglas	Eagle	
F- 15	LA	N.Orl	FoJBMM	McDonnell-Douglas	Eagle	
F- 15	WA	Tacoma	MAFB	McDonnell-Douglas	Eagle	
F- 15A	AZ	Tucso	PAM	McDonnell-Douglas	Eagle	74-118
F- 15A	CO	CSpri	EJPSCM	McDonnell-Douglas	Eagle	76-024
F- 15A	HI	Honolulu	HAFB	McDonnell-Douglas	Eagle	76018
F- 15A	IL	Ranto	OCAM	McDonnell-Douglas	Eagle	71-0286
F- 15A	FL	Panam	TAFB	McDonnell-Douglas	Eagle	74-0095
F- 15A	FL	Shali	USAFAM	McDonnell-Douglas	Eagle	74-124, OT
F- 15A	GA	Warner Robin	MoF	McDonnell-Douglas	Eagle	73-85, RG
F- 15A	MO	SLoui	MOANGSLL	McDonnell-Douglas	Eagle	
F- 15A	OH	Dayto	USAFM	McDonnell-Douglas	Eagle	72-119
F- 15A	OH	Lockb	RANGB	McDonnell-Douglas	Eagle	77-68
F- 15A	OR	Klamath Falls	OANG	McDonnell-Douglas	Eagle	
F- 15A	OR	Mc Minnville	EAEC	McDonnell-Douglas	Eagle	76-0014
F- 15A	TX	San A	LAFB	McDonnell-Douglas	Eagle	71-280
F- 15A	TX	Wichi	SAFB	McDonnell-Douglas	Eagle	
F- 15A	UT	Ogden	HAFBM	McDonnell-Douglas	Eagle	
F- 15A(YF)	VA	Hampt	LAFB	McDonnell-Douglas	Eagle	
F- 15B	AZ	Phoen	LAFB	McDonnell-Douglas	Eagle	
F- 15B/E	NC	Goldsboro	SJAFB	McDonnell-Douglas	Eagle	77-0161
F- 15C	FL	Panama City	VMP	McDonnell-Douglas	Eagle	
F- 16	CO	CSpri	USAFA	General Dynamics	Fighting Falcon	
F- 16	DE	Dover	AMCM	General Dynamics	Fighting Falcon	
F- 16	FL	Pinellas Park	FLP	General Dynamics	Fighting Falcon	80-0528
F- 16	NM	Albuq	KAFB	General Dynamics	Fighting Falcon	
F- 16	NM	Albuq	KAFB	General Dynamics	Fighting Falcon	
F- 16	ND	Fargo	FANG	General Dynamics	Fighting Falcon	
F- 16	NV	Fallon	NASF	General Dynamics	Fighting Falcon	
F- 16	NY	NYC	ISASM	General Dynamics	Fighting Falcon	
F- 16 Cockpit	OH	Dayton	USAFM	General Dynamics	Fighting Falcon	
F- 16	OK	Weatherford	GTSM	General Dynamics	Fighting Falcon	
F- 16	WI	Madison	MTFMDCRA	General Dynamics	Fighting Falcon	
F- 16A	AL	Mobile	BMP	General Dynamics	Fighting Falcon	79-0334
F- 16A	MI	Selfridge	SMAM	General Dynamics	Fighting Falcon	78-0059
F- 16A	NC	Sumter	SAFB	General Dynamics	Fighting Falcon	
F- 16A	VA	Hampt	LAFB	General Dynamics	Fighting Falcon	
F- 16A(YF)	OH	Dayto	USAFM	General Dynamics	Fighting Falcon	75-745, "Thunderbirds"
F- 16A	OR	Klamath Falls	OANG	General Dynamics	Fighting Falcon	81-759

Type	State	City	Location	Manufacturer	Name	Notes
F-16A	OR	Medford	RVIA	General Dynamics	Fighting Falcon	81-759
F-16A	UT	Ogden	HAFBM	General Dynamics	Fighting Falcon	Side # 399FW, Tail HL
F-16A(YF)	VA	Hampt	VA&SC	General Dynamics	Fighting Falcon	1567
F-16B	CA	Rosam	EAFB	General Dynamics	Fighting Falcon	
F-16C	FL	Shali	USAFAM	General Dynamics	Fighting Falcon	80-573, ET
F-16N	CA	Palm Sprgs	PoFAM	General Dynamics	Fighting Falcon	
F-16N	CA	El Cajon	SDAMGF	General Dynamics	Fighting Falcon	
F-16N	CA	SRosa	PCAM	General Dynamics	Fighting Falcon	
F-16N	TX	FWort	NASFWJRB	General Dynamics	Fighting Falcon	
F-17(YF) Mock-Up	NY	NYC	ISASM	Northrop	Hornet	
F-17(YF)(F/A18)	AL	Mobile	BMP	Northrop	Hornet	AC1002
F-17(YF)(F/A18)	CA	Ridgecrest	CLNWC	Northrop	Hornet	
F-17(YF)(F/A18)	CA	Hawth	WMoF	Northrop	Hornet	
F-17(YF)(F/A18)	CA	Miramar	FLAM	Northrop	Hornet	SH, VMF AT-101
F-17(YF)(F/A18)	CA	Lancaster	AVC	Northrop	Hornet	
F-17(YF)(F/A18)	FL	Jacks	NASCF	Northrop	Hornet	162462, AC401, VFA-105
F-17(YF)(F/A18)	FL	Pensa	USNAM	Northrop	Hornet	201570
F-17(YF)(F/A18)	GA	Hampton	AAHF	Northrop	Hornet	
F-17(YF)(F/A18)	MD	Lexington	PRNAM	Northrop	Hornet	151353, Side # 120, SD Tail
F-17(YF)(F/A18)	MI	Kalamazoo	KAHM	Northrop	Hornet	161984
F-17(YF)(F/A18)	NV	Fallon	NASF	Northrop	Hornet	
F-17(YF)(F/A18)	TX	FWort	NASFWJRB	Northrop	Hornet	
F-17(YF)(F/A18)	UT	Ogden	HAFBM	Northrop	Hornet	
F-17A-25 (F/A18)	GA	Warner Robin	MoF	Northrop	Hornet	FS-604A
F-17A(CF)(F/A18)	BC-C	La Baie	ADM	Northrop	Hornet	
F-17A(CF)(F/A18)	ON-C	Ottawa	CAM	Northrop	Hornet	
F-17A(L)(F/A18)	WA	Seatt	MoF	Northrop	Hornet	
F-17A(YF)(F/A18)	FL	Pensa	USNAM	Northrop	Hornet	162462
F-20	CA	LAnge	CMoS&I	Northrop	Tigershark	
F-20	CA	Rosam	EAFB	Northrop	Tigershark	
F-23(YF)	CA	Hawth	WMoF	Northrop	Black Widow II	
F-23(YF)	OH	Dayton	USAFM	Northrop	Black Widow II	
F-80	AK	Anchr	KANGB	Lockheed	Shooting Star	
F-80	IN	Columbus	VFW	Lockheed	Shooting Star	
F-80	NM	Albuquerque	KAFB	Lockheed	Shooting Star	48501
F-80	SC	McEnt	MEANGB	Lockheed	Shooting Star	
F-80	TX	Beevi	CourtHse	Lockheed	Shooting Star	
F-80 (P)	IN	South Bend	MHP	Lockheed	Shooting Star	
F-80 (P)	KS	Liber	MAAM	Lockheed	Shooting Star	
F-80 (P)	MI	Kalam	KAHM	Lockheed	Shooting Star	44-85152
F-80 (P)	NC	Charl	CHAC	Lockheed	Shooting Star	
F-80 (P)	NC	CPoin	CPMB	Lockheed	Shooting Star	
F-80 (P)(TV-1)	WA	Seatt	MoF	Lockheed	Shooting Star	47-1388, 33841
F-80 (XP)	DC	Washi	NA&SM	Lockheed	Shooting Star	
F-80 Cockpit	MI	Kalam	KAHM	Lockheed	Shooting Star	
F-80-1D	FL	Shali	USAFAM	Lockheed	Shooting Star	49713
F-80A	CA	Chino	PoFAM	Lockheed	Shooting Star	
F-80A Mock-Up	UT	Ogden	HAFBM	Lockheed	Shooting Star	
F-80A(P)	AZ	Mesa	WAFB	Lockheed	Shooting Star	
F-80A(P)	CA	Chino	PoFAM	Lockheed	Shooting Star	
F-80A(P)	CA	Rosamond	EAFB	Lockheed	Shooting Star	
F-80A(P)	FL	Pensa	USNAM	Lockheed	Seastar	44-85235, 29689
F-80A(P)	GA	Warner Robin	MoF	Lockheed	Shooting Star	
F-80A(P)	OH	Newbu	WASAC	Lockheed	Shooting Star	689
F-80B	NM	Clovi	CAFB	Lockheed	Shooting Star	
F-80B(P)	AZ	Tucso	PAM	Lockheed	Shooting Star	45-8612
F-80B(P)	CA	Sacra	McCelAFB	Lockheed	Shooting Star	45-8704
F-80B	CA	Atwater	CAM	Lockheed	Shooting Star	45-8490, Side FT-490
F-80C	CA	Chino	YAM	Lockheed	Shooting Star	
F-80C	FL	Shali	USAFAM	Lockheed	Shooting Star	53-2610
F-80C	GA	Warner Robin	MoF	Lockheed	Shooting Star	45-8357 FN
F-80C	KS	Wichita	K&HAP	Lockheed	Shooting Star	45-8612, "City of Wichita"
F-80C	NC	Charl	CHAC	Lockheed	Shooting Star	
F-80C	NM	Alamo	HAFB	Lockheed	Shooting Star	
F-80C (P)	PA	Willo	WGNAS	Lockheed	Shooting Star	33824, 28
F-80C	OH	Dayto	USAFM	Lockheed	Shooting Star	49-696
F-80C	OH	Lockb	RANGB	Lockheed	Shooting Star	47-171
F-80C	OK	Oklahoma City	45thIDM	Lockheed	Shooting Star	
F-80C	TX	Austi	BAFB	Lockheed	Shooting Star	
F-80C	WA	Seattle	MoF	Lockheed	Shooting Star	3841
F-80C(EF)	CA	Rosam	EAFB	Lockheed	Shooting Star	49-851
F-80C(GF)	WI	Oshko	EAAAAM	Lockheed	Shooting Star	48-868
F-80C(QF)	KS	Liber	MAAM	Lockheed	Shooting Star	
F-80F	NM	Alamo	CityPark	Lockheed	Shooting Star	
F-80F	NY	NYC	ISASM	Lockheed	Shooting Star	
F-80L	TX	Dalla	DNAS	Lockheed	Shooting Star	
F-80L	TX	FWort	NASFWJRB	Lockheed	Shooting Star	
F-80R(XP)	OH	Dayto	USAFM	Lockheed	Shooting Star	44-85200
F-82(P)	CA	El Cajon	CAFAG1	North American	Twin Mustang	
F-82(P)	TX	Midla	CAF-P82	North American	Twin Mustang	N 12102
F-82B(P)	OH	Dayto	USAFM	North American	Twin Mustang	44-65168 naca-132
F-82E(EF)(P)	TX	San A	LAFB	North American	Twin Mustang	46-262
F-82E(P)	KS	Kansi	D.Arnold	North American	Twin Mustang	46-256 Dave Arnold Kansas City KS
F-84	AR	Little Rock	LRAFB	Republic	Thunderjet	0-37543
F-84	CO	Puebl	FWAM	Republic	Thunderjet	71562
F-84	IA	Des Moines	ING	Republic	Thunderjet	40-26497
F-84	IA	SBluf	MAAM	Republic	Thunderjet	
F-84	IN	Ft. W	MC	Republic	Thunderjet	50-19514
F-84	TX	FWort	PMoT	Republic	Thunderjet	
F-84 (XP)	MD	Silve	PEGF	Republic	Thunderjet	
F-84(RF)	AR	FSmit	EANG	Republic	Thunderjet	
F-84(RF)	IA	SBluf	MAAM	Republic	Thunderjet	
F-84A(YP) Fuse	CA	Chino	PoFAM	Republic	Thunderjet	
F-84B	AZ	Grand	PoFGCVA	Republic	Thunderjet	45-59566
F-84B	AZ	Tucso	PAM	Republic	Thunderjet	45-59554
F-84B	NY	Garde	CoAM	Republic	Thunderjet	45-59504
F-84B-35-RE	PA	Readi	MAAM	Republic	Thunderjet	
F-84B	TX	Lackland	H&TM	Republic	Thunderjet	
F-84C	AZ	Tucso	PAM	Republic	Thunderjet	47-1433
F-84C	CA	Riverside	MFAM	Republic	Thunderjet	47-1595
F-84C	KS	Wichi	K&HAP	Republic	Thunderjet	47-1513
F-84C	NM	Clovi	CAFB	Republic	Thunderjet	
F-84C	OH	Sprin	OHANG	Republic	Thunderjet	
F-84C	OH	Sprin	SMAM	Republic	Thunderjet	
F-84C	WI	Oshko	EAAAAM	Republic	Thunderjet	51-9456
F-84D	GA	Savan	SMAM	Republic	Thunderjet	

Type	State	City	Place	Mfr	Name	Serial	Notes
F-84E	AZ	Tucson	AM 109	Republic	Thunderstreak	46-0294	
F-84E	CA	Chino	PoFAM	Republic	Thunderjet	FU-849	
F-84E	HI	Oahu	HAFB	Republic	Thunderjet		
F-84E	OH	Dayto	USAFM	Republic	Thunderjet	50-1143	
F-84E	OH	Lockb	RANGB	Republic	Thunderjet	49-2348	
F-84E	OH	Newbu	WASAC	Republic	Thunderjet		
F-84E(RF)	AR	Littl	LRAFB	Republic	Thunderjet		
F-84E-25-RE	GA	Warner Robin	MoF	Republic	Thunderjet	51-604A	
F-84F	AL	Birmingham	SMoF	Republic	Thunderstreak		
F-84F	AL	Birmingham	SMoF	Republic	Thunderstreak		
F-84F	AL	Montg	CityPark	Republic	Thunderstreak		
F-84F	AR	Harri	VWF	Republic	Thunderstreak		
F-84F	AZ	Peori	VWF	Republic	Thunderstreak		
F-84F	AZ	Phoen	LAFB	Republic	Thunderstreak		
F-84F	AZ	Tucso	PAM	Republic	Thunderstreak	52-6563	Thunderbird Painted
F-84F	AZ	Tucso	TANG	Republic	Thunderstreak		
F-84F	CA	Atwater	CAM	Republic	Thunderstreak	51-9433, Side FS-433	
F-84F	CA	Fairf	TAFB	Republic	Thunderstreak	52-6359	FS-359
F-84F	CA	Riverside	MFAM	Republic	Thunderstreak	51-9432	
F-84F	CA	Rosam	EAFB	Republic	Thunderstreak	51-9350	
F-84F	CA	Sacra	McCelAFB	Republic	Thunderstreak	54-1772	
F-84F	CA	Santa Rosa	PCAM	Republic	Thunderstreak	52-6475, AF	
F-84F	FL	Shali	USAFAM	Republic	Thunderstreak	51-495	FS-495
F-84F	FL	Titusville	VAC	Republic	Thunderstreak		
F-84F	FL	Wauch	AL P-2	Republic	Thunderstreak		
F-84F	GA	Athen	VFW 2872	Republic	Thunderstreak		
F-84F	GA	Calhoun	MAM	Republic	Thunderstreak		
F-84F	GA	Corde	ALP-38	Republic	Thunderstreak		
F-84F	GA	Corde	GVMSP	Republic	Thunderstreak		
F-84F	GA	Dobbi	DAFB	Republic	Thunderstreak		
F-84F	GA	Marie	CCYM	Republic	Thunderstreak		
F-84F	IA	Corre	CityPark	Republic	Thunderstreak		
F-84F	IA	Fairf	CityPark	Republic	Thunderstreak		
F-84F	IA	FtDod	FtDIAANG	Republic	Thunderstreak		
F-84F	IA	Grime	GANG	Republic	Thunderstreak		
F-84F	IA	Sergant Bluff	SCANG	Republic	Thunderstreak		
F-84F	ID	Mount	MHAFB	Republic	Thunderstreak		
F-84F	IL	Cahok	PCUSL	Republic	Thunderstreak		
F-84F	IL	Grani	AMVETS51	Republic	Thunderstreak		
F-84F	IL	Peori	PANG	Republic	Thunderstreak		
F-84F	IL	Perki	CityPark	Republic	Thunderstreak		
F-84F	IL	Ranto	OCAM	Republic	Thunderstreak	51-531	
F-84F	IL	Sprin	SMAM	Republic	Thunderstreak	2844	
F-84F	IL	Wenan	ALP1130	Republic	Thunderstreak		
F-84F	IN	Hagerstown	WWB	Republic	Thunderstreak	52-6993	
F-84F	IN	Hoagl	CityPark	Republic	Thunderstreak		
F-84F	IN	Monro	CityPark	Republic	Thunderstreak		
F-84F	IN	Montp	CityPark	Republic	Thunderstreak		
F-84F	IN	Peru	GAFB	Republic	Thunderstreak		
F-84F	IN	South	CityPark	Republic	Thunderstreak		
F-84F	IN	Terre Haute	THANG	Republic	Thunderstreak	027202	
F-84F	KS	Lynn	ALP237	Republic	Thunderstreak		
F-84F	KS	Wichita	KAM	Republic	Thunderstreak		
F-84F	KY	Frank	BNGC	Republic	Thunderstreak		
F-84F	LA	Alexandria	EHP	Republic	Thunderstreak	27080, FS-080, EL 23 TFW	
F-84F	LA	Bossi	BAFB	Republic	Thunderstreak	11386	
F-84F-25-GK	MI	Belleville	YAF	Republic	Thunderstreak	51-9361	
F-84F-35-GK	MI	Belleville	YAF	Republic	Thunderstreak	51-9501, N5006	
F-84F	MI	Escan	CityPark	Republic	Thunderstreak		
F-84F	MI	Lapee	YAFDLA	Republic	Thunderstreak		
F-84F	MI	Mt Clemens	SMAM	Republic	Thunderstreak	51-1664	
F-84F	MT	Great Falls	MAFB	Republic	Thunderstreak	52-6969	
F-84F	NE	Creig	CityPark	Republic	Thunderstreak		
F-84F	NJ	Wrightstown	McGAFB	Republic	Thunderstreak	27066, NJANG	
F-84F	NM	Alamo	HAFB	Republic	Thunderstreak		
F-84F	NM	Artes	CityPark	Republic	Thunderstreak		
F-84F	NM	STere	WEAM	Republic	Thunderstreak		
F-84F	NV	Indian Springs	City Park	Republic	Thunderstreak	948051	
F-84F	NY	Garde	CoAM	Republic	Thunderstreak	948051	
F-84F	NY	NYC	ISASM	Republic	Thunderstreak		
F-84F	NY	Scotia	ESAM	Republic	Thunderstreak	51-1620	
F-84F	NC	Asheboro	PFAC	Republic	Thunderstreak		
F-84F	OH	Dayto	USAFM	Republic	Thunderstreak	52-6526	
F-84F	OH	Lockb	RANGB	Republic	Thunderstreak	51-1346	
F-84F	OH	Mansf	MANG	Republic	Thunderstreak		
F-84F	OH	Newbu	WASAC	Republic	Thunderstreak	52-6524	
F-84F	OH	Sprin	OHANG	Republic	Thunderstreak	51-1797	
F-84F	OH	Sprin	SMAM	Republic	Thunderstreak	92348	
F-84F	OH	Swant	TANG	Republic	Thunderstreak		
F-84F	PA	Pitts	PANG	Republic	Thunderstreak		
F-84F	SD	Rapid	SDA&SM	Republic	Thunderstreak	52-8886	
F-84F	TX	Abile	DLAP	Republic	Thunderstreak	51-9364	
F-84F	TX	Amarillo	EFA&SM	Republic	Thunderstreak	52-6553	
F-84F	TX	D Rio	LAFB	Republic	Thunderstreak		
F-84F	TX	Houst	ALP490	Republic	Thunderstreak		
F-84F	TX	Muens	CityPark	Republic	Thunderstreak		
F-84F	UT	Ogden	HAFBM	Republic	Thunderstreak		
F-84F	VA	Hampt	VA&SC	Republic	Thunderstreak	51-1786	FS-786
F-84F	VA	Richm	DGSC	Republic	Thunderstreak		
F-84F	VA	Richm	SMAM	Republic	Thunderstreak		
F-84F	VA	VBeac	VANG	Republic	Thunderstreak		
F-84F	WI	CDoug	WNGML&M	Republic	Thunderstreak		
F-84F	WI	Kenosha	GTAC	Republic	Thunderstreak	52-6370	
F-84F	WI	Oshko	EAAAAM	Republic	Thunderstreak	47-1498	
F-84F	WY	Cheye	WYANG	Republic	Thunderstreak		
F-84F	IA	Cedar	CityPark	Republic	Thunderstreak	51-9444	
F-84F (2ea)	KS	Topek	CAM	Republic	Thunderstreak	0-26458	
F-84F(RF)	AL	Ozark	CityPark	Republic	Thunderflash		
F-84F(RF)	AR	Littl	LRAFB	Republic	Thunderflash		
F-84F(RF)	AZ	Tucso	PAM	Republic	Thunderflash	51-1944	
F-84F(RF)	GA	Warner Robin	MoF	Republic	Thunderflash		
F-84F(RF)	IA	Harla	CityPark	Republic	Thunderflash		
F-84F(RF)	IA	Ida Grove	CityPark	Republic	Thunderflash	Tail 8BC	
F-84F	IA	Sergant Bluff	SCANG	Republic	Thunderstreak		
F-84F(RF)	MD	Middl	GLMAM	Republic	Thunderflash		
F-84F(RF)	MI	Belle	VFW4434	Republic	Thunderflash		

Type	State	City	Code	Manufacturer	Name	Serial/Notes
F-84F(RF)	MI	Mt Clemens	SMAM	Republic	Thunderstreak	51-1896
F-84F(RF)	MI	Lapee	YAFDLA	Republic	Thunderflash	
F-84F(RF)	MI	Ypsil	YAF	Republic	Thunderflash	
F-84F(RF)	MS	Hatti	CityPark	Republic	Thunderflash	
F-84F(RF)	MS	Jacks	JANG	Republic	Thunderflash	
F-84F(RF)	NC	Inca	IJHS	Republic	Thunderflash	
F-84F(RF)	NE	David	ALP125	Republic	Thunderflash	
F-84F(RF)	NE	Linco	LANG	Republic	Thunderflash	51-11259, Tail NEBR 0-11259
F-84F(RF)	NE	Nelig	CityPark	Republic	Thunderflash	
F-84F(RF)	NE	Valle	CityPark	Republic	Thunderflash	
F-84F(RF)	NE	York	CityPark	Republic	Thunderflash	
F-84F(RF)	OH	Dayto	USAFM	Republic	Thunderflash	49-2430
F-84F(RF)	OH	Newbu	WASAC	Republic	Thunderflash	52-7262
F-84F(RF)	TN	Nashv	NANG	Republic	Thunderflash	
F-84F(RF)	TX	Abile	DLAP	Republic	Thunderflash	51-1123
F-84F(RF)	TX	Austi	BAFB	Republic	Thunderflash	
F-84F(RF)	TX	Midla	CAFFM	Republic	Thunderflash	
F-84F-20-RE	GA	Warner Robin	MoF	Republic	Thunderflash	52-7244
F-84F-30	NC	Asheb	AMA	Republic	Thunderstreak	
F-84F-30	VA	Hampt	APM	Republic	Thunderstreak	51-1786
F-84F-35RE	MI	Kalam	KAHM	Republic	Thunderstreak	52-6486
F-84F-45-RE	GA	Warner Robin	MoF	Republic	Thunderflash	52-6701A FS-701
F-84F-RE	NE	Ashland	SACM	Republic	Thunderstreak	51-1714
F-84G	IL	Ellington	EFM	Republic	Thunderjet	
F-84G	IL	Ranto	OCAM	Republic	Thunderjet	
F-84G	NY	Niagara Falls	NAM	Republic	Thunderjet	
F-84G	NC	Charl	CHAC	Republic	Thunderjet	
F-84G	UT	Ogden	HAFBM	Republic	Thunderjet	23275, FS-275
F-84H(XF)	OH	Dayton	USAFM	Republic	Thunderscreech	51-17059
F-84K(RF)	CA	Chino	PoFAM	Republic	Thunderjet	
F-84K(RF)	CO	Denve	WOR	Republic	Thunderjet	
F-84K(RF)-17-RE	OH	Dayton	USAFM	Republic	Thunderjet	52-7259, "Ypsi Gypsy Rose"
F-84K(RF)-17-RE	MI	Belleville	YAF	Republic	Thunderjet	52-7259
F-84K(RF)-17-RE	MI	Ypsil	YAF	Republic	Thunderjet	52-7260
F-84K(RF)	MI	Ypsil	YAF	Republic	Thunderjet	52-7259
F-84K(RF)	MI	Ypsil	YAF	Republic	Thunderjet	
F-84K(RF)	OH	Dayto	USAFM	Republic	Thunderflash	51-1847
F-85(XF)	OH	Dayto	USAFM	McDonnell	Goblin	46-523
F-85(XF)-MC	NE	Ashland	SACM	McDonnell	Goblin	46-524
F-86(QF)	CA	Ridgecrest	CLNWC	North American	Sabre	
F-86	CA	San Diego	SDAM	North American	Sabre	
F-86	CA	Santa Maria	SMMoF	North American	Sabre	
F-86	D.C.	Washington	USS&AH	North American	Sabre	
F-86	ID	Idaho	IFA	North American	Sabre	
F-86	IL	Danville	MAM	North American	Sabre	
F-86	IL	Joliet	RFA	North American	Sabre	52-4986, NX188RL, FU-584, "Mig Mad Marine"
F-86	KS	Wichi	AEC	North American	Sabre	
F-86	KY	Middleboro	LS	North American	Sabre	31361, FU-361
F-86	MI	Frankenmuth	MOM&SM	North American	Sabre	
F-86	MI	Kalam	KAHM	North American	Sabre	52-5143
F-86	NC	CPoin	CPMB	North American	Sabre	
F-86	NM	STere	WEAM	North American	Sabre	
F-86	NV	Fallon	NASF	North American	Sabre	
F-86	NV	LasVe	NAFB	North American	Sabre	
F-86	OH	Cinncinnati	CMALF	North American	Sabre	
F-86	OK	Weatherford	GTSM	North American	Sabre	
F-86	AB-C	Bagotville	CFB	Canadair	Sabre	19454
F-86	BC-C	Sidney		Canadair	Sabre	23060
F-86	ON-C	Belle	ZPark	Canadair	Sabre	23053, Golden Hawks Colours
F-86	ON-C	Borden	BIBM	Canadair	Sabre	23228
F-86	ON-C	Brockville		Canadair	Sabre.	23649
F-86	ON-C	Kingston	RMC	Canadair	Sabre	23221
F-86	ON-C	Hamilton	CWH	Canadair	Sabre	23651, GH
F-86	ON-C	Oshawa		Canadair	Sabre	23047, "City of Oshawa", 416
F-86	ON-C	Petersburg	RP&Z	Canadair	Sabre	23428
F-86	ON-C	Sarnia	GP	Canadair	Sabre	23164, Golden Hawks Colours, RCAF 428
F-86 Mk VI	ON-C	Trenton	MP	Canadair	Sabre	23641, Golden Hawks Colours
F-86	ON-C	Trenton	RCAFMM	Canadair	Sabre	23257, RCAF 428 Golden Hawks Colours
F-86	TN	Sevierville	TMoA	North American	Sabre	
F-86	TX	FWort	PMoT	North American	Sabre	
F-86	TX	FWort	VFM	North American	Sabre	
F-86	TX	Tulia	VFWP1798	North American	Sabre	
F-86	WA	Seatt	MoF	North American	Sabre	
F-86	WI	Monroe	TP	North American	Sabre	
F-86 Mk 3	MB-C	Winni	WCAM	Canadair	Sabre	
F-86 Mk.V	NS -C	Halifax	HAM	Canadair	Sabre	"Golden Hawks"
F-86 Mk.V	ON-C	Oshawa	OA	Canadair	Sabre	"Golden Hawks"
F-86 Mk VI	ON-C	Peterborough	RP	Canadair	Sabre	
F-86 Mk V	WI	Oshko	EAAAAM	North American	Sabre	N8687D, "The Huff"
F-86 Mk V/VI	WI	Oshko	EAAAAM	North American	Sabre	N86JR
F-86A	AK	Ancho	KANGB	North American	Sabre	
F-86A	CA	Fresn	FANG	North American	Sabre	
F-86A	CT	Winds	NEAM	North American	Sabre	
F-86A	MD	Silve	PEGF	North American	Sabre	
F-86A	MI	Mt Clemens	SMAM	North American	Sabre	52-4387
F-86A	MT	Great	GFANG	North American	Sabre	47-00637
F-86A	OH	Dayto	USAFM	North American	Sabre	49-1067
F-86A	TX	San A	LAFB	North American	Sabre	59-1605
F-86A	UT	Salt	SLCANG	North American	Sabre	
F-86A(P)	WA	Seatt	MoF	North American	Sabre	
F-86C	GA	Calhoun	MAM	North American	Sabre	15896
F-86D	AZ	Chand	CityPark	North American	Sabre	
F-86D	AZ	Globe	VWF1704	North American	Sabre	
F-86D	AZ	Tucso	DMAFB	North American	Sabre	
F-86D	CA	Sacra	McCelAFB	North American	Sabre	51-2968
F-86D	CA	West	VWF	North American	Sabre	
F-86D	CO	Auror	BANGB	North American	Sabre	
F-86D	FL	Clear	FMAM	North American	Sabre	
F-86D	FL	Panam	TAFB	North American	Sabre	54-5244
F-86D	FL	Shali	USAFAM	North American	Sabre	51-2831, FU-831
F-86D	LA	N.Orl	FoJBMM	North American	Sabre	
F-86D	LA	N.Orl	NONAS	North American	Sabre	
F-86D-60-NA	MI	Belleville	YAF	North American	Sabre	53-1060, N201504
F-86D	NV	Reno	NAHS	North American	Sabre	
F-86D	OH	Dayto	USAFM	North American	Sabre	50-477
F-86D	OK	Oklah	45IDM	North American	Sabre	52-4043

F-86D	OK	Oklah	45IDM	North American	Sabre	
F-86D	OK	Tinke	TANG	North American	Sabre	
F-86D	OK	Tulsa	TANG	North American	Sabre	
F-86D	TN	Knoxv	CityPark	North American	Sabre	
F-86D	TX	Austi	AGDTAG	North American	Sabre	
F-86D	TX	FWort	SAM	North American	Sabre	
F-86D	TX	Paris	FTAM	North American	Sabre	
F-86D	WA	Tacoma	MAFB	North American	Sabre	
F-86D	WI	Monroe	Park	North American	Sabre	NAtch
F-86E	AZ	Mesa	WAFB	North American	Sabre	
F-86E	CA	P.Hue	CIANGB	North American	Sabre	
F-86E	CA	PHuen	CIANGB	North American	Sabre	
F-86E	HI	Honolulu	HAFB	North American	Sabre	50-00653
F-86E	HI	Honolulu	HANG	North American	Sabre	52-04191
F-86E	IN	India	VFWP7119	North American	Sabre	
F-86E	LA	Alexandria	EAB	North American	Sabre	24931, FU-931
F-86E-15NA	NC	Golds	SJAFB	North American	Sabre	51-12972, N1028
F-86E	NM	Alamo	HAFB	North American	Sabre	
F-86E	OH	Newbu	WASAC	North American	Sabre	50-11123
F-86E	TX	Dalla	CFM	North American	Sabre	51-12821, N4689H, FU-821, 23293
F-86E	WA	Spoka	FAFBHM	North American	Sabre	
F-86E	WY	Cheye	WYANG	North American	Sabre	
F-86F	AL	Birmingham	SMoF	North American	Sabre	
F-86F	AZ	Mesa	CFM	North American	Sabre	
F-86F	AZ	Phoen	LAFB	North American	Sabre	
F-86F	CA	Chino	PoFAM	North American	Sabre	
F-86F	CA	El Cajon	SDAMGF	North American	Sabre	
F-86F(QF)	CA	Paso Robles	EWM	North American	Sabre	555082, N454
F-86F	CA	Rosam	EAFB	North American	Sabre	52-5241
F-86F	CA	Sacra	McCelAFB	North American	Sabre	51-13082
F-86F-30NA	CO	Auror	BANGB	North American	Sabre	52-4913, AF. JASDF, Side # 609
F-86F(RF)	CO	Auror	BANGB	North American	Sabre	
F-86F	CO	Auror	BANGB	North American	Sabre	
F-86F	FL	Clear	FMAM	North American	Sabre	
F-86F	FL	Miami	WOM	North American	Sabre	
F-86F	FL	Titusville	VAC	North American	Sabre	
F-86F	GA	Warner Robin	MoF	North American	Sabre	53-1511
F-86F(RF)	IL	Sugar Grove	ACM	North American	Sabre	51-13990
F-86F	IL	Sprin	S.ArmyNG	North American	Sabre	50-27051 IL
F-86F	IL	Sprin	SMAM	North American	Sabre	51-10822 IL
F-86F	IN	Ft. W	FWAS	North American	Sabre	Sn 52-5139, NX86F, "No Jokes" 90 Willy 10"
F-86F	MI	Ypsil	YAF	North American	Sabre	
F-86F	OR	Clack	CANG	North American	Sabre	
F-86F(QF)	OR	Clack	CANG	North American	Sabre	
F-86F(RF)	QC-C	La Baie	ADM	Canadair	Sabre	
F-86F-25	PA	Readi	MAAM	North American	Sabre	51-13417 N 51RS
F-86F-30	TX	Grand Prairie	TACM	North American	Sabre	
F-86F	WA	Seattle	MoF	North American	Sabre	51-13371, 371, FU-371
F-86F	WA	Eastsound	FHC	North American	Sabre	49-1217, G-BZNL
F-86H	AZ	Tucso	PAM	North American	Sabre	53-1525
F-86H	CA	Victorville	GAFB	North American	Sabre	
F-86H	CA	Atwater	CAM	North American	Sabre	53-1230, Tail A
F-86H-10NA	CA	Riverside	MFAM	North American	Sabre	53-1304
F-86H	CA	Victorville	GAFB	North American	Sabre	53-1378A, AF
F-86H	CO	Denve	WOR	North American	Sabre	
F-86H	DE	New C	NCANG	North American	Sabre	
F-86H	FL	Ft. Lauderdale	HP	North American	Sabre	53-1255
F-86H	IN	Churu	CityPark	North American	Sabre	56-298, 64, 66N
F-86H	IN	Peru	GAFB	North American	Sabre	
F-86H	KS	Liber	MAAM	North American	Sabre	
F-86H	KS	Topek	CAM	North American	Sabre	
F-86H	MA	Bedfo	HAFB	North American	Sabre	
F-86H	MD	Balti	BANG	North American	Sabre	
F-86H	MD	Ellic	VFWP7472	North American	Sabre	
F-86H	MO	LaPla	CityPark	North American	Sabre	
F-86H	NC	Golds	CityPark	North American	Sabre	53-1370
F-86H	ND	Hetti	CityPark	North American	Sabre	
F-86H	ND	James	CityPark	North American	Sabre	
F-86H	ND	Walha	CityPark	North American	Sabre	
F-86H	NE	Mc Co	CityPark	North American	Sabre	
F-86H	NM	Clovi	CAFB	North American	Sabre	
F-86H	NY	Centr	ALP915	North American	Sabre	
F-86H	NY	Manch	ALP	North American	Sabre	
F-86H	NY	Syrac	SMAMB	North American	Sabre	
F-86H	OH	Cinci	CityPark	North American	Sabre	
F-86H	OH	Dayto	USAFM	North American	Sabre	53-1352
F-86H	PA	Beave	CityPark	North American	Sabre	
F-86H	SC	Flore	FA&MM	North American	Sabre	
F-86H	SC	Green	CityPark	North American	Sabre	
F-86H	SC	McEnt	MEANGB	North American	Sabre	
F-86H	SD	Rapid	SDA&SM	North American	Sabre	53-1375
F-86H	VA	Hampt	LAFB	North American	Sabre	
F-86H	WI	Argyl	CityPark	North American	Sabre	
F-86HL-26	WI	CDoug	WNGML&M	North American	Sabre	51-3064, FU-064
F-86H	WI	Oshko	EAAAAM	North American	Sabre	52-1993
F-86H	WVA	Vienn	CityPark	North American	Sabre	
F-86H(QF)	CA	Chino	PoFAM	North American	Sabre	
F-86H-10-NH	NM	Manch	CityPark	North American	Sabre	
F-86H-NH	NE	Ashland	SACM	North American	Sabre	53-1375
F-86L	AL	Mobil	BMP	North American	Sabre Dog	51-2993
F-86L	AL	Montg	MAFB	North American	Sabre Dog	
F-86L Cockpit	AZ	Grand	PoFGCVA	North American	Sabre Dog	49-1217
F-86L	AZ	Tucso	PAM	North American	Sabre Dog	56-965, FU-965
F-86L	CA	Fairf	TAFB	North American	Sabre Dog	30704, FU-704
F-86L	CA	Fresn	FANG	North American	Sabre Dog	
F-86L	CA	Riverside	MFAM	North American	Sabre Dog	50-0560
F-86L	CO	CSpri	EJPSCM	North American	Sabre Dog	53-0782
F-86L	FL	Panam	TAFB	North American	Sabre Dog	52-10133
F-86L	FL	Wauchula	FMAM	North American	Sabre Dog	53-0658
F-86L	GA	Macon	MACF	North American	Sabre Dog	
F-86L	GA	Savan	SMAM	North American	Sabre Dog	
F-86L	GA	Valdo	CityPark	North American	Sabre Dog	
F-86L	HI	Oahu	HAFB	North American	Sabre Dog	
F-86L	HI	Honolulu	HANG	North American	Sabre Dog	52-02841
F-86L	IA	Iowa	CityPark	North American	Sabre Dog	53-0750
F-86L	ID	IFall	CityPark	North American	Sabre Dog	

Model	State	City	Org	Manufacturer	Name	Serial
F-86L	IL	Brook	Village	North American	Sabre Dog	
F-86L-50	KS	Wichi	K&HAP	North American	Sabre Dog	52-4256
F-86L	MI	Ypsil	YAF	North American	Sabre Dog	
F-86L	MS	Hazle	VFW2567	North American	Sabre Dog	
F-86L	MT	Butte	CityPark	North American	Sabre Dog	53-997
F-86L	NC	Charl	CANG	North American	Sabre Dog	
F-86L	ND	Grand	CityPark	North American	Sabre Dog	
F-86L	NE	Linco	LANG	North American	Sabre Dog	53-0831, Tail ANG 0-23760
F-86L	NJ	Lumberton	AVM	North American	Sabre Dog	FU-110
F-86L	NV	Battl	BMAM	North American	Sabre Dog	53-1045
F-86L	NY	Monro	Village	North American	Sabre Dog	
F-86L	OH	Newbu	WASAC	North American	Sabre Dog	30959
F-86L	OR	Nyssa	CityPark	North American	Sabre Dog	
F-86L	OR	Vale	CityPark	North American	Sabre Dog	
F-86L	PA	Imper	VFWP7714	North American	Sabre Dog	
F-86L	PA	Pitts	PANG	North American	Sabre Dog	
F-86L	SC	McEnt	MEANGB	North American	Sabre Dog	
F-86L	TN	Nashv	CityPark	North American	Sabre Dog	
F-86L	TX	Abile	DLAP	North American	Sabre Dog	
F-86L	TX	Dalla	DNAS	North American	Sabre Dog	
F-86L	TX	Denis	VFWP2773	North American	Sabre Dog	
F-86L	TX	FWort	NASFWJRB	North American	Sabre Dog	
F-86L	TX	FWort	SAM	North American	Sabre Dog	
F-86L	TX	Sherm	ALP29	North American	Sabre Dog	
F-86L	UT	Ogden	HAFBM	North American	Sabre Dog	
F-86L	WA	Bridg	CityPark	North American	Sabre Dog	
F-86L	WI	Apple	ALP38	North American	Sabre Dog	
F-86L	WVA	Milto	CityPark	North American	Sabre Dog	
F-86L	WY	Cheye	WYANG	North American	Sabre Dog	
F-86L (3 ea)	AL	Montg	CityPark	North American	Sabre Dog	
F-86L-26	VA	Hampt	APM	North American	Sabre Dog	51-3064, FU-064
F-89 Fuse Only	TN	Memph	LS	Northrop	Scorpion	
F-89 Fuse Only	TN	Peru	GAM	Northrop	Scorpion	
F-89B	IA	Nampa	CityPark	Northrop	Scorpion	49-2457
F-89D	CA	Rosam	EAFB	Northrop	Scorpion	52-1959
F-89D	FL	Panam	TAFB	Northrop	Scorpion	52-1862
F-89D	GA	Warner Robin	MoF	Northrop	Scorpion	53-2463
F-89D	VT	Burli	BANG	Northrop	Scorpion	
F-89H	MN	Minne	MAGM	Northrop	Scorpion	53-2677, 373
F-89H	TX	Abile	DLAP	Northrop	Scorpion	54-298
F-89H	UT	Ogden	HAFBM	Northrop	Scorpion	54-0322
F-89J	AZ	Tucso	PAM	Northrop	Scorpion	53-2674
F-89J	CA	Atwater	CAM	Northrop	Scorpion	52-1927
F-89J	CA	Riverside	MFAM	Northrop	Scorpion	52-1949
F-89J	CO	CSpri	EJPSCM	Northrop	Scorpion	52-1941
F-89J	CT	Winds	NEAM	Northrop	Scorpion	52-2494
F-89J	FL	Panam	TAFB	Northrop	Scorpion	54-8422
F-89J	FL	Shali	USAFAM	Northrop	Scorpion	53-2610
F-89J	ME	Bangor	MAM	Northrop	Scorpion	
F-89J	ME	Water	CityPark	Northrop	Scorpion	52-1856
F-89J	MT	Great Falls	GFANG	Northrop	Scorpion	53-2467
F-89J	MT	Helena	CoT	Northrop	Scorpion	53-2453
F-89J	ND	Fargo	FANG	Northrop	Scorpion	53-2465
F-89J	OH	Dayto	USAFM	Northrop	Scorpion	52-1911
F-89J	OR	Mc Minnville	EAEC	Northrop	Scorpion	53-2534
F-89J	SC	Flore	FA&MM	Northrop	Scorpion	53-2646
F-89J	TX	FWort	SAM	Northrop	Scorpion	
F-89J	TX	Midla	CAFFM	Northrop	Scorpion	52-1868
F-89J	VT	Nurli	BANG	Northrop	Scorpion	52-1883
F-89J	WI	Oshko	EAAAAM	Northrop	Scorpion	53-3546
F-89J (2ea)	CA	Chino	PoFAM	Northrop	Scorpion	
F-89J-50	VA	Hampt	APM	Northrop	Scorpion	52-2129
F-90(XF)	OH	Dayton	USAFM			
F-91(XF)	OH	Dayto	USAFM	Republic	Thunderceptor	46-680
F-92A(XF)	OH	Dayto	USAFM	Convair		46-682
F-94	PA	Water	I79&RT19	Lockheed	Starfire	
F-94A	NY	Niagara Falls	NAM	Lockheed	Starfire	49-2500
F-94A	OH	Dayto	USAFM	Lockheed	Starfire	49-500
F-94A	OH	Dayto	USAFM	Lockheed	Starfire	49-2498
F-94A(YF)	CA	Rosam	EAFB	Lockheed	Starfire	
F-94B	NY	Syrac	SMAMB	Lockheed	Starfire	
F-94C	AZ	Tucso	PAM	Lockheed	Starfire	51-5623
F-94C	CO	CSpri	EJPSCM	Lockheed	Starfire	50-1006
F-94C	CT	Winds	NEAM	Lockheed	Starfire	51-13575
F-94C	MN	Chish	MMoM	Lockheed	Starfire	
F-94C	MN	Minne	MAGM	Lockheed	Starfire	51-13563
F-94C	NC	Fayet	VFWP670	Lockheed	Starfire	
F-94C	ND	Fargo	FANG	Lockheed	Starfire	
F-94C	OH	Dayto	USAFM	Lockheed	Starfire	50-980
F-94C	PA	Cory	VFWP264	Lockheed	Starfire	
F-94C	VT	Burli	BANG	Lockheed	Starfire	
F-100	FL	Clear	FMAM	North American	Super Sabre	
F-100	MD	Middl	GLMAM	North American	Super Sabre	
F-100	NB	Fairb	A	North American	Super Sabre	
F-100	NM	Melrose	MBR	North American	Super Sabre	
F-100	TX	FWort	PMoT	North American	Super Sabre	
F-100	TX	Galve	LSFM	North American	Super Sabre	56-3154
F-100 Cockpit	CT	Winds	NEAM	North American	Super Sabre	
F-100(CF)	CA	Atwater	CAM	Avro	Canuck	
F-100(CF)	CO	CSpri	EJPSCM	Avro	Canuck	100779
F-100(CF)	AB-C	Calga	AMoC	Avro	Canuck	18126
F-100(CF)	AB-C	Edmonton	AAM	Avro	Canuck	
F-100(CF)	AB-C	Nanton	NLSAM	Avro	Canuck	
F-100(CF)	NS-C	Halifax	ACAM	Avro	Canuck	
F-100(CF)	ON-C	Belle	BA	Avro	Canuck	
F-100(CF)	ON-C	Campbellford		Avro	Canuck	181106
F-100(CF)	ON-C	Hamilton	RCAF	Avro	Canuck	
F-100(CF)	ON-C	Missi	DR	Avro	Canuck	
F-100(CF)	ON-C	Mt.Vie	MVRCAF	Avro	Canuck	
F-100(CF)	ON-C	Toronto	WP	Avro	Canuck	
F-100(CF)	ON-C	Bagotville	CFB-3WB	Avro	Canuck	100741
F-100(CF)	PE-C	Summe	PEIHAS	Avro	Canuck	
F-100(CF)	SK-C	MJaw	WDM	Avro	Canuck	
F-100(CF) Mk.V	MB-C	Winni	WCAM	Avro	Canuck	
F-100(CF) Mk C	MB C	Winnipeg	WRACFB	Avro	Canuck	
F-100(CF) Mk V	NS -C	Halifax	HAM	Avro	Canuck	18747, #2 OTU

Type	Loc	City	Facility	Manufacturer	Model	Notes
F-100(CF) Mk V	ON-C	CFB Borden	BHT	Avro	Canuck	18488, "RCAF"
F-100(CF) Mk.V	ON-C	CFB Borden	BHT	Avro	Canuck	100785, C
F-100(CF) Mk V	ON-C	Hamilton	CWH	Avro	Canuck	
F-100(CF)	ON-C	Burlington	WP	Avro	Canuck	
F-100(CF)	ON-C	Burlington	WP	Avro	Canuck	
F-100(CF)	ON-C	Goose Bay	5WGB	Avro	Canuck	
F-100(CF)	ON-C	Kingston	RMC	Avro	Canuck	100731
F-100(CF)	ON-C	North Bay	CFBNB	Avro	Canuck	
F-100(CF)	ON-C	North Bay	LP	Avro	Canuck	
F-100(CF) Mk IV	ON-C	Trenton	RCAFMM	Avro	Canuck	18774
F-100(CF)	Quebec-C	St Hubert	CFB	Avro	Canuck	100760, CAF 760
F-100(CF)	Quebec-C	St Jean	CFB	Avro	Canuck	104784, CAF 746
F-100(CF) Mk 38	BC-C	Langley	CMoF&T	Avro	Canuck	18138
F-100(YF)	MS	Bilox	KAFB	Avro	Canuck	52-5755
F-100A	CA	Rosam	EAFB	North American	Super Sabre	52-1688
F-100A	CA	Rosam	EAFB	North American	Super Sabre	52-5760
F-100A(YF)	CA	Rosam	EAFB	North American	Super Sabre	#2
F-100A(YF)	CA	Rosam	EAFB	North American	Super Sabre	#2
F-100A	CO	Auror	BANGB	North American	Super Sabre	
F-100A	CT	Winds	NEAM	North American	Super Sabre	
F-100A	MI	Grand	CityPark	North American	Super Sabre	
F-100A	NM	Albuq	AANG	North American	Super Sabre	
F-100A	NM	Melro	Village	North American	Super Sabre	
F-100A	OH	Sprin	OHANG	North American	Super Sabre	
F-100A	TX	San A	GAFB	North American	Super Sabre	
F-100A	TX	San A	LAFB	North American	Super Sabre	52-5759
F-100A	UT	Ogden	HAFBM	North American	Super Sabre	
F-100A	WI	Oshko	EAAAAM	North American	Super Sabre	53-1553
F-100C	AL	Montg	MAFB	North American	Super Sabre	
F-100C	AZ	Phoen	LAFB	North American	Super Sabre	
F-100C	AZ	Tucso	PAM	North American	Super Sabre	54-1823
F-100C	CA	Riverside	MFAM	North American	Super Sabre	54-1786
F-100C	FL	Shali	USAFAM	North American	Super Sabre	54-954 SS
F-100C	GA	Kenne	AFAMA	North American	Super Sabre	
F-100C	GA	Warner Robin	MoF	North American	Super Sabre	54-1851 FW 851
F-100C	IA	Sioux	SCANG	North American	Super Sabre	
F-100C	ID	Mount	MHAFB	North American	Super Sabre	
F-100C	IL	Ranto	OCAM	North American	Super Sabre	54-1784
F-100C	IN	Peru	GAFB	North American	Super Sabre	56-3232 712Th FW
F-100C	KS	Wichita	K&HAP	North American	Super Sabre	54-1993
F-100C	OH	Dayto	USAFM	North American	Super Sabre	54-1753
F-100C	TX	Abile	DLAP	North American	Super Sabre	54-1752
F-100C	VA	Hampt	CityPark	North American	Super Sabre	
F-100C	WI	CDoug	WNGML&M	North American	Super Sabre	
F-100D	AZ	Glend	CityPark	North American	Super Sabre	
F-100D	AZ	Tucso	TANG	North American	Super Sabre	
F-100D	CA	Victorville	GAFB	North American	Super Sabre	
F-100D	CA	Chino	PoFAM	North American	Super Sabre	
F-100D	CA	Sacra	McCelAFB	North American	Super Sabre	56-3288
F-100D	CO	Puebl	FWAM	North American	Super Sabre	55-3503
F-100D	CT	Winds	BANGB	North American	Super Sabre	55-3805
F-100D	FL	Clearwater	FMAM	North American	Super Sabre	
F-100D	FL	Homes	HAFB	North American	Super Sabre	
F-100D	FL	Kissimmee	FTWM	North American	Super Sabre	
F-100D	FL	Panam	TAFB	North American	Super Sabre	
F-100D	GA	Marie	DAFB	North American	Super Sabre	
F-100D	IL	Ranto	OCAM	North American	Super Sabre	54-1785
F-100D	IN	Terre Haute	THANG	North American	Super Sabre	
F-100D	LA	N.Orl	FoJBMM	North American	Super Sabre	
F-100D	LA	N.Orl	NONAS	North American	Super Sabre	
F-100D	MA	Otis	OANG	North American	Super Sabre	
F-100D	MA	Westf	MAANG	North American	Super Sabre	
F-100D	MD	Silve	PEGF	North American	Super Sabre	
F-100D	ME	Westf	MAANG	North American	Super Sabre	
F-100D	MI	Mt Clemens	SMAM	North American	Super Sabre	56-3025
F-100D	MO	SLoui	MOANGSLL	North American	Super Sabre	
F-100D	NM	Alamo	HAFB	North American	Super Sabre	
F-100D	NM	Clovi	CAFB	North American	Super Sabre	
F-100D	NV	LasVe	NAFB	North American	Super Sabre	
F-100D	NY	Niaga	NFANG	North American	Super Sabre	
F-100D	OH	Colum	CDCSC	North American	Super Sabre	
F-100D	OH	Dayto	USAFM	North American	Super Sabre	55-3754
F-100D	OH	Lockb	RANGB	North American	Super Sabre	55-2884 Model 224
F-100D	OH	Sprin	SMAM	North American	Super Sabre	
F-100D	OH	Swant	TANG	North American	Super Sabre	
F-100D	OK	Tulsa	TANG	North American	Super Sabre	
F-100D	SC	Myrtl	MBAFB	North American	Super Sabre	
F-100D	TX	FWort	SAM	North American	Super Sabre	
F-100D	TX	San A	BAFB	North American	Super Sabre	
F-100D	TX	San A	KAFB	North American	Super Sabre	
F-100D	TX	San A	KANG	North American	Super Sabre	
F-100D	TX	San A	MoFM	North American	Super Sabre	
F-100D (2 EA)	CO	Denve	WOR	North American	Super Sabre	
F-100D(GF)	CO	Denve	WOR	North American	Super Sabre	
F-100D(GF)	TX	Wichi	SAFB	North American	Super Sabre	
F-100D-5	VA	Hampt	APM	North American	Super Sabre	54-2145, "Thunderbirds"
F-100F	AZ	Tucso	DMAFB	North American	Super Sabre	
F-100F-16	IN	Ft Wayne	Mercury	North American	Super Sabre	Sn 56-3948, N2011V, FW-948, "Victor in Valor"
F-100F	MI	Mt Clemens	SMAM	North American	Super Sabre	56-3894
F-100F	NJ	Pomon	ANG	North American	Super Sabre	
F-100F	NM	Las Cruces	LCIA	North American	Super Sabre	
F-100F	OH	Dayton	USAFM	North American	Super Sabre	
F-100F	TX	Burnet	HLS-CAF	North American	Super Sabre	
F-101	AL	Birmingham	SMoF	McDonnell	Voodoo	
F-101	FL	Callo	CityPark	McDonnell	Voodoo	
F-101	ID	Pocatello	Airport	McDonnell	Voodoo	57-0430
F-101	MI	Mt Clemens	FHCMP	McDonnell	Voodoo	57-0430
F-101	MO	SLoui	SLAM	McDonnell	Voodoo	
F-101	WY	RockS	CityPark	McDonnell	Voodoo	58-0312
F-101 (Black)	MN	Minne	MAGM	McDonnell	Voodoo	67
F-101(CF)	AB-C	Abbotsford	CFB	McDonnell	Voodoo	101055
F-101(CF)	AB-C	Bagotville	CFB-3WB	McDonnell	Voodoo	101027
F-101(CF)	AB-C	Cold Lake	CFB	McDonnell	Voodoo	101056
F-101(CF)	AB-C	Wetaskiwin	CFB	McDonnell	Voodoo	101038
F-101(CF)	BC-C	Lazo	CFB Comox	McDonnell	Voodoo	101030
F-101(CF)	BC-C	Lazo	CFB Comox	McDonnell	Voodoo	101057

Model	Loc	City	Code	Mfr	Name	Serial/Notes
F-101(CF)	MB-C	Winnipeg	CFB	McDonnell	Voodoo	101034
F-101(CF)	ON-C	CFB Borden	BHT	McDonnell	Voodoo	101011
F-101(CF)	ON-C	Haliburton		McDonnell	Voodoo	A683
F-101(CF)	ON-C	Levis	CFB	McDonnell	Voodoo	101015
F-101(CF)	ON-C	Lindsay	LA	McDonnell	Voodoo	101002
F-101(CF)	ON-C	Malton		McDonnell	Voodoo	18619
F-101(CF)	ON-C	Mt Hope		McDonnell	Voodoo	18506
F-101(CF)	ON-C	North Bay	CFBNB	McDonnell	Voodoo	101054
F-101(CF)	ON-C	Ottawa	OIA	McDonnell	Voodoo	101025
F-101(CF)	ON-C	Ottawa	OIA	McDonnell	Voodoo	101045
F-101(CF)	ON-C	Trenton	RCAFMM	McDonnell	Voodoo	101040
F-101(CF)	NB-C	Hillsborough	P	McDonnell	Voodoo	101028, 416 LYNX Squadron, Side # 28
F-101(CF)	NF-C	Gander	NAAM	McDonnell	Voodoo	
F-101(CF)	NF-C	Goose Bay	CFB	McDonnell	Voodoo	101003
F-101(CF)	NS-C	Bedford	CBF	McDonnell	Voodoo	101043
F-101(CF)	NS-C	Chatham	CFBC	McDonnell	Voodoo	101053, 416 LYNX Squadron
F-101(CF)	NS-C	Cornwallis	CFRSC	McDonnell	Voodoo	101006, 416 LYNX Squadron, Side # 6
F-101(CF)	PEI-C	Summerside	CFB	McDonnell	Voodoo	101037
F-101(RF)	TX	Beaum	BDZMP	McDonnell	Voodoo	
F-101A	CO	Puebl	FWAM	McDonnell	Voodoo	53-2418
F-101A	FL	Kissi	FTWAM	McDonnell	Voodoo	
F-101A	NM	Clovi	CAFB	McDonnell	Voodoo	
F-101B	AB-C	Edmonton	AAM	McDonnell	Voodoo	101021
F-101B	AB-C	Edmonton	AAM	McDonnell	Voodoo	101032
F-101B-110-MC	AB-C	Edmonton	AAM	McDonnell	Voodoo	101060, 57-433, 101-590
F-101B	AZ	Tucso	PAM	McDonnell	Voodoo	57-282
F-101B	CA	Atwater	CAM	McDonnell	Voodoo	57-0412
F-101B	CA	Fairf	TAFB	McDonnell	Voodoo	
F-101B	CA	Riverside	MFAM	McDonnell	Voodoo	59-0418
F-101B	CA	Rosam	EAFB	McDonnell	Voodoo	58-288
F-101B	CA	Sacra	McCelAFB	McDonnell	Voodoo	57-427
F-101B	CO	CSpri	EJPSCM	McDonnell	Voodoo	58-274
F-101B	CO	Denve	WOR	McDonnell	Voodoo	
F-101B	DE	Dover	DAFB	McDonnell	Voodoo	
F-101B	FL	Kissimmee	FTWM	McDonnell	Voodoo	60417
F-101B	FL	Lakel	SFAF	McDonnell	Voodoo	59-400
F-101B	FL	Panam	CP	McDonnell	Voodoo	60417
F-101B	FL	Panam	GCCC	McDonnell	Voodoo	70438
F-101B	FL	Panam	TAFB	McDonnell	Voodoo	57-0332
F-101B	FL	Panam	TAFB	McDonnell	Voodoo	59-0400
F-101B-115-MC	FL	Titusville	VAC	McDonnell	Voodoo	59-0400
F-101B	IL	Ranto	OCAM	McDonnell	Voodoo	56-0273
F-101B	IN	Peru	GAFM	McDonnell	Voodoo	
F-101B	KS	Topek	CAM	McDonnell	Voodoo	
F-101B	MI	Mt Clemens	ALP4	McDonnell	Voodoo	57-0430
F-101B	ND	Fargo	FANG	McDonnell	Voodoo	
F-101B	ND	Grand	GFAFB	McDonnell	Voodoo	
F-101B	OH	Dayto	USAFM	McDonnell	Voodoo	58-325
F-101B	OH	Oberl	OFAA	McDonnell	Voodoo	
F-101B	OR	Portl	ORANGP	McDonnell	Voodoo	
F-101B	SD	Rapid	SDA&SM	McDonnell	Voodoo	
F-101B	TN	Chatt	CANG	McDonnell	Voodoo	
F-101B	TX	Abile	DLAP	McDonnell	Voodoo	57-287
F-101B	TX	San A	LAFB	McDonnell	Voodoo	56-241
F-101B	UT	Ogden	HAFBM	McDonnell	Voodoo	
F-101B	WA	Spoka	FAFBHM	McDonnell	Voodoo	
F-101B (2 ea)	MI	Marqu	KISAFB	McDonnell	Voodoo	
F-101B(CF)	AB-C	Calga	AMoC	McDonnell	Voodoo	
F-101B(CF)	CO	CSpri	EJPSCM	McDonnell	Voodoo	101044
F-101B(CF)	ME	Bango	BANG	McDonnell	Voodoo	
F-101B(CF)	NS	Halifax	ACAM	McDonnell	Voodoo	
F-101B(CF)	NS-C	Shearwater	SAM	McDonnell	Voodoo	
F-101B(CF)	NF-C	Gander	NAAM	McDonnell	Voodoo	101065
F-101B(CF)	ON-C	Ottaw	CAM	McDonnell	Voodoo	101025
F-101B(CF)	ON-C	Trenton	RCAFMM	McDonnell	Voodoo	101046
F-101B(EB)	MN	Minne	MAGM	McDonnell	Voodoo	58-350
F-101B(NF)-40-MC	MI	Belleville	YAF	McDonnell	Voodoo	56-235
F-101B(NF)	MI	Ypsil	YAF	McDonnell	Voodoo	
F-101B(RF)	NV	Reno	MANG	McDonnell	Voodoo	
F-101B-55	VA	Hampt	APM	McDonnell	Voodoo	56-0246
F-101B-MC	NE	Ashland	SACM	McDonnell	Voodoo	59-40462
F-101C	FL	Shali	USAFAM	McDonnell	Voodoo	60250
F-101C	GA	Warner Robin	MoF	McDonnell	Voodoo	41518-5656
F-101C	TX	Wichi	SAFB	McDonnell	Voodoo	
F-101C(RF)	AL	Montg	MAFB	McDonnell	Voodoo	
F-101C(RF)	AR	Littl	LRAFB	McDonnell	Voodoo	56-231
F-101C(RF)	AZ	Dougl	CityPark	McDonnell	Voodoo	
F-101C(RF)	AZ	Gila	CityPark	McDonnell	Voodoo	
F-101C(RF)	AZ	Tucso	PAM	McDonnell	Voodoo	56-214
F-101C(RF)	GA	Warner Robin	MoF	McDonnell	Voodoo	56-229
F-101C(RF)	KY	Frank	BNGC	McDonnell	Voodoo	
F-101C(RF)	MD	Silve	PEGF	McDonnell	Voodoo	
F-101C(RF)	MI	Mt Clemens	SMAM	McDonnell	Voodoo	56-048; C/N697
F-101C(RF)	MS	Bilox	KAFB	McDonnell	Voodoo	
F-101C(RF)	MS	Hatti	CityPark	McDonnell	Voodoo	
F-101C(RF)	MS	Jacks	JANG	McDonnell	Voodoo	
F-101C(RF)	NY	Niaga	NFANG	McDonnell	Voodoo	
F-101C(RF)	OH	Dayto	USAFM	McDonnell	Voodoo	56-166
F-101C(RF)	SC	Sumte	SAFB	McDonnell	Voodoo	
F-101C(RF)	TX	Austi	BAFB	McDonnell	Voodoo	
F-101D	WA	Tilli	CMANGP	McDonnell	Voodoo	50-70294
F-101F	FL	Clear	FMAM	McDonnell	Voodoo	
F-101F	GA	Warner Robin	MoF	McDonnell	Voodoo	58-276
F-101F	MD	Middl	GLMAM	McDonnell	Voodoo	
F-101F	MN	Proct	CityPark	McDonnell	Voodoo	
F-101F	MT	Great	MAFB	McDonnell	Voodoo	59-0419
F-101F	NC	Charlotte	CAM	McDonnell	Voodoo	56-0243
F-101F	ND	Fargo	FANG	McDonnell	Voodoo	
F-101F	NY	Buffa	B&ECNP	McDonnell	Voodoo	80338
F-101F	NY	Buffa	City	McDonnell	Voodoo	
F-101F	NY	Niaga	NFANG	McDonnell	Voodoo	
F-101F	NY	Scotia	ESAM	McDonnell	Voodoo	59-413
F-101F	TX	Ellin	EANGB	McDonnell	Voodoo	
F-101F	TX	San A	LAFB	McDonnell	Voodoo	58-290
F-101F(CF)	MB-C	Winni	WRCAF	McDonnell	Voodoo	101008
F-101F(CF)	WA	Tacoma	MAFB	McDonnell	Voodoo	022

Model	State	City	Code	Mfr	Name	Serial
F-101F(TF)	SC	Flore	FA&MM	McDonnell	Voodoo	
F-101H(RF)	AZ	Tucso	PAM	McDonnell	Voodoo	56-11
F-101H(RF)	KY	Louis	LANG	McDonnell	Voodoo	56-001
F-102	NY	Scotia	ESAM	Convair	Delta Dagger	61515
F-102	WA	Spoka	FAFBHM	Convair	Delta Dagger	
F-102(YF)	LA	N.Orl	FoJBMM	Convair	Delta Dagger	
F-102A	AB-C	Stephanville	HF	Convair	Delta Dagger	
F-102A	AK	Ancho	EAFB	Convair	Delta Dagger	
F-102A	AK	Palme	MOAT&I	Convair	Delta Dagger	
F-102A	AZ	Phoen	LAFB	Convair	Delta Dagger	
F-102A	AZ	Tucso	PAM	Convair	Delta Dagger	56-1393
F-102A	AZ	Tucso	TANG	Convair	Delta Dagger	
F-102A	CA	Chino	PoFAM	Convair	Delta Dagger	
F-102A	CA	El Cajon	SDAMGF	Convair	Delta Dagger	
F-102A	CA	Fairf	TAFB	Convair	Delta Dagger	
F-102A	CA	Fresn	FANG	Convair	Delta Dagger	
F-102A	CA	Riverside	MFAM	Convair	Delta Dagger	56-1114, "Keith's Kitten"
F-102A	CA	Sacra	McCelAFB	Convair	Delta Dagger	51-1140
F-102A	CO	CSpri	EJPSCM	Convair	Delta Dagger	56-1109
F-102A	CT	Winds	NEAM	Convair	Delta Dagger	56-1264
F-102A	FL	Panam	TAFB	Convair	Delta Dagger	57-858
F-102A	GA	Warner Robin	MoF	Convair	Delta Dagger	57-907
F-102A	HI	Oahu	HAFB	Convair	Delta Dagger	54-01373
F-102A	ID	Boise	BANG	Convair	Delta Dagger	
F-102A	MN	Minne	MAGM	Convair	Delta Dagger	50-61432
F-102A	MT	Helena	CoT	Convair	Delta Dagger	0-6116
F-102A	MT	Great	LP	Convair	Delta Dagger	56-1105
F-102A	ND	Fargo	FANG	Convair	Delta Dagger	
F-102A	ND	Grand	GFAFB	Convair	Delta Dagger	
F-102A	ND	Minot	MAFB	Convair	Delta Dagger	
F-102A	NY	Syrac	SMAMB	Convair	Delta Dagger	
F-102A	NY	WHamp	SMAM	Convair	Delta Dagger	
F-102A	OH	Dayto	USAFM	Convair	Delta Dagger	56-1416
F-102A	OR	Mc Minnville	TNSAM	Convair	Delta Dagger	56-1368
F-102A	PA	Pitts	PANG	Convair	Delta Dagger	
F-102A	SC	McEnt	MEANGB	Convair	Delta Dagger	
F-102A	SD	Rapid	SDA&SM	Convair	Delta Dagger	
F-102A	SD	Sioux	SDANGSF	Convair	Delta Dagger	
F-102A	TX	Ellin	EANGB	Convair	Delta Dagger	
F-102A	TX	Midla	CAFFM	Convair	Delta Dagger	
F-102A	TX	San A	KAFB	Convair	Delta Dagger	
F-102A	TX	Wichi	SAFB	Convair	Delta Dagger	
F-102A	UT	Ogden	HAFBM	Convair	Delta Dagger	75833, FC-833
F-102A	VT	Nurli	BANG	Convair	Delta Dagger	
F-102A	WA	Tacoma	McCordAFB	Convair	Delta Dagger	57-0858
F-102A	WI	CDoug	WNGML&M	Convair	Delta Dagger	
F-102A(TF)	AL	Birmingham	SMoF	Convair	Delta Dagger	
F-102A(GF)	CO	Denve	WOR	Convair	Delta Dagger	
F-102A(TF)	AZ	Tucso	PAM	Convair	Delta Dagger	54-1366
F-102A(TF)	CA	Lanca	MoFM	Convair	Delta Dagger	
F-102A(TF)	CA	Rosam	EAFB	Convair	Delta Dagger	54-1353
F-102A(TF)	FL	Panam	TAFB	Convair	Delta Dagger	
F-102A(TF)-35-CO	MI	Belleville	YAF	Convair	Delta Dagger	56- 2317, "La Tina"
F-102A(GTF)	MI	Mt Clemens	SMAM	Convair	Delta Dagger	54-1351
F-102A(TF)	PA	Annvi	AANG	Convair	Delta Dagger	
F-102A(YF)	LA	N.Orl	NONAS	Convair	Delta Dagger	
F-102A(YF)	NC	Charlotte	CAM	Convair	Delta Dagger	53-1788
F-102A(YF)	SC	Flore	FA&MM	Convair	Delta Dagger	
F-102A-80-CO	NY	Baldw	CityPark	Convair	Delta Dagger	61515
F-102A-CO	NE	Ashland	SACM	Convair	Delta Dagger	54-1405
F-102D	FL	Clear	FMAM	Convair	Delta Dagger	
F-104	AR	Little Rock	CRNGA	Lockheed	Starfighter	AUG00
F-104	AZ	Presc	ERAU	Lockheed	Starfighter	
F-104	CA	Moffe	NASAAVC	Lockheed	Starfighter	
F-104	FL	Clearwater	SI	Lockheed	Starfighter	Sn 104632, N103RB
F-104	FL	Clearwater	SI	Lockheed	Starfighter	Sn 104850, N 104RD
F-104	FL	Kissi	FTWAM	Lockheed	Starfighter	
F-104	MT	Dutton	AM	Lockheed	Starfighter	57-1332
F-104	ND	Fargo	NDSU	Lockheed	Starfighter	
F-104	OK	Oklah	A&SM	Lockheed	Starfighter	
F-104	OK	Oklah	KCASM	Lockheed	Starfighter	
F-104	TX	Dalla	CFM	Lockheed	Starfighter	56-0780
F-104(CF)	AB-C	Cold Lake	CFB	Lockheed	Starfighter	12702
F-104(CF)	AB-C	Cold Lake	CFB	Lockheed	Starfighter	
F-104(CF)	AB-C	Wetaskiwin	CFB	Lockheed	Starfighter	104763
F-104(CF)	AB-C	Grand Center	City	Lockheed	Starfighter	
F-104(CF)	MB-C	Winnipeg	WRACFB	Lockheed	Starfighter	104753
F-104(CF)	NS	Halifax	ACAM	Canadair	Starfighter	
F-104(CF)	ON-C	CFB Borden	BHT	Lockheed	Starfighter	104792
F-104(CF)	ON-C	Ottaw	CAM	Lockheed	Starfighter	12700
F-104(CF)	Quebec-C	St Jean	CFB	Lockheed	Starfighter	CAF 784
F-104A	CA	Fairf	TAFB	Lockheed	Starfighter	56-0752
F-104A	CO	CSpri	USAFA	Lockheed	Starfighter	55-2967
F-104A	DC	Washi	NA&SM	Lockheed	Starfighter	
F-104A	GA	Warner Robin	MoF	Lockheed	Starfighter	56-0817 FG-817
F-104C	IL	Ranto	OCAM	Lockheed	Starfighter	56-0732
F-104A	LA	Alexandria	RE	Lockheed	Starfighter	56-0791
F-104A	OH	Dayto	USAFM	Lockheed	Starfighter	56-0754
F-104A	OH	Dayto	USAFM	Lockheed	Starfighter	56-0879
F-104A	TX	Abile	DLAP	Lockheed	Starfighter	56-0748
F-104A(2ea)	CA	Rosam	EAFB	Lockheed	Starfighter	56-0801
F-104A(NF)	CA	Rosam	EAFB	Lockheed	Starfighter	56-0760
F-104B	CA	Sacra	McCelAFB	Lockheed	Starfighter	57-1303
F-104B	KS	Hutchinson	C	Lockheed	Starfighter	57-1301
F-104B	SC	Flore	FA&MM	Lockheed	Starfighter	
F-104C	AZ	Phoen	LAFB	Lockheed	Starfighter	56-0892
F-104C	AZ	Phoen	PANG	Lockheed	Starfighter	56-0891
F-104C	CA	Victorville	GAFB	Lockheed	Starfighter	56-0934
F-104C	CA	Van Nuys	VNAFB	Lockheed	Starfighter	56-0932
F-104C	CO	CSpri	EJPSCM	Lockheed	Starfighter	56-0936
F-104C	CO	Denve	WOR	Lockheed	Starfighter	56-0910
F-104C	CT	Winds	NEAM	Lockheed	Starfighter	56-0901
F-104C	FL	Panam	TAFB	Lockheed	Starfighter	56-0919
F-104C	IL	Chica	MoS&I	Lockheed	Starfighter	
F-104C	KS	Liber	MAAM	Lockheed	Starfighter	56-0933
F-104C	MI	Kalam	KAHM	Lockheed	Starfighter	56-0898

F-104C	MS	Bilox	KAFB	Lockheed	Starfighter	56-0938	
F-104C	ND	Fargo	FANG	Lockheed	Starfighter	56-0926	
F-104C	NM	Alamo	HAFB	Lockheed	Starfighter	56-0886	
F-104C	OH	Dayto	USAFM	Lockheed	Starfighter	56-0914	
F-104C	SC	McEnt	MEANGB	Lockheed	Starfighter	57-0920, 60920	
F-104C	TN	Chatt	CANG	Lockheed	Starfighter		
F-104C	TN	Knoxv	KANG	Lockheed	Starfighter	56-0890	8th FG
F-104C	TX	San A	LAFB	Lockheed	Starfighter	56-0929	
F-104C	TX	Wichi	SAFB	Lockheed	Starfighter	56-0912	
F-104C	VA	Hampt	VA&SC	Lockheed	Starfighter	57-0916	FG-916
F-104C	WA	Everett	MoF	Lockheed	Starfighter	56-0934, N56-934, N820NA	
F-104C(TF)	FL	Shali	USAFAM	Lockheed	Starfighter	57-1331	
F-104D	AZ	Tucso	PAM	Lockheed	Starfighter	57-1323	
F-104D	CA	Atwater	CAM	Lockheed	Starfighter	57-1312, FG-312	
F-104D	CA	Burba	VWF	Lockheed	Starfighter		
F-104D	CA	LAnge	CMoS&I	Lockheed	Starfighter	57-1333	
F-104D	NJ	Jackson	AP	Lockheed	Starfighter	57-1320	
F-104D(CF)	ON-C	Hamilton	CWH	Lockheed	Starfighter	10-4756, Tiger Paint	
F-104D(CF)	ON-C	Hamilton	CWH	Lockheed	Starfighter	104641	
F-104D(CF)	ON-C	Trenton	RCAFMM	Lockheed	Starfighter	10646, Side # 646, 2 Seater	
F-104D(CF)	WI	Oshko	EAAAAM	Lockheed	Starfighter	N104JR	
F-104D(TF)	TX	San A	LAFB	Lockheed	Starfighter	57-1319	
F-104D-10	IN	Hunti	WoF	Lockheed	Starfighter	57-1322, Total Built: F-104D=21; D-10=8	
F-104G	CA	Chino	PoFAM	Lockheed	Starfighter	FX82	
F-104G(TF)	CA	Paso Robles	EWM	Lockheed	Starfighter	NASA 824NA	
F-104G	NJ	Lumberton	AVM	Lockheed	Starfighter	56-0933, D-8090, Side FX-81	
F-105	AL	Birmingham	SMoF	Republic	Thunderchief		
F-105B-IRE	AL	Mobil	CityPark	Republic	Thunderchief	54-0102	
F-105	CA	Chino	YAM	Republic	Thunderchief	60-471	
F-105	CT	Windsor	ANG	Republic	Thunderchief		
F-105	KS	Liber	MAAM	Republic	Thunderchief		
F-105	MO	Chill	CityPark	Republic	Thunderchief		
F-105	MS	Jacks	AmLgl	Republic	Thunderchief		
F-105	NC	Kings	CityPark	Republic	Thunderchief		
F-105	NC	Wilmi	VFWP2573	Republic	Thunderchief		
F-105(CF)	ON-C	Campbellford	MMM	Avro	Arrow	181106	
F-105(CF)	ON-C	Ottawa	CAM	Avro	Arrow		
F-105(CF) Mk 1	ON-C	Toronto	TAM	Avro	Arrow		
F-105	SC	Sumte	SAFB	Republic	Thunderchief		
F-105	TX	Dalla	CFM	Republic	Thunderchief		
F-105	TX	Slanton	TAM	Republic	Thunderchief		
F-105B	CA	Atwater	CAM	Republic	Thunderchief	57-837	
F-105B	CA	Chino	PoFAM	Republic	Thunderchief	57-5803	
F-105B	CA	Riverside	MFAM	Republic	Thunderchief	62-4301	
F-105B	CA	Sacra	McCelAFB	Republic	Thunderchief		
F-105B	CT	Winds	NEAM	Republic	Thunderchief		
F-105B	FL	Clear	FMAM	Republic	Thunderchief		
F-105B	IL	Ranto	OCAM	Republic	Thunderchief	40104	
F-105B-15-RE	MI	Belleville	YAM	Republic	Thunderchief	57-5793	
F-105B	NC	Hickory	HRA	Republic	Thunderchief	54-0107	
F-105B	NJ	Trent	MGANG	Republic	Thunderchief		
F-105B	NY	Garde	CoAM	Republic	Thunderchief	5783	
F-105B	SC	Ander	ACA	Republic	Thunderchief		
F-105B	SD	Rapid	SDA&SM	Republic	Thunderchief		
F-105B	UT	SaltL	SLANG	Republic	Thunderchief		
F-105B	WA	Spoka	FAFBHM	Republic	Thunderchief		
F-105B	WI	CDoug	WNGML&M	Republic	Thunderchief		
F-105B(JF)	TX	San A	LAFB	Republic	Thunderchief	54-105	
F-105D	AL	Montg	MAFB	Republic	Thunderchief		
F-105D	AZ	Gila	GBAFAF	Republic	Thunderchief		
F-105D	AZ	Tucso	DMAFB	Republic	Thunderchief		
F-105D	AZ	Tucso	PAM	Republic	Thunderchief	61-86	
F-105D	CA	Victorville	GAFB	Republic	Thunderchief		
F-105D	CA	Fairf	TAFB	Republic	Thunderchief		
F-105D	CA	Riverside	MFAM	Republic	Thunderchief	62-4383	
F-105D	CA	Rosam	EAFB	Republic	Thunderchief	61-146	
F-105D	CA	Sacra	McCelAFB	Republic	Thunderchief	62-4301	
F-105D	CA	San B	NAFB	Republic	Thunderchief		
F-105D	CO	CSpri	USAFA	Republic	Thunderchief		
F-105D	CT	Winds	BANGB	Republic	Thunderchief		
F-105D	DC	Washi	AAFB	Republic	Thunderchief		
F-105D	DC	Washi	BAFB	Republic	Thunderchief		
F-105D	FL	Shali	USAFAM	Republic	Thunderchief	58-771 JV	
F-105D	GA	Warner Robin	MoF	Republic	Thunderchief		
F-105D	IL	Sugar Grove	ACM	Republic	Thunderchief	61-0099	
F-105D	IN	Peru	GAFB	Republic	Thunderchief	61-088	
F-105D	KS	Topek	CAM	Republic	Thunderchief		
F-105D	MD	Andrews	APG	Republic	Thunderchief	AF 61041	
F-105D	MD	Silve	PEGF	Republic	Thunderchief		
F-105D	MS	Bilox	KAFB	Republic	Thunderchief		
F-105D	NC	Fayet	PAFB	Republic	Thunderchief		
F-105D	NC	Golds	SJAFB	Republic	Thunderchief	61-056, SJ	
F-105D	NM	Alamo	HAFB	Republic	Thunderchief		
F-105D	NM	Albuq	NAM	Republic	Thunderchief		
F-105D	OH	Colum	CDCSC	Republic	Thunderchief		
F-105D	OH	Dayto	USAFM	Republic	Thunderchief	60-504	
F-105D	OK	Enid	VAFB	Republic	Thunderchief		
F-105D	OK	Tinke	TANG	Republic	Thunderchief		
F-105D	TN	Arnol	AAFS	Republic	Thunderchief		
F-105D	TX	Abile	DLAP	Republic	Thunderchief	59-1738	
F-105D	TX	FWort	CAFB	Republic	Thunderchief		
F-105D	TX	FWort	NASFWJRB	Republic	Thunderchief		
F-105D	TX	FWort	PMoT	Republic	Thunderchief		
F-105D	TX	San A	LAFB	Republic	Thunderchief	62-4387	
F-105D	TX	Slanton	TAMCC	Republic	Thunderchief	63-0091	
F-105D	TX	Wichi	SAFB	Republic	Thunderchief		
F-105D	UT	Ogden	HAFBM	Republic	Thunderchief		
F-105D	VA	Hampt	LAFB	Republic	Thunderchief		
F-105D	VA	Richm	SMAM	Republic	Thunderchief		
F-105D Simulator	NY	Garde	CoAM	Republic	Thunderchief		
F-105D(GF)	CO	Denve	WOR	Republic	Thunderchief		
F-105D15	VA	Hampt	APM	Republic	Thunderchief	61-73	
F-105F	IL	Ranto	OCAM	Republic	Thunderchief	63-8287, "Root Rat Pak", RK	
F-105F	KS	Wichi	K&HAP	Republic	Thunderchief	62-4253	
F-105F	TX	Dallas	FoF	Republic	Thunderchief	63-8343	
F-105F	TX	FWort	SAM	Republic	Thunderchief		

Model	State	City	Location	Manufacturer	Name	Notes
F-105G	CA	Victorville	GAFB	Republic	Thunderchief	
F-105G	CA	Sacramento	MHMAFB	Republic	Thunderchief	63-8278
F-105G	GA	Marie	DAFB	Republic	Thunderchief	
F-105G	GA	Warner Robin	MoF	Republic	Thunderchief	62-4438 HI
F-105G	LA	Alexandria	EAP	Republic	Thunderchief	63-296, MD, AD
F-105G	MD	Middl	GLMAM	Republic	Thunderchief	
F-105G	NV	LasVe	NAFB	Republic	Thunderchief	
F-105G	NY	Scotia	ESAM	Republic	Thunderchief	62-4444
F-105G	OH	Dayto	USAFM	Republic	Thunderchief	63-8320
F-105G	UT	Ogden	HAFBM	Republic	Thunderchief	"Wild Weasel"
F-105G (2 ea)	AZ	Tucso	PAM	Republic	Thunderchief	62-4427
F-105H	GA	Warner Robin	MoF	Republic	Thunderchief	63-8309
F-106	AL	Birmingham	SMoF	Convair	Delta Dart	
F-106	CT	Windsor	ANG	Convair	Delta Dart	
F-106	FL	Titusville	VAC	Convair	Delta Dart	
F-106	DE	Dover	DAFB	Convair	Delta Dart	
F-106	UT	Ogden	DAFB	Convair	Delta Dart	
F-106 Simulator	DE	Dover	DAFB	Convair	Delta Dart	
F-106A	AZ	Tucso	PAM	Convair	Delta Dart	59-3
F-106A	CA	Fresn	FANG	Convair	Delta Dart	
F-106A	CO	CSpri	EJPSCM	Convair	Delta Dart	59-0134
F-106A	CO	Denve	WOR	Convair	Delta Dart	
F-106A	DC	Washi	AAFB	Convair	Delta Dart	
F-106A	FL	Clearwater	FMAM	Convair	Delta Dart	
F-106A	FL	Jacks	JIA	Convair	Delta Dart	70230 13
F-106A	FL	Panam	TAFB	Convair	Delta Dart	59-145
F-106A	GA	Warner Robin	MoF	Convair	Delta Dart	59-123
F-106A	HI	Honolulu	HANG	Convair	Delta Dart	53366
F-106A(NF)	MI	Mt Clemens	CityPark	Convair	Delta Dart	56-451
F-106A	MT	Great Falls	GFANG	Convair	Delta Dart	72492
F-106A	ND	Minot	MAFB	Convair	Delta Dart	
F-106A	NY	Rome	GAFBM	Convair	Delta Dart	
F-106A	OH	Dayto	USAFM	Convair	Delta Dart	58-787
F-106A	SC	Charl	CAFB	Convair	Delta Dart	
F-106A	WA	Tacoma	MAFB	Convair	Delta Dart	56-0459
F-106A Cockpit	MI	Kalam	KAHM	Convair	Delta Dart	
F-106B	CA	Rosamond	EAFB	Convair	Delta Dart	
F-106B	NJ	Pomon	ANG	Convair	Delta Dart	
F-106B	TX	San A	KAFB	Convair	Delta Dart	
F-106B(NF)	VA	Hampt	VA&SC	Convair	Delta Dart	N816NA, 816
F-107A	AZ	Tucso	PAM	North American	Mach 2 Jet Fighter	55- 5118, Man Sn 212-1, 1st F-107
F-107A	OH	Dayto	USAFM	North American	Mach 2 Jet Fighter	55- 5119
F-107(LF)	WA	Seattle	MoF	Let		N2170D
F-111A(EF)	NM	Clovi	CAFB	General Dynamics	Raven (ECM)	
F-111A(EF)	OH	Dayton	USAFM	General Dynamics	Raven (ECM)	
F-111	AL	Huntsville	AC	General Dynamics	Aardvark	
F-111A	AL	Birmingham	SMoF	General Dynamics	Aardvark	
F-111A	CA	Rosam	EAFB	General Dynamics	Aardvark	63-9766
F-111A	IL	Ranto	OCAM	General Dynamics	Aardvark	63-9767, NA, 474th TacFW
F-111A	NV	Battl	BMAM	General Dynamics	Aardvark	66-12
F-111A	OH	Dayto	USAFM	General Dynamics	Aardvark	67-0057
F-111A(FB)	NB	Bellevue	SACM	General Dynamics	Aardvark	Fighter/Bomber
F-111A(FB)	SD	Rapid	SDA&SM	General Dynamics	Aardvark	68-0248, Fighter/Bomber
F-111A	TX	Wichi	SAFB	General Dynamics	Aardvark	
F-111A(FB)	CA	Sacra	McCelAFB	General Dynamics	Aardvark	67-159, Fighter/Bomber
F-111A(NF)	CA	Rosam	EAFB	General Dynamics	Aardvark	63-9778
F-111A(RF)	ID	Mount	MHAFB	General Dynamics	Aardvark	RAAF
F-111E	AZ	Tucso	PAM	General Dynamics	Aardvark	63-33
F-111E	FL	Shali	USAFM	General Dynamics	Aardvark	68-58 ET
F-111E	GA	Warner Robin	MoF	General Dynamics	Aardvark	68-255
F-111E	UT	Ogden	HAFBM	General Dynamics	Aardvark	"My Lucky Blonde"
F-111F	NM	Clovis	CP	General Dynamics	Aardvark	
F-111F	NM	Portales	CP	General Dynamics	Aardvark	
F-111F	OH	Dayto	USAFM	General Dynamics	Aardvark	
F-116A(CF)	ONT-C	Ottawa	CAM	Canadair		
F-117A	NV	LasVe	NAFB	Lockheed	Nighthawk	
F-117A(YF)	OH	Dayto	USAFM	Lockheed	Nighthawk	79-10781
F2F	SC	Mt Pl	PPM	Grumman	Flying Barrel	
F2H-2	CA	Miramar	FLAM	McDonnell	Banshee	
F2H-2	TX	C Christi	USS Lexi	McDonnell	Banshee	
F2H-2N	MO	SLoui	SLAM	McDonnell	Banshee	
F2H-2P	FL	Pensa	USNAM	McDonnell	Banshee	126673, MW-2, VMJ-1, Photo Recon
F2H-2P	NY	Horseheads	NWM	McDonnell	Banshee	125690, VFP-61
F2H-3	AB-C	Calga	NMoA	McDonnell	Banshee	At Naval Museum
F2H-3	NS-C	Shear	CFBS	McDonnell	Banshee	
F2H-3	ON-C	Ottaw	CAM	McDonnell	Banshee	126464
F2H-3	VA	VBeac	ONAS	McDonnell	Banshee	7693, AD 300
F2H-4(F-2D)	FL	Pensa	USNAM	McDonnell	Banshee	126419, 127663
F3B	NY	NYC	ISASM	McDonnell	Demon	
F3D (F-10B)	CA	Rosam	EAFB	Douglas	Skynight	125850
F3D (F-10B)	KS	Topek	CAM	Douglas	Skynight	
F3D (F-10B)	NY	NYC	ISASM	Douglas	Skynight	
F3D-2(F-10B)	AZ	Tucso	PAM	Douglas	Skynight	124629
F3D-2(F-10B)	CA	Miramar	FLAM	Douglas	Skynight	L,T VMF(AW)-531
F3D-2(F-10B)	FL	Pensa	USNAM	Douglas	Skynight	124598
F3D-2(F-10B)	RI	NKing	QAM	Douglas	Skynight	124620
F3F-2	CA	Carls	CAJRM	Grumman	Flying Barrel	8F8
F3F-2	CA	San Diego	SDAM	Grumman	Flying Barrel	0964
F3F-2	FL	Pensa	USNAM	Grumman	Flying Barrel	0976, VMF-2, #16
F3F-2	NY	NYC	ISASM	Grumman	Flying Barrel	
F3F-2	TX	Galve	LSFM	Grumman	Flying Barrel	
F3F-2 (2ea)	CA	Chino	PoFAM	Grumman	Flying Barrel	N20RW, 972
F3F-3	NY	Garden City	CoAM	Grumman	Flying Barrel	
F3H	NY	NYC	ISASM	McDonnell	Demon	
F3H	FL	Clearwater	FMAM	McDonnell	Demon	
F3H-2(F-3B)	AZ	Tucso	PAM	McDonnell	Demon	145221
F.4	AL	Gunte	LGARFM	Martinsyde	Buzzard	
F4B-3(P-12E)	NC	Havelock	HTC	Boeing	Biplane	
F4B-4(P-12E)	AL	Mobile	BMP	Boeing	Biplane	9022
F4B-4(P-12E)	FL	Pensacola	PSAM	Boeing	Biplane	9029, 6-F-1, Felix the Cat Sq
F4B-4(P-12E)	DC	Washi	NA&SM	Boeing	Biplane	
F4D-1(F-6A)	AZ	Tucson	PAM	Douglas	Skyray	Sn 134748, Man Sn 10342
F4D-1(F-6A)	CO	Puebl	FWAM	Douglas	Skyray	1-34936
F4D-1(F-6A)	CT	Winds	NEAM	Douglas	Skyray	134836
F4D-1(F-6A)	FL	Pensa	USNAM	Douglas	Skyray	134806
F4D-1(F-6A)	MD	Lexin	PNA&EM	Douglas	Skyray	

Model	State	City	Code	Manufacturer	Name	Serial/Notes
F4D-1(F-6A)	VA	Quantico	MCAGM	Douglas	Skyray	139177
F4F-2(F-6A)	CA	PalmS	PSAM	Grumman	Wildcat	N47201
F4F	WI	Janesville	YAFS4D	Grumman	Wildcat	
F4F-2(XF)	FL	Titusville	VAC	Grumman	Wildcat	0383
F4F-3	IL	Aurora	RH	Grumman	Wildcat	
F4F-3	IL	Chica	O'Hare	Grumman	Wildcat	15
F4F-3	KS	New Century	CAF-HoAW	Grumman	Wildcat	
F4F-3(FM-2)	WA	Everett	MoF	Grumman	Wildcat	74512
F4F-3(FM-2)	WA	Olympia	OFM	Grumman	Wildcat	
F4F-3(FM-2)	FL	Pensa	USNAM	Grumman	Wildcat	3872, 72-F-7
F4F-3A(FM-2)	CA	Miramar	FLAM	Grumman	Wildcat	
F4F-3A(FM-2)	CA	San Diego	SDAM	Grumman	Wildcat	3696
F4F-3A(FM-2)	NY	Garde	CoAM	Grumman	Wildcat	5948
F4F-3A(FM-2)	TX	Breck	BAM	Grumman	Wildcat	
F4F-4(FM-2)	DC	Washi	NA&SM	Grumman	Wildcat	
F4F-4(FM-2)	VA	Quant	MCAGM	Grumman	Wildcat	12114
F4U	CA	Palm Sprg	PSAM	Chance-Vought	Corsair	NX62290, 301, S
F4U	DC	Washi	NM	Chance-Vought	Corsair	
F4U	FL	Titus	VACM	Chance-Vought	Corsair	
F4U	ND	Fargo	FAM	Chance-Vought	Corsair	
F4U	TX	Breck	BAF	Chance-Vought	Corsair	97302, NX 65HP, WF, VMF(N)-513
F4U	TX	Addison	CFM	Chance-Vought	Corsair	
F4U 1/3 Scale	ON-C	Wellington	G	Chance-Vought	Corsair	
F4U(F2G-1)	AZ	Mesa	CFM	Goodyear	Corsair	NATC 454
F4U(F2G-1D)	ND	Fargo	FAM	Goodyear	Corsair	N5588N, #5, Red & White
F4U(F2G-1)	OH	Newbu	WASAC	Goodyear	Corsair	N5577N
F4U(F2G-1)	TX	Galve	LSFM	Goodyear	Corsair	N5588N, 88457
F4U(F2G-1)	WA	Seattle	MoF	Goodyear	Corsair	88382, NATC 454, NX4324
F4U(F2G-2)	OH	Cleveland	FCAAM	Goodyear	Corsair	#74
F4U(FG-1D)	CO	Denver	WOR	Goodyear	Corsair	
F4U(FG-1D)	CT	Strat	SMA	Goodyear	Corsair	
F4U(FG-1D)	FL	Kissi	FTWAM	Goodyear	Corsair	
F4U(FG-1D)	FL	Pensa	USNAM	Goodyear	Corsair	N766JD, 92246
F4U(FG-1D)	IL	Danville	MAM	Goodyear	Corsair	
F4U(FG-1D)	KY	Louisville	CCA	Goodyear	Corsair	67060
F4U(FG-1D)	MI	Kalam	KAHM	Goodyear	Corsair	92509, 611
F4U(FG-1D)	MI	Mt Clemens	SMAM	Goodyear	Corsair	92085, Side # 9
F4U(FG-1D)	NY	Farmingdale	AAM	Goodyear	Corsair	115
F4U(FG-1D) Forward Fuse	OH	Akron	GWoR	Goodyear	Corsair	(Cockpit/Canopy, Wing Stubs, Cowling)
F4U(FG-1D)	OH	Newbu	WASAC	Goodyear	Corsair	
F4U(FG-1D)	OR	Mc Minnville	EAEC	Goodyear	Corsair	3356, N67HP
F4U(FG-1D)	PA	Tough	CFCM	Goodyear	Corsair	
F4U(FG-1D)	SC	Mt Pl	PPM	Chance-Vought	Corsair	
F4U(FG-1D)	TX	Lanca	CAF-DFW	Goodyear	Corsair	N9964Z
F4U(FG-1D)	TX	Midla	CAFFM	Goodyear	Corsair	
F4U(FG-1D)	VA	Quant	MCAGM	Goodyear	Corsair	13486
F4U(FG-1D	VA	Suffolk	FF	Goodyear	Corsair	82640, 4487, N46RL, VF-17
F4U(FG-1D)	WA	Bellevile	AM	Goodyear	Corsair	88303, N700G
F4U(FG-1D)	WA	Olympia	OFM	Goodyear	Corsair	Side # 115
F4U(FG-1D)	WA	Seatt	MoF	Goodyear	Corsair	88382
F4U-1	MA	Stow	BCF	Chance-Vought	Corsair	
F4U-1	VA	Chesapeake	CAFODW	Chance-Vought	Corsair	
F4U-1A	CA	Chino	PoFAM	Chance-Vought	Corsair	
F4U-1D	MD	Silve	PEGF	Chance-Vought	Corsair	
F4U-1D	VA	Hampt	VA&SC	Chance-Vought	Corsair	50375, 56, "Sun Setter"
F4U-4	AZ	Tucso	PAM	Chance-Vought	Corsair	Sn 97142, N22SN
F4U-4	CA	Chino	YACM	Chance-Vought	Corsair	97390, N47991, 97390
F4U-4	FL	Miami	WOM	Chance-Vought	Corsair	NX24OCA
F4U-4	FL	Pensa	USNAM	Chance-Vought	Corsair	97349, WR 18, #86
F4U-4	FL	Polk	FoF	Chance-Vought	Corsair	N5215V, 5, "Angel of Okinawa"
F4U-4	ND	Wahpe	TSA	Chance-Vought	Corsair	
F4U-4	NM	STere	WEAM	Chance-Vought	Corsair	JM 53
F4U-4	VA	Quant	MCAGM	Chance-Vought	Corsair	97369
F4U-4	WI	Oshko	EAAAM	Chance-Vought	Corsair	N6667, 9413
F4U-4B Rep ½ Scale	MI	Kalam	KAHM	Goodyear	Corsair	
F4U-4(XF)	CT	Winds	NEAM	Chance-Vought	Corsair	
F4U-5	FL	Kissi	FTWAM	Chance-Vought	Corsair	
F4U-5	IL	Springfield	ACM	Chance-Vought	Corsair	124486
F4U-5N	CA	Miramar	FLAM	Chance-Vought	Corsair	
F4U-5N	IN	Valparaiso	IAM	Chance-Vought	Corsair	122179
F4U-5	KS	Liber	MAAM	Chance-Vought	Corsair	
F4U-5N	TX	Galve	LSFM	Chance-Vought	Corsair	N43RW, 121881
F4U-7	OR	Tillamook	TAM	Chance-Vought	Corsair	
F4U-7(AU-1)	AL	Mobil	BMP	Chance-Vought	Corsair	133704, LO10, VMA-212, "Marines" Rear Fuse
F5D-1(X-4)	OH	Wapak	NAA&SM	Douglas	Skylancer	142350
F6C *See P-1*						
F6C-4	VA	Quant	MCAGM	Curtiss	Hawk	A-7412
F6F	CA	PalmS	PSAM	Grumman	Hellcat	
F6F	CA	Point Mugu	PMMP	Grumman	Hellcat	79063
F6F	MD	Andrews	APG	Grumman	Hellcat	77722, Tail 22 White Diamond
F6F	SC	Mt Pl	PPM	Grumman	Hellcat	
F6F	TX	Midla	CAF-JK	Grumman	Hellcat	N1078Z
F6F-3	CA	Carls	CAJM	Grumman	Hellcat	41930, N30FG, 5
F6F-3	CA	Chino	PoFAM	Grumman	Hellcat	
F6F-3	CA	San Diego	SDAM	Grumman	Hellcat	42874, 21
F6F-3	MD	Silver Hill	PEGF	Grumman	Hellcat	N7537U
F6F-3	FL	Miami	WOM	Grumman	Hellcat	66237, #17
F6F-3	FL	Pensa	USNAM	Grumman	Hellcat	
F6F-3	MD	Silve	PEGF	Grumman	Hellcat	
F6F-3	VA	Quant	MCAGM	Grumman	Hellcat	41476
F6F-4	VA	Quant	MCAGM	Grumman	Hellcat	
F6F-5	CA	Chino	PoFAM	Grumman	Hellcat	93879, N4994V, 31
F6F-5	CA	Chino	YACM	Grumman	Hellcat	78645, N9265A, 78645
F6F-5	CA	Palm Sprg	PoF	Grumman	Hellcat	NX4964W, 58644, 36
F6F-5	CA	Camarillo	CAF-SCW	Grumman	Hellcat	N1078Z, 70222
F6F-5	CT	Winds	NEAM	Grumman	Hellcat	
F6F-5	FL	Pensa	USNAM	Grumman	Hellcat	94203
F6F-5	MI	Kalam	KAHM	Grumman	Hellcat	79683, 47-8960, N4PP, 4
F6F-5	NY	Garde	CoAM	Grumman	Hellcat	94263
F6F-5	RI	NKing	QAM	Grumman	Hellcat	70185
F6F-5	WA	Eastsound	FHC	Grumman	Hellcat	79863, N79863
F6F-5 Replica	NY	NYC	ISASM	Grumman	Hellcat	
F6F-5N	TX	Galve	LSFM	Grumman	Hellcat	N4998V, 94204, 32
F6F-5N	TX	Midla	CAFFM	Grumman	Hellcat	
F7C-1	FL	Pensa	USNAM	Curtiss	Sea Hawk	A-7667
F7F	CA	Rialto	KA			80375

Model	State	City	Museum	Manufacturer	Name	Notes
F7F-3	CA	Palm Sprg	PSAM	Grumman	Tigercat	45-80411, NX207F, Tail BP", "King of Cats"
F7F-3	FL	Miami	WOM	Grumman	Tigercat	N7626C
F7F-3 (2 ea)	FL	Pensa	USNAM	Grumman	Tigercat	N 7654C 80373
F7F-3N	AZ	Tucso	PAM	Grumman	Tigercat	80410
F7F-3N	CA	Chino	PoFAM	Grumman	Tigercat	
F7F-3P	MI	Kalam	KAHM	Grumman	Tigercat	803903
F7U-3	CA	Alameda	USSHM	Chance-Vought	Cutlass	129565
F7U-3	OH	Newbu	WASAC	Chance-Vought	Cutlass	129685
F7U-3	PA	Willo	WGNAS	Chance-Vought	Cutlass	9462
F7U-3	WA	Everett	MoF	Chance-Vought	Cutlass	129554
F7U-3M	FL	Pensa	USNAM	Chance-Vought	Cutlass	129655
F8C/K-2	SC	Beauf	MAS	Vought	Crusader	146963, DC5, VMF(AW)-122
F8F (G-58B)	CA	Palm SPrg	PSAM	Grumman	Bearcat	Sn 1262, NL700A, "Bob's Bear"
F8F-1				Grumman	Bearcat	95255, N41089, VF-6A, Tail S, Side # 204
F8F-1A	CA	Chino	PoFAM	Grumman	Bearcat	
F8F-1	TX	Breck	BAM	Grumman	Bearcat	
F8F-1B	CA	Chino	YACM	Grumman	Bearcat	122095, N2209, 122095
F8F-1D(XF)	MI	Kalam	KAHM	Grumman	Bearcat	90454, N9G
F8F-2	CA	Camarillo	CAF-SCW	Grumman	Bearcat	N7825C, Side Number 201
F8F-2	CA	Chino	PoFAM	Grumman	Bearcat	
F8F-2	FL	Pensa	USNAM	Grumman	Bearcat	121710, B, 100
F8F-2	MD	Silve	PEGF	Grumman	Bearcat	"Conquest I"
F8F-2	TX	Galve	LSFM	Grumman	Bearcat	N1030B, 121776
F8F-2	TX	Midla	CAFFM	Grumman	Bearcat	
F8F-2	WA	Eastsound	HFM	Grumman	Bearcat	
F8F-2	WI	Oshko	EAAAAM	Grumman	Bearcat	122619
F8U-1(F-8A)	CA	Alameda	USSHM	Vought	Crusader	143703
F8U-1	CA	Chino	PoFAM	Vought	Crusader	16
F8U-1(F-8J)	CA	El Cajon	SDAMGF	Vought	Crusader	
F8U-1	CA	SRosa	PCAM	Vought	Crusader	
F8U-1	FL	Jacks	NASCF	Vought	Crusader	14135,1 AD, 201, VF-174
F8U-1	GA	Calho	Mercer A	Vought	Crusader	
F8U-1	PA	Willo	WGNAS	Vought	Crusader	143806
F8U-1	SC	MtPleasant	PPM	Vought	Crusader	
F8U-1(XF)	WA	Everett	MoF	Vought	Crusader	138899
F8U-1(F-8)	CO	Puebl	FWAM	Vought	Crusader	145349
F8U-1(F-8)	NV	FAllon	NASF	Vought	Crusader	
F8U-1(F-8A)	AZ	Tucso	PAM	Vought	Crusader	144427, AC, 207, VF- 32
F8U-1(F-8A)	TX	FWort	PMoT	Vought	Crusader	
F8U-1(F-8A)	VA	VBeac	ONAS	Vought	Crusader	149150, AD, VF-101
F8U-1(F-8C)	CA	SRosa	PCAM	Vought	Crusader	
F8U-1(F-8H)	KS	Liber	MAAM	Vought	Crusader	
F8U-1(F-8J)	CA	San Diego	SDAM	Vought	Crusader	150297
F8U-1(F-8J)	HI	Kaneohe	KBMCAS	Vought	Crusader	146973, VMF AW235DB
F8U-1(F-8J)	MI	Kalam	KAHM	Vought	Crusader	150904
F8U-1(F-8J) Cockpit	OR	Tillamook	TAM	Vought	Crusader	
F8U-1(F-8K)	AZ	Phoenix	DVA	Vought	Crusader	
F8U-1(F-8K)	CA	Alameda	USSHM	Vought	Crusader	146931
F8U-1(F-8K)	FL	Titusville	VAC	Vought	Crusader	
F8U-1(F-8K)LTV	CT	Winds	NEAM	Vought	Crusader	
F8U-1(F-8L)	CA	Ridegrest	CLNWC	Vought	Crusader	
F8U-1(RF-8G)	CA	Rosam	EAFB	Vought	Crusader	
F8U-1(RF-8G)	DC	Dulle	DA	Vought	Crusader	
F8U-1P(F-8A)	FL	Pensa	USNAM	Vought	Crusader	144347, NP201, VF- 24
F8U-1P(F-8G(RF))	AL	Mobile	BMP	Vought	Crusader	146898
F8U-1P(F-8G(RF))	FL	Pensa	USNAM	Vought	Crusader	146898
F8U-1P(RF-8G)	CA	Miramar	FLAM	Vought	Crusader	WS, VMF-323, 14467, #21
F9-5	TX	Hawki	RRSA			
F9C-2	FL	Pensa	USNAM	Curtiss	Sparrowhawk	9056
F9F	FL	Titusville	VAC	Grumman	Panther	
F9F	KS	Topek	CAM	Grumman	Panther	
F9F	MD	Lexington	PRNAM	Grumman	Panther	144276, AD Tail
F9F	MD	Middl	GLMAM	Grumman	Panther	
F9F	MS	Petal	MWHMM	Grumman	Panther	
F9F	NY	NYC	ISASM	Grumman	Panther	
F9F	NY	Tonaw	CityPark	Grumman	Panther	
F9F	SC	Mt Pl	PPM	Grumman	Panther	
F9F	TX	FWort	PMoT	Grumman	Panther	
F9F	WI	Janes	CityPark	Grumman	Panther	
F9F	WI	Janesville	VFW 75	Grumman	Panther	
F9F-2	CT	Winds	NEAM	Grumman	Panther	
F9F-2	FL	Pensa	USNAM	Grumman	Panther	123050
F9F-2	MI	Kalamazoo	KAHM	Grumman	Panther	123072
F9F-2	PA	Willo	WGNAS	Grumman	Panther	127120, V209, VF-113
F9F-2	TX	Dalla	CFM	Grumman	Panther	N9525A, 123078, A 112, VF- 21 From: USS Kearsage, Boxer
F9F-2	VA	Quant	MCAGM	Grumman	Panther	123526
F9F-2	VA	VBeac	ONAS	Grumman	Panther	123612, AD 200
F9F-5P	AL	Mobile	BMP	Grumman	Panther	126285, F21, "F21"
F9F-4 (2 ea)	AZ	Tucso	PAM	Grumman	Panther	125183
F9F-5	FL	Tittusville	VACM	Grumman	Panther	
F9F-5P	CA	Alameda	USSHM	Grumman	Panther	125316
F9F-5P	CA	Chino	PoFAM	Grumman	Panther	
F9F-5P	FL	Pensa	USNAM	Grumman	Panther	94203
F9F-5P	FL	Pensa	VC	Grumman	Panther	
F9F-5P	MN	Winoma	MCA	Grumman	Panther	125952
F9F-6(TF)	CA	San Diego	SDACM	Grumman	Cougar	
F9F-6	FL	Pensa	USNAM	Grumman	Cougar	128109, A, 211, VF-142
F9F-6	MN	Brain	CWCRA	Grumman	Cougar	
F9F-6P	NC	Havelock	HTC	Grumman	Cougar	
F9F-7	NY	Garde	CoAM	Grumman	Cougar	124382
F9F-8(TAF-9J)	AZ	Tucso	PAM	Grumman	Cougar	Sn 141121
F9F-8	CO	Puebl	FWAM	Grumman	Cougar	138876
F9F-8	FL	Jacks	NASCF	Grumman	Cougar	131230, O, 401, VF- 81
F9F-8	MD	Lewington	PRNAM	Grumman	Cougar	51-44276, AD 310
F9F-8	WA	Seatt	MoF	Grumman	Cougar	131232
F9F-8(TAF-9J)	AZ	Tucso	PAM	Grumman	Cougar	368 141121
F9F-8(TAF-9J)	CA	San Diego	SDACM	Grumman	Cougar	
F9F-8P	CA	Miramar	FLAM	Grumman	Cougar	TN VMCJ-3
F9F-8T(TF-9J)	AZ	Tucso	PAM	Grumman	Cougar	Sn 147397
F9F-8T	TX	C Christi	USS Lexi	Grumman	Cougar	
F9J(TF)	MI	Kalamazoo	KAHM	Grumman	Cougar	147283
F9F-P(RF-9J)	AZ	Tucso	PAM	Grumman	Cougar	110 144426
F11F	FL	Pensa	NASP	Grumman	Tiger	1, "Blue Angels"
F11F	FL	Pensa	PRA	Grumman	Tiger	3, "Blue Angels"
F11F	MI	Ypsil	YAF	Grumman	Tiger	
F11F	SC	Flore	FA&MM	Grumman	Tiger	

F11F-1	SC	MtPleasant	PPM	Grumman	Tiger		
F11F-1	AZ	Grand	PoFGCVA	Grumman	Tiger	141868, "Blue Angles #2"	
F11F-1	AZ	Tucso	PAM	Grumman	Tiger	141824	
F11F-1	KS	Topek	CAM	Grumman	Tiger	5, "Blue Angels"	
F11F-1(F-11A)	MI	Kalam	KAHM	Grumman	Tiger	141872	
F11F-1	NY	NYC	ISASM	Grumman	Tiger	AF 210	
F11F-1	OH	Newbu	WASAC	Grumman	Tiger	141849	
F11F-1F	NY	NYC	ISASM	Grumman	Tiger		
Fa 330	AZ	Tucson	PAM	Focke-Achgelis	Rotor Kite	Towed Behind U-Boats	
Fa 330	MD	Silve	PEGF	Focke-Achgelis	Rotor Kite		
Fa 330A-1	OH	Dayto	USAFM	Focke-Achgelis	Sandpiper		
Fairchild 100B	AK	Ancho	AAHM	Fairchild	American Pilgrim	N709Y, "American Pilgrim"	
Fairchild F-45	MN	Blaine	GWFM	Fairchild	F-45		
Fairchild F-45	WY	Jackson	GWFM	Fairchild	F-45		
Fairchild F-27A	NV	Las Vegas	LBAHSM	Fairchild	Friendship	Model 27, Sn 48, N753L, "Bonanaza Airlines"	
Fairey Battle 1T	ON-C	Ottaw	CAM	Fairey	Battle		
Fairey Firefly Mk.5	ON-C	Hamilton	CWH	Fairey	Firefly	C-GBD6	
Fairey Firefly Mk.I	NS-C	Shear	CFBS	Fairey	Firefly		
Fairchild XAUM	NY	Garden	CoAM	Fairchild	Petrel	E278	
Fairey Swordfish	NS-C	Shear	CFBS	Fairey	Swordfish		
Fairey Swordfish	ON-C	Ottaw	CAM	Fairey	Swordfish		
Fairey Swordfish Mk.II	CA	S.Mon	MoF	Fairey	Swordfish	HS 164, N2F	
Fairey Swordfish Mk.IV	FL	Polk	FoF	Fairey	Swordfish		
Falck Racer	WI	Oshko	EAAAAM	Falck	Racer		
Fanjet Falcon 20	MD	Silve	PEGF	Dassault	Fanjet Falcon	"Federal Express"	
Farley Vincent-Starflight	LA	Patte	WWMAM	Farley	Starflight		
Farman Sport	MD	Silve	PEGF	Farman	Sport		
FB-111A	CA	Atwater	CAM	General Dynamics	Aardvark	69-6507	
FB-111A	CA	Riverside	MFAM	General Dynamics	Aardvark	68-0245, "Ready Teddy"	
FB-111A	LA	Bossi	BAFB	General Dynamics	Aardvark	SAC Bomber	
FB-111A	NE	Ashland	SACM	General Dynamics	Aardvark	68-267, SAC Bomber	
FB-5	CA	Chino	PoFAM	Boeing	Model 55	Model 55	
FB-5	VA	Quant	MCAGM	Boeing	Model 55		
FC- 2	DC	Washi	NA&SM	Fairchild			
FC- 2	MB-C	Winni	WCAM	Fairchild			
FC- 2W-2	ON-C	Ottaw	CAM	Fairchild		NC 6621	
FC- 2W-2	VA	Sands	VAM	Fairchild		"Stars & Stripes"	
FC- 2W-2	WI	Oshko	EAAAAM	Fairchild		NC 3569	
FC-2-W2	WY	Jackson	GWFM	Fairchild			
FC-22	CA	San Carlos	HAM	Fairchild			
FC-22	IA	Ottumwa	APM	Fairchild		512, N11649	
FC-24	CA	Camarillo	CAF-SCW	Fairchild			
FC-24	CA	San Carlos	HAM	Fairchild			
FC-24	CA	Santa Paula	SPAA	Fairchild			
FC-24W	WA	Seattle	MoF	Fairchild		206, N37161	
FC-24	WA	Vancouver	PAM	Fairchild			
FC-24 *See C 61(UC)*				Fairchild			
FC-24-C8F	OH	Dayto	USAFM	Fairchild		For Mil Version See UC-61J	
FC-27	WY	Greyb	H&PA	Fairchild			
FC-71	AB-C	Wetas	RM	Fairchild	Super 71	USAAF as C-8 or UC-96	
FC-71	IA	Ottumwa	APM	Fairchild	Super 71	603, N9726	
FC-71	MB-C	Winni	CC	Fairchild		USAAF as C-8 or UC-96	
FC-71(C-8)	MB-C	Winni	WCAM	Fairchild	Super 71		
FC-71C	AB-C	Edmonton	AAM	Fairchild	Super 71	17	
FC-82A	BC-C	Langley	CMoF&T	Fairchild	Packet		
FC-82A	ON-C	Ottaw	CAM	Fairchild	Packet		
FE-8	DC	Washi	NA&SM	RAF			
FE-8	MD	Silve	PEGF	RAF			
FE-8	ME	OwlsH	OHTM	RAF			
Ferret Scout Car	ON-C	Oshaw	OAM&IM	Ferret	Scout Car		
FF-1	FL	Pensa	USNAM	Grumman	Goblin	9351 5-F-1	
FH-1	DC	Washi	NA&SM	McDonnell	Phantom		
FH-1	FL	Pensa	USNAM	McDonnell	Phantom	111793	
FH-1	NY	Horseheads	NWM	McDonnell	Phantom	111768, Side #5, Tail MW	
FH-1099	CA	SCarl	HAM	Fairchild-Hiller	CAMEL	LargestJet Helicopter	
FH-1100	CA	SCarl	HAM	Fairchild-Hiller	Light Utility 1	Commercial Helicopter	
Fi-103(V-1)	CA	Chino	PoFAM	Fiesler	Flying Bomb		
Fi-103(V-1)	IN	Green	CityPark	Fiesler	Flying Bomb(Buzz)		
Fi-103(V-1)	KS	Hutch	KC&SC	Fiesler	Flying Bomb(Buzz)		
Fi-103(V-1) FZG-76	NS	Halifax	ACAM	Fiesler	Flying Bomb		
Fi-103(V-1)	OH	Dayton	USAFM	Fiesler	Flying Bomb		
Fi-103(V-1)	TX	RioHo	TAM	Fiesler	Flying Bomb(Buzz)		
Fi-103(V-1)	VA	Suffolk	FF	Fiesler	Flying Bomb(Buzz)		
Fi-156	MD	Silve	PEGF	Fiesler	Storch	"Ms. 500"	
Fi-156	NM	STere	WEAM	Fiesler	Storch		
Fi-156	OH	Dayto	USAFM	Fiesler	Storch	4389	
Fi-156	TX	Midland	CAFM	Fiesler	Storch	N40FS	
Fi-156	TX	RioHo	TAM	Fiesler	Storch	N43FS	
Fi-156A-1	VA	Suffolk	FF	Fiesler	Storch	2631.751	
Fi-156	WA	Eastsound	FHC	Fiesler	Storch	4362, N43fFS	
Fi-156C-2	WI	Oshko	EAAAAM	Fiesler	Storch	NX464FB	
Fiat G.91 Pan	WA	Seatt	MoF	Fiat	Pan	MM6244, NC10	
Fike Model A	OR	Eugen	OAM	Fike	Homebuilt	19	
Fike Model C	WI	Oshko	EAAAAM	Fike	Homebuilt	13390	
Fisher Kola 202	KS	Liberal	MAAM	Fisher	Kola		
Fisher F-303	FL	Lakeland	SNFAM	Fisher	Classic		
F- 86	TX	Galveston	SP	North American	Fury		
FJ-1A	CA	Chino	YAM	North American	Fury		
FJ-1	CT	Winds	NEAM	North American	Fury		
FJ-1	FL	Pensa	USNAM	North American	Fury	120351, S104	
FJ-1	KY	Louisville	CCA	North American	Fury		
FJ-2	CA	Alameda	USSHM	North American	Fury	132057	
FJ-2	FL	Pensa	USNAM	North American	Fury	N132023	
FJ-2	NM	STere	WEAM	North American	Fury		
FJ-2	SC	Mt Pl	PPM	North American	Fury		
FJ-3	AL	Everg	MAE	North American	Fury		
FJ-3	CA	Chino	PoFAM	North American	Fury		
FJ-3	CA	Miramar	FLAM	North American	Fury	WS, VMF-323	
FJ-3	NC	Hickory	HRA	North American	Fury		
FJ-3	NY	NYC	ISASM	North American	Fury		
FJ-3	SC	Beauf	MAS	North American	Fury	134841, DN9, VMF-333	
FJ-3	VA	Quantico	MCAGM	North American	Fury	136119	
FJ-3M	FL	Pensa	USNAM	North American	Fury	N136008	
FJ-4B	GA	Cordele	GVMSP	North American	Fury		
FJ-4B	NY	Buffa	B&ECNP	North American	Fury		
FJ-4B	NY	Buffa	City	North American	Fury		

FJ-4B	PA	Willo	WGNAS	North American	Fury	143568
FJ-4B(AF-1E)	AZ	Tucso	PAM	North American	Fury	139531, FU-525
Flaglor Sky Scooter	AZ	Tucso	PAM	Flagor	Sky Scooter	1000, N6WM
Flagg	MO	Maryland Hts	HARM	Flagg	Biplane	
Fleet	NM	Kirkl	KA	Fleet		
Fleet	TX	Brown	RGVW-CAF	Fleet		N16BR
Fleet	ON-C	Collingwood	CCAF	Fleet	Canuck	48, C-FDPV
Fleet 7C	AB-C	Nanto	NLS&AM	Fleet	Fawn	
Fleet 7C	IA	Ottumwa	APM	Fleet	Fawn	
Fleet 7C	ID	Athol	NAM	Fleet	Fawn	
Fleet 7C II	ON-C	Hamilton	CWH	Fleet	Fawn	
Fleet 7C II	ON-C	Windsor	CAHS	Fleet	Fawn	
Fleet 21K	ON-C	Hamilton	CWH	Fleet		
Fleet	MB-C	Brandon	CATPM	Fleet	Fort	
Fleet 50K	ON-C	Ottaw	CAM	Fleet	Fort	
Fleet 60K	ON-C	Hamilton	CWH	Fleet	Fort	
Fleet 60K	SK-C	MJaw	WDM	Fleet	Fort	
Fleet 80K	ON-C	Ottaw	CAM	Fleet	Fort	
Fleet Biplane (2 ea)	VA	Bealt	FCA	Fleet		Sn 347
Fleet Model 1	VA	Sandston	VAM	Fleet	Finch	N605M
Fleet Model 2	AZ	Tucso	PAM	Fleet	Finch	N605M
Fleet Model 2	BC-C	Langley	CMoF&T	Fleet	Finch	
Fleet Model 2	CA	S.Mar	SMMoF	Fleet	Finch	
Fleet Model 2	CA	S.Mon	MoF	Fleet	Finch II	325, N1328V
Fleet Model 2	CA	San Diego	SDAM	Fleet	Finch	N648M
Fleet Model 2	NY	Garde	CoAM	Fleet	Finch	NC614M
Fleet Model 2	NY	Ghent	POMAM	Fleet	Finch	
Fleet Model 2	OH	Madis	CFR	Fleet	Finch	
Fleet Model 2	ON-C	Ottaw	CAM	Fleet	Finch	
Fleet Model 2	SK-C	MJaw	WDM	Fleet	Finch	
Fleet Model 2	TX	Brown	CAFRGVW	Fleet	Finch	
Fleet Model 16	AB-C	Wetas	RM	Fleet	Finch	
Fleet Model 16B	NY	Bayport	BA	Fleet	Finch II	
Fleet Model 16B	NY	Mayvi	DA	Fleet	Finch	
Fleet Model 16B	NY	Rhine	ORA	Fleet	Finch	
Fleet Model 16B	ON-C	Hamilton	CWH	Fleet	Finch	C-FFLA, 4738
Fleet Model 16B	ON-C	Ottaw	CAM	Fleet	Finch	4510
Fleetwings Seabird	WY	Jackson	GWFM	Fleetwings	Seabird	
Flight Simulator	BC-C	Langley	CMoF&T			
Fly Baby	KS	Liberal	MAM		Fly Baby	
Flying Boat	CT	Winds	NEAM			
FM-2(F4F)	CA	Chino	YACM	General Motors	Wildcat	85564, N4629V
FM-2(F4B-4)	CA	El Cajon	CAFFFM	General Motors	Wildcat	
FM-2(F4F)	CA	SCarl	CAF-BR	General Motors	Wildcat	N5833
FM-2(F4F)	CT	Winds	NEAM	General Motors	Wildcat	
FM-2(F4F)	FL	Pensa	USNAM	General Motors	Wildcat	16278, 7
FM-2(F4F)	FL	Polk	FoF	General Motors	Wildcat	
FM-2(F4F)	MI	Kalam	KAHM	General Motors	Wildcat	86581
FM-2(F4F)	OR	Tillamook	TAM	General Motors	Wildcat	N58918
FM-2(F4F)	PA	Tough	CFCM	General Motors	Wildcat	N315E, Side # F-13
FM-2(F4F)	TX	Dalla	CFM	General Motors	Wildcat	17
FM-2(F4F)	TX	Galve	LSFM	General Motors	Wildcat	N551TC, 47160
FM-2(F4F)	TX	Midla	CAFFM	General Motors	Wildcat	N681S
FM-2(F4F)	WA	Seatt	MoF	General Motors	Wildcat	4512
FM-2(F4F)	WI	Oshko	EAAAAM	General Motors	Wildcat	86956
FO-141	CA	Riverside	MFAM	Folland	Gnat	E1076, "Green Mountain Boys"
Fokker D.VA	AZ	Mesa	CFM	Fokker	D.VIII	N111CV
Fokker D.VA	ME	Owls Head	OHTM	Fokker	D.VIII	
Fokker D.VII	AL	Birmingham	SMoF	Fokker	D.VII	Project
Fokker D.VII	AL	Gunte	LGARFM	Fokker	D.VII	
Fokker D.VII	AZ	Mesa	CFM	Fokker	D.VII	
Fokker D.VII	WA	Seattle	MoF	Fokker	D.VII	N38038
Fokker D.VII -	CA	Chino	PoFAM	Fokker	D.VII	
Fokker D.VII	CO	Denve	WOR	Fokker	D.VII	
Fokker D.VII	DC	Washi	NA&SM	Fokker	D.VII	
Fokker D.VII	FL	Orlan	CSS	Fokker	D.VII	
Fokker D.VII	FL	Orlan	OFW	Fokker	D.VII	
Fokker D.VII	FL	Pensa	USNAM	Fokker	D.VII	1975, 18
Fokker D.VII	NY	Rhine	ORA	Fokker	D.VII	
Fokker D.VII	NY	River	RE	Fokker	D.VII	
Fokker D.VII	OH	Dayto	USAFM	Fokker	D.VII	D7625118
Fokker D.VII	ON-C	Chelt	TGWFM	Fokker	D.VII	
Fokker D.VII	ON-C	Ottaw	CAM	Fokker	D.VII	10347, 18
Fokker D.VII	PQ-C	Knowl	BCHS	Fokker	D.VII	
Fokker D.VII	TX	Kingbury	VAHF	Fokker	D.VII	Project
Fokker D.VIII	AL	Gunte	LGARFM	Fokker	D.VIII	N111CV
Fokker D.VIII	AZ	Mesa	CFM	Fokker	D.VIII	N111CV
Fokker D.VIII	WA	Seattle	MoF	Fokker	D.VIII	NX7557U
Fokker D.VIII	NY	Rhine	ORA	Fokker	D.VIII	
Fokker D.VIII	TX	Bealt	FCA	Fokker	D.VIII	
Fokker D.VIII	TX	Dalla	CFM	Fokker	D.VIII	
Fokker DR.I	AB-C	Calga	AMoC	Fokker	Triplane	Dreidecker
Fokker DR.I	AL	Gunte	LGARFM	Fokker	Triplane	Dreidecker
Fokker DR.I	AZ	Mesa	CFM	Fokker	Triplane	Dreidecker
Fokker DR.I	WA	Seattle	MoF	Fokker	Triplane	535, NX2203
Fokker DR.I	CA	Chino	PoFAM	Fokker	Triplane	Dreidecker
Fokker DR.I	CA	S.Mon	MoF	Fokker	Triplane	Dreidecker
Fokker DR.I Rep	CA	San Diego	SDAM	Fokker	Triplane	Dreidecker
Fokker DR.I	CT	Winds	NEAM	Fokker	Triplane	Dreidecker
Fokker DR.I	FL	Orlan	CSS	Fokker	Triplane	Dreidecker
Fokker DR.I	FL	Orlan	OFW	Fokker	Triplane	Dreidecker
Fokker DR.I	ID	Athol	NAM	Fokker	Triplane	Dreidecker
Fokker DR.I	ID	Cadwe	WAM	Fokker	Triplane	Dreidecker
Fokker DR.I	IL	Rantoul	OCM	Fokker	Triplane	Dreidecker
Fokker DR.I	ME	OwlsH	OHTM	Fokker	Triplane	Dreidecker
Fokker DR.I	NY	EGall	GA	Fokker	Triplane	Dreidecker
Fokker DR.I	NY	Rhine	ORA	Fokker	Triplane	Dreidecker
Fokker DR.I	OH	Dayto	USAFM	Fokker	Triplane	Dreidecker, N1387B
Fokker DR.I	OH	Madis	CFR	Fokker	Triplane	Dreidecker
Fokker DR.I	OK	Oklah	KCASM	Fokker	Triplane	Dreidecker
Fokker DR.I	ON-C	Chelt	TGWFM	Fokker	Triplane	Dreidecker
Fokker DR.I	OR	Eugene	OA&SM	Fokker	Triplane	Dreidecker
Fokker DR.I	OR	McMinnville	EAEC	Fokker	Triplane	Dreidecker
Fokker DR.I	PA	Bethel	GAAM	Fokker	Triplane	Dreidecker
Fokker DR.I	TX	Kingbury	VAHF	Fokker	Triplane	Dreidecker Project
Fokker DR.I	WA	Seatt	Restaura	Fokker	Triplane	Dreidecker, FI 102/17

Aircraft	State	City	Museum	Manufacturer	Type	Notes
Fokker DR.I	WA	Vancouver	Pam	Fokker	Triplane	Dreidecker
Fokker DR.I	WI	Oshko	EAAAAM	Fokker	Triplane	Dreidecker, Redfern, N 105RF
Fokker DR.I	WI	Oshko	EAAAAM	Fokker	Triplane	Dreidecker, Sorrell, N 4435C
Fokker E.III	AL	Gunte	LGARFM	Fokker	Eindecker	
Fokker E.III	AZ	Mesa	CFM	Fokker	Eindecker	
Fokker E.III	WA	Seattle	MoF	Fokker	Eindecker	208 226, N3363G
Fokker E.III Rep	CA	San Diego	SDAM	Fokker	Eindecker	
Fokker F.VIIA	MI	Dearb	HFM	Fokker	Trimoter	1
Fokker F.XI	MB-C	Winni	WCAM	Fokker	F.XI	
Fokker SU	MB-C	Winni	WCAM	Fokker	Super Universal	
Fokker SU Frame	AK	Fairb	APAM	Fokker	Super Universal	NC 9792
Folkerts Gullwing	WI	Oshko	EAAAAM	Folkerts	Gullwing	
Ford 4-AT	CA	MHill	Restaura	Ford	Tri-Motor	
Ford 4-AT	WY	Jackson	GWFM	Ford	Tri-Motor	
Ford 4-AT-15	MI	Dearb	HFM	Ford	Tri-Motor	NX 4542,Byrd Antarctic Expedition, "Floyd Bennett"
Ford 4-AT-B	OH	Port	IA	Ford	Tri-Motor	
Ford 4-AT-E	WI	Oshko	EAAAAM	Ford	Tri-Motor	NC 8407
Ford 5-AT	AK	Ancho	AAHM	Ford	Tri-Motor	Wreckage
Ford 5-AT	AZ	Grand	PoFGCVA	Ford	Tri-Motor	N414H, "Scenic Airways"
Ford 5-AT	DC	Washi	NA&SM	Ford	Tri-Motor	
Ford 5-AT	FL	Polk	FoF	Ford	Tri-Motor	
Ford 5-AT	MI	Kalamazoo	KAHM	Ford	Tri-Motor	
Ford 5-AT	MN	Blaine	GH	Ford	Tri-Motor	
Ford 5-AT	NV	L.Veg	MIA	Ford	Tri-Motor	
Ford 5-AT	NV	LasVe	MIAHM	Ford	Tri-Motor	
Ford 5-AT	OR	Mc Minnville	EAEC	Ford	Tri-Motor	8, N9645
Ford 5-AT(RR-5)	FL	Pensa	USNAM	Ford	Tri-Motor	46, NC7861, 9206
Ford 5-AT-B	CA	San Diego	SDAM	Ford	Tri-Motor	N9637
Ford Flivver	FL	Kissimmee	SNFAM	Ford	Flivver	
Ford Flivver	FL	India	FAHS	Ford	Flivver	
Ford Flivver	MI	Dearb	HFM	Ford	Flivver	268
Ford Flivver	WI	Oshko	EAAAAM	Ford	Flivver	268
Formula One Racer	CA	Chino	PoFAM		Racer	"Miss Cosmic Wind"
Formula One Racer	WA	Vancouver	PAM		Racer	
Fouga Magister	FL	Kissimmee	FTWAM			
Fouga Magister	FL	Miami	WOM			
Fouga Magister	TX	Ft Worth	VFM			
Found 100	BC-C	Langley	CMoF&T	Found	Centennail	
Found FBA-2C	ON-C	Ottaw	CAM	Found	FBA-2C	
Fournier RF-4D	WA	Everett	MoF	Fournier	Glider	4064, N1700
Fowler-Gage Tractor	MD	Silve	PEGF	Fowler-Gage	Tractor	
FP-303	FL	Lakel	SFAF	Fisher	Ultralight	
FP-404	NJ	Lumberton	AVM	Fisher	Kit Biplane	
FR-1	CA	Chino	PoFAM	Ryan	Fireball	
Frasca IFR Simulator	ON-C	Sault Ste Marie	CBHC	Frasca	Simulator	
Froebe Helicopter	MB-C	Winni	WCAM	Froebe	Helicopter	
Fulton FA-3	OH	Cleveland	FCAAM	Fulton	Airphibian	
Fulton FA-3-101	MD	Silve	PEGF	Fulton	Airphibian	
Funk 1930	FL	Kissi	FTWAM	Funk		
Funk Model B	CA	Oakla	OWAM	Funk		
Funk Model B	IA	Ottumwa	APM	Funk		60, N24134
Funk Model B	KS	Wichita	KAM	Funk		
Funk Model B	NY	Rhine	ORA	Funk		
Funk Model B	OK	Fredi	AAM	Funk		
Funk Model B	WI	Oshko	EAAAAM	Funk		NC24116
Funk Model B-75	KS	Liber	MAAM	Funk		
Funk Model F-23	TX	RioHo	TAM	Funk		SM SN5, N1128Z
Fw 44	TX	Brown	RGVW-CAF	Focke-Wulf	Stieglitz	N 2497
Fw 44-J	AZ	Tucso	PAM	Focke-Wulf	Stieglitz	2827 N 133JM
Fw 190D	FL	Kissimmee	W1F	Focke-Wulf		Werk Nr 931862
Fw 190A-3	TX	RioHo	TAM	Focke-Wulf		SN5467, "Yellow 9"
Fw 190A-6	TX	Slanton	TAMCC	Focke-Wulf		550470
Fw 190A-8	TX	RioHo	TAM	Focke-Wulf		SN732183, "Blue 4"
Fw 190A-8	TX	San Antonio	TAM	Focke-Wulf		SN732070
Fw 190D-12	AZ	Mesa	CFM	Focke-Wulf		N190D, 10
Fw 190D-9	OH	Dayto	USAFM	Focke-Wulf		60- 1088
Fw 190D-13	AX	Mesa	GU	Focke-Wulf		
Fw 190F-8	MD	Silve	PEGF	Focke-Wulf		
Fw 190F-8	FL	Kissimmee	FTWRM	Focke-Wulf		SN931862, "White 1"
Fw Ta 152H	MD	Silve	PEGF	Focke-Wulf		
G-1B(YG)	CA	Chino	YACM	Kellett	Autogyro	37-381
G-1B(YG)	CT	Washi	TFC	Kellett	Autogyro	
G-6	CA	Chino	YAM	Schultz	Glider	
G-21 (OA-13), (JRF)	CA	Palm Springs	PoFAM	Grumman	Goose	
G-21	DC	Washi	NA&SM	Grumman	Goose	
G-21	NY	Garde	CoAM	Grumman	Goose	1051
G-21	NY	Horsehead	NWM	Grumman	Goose	
G-21	ONT-C	Ottawa	CAM	Grumman	Goose	
G-22	MD	Silver Hill	PEGF	Grumman	Gulfhawk II	
G-44	AK	Ancho	AAHM	Grumman	Widgeon	
G-63	NY	Garde	CoAM	Grumman	Kitten	NX31808
G4M	CA	S.Mon	MoF	Mitsubishi	Betty	
G4M3	MD	Silve	PEGF	Mitsubishi	Betty	
GA-22	WI	Oshko	EAAAAM	Goodyear	Drake	N5516M
GA-36	NY	Amherst	AM	Cunningham-Hall		
GA-36	NY	Niagara Falls	NAM	Cunningham-Hall		
GA-400-R-2J	WI	Oshko	EAAAAM	Goodyear	Gismo	N69N
Gazda Helicospeeder	CA	SCarl	HAM	Gazda	Helicospeeder	
GB Penquin Trainer	WI	Oshko	EAAAAM	Gunderson/Burke	Penquin Trainer	N41047
GB-2	FL	Pensa	USNAM	Beech	Traveller	23688
GeeBee R-1	CT	Winds	NEAM	Grandville Aircraft	GeeBee Racer	711, NR2100
GeeBee R-1 Model A	CT	Winds	NEAM	Grandville Aircraft	GeeBee Racer	
GeeBee R-1 Z Replica	CA	S.Mon	MoF	Grandville Aircraft	GeeBee Racer	NR77V, #4, Model Z
GeeBee R-1 Replica	OH	Cleveland	FCAAM	Grandville Aircraft	GeeBee Racer	
GeeBee R-5 Model E	CT	Winds	NEAM	Grandville Aircraft	GeeBee Racer	
GeeBee R-6H	MEXI	CLedr	CL	Grandville Aircraft	GeeBee Racer	
GEM Little Carrier	VA	FtEus	USATM			
GEM X-2	VA	FtEus	USATM			
Gemini	CA	San Diego	SDAM	McDonnell	Module	
Gemini	KS	Hutch	KC&SC	McDonnell	Space Capsule	
Gemini	KY	Louis	MoH&S	McDonnell	Trainer	
Gemini	MO	SLoui	MDPR	McDonnell	Space Capsule	
Gemini	OH	Dayton	USAFM	McDonnell	Space Capsule	
Gemini	OK	Oklah	KCASM	McDonnell	Space Capsule	
Gemini 11	CA	LAnge	CMoS&I	McDonnell	Space Capsule	
Gemini Grissom	IN	Mitch	SMSP	McDonnell	Space Capsule	

Name	State	City	Code	Manufacturer	Type	Notes
Gemini GT-3	NY	NYC	ISASM	McDonnell	Space Capsule	"Gemini"
Gemini VIII	OH	Wapak	NAA&SM	McDonnell		
Gemini XI	WA	Seatt	PSC	McDonnell		
GH-1	WA	Everett	MoF	Howard		
GH-2	MI	Kalam	KAHM	Howard	Nightingale	32347
GH-2	MI	Ypsil	YAF	Howard	Nightingale	
GH-3	TX	C Christi	USS Lexi	Howard	Nightingale	
Gibson Twin	BC-C	Sidne	BCAM	Gibson	Twin	
GK-1	FL	Pensa	USNAM	Fairchild		7033
GK-1	OR	Tillamook	TAM	Fairchild		
Glasair	CA	Oakla	OWAM	Hamilton	Glasair	
Glasair II-FT	AL	Birmingham	SMoF	Hamilton	Glasair	
Glasair Ham-2	WI	Oshko	EAAAAM	Hamilton	Glasair	N88TH
Glasflugel BS-1	TX	Dallas	FoF	Glasflugel		
Glider	CA	Calis	Nance's		Glider	
Glider	CA	San F	TE		Glider	
Glider 1942	CO	Denve	JWDAS		Glider	
Gliders 6 ea	PA	Water	TGAM		Glider	
Globe GC-1B	KS	Liber	MAAM	Globe	Swift	
Globe GC-1B	OK	Fredi	AAM	Globe	Swift	
Globe KD2G-2	WI	Oshko	EAAAAM	Globe		
Globe KD6D-2	AZ	Grand Canyon	PoFGCVA	Globe		
Go 229	MD	Silve	PEGF	Gotha		
Goddard Model A	NY	Garde	CoAM	Goddard	Rocket	
Gonzales Biplane	CA	Fairc	TAFB	Gonzales		
Gonzales Biplane	CA	Fairf	TAFB	Gonzales		
Gonzales Biplane	CA	San Carlos	HAM	Gonzales		
Goodyear 195	FL	Pensa	USNAM	Goodyear	Inflat A-Plane	Model XA029
Goodyear 195	MD	Lexin	PNA&EM	Goodyear	Inflat A-Plane	
Goodyear Blimp K Car	CT	Winds	NEAM	Goodyear	Blimp.K Car	
Goodyear Blimp K Car	DC	Dulle	DA	Goodyear	Blimp K Car	
Goodyear Gondola	MD	Silver Hill	PEGF	Goodyear	Gondola	"Pilgram"
Gossamer Albatross II	WA	Seatt	MoF	Gossamer	Albatross II	GA-11
Gossamer Condor	DC	Washi	NA&SM	Gossamery	Condor	
Gostave 21	CT	Bridg	CoveRest	Gostave	Whitehead	
Graflite	WI	Oshko	EAAAAM	Kotula-Lundy	Graflite	N780GF
Great Lakes 2T-1A	AL	Birmingham	SMoF	Great Lakes	Sport Trainer	
Great Lakes 2T-1A	CA	El Cajon	SDAMGF	Great Lakes	Sport Trainer	
Great Lakes 2T-1A	CA	S.Mar	SMMoF	Great Lakes	Sport Trainer	
Great Lakes 2T-1A	IA	Ottumwa	APM	Great Lakes	Sport Trainer	252, N11339
Great Lakes 2T-1A	NY	Rhine	ORA	Great Lakes	Sport Trainer	
Great Lakes 2T-1A	OH	Cleveland	FCAAM	Great Lakes	Sport Trainer	#8
Great Lakes 2T-1A	ON-C	Sault Ste Marie	CBHC	Great Lakes	Sport Trainer	C-APL
Great Lakes 2T-1A	PA	Bethel	GAAM	Great Lakes	Sport Trainer	N75M
Great Lakes 2T-1A-2	AL	Birni	Southe	Great Lakes	Sport Trainer	
Great Lakes 2T-1AE	CT	Winds	NEAM	Great Lakes	Sport Trainer	461
Great Lakes 2T-1AE	NM	STere	WEAM	Great Lakes	Sport Trainer	
Great Lakes 2T-1AE	WI	Oshko	EAAAAM	Great Lakes	Sport Trainer	N3182
Great Lakes Special	KS	Ashla	HKAM	Great Lakes	Special	N21E
Greenwood Witch	TX	RioHo	TAM	Greenwood	Witch	N3147N
Grob 103	NM	Hobbs	NSF	Grob	Glider	
Groud Trainer	WI	Oshkosh	EAAAAM	Grooud	Trainer	
Gruneau 2	MB-C	Winni	WCAM	Gruneau	Glider	
Grumman AgCat	GA	Woodstock	NGWS	Grumman	AgCat	
Grumman Echo Cannister	NY	Garde	CoAM	Grumman	Echo Cannister	7
Grumman LM -13	NY	Garde	CoAM	Grumman	LM Ascent Stage	
Grumman LRV Molab	NY	Garde	CoAM	Grumman	LRV Mo Lab	
Grumman LTA-1	NY	Garde	CoAM	Grumman		
Grunau Baby IIb	BC-C	Langley	CMoF&T	Grunau	Baby IIb	
Grunau Baby IIb	MD	Silve	PEGF	Grunau	Baby IIb	
Gulfstream Peregrine	OK	Oklah	A&SM	Gulfstream	Peregrine	
Gulfstream Peregrine	OK	Oklah	KCASM	Gulfstream	Peregrine	
Gulfstream SC	OK	Oklah	SFG	Gulfstream	Shrike Commander	
Gun 3" M5	IN	Atterbury	CAM&MC		Howitzer	
Gun 3" M9 Army	IL	Sprin	S.ArmyNG		Howitzer	
Gun 5" Navy	IL	Edgew	KAALP		Howitzer	
Gun 8" M115	IN	Atterbury	CAM&MC		Howitzer	
Gun 8"	MO	SLoui	NPRC		Howitzer	
Gun 8"	OH	Hubbard	WWIIVM		Howitzer	
Gun 8" M110A2	OH	Groveport	MMM		Howitzer	
Gun 8" M110A2	TX	Pampa	FM		Howitzer	
Gun WWI Howitzer	IL	Salem			Howitzer	
Gun M1918A3	IN	Atterbury	CAM&MC		Schneider	155mm
Guns	VA	Quantico	MCAGM			
Gyrodyne 2C	NY	Garde	CoAM	Gyrodyne	Gyrodyne 2C	N6594K
GZ-22	OH	N Canton	MAM		Gondola	
H- 1 Racer Rep	OR	Cottage Grove	WT	Hughes	Racer Rep	NX258Y
H- 1	DC	Washi	NA&SM	Hughes	Racer	NX258Y
H- 1	OR	McMinnville	EAEC	Hughes	Racer Rep	
H- 1 (AH)	AL	Huntsville	AC	Bell	Huey Cobra	Bell 209
H- 1 (AH)	CA	San Diego	SDAM	Bell	Huey Cobra	Bell 209
H- 1 (AH)	HI	Honolulu	USAM	Bell	Huey Cobra	
H- 1 (AH)	HI	Oahu	USAM	Bell	Huey Cobra	
H- 1 (AH)	IA	Des Moines	ING	Bell	Huey Cobra	0-45454
H- 1 (AH)	IA	Greenfield	IAM	Bell	Huey Cobra	Bell 209
H- 1 (AH)	KS	Topeka	MoKNG	Bell	Huey Cobra	
H- 1 (AH)	KY	FKnox	PMoC&A	Bell	Huey Cobra	Bell 209
H- 1 (AH)	MD	Lexington	USNTPS	Bell	Huey Cobra	Bell 209, 0-15645, Side # 55, ARMY TPS Tail
H- 1 (AH)	MI	Mt Clemens	SMAM	Bell	Huey Cobra	67-15675
H- 1 (AH)	MO	SLoui	SLUPC	Bell	Huey Cobra	Bell 209
H- 1 (AH)	MO	Springfield	AMMO	Bell	Huey Cobra	Bell 209
H- 1 (AH)	SC	Citadel	CC	Bell	Huey Cobra	Bell 209
H- 1 (AH)	SC	MtPleasant	PPM	Bell	Huey Cobra	159210
H- 1 (AH)	WA	Vancouver	PAM	Bell	Huey Cobra	77-22791, Bell 209
H- 1 (AH)	WI	Madison	MTFMDCRA	Bell	Huey Cobra	Bell 209
H- 1 (AH)	WI	Oshkosh	EAAAAM	Bell	Huey Cobra	Bell 209
H- 1 (AH)Cockpit	PA	WChes	AHM	Bell	Huey Cobra	Bell 209
H- 1A(AH)	NJ	Lumberton	AVM	Bell	Huey Cobra	
H- 1A(AH)	OH	Norwalk	FMoMH	Bell	Huey Cobra	66-00825
H- 1F(AH)	AL	Huntsville	RA	Bell	Huey Cobra	
H- 1F(AH)	AL	Ozark	AAM	Bell	Huey Cobra	
H- 1F(AH)	NY	Niagara Falls	NAM	Bell	Huey Cobra	65-09834
H- 1G(AH)	AL	Ozark	USAAM	Bell	Huey Cobra	66-15246	Bell 209
H- 1G(AH)	GA	Hampton	AAHF	Bell	Huey Cobra	
H- 1J(AH)	CA	Miramar	FLAM	Bell	Huey Cobra	
H- 1P(TAH)	GA	Hampton	AAHF	Bell	Huey Cobra	

H- 1S(AH)	OH	N Canton	MAM	Bell	Huey Cobra	70-16084	
H- 1S(AH)	AR	Fayet	AAM	Bell	Huey Cobra	70-16050	
H- 1S(AH)	HI	Waikiki	FRAM	Bell	Huey Cobra	67-15796	
H- 1S(AH) 2ea	HI	Wheeler	WAFB	Bell	Huey Cobra	0-15036 & 33068	
H- 1S(AH)	KS	Liberal	MAAM	Bell	Huey Cobra		
H- 1S(AH)	NJ	Teterboro	AHoFNJ	Bell	Huey Cobra	69-16437	
H- 1S(AH)	RI	NKing	QAM	Bell	Huey Cobra	66-15317	Bell 209
H- 1S(AH)	TX	C Cristi	USS Lexi	Bell	Huey Cobra		
H- 1 (HH)	MI	Grand Rapids	GFM	Bell	Iroquois (Huey)		
H- 1 (HH)	TX	Pampa	PAAF	Bell	Iroquois (Huey)		
H- 1H(HH)	AK	Fairb	APAM	Bell	Iroquois (Huey)	66- 934	
H- 1H(HH)	AR	Fayet	AAM	Bell	Iroquois (Huey)	70-16050	
H- 1H(HH)	AZ	Tucso	PAM	Bell	Iroquois (Huey)	64-13895	
H- 1H(HH)	CA	Marys	FWM	Bell	Iroquois (Huey)		
H- 1H(HH)	CA	Sacra	McCelAFB	Bell	Iroquois (Huey)	70- 2467, "Huey Slick"	
H- 1H(HH)	FL	Clear	FMAM	Bell	Iroquois (Huey)		
H- 1H(HH)	FL	Eglin	USAFAC	Bell	Iroquois (Huey)		
H- 1H(HH)	IL	Linco	HIFM	Bell	Iroquois (Huey)		
H- 1H(HH)	MD	Silve	PEGF	Bell	Iroquois (Huey)		
H- 1H(HH)	OR	Tillamook	TAM	Bell	Iroquois (Huey)		
H- 1H(HH)	RI	NKing	QAM	Bell	Iroquois (Huey)	64-13402	
H- 1H(HH)	UT	Ogden	HAFBM	Bell	Iroquois (Huey)		
H- 1K(HH)	FL	Pensa	USNAM	Bell	Iroquois (Huey)	157188, 301, HAL-3	
H- 1L(TH)	MD	Lexington	PRNAM	Bell	Iroquois (Huey)	157842, NATC Tail	
H- 1L(TH)	PA	WChester	AHM	Bell	Iroquois (Huey)		
H- 1L(TH)	TX	Dallas	FoF	Bell	Iroquois (Huey)	157838, N7UW	
H- 1 (UH)	AL	Birmingham	SMoF	Bell	Iroquois (Huey)		
H- 1 (UH)	AL	Starke	BMP	Bell	Iroquois (Huey)		
H- 1 (UH)	AL	Tuscalloosa	I-20/59	Bell	Iroquois (Huey)		
H- 1 (UH)	CA	Los Alamitos	NAS	Bell	Iroquois (Huey)		
H- 1 (UH)	CA	Paso Robles	EWM	Bell	Iroquois (Huey)	61-3859	
H- 1 (UH)	CA	Ridgecrest	CLNWC	Bell	Iroquois (Huey)		
H- 1 (UH)	CO	Puebl	FWAM	Bell	Iroquois (Huey)		
H- 1 (UH)	DE	Dover	AMCM	Bell	Iroquois (Huey)		
H- 1 (UH)	FL	Shali	USAFAM	Bell	Iroquois (Huey)		
H- 1 (UH)	FL	Tittusville	VACM	Bell	Iroquois (Huey)		
H- 1 (UH)	HI	Oahu	WAFB	Bell	Iroquois (Huey)		
H- 1 (UH)	IA	Des Moines	ING	Bell	Iroquois (Huey)	0-38825	
H- 1 (UH)	IL	Sugar Grove	ACM	Bell	Iroquois (Huey)	68-16215	
H- 1 (UH)	IL	Sugar Grove	ACM	Bell	Iroquois (Huey)	68-16265	
H- 1 (UH)	IN	South Bend	MHP	Bell	Iroquois (Huey)		
H- 1 (UH)	KS	Topeka	MoKNG	Bell	Iroquois (Huey)		
H- 1 (UH)	KY	FKnox	FC	Bell	Iroquois (Huey)		
H- 1 (UH)	MI	Monro		Bell	Iroquois (Huey)		
H- 1 (UH)	MI	Sterling Hts	FHCMP	Bell	Iroquois (Huey)	15719	
H- 1 (UH)	MT	Helena	HA	Bell	Iroquois (Huey)		
H- 1 (UH)	NV	Fallon	NASF	Bell	Iroquois (Huey)		
H- 1 (UH)	OH	Groveport	MMM	Bell	Iroquois (Huey)	56-17048, Joe Sepesy	
H- 1 (UH)	OH	Norwalk	FMoMH	Bell	Iroquois (Huey)	66-00992	
H- 1 (UH)	SC	Mt Pleasant	PP	Bell	Iroquois (Huey)		
H- 1 (UH)	TN	Caryville	I-75&US25W	Bell	Iroquois (Huey)		
H- 1 (UH)	TX	Dalla	CFM	Bell	Iroquois (Huey)	91E	
H- 1 (UH)	TX	FWort	NASFWJRB	Bell	Iroquois (Huey)		
H- 1 (UH)	TX	FWort	VFM	Bell	Iroquois (Huey)		
H- 1 (UH)	WI	Madison	MTFMDCRA	Bell	Iroquois (Huey)		
H- 1 (UH)	VA	Quantico	MCAGM	Bell	Iroquois (Huey)	154760	
H- 1(UH)	TX	Sweetwater	CP	Bell	Iroquois (Huey)		
H- 1A(UH)	CA	SRosa	PCAM	Bell	Iroquois (Huey)		
H- 1A(UH)	NC	Fayet	FBADM	Bell	Iroquois (Huey)	59-1711	
H- 1A(UH)	NY	NYC	ISASM	Bell	Iroquois (Huey)		
H- 1B(UH)	AL	Mobile	BMP	Bell	Iroquois (Huey)	21966	
H- 1B(UH)	AL	Ozark	USAAM	Bell	Iroquois (Huey)	60- 3553	
H- 1B(UH)	CA	El Cajon	SDAMGF	Bell	Iroquois (Huey)		
H- 1B(UH)	CT	Strat	NHM	Bell	Iroquois (Huey)		
H- 1B(UH)	CT	Winds	NEAM	Bell	Iroquois (Huey)		
H- 1B(UH)	DC	Washi	AAFB	Bell	Iroquois (Huey)		
H- 1B(UH)	GA	Hampton	AAHF	Bell	Iroquois (Huey)		
H- 1B(UH)	IA	SBluf	MAAM	Bell	Iroquois (Huey)		
H- 1B(UH)	IL	Ranto	OCAM	Bell	Iroquois (Huey)	60686	
H- 1B(UH)	IN	Vince	IMM	Bell	Iroquois (Huey)		
H- 1B(UH)	KS	Topek	CAM	Bell	Iroquois (Huey)		
H- 1B(UH)	KY	FKnox	PMoC&A	Bell	Iroquois (Huey)		
H- 1B(UH)	MI	Battle Creek	BCANG	Bell	Iroquois (Huey)		
H- 1B(UH)	MO	SLoui	NPRC	Bell	Iroquois (Huey)		
H- 1B(UH)	OK	FtSil	USAFAM	Bell	Iroquois (Huey)		
H- 1B(UH)	OK	Oklah	45IDM	Bell	Iroquois (Huey)	62-4588	
H- 1B(UH)	OH	N Canton	MAM	Bell	Iroquois (Huey)		
H- 1B(UH)	SC	Columbia	FJM	Bell	Iroquois (Huey)		
H- 1B(UH)	VA	FtEus	USATM	Bell	Iroquois (Huey)		
H- 1B(UH)	WA	Tacom	FL	Bell	Iroquois (Huey)		
H- 1C(UH)	NY	Horseheads	NWM	Bell	Iroquois (Huey)		
H- 1D(UH)	AL	Ozark	USAAM	Bell	Iroquois (Huey)	60-6030	
H- 1D(UH)	CA	San Diego	SDAM	Bell	Iroquois (Huey)	432	
H- 1D(UH)-BF	MI	Belleville	YAF	Bell	Iroquois (Huey)	66-16006, N5700	
H- 1D(UH)-BF	MI	Oscoda	YAF	Bell	Iroquois (Huey)	66-16048, N13YA	
H- 1D(UH)	WA	Seatt	MoF	Bell	Iroquois (Huey)		
H- 1E(UH)	WI	Brist	Museum	Bell	Iroquois (Huey)		
H- 1F(UH)	AZ	Green	TMM	Bell	Iroquois (Huey)		
H- 1F(UH)	AZ	Tucso	PAM	Bell	Iroquois (Huey)	66-1211	
H- 1F(UH)	CA	Riverside	MAFB	Bell	Iroquois (Huey)	63-13143	
H- 1F(UH)	MO	Knob	WAFB	Bell	Iroquois (Huey)		
H- 1F(UH)	MT	Great	MAFB	Bell	Iroquois (Huey)	65-956	
H- 1F(UH)	ND	Grand	GFAFB	Bell	Iroquois (Huey)		
H- 1F(UH)	ND	Minot	MAFB	Bell	Iroquois (Huey)		
H- 1F(UH)	NM	Albuq	KAFB	Bell	Iroquois (Huey)		
H- 1F(UH)	SD	Rapid	SDA&SM	Bell	Iroquois (Huey)	66-7591	
H- 1F(UH)	WY	Cheye	FEWAFB	Bell	Iroquois (Huey)		
H- 1F2(UH)	GA	Warner Robin	MoF	Bell	Iroquois (Huey)	65-7959	
H- 1H(UH)	CA	S.Mon	MoF	Bell	Iroquois (Huey)		
H- 1H(UH)	FL	Lakeland	SNFAM	Bell	Iroquois (Huey)		
H- 1H(UH)	CA	S.Mon	MoF	Bell	Iroquois (Huey)	0-38801	
H- 1H(UH)	FL	Lakeland	SNFAM	Bell	Iroquois (Huey)	0-38801	
H- 1H(UH)	HI	Wheeler	WAFB	Bell	Iroquois (Huey)	0-15127	
H- 1H(UH)	HI	Wheeler	WAFB	Bell	Iroquois (Huey)	27548	
H- 1H(UH)	GA	Hampton	AAHF	Bell	Iroquois (Huey)		

H- 1H(UH)	KS	Topek	CAM	Bell	Iroquois (Huey)	TA-897
H- 1H(UH)	NM	Angel Fire	VVNM	Bell	Iroquois (Huey)	SN64-13670
H- 1H(UH)	NY	Buffalo	B&ECN$SP	Bell	Iroquois (Huey)	SN63-12982
H- 1H(UH)	OH	Norwalk	FMoMH	Bell	Iroquois (Huey)	67-17658
H- 1H(UH)	OR	Mc Minnville	EAEC	Bell	Iroquois (Huey)	
H- 1H(UH)	PA	Beaver Falls	AHM	Bell	Iroquois (Huey)	
H- 1H(UH)	PA	Smethport	AAAM	Bell	Iroquois (Huey)	
H- 1H(UH)	RI	NKing	QAM	Bell	Iroquois (Huey)	65-09996
H- 1H(UH)	SC	MtPleasant	PPM	Bell	Iroquois (Huey)	10132
H- 1H(UH)	TX	Grand Prairie	TACM	Bell	Iroquois (Huey)	
H- 1H(UH)	TX	W Houston	Airport	Bell	Iroquois (Huey)	
H- 1H(UH)	TX	RioHo	TAM	Bell	Iroquois (Huey)	SN64-13624, 24A
H- 1H(UH)	WI	Kenos	KMM	Bell	Iroquois (Huey)	66-01169, "123 AVBN AMDIV"
H- 1H(UH)	WI	Kenos	KMM	Bell	Iroquois (Huey)	66-16122
H- 1H(UH)	WI	Kenos	KMM	Bell	Iroquois (Huey)	65-9534
H- 1HA(UH)	NC	Charl	CHAC	Bell	Iroquois (Huey)	
H- 1HA(UH)	NC	CPoin	CPMB	Bell	Iroquois (Huey)	
H- 1HB(UH)	NC	Charl	CHAC	Bell	Iroquois (Huey)	
H- 1HB(UH)	NC	CPoin	CPMB	Bell	Iroquois (Huey)	
H- 1M(UH)	AL	Huntsville	RA	Bell	Iroquois (Huey)	
H- 1M(UH)	AR	Littl	LRAFB	Bell	Iroquois (Huey)	
H- 1M(UH)	AZ	Tucso	PAM	Bell	Iroquois (Huey)	65-9430
H- 1M (UH)	IN	Atterbury	CAM&MC	Bell	Iroquois (Huey)	0-15084
H- 1M(UH)	FL	Pensa	VMP	Bell	Iroquois (Huey)	314 HL-3
H- 1M(UH)	GA	Hampton	AAHF	Bell	Iroquois (Huey)	
H- 1M(UH)	KS	Topek	CAM	Bell	Iroquois (Huey)	
H- 1M(UH)	MD	Silve	PEGF	Bell	Iroquois (Huey)	
H- 1M(UH)	NM	Las Cruces	WSMP	Bell	Iroquois (Huey)	
H- 1M(UH)	NY	NYC	ISASM	Bell	Iroquois (Huey)	
H- 1M(UH)	NY	Scotia	ESAM	Bell	Iroquois (Huey)	65-9435
H- 1M(UH)	PA	Fall River	PL	Bell	Iroquois (Huey)	
H- 1M(UH)	RI	NKing	QAM	Bell	Iroquois (Huey)	66-15083
H- 1M(UH)	SC	MtPleasant	PPM	Bell	Iroquois (Huey)	65-10132
H- 1M(UH)	TX	Amari	EFA&SM	Bell	Iroquois (Huey)	
H- 1M(UH)	VA	Hampt	VA&SC	Bell	Iroquois (Huey)	
H- 1P(UH)	FL	FtWal	HF	Bell	Iroquois (Huey)	64-15493
H- 1P(UH)	GA	Warner Robin	MoF	Bell	Iroquois (Huey)	
H- 1P(UH)	OH	Dayto	USAFM	Bell	Iroquois (Huey)	64-15476
H- 1V(UH)	FL	Tittusville	VACM	Bell	Iroquois (Huey)	
H- 1V(UH)	PA	Willow	WGNAS	Bell	Iroquois (Huey)	
H- 3C(CH)	AZ	Tucso	DMAFB	Sikorsky	Jolly Green Giant	
H- 3C(CH)	UT	Ogden	HAFBM	Sikorsky	Jolly Green Giant	
H- 3E(CH)	CA	Chino	YAM	Sikorsky	Jolly Green Giant	
H- 3E(CH)	CA	Rosam	EAFB	Sikorsky	Jolly Green Giant	62-12581
H- 3E(CH)	CA	Sacra	McCelAFB	Sikorsky	Jolly Green Giant	65-5690
H- 3E(CH)	GA	Warner Robin	MoF	Sikorsky	Jolly Green Giant	65-12797
H- 3E(CH)	OH	Dayto	USAFM	Sikorsky	Jolly Green Giant	63- 9676
H- 3F(HH)	NY	Horsehead	NWM	Sikorsky	Pelican	
H- 3F(HH)	SC	Mt Pleasant	PPM	Sikorsky	Pelican	149932, Side 55
H- 3F(HH)(S-61)	IL	Chica	MoS&I	Sikorsky	Pelican	
H- 3F(HH)(S-61)	FL	FtWal	HF	Sikorsky	Pelican	65-12784, AH
H- 3F(HH)(S-61)	AZ	Tucso	PAM	Sikorsky	Pelican	1476
H- 3F(HH)(S-61)	FL	Pensa	USNAM	Sikorsky	Pelican	CGNR1486
H- 3F(HH)(S-61)	FL	Clear	FMAM	Sikorsky	Pelican	
H- 3F(HH)(S-61)	PA	WChester	AHM	Sikorsky	Pelican	
H- 3F(HH)(S-61)	WI	Janesville	BHTSAC	Sikorsky	Pelican	
H- 3F(HH)(S-61)	WI	Kenosha	KMM	Sikorsky	Pelican	1485
H- 3F(HH)(S-61)	WI	Kenosha	KMM	Sikorsky	Pelican	44043
H- 3S(OH)	NY	NYC	ISASM	Bell	Souix	
H- 4A(OH)	AL	Ozark	USAAM	Ryan	Jet Ranger	62-4201
H- 5 (HH)(S-51)	AK	Palme	MOAT&I	Sikorsky	Dragonfly	
H- 5 (R)	AL	Ozark	USAAM	Sikorsky	Dragonfly	51-24352
H- 5A(OH)(S-51)	AL	Ozark	USAAM	Sikorsky	Dragonfly	62-4206
H- 5A(YH)(S-51)	OH	Dayto	USAFM	Sikorsky	Dragonfly	43-46620
H- 5G(S-51)	AZ	Tucso	PAM	Sikorsky	Dragonfly	48-548, N9845Z
H- 5G(S-51)	NM	Albuq	KAFB	Sikorsky	Dragonfly	
H- 5H(S-51)	CT	Winds	NEAM	Sikorsky	Dragonfly	
H- 6A(OH)	AL	Ozark	USAAM	Hughes	Cayuse	65-12917
H- 6A(OH)	AL	Birmingham	SMoF	Hughes	Cayuse	
H- 6A(YO)	AL	Ozark	USAAM	Hughes	Cayuse	62-4213
H- 6A(OH)	CA	Marys	FWM	Hughes	Cayuse	
H- 6A(OH)	CA	Riverside	MFAM	Hughes	Cayuse	68-17252
H- 6A(OH)	CA	S.Mon	MoF	Hughes	Cayuse	
H- 6A(OH)	CO	CO.Sp	FCBA	Hughes	Cayuse	
H- 6A(OH)	GA	Hampton	AAHF	Hughes	Cayuse	
H- 6A(OH)	KS	Liber	MAAM	Hughes	Cayuse	
H- 6A(OH)	KS	Topeka	MoKNG	Hughes	Cayuse	
H- 6A(OH)	LA	Reser	AMHFM	Hughes	Cayuse	
H- 6A(OH)	NY	Horseheads	NWM	Hughes	Cayuse	67-16668
H- 6A(OH)	NY	Scotia	ESAM	Hughes	Cayuse	68-17343
H- 6A(OH)	OK	Oklah	45IDM	Hughes	Cayuse	
H- 6A(OH)	PA	WChes	AHM	Hughes	Cayuse	
H- 6A(OH)	RI	NKing	QAM	Hughes	Cayuse	67-16570
H- 6A(OH)	UT	Ogden	HAFBM	Hughes	Cayuse	
H- 6A(OH)	VA	FtEus	USATM	Hughes	Cayuse	
H- 6A(R)	OH	Dayto	USAFM	Sikorsky		
H-12	OK	Lexington	CPT	Hiller	Raven	
H-12 (UH)	CA	SCarl	HAM	Hiller	Raven	Model 360
H-12(UH)	CO	Denve	JWDAS	Hiller	Raven	
H-12 (UH)	HI	Oahu	WAFB	Hiller	Raven	
H-12 (UH)	IN	Mentone	LDBAM	Hiller	Raven	
H-12 (UH)(U-23)	CA	Chino	PoFAM	Hiller	Raven	
H-12 (UH)(U-23)	MI	Kalam	KAHM	Hiller	Raven	51-4007
H-12 (HTE-2)	CA	SCarl	HAM	Hiller		
H-12A(HTE-1)	FL	Pensa	USNAM	Hiller	Raven HTE	41-4017, N3HK, 128647
H-12B(UH)	CA	SCarl	HAM	Hiller	Raven	Model 360
H-12C(UH)	AZ	Tucso	PAM	Hiller	Raven J	345, N7725C, Model 360
H-12C(UH)	CA	Redwo	HAM	Hiller	Raven	Model 360
H-12D(UH)(H-23)	PA	WChes	AHM	Hiller	Raven	Model 360
H-12E(UH)	OR	McMinnville	EAM	Hiller	Raven	2100, N1H
H-12E(UH)	OR	McMinnville	EAM	Hiller	Raven	2049, N5363V
H-12E(UH)(U-23)	WY	Greyb	H&PA	Hiller	Raven	
H-12E-E4(UH)NASA	CA	SCarl	HAM	Hiller	Raven	Model 360
H-12L(UH)	CA	Redwo	HAM	Hiller	Raven	
H-13	AL	Starke	CBM	Bell	Sioux	Bell 47, 0-21455
H-13	GA	Hampton	AAHF	Bell	Sioux	Bell 47
H- 1H(UH)	IN	Fairmount	AMP313	Bell	Iroquois (Huey)	68-16504, 05/19/85

H-13	IN	Mentone	LDBAM	Bell	Sioux	Bell 47
H-13	KS	Liber	MAAM	Bell	Sioux	Bell 47
H-13	NJ	Teter	AHoFNJ	Bell	Sioux	Bell 47
H-13	SD	Rapid	SDA&SM	Bell	Sioux	
H-13	WI	Kenos	KMM	Bell	Souix	
H-13 (HTL-2)	MI	Ypsil	YAF	Bell	Air Ambulance	
H-13 (OH)	CA	SanLu	CSLO	Bell	Sioux	Bell 47
H-13 (OH)	CO	CO.Sp	FCBA	Bell	Sioux	
H-13B(OH)	AL	Ozark	USAAM	Bell	Sioux	48- 827, Bell 47
H-13B(OH)	VA	FtEus	USATM	Bell	Sioux	Bell 47
H-13E(HTL-4)	FL	Pensa	USNAM	Bell	Air Ambulance	128911
H-13E(HTL-4)	VA	Quant	MCAGM	Bell	Air Ambulance	128635
H-13E(OH)	AL	Ozark	USAAM	Bell	Sioux 51-14193	Bell 47
H-13E(OH)	KY	FKnox	PMoC&A	Bell	Sioux	Bell 47
H-13E(OH)	NM	Albuq	KAFB	Bell	Sioux	Bell 47
H-13E(OH)	OK	Oklah	45IDM	Bell	Sioux	Bell 47
H-13E(OH)	VA	FtEus	USATM	Bell	Sioux	Bell 47
H-13E(OH)	WA	Seattle	MoF	Bell	Sioux	51-14030, N795
H-13H(VH)	CA	Atwater	CAM	Bell	Sioux	Bell 47
H-13(UH)	CO	Denve	JWDAS	Bell	Sioux	
H-13J(UH)	OH	Dayto	USAFM	Bell	Sioux	57-2728,Bell 47
H-13J(VH)	MD	Silve	PEGF	Bell	Sioux	Bell 47, "Eisenhower"
H-13M(TH)	GA	Warner Robin	MoF	Bell	Sioux	142376, Bell 47
H-13M(TH)(HTL-6)	FL	Pensa	USNAM	Bell	Sioux	142377, 18, Bell 47
H-13N(TH)(HTL-7)	AZ	Tucso	PAM	Bell	Sioux	Sn 145842
H-13P(UH)	GA	Warner Robin	MoF	Bell	Sioux	143143, Bell 47
H-13S(OH)	NY	NYC	ISASM	Bell	Sioux	Bell 47
H-13T	UT	Ogden	HAFBM	Bell	Sioux	Bell 47
H-13T(TH)	AL	Ozark	USAAM	Bell	Sioux	67-17024, Bell 47
H-13T(TH)	IL	Linco	HIFM	Bell	Sioux	Bell 47
H-19 (CH)	AL	Mobile	BMP	Sikorsky	Chickasaw	554239
H-19 (CH)	CA	Ramona	CR	Sikorsky	Chickasaw	
H-19 (CH)	CA	SanLu	CSLO	Sikorsky	Chickasaw	
H-19 (UH)	TX	RioHo	TAM	Sikorsky	Chickasaw	0-13948
H-19 (UH)	TX	RioHo	TAM	Sikorsky	Chickasaw	
H-19B(UH)	AZ	Tucso	PAM	Sikorsky	Chickasaw	52-7537, N2256G
H-19B(UH)	OH	Dayto	USAFM	Sikorsky	Chickasaw	52-7587, "Whirl-O-Way"
H-19B(UH)-SI(S-55)	BC-C	Langley	CMoF&T	Sikorsky	Chickasaw	53-4414
H-19B(UH) (S-55)	MT	Helena	MHSM	Sikorsky	Chickasaw	
H-19B(UH)-ST	NE	Ashland	SACM	Sikorsky	Chickasaw	53-4426
H-19C(UH)	VA	FtEus	USATM	Sikorsky	Chickasaw	
H-19D(UH)	AL	Ozark	USAAM	Sikorsky	Chickasaw	55-5239
H-19D(UH)	CA	Ramona	CR	Sikorsky	Chickasaw	
H-19D(UH)	FL	Tittusville	VACM	Sikorsky	Chickasaw	
H-19D(HH)	GA	Warner Robin	MoF	Sikorsky	Chickasaw	55-3328
H-19D(UH)	ND	Grand	GFAFB	Sikorsky	Chickasaw	
H-19E(CH)(HRS-2)	FL	Pensa	USNAM	Sikorsky	Chickasaw	130151
H-19E(CH)(HRS-3)	FL	Pensa	USNAM	Sikorsky	Chickasaw	142432
H-19F(UH)	NM	Albuq	KAFB	Sikorsky	Chickasaw	
H-19G(HH)(H04S-1)	SC	Flore	FA&MM	Sikorsky	Chickasaw	USCG
H-20 (XH)	OH	Dayto	USAFM	McDonnell		46-689, "Lt Henery"
H-21	BC-C	Langley	CMoF&T	Piasecki	Workhorse	Model 44B
H-21	PA	WChester	AHM	Piasecki	Workhorse	
H-21B(UH)	CA	River	MFAM	Piasecki	Workhorse	53-4326
H-21B(CH)	AL	Mobil	BMP	Piasecki	Workhorse	515859
H-21B(CH)	CA	Fairf	TAFB	Piasecki	Workhorse	
H-21B(CH)	CA	Ramona	CR	Piasecki	Workhorse	
H-21B(CH)	CO	Puebl	FWAM	Piasecki	Workhorse	53-4347
H-21B(CH)	GA	Warner Robin	MoF	Piasecki	Workhorse	52-8685
H-21B(CH)	NM	Albuq	KAFB	Piasecki	Workhorse	
H-21B(CH)	OH	Dayto	USAFM	Piasecki	Workhorse	51-15857
H-21B(CH)	PA	Readi	MAAM	Piasecki	Workhorse	
H-21B(CH)	SC	Flore	FA&MM	Piasecki	Workhorse	
H-21B(CH)	TX	FWort	PMoT	Piasecki	Workhorse	
H-21B(CH)	UT	Ogden	HAFBM	Piasecki	Workhorse	
H-21C	WA	Everett	MoF	Piasecki	Workhorse	53-4366, N6797, 53-4329
H-21B(CH)(PD-22)	WI	Oshko	EAAAM	Piasecki	Workhorse	N57968, 28683
H-21B-PH(CH)	BC-C	Langley	CMoF&T	Piasecki	Workhorse	53-4366, N6792, Model 142
H-21B-PH(CH)	NE	Ashland	SACM	Piasecki	Workhorse	52-8676
H-21C(CH)	AZ	Tucso	PAM	Piasecki	Workhorse	56-2159
H-21C(CH)	CA	Rosam	EAFB	Piasecki	Workhorse	52-8623
H-21C(CH)	CA	Sacra	McCelAFB	Piasecki	Workhorse	51-15886
H-21C(CH)	CO	Denve	WOR	Piasecki	Workhorse	
H-21C(CH)	NY	NYC	ISASM	Piasecki	Workhorse	
H-21C(CH)	RI	NKing	QAM	Piasecki	Workhorse	51-15892
H-21C(CH)	VA	FtEus	USATM	Piasecki	Workhorse	
H-23 (OH)	CA	SanLu	CSLO	Hiller	Raven	
H-23 (OH)	GA	Hampton	AAHF	Hiller	Raven	
H-23 (OH)	LA	New Orleans	FoJBMM	Hiller	Raven	51-16336
H-23 (OH)	NY	NYC	ISASM	Hiller	Raven	
H-23A(OH)	AL	Ozark	USAAM	Hiller	Raven	51-3975, G
H-23A(OH)	CA	SCarl	HAM	Hiller	Raven	
H-23B(OH)	CA	Ramona	CR	Hiller	Raven	
H-23B(OH)	CA	SCarl	HAM	Hiller	Raven	
H-23B(OH)	GA	Hampton	AAHF	Hiller	Raven	
H-23B(OH)	KY	FKnox	PMoC&A	Hiller	Raven	
H-23B(OH)	TX	FWort	PMoT	Hiller	Raven	
H-23C(OH)	CA	SCarl	HAM	Hiller	Raven	
H-23C(OH)	GA	Warner Robin	MoF	Hiller	Raven	56-421
H-23C(OH)	OK	Oklah	45IDM	Hiller	Raven	55-4124
H-23C(OH)	VA	FtEus	USATM	Hiller	Raven	
H-23D(OH)	CA	SCarl	HAM	Hiller	Raven	
H-23F(OH)	AL	Ozark	USAAM	Hiller	Raven	62-12508
H-23F(OH)	CA	SCarl	HAM	Hiller	Raven	
H-23F(OH)	OK	FtSil	USAFAM	Hiller	Raven	62-3791
H-23G(OH)	CT	Winds	NEAM	Hiller	Raven	
H-23G(OH)	HI	Wheeler	WAFB	Hiller	Raven	64-15245
H-25 (UH)	MI	Kalam	KAHM	Piasecki	Army Mule	
H-25A	AL	Ozark	USAAM	Piasecki	Army Mule	51-16616
H-25A(UH)	VA	FtEus	USATM	Piasecki	Army Mule	
H-25C(OH)	GA	Warner Robin	MoF	Piasecki	Army Mule	
H-26 (XH)	OH	Dayto	USAFM	American Helicopter	Jet Jeep	
H-26A(XH)	AL	Ozark	USAAM	American Helicopter	Jet Jeep	50-1840
H-30(YH)	CA	Ramona	CR	Jovair	McCulloch	
H-32(YH) See HOE						
H-32	CA	Ramona	CR	Hiller	Hornet	

Model	State	City	Museum	Mfr	Name	Serial/Notes
H-31(YH)(LZ-5)	CA	SCarl	HAM	Doman	Carbie	
H-34(HSS-1)	CA	Alameda	USSHM	Sikorsky	Seahorse	140136
H-34	CA	Alameda Pt	USSHM	Sikorsky	Seahorse	
H-34	CA	Chino	PoFAM	Sikorsky	Seahorse	
H-34	FL	Kissi	FTWAM	Sikorsky	Seahorse	
H-34	GA	Calhoun	MAM	Sikorsky	Seahorse	
H-34 (CH)	AL	Ozark	USAAM	Sikorsky	Choctaw	65-7992
H-34 (CH)	CA	Chino	YAM	Sikorsky	Choctaw	
H-34 (CH)	CA	Fairf	TAFB	Sikorsky	Choctaw	
H-34 (CH)	CA	SanLu	CSLO	Sikorsky	Choctaw	
H-34 (CH)	MN	Blaine	AWAM	Sikorsky	Choctaw	14173
H-34 (CH)	SC	Flore	FA&MM	Sikorsky	Choctaw	
H-34 (HH)	NM	Albuq	KAFB	Sikorsky	Seahorse	
H-34 (UH)	NY	NYC	ISASM	Sikorsky	Seahorse	
H-34 (UH)	TX	FWort	NASFWJRB	Sikorsky	Seahorse	
H-34A	FL	Clear	FMAM	Sikorsky	Seahorse	
H-34A(CH)	AL	Ozark	USAAM	Sikorsky	Choctaw	53-4526
H-34A(CH)	WY	Greyb	H&PA	Sikorsky	Choctaw	
H-34A(VCH)	AL	Ozark	USAAM	Sikorcky	Army One	56-4320
H-34C(CH)	NC	Charlotte	CAM	Sikorsky	Choctaw	55-4496
H-34C(CH)	VA	FtEus	USATM	Sikorsky	Choctaw	
H-34C(VH)	AZ	Tucso	PAM	Sikorsky	Seahorse	57-1684
H-34C(VH)	CA	Rosam	EAFB	Sikorsky	Seahorse	57-1726
H-34D(LH)	CT	Winds	NEAM	Sikorsky	Seahorse	
H-34D(UH)	CA	Miramar	FLAM	Sikorsky	Seahorse	YP, HMM-163
H-34D(UH)	MD	Silve	PEGF	Sikorsky	Seahorse	
H-34D(UH)	PA	Willow	WGNAS	Sikorsky	Seahorse	
H-34D(UH)	PA	Readi	MAAM	Sikorsky	Seahorse	
H-34D(UH)(HUS-1)	FL	Pensa	USNAM	Sikorsky	Seahorse	X0, 657, 150227, 1
H-34E(HH)	GA	Warner Robin	MoF	Sikorsky	Seahorse	
H-34G(UH)	CA	Rosam	EAFB	Sikorsky	Seahorse	137856
H-34J	UT	Ogden	HAFBM	Sikorsky	Seahorse	
H-34J(HH)	AZ	Phoen	LAFB	Sikorsky	Seahorse	
H-34(HH)	GA	Warner Robin	MoF	Sikorsky	Seabat	148963
H-34(SH)	SC	MtPleasant	PPM	Sikorsky	Seabat	14171
H-37 (CH)(HR2S-1)	FL	Pensa	USNAM	Sikorsky	Mojave	145864
H-37B(CH)	AL	Ozark	USAAM	Sikorsky	Mojave	55-644
H-37B(CH)	AZ	Tucso	PAM	Sikorsky	Mojave	56-1005, "Tired Dude"
H-37B(CH)	CA	Ramona	CR	Sikorsky	Mojave	
H-37B(CH)	VA	FtEus	USATM	Sikorsky	Mojave	
H-41A(YH)	AL	Ozark	USAAM	Cessna	Seneca	56-4244
H-43 (HH)(HOK-1)	CA	Atwater	CAM	Kaman	Huskie	62-4513
H-43 (HH)(HOK-1)	CA	Ramona	CR	Kaman	Huskie	
H-43 (HOK-1)	OR	Tillamook	TAM	Kaman	Huskie	
H-43B(HH)(HOK-1)	CT	Winds	NEAM	Kaman	Huskie	289
H-43B(HH)(HOK-1)	DE	Dover	AMCM	Kaman	Huskie	4532
H-43B(HH)(HOK-1)	GA	Warner Robin	MoF	Kaman	Huskie	58-1853
H-43B(HH)(HOK-1)	NM	Albuq	KAFB	Kaman	Huskie	
H-43B(HH)(HOK-1)	TX	FWort	PMoT	Kaman	Huskie	
H-43B(OH)(HOK-1)	UT	Ogden	HAFBM	Kaman	Huskie	
H-43D(OH)(HOK-1)	AZ	Tucso	PAM	Kaman	Huskie	139974
H-43F(HH)(HOK-1)	AZ	Tucso	PAM	Kaman	Huskie	62-4531
H-43F(HH)(HOK-1)	OH	Dayto	USAFM	Kaman	Huskie	60-263
H-43F(HH)(HOK-1)	OR	Tillamook	TAM	Kaman	Huskie	60-263
H-44 (XH)	MD	Silve	PEFG	Hiller	Commuter	
H-44(UH)	CA	SCarl	HAM	Hiller	Commuter	
H-47 (CH)	CA	SanLu	CSLO	Boeing-Vertol	Chinook	
H-47 (CH)	CO	Puebl	FWAM	Boeing-Vertol	Chinook	
H-47A(CH)	AL	Huntsville		Boeing-Vertol	Chinook	
H-47A(CH)	AL	Ozark	USAAM	Boeing-Vertol	Chinook	60-3451 (64-13149) "Easy Money"
H-47(HK)	OK	Tulsa	TA&SC	Bell		
H-50A(OH)	SC	MtPleasant	PPM	Gyrodyne	Drone	
H-50C(OH)	CT	Winds	NEAM	Gyrodyne	Drone	
H-50C(OH)	GA	Warner Robin	MoF	Gyrodyne	Drone	
H-50C(OH)	MD	Lexington	PRNAM	Gyrodyne	Drone	DS-1679
H-50C(QH)	NC	Charlotte	CAM	Gyrodyne	Drone	1355
H-50C(QH)	PA	WChester	AHM	Gyrodyne	Drone	
H-51A(XH)	AL	Ozark	USAAM	Lockheed	Rigid Rotor	61-51262
H-51A(XH)	AL	Ozark	USAAM	Lockheed	Compound	61-51263
H-52A(HH)	AZ	Tucso	PAM	Sikorsky	Seaguard USCG	62-71, N8224Q, 1390,USCG Polar Star
H-52A(HH)	CT	Winds	NEAM	Sikorsky	Seaguard USCG	1428, Polar Star
H-52A(HH)	FL	Pensa	USNAM	Sikorsky	Seaguardian	USCG Polar Star, CGNR1355
H-52A(HH)	IL	Chica	MoS&I	Sikorsky	Seaguard USCG	Polar Star
H-52A(HH)	MI	Mt Clemens	SMAM	Sikorsky	Seaguard USCG	1466, Polar Star
H-52A(HH)	NJ	Teterboro	AHoFNJ	Sikorsky	Seaguard USCG	
H-52A(HH)	NY	NYC	ISASM	Sikorsky	Seaguard USCG	Polar Star, 1429
H-52A(HH)	PA	Readi	MAAM	Sikorsky	Seaguard USCG	Polar Star
H-52A(HH)(S-62)	PA	WChester	AHM	Sikorsky	Seaguard USCG	
H-52A(HH)(S-62)	WA	Everett	MoF	Sikorsky	Seaguard USCG	CGNR1415
H-53a(CH)	CA	Miramar	FLAM	Sikorsky	Sea Stallion	
H-53a(CH)	FL	Pensa	USNAM	Sikorsky	Sea Stallion	151687
H-53a(CH)	HI	Kaneohe	MB	Sikorsky	Sea Stallion	
H-53a(CH)	KS	Topeka	CAM	Sikorsky	Sea Stallion	
H-53a(CH)	MD	Lexington	PRNAM	Sikorsky	Sea Stallion	151686
H-53a(UH)	PA	Willow	WGNAS	Sikorsky	Sea Stallion	
H-53a(CH)	VA	Norfolk	NASN	Sikorsky	Sea Stallion	
H-53a(CH)	VA	Quantico	MCAGM	Sikorsky	Sea Stallion	151692
H-53D(RH)	HI	Kaneohe	KBMCAS	Sikorsky	Sea Stallion	158748, 1st MAW ASE
H-53D(RH)	NJ	Lumberton	AVM	Sikorsky	Sea Stallion	158690
H-54 (CH)	KS	Topeka	MoKNG	Sikorsky	Tarhe (Skycrane)	
H-54 (CH)	MS	McLaurin	AFM	Sikorsky	Tarhe (Skycrane)	
H-54 (CH)	VA	FtEus	USATM	Sikorsky	Tarhe (Skycrane)	
H-54 (CH)	WI	Brist	Museum	Sikorsky	Tarhe (Skycrane)	
H-54 (CH)	WI	Kenos	KMM	Sikorsky	Tarhe (Skycrane)	446, "The Bull Stops Here"
H-54 (CH)	WI	Kenos	KMM	Sikorsky	Tarhe (Skycrane)	486
H-54 (S-64)	OR	McMinnville	EAEC	Sikorsky	Tarhe (Skycrane)	
H-54A(CH)	AZ	Tucso	PAM	Sikorsky	Tarhe (Skycrane)	68-18437, 64039
H-54A(CH)	KS	Topek	CAM	Sikorsky	Tarhe (Skycrane)	
H-54B(CH)	AL	Birmingham	SMoF	Sikorsky	Tarhe (Skycrane)	
H-54B(CH)	CT	Winds	NEAM	Sikorsky	Tarhe (Skycrane)	
H-54B(S-64)	WY	Greyb	H&PA	Sikorsky	Tarhe (Skycrane)	
H-54D(CH)	GA	Spart	GSMA	Sikorsky	Tarhe (Skycrane)	
H-55A(TH)	AL	Ozark	USAAM	Hughes	Osage	67-16795
H-55A(TH)	AZ	Tucso	PAM	Hughes	Osage	67-18350
H-55A(TH)	AZ	Tucso	PAM	Hughes	Osage	67-18273
H-55A(TH)	AZ	Tucso	PAM	Hughes	Osage	67-18203

137

H-55A(TH)	AZ	Tucson	PAM	Hughes	Osage	67-18017
H-55A(TH)	AZ	Tucson	PAM	Hughes	Osage	67-118133
H-55A(TH)	PA	WChester	AHM	Hughes	Osage	
H-55A(TH)	OR	McMinnville	EAM	Hughes	Osage	38-0002, N79P, Huges 269A
H-55A(TH)	VA	FtEus	USATM	Hughes	Osage	
H-56A(AH)	AL	Ozark	USAAM	Lockheed	Cheyenne	66- 8830
H-56A(AH)	VA	FtEus	USATM	Lockheed	Cheyenne	
H-57A(TH)	FL	Pensa	USNAM	Bell	Sea Ranger	157363 O4-E
H-58(OH)	DE	Dover	AMCM	Bell	Kiowa	
H-58(OH)	HI	Oahu	WAFB	Bell	Kiowa	
H-58(OH)	KY	Lexington	AMoK	Bell	Kiowa	
H-58(OH)	LA	New Orleans	FoJBMM	Bell	Kiowa	70-15426
H-58(OH)	KS	Topeka	MoKNG	Bell	Kiowa	
H-58(OH)	MB-C	Winnipeg	WRCAFB	Bell	Kiowa	
H-58(OH)	ON-C	Kingston	CFB	Bell	Kiowa	
H-58(OH)	ON-C	Trenton	CFB	Bell	Kiowa	136408
H-58(OH)	RI	NKing	QAM	Bell	Kiowa	
H-58(OH)	TX	Denton	H10FM	Bell	Kiowa	
H-58A(OH)	HI	Wheeler	WAFB	Bell	Kiowa	0-15358
H-58A(OH)	CA	Riverside	MAFM	Bell	Kiowa	70-15258
H-58A(OH)	OK	Oklah	45IDM	Bell	Kiowa	
H-58A(OH)	OH	N Canton	MAM	Bell	Kiowa	
H-58A(OH)	TX	FWort	NASFWJRB	Bell	Kiowa	
H-58A(OH)	TX	FWort	VFM	Bell	Kiowa	
H-61A(YU)	AL	Ozark	USAAM	Boeing-Vertol	UTTAS	73-21656
H-63 (YAH)	AL	Ozark	USAAM	Bell	Model 409	74-22247, Bell 409
H-63 (YAH)	KS	Liber	MAAM	Bell	Model 409	Bell 309
H-64 (YAH)	VA	FtEus	USATM	Hughes	Apache	
H-64A(AH)	AL	Huntsville	RA	Hughes	Apache	
H-64A(YAH)	AL	Ozark	USAAM	Hughes	Apache	74-22249
H-65 (AH)	KY	FKnox	FC	Hughes		
HA-200A	FL	Titusville	VACM	Hispano	Cairo	
HA-200B	MD	Silve	PEGF	Hispano	Cairo	
HA-1112	AZ	Grand Canyon	PoFGCVA	Hispano	Buchon	
HA-1112	MB-C	Winni	WCAM	Hispano	Buchon	
HA-1112	MI	Kalam	KAHM	Hispano	Buchon	C4K-19
HA-1112	TX	Midla	CAFFM	Hispano	Buchon	
HA-1112	WI	Oshko	EAAAAM	Hispano	Buchon	N109BF
Halberstadt CL-IV	AL	Gunte	LGARFM	Halberstadt		
Halberstadt CL.II	OH	Dayto	USAFM	Halberstadt		
Halberstadt D.III	AL	Gunte	LGARFM	Halberstadt		
Half Track M3	AL	Starke	CBM		Armored Vehicle	
Half Track M3	LA	New Orleans	DDM		Armored Vehicle	
Half Track M16	OH	Hubbard	WWIIVM		Armored Vehicle	A-27
Hanson-Meyer Quickie	CT	Winds	NEAM	Hanson-Meyer	Quickie	
Harbinger Sailplane	ON-C	Ottaw	CAM	Harbinger	Sailplane	
Hardly Abelson	WI	Oshlosh	EAAAAM	Hardly	Abelson	
Harlow PJC-2	WI	Oshko	EAAAAM	Harlow		N3947B
Harrison Mini-Mack	AL	Birmingham	SMoF	Harrison	Mini-Mack	
Hartman 1910	NE	Minde	HWPV	Hartman		
Hawk	CO	CSpri	EJPSCM			
Hawk 2	WI	Oshko	EAAAAM	Haufe Dale	Hawk 2	N18278
Hawk Major M.2.W	WI	Oshko	EAAAAM	Miles	Hawk Major	CF-NXT
Hawker FB.1	NY	NYC	ISASM	Hawker	Sea Hawk	
Hawker FB.1	WI	Oshko	EAAAAM	Hawker	Sea Hawk	N83SH
Hawker FB.11	AB-C	Calga	AMoC	Hawker	Sea Fury	
Hawker FB.11	AB-C	Calga	NMoA	Hawker	Sea Fury	
Hawker FB.11	WA	Olympia	OFM	Hawker	Sea Fury	
Hawker FB.11	ON-C	Ottaw	CAM	Hawker	Sea Fury	
Hawker FB.11	TX	Breck	BAM	Hawker	Sea Fury	
Hawker FB.11 Fuse	TN	Memph	LS	Hawker	Sea Fury	
Hawker FB.11	WA	Olympia	OFM	Hawker	Sea Hawk	Side # 737
Hawker Hind	ON-C	Ottaw	CAM	Hawker	Hind	
Hawker Hunter	TX	Grand Prairie	TACM	Hawker	Hunter	
Hawker Hunter	TX	Ft Worth	VFM	Hawker	Hunter	
Hawker Hunter Mk.9	ON-C	Trenton	RCAFMM	Hawker	Hunter	J-4029, Tail 30
Hawker Hunter Mk.51	WI	Oshko	EAAAAM	Hawker	Hunter	N611JR
Hawker Hunter Mk.58A	PA	Readi	MAAM	Hawker	Hunter	
Hawker Hunter Mk.58A Rep	ON-C	Hamilton	CWH	Hawker	Hunter	
Hawker	AB-C	Wetas	RM	Hawker	Hurricane	
Hawker Hurricane	MB-C	Brandon	CATPM	Hawker	Hurricane	
Hawker Hurricane Mk.IIB	ON-C	Hamilton	CWH	K-W Surplus, Kitchener	Hurricane	C-GCWH, P3069, YOA Replica
Hawker Hurricane	ON-C	Ottaw	CAM	Hawker	Hurricane	5584
Hawker Hurricane Rep	ON-C	Toronto	TAM	Hawker	Hurricane	
Hawker Hurricane	SK-C	MJaw	WDM	Hawker	Hurricane	
Hawker Hurricane	TX	Addison	CFM	Hawker	Hurricane	
Hawker Hurricane	TX	Hawki	RRSA	Hawker	Hurricane	
Hawker Hurricane Mk.II	CA	Santa Monica	MoF	Hawker	Hurricane	5481, N678DP, Side #P2970, Tail USX
Hawker Hurricane Mk.II	OH	Dayto	USAFM	Hawker	Hurricane	5390
Hawker Hurricane Mk.II	VA	Suffolk	FF	Hawker	Hurricane	RCAF5667, N2549
Hawker Hurricane Mk.IIB	BC-C	Langley	CMoF&T	Hawker	Hurricane	Partial Static Project
Hawker Hurricane Mk.IIB	TX	Galve	LSFM	Hawker	Hurricane	N68RW, CCF-96
Hawker Hurricane Mk.IIC	MD	Silve	PEGF	Hawker	Hurricane	
Hawker Hurricane Mk.X	CA	Chino	PoFAM	Hawker	Hurricane	
Hawker Hurricane Mk.XII	CA	S.Mon	MoF	Hawker	Hurricane	N678DP, "Little Willie"
Hawker Hurricane Mk.XIIb	AB-C	Calga	AMoC	Hawker	Hurricane	
Hawker Hurricane Mk.XXII	CA	S.Mon	MOF	Hawker	Hurricane	
Hawker Hurricane Rep	AB-C	Edmonton	AAM	Hawker	Hurricane	
Hawker Tempest Mk.2	FL	Lakeland	SNF	Hawker	Tempest	
Hawker-Siddeley Kestrel	DC	Washi	NA&SM	Hawker-Siddeley	Kestral	
Haye Valmer	BC-C	Langley	CMoF&T	Haye	Valmer	
HD-1	CA	Chino	PoFAM	Hanriot	Scout	
HD-1	FL	Pensa	USNAM	Hanriot	Scout	A5625
HD-1	NY	Rhine	ORA	Hanriot	Scout	
HD-4 Remains	NS-C	Badde	AGBNHP	Hanriot	Hydrofoil	19
He 100	CA	Chino	PoFAM	Heinkel		
He 111/CASA 2.111	WA	Eastsound	FHC	Heinkel	Dresden	N11105
He 111/CASA 2.111	WA	Seattle	MoF	Heinkel	Dresden	G
He 111/CASA 2.111D	OH	Dayto	USAFM	Heinkel	Dresden	
He 111/CASA 2.111E	TX	Dalla	CFM	Heinkel	Dresden	N99230
He 162	ON-C	Ottaw	CAM	Heinkel	Volksjager	120076
He 162	ON-C	Ottaw	CAM	Heinkel	Volksjager	120086
He 162A	MD	Silve	PEGF	Heinkel	Volksjager	
He 162A-1	CA	Chino	PoFAM	Heinkel	Volksjager	
He 219A-3	MD	Silve	PEGF	Heinkel	Uhu	
Headwind JD-HWL-7	AR	Little Rock	AEC	Headwind	Ultrlight	

Heath Feather	WI	Oshko	EAAAAM	Heath	Feather	
Heath Center Wing 115	KY	Lexington	AVoK	Heath	Center Wing 115	NR2881
Heath Parasol	CT	Winds	NEAM	Heath	Parasol	
Heath Parasol	MI	Kalamazoo	KAHM	Heath	Parasol	
Heath Parasol	NC	Hende	WNCAM	Heath	Parasol	
Heath Parasol	NY	Rhine	ORA	Heath	Parasol	
Heath Super Parasol	VA	Sands	VAM	Heath	Parasol	Sn 31919
Heath Parasol	WA	Seattle	MoF	Heath	Parasol	
Heath Parasol 5	WI	Oshko	EAAAAM	Heath	Parasol	
Heath Parasol 5	NE	Minde	HWPV	Heath	Parasol	
Heath Parasol Rep	NY	Mayvi	DA	Heath	Parasol	
Heath Super Parasol	FL	Lakel	SFAF	Heath	Super Parasol	N88EG
Heath Super Parasol	WI	Oshko	EAAAAM	Heath-Scimone	Super Parasol	N953M
Hegy R.C.H.L	WI	Oshko	EAAAAM	Hegy		N9360, "El Chuparosa"
Helio 1A	MD	Silve	PEGF	Helio	Courier	
Helton Lark 95	AZ	Tucson	PAM	Helton	Lark 95	Man Sn 9512, N1512H
Henderschott	WI	Oshko	EAAAAM	Henderschott	Monoplane	
Henderson Highwing	WI	Oshko	EAAAAM	Folkerts	Henderson	8902
Henri Farman III	ME	Owls Head	OHTM	Henri Farman		
Herring-Curtiss	NY	Garde	CoAM	Herring-Curtiss	Golden Glider	
Hill Hummer	WI	Oshko	EAAAAM	Hill	Hummer	N90381, "Pete"
Hiller Flying Crane	CA	Redwo	HAM	Hiller	Flying Crane	
Hiller Flying Platform	AZ	Tucson	PAM	Hiller	Flying Platform	
Hiller Helicopter	CA	Chino	PoFAM	Hiller		
Hiller 360	CA	San Carlos	HAM	Hiller	360	
Hispano-Suiza	NY	River	TFAC	Hispano-Suiza		
Hisso Standard	MO	Maryland Hts	HARM	Hisso	Standard	
HJD-1(X)	MD	Silve	PEGF	McDonnell	Whirlaway	
HJD-1H(X)	MD	Silve	PEGF	McDonnell	Whirlaway	
HK-1	OR	McMinnville	EAEC	Hughes	Spruce Goose	NX37602
HM-14	WI	Oshko	EAAAAM	Mignet	Flying Flea	Pou du Ciel
HM-	FL	Lakeland	SNF	Midget	Flying Flea	
HM-290	BC-C	Langley	CMoF&T	Mignet	Flying Flea	
HM-293	MI	Belleville	YAF	Mignet	Flying Flea	F-312 ,N4067
HM-360	WI	Oshko	EAAAAM	Mignet	Flying Flea	N360HM
HO-3B(YHO)	AL	Ozark	USAAM	Brantley		58-1496
HO-45	AK	Fairb	APAM	Hamilton	Metalplane	NC10002
HO-49	FL	Pensa	USNAM			1049
HO-6A(YH)	AL	Ozark	USAAM	Hughes	Cayuse	62- 4213
HO3S	VA	Quant	MCAGM	Sikorsky	Dragonfly	124344
HO3S-1(S-51)	BC-C	Langley	CMoF&T	Sikorsky	Dragonfly	N2842D, 124345, CF-FDF
HO3S-1(S-51)	NC	Charlotte	CAM	Sikorsky	Dragonfly	125136
HO3S-1G	AZ	Tucso	PAM	Sikorsky	Dragonfly	CG, 232, N4925E
HO4S	TX	Slanton	TAMCC	Sikorsky	Chickasaw	
HO4S (S-55)	FL	Pensa	USNAM	Sikorsky	Chickasaw	CGNR1258, 130151
HO4S-3	NS-C	Shear	CFBS	Sikorsky	Chickasaw	
HO4S-3	ON-C	Ottaw	CAM	Sikorsky	Chickasaw	
HO5S-1G(S-52)	FL	Pensa	USNAM	Sikorsky	Dragonfly	N8003E, 125519
HO5S-1G(S-52)	PA	WChester	AHM	Sikorsky	Dragonfly	
HO5S-1G(S-52)	VA	Quantico	MCAGM	Sikorsky	Dragonfly	128610
HOE-1	CA	Hawth	WMoF	Hiller	Hornet	
HOE-1	MD	Silve	PEGF	Hiller	Hornet	
HOE-1(HJ-1)	CA	SCarl	HAM	Hiller	Hornet	
HOE-1(YH-32)	AL	Ozark	USAAM	Hiller	Hornet	55- 4965, "Sally Rand"
HOE-1(YH-32)	CA	SCarl	HAM	Hiller	Hornet	
HOE-1(YH-32)	WA	Everett	MoF	Hiller	Hornet	55-4969
HOK-1	NC	Charlotte	CAM	Hiller	Hornet	139990
Homebuilt	AZ	Tucso	PAM		Homebuilt	
Homebuilt	NS-C	Halifax	ACAM		Scamp 1	
Horton Ho II	MD	Silve	PEGF	Horton	Flying Wing Glider	
Horton Ho III	MD	Silve	PEGF	Horton	Flying Wing Glider	
Horton Ho III-H	MD	Silve	PEGF	Horton	Flying Wing Glider	
Horton Ho IV	CA	Chino	PoFAM	Horton	Flying Wing Glider	
Horton Ho VI	MD	Silve	PEGF	Horton	Flying Wing Glider	
Hovercraft	NY	River	TFAC	Hovercraft	Hovercraft	
Howard 250	CA	Chino	PoFAM	Howard	Ero	
Howard Pete	WI	Oshko	EAAAAM	Howard	Pete	N111PL, "Little Audrey"
HP-10	WI	Oshko	EAAAAM	Helisoar	Glider	N319Y
HP-18-LK Sailplane	WI	Oshko	EAAAAM	Bryan-Harris	Sailplane	N96326
HP-52	BC-C	Langley	CMoF&T	Handley-Page	Hampden	I, P, 5436
HP-52	ON-C	Trenton	RCAFMM	Handley-Page	Hampden	NA337
HRP-1	CT	Winds	NEAM	Piasecki	Rescuer	
HRP-1(X)	MD	Silve	PEGF	Piasecki	Rescuer	37969
HRP-3	IN	S Bend	JA			147608
HRS-1(S-55)	VA	Quant	MCAGM	Sikorsky	Chickasaw	127828
HRS-3(S-55)	CA	Miramar	FLAM	Sikorsky	Chickasaw	WW, MALS-16
HS-2L	ON-C	Ottaw	CAM	Curtiss		A-1876
HTK-1(K-125)	FL	Pensa	USNAM	Kaman		129313
HU- 1	CA	Chino	YACM	Piasecki	Helicopter	147610, 147610
HU-16	AZ	Tucson	SA	Grumman	Albatross	MSN 090, N7026C
HU-16	AZ	Tucson	SA	Grumman	Albatross	Sn 131904, N7026X
HU-16	AZ	Tucson	SA	Grumman	Albatross	Sn 141271, N70258, MSN 418
HU-16	AZ	Tucson	SA	Grumman	Albatross	Sn 137933, N70275, MSN 406
HU-16	AZ	Tucson	TI	Grumman	Albatross	Sn 2132, N226GR, MSN 359
HU-16	AZ	Tucson	TI	Grumman	Albatross	N115FB, MSN 462
HU-16	AZ	Tucson	WIA	Grumman	Albatross	sn 51-043, N7049D, MSN 119
HU-16	CT	New England	NEAM	Grumman	Albatross	USCG 7218, MSN 310
HU-16	FL	Ft Lauderdale FL		Grumman	Albatross	N48318, MSN 244
HU-16	FL	Ft Lauderdale FL		Grumman	Albatross	N113LA, MSN 219
HU-16	FL	Ft Lauderdale FL		Grumman	Albatross	N43846, MSN 381
HU-16	FL	Ft Lauderdale FL		Grumman	Albatross	N928J, MSN 401
HU-16	FL	Ft Lauderdale FL		Grumman	Albatross	N42MY, MSN 464
HU-16	FL	Lantana		Grumman	Albatross	N43GL, MSN 367
HU-16	FL	Opa Locka		Grumman	Albatross	N49115, MSN 327
HU-16	FL	Opa Locka		Grumman	Albatross	Sn 141265, N7025V, MSN 412
HU-16	ID	Driggs	TAC	Grumman	Albatross	Sn 1906
HU-16	KS	Liber	MAAM	Grumman	Albatross	
HU-16	MA	Cape Cod	CGAS	Grumman	Albatross	USCG 7250, MSN 340
HU-16	NY	Brooklyn	NARF	Grumman	Albatross	
HU-16	NV	Carson City		Grumman	Albatross	Sn 51-067, N3395F, MSN 146
HU-16	NV	Carson City		Grumman	Albatross	N120FB, MSN 331
HU-16	NV	Carson City		Grumman	Albatross	N117FB, MSN 461
HU-16	NV	Carson City		Grumman	Albatross	Sn 141278, N20861, MSN 425
HU-16	VA	VA Beach	MAFB	Grumman	Albatross	USCG 7209, MSN 282
HU-16 (SA-16)	CA	Atwater	CAM	Stits	Albatross	
HU-16 (SA-16)	KS	Liber	MAAM	Stits	Albatross	

Model	State	City	Museum	Manufacturer	Type	Notes
HU-16 (SA-16)	OK	Fredi	AAM	Stits	Albatross	
HU-16A	CA	SRosa	PCAM	Grumman	Albatross	
HU-16A	FL	Lakel	SFAF	Grumman	Albatross	N693S
HU-16A	NM	Albuq	KAFB	Grumman	Albatross	USCG 1280, MSN 302
HU-16A(SA-16)	AZ	Mesa	CAFM	Grumman	Albatross	51-22, MSN 096
HU-16A(SA-16)	AZ	Tucso	PAM	Grumman	Albatross	51-22, MSN 096
HU-16B	CA	Sacra	McCelAFB	Grumman	Albatross	51-7209
HU-16B	GA	Warner Robin	MoF	Grumman	Albatross	51-7144
HU-16B	IL	Ranto	OCAM	Grumman	Albatross	51-7200
HU-16B	MD	Balti	BANG	Grumman	Albatross	
HU-16B	OH	Dayto	USAFM	Grumman	Albatross	51-5282
HU-16B	SC	Flore	FA&MM	Grumman	Albatross	Sn 51-7212, MSN 281
HU-16B	TX	FWort	PMoT	Grumman	Albatross	50-17176
HU-16B	TX	Midla	CAFFM	Grumman	Albatross	
HU-16B-GR	NE	Ashland	SACM	Grumman	Albatross	51-6
HU-16E	AL	Mobil	BMP	Grumman	Albatross	2129
HU-16E	AZ	Phoen	LAFB	Grumman	Albatross	
HU-16E	CA	Riverside	MFAM	Grumman	Albatross	1293, "Cape Cod"
HU-16E	CT	Winds	NEAM	Grumman	Albatross	
HU-16E	FL	Pensa	USNAM	Grumman	Albatross	CGNR7236, 7236
HU-16E	NY	NYC	ISASM	Grumman	Albatross	
HU-16E	TX	Abile	DLAP	Grumman	Albatross	51-7251
Huber 101-1 Aero	WA	Seattle	MoF	Huber	Aero	001
Huff-Daland Duster	AL	Birmi	Southe	Huff-Daland	Duster	
Hughes Helicopter	WI	Kenos	KMM	Hughes	Helicopter	
HUP-1(UH-25)	CA	Alameda	USSHM	Piasecki	Retriever	124915
HUP-1	CA	Ramona	CR	Piasecki	Retriever	
HUP-1	CT	Winds	NEAM	Piasecki	Retriever	7228
HUP-1	FL	Kissi	FTWAM	Piasecki	Retriever	
HUP-2(H-25A)	AZ	Tucso	PAM	Piasecki	Retriever	Sn 134434, N8SA
HUP-2	AZ	Tucso	PAM	Piasecki	Retriever	N8SA
HUP-2	CA	Rosam	EAFB	Piasecki	Retriever	130059
HUP-2	CA	Miramar	FLAM	Piasecki	Retriever	
HUP-2	PA	WChes	AHM	Piasecki	Retriever	
HUP-2(H-25)	CA	Ramona	CR	Piasecki	Retriever	
HUP-2(H-25)	CT	Winds	NEAM	Piasecki	Retriever	
HUP-3	KS	Liber	MAAM	Piasecki	Retriever	
HUP-3	MI	Kalam	KAHM	Piasecki	Retriever	146700, 51-16607
HUP-3	ON-C	Ottaw	CAM	Piasecki	Retriever	51-16623
HUP-3 PD-18	BC-C	Langley	CMoF&T	Piasecki	Retriever	51-16621
HUP-3(PD-18)	AB-C	Calga	AMoC	Piasecke	Retriever	
HUP-3(H-25A)	AZ	Tucso	PAM	Piasecki	Retriever	Sn 147595, 51-16608
HUP-3(UH-25C)	FL	Pensa	USNAM	Piasecki	Retriever	N4953S, 147607
Hutter 17	NY	Elmir	NSM	Hutter		WB153624, CF-RCD, 1934
HV2A	MD	Silve	PEGF	Herrick	Convertaplane	
Hwaker Hurricane	WY	Jackson	GWFM	Hawker	Hurricane	
Hydro-Kite Gallauder	DC	Washi	NA&SM	Gallauder	Hydro-Kite	
Hyper Light Hang Glider	AZ	Tucso	PAM	Hyper Light	Hyper Light	
I-15bis	VA	Suffolk	FF	Polikarpov		#7
I-16 Rata	VA	Suffolk	FF	Polikarpov	Rata	
I-16 Rata	WA	Eastsound	FHC	Polikarpov	Rata	
Icarus Hang Glider	AZ	Tucso	PAM	Icarus	Hang Glider	
Icarus I	MD	Silve	PEGF	Icarus		
ICBM	AL	Mobile	BMP	Redstone	Arsenal Redstone	
ICBM	OH	Dayton	USAFM	Redstone	Hard Mobile Launcher	
Ikarus Aero 3A	CA	Oakla	OWAM	Ikarus	Aero	
Ikenga 530Z Autogiro	MD	Silve	PEGF	Gittens	Autogiro	
Ilyushin IL-14P	CA	Santa Rosa	PCAM	Ilyushin	Model SO	1954
Ilyushin IL-2m3	MD	Silver Hill	PEGF	Ilyushin	Shturmovik	
Ilyushin	NV	Reno	Steade	Ilyushin	Model SO	
Ingram/Foster Biplane	NM	Albuq	AA	Ingram-Foster	Biplane	
Insitu Aerosonde	WA	Seattle	MoF	Insitu	Aerosonde	
J-1	CA	San Diego	SDAM	Standard		1598, N2826D
J-1	FL	Polk	FoF	Standard		
J-1	MD	Silve	PEFG	Standard		
J-1	MD	Silve	PEGF	Standard		
J-1	ME	OwlsH	OHTM	Standard		
J-1	ND	WFarg	Bonanzav	Standard		
J-1	NY	Buffa	B&ECHM	Standard		
J-1	NY	Rhine	ORA	Standard		
J-1	OH	Dayto	USAFM	Standard		1141
J-1 Fabric Covered	OH	Dayto	USAFM	Standard		Fabric Covered
J-1	PA	Bethel	GAAM	Standard		
J-1	WI	Oshko	EAAAAM	Standard		N6948
J-2	AZ	Tucso	PAM	McCulloch	Super Gyroplane	Man Sn 019, N4309G
J-2	CA	El Cajon	FFM	Taylor	Cub	
J-2	FL	Miami	WOM	McCulloch	Gyro-Plane	
J-2	IA	Greenfield	IAM	Taylor	Cub	
J-2	IL	Harva	BA	Taylor	Cub	
J-2	KS	Liber	MAAM	McCulloch	Gyro-Plane	
J-2	MD	College Park	CPAM	Taylor	Cub	NC16769
J-2	MD	Hager	HRegAirP	Taylor	Cub	
J-2	NC	Hende	WNCAM	Piper	Cub	NC16315
J-2	ND	Minot	DTAM	Piper	Cub	
J-2	NE	Minde	HWPV	Taylor	Cub	
J-2	NY	Mayvi	DA	Taylor	Cub	
J-2	NY	Niagara Falls	NAM	Taylor	Cub	NC17834
J-2	NY	Rhine	ORA	Taylor	Cub	
J-2	OK	Fredi	AAM	Taylor	Cub	
J-2	PA	Readi	MAAM	Taylor	Cub	
J-2	WA	Seatt	MoF	Wizard	Ultralight	
J-2	WI	Oshkosh	EAAAAM	Piper	Cub	
J-2A	MD	Silve	PEGF	Taylor	Cub	
J-3	AL	Birmingham	SMoF	Piper	Cub	Project
J-3	AR	Fayet	AAM	Piper	Cub	NC38668
J-3	CA	San Diego	SDAM	Piper	Cub	NC333ED
J-3	CO	GJunc	CAF-RMW	Piper	Cub	N53503
J-3	CT	Winds	NEAM	Piper	Cub	
J-3	FL	Ameli	IAT	Piper	Cub	
J-3	FL	Kissi	FTWAM	Piper	Cub	
J-3	FL	Pensa	USNAM	Piper	Cub	8375H NC
J-3	IA	Greenfield	IAM	Piper	Cub	
J-3	ID	Zellw	BWA	Piper	Cub	
J-3	IN	Auburn	HW	Piper	Cub	
J-3	MB-C	Brand	CATPM	Piper	Cub	
J-3	MD	Silve	PEGF	Piper	Cub	

J-3	MO	Missoula	MMF	Piper	Cub	
J-3	ND	Minot	DTAM	Piper	Cub	
J-3	NM	STere	WEAM	Piper	Cub	
J-3	NY	Mayvi	DA	Piper	Cub	
J-3	NY	Rhine	ORA	Piper	Cub	
J-3	NY	River	RE	Piper	Cub	
J-3	NC	Asheboro	PFAC	Piper	Cub	Flitfire
J-3	OH	Dayton	USAFM	Piper	Cub	
J-3	TX	Dalla	CFM	Piper	Cub	N24935
J-3	TX	Kingbury	VAHF	Piper	Cub	Project
J-3	TX	Ladero	Airport	Piper	Cub	
J-3	UT	Heber	HVAM	Piper	Cub	
J-3	VA	Bealt	FCA	Piper	Cub	
J-3	VA	Richm	SMoV	Piper	Cub	
J-3	WA	Vancouver	PAM	Piper	Cub	
J-3	WA	Yakima	MMoA	Piper	Cub	
J-3	WI	Oshkosh	EAAAAM	Piper	Cub	
J-3 (3ea)	FL	Zellw	BWA	Piper	Cub	
J-3 CP-65	OK	Fredi	AAM	Piper	Cub	
J-3C	CA	Palm Sprg	PSAM	Piper	Cub	N28118
J-3C	KS	Liber	MAAM	Piper	Cub	
J-3C	ME	OwlsH	OHTM	Piper	Cub	
J-3C	WA	Seattle	MoF	Piper	Cub	15641, N88023
J-3C-65	MI	Kalamazoo	KAHM	Piper	Cub	
J-3C	PA	Harri	SMoP	Piper	Cub	
J-3C-65	NC	Hende	WNCAM	Piper	Cub	N3450K
J-3C-65	OR	Mc Minnville	EAEC	Piper	Cub	G-31, N46471
J-3C-65	TX	RioHo	TAM	Piper	Cub	SN5660, N32851
J-4A	BC-C	Langley	CMoF&T	Piper	Cub Coupe	
J-4A	KS	Liber	MAAM	Piper	Cub Coupe	
J-4A	OK	Fredi	AAM	Piper	Cub Coupe	
J-4A	WI	Oshko	EAAAAM	Piper	Cub Coupe	N30340
J-4A	AZ	Tucson	PAM	Piper	Cub Coupe	Man Sn 4-469, NC22783
J-4F	KS	Liber	MAAM	Piper	Cub Coupe	
J-4F	OK	Fredi	AAM	Piper	Cub Coupe	
J-5	GA	Woodstock	AAM	Piper	Cruiser	
J-5	GA	Woodstock	AAM	Piper	Cruiser	
J-5	GA	Woodstock	AAM	Piper	Cruiser	
J-5	NC	Hende	WNCAM	Piper	Cruiser	NC38499
J-5	OH	Madis	CFR	Piper	Cruiser	
J-5	VA	Sands	VAM	Piper	Cruiser	
J-5C(AE-1)	TX	San A	ILP&AAM	Piper	Super Cruiser	
J-10-JET	CA	Redwo	HAM			Model 360
J-29	MD	Silve	PEGF	Saab	Tunman	Swept Wing Fighter
J-35	GA	Woodstock	AAM	CuMaulaCraftMan		
J1N1-S	MD	Silve	PEGF	Nakajima	Moonlight	
J2F-6	AK	Ancho	AAHM	Grumman	Duck	
J2F-6	CA	Chino	PoFAM	Grumman	Duck	
J2F-6	CA	San Diego	SDAM	Grumman	Duck	N1273N, 33594
J2F-6	FL	Miami	WOM	Grumman	Duck	N1214N, I-J-7
J2F-6	FL	Pensa	USNAM	Grumman	Duck	33581, 149
J2F-6	FL	Polk	FoF	Grumman	Duck	
J2F-6	OR	Tillamook	TAM	Grumman	Duck	N3960C
J2F-6	WI	Oshko	EAAAAM	Grumman	Duck	36976
J2M3	CA	Chino	PoFAM	Mitsubishi	Raiden	
J4F-1	FL	Lakeland	SNF	Grumman	Widgeon	
J4F-1	FL	Pensa	USNAM	Grumman	Widgeon	1260, N212ST, V 212, Model G-44
J4F-2	AZ	Tucso	PAM	Grumman	Widgeon	32976, Model G-44
J4F-1	ON-C	Hamilton	CWH	Grumman	Widgeon	
J7W1	MD	Silve	PEGF	Mitsubishi	Kyushu	
J8M1	CA	Chino	PoFAM	Mitsubishi	Shusui	
JC-1	MD	Silve	PEGF		Weedhopper	
JC-1	WI	Oshko	EAAAAM	Chase-Church	Midwing	N9167
JC-24-B	WI	Oshko	EAAAAM	Weedhopper	Weedhopper	
JN-2D-1	WI	Oshko	EAAAAM	Curtiss	Jenny	N1005Z
JN-4D	AB-C	Wetas	RM	Curtiss	Jenny	
JN-4D	AL	Ozark	USAAM	Curtiss	Jenny	
JN-4D	CA	Chino	YACM	Curtiss	Jenny	N1563, D-51
JN-4D	CA	Paso Robles	EWM	Curtiss	Jenny	A-996
JN-4D	CA	S.Mon	MoF	Curtiss	Jenny	A-996
JN-4D	CA	San Diego	SDAM	Curtiss	Jenny	N5391, 3826, 38262
JN-4D	CA	San Francisco	CFAMA	Curtiss	Jenny	
JN-4D	CO	Denve	DIA	Curtiss	Jenny	SC1918, #65
JN-4D	CT	Washi	TFC	Curtiss	Jenny	
JN-4D	FL	Pensa	USNAM	Curtiss	Jenny	490, A, 995
JN-4D	FL	Polk	FoF	Curtiss	Jenny	
JN-4D	IL	Chica	MoS&I	Curtiss	Jenny	
JN-4D	KS	Topek	CAM	Curtiss	Jenny	N-101JN
JN-4D	MD	College Park	CPAM	Curtiss	Jenny	
JN-4D	MD	Silve	PEGF	Curtiss	Jenny	
JN-4D	ME	OwlsH	OHTM	Curtiss	Jenny	
JN-4D	MO	Maryland Hts	HARM	Curtiss	Jenny	
JN-4D	NE	Minde	HWPV	Curtiss	Jenny	
JN-4D	NY	Garde	CoAM	Curtiss	Jenny	1187
JN-4D	NY	Hammo	CM	Curtiss	Jenny	
JN-4D	NY	Rhine	ORA	Curtiss	Jenny	
JN-4D	NY	Niagara Falls	NAM	Curtiss	Jenny	3059
JN-4D	OH	Dayto	USAFM	Curtiss	Jenny	2805
JN-4D	OK	Tulsa	TA	Curtiss	Jenny	
JN-4D	ON-C	Ottaw	CAM	Curtiss	Jenny	39158
JN-4D	OR	Mc Minnville	EAEC	Curtiss	Jenny	
JN-4D	PA	Bethel	GAAM	Curtiss	Jenny	
JN-4D	SK-C	MJaw	WDM	Curtiss	Jenny	
JN-4D	TX	San A	LAFB	Curtiss	Jenny	
JN-4D	TX	San A	MoFM	Curtiss	Jenny	
JN-4D	TX	San A	SAMoT	Curtiss	Jenny	
JN-4D	UT	Ogden	HAFB	Curtiss	Jenny	
JN-4D	VA	Quantico	MCAGM	Curtiss	Jenny	
JN-4D	WA	Eastsound	FHC	Curtiss	Jenny	3712, N31712
JN-4D	WA	Seatt	MoF	Curtiss	Jenny	
JN-4D	WA	Stevenson	CGIC	Curtiss	Jenny	
JN-4D	WI	Oshko	EAAAAM	Curtiss	Jenny	N5357
JN-4D	WI	Oshko	EAAAAM	Curtiss	Jenny	2525
JN-6H	MN	Minne	MAGM	Curtiss	Jenny	
JRF-3(OA-13), (G-21)	FL	Pensa	USNAM	Grumman	Goose	V190, Model G-21A

141

Aircraft	ST	City	Code	Manufacturer	Model	Notes
JRS-1 (S-43)	AZ	Tucso	PAM	Sikorsky	Cargo Trans	4325, NC16934, 1059
JRS-1 (S-43)	MD	Silve	PEGF	Sikorsky	Cargo Trans	
Ju 52	DC	Dulle		Junkers	Aunti Ju	
Ju 52	IL	Chica	CAF-GLW	Junkers	Aunti Ju	N352JU
Ju 52/1M	MB-C	Winni	WCAM	Junkers	Aunti Ju	
Ju 52/3M	OH	Dayto	USAFM	Junkers	Aunti'Ju	
Ju 87/B (7/8 Scale)	NY	Elmir	CRA	Junkers	Stuka	
Ju 87B	IL	Chica	MoS&I	Junkers	Stuka	
Ju 88D/1	OH	Dayto	USAFM	Junkers	Zerstorer	430650
Ju 388L	MD	Silve	PEGF	Junkers	1945 Recon.	
Junkers D.1	AL	Gunte	LGARFM	Junkers		1st All Metal Fighter
Junkers F-13	MB-C	Winni	WCAM	Junkers		
Junkers J1	ON-C	Ottaw	CAM	Junkers		586
Junkers W 34f/fi	ON-C	Ottaw	CAM	Junkers		1934
Junkin Brukner	OH	Troy	WHS	Junkin Brukner	Baby Flying Boat	
Jurga-Tepete	FL	Lakeland	SNFAM	Jurga-Tepete		
K-16 V-STOL	CT	Winds	NEAM			
K-225	CT	Winds	NEAM	Kaman		
K-225	DC	Dulle		Kaman		
K-47 CAR	FL	Pensa	USNAM		Dirigible	
K-84	WY	Jackson	GWFM	Keystone-Loening	Commuter	
K-84 Biplane	AK	Palme	MOAT&I	Schleicher	2 Place Glider	
KA-4	NM	Moriarty	SSM	Schleicher	2 Place Glider	
KA-6	NM	Moriarty	SSM	Schleicher	2 Place Glider	
Kaminskas RK3	CA	San Diego	SDAM	Kaminskas	Jungster VI	N8355
Kaminskas RK3	WI	Oshko	EAAAAM	Kaminskas	Jungster III	N76AQ,"Johnathan Livingston Seagull"
Karnov Ka-26	CA	Ramona	CR	Karnov	Hoodlum	
KAQ-1	CA	Atwater	CAM	Kawasaki	Drone	
Karp Pusher	WI	Oshkosh	EAAAAM	Karp	Pusher	
Kasperwing 180-B	WA	Everett	MoF	Kasperwing		
Kaviler	OK	Oklah	A&SM		Kaviler	
KD-1A	PA	Readi	MAAM	Kellett	Autogiro	
KD-3G	FL	Pensa	USNAM			
Ki- 43	OR	Tillamook	TAM	Nakajima	Oscar (Hayabusa)	Peregrine Falcon
Ki-43B	TX	Ft Worth	TAF	Nakajima	Oscar (Hayabusa)	Peregrine Falcon (2ea)
Ki- 43B	WA	Eastsound	FHC	Nakajima	Oscar (Hayabusa)	750, N750
Ki- 43B	WI	Oshko	EAAAAM	Nakajima	Oscar (Hayabusa)	Peregrine Falcon
Ki-45	MD	Silver Hill	PEGF	Kawasaki	Nick	
Ki- 46	MD	Silve	PEGF	Mitsubishi	Dinah	
Ki- 61	CA	S.Mon	MoF	Kawasaki	Tony (Hein)	Army Type 3 Hein
Ki- 61	FL	Miami	WOM	Kawasaki	Tony (Hein)	N759, Army Type 3 Hein
Ki- 61	FL	Polk	FoF	Kawasaki	Tony (Hein)	Army Type 3 Hein
Ki- 61 Rep	TX	SMarc	CTWCAF	Kawasaki	Tony (Hein)	
Ki-115	MD	Silve	PEGF	Nakajima	Tsurugi	Suicide Plane
Kiceniuk Icarus V	WI	Oshko	EAAAAM	Kiceniuk	Icarus V	
Kikka	MD	Silve	PEGF		Kikka	
Kinner Sportster	IA	Ottumwa	APM	Kinner	Sportster	
Kitfox Model 1	FL	Lakel	SFAF	Denny Aerocraft	Speedster	N3LB
Kitfox Model 4				Denny Aerocraft	Speedster	N177CA
Klemm 35	CA	Santa Maria	SMMoF	Klemm		
Knight Twister Imperial	WI	Oshko	EAAAAM	Payne	Twister Imperial	N5DF, "White Knight",
Kola 202	KS	Liber	MAAM	Kola		
KR-21(C-6)	FL	Kissi	FTWAM	Fairchild	Challanger	FC Took Over Kreider-Reisner
KR-21B(C-6)	WI	Oshko	EAAAAM	Fairchild	Challanger	N954V
KR-34	FL	Kissi	FTWAM	Kreider Reiser	Challanger	
KR-34	WY	Jackson	GWFM	Fairchild	Challanger	FC Took Over Kreider-Reisner
KR-34C(C-4)	MB-C	Winnipeg	WRCAFB	Fairchild	Challanger	
KR-34C(C-4)	NS-C	Greenwood	GMAM	Fairchild	Challanger	
KR-34C(C-4)	ON-C	Sault Ste Marie	CBHC	Fairchild	Challanger	Sn 900, C-FADH,
KR-34C	MD	Silve	PEGF	Fairchild	Challanger	Kreider Reiser Formerly
Kreutzer K-5	WY	Jackson	GWFM	Kreutzer	Tri-Motor Aircoach	
Krier Kraft	KS	Ashla	HKAM	Kraft	Kraft	N5400E
Kurir	NY	Horseheads	NWM	Kurir	Kurir	50-133
L- 1	TX	FWort	BCVintag	Piaggio	Royal Gull	
L- 1A(O-49)	BC-C	Langley	CMoF&T	Vultee	Vigilant	40-283, Stinson 74
L- 1A(O-49)	FL	Polk	FoF	Vultee	Vigilant	
L- 1A(O-49)	OH	Dayto	USAFM	Vultee	Vigilant	41-19039
L- 1A(O-49)	TX	San A	ILP&AAM	Vultee	Vigilant	
L- 2	FL	Kissi	FTWAM	Taylorcraft	Grasshopper	
L- 2	KS	Liber	MAAM	Taylorcraft	Grasshopper	
L- 2	KS	New Century	CAF-HoAW	Taylorcraft	Grasshopper	N50573
L- 2	KS	New Century	CAF-HoAW	Taylorcraft	Grasshopper	N75891
L- 2	NY	Geneseo	1941AG	Taylorcraft	Grasshopper	
L- 2	NC	Hendersonville	WNCAM	Taylorcraft	Grasshopper	
L- 2	OK	Fredi	AAM	Taylorcraft	Grasshopper	
L- 2	TX	Brown	CAFRGVW	Taylorcraft	Grasshopper	
L- 2	TX	San A	ILP&AAM	Taylorcraft	Grasshopper	
L- 2	TX	Slanton	TAM	Taylorcraft	Grasshopper	95-04
L- 2	WA	Evere	CAF-EW	Taylorcraft	Grasshopper	N53768
L- 2	WA	Olympia	OFM	Taylorcraft	Grasshopper	Side # 8B
L- 2A	AL	Ozark	USAAM	Taylorcraft	Grasshopper	
L- 2A	PA	Tough	CFCM	Taylorcraft	Grasshopper	
L- 2A(D)	IA	Ottumwa	APM	Taylorcraft	Grasshopper	
L- 2B	CA	El Cajon	SDAMGF	Taylorcraft	Grasshopper	
L- 2D	OH	N Canton	MAM	Taylorcraft	Grasshopper	
L- 2M	AZ	Tucso	PAM	Taylorcraft	Grasshopper	43-26402, N59068
L- 2M	CA	Sacra	McCelAFB	Taylorcraft	Grasshopper	43- 5745, N53792
L- 2M	IL	Springfield	ACM	Taylorcraft	Grasshopper	43-26564
L- 2M	GA	Woodstock	NGWS	Taylorcraft	Grasshopper	
L- 2M	GA	Woodstock	NGWS	Taylorcraft	Grasshopper	
L- 2M	GA	Woodstock	NGWS	Taylorcraft	Grasshopper	
L- 2M	OH	Dayto	USAFM	Taylorcraft	Grasshopper	43-26753
L- 2M	TX	RioHo	TAM	Taylorcraft	Grasshopper	N47344
L- 3B	MO	SChar	CAF-MW	Aeronca	Grasshopper	N36681
L- 3B(O-58B)	AZ	PBluf	RWCAF	Aeronca	Grasshopper	
L- 3B(O-58B)	AZ	Tucso	PAM	Aeronca	Grasshopper	43-27206, N46067
L- 3B(O-58B)	CA	Shafter	MFAM	Aeronca	Commuter	
L- 3B(O-58B)	CA	SRosa	PCAM	Aeronca	Commuter	
L- 3B(O-58B)	GA	Warner Robin	MoF	Aeronca	Grasshopper	
L- 3B(O-58B)	IA	Ottumwa	APM	Aeronca	Grasshopper	058B12783, N50334
L- 3B(O-58B)	IN	Huntington	WoF	Aeronca	Grasshopper	43-1520
L- 3B(O-58B)	KS	Liber	MAAM	Aeronca	Grasshopper	Aeronca 65C
L- 3B(O-58B)	MI	Kalam	KAHM	Aeronca	Grasshopper	43-26772
L- 3B(O-58B)	NY	Horseheads	NWM	Aeronca	Grasshopper	
L- 3B(O-58B)	OH	Dayto	USAFM	Aeronca	Grasshopper	42-36200
L- 3B(O-58B)	OK	Fredi	AAM	Aeronca	Grasshopper	Aeronca 65C

Model	State	City	Code	Mfr	Name	Serial/Reg
L-3B(O-58B)	TX	Brown	CAFRGVW	Aeronca	Grasshopper	
L-3B(O-58B)	TX	Dalla	CFM	Aeronca	Grasshopper	
L-3B(O-58B)	TX	FWort	BCVintag	Aeronca	Defender	
L-3B(O-58B)	TX	San A	ILP&AAM	Aeronca	Grasshopper	
L-3B(O-58B)	WA	Seatt	MoF	Aeronca	Grasshopper	9223, N47427
L-3E	IA	CBluf	CAF-GPW	Aeronca	Grasshopper	N36687
L-4	CA	Atwater	CAM	Piper	Grasshopper	
L-4	CA	Corno	CAF-IES	Piper	Grasshopper	N35786
L-4	CA	Fairf	TAFB	Piper	Grasshopper	
L-4	CO	Denve	JWDAS	Piper	Grasshopper	
L-4	FL	Polk	FoF	Piper	Grasshopper	
L-4	IN	Valparaiso	IAM	Piper	Grasshopper	
L-4	KY	Lexington	AVoK	Piper	Grasshopper	NC42008
L-4Rep	MI	Saginaw	YAF	Homebuilt	Grasshopper	
L-4	MN	Minne	MAGM	Piper	Grasshopper	
L-4	NC	Asheboro	PFAC	Piper	Grasshopper	
L-4	ND	Wahpe	TSA	Piper	Grasshopper	
L-4(O-59A)	OH	Dayton	USAFM	Piper	Grasshopper	
L-4	OK	FtSil	USAFAM	Piper	Grasshopper	
L-4	TX	Brown	CAFRGVW	Piper	Grasshopper	
L-4	TX	C Christi	USS Lexi	Piper	Grasshopper	
L-4	TX	LV	LVAM	Piper	Grasshopper	
L-4	TX	San A	ILP&AAM	Piper	Grasshopper	
L-4	UT	Ogden	HAM	Piper	Grasshopper	
L-4	VA	FtEus	USATM	Piper	Grasshopper	
L-4	WA	Vancouver	PAM	Piper	Grasshopper	
L-4A	OH	Dayto	USAFM	Piper	Grasshopper	42-36446
L-4B	AL	Ozark	USAAM	Piper	Grasshopper	43-515
L-4B	FL	Pensa	USNAM	Piper	Grasshopper	
L-4B	GA	Hampton	AAHF	Piper	Grasshopper	
L-4B	OK	Oklah	45IDM	Piper	Grasshopper	
L-4H	MI	Kalamazoo	KAHM	Piper	Grasshopper	44-79817
L-4J	FL	Tittusville	VACM	Piper	Grasshopper	
L-4J	OK	Fredi	AAM	Piper	Grasshopper	
L-4J	TX	Dalla	CFM	Piper	Grasshopper	N9073C
L-5	CA	Chino	YAM	Stinson	Sentinel	
L-5	CA	El Cajon	CAFFFM	Stinson	Sentinel	N59AF
L-5	CA	Fairf	TAFB	Stinson	Sentinel	
L-5	CA	Riverside	MFAM	Stinson	Sentinel	63085
L-5	CO	Denve	JWDAS	Stinson	Sentinel	
L-5	KS	Liber	MAAM	Stinson	Sentinel	
L-5	LA	New Orleans	DDM	Stinson	Sentinel	
L-5	MD	Silve	PEGF	Stinson	Sentinel	
L-5	NC	Charl	CHAC	Stinson	Sentinel	
L-5	OH	Colum	CAF-OVW	Stinson	Sentinel	N5138B
L-5	OH	Dayto	USAFM	Stinson	Sentinel	42-98667
L-5	OK	Fredi	AAM	Stinson	Sentinel	
L-5	PA	Pitts	CAF-KW	Stinson	Sentinel	N25818
L-5	SD	Rapid	SDA&SM	Stinson	Sentinel	45-35046
L-5	TX	Abile	PSCAF	Stinson	Sentinel	
L-5	TX	Burnet	HLS-CAF	Stinson	Sentinel	
L-5	TX	Brown	RGVW-CAF	Stinson	Sentinel	
L-5	TX	Ft Worth	VFM	Stinson	Sentinel	
L-5	TX	Galve	LSFM	Stinson	Sentinel	1039, N68MH
L-5	TX	Midla	CAFFM	Stinson	Sentinel	
L-5	TX	San A	ILP&AAM	Stinson	Sentinel	
L-5	TX	SMarc	CTWCAF	Stinson	Sentinel	
L-5	VA	Chesa	CAF-ODS	Stinson	Sentinel	N61100
L-5	VA	Manas	CAF-NCS	Stinson	Sentinel	N1156V
L-5	VA	Suffolk	FF	Stinson	Sentinel	41-7588
L-5	VA	Chesapeake	CAFODW	Stinson	Sentinel	
L-5A	MN	StPau	CAF-SMW	Stinson	Sentinel	N68591
L-5B	AZ	Tucso	PAM	Stinson	Sentinel	44-16907, N4981V
L-5E	CA	Atwater	CAM	Stinson	Sentinel	
L-5E	CA	Chino	PoFAM	Stinson	Sentinel	
L-5E	CA	Okdal	CAF-CCVS	Stinson	Sentinel	N5625V
L-5E	CA	Paso Robles	EWM	Stinson	Sentinel	44-17944, N45CV
L-5E-1VW	WI	Oshko	EAAAAM	Stinson	Sentinel	4297
L-5E(OY-2)	OH	Columbus	CAF-OVW	Stinson	Sentinel	44-181143, N5138B (04013)
L-5G	CA	Chino	PoFAM	Stinson	Sentinel	
L-5Spatz-55	NS-C	Halifax	ACAM			
L-6	AZ	Tucso	PAM	Interstate	Cadet	
L-6	KS	Liber	MAAM	Interstate	Cadet	
L-6	OH	Dayto	USAFM	Interstate	Cadet	43-2680
L-6	OK	Fredi	AAM	Interstate	Cadet	N37214
L-6	TX	Brown	CAFRGVW	Interstate	Cadet	
L-6	TX	Corpus Christi	CAF-TCW	Interstate	Cadet	
L-6	TX	Denton	H10FM	Interstate	Cadet	
L-6	TX	San A	ILP&AAM	Interstate	Cadet	
L-6(S-1A)	AK	Palme	MOAT&I	Interstate	Cadet	1941
L-9B	PA	Pitts	CAF-KW			N26295
L-13	CA	Atwater	CAM	Convair	Scorpion	
L-13	MN	Minne	JJ	Convair	Scorpion	
L-13	WA	Eastsound	HFM	Convair	Scorpion	
L-13A	CA	Chino	PoFAM	Convair	Scorpion	
L-13A	MI	Fairf	YAFNE	Convair	Scorpion	
L-13A	NJ	Fairfield	YAM	Convair	Scorpion	47-389, N65893
L-13A	NM	STere	WEAM	Convair	Scorpion	
L-13B	WA	Seatt	MoF	Convair	Scorpion	
L-15(YL)A	AL	Ozark	USAAM	Boeing	Scout	47-429
L-16A	CA	Paso Robles	EWM	Aeronca	Chief	47-0787, N82107
L-16	CO	Denve	JWDAS	Aeronca	Chief	
L-16	IL	Linco	HIFM	Aeronca	Chief	
L-16	KS	Liber	MAAM	Aeronca	Chief	
L-16	NY	Geneseo	1941AG	Aeronca	Chief	
L-16	OK	Fredi	AAM	Aeronca	Chief	
L-17	CO	Denve	JWDAS	Ryan	Navion	
L-17	GA	Calhoun	MAM	Ryan	Navion	
L-17	GA	Hampton	AAHF	Ryan	Navion	
L-17	IL	Linco	HIFM	Ryan	Navion	
L-17	KS	Liber	MAAM	Ryan	Navion	
L-17	GA	Hampton	AAHF	Ryan	Navion	
L-17	GA	Woodstock	AAM	Ryan	Navion	
L-17	NY	Geneseo	1941AG	Ryan	Navion	
L-17	TX	Midla	CAF-Hq	Ryan	Navion	N444AC
L-17A	AL	Ozark	USAAM	Ryan	Navion	47-1344

L-17A	CA	Paso Robles	EWM	North American	Navion	47-1333, N91668
L-17A	OH	Dayto	USAFM	Ryan	Navion	47-1347
L-17A	OK	Oklah	45IDM	Ryan	Navion	
L-17A	TX	Denton	H10FM	Ryan	Navion	
L-17A	TX	Slanton	TAMCC	Ryan	Navion	
L-17B	FL	Deland	FW-CAF	Ryan	Navion	
L-17B	IN	Crown	CPV	Ryan	Navion	
L-17B	OH	N Canton	MAM	North American	Navion	
L-17B	TX	Burnet	HLSCAF	North American	Navion	
L-19	CA	El Cajon	SDAMGF	Cessna	Bird Dog	
L-19	CO	Denve	JWDAS	Cessna	Bird Dog	
L-19	MN	Winoma	WTI	Cessna	Bird Dog	N1983AP
L-19	NY	River	RE	Cessna	Bird Dog	
L-19	OK	FtSil	USAFAM	Cessna	Bird Dog	
L-19	OK	Oklah	45IDM	Cessna	Bird Dog	56-367
L-19	ON-C	Petawawa	CFBPMM	Cessna	Bird Dog	
L-19	WA	Eastsound	HFM	Cessna	Bird Dog	
L-19(OE-1)(O-1)	FL	Pensa	USNAM	Cessna	Bird Dog	51-14981
L-19(OE-2)(O-2)	KS	Wichita	KAM	Cessna	Bird Dog	21469
L-19(OE-2)(O-2)	VA	Quantico	MCAGM	Cessna	Bird Dog	140090
L-19(OE-2)(O-2)	WA	Everett	MoF	Cessna	Bird Dog	67-21363
L-19A	AL	Ozark	USAAM	Cessna	Bird Dog	50-1327
L-19A	AL	Ozark	USAAM	Cessna	Bird Dog	51- 4943
L-19A	AZ	Grand	PoFGCVA	Cessna	Bird Dog	51-12129
L-19A	GA	Hampton	AAHF	Cessna	Bird Dog	
L-19A	GA	Warner Robin	MoF	Cessna	Bird Dog	
L-19A	KY	FKnox	PMoC&A	Cessna	Bird Dog	
L-19A(O-1)	CA	SanLu	CSLO	Cessna	Bird Dog	
L-19A(O-1)	IN	India	IMoMH	Cessna	Bird Dog	
L-19A(O-1)	CA	SanLu	CSLO	Cessna	Bird Dog	53-8029
L-19A(O-1)	VA	FtEus	USATM	Cessna	Bird Dog	12745
L-19A(O-1A)	MD	Silve	PEGF	Cessna	Bird Dog	
L-19A(O-1E)	FL	FtWal	HF	Cessna	Bird Dog	56-4208
L-19A(O-1E)	GA	Warner Robin	MoF	Cessna	Bird Dog	51-12857
L-19A-CE	MI	Oscoda	YAM	Cessna	Bird Dog	51-12107, N3302T
L-19A	NC	Asheboro	PFAC	Cessna	Bird Dog	
L-19A(O-1G)	OH	Dayto	USAFM	Cessna	Bird Dog	51-11917
L-19D(TL)	AL	Ozark	USAAM	Cessna	Bird Dog	55- 4681
L-19D	GA	Hampton	AAHF	Cessna	Bird Dog	
L-21 (PA-18)	CA	Atwater	CAM	Piper	Super Cub	
L-21 (PA-18)	GA	Calhoun	MAM	Piper	Super Cub	
L-21 (PA-18)	VA	FtEus	USATM	Piper	Super Cub	
L-21A(TL)(PA-18)	AL	Ozark	USAAM	Piper	Super Cub	51-15782
L-21B(PA-18)	NY	Geneseo	1941AG	Piper	Super Cub	
L-21B(PA-18)	PA	Beave	AHM	Piper	Super Cub	
L-21B(PA-18)	PA	Readi	MAAM	Piper	Super Cub	53- 7720, N50084
L-29	FL	Miami	WOM	Aero	Delfin	
L-29	ND	Minot	DTAM	Aero	Delfin	
L-29	OR	Tillamook	TAM	Aero	Delfin	
L-29	WI	Amery	AMA	Aero	Delfin	
L-38	MO	StCha	CAFMW			
L-38A (Not Correct)	IL	Ranto	OCAM	Northrop	Talon	
L-39	KS	New Century	CAF-HoAW	Aerovodochody	Albatross	
L-39	MN	Anoka	Airport	Aerovodochody	Albatross	N139BH
L-39	WA	Eastsound	HFM	Aerovodochody	Albatross	
L-39A	WA	Olympia	OFM	Aerovodochody	Albatross	
L-106	WA	Seatt	MoF	Lamson	Alcor Glider	18, N924LR
L-049(C-69)	AZ	Tucso	PAM	Lockheed	Columbine	Sn 42-94549, 48-614, N90831
L-1011	NV	Las Vegas	LBAHSM	Lockheed	Tri-Star	
L-1049(EC-121D)	CA	Sacra	McCelAFB	Lockheed	Super Constellation 53-552	
L-1049(EC-121K)	DC	Dulle		Lockheed	Super Constellation USAF	
L-1049(EC-121K)	IL	Ranto	OCAM	Lockheed	Super Constellation 141311, USAF	
L-1049(EC-121K)	OK	Tinke	TAFB	Lockheed	Super Constellation USAF	
L-1049(EC-121S)	TX	San A	LAFB	Lockheed	Super Constellation 54- 155,	
L-1049(EC-121T)	CO	CSpri	EJPSCM	Lockheed	Super Constellation 52-3425, USAF	
L-1049(EC-121T)	KS	Topek	CAM	Lockheed	Super Constellation 52-3418	
L-1049(EC-121T)	MO	Kansas City	AHM	Lockheed	Super Constellation N6937C	
L-1049(WF-2)	FL	Pensa	USNAM	Lockheed	Super Constellation Navy	
L-1649A	FL	Orlando	OSA	Lockheed	Starliner	N974R, "Jenny's Star"
L-1649A	ME	Aubur	SLP	Lockheed	Starliner	N8083H, "Jason's Star"
L-1649A	ME	Aubur	SLP	Lockheed	Starliner	N7316C, "Brian's Star"
L-450F LTVE	TX	FWort	SAM			
L10A	CA	Oakla	OWAM	Lockheed	Electra	N3828
L10A	CT	Winds	NEAM	Lockheed	Electra	
L10A	MB-C	Winni	WCAM	Lockheed	Electra	
L10A	ON-C	Ottaw	CAM	Lockheed	Electra	
L12A	KY	Lexington	AMoK	Lockheed	Electra	1203, N12EJ
L12A	ON-C	Ottaw	CAM	Lockheed	Electra	
L14	CT	Winds	NEAM	Lockheed	Super Electra	
L18(C-60)	HI	Honol	HIA	Lockheed	Lodestar	
L18(C-60)	TX	Denton	H10FM	Lockheed	Lodestar	
L18(C-60)	WY	Greyb	H&PA	Lockheed	Lodestar	
L18-50	TX	Midla	CAFFM	Lockheed	Lodestar	
L-24 See U-10						
L.25J	PA	Beave	AHM	British Aircraft	Swallow	
Laird Swallow	KS	Wichi	KAM	Laird	Swallow	
Lancair 200	WI	Oshko	EAAAAM	Lancair	Lancair 200	N384L, Neibauer
Langley Aerodrome A	MD	Silve	PEGF	Langley	Aerodrome	
Langley Aerodrome N0. 5	MD	Silve	PEGF	Langley	Aerodrome	
Langley Aerodrome	VA	Hampton	VA&SM	Langley	Aerodrome	
Latter	PA	Tough	CFCM	Latter		
Lazair	FL	Lakel	SFAF	Lazair		
Lazair SS EC Ultralight	MD	Silve	PEGF	Lazair	Ultralight	
LC-DW500	CT	Winds	NEAM	Laird	Super Solution	
LC-DW500	MD	Silve	PEFG	Laird	Super Solution	
LC-DW500	MI	Dearb	HFM	Laird	Super Solution	
LC-DW500	WI	Oshko	EAAAAM	Laird	Super Solution	NR12048
LC-DW500 Fuse	MD	Silve	PEGF	Laird	Super Solution	
LCVP	LA	New Orleans	DDM	Higgins	Boat	
LCVP	DC	Washington	NM	Higgins	Boat	
Le Rhone	FL	Pensa	USNAM	Le Rhone		
Leak Avid Flyer	KS	Liber	MAAM	Leak	Avid Flyer	
Leak Avid Flyer	OK	Fredi	AAM	Leak	Avid Flyer	
Learjet 23	AZ	Tucson	PAM	Gates	Learjet	Man Sn 23-015, N88B
Learjet 23	KS	Wichita	KAM	Gates	Learjet	
Learjet 23	MI	Kalamazoo	KAHM	Gates	Learjet	23-083

Aircraft	State	City	Museum	Manufacturer	Model	Notes
Learjet 23	VA	Richm	SMoV	Gates	Learjet	
Learjet 25	AL	Ozark	AA&TC	Gates	Learjet	
LeBel VTO	CA	Chino	PoFAM	LeBel		
LEM Grumman	NY	NYC	ISASM	Grumman	LEM	
Les Broussard 1956	MI	Hamil	ML	Les Broussard		
LF-107 Glider	WA	Everett	MoF	Let	Lunak	N2170D
LF-2100	WA	Seatt	MoF	Learfan		001, N626BL
LF-2100	WI	Oshko	EAAAAM	Learfan		N327ML
Lilienthal Glider	CA	Chino	PoFAM	Lilienthal	Glider	
Lilienthal Glider	CA	San Diego	SDAM	Lilienthal	Glider	
Lilienthal Glider	DC	Washi	NA&SM	Lilienthal	Glider	
Lilienthal Glider	ME	Owls Head	OHTM	Lilienthal	Glider	
Lilienthal Glider	NY	Garde	CoAM	Lilienthal	Glider	
Lilienthal Glider	WA	Seatt	MoF	Lilienthal	Glider	
Linburgs Monocoupe	MO	SLoui	SLLIA	Linburgs	Monocoupe	
Lincoln Biplane	WI	Oshko	EAAAAM	Lincoln	Biplane	
Lincoln Page LP3A	IL	Paris	HAAM	Lincoln		
Lincoln PT-K	WI	Oshko	EAAAAM	Lincoln	Biplane	N275N
Lincoln Sports	NS	Halifax	ACAM	Lincoln	Sports Biplane	
Link ANT-18 Trainer	CT	Winds	NEAM	Link	Trainer	
Link Trainer	AL	Birmingham	SMoF	Link	Trainer	
Link Trainer	AB-C	Calgary	AMoC	Link	Trainer	
Link Trainer	AB-C	Nanton	NLSAM	Link	Trainer	
Link Trainer	AB-C	Wetas	RM	Link	Trainer	
Link Trainer	AR	Little Rock	AEC	Link	Trainer	
Link Trainer	AR	Walnut Ridge	WRAFSM	Link	Trainer	
Link Trainer	CA	Oakla	OWAM	Link	Trainer	
Link Trainer	CA	San Diego	SDAM	Link	Trainer	
Link Trainer	CO	Denver	DIA/UAL	Link	Trainer	
Link Trainer	DE	Dover	DAFB	Link	Trainer	
Link Trainer	FL	Tittusville	VACM	Link	Trainer	
Link Trainer	KS	Liber	MAAM	Link	Trainer	
Link Trainer	KY	Lexington	AMoK	Link	Trainer	
Link Trainer	MI	Kalam	KAHM	Link	Trainer	
Link Trainer	MI	OScoda	YAF	Link	Trainer	
Link Trainer	MN	Duluth	CAF-LSS	Link	Trainer	
Link Trainer	MN	Minneapolis	MSPIA	Link	Trainer	
Link Trainer	NF-C	Gander	NAAM	Link	Trainer	
Link Trainer	NJ	Milli	MAAFM	Link	Trainer	
Link Trainer	NJ	Milvi	MAAFM	Link	Trainer	
Link Trainer	NM	STere	WEAM	Link	Trainer	
Link Trainer	NS	Halifax	ACAM	Link	Trainer	
Link Trainer	NY	Binghamton	LFSC	Link	Trainer	
Link Trainer	NY	Binghamton	BRA	Link	Trainer	
Link Trainer	NY	Ghent	POMAM	Link	Trainer	
Link Trainer C-3	OH	N Canton	MAM	Link	Trainer	
Link Trainer	ON-C	Hamilton	CWHM	Link	Trainer	
Link Trainer	ON-C	Sault Ste Marie	CBHC	Link	Trainer	
Link Trainer	OR	Eugen	OAM	Link	Trainer	
Link Trainer	PA	Lock Haven	PAM	Link	Trainer	
Link Trainer	TX	Dalla	CFM	Link	Trainer	
Link Trainer	VA	Quantico	MCAGM	Link	Trainer	
Link Trainer	WA	Vancouver	PAM	Link	Trainer	N192GP
Link Trainer Mk.IV	AB-C	Edmonton	AAM	Link	Trainer	
Lippisch DM-1	MD	Silve	PEGF	Lippisch		
Little Looper	CA	San Carlos	HAM	Aerobatic	"Little Looper"	
Little Rocket	FL	Lakel	SFAF	Little Rocket	Racer	N345JA
Liverpuffin 11	PA	Tough	CFCM	Liverpuffin		
LK-10 Glider	CA	Chino	PoFAM	Laister-Kauffman	Glider	
LN2S-3(Model 73)	KS	Liber	MAAM	Boeing-Stearman	Kaydet	
LNA-40 Super	WI	Oshko	EAAAAM	Heath	Super	N16GR
LNE-1	AL	Birmingham	SMoF	Pratt-Read	Glider	31543, Sn 39, N60432
LNE-1	CA	San Martin	WoHM	Pratt-Read	Glider	31543, Sn 39, N60432
LNE-1	FL	Pensa	USNAM	Pratt-Read	Glider	N60745
LNE-1(HH-2D)	FL	Pensa	USNAM	Pratt-Read	Glider	149031
LNE-1	KY	Lexington	AMoK	Pratt-Read	Glider	PRG-01-73, N60235
LNE-1 Cockpit	MD	Ft Meade	QM	Pratt-Read	Glider	
LNE-1	NY	Elmira	NSM	Pratt-Read	Glider	31561, Sn 57, N5346G
LNE-1	ND	Fargo	BAM	Pratt-Read	Glider	31569, Sn 65, N56660
LNE-1(TG-3A)	OH	Dayto	USAFM	Pratt-Read	Glider	31523, Sn 19, N69215
LNE-1(HH-2D)	IN	Auburn	HW	Pratt-Read	Glider	
LNE-1(X)	NY	Horseheads	NWM	Pratt-Read	Glider	31506, NC4467U
LNE-1(PR-G1)	WA	Everett	MoF	Pratt-Read	Glider	31517, Sn 13, N60353
LNS-1 Schweizer	FL	Pensa	USNAM	Schweizer	Glider	S- 4385
LNS-1 Schweizer	FL	Pensa	USNAM	Schweizer	Glider	04384, #6
Shafor Ganagobie	WI	Oshko	EAAAAM	Shafor	Ganagobie	N60G
Lockheed 402-2	NJ	Teter	AHoFNJ	Lockheed	Bushmaster	N160IL
Lockheed Hudson Mk IIIa	NF-C	Gander	NAAM	Lockheed	Hudson	
Lockheed Mk.6 (Fuse)	NS	Halifax	ACAM	Lockheed	Hudson	
Lockheed Q-5	AZ	Grand Canyon	PoFGCVA	Lockheed		
Lockheed Satellite	OH	Dayton	USAFM	Lockheed	Satellite	
Lockheed Sirius 8	DC	Washi	NA&SM	Lockheed	Sirius	
Lockheed Vega 5	KS	Liber	MAAM	Lockheed	Vega	
Lockheed Vega 5	MI	Dearb	HFM	Lockheed	Vega	N965Y
Lockheed Vega 5	OK	Fredi	AAM	Lockheed	Vega	
Lockheed Vega 5B	DC	Washi	NA&SM	Lockheed	Vega	
Lockheed Vega 5C	DC	Washi	NA&SM	Lockheed	Vega	"Winnie Mae"
Lockheed Vega 5C	WI	Oshko	EAAAAM	Lockheed	Vega	NC105W
Loehle 5151 Mustang	GA	Woodstock	NGWS	Loehle	Mustang Kit	
Long Eze	AZ	Tucso	PAM	Rutan	Long Eze	N82ST
Longster	MI	Kalamazoo	KAHM	Longster	Homebuilt	
Longwing Eaglerock	AL	Birmingham	SmoF	Longwing	Eaglerock	
Loving's-Love	FL	Lakeland	SNF	Loving-Wayne	Love	
Loving-Wayne WR-1 Love	WI	Oshko	EAAAAM	Loving-Wayne	Love	N351C
LP-3	CA	Chino	YACM	Lincoln	Page	156, N3830
LST	MI	Muskegon	USS S		Landing Ship Tank	
LTV4	OH	Hubbard	WWIIVM		Water Buffalo	D11
LTV4	TX	Frede	NMofPW			
Lunar Excursion Module	OK	Oklah	KCASM		Lunar Module	
Lunar Lander	KS	Hutch	KC&SC			
Lunar Orbiter	WA	Seatt	PSC			
Lunar Rover	KS	Hutch	KC&SC			
Lusac-11	OH	Dayto	USAFM	Packard LePere		SC-42133
Luscombe 8	KS	Liber	MAAM	Luscombe	Observer	
Luscombe 8	MN	Winoma	WTI	Luscombe	Silvaire	NC13308
Luscombe 8A	BC-C	Sidne	BCAM	Luscombe	Silvaire	

Aircraft	State	City	Museum	Manufacturer	Model	Notes
Luscombe 8A	IL	Urban	RFIA	Luscombe	Silvaire	
Luscombe 8A	KS	Liber	MAAM	Luscombe	Silvaire	990
Luscombe 8A	ME	Bangor	MAM	Luscombe	Silvaire	
Luscombe 8A	OH	Madis	CFR	Luscombe	Silvaire	
Luscombe 8A	OK	Fredi	AAM	Luscombe	Silvaire	
Luscombe 8A	TX	Kingbury	VAHF	Luscombe	Silvaire	
Luscombe 8E	GA	Woodstock	AAM	Luscombe	Silvaire	
Luscombe 8E	NY	River	RE	Luscombe	Silvaire	
Luscombe 8F	IA	Ottumwa	APM	Luscombe	Phantom I	6735, N805B
Luscombe 8F	WI	Oshko	EAAAAM	Luscombe	Phantom I	NC1025
Luscombe 8F	OK	Fredi	AAM	Luscombe	Phantom I	
Lysander	MB-C	Brand	CATPM	Westland	Lizzie	
Lysander	MD	Silve	PEGF	Westland	Lizzie	
Lysander	TX	Lubbock	SWM	Lysander	Lizzie	
M-1	OH	Dayto	USAFM	Ryan	Messenger	68-533
M-1	PA	Bethel	GAAM	Ryan	Messenger	NX2073
M-1	WA	Seatt	MoF	Ryan	Messenger	HN-1, N46853
M-2	DC	Washi	NASM	Douglas	Mail Plane	
M-6	NY	Garden	CoAM	Douglas	Nike Hercules	
M.J.5 Sirocco	WI	Oshko	EAAAAM	Jurca	Sirocco	N8038E
M2-F3(HL-10)	DC	Washi	NA&SM	Northrop	Lifting Body	
M6A1	MD	Silve	PEGF	Aichi	Seiran	
MA14/LJ-5B	VA	Hampt	APM	NA-McDonnell Douglas	Spacecraft	
Mace Model III	WI	Oshkosh	EAAAAM	Mace		
Mahoney Sorceress	MD	Silve	PEGF	Mahoney	Sorceress	
Manhigh II Gondola	OH	Dayton	USAFM	Manhigh	Gondola II	
Marcoux-Bromberg Special	CT	Winds	NEAM	Marcoux-Bromberg	Special	
Marske Pioneer II	CA	Santa Martin	WoHAM	Marske	Pioneer II Glider	Year 1985, Flying Wing Glider
Marinac Flying Mercury	WI	Oshko	EAAAAM	Marinac	Flying Mercury	
Martin 162A	MD	Balti	BMoI	Martin	Martin 162A	
Martin 2-0-2A	NJ	Teter	AHoFNJ	Martin	Martinliner	14074, N93204
Martin 4-0-4	MD	Middle River	GMAM	Martin	Martinliner	
Martin 4-0-4	MO	Kansas City	AHM	Martin	Martinliner	SN 14142, N145S
Martin 4-0-4	MT	Billings		Martin	Martinliner	
Martin 4-0-4	PA	Readi	MAAM	Martin	Martinliner	"Silver Falcon"
Martin J.V. K-III	MD	Silve	PEGF	Martin	Kitten	
Maupin-Lanteri Black Dia	MD	Silve	PEGF	Maupin-Lanteri	Black Diamond	
Maurice Farman S.11	ON-C	Ottaw	CAM	Maurice	Farman	
MB-2	OH	Dayton	USAFM			
MC- 1C	CA	Chino	YACM	McCulloch	Helicopter	3818
MC- 4C	AZ	Tucso	PAM	McCulloch		133817, N4072K
MC- 12 Cricket	WI	Oshko	EAAAAM	Rombaugh	Cricket	N1377L
M.C. 200	OH	Dayto	USAFM	Macchi	Seatta	McCulloch
MC-202	DC	Washi	NA&SM	McCulloch		
McAllister Yakima Clipper	WA	Seatt	MoF	McAllister	Yalima Clipper	N10655
McCook Wind Tunnel	OH	Dayton	USAFM	McCook	Wind Tunnel	
McDowall Monoplane	ON-C	Ottaw	CAM	McDowall	Monoplane	
Me 108	CA	Chino	PoFAM	Messerschmitt	Taifun	5
Me 108	FL	Miami	WOM	Messerschmitt	Taifun	
Me 108	NM	Hobbs	CAF-NMW	Messerschmitt	Taifun	N2231
Me 108	NY	Geneseo	1941AG	Messerschmitt	Taifun	N2231
Me 108	WA	Everett	MoF	Messerschmitt	Taifun	
Me 108B	TX	Midla	CAFFM	Messerschmitt	Taifun	
Me 109	FL	FtLau	WJAIS&L	Messerschmitt	GUSTOV	
Me 109	NY	Ghent	POMAM	Messerschmitt	GUSTOV	
Me 109	NY	Shirley	DLIA	Messerschmitt	GUSTOV	
Me 109	OR	McMinnville	EAEC	Messerschmitt	GUSTOV	
Me 109	TX	Midla	CAF-Hq	Messerschmitt	GUSTOV	N109KE
Me 109 Mock Up	KS	Topek	CAM	Messerschmitt	GUSTOV	
Me 109E	AZ	Mesa	CFM	Messerschmitt	GUSTOV	
Me 109E-3	WA	Seattle	MoF	Messerschmitt	GUSTOV	186, NX109J
Me 109F-4	TX	Slanton	TAMCC	Messerschmitt	Throp	8461
Me 163	GA	Savan	MEHM	Messerschmitt	Komet	
Me 163	OH	Dayton	USAFM	Messerschmitt	Komet	
Me 163B	CA	Chino	PoFAM	Messerschmitt	Komet	
Me 163B	MD	Silve	PEGF	Messerschmitt	Komet	
Me 163B (2 ea)	ON-C	Ottaw	CAM	Messerschmitt	Komet	191095
Me 163B (2 ea)	ON-C	Ottaw	CAM	Messerschmitt	Komet	191916
Me 208	FL	Tittusville	VACM	Messerschmitt	Ramier	
Me 208	NY	Geneseo	1941AG	Messerschmitt	Ramier	187, Nord 1101
Me 208	RI	NKing	QAM	Messerschmitt	Ramier	187, Nord 1101
Me 262 A	DC	Washi	NA&SM	Messerschmitt	Stormbird	Sturmvogel
Me 262 A	WA	Everett	TMP	Messerschmitt	Stormbird 13	Sturmvogel
Me 262 A	WA	Everett	TMP	Messerschmitt	Stormbird 13	Sturmvogel
Me 262 A	WA	Everett	TMP	Messerschmitt	Stormbird 13	Sturmvogel
Me 262 A	WA	Everett	TMP	Messerschmitt	Stormbird 13	Sturmvogel
Me 262 A	WA	Everett	TMP	Messerschmitt	Stormbird 13	Sturmvogel
Me 262-1a/U3	WA	Eastsound	FHC	Messerschmitt	Stormbird 09	Sturmvogel
Me 262A	OH	Dayto	USAFM	Messerschmitt	Stormbird	Sturmvogel 121442
Me 262B-1A	PA	Willo	WGNAS	Messerschmitt	Stormbird 13	Sturmvogel
Me 262B-1B	TX	Ft Worth	TAF	Messerschmitt	Stormbird 13	Sturmvogel
Me 410 A-3	MD	Silve	PEGF	Messerschmitt	Hornisse	
Mead C-III	SK-C	MJaw	WDM	Mead		
Mead Glider	AB-C	Wetas	RM	Mead	Glider	
Mead Primary Glider	IA	Greenfield	IAM	Mead	Glider	
Mead Primary Glider 1932	NY	Mayvi	DA	Mead	Primary Glider	
Mead Rhon Ranger	CT	Winds	NEAM	Mead	Rhon Ranger	
Melberg Biplane	NY	Mayvi	DA	Melberg	Biplane	1939
Mercury Capsule MR-2	CA	LAnge	CMoS&I	McDonnell	Mercury Capsule	
Mercury Capsule	CA	Chino	PoFAM	McDonnell	Mercury Capsule	
Mercury Capsule	CA	San Diego	SDAM	McDonnell	Mercury Capsule	
Mercury Capsule	OH	Dayton	USAFM	McDonnell	Mercury Capsule	
Mercury 7 Capsule	IL	Chicago	MoS&I	Mercury	Mercury Capsule	
Mercury 7 Capsule	KS	Hutch	KC&SC	McDonnell	Mercury Capsule	
Mercury Capsule Replica	MO	SLoui	MDPR	McDonnell	Mercury Capsule	
Mercury Capsule	NY	NYC	ISASM	Mercury	Mercury Capsule	"Aurora 7"
Mercury Capsule Replica	NC	Charlotte	CAM	McDonnell	Mercury Capsule	
Mercury Capsule	OH	Colum	CoS&I	McDonnell	Mercury Capsule	
Mercury Capsule Rep	OK	Oklah	KCASM	McDonnell	Mercury Capsule	
Mercury 6 Capsule	TX	Houst	HMoNS	Mercury	Mercury Capsule	
Mercury Capsule Replica	WA	Seatt	MoF	McDonnell	Mercury Capsule	
Mercury Air Shoestring	CA	San Diego	SDAM	Mercury	Air Shoestring	N16V
Mercury Chick	NY	Hammo	CM	Mercury	Chick	
Mercury S-1 Racer	NY	Hammo	CM	Mercury	Racer	
Merlin Hang Glider	NY	Garde	CoAM	Merlin	Hang Glider	
Meteor 1919	CA	Oakla	MDoH	Meteor	Meteor	

Name	State	Location	Code	Manufacturer	Model	Notes
Meyer Little Toot	WI	Oshko	EAAAAM	Meyers	Little Toot	N217J, "Petit Papillon",
Meyers M-1 Special	WI	Oshko	EAAAAM	Meyers	Special	N42963
Meyers OTW	FL	Pensa	USNAM	Meyers	OTW	N26482
Meyers OTW	KS	Topek	CAM	Meyers	OTW	
Meyers OTW	OH	Madis	CFR	Meyers	OTW	
Meyers OTW	TX	Kingbury	VAHF	Meyers	OTW	
Meyers OTW	WA	Vanco	PAM	Meyers	OTW	
Meyers OTW-145	WI	Oshko	EAAAAM	Meyers	OTW	N34357
Meyers Racer	RI	NKing	QAM	Orlokwski	Racer	N426A, "Mr D. Robert",
Midget Mustang	NC	Charl	CHAC	Midget	Mustang	
Midget Mustang	NC	CPoin	CPMB	Midget	Mustang	
MiG-15	AL	Birmingham	SMoF	Mikoyan-Gurevich	Midget	
MiG-15	AZ	Grand	PoFGCVA	Mikoyan-Gurevich	Midget	1301
MiG-15	AZ	Mesa	CFM	Mikoyan-Gurevich	Midget	1301
MiG-15	AZ	Phoenix	DVA	Mikoyan-Gurevich	Midget	2 Seater
MiG-15	CA	Chino	PoFAM	Mikoyan-Gurevich	Midget	1301
MiG-15	CA	Miramar	FLAM	Mikoyan-Gurevich	Midget	
MiG-15	CA	San Diego	SDAM	Mikoyan-Gurevich	Midget	
MiG-15	CA	SRosa	PCAM	Mikoyan-Gurevich	Midget	
MiG-15	CT	Winds	NEAM	Mikoyan-Gurevich	Midget	83277
MiG-15	FL	Miami	WOM	Mikoyan-Gurevich	Midget	
MiG-15	ID	Driggs	TAC	Mikoyan-Gurevich	Midget	358
MiG-15	KS	Topek	CAM	Mikoyan-Gurevich	Midget	B01016, N15YY
MiG-15	MD	Silve	PEGF	Mikoyan-Gurevich	Midget	
MiG-15	MI	Kalam	KAHM	Mikoyan-Gurevich	Midget	1B-01621
MiG-15	NJ	Cape May	NASWF	Mikoyan-Gurevich	Midget	N51MG
MiG-15	NV	FAllon	NASF	Mikoyan-Gurevich	Midget	
MiG-15	NV	Reno	SAFB	Mikoyan-Gurevich	Midget	
MiG-15	OH	Dayto	USAFM	Mikoyan-Gurevich	Midget	20-15357
MiG-15	TX	Amirillo	EFA&SM	Mikoyan-Gurevich	Midget	#509
MiG-15	UT	Heber	HVAM	Mikoyan-Gurevich	Midget	
MiG-15	VA	Quant	MCAGM	Mikoyan-Gurevich	Midget	1317
MiG-15	ONT-C	Ottawa	CAM	Mikoyan-Gurevich	Midget	1317
MiG-15	WA	Seattle	MoF	Mikoyan-Gurevich	Midget	79
MiG-15	WI	Oshko	EAAAAM	Mikoyan-Gurevich	Midget	N15MG
MiG-15 (2 Seater)	MN	Minneapolis	MAGM	Mikoyan-Gurevich	Midget	
MiG-15 (2 Seater)	NM	STere	WEAM	Mikoyan-Gurevich	Midget	640
MiG-15bis	AZ	Tucso	PAM	Mikoyan-Gurevich	Midget	Man Sn 1A-06-038, 822, VK-1 Engine
MiG-15UTI	AZ	Tucso	PAM	Mikoyan-Gurevich	Midget	38, N38BM
MiG-15UTI	OR	Mc Minnville	EAEC	Mikoyan-Gurevich	Midget	IA-242271, 38, NX271JM
MiG-15UTI/SB	TX	Dalla	CFM	Mikoyan-Gurevich	Midget	
MiG-17	AL	Huntsville	AC	Mikoyan-Gurevich	Fresco	
MiG-17	AZ	Mesa	CFM	Mikoyan-Gurevich	Fresco	
MiG-17	CA	Chino	PoFAM	Mikoyan-Gurevich	Fresco	
MiG-17	CA	Oakland	CAF-GGW	Mikoyan-Gurevich	Fresco	
MiG-17	CA	San Diego	SDAM	Mikoyan-Gurevich	Fresco	
MiG-17	FL	Tittusvill	VACM	Mikoyan-Gurevich	Fresco	
MiG-17	KS	New Century	CAF-HoAW	Mikoyan-Gurevich	Fresco	Ic1717, N1717M
MiG-17	KS	Topek	CAM	Mikoyan-Gurevich	Fresco	611
MiG-17	NV	Fallon	NASF	Mikoyan-Gurevich	Fresco	
MiG-17	NV	Reno	SAFB	Mikoyan-Gurevich	Fresco	
MiG-17	NY	Horseheads	NWM	Mikoyan-Gurevich	Fresco	
MiG-17	OH	Dayto	USAFM	Mikoyan-Gurevich	Fresco	799
MiG-17	OH	N Canton	MAM	Mikoyan-Gurevich	Fresco	
MiG-17(Lim-5)	TN	Sevierville	TMoA	Mikoyan-Gurevich	Fresco	IC1706
MiG-17(Lim-5R)	TN	Sevierville	TMoA	Mikoyan-Gurevich	Fresco	IC1728
MiG-17	TX	Dalla	CFM	Mikoyan-Gurevich	Fresco	
MiG-17	UT	Ogden	CFM	Mikoyan-Gurevich	Fresco	
MiG-17	WA	Seattle	MoF	Mikoyan-Gurevich	Fresco	1406016, IFJ-10
MiG-17A	GA	Warner Robin	MoF	Mikoyan-Gurevich	Fresco	54- 713 85
MiG-17F	AZ	Tucso	PAM	Mikoyan-Gurevich	Fresco C	1C 1905
MiG-17F	NY	Scotia	ESAM	Mikoyan-Gurevich	Fresco C	605
MiG-17F	RI	NKing	QAM	Mikoyan-Gurevich	Fresco C	1F0325
MiG-17PF	AZ	Tucso	PAM	Mikoyan-Gurevich	Fresco D	Man Sn 1A06038, 634
MiG-17PF	CA	Sacra	McCelAFB	Mikoyan-Gurevich	Fresco D	1186
MiG-19	CA	Riverside	MFAM	Mikoyan	Farmer	0301, A-5(F-9) Fantan, F-6 = China
MiG-19	CA	Riverside	MFAM	Mikoyan	Farmer	0409
MiG-19	NV	Reno	SAFB	Mikoyan	Farmer	
MiG-19S	OH	Dayto	USAFM	Mikoyan	Farmer	TB, 972, A-5(F-9) Fantan, F-6 = China
MiG-21 PFM	AZ	Tucson	PAM	Mikoyan	Fishbed	N21MF
MiG-21	AL	Birmingham	SMoF	Mikoyan	Fishbed	
MiG-21	CA	Riverside	MAFM	Mikoyan	Fishbed	1101
MiG-21	FL	Kissi	YAF	Mikoyan	Fishbed	
MiG-21	FL	Shali	USAFAM	Mikoyan	Fishbed	85 , RED
MiG-21	LA	Bossier City	BAFB	Mikoyan	Fishbed	
MiG-21	MD	Silver Hill	PEGF	Mikoyan	Fishbed	
MiG-21PF	MI	Kalam	KAHM	Mikoyan	Fishbed	4107
MiG-21	NE	Ashland	SACM	Mikoyan	Fishbed	
MiG-21	NY	Horseheads	NWM	Mikoyan	Fishbed	
MiG-21	OH	Dayto	HAFBM	Mikoyan	Fishbed	
MiG-21	OH	Dayto	USAFM	Mikoyan	Fishbed	560-301, "City of Moscow"
MiG-21	OK	Wetherford	GTSM	Mikoyan	Fishbed	
MiG-21 MF	ON-C	Trenton	RCAFMM	Mikoyan	Fishbed	23 45
MiG-21	TX	Dalla	CFM	Mikoyan	Fishbed	
MiG-21	UT	Ogden	HAFBM	Mikoyan	Fishbed	
MiG-21-D	VA	Quantico	MCAGM	Mikoyan	Fishbed	507
MiG-21 PF	WA	Seatt	MoF	Mikoyan	Fishbed	TT1697, 4315
MiG-21 PFM	WA	Seatt	MoF	Mikoyan	Fishbed	5411
MiG-21(F-7)	WI	Oshko	EAAAAM	Mikoyan	Fishbed	N21MG
MiG-21F	CA	Sacra	McCelAFB	Mikoyan	Fishbed	201
MiG-21PFM	NM	STere	WEAM	Mikoyan	Fishbed	4105
MiG-21PFM	NY	NYC	ISASM	Mikoyan	Fishbed	4105
MiG-21PFM	NY	Scotia	ESAM	Mikoyan	Fishbed	2406
MiG-21U	TN	Sevierville	TMoA	Mikoyan	Fishbed	
MiG-23	CA	Riverside	MAFM	Mikoyan	Flogger	5744
MiG-23	NV	Fallon	NASF	Mikoyan	Flogger	353
MiG-23	OH	Dayton	USAFM	Mikoyan	Flogger	
MiG-23	QC-C	La Baie	ADM	Mikoyan	Flogger	
MiG-29 Flogger D	CA	Chino	YAM	RS Systems	Target Drone	
MiG-29	OH	Dayton	USAFM	Mikoyan		
Miles Atwood	CA	Chino	PoFAM	Miles Atwood	Air Racer	
Miller Fly Rod	KS	Liberal	MAM	Miller	Fly Rod	
Milliken Special	ME	OwlsH	OHTM	Milliken	Special	
Mini-Cab	WA	Vancouver	PAM			
Minimora	NY	Elmir	NSM	Minimora		56, N16923
Mitchell Wing B-10 Buzzard	AL	Birmi	Southe	Mitchell	Buzzard	Wing Ultralight

Model	State	City	Museum	Manufacturer	Type	Serial/Reg
MMC-845	CA	Rosam	EAFB			1454
Monerai S	AL	Birmi	Southe	Monerai	Powered Sailplane	
Monerai S	CT	Winds	NEAM	Monerai	Powered Sailplane	
Mong Sport	IL	Rantoul	OCAM	Mong	Sport	N1174
Mong Sport	WI	Oshko	EAAAAM	Mong	Sport	
Moni Motor Glider	FL	Lakel	SFAF	Monnett	Motor Glider	N46431
Moni Motor Glider	KS	Liber	MAAM	Monnett	Motor Glider	
Moni Motor Glider	MD	Silve	PEGF	Monnett	Motor Glider	
Moni Motor Glider	WI	Oshko	EAAAAM	Monnett	Motor Glider	N153MX
Moni Motor Glider	WI	Oshko	EAAAAM	Monnett	Motor Glider	N82MX
Moni Motor Glider	WI	Oshko	EAAAAM	Monnett	Motor Glider	N107MX
Monnett Sonerai II	AL	Birmingham	SMoF	Monnett	Sonerai II	N11ME
Monnett Sonerai II	IN	LaPorte	DPAM	Monnett	Sonerai II	
Monnett Sonerai II	KS	Wichita	KAM	Monnett	Sonerai II	
Monnett Sonerai II	WI	Oshko	EAAAAM	Monnett	Sonerai II	N11ME
Monocoupe	PA	Readi	Restrant	Monocoupe		
Monocoupe	WY	Greyb	H&PA	Monocoupe		
Monocoupe 90A	PA	Bethel	GAAM	Monocoupe		NC11750
Monocoupe 90A	WI	Oshko	EAAAAM	Monocoupe		N11783
Monocoupe 110	CA	Oakla	OWAM	Monocoupe	Special	
Monocoupe 110	ID	Athol	NAM	Monocoupe	Special	
Monocoupe 110	MD	College Park	CPAM	Monocoupe	Special	NC 12345
Monocoupe 110	ND	Minot	DTAM	Monocoupe	Special	
Monocoupe 110	WI	Oshko	EAAAAM	Monocoupe	Special	N15E
Monocoupe 110	WI	Oshko	EAAAAM	Monocoupe	Special	NC533W
Monocoupe 113	NY	Rhine	ORA	Monocoupe		N7808
Monocoupe 113	WI	Oshko	EAAAAM	Monocoupe		
Monocoupe 90	IA	Ottumwa	APM	Monocoupe		504, NC170K
Monoprep	IA	Ottumwa	APM			6077, NC179K
Monte Copter 15	CA	Ramona	CR	Monte	Copter 15	
Montgomery Glider	CA	Hawth	WMoF	Montgomery	Evergreen Glider	
Montgomery Glider	CA	San Diego	SDAM	Montgomery	Evergreen Glider	
Montgomery Gull Glider	CA	SCarl	HAM	Stearman-Hammond	Gull Glider	
Montgomery Santa Clara	CA	SCarl	HAM	Montgomery	Glider	
Montgmery Evergreen	CA	SCarl	HAM	Montgomery	Evergreen Glider	
Mooney	FL	Dayto	ERAU	Mooney		
Mooney	MO	SLoui	SLDPA	Mooney		
Mooney M.18C	AL	Birmingham	SmoF	Mooney	Mite	
Mooney M.18C	BC-C	Langley	CMoF&T	Mooney	Mite	
Mooney M.18C	IA	Ottumwa	APM	Mooney	Mite	210, NC329M
Mooney M.18C	KS	Liber	MAAM	Mooney	Mite	
Mooney M.18C	KS	Wichita	KAM	Mooney	Mite	
Mooney M.18C	OK	Fredi	AAM	Mooney	Mite	
Mooney M.18C	WA	Vancouver	PAM	Mooney	Mite	
Mooney M.20B	KS	Liber	MAAM	Mooney	Mite	
Mooney M.20B	OK	Fredi	AAM	Mooney	Mite	
Morrisey Bravo	IA	Ottumwa	APM	Morrisey	Bravo	TRGR-1, N37HM
Mosquito H. Glider	CT	Winds	NEAM		Mosquito HG	
MPA	PA	Tough	CFCM			
MQM-107	FL	Panam	TAFB		Drone	
MQM-107	OH	Dayton	USAFM		Drone	
MQM-57	AZ	Tucso	PAM	Northrop	Drone	
MQM-74	CA	Chino	PoFAM	Northrop	Chukar II Drone	
MS 181	WI	Oshko	EAAAAM	Morane-Saulnier		N304JX
MS 230	BC-C	Langley	CMoF&T	Morane-Saulnier		
MS 230	CA	San Diego	SDAM	Morane-Saulnier		N7461
MS 230	FL	Polk	FoF	Morane-Saulnier		
MS 230	IL	Chica	MoS&I	Morane-Saulnier		
MS A-1	NY	Rhine	ORA	Morane-Saulnier		
MS Alcyon 733	MI	Kalamazoo	KAHM	Morane-Saulnier		
MS BB	AL	Gunte	LGARFM	Morane-Saulnier		
MSK	NM	Moriarty	SSM	Kensure	Glider	
Muller Arrow	BC-C	Langley	CMoF&T	Muller	Hang Glider	
Mummert 13223	MI	Detro		Mummert	Mercury	
Mutual Aviation Blackbird	CA	El Cajon	SDAMGF	Mutual Aviation	Blackbird	
MXY7	AZ	Grand Canyon	PoFGCVA	Yokosuka	Ohka II	
MXY7	MD	Silve	PEGF	Yokosuka	Ohka II	
MXY7-K1	OH	Dayto	USAFM	Yokosuka	Ohka II	
MXY7-K1 Trainer	OH	Dayto	USAFM	Yokosuka	Ohka II	
MXY7-K2	MD	Silve	PEGF	Yokosuka	Ohka II	
Mystery Aircraft	TX	RioHo	TAM	Mystery Aircraft		
N-1M	MD	Silve	PEGF	Northrop	Flying Wing	
N-62 JAMCO	WA	Seatt	MoF	JAMCO		
N-9H	FL	Pensa	USNAM	Burgess	Curtiss	N-9
N.A. Model A	TX	RioHo	TAM	North American		
N1K1	FL	Pensa	USNAM	Kawanishi	George	343-A-19
N1K1-J	WA	Seattle	MoF	Kawanishi	George	
N1K2-J	FL	Pensa	USNAM	Kawanishi	George	343-A-19
N1K2-J	MD	Silve	PEGF	Kawanishi	George	
N1K2-J	OH	Dayto	USAFM	Kawanishi	George	5312
N2C-2	FL	Pensa	USNAM	Curtiss	Fledgling	A8529
N2S	NC	Hendersonville	WNCAM	Boeing-Stearman	Kaydet	
N2S-2	WA	Olympia	OFM	Boeing-Stearman	Kaydet	
N2S-2	AR	Fayet	AAM	Boeing-Stearman	Kaydet	N5862
N2S-2(PT-17)	TX	Dalla	CFM	Boeing-Stearman	Kaydet	214
N2S-3				Boeing-Stearman	Kaydet	03401, Side # 401
N2S-3	CA	San Diego	SDAM	Boeing-Stearman	Kaydet	N1301M, 5414, 39
N2S-3	FL	Pensa	USNAM	Boeing-Stearman	Kaydet	569, 41
N2S-3(PT-17)	IL	Glenview	VM	Boeing-Stearman	Kaydet	
N2S-3(PT-17)	IN	Auburn	HW	Boeing-Stearman	Kaydet	
N2S-3(PT-17)	IN	India	CMoI	Boeing-Stearman	Kaydet	
N2S-3(PT-17)	NY	Horseheads	NWM	Boeing-Stearman	Kaydet	07190
N2S-3	VA	Quant	MCAGM	Boeing-Stearman	Kaydet	07481
N2S-4(PT-17)	FL	Lakel	SFAF	Stearman	Kaydet	Model 73
N2S-4(PT-17)	WA	Vashon	OTA	Stearman	Kaydet	Model 73, N68827
N2S-4(A75L3)	WY	Jackson	GWFM	Boeing Stearman	Kaydet	
N2S-4(A75N1)	CA	S.Mon	MoF	Boeing-Stearman	Kaydet	
N2S-4(A75N1)	FL	Lakeland	SNFAM	Boeing-Stearman	Kaydet	
N2S-5	WA	Seattle	MoF	Boeing-Stearman	Kaydet	
N2S-5	FL	Pensa	USNAM	Boeing-Stearman	Kaydet	43156
N2S-5	MD	Silve	PEGF	Boeing-Stearman	Kaydet	
N2S3(B-75N-1)	PA	Readi	MAAM	Boeing-Stearman	Kaydet	
N4S	NC	Hendersonville	WNCAM	Stearman	Kaydet	
N2T-1	FL	Pensa	USNAM	Timm	Tuter	32478, 312
N2T-1	MI	Kalam	KAHM	Timm	Tuter	32622
N2Y-1	FL	Pensa	USNAM	Consolidated	Fleet I	A8605

148

N3N	AZ	Tucso	PAM	Naval Aircraft Factory	Yellow Peril	N45084, 4497
N3N	CO	Denve	JWDAS	Naval Aircraft Factory	Yellow Peril	
N3N	ID	Driggs	TAC	Naval Aircraft Factory	Yellow Peril	
N3N	ID	Twin	NWWI	Naval Aircraft Factory	Yellow Peril	
N3N	MI	Kalam	KAHM	Naval Aircraft Factory	Yellow Peril	2951
N3N	NV	Carso	YF	Naval Aircraft Factory	Yellow Peril	
N3N	SC	Mt Pl	PPM	Naval Aircraft Factory	Yellow Peril	
N3N	TX	C Christi	CCMOS&H	Naval Aircraft Factory	Yellow Peril	
N3N	TX	C Christi	USS Lexi	Naval Aircraft Factory	Yellow Peril	2959, 703
N3N	TX	Houst	CAF-WHS	Naval Aircraft Factory	Yellow Peril	N44741, "The Real Thing",
N3N-3	CA	Chino	YACM	Naval Aircraft Factory	Yellow Peril	2621, N44757, 2621
N3N-3	CA	Chino	YACM	Naval Aircraft Factory	Yellow Peril	2685, N45265, 2685
N3N-3	CA	Chino	YACM	Naval Aircraft Factory	Yellow Peril	2804, N45070, 2804
N3N-3	CA	Chino	YACM	Naval Aircraft Factory	Yellow Peril	2827, N45280, 2827
N3N-3	CA	Chino	YACM	Naval Aircraft Factory	Yellow Peril	4480, N695M, 4480
N3N-3	FL	Pensa	USNAM	Naval Aircraft Factory	Yellow Peril	2693
N3N-3	FL	Pensa	USNAM	Naval Aircraft Factory	Yellow Peril	N6399T, 3046
N3N-3	MI	Ypsil	YAF	Naval Aircraft Factory	Yellow Peril	
N3N-3	MO	Maryland Hts	HARM	Naval Aircraft Factory	Yellow Peril	
N3N-3	PA	Readi	MAAM	Naval Aircraft Factory	Yellow Peril	Side # 46
N3N-3	TX	Galve	LSFM	Naval Aircraft Factory	Yellow Peril	N3NZ, 1974
N9M-B	CA	Chino	PoFAM	Northrop	Flying Wing	004, N9MB
N22S	AZ	Tucson	PAM	A/C Factories	Nomad	Man Sn F163, N6328, VH-HVZ, Searchmaster
Nangchang CJ-6A	CA	Santa Rosa	PCAM			
Nangchang C-5-6A	PA	Beaver Falls	AHM			
NASA Parasev	MD	Silve	PEGF	NASA	Paresev	
Navion	CA	Chino	PoFAM	Ryan	Navion	
Navion	GA	Calho	Mercer A	Ryan	Navion	
Navion B	MN	Anoka	Airport	Ryan	Navion	B488DS
NB-8G	MO	Maryland Hts	HARM	Nicolas-Beazley	NB-8G	
NC-9-A	FL	Pensa	USNAM	Pilgram	Gondola	
NC5-Rotormatic	CA	SCarl	HAM		Rotormatic	
NE-1(J3C-65)	PA	Readi	MAAM	Piper	Cub	
Nelson Dragonfly	CA	Santa Martin	WoHAM	Nelson	Dragonfly	
Nelson Hummingbird	CA	SCarl	HAM	Nelson	Hummingbird	
Nesmith	FL	Lakeland	SNFAM	Nesmith	Cougar	
Nesmith	IA	Ottumwa	APM	Nesmith	Cougar	L-1, N10162
NF-11(TT-20)	CA	Rosam	EAFB	Gloster	Meteor	
Nieuport 11	NY	Rhine	ORA	Nieuport		
Nieuport 11 7/8 Scale	CA	Riverside	MAFM	Nieuport		
Nieuport 11	CA	Santa Martin	WoHAM	Nieuport		
Nieuport 11	CA	San Diego	SDAM	Nieuport	Bebe	N1486
Nieuport 11	NC	Hende	WNCAM	Nieuport	Bebe	N8217V
Nieuport 11	OK	Oklah	KCASM	Nieuport	Bebe	
Nieuport 12	ON-C	Ottaw	CAM	Nieuport		
Nieuport 17	ON-C	Ottaw	CAM	Nieuport	Bebe	
Nieuport 17	ON-C	Ottaw	CWM	Nieuport	Bebe	
Nieuport 17	OR	Eugene	OA&SM	Nieuport	Bebe	
Nieuport 24	WA	Seattle	MoF	Nieuport		N24RL
Nieuport 24	WI	Oshko	EAAAAM	Nieuport		N65113, McGlothen
Nieuport 27	AZ	Mesa	CFM	Nieuport		N5597M, H
Nieuport 27	NY	River	RE	Nieuport		
Nieuport 27	WA	Seattle	MoF	Nieuport		N5597M, H
Nieuport 28	AL	Gunte	LGARFM	Nieuport		
Nieuport 28	AZ	Mesa	CFM	Nieuport		
Nieuport 28	CA	San Diego	SDAM	Nieuport		N28GH, 6
Nieuport 28	FL	Pensa	USNAM	Nieuport		5769, 21
Nieuport 28	ME	OwlsH	OHTM	Nieuport		
Nieuport 28	OH	Dayto	USAFM	Nieuport		N8539
Nieuport 28	WA	Seattle	MoF	Nieuport		14
Nieuport 28C-1	AL	Ozark	USAAM	Nieuport		
Nieuport 28C-1	MD	Silve	PEGF	Nieuport		
Nieuport 28C1	CA	Chino	PoFAM	Nieuport		
Nieuport 17 7/8 Scale	BC-C	Sidne	BCAM	Nieuport		
Nimbus II	KY	Lexington	AMoK	Scherp-Hirth	Nimbus II	N257JB
Nimbus II	WI	Oshko	EAAAAM	Scherp-Hirth	Nimbus II	N257JB
Nixon Special	CT	Winds	NEAM	Nixon	Special	
Nord 1002	FL	FtLau	WJAIS&L	Nord	Taifun	
Nord 1002	PA	Readi	MAAM	Nord	Taifun	
Nord 1101	OR	Tillamook	TAM	Nord	Noralpha	
Nord 1101	PA	Readi	MAAM	Nord	Noralpha	N1101M
Northrop Alhpa 4A	DC	Washi	NA&SM	Northrop	Alpha	"TWA"
Northrop Delta Fuse	ON-C	Ottaw	CAM	Northrop	Delta	
Northrop Gama	DC	Washi	NA&SM	Northrop	Gama "Polar Star"	
Northrup	IA	Greenfield	IAM	Northrop	Primary GLider	
NR-1W	ID	StMar	D.Freema	Nicholas-Beazley		
NR-1W	NY	Bayport	BA	Nicholas-Beazley		
NR-1W	NY	Rhine	ORA	Nicholas-Beazley		
NT-1	FL	Pensa	USNAM	New Standard		A8588
NW Porterfield	KS	Liber	MAAM	Northwest-Porterfield		
O-1E	MN	Blaine	AWAM			
O-2A	AZ	Tucso	PAM	Cessna	Super Skymaster	68-6901, N37581
O-2A	CA	Atwater	CAM	Cessna	Super Skymaster	67-21413
O-2A	CA	Fairf	TAFB	Cessna	Super Skymaster	
O-2A	OH	Dayton	USAFM	Cessna	Super Skymaster	62-1345
O-2A	CO	Denve	69thB	Cessna	Super Skymaster	
O-2A	CO	Denve	JWDAS	Cessna	Super Skymaster	
O-2A	FL	FtWal	HF	Cessna	Super Skymaster	67-21368
O-2A	FL	Shali	USAFAM	Cessna	Super Skymaster	86864
O-2A	HI	Oahu	WAFB	Cessna	Super Skymaster	
O-2A	IL	Ranto	OCAM	Cessna	Super Skymaster	61411
O-2A	IN	Peru	GAFB	Cessna	Super Skymaster	68-6871
O-2A	MD	Silve	PEGF	Cessna	Super Skymaster	
O-2A	MI	Mt Clemens	SMAM	Cessna	Super Skymaster	67-21340
O-2A	MN	Blaine	AWAM	Cessna	Super Skymaster	
O-2A	NC	Asheboro	PFAC	Cessna	Super Skymaster	"Navy"
O-2A	NC	Asheboro	PFAC	Cessna	Super Skymaster	"Air Force"
O-2A	OH	Dayto	USAFM	Cessna	Super Skymaster	67-21331
O-2A	OH	Lockb	RANGB	Cessna	Super Skymaster	69-7630
O-2A	OH	N Canton	MAM	Cessna	Super Skymaster	
O-2A	RI	NKing	QAM	Cessna	Super Skymaster	68-10997
O-2A	SC	Sumte	SAFB	Cessna	Super Skymaster	
O-2A	SD	Rapid	SDA&SM	Cessna	Super Skymaster	
O-2A	TX	Abile	DLAP	Cessna	Super Skymaster	67-21326
O-2A	TX	San A	KAFB	Cessna	Super Skymaster	
O-2A	UT	Ogden	HAFBM	Cessna	Super Skymaster	

O-2A	WA	Everett	MoFRC	Cessna	Super Skymaster	67-21363, N18BB
O-2A	WI	CDoug	WNGML&M	Cessna	Super Skymaster	
O-2A (2 ea)	GA	Warner Robin	MoF	Cessna	Super Skymaster	68- 6894
O-2A(GO)	TX	Austi	BAFB	Cessna	Super Skymaster	
O-2B	CA	Riverside	MFAM	Cessna	Super Skymaster	67-21465
O-2B	IN	Indianapolis	AMHF	Cessna	Super Skymaster	"Twigger Happy", 997
O-2B	IN	Indianapolis	AMHF	Cessna	Super Skymaster	Project
O-2B	KS	Wichi	KAM	Cessna	Super Skymaster	
O-3A(YO)	AZ	Tucso	PAM			69-18006
O-3A(YO)	CA	Hawth	WMoF			
O-38F	OH	Dayto	USAFM	Douglas		3-30324
O-46A	OH	Dayto	USAFM	Douglas		35-179
O-47	CA	Chino	PoFAM	North American	Observation Plane	
O-47A	MN	Minne	MAGM	North American	Observation Plane	38-295
O-47A(RO)	MD	Silve	PEGF	North American	Observation Plane	
O-47B	KS	Topek	CAM	North American	Observation Plane	
O-47B	OH	Dayto	USAFM	North American	Observation Plane	37-328, 39-112
O-52	CA	Chino	YACM	Curtiss	Owl	40- 2769, N61241
O-52	OH	Dayto	USAFM	Curtiss	Owl	40- 2763
O-52	OH	Newbu	WASAC	Curtiss	Owl	
O1-A	CO	Denver	69thB	FAC		
OA- 1A	OH	Dayto	USAFM		Loening	26- 431
OA-10A(PBY-5A)	OH	Dayto	USAFM	Consolidated	Catalina	44-33879, 46595
OA-12A(J2F-6)	OH	Dayto	USAFM	Grumman	Duck	48-563, 33587
Ohka 11 MXY7	AZ	Grand	PoFGCVA	Kugisho	Baka	I-18
Ohka 11 MXY7	CA	Chino	YACM	Kugisho	Baka	I-18 Yokosuka
Ohm Special Racer	NY	Hammo	CM	Ohm	Special Racer	
Oldfield Special BGL	WI	Oshko	EAAAM	Oldfield	Special BGL	N11311
Olmstead Pusher	MD	Silve	PEGF	Olmstead	Pusher	
OMAC-1	WA	Seatt	MoF			
OPAS Buhl	ON-C	Sault Ste Marie	CBHC			
OQ- 1	CA	San Diego	SDAM	Radioplane	Drone	
OQ- 2	BC-C	Langley	CMoF&T	Radioplane	Drone	
OQ- 2A	MI	Kalamazoo	KAHM	Radioplane	Drone	
OQ- 2A	OH	Dayton	USAFM	Radioplane	Drone	
OQ- 2A	WI	Oshko	EAAAM	Radioplane	Drone	
OQ- 3	AZ	Tucso	PAM	Radioplane	Drone	
OQ- A	WI	Oshko	EAAAM	Globe	Drone	26, "Wimpy"
OQ-14	OH	Dayton	USAFM			
OQ-19(MQM-33)	AZ	Tucso	PAM	Northrop	Drone	KD2R-5
OQ-19(MQM-33)	CA	Hawthorne	WMoF	Northrop	Drone	KD2R-5
OQ-19(MQM-33)	KS	Liber	MAAM	Northrop	Drone	
OQ-19D	WI	Oshko	EAAAM	Northrop	Drone	
Ornithopter 1510	CA	San Diego	SDAM	Ornithopter		
OS2U	AL	Mobil	BMP	Vought	Kingfisher	BU0951, 60
OS2U	NC	Wilmi	USSNCBC	Vought	Kingfisher	
OS2U	VA	Suffolk	FF	Vought	Kingfisher	Storage in Virginia Beach
OS2U-3	CA	Chino	YACM	Vought-Skirosky	Kingfisher	9643, 9643
OS2U-3	FL	Pensa	USNAM	Vought-Skirosky	Kingfisher	7534, 5926
OS2U-3	MD	Silve	PEGF	Vought-Skirosky	Kingfisher	
OV- 1	GA	Dobbi	DAFB	Grumman	Mohawk	
OV- 1	MN	Blaine	AWAM	Grumman	Mohawk	61-5936
OV- 1	OR	Mc Minnville	EAEC	Grumman	Mohawk	
OV- 1B	GA	Hampton	AAHF	Grumman	Mohawk	
OV- 1B	NY	Garden City	CoAM	Grumman	Mohawk	59-2633
OV- 1	NY	Horseheads	NWM	Grumman	Mohawk	62-5856, N6744
OV- 1A(JOV)	MN	Blaine	AWAM	Grumman	Mohawk	62-5856, N6744
OV- 1A	VA	FtEus	USATM	Grumman	Mohawk	
OV- 1B	MN	Blaine	AWAM	Grumman	Mohawk	62-5856, N6744
OV- 1B (2 ea)	AL	Ozark	USAAM	Grumman	Mohawk	59-2631
OV- 1B	TX	Amarillo	EFA&SM	Grumman	Mohawk	
OV- 1C	AZ	Tucso	PAM	Grumman	Mohawk	61-2724, "Dirty Dawg"
OV- 1C	FL	Clear	FMAM	Grumman	Mohawk	
OV- 1C(JOV)	MN	Blaine	AWAM	Grumman	Mohawk	61-2718, N-2036P
OV- 1C	NY	Horseheads	NWM	Grumman	Mohawk	62-05856
OV- 1D	AZ	FtHua	FH	Grumman	Mohawk	
OV- 1D	CO	Denver	69thB	Grumman	Mohawk	
OV- 1D	FL	Tittusville	VACM	Grumman	Mohawk	
OV- 1D	GA	Spart	GSMA	Grumman	Mohawk	
OV- 1D	MI	Kalam	KAHM	Grumman	Mohawk	68-16993, 993
OV- 1D	NC	Charlotte	CAM	Grumman	Mohawk	
OV- 1D	PA	Beaver Falls	AHM	Grumman	Mohawk	62-5856, N6744
OV- 1D	WI	Kenos	KMM	Grumman	Mohawk	67-18900, "Valdez II"
OV- 1D	WI	Kenos	KMM	Grumman	Mohawk	68-16992
OV- 1D	WI	Kenos	KMM	Grumman	Mohawk	
OV-2-5	OH	Dayton	USAFM			
OV- 3A(YO)	AL	Ozark	USAAM	Lockheed	Silent One	69-18000
OV-10	FL	Esther	HAP	Grumman	Bonco	
OV-10	KS	Liber	MAAM	Grumman	Bonco	
OV-10	NC	Charlotte	CAM	Grumman	Bonco	155472
OV-10A	AZ	Tucso	DMAFB	Grumman	Bonco	
OV-10A	OH	Dayto	USAFM	Grumman	Bronco	68-3787
OV-10A(YO)	MI	Belleville	YAF	North American	Bonco	152881
OV-10D	AZ	Tucso	PAM	Grumman	Bonco	155499
OV-10D	CA	Miramar	FLAM	Grumman	Bonco	UU, VMO-2
OW-8	IA	Ottumwa	APM	Welch		
OY-1	CA	Miramar	FLAM	Convair	Sentinel	
OY-1	FL	Pensa	USNAM	Convair	Sentinel	60645
OY-1/2	VA	Quant	MCAGM	Convair	Sentinel	120454
P- 1(F6C-1)	FL	Pensa	USNAM	Curtiss	Hawk	N6969A
P- 1(F6C-1)	MO	SLoui	SLDPA	Curtiss	Hawk	
P- 1(F6C-4)	MD	Silve	PEGF	Curtiss	Hawk	
P- 3A	FL	Jacks	NASJ	Lockheed	Orion	151374, LQ, 56
P- 3A	FL	Pensa	USNAM	Lockheed	Orion	152152, PJ, 1, VP-96
P- 3A	HI	Oahu	BPNAS	Lockheed	Orion	
P- 3A	HI	Kaneohe	KBMCAS	Lockheed	Orion	
P- 3A	ME	Bangor	MAM	Lockheed	Orion	
P- 3B	MI	Mt Clemens	SMAM	Lockheed	Orion	152748, VP-93
P- 3B	PA	Willow	WGNAS	Lockheed	Orion	
P- 6 7/8 Scale	CA	Riverside	MAFM	Curtiss	Hawk	AC 32-240, N90DS
P- 6E(F6C)	OH	Dayto	USAFM	Curtiss	Hawk	32-261
P- 6E(F6C)	WI	Oshko	EAAAAM	Curtiss	Hawk	NX 606PE
P- 9 Pober Pixie EAA	KS	Liber	MAAM	Pober	Pixie	
P-10 Cuby	WI	Oshko	EAAAAM	Wag-Aero	P-10 Cuby	NC23254, "Lil' Gonk"
P-12 (F4B)	WA	Seatt	MoF	Boeing		N872H
P-12E(F4B-4)	CA	Chino	PoFAM	Boeing		

Model	State	City	Code	Mfr	Type	Notes
P-12E(F4B-4)	OH	Dayto	USAFM	Boeing		31-599
P-26A	CA	Chino	PoFAM	Boeing	Peashooter	Model 266
P-26A	MD	Silver Hill	PEGF	Boeing	Peashooter	Model 266
P-26A	OH	Dayto	USAFM	Boeing	Peashooter	Model 266
P-35A	FL	Miami	WOM	Seversky		N28211
P-35A	OH	Dayto	USAFM	Seversky		36-404
P-36A	OH	Dayto	USAFM	Curtiss	Hawk	38-1
P-38	CA	Camarillo	CAF-SCW	Lockheed	Lightning	
P-38	FL	Kissi	FTWAM	Lockheed	Lightning	44-53242, N57496
P-38	WA	Eastsound	FHC	Lockheed	Lightning	44-27231, N79123, "Magre"
P-38 Replica	IL	Wheeling	94 Aero Sq	Lockheed	Lightning	
P-38-L5	TX	Galve	LSFM	Lockheed	Lightning	44-53095, N9005R, 100, "Putt Putt Maru"
P-38F-1-LO	KY	Middl	LS	Lockheed	Lightning	41-3630, N5757, 17630, "Glacier Girl"
P-38J	MD	Silve	PEGF	Lockheed	Lightning	42-67762
P-38J 5/8 Rep	MI	Kalamazoo	KAHM	Lockheed	Lightning	
P-38J-20-LO	CA	Chino	PoFAM	Lockheed	Lightning	44-23314, N29Q, "Joltin Josie"
P-38J	UT	Ogden	HAFBM	Lockheed	Lightning	42-67638
P-38L	AZ	Mesa	CFM	Lockheed	Lightning	44-53286, "Marge"
P-38L	TX	SMarc	CTWCAF	Lockheed	Lightning	42-104088, N38LL, "Scatterbrain Kidd II"
P-38L	WI	Popla	RBM	Lockheed	Lightning	44-53087, N3800L, "Marge"
P-38L(F-5G)	CA	S.Mon	MoF	Lockheed	Lightning	44-26996, N5596V
P-38L-5-LO	OR	Tillamook	TAM	Lockheed	Lightning	44-53186, N38V
P-38L-5-LO	OH	Dayto	USAFM	Lockheed	Lightning	44-53232, NX66678, FAH505
P-38L-5-LO	PA	Tough	CFCM	Lockheed	Lightning	44-53193, N3005
P-38L-5-LO(F-5G)	CA	Chino	YACM	Lockheed	Lightning	44-27183, N718
P-38L-5-LO(F-5G)	NJ	Trent	MGAFB	Lockheed	Lightning	44-53015, "Pudgy V"
P-38L-5-LO(F-5G)	NM	STere	WEAM	Lockheed	Lightning	44-27087, N577JB, Relammpago/N345/Black
P-38L-5-LO(F-5G)	OR	Mc Minnville	EAEC	Lockheed	Lightning	44-27083, 197425-501, N503MH
P-38L-5-LO(F-5G)	WI	Oshko	EAAAAM	Lockheed	Lightning	44-53087, N3800L, 8342, "Marge"
P-38L-5-LO	FL	Miami	WOM	Lockheed	Lightning	44-26761, N2897S
P-38M-5-LO	WA	Seattle	MoF	Lockheed	Lightning	44-53097, NL3JB, 4-JS, Displ:53097/4-JS
P-39	FL	Polk	FoF	Bell	Airacobra	
P-39	OH	Newbu	WASAC	Bell	Airacobra	
P-39	VA	Suffolk	FF	Bell	Airacobra	Storage in Virginia Beach
P-39N	PA	Beave	AHM	Bell	Airacobra	42-18814
P-39N-0	CA	Chino	YACM	Bell	Aircobra	42-8740, N81575
P-39N-5-BE	CA	Chino	PoFAM	Bell	Airacobra	
P-39Q	CA	Riverside	MFAM	Bell	Airacobra	42-20000
P-39Q	MD	Silve	PEGF	Bell	Airacobra	
P-39Q	MI	Kalam	KAHM	Bell	Airacobra	44-3908
P-39Q-8-DC	NY	Buffa	B&ECNP	Bell	Airacobra	42-19995, "Snooks 2"
P-39Q	NY	Niagara Falls	NAM	Bell	Airacobra	"Galloping Gertie"
P-39Q	OH	Dayto	USAFM	Bell	Airacobra	44-3887
P-39Q	OH	N Canton	MAM	Bell	Airacobra	42-18828
P-39Q	TX	Midla	CAFFM	Bell	Airacobra	
P-39Q	TX	SMarc	CTWCAF	Bell	Airacobra	N6968
P-39Q	VA	Hampt	VA&SC	Bell	Airacobra	220027
P-39Q-20	CA	S.Mon	MoF	Bell	Airacobra	
P-40 Mock-Up	Hi	Wheeler	WAFB	Curtiss	Warhawk	41-18P, #155, 12 Mock-Ups
P-40	KS	Tipton	NAM	Curtiss	Warhawk	Kenneth Kake
P-40	ND	Fargo	FAM	Curtiss	Kittyhawk	
P-40	ON-C	Ottaw	CAM	Curtiss	Kittyhawk	1076
P-40	TX	Burne	CAF-OC	Curtiss	Warhawk	N1226N
P-40	TX	Hawki	RRSA	Curtiss	Warhawk	P-40D&E in RAF/RCAF=Kittyhawk
P-40	WI	Janesville	YAFS4D	Curtiss	Warhawk	
P-40 Replica	HI	Oahu	WAFB	Curtiss	Warhawk	
P-40C	FL	Pensa	USNAM	Curtiss	Warhawk	AK255
P-40C	GA	Marie	DAFB	Curtiss	Warhawk	AK295
P-40C	WA	Eastsound	FHC	Curtiss	Warhawk	41-13390, N2689
P-40E	AK	Anchorage	AAHM	Curtiss	Warhawk	
P-40E	CA	Chino	YACM	Curtiss	Warhawk	AK827, N40245
P-40E	CA	San Diego	SDAM	Curtiss	Warhawk	AK979, N40FT
P-40E Rep	CO	CSpri	EJPSCM	Curtiss	Warhawk	
P-40E Mk.1	MD	Silver Hill	PEGF	Curtiss	Warhawk	AK875
P-40E	FL	Kissi	FTWAM	Curtiss	Warhawk	
P-40E	GA	Douglas	TW	Curtiss	Warhawk	41-35927 Tom Wilson
P-40E	GA	Douglas	TW	Curtiss	Warhawk	41-5709 Tom Wilson
P-40E	ID	Boise	JP	Curtiss	Warhawk	AK863, John Paul
P-40E	IL	Aurora	RH	Curtiss	Kittyhawk	
P-40E	IL	Batavia	RWH	Curtiss	Warhawk	AK899, N9837A, Richard W Hansen
P-40E	IL	Herscher	HWP	Curtiss	Warhawk	AL137, N88917, Harlan W Porter
P-40E	IL	Urban	RFIA	Curtiss	Warhawk	AK905, NX40PE
P-40E	LA	BRoug	LNWM	Curtiss	Warhawk	Tail # 191, "Joy"
P-40E	MN-C	Carman	BD	Curtiss	Kittyhawk	
P-40E	MN	Granite Falls	RF	Curtiss	Warhawk	AK753, N4420K, Ron Fagan
P-40E	MT	Kalispell	JS	Curtiss	Warhawk	AK752, N440PE, James E Smith
P-40E	NM	STere	WEAM	Curtiss	Warhawk	AL152, N95JB
P-40E	OH	Dayto	USAFM	Curtiss	Warhawk	AK987
P-40E	TX	Midla	CAFFM	Curtiss	Kittyhawk	42-105867, N1226N
P-40E	VA	Suffolk	FF	Curtiss	Kittyhawk	41-35927, In Auckland New Zealand
P-40K	OR	Mc Minnville	TASM	Curtiss	Warhawk	FR293
P-40K	KY	Louisville	DT	Curtiss	Warhawk	42-9733, N4436J, Dick Thurman
P-40K	GA	Douglas	TW	Curtiss	Warhawk	42-10083 Tom Wilson
P-40K	ID	Cadwe	WAM	Curtiss	Warhawk	AK933, N94466
P-40K	KY	Louisville	BS	Curtiss	Warhawk	42-10266, N40K Bill Stebbins
P-40M	NY	Long Island	JC	Curtiss	Warhawk	43-5795, N1232N, Jeff Clyman
P-40M	TX	RioHo	TAM	Curtiss	Warhawk	43-5778
P-40N	AZ	Mesa	CFM	Curtiss	Warhawk	
P-40N	CA	Chino	PoFAM	Curtiss	Warhawk	42-105951
P-40N	CA	Chino	PoFAM	Curtiss	Warhawk	42-106101
P-40N	CA	PalmS	PSAM	Curtiss	Warhawk	42-104959
P-40N	CA	PalmS	PSAM	Curtiss	Warhawk	42-104961
P-40N	CA	PalmS	PSAM	Curtiss	Warhawk	42-105710
P-40N	FL	Arcadia	HT	Curtiss	Warhawk	43-24362 Hall Thompson
P-40N	GA	Douglas	TW	Curtiss	Warhawk	42-46111
P-40N	ID	Boise	JP	Curtiss	Warhawk	42-106396, N1195N, John Paul
P-40N	ID	Cadwe	WAM	Curtiss	Warhawk	
P-40N	ID	Nampa	WAM	Curtiss	Warhawk	
P-40N	MA	Bedfo	HAFB	Curtiss	Warhawk	
P-40N	MI	Kalam	KAHM	Curtiss	Warhawk	44-7619, N222SU
P-40N	NC	Fayet	PAFB	Curtiss	Warhawk	42-105702
P-40N	NY	Farmingdale	AAM	Curtiss	Warhawk	
P-40N	OH	N Canton	MAM	Curtiss	Warhawk	42-104818
P-40N	PA	Beave	AHM	Curtiss	Warhawk	
P-40N	TX	Dalla	CFM	Curtiss	Warhawk	44-7369, 40, 40
P-40N	TX	SMarc	CTWCAF	Curtiss	Warhawk	

Model	ST	City	Code	Manufacturer	Name	Notes
P-40N	WA	Seattle	MoF	Curtiss	Warhawk	44-4192, NL10626
P-40N(TP)	CA	Palm Sprg	PSAM	Curtiss	Warhawk	44-7284, NX999CD, "Miss Josephine"
P-40N(TP)	FL	Miami	WOM	Curtiss	Warhawk	44-47923, N923
P-40N Replica	CA	Riverside	MFAM	Curtiss	Warhawk	
P-40N-5-CU	GA	Warner Robin	MoF	Curtiss	Warhawk	42-105927
P-47 ½ Scale	AZ	Tucson	PAM	Gettings	Thunderbolt	N555TN, Experimental
P-47	CA	PalmS	PSAM	Republic	Thunderbolt	45-49205 "Big Chief"
P-47	CA	Rialt	KA	Republic	Thunderbolt	45-49385, NX47D
P-47	IL	Wheeling	94th Aero Sq	Republic	Thunderbolt	
P-47	OR	Tillamook	TAM	Republic	Thunderbolt	44-32817, N767WJ
P-47	TX	Midla	CAF-LF	Republic	Thunderbolt	N47TG
P-47D-2	AZ	Mesa	CFM	Republic	Thunderbolt	42-8205 N14519, 88, "Big Stud"
P-47D	CA	Chino	YAM	Republic	Thunderbolt	
P-47D	CA	Palm SPrg	PSAM	Republic	Thunderbolt	45-49205, NX47RP, Side # HVP, "Big Chief"
P-47D	CA	Farmingdale	AAM	Republic	Thunderbolt	44-90447, NX1345B, I-LH, 350FS,353FG
P-47D	CT	Winds	NEAM	Republic	Thunderbolt	45-49458, 54, "Norma"
P-47D	FL	Shali	USAFAM	Republic	Thunderbolt	44-89320, 26
P-47D	IL	Danville	MA	Republic	Thunderbolt	44-90471
P-47D	MI	Kalam	KAHM	Republic	Thunderbolt	45- 49181, N444SU
P-47D	NY	Farmingdale	AAM	Republic	Thunderbolt	
P-47D	OH	Dayto	USAFM	Republic	Thunderbolt	42-23278
P-47D	TN	Sevierville	TMoA	Republic	Thunderbolt	44-90438, NX647D
P-47D	TN	Sevierville	TMoA	Republic	Thunderbolt	44-90460, N9246B, Side #40, "Hun Hunter XVI"
P-47D	TX	Midla	CAFFM	Republic	Thunderbolt	
P-47D	WA	Bellevue	AM	Republic	Thunderbolt	
P-47D 3/8 Scale	WA	Seattle	MoF	Republic	Thunderbolt	42-8205 N14519, 88, "Big Stud"
P-47D Replica	SC	Sumte	SAFB	Republic	Thunderbolt	
P-47D-30	OH	Dayto	USAFM	Republic	Thunderbolt	45-49167
P-47D-30-NA	GA	Warner Robin	MoF	Republic	Thunderbolt	44-32691 LH-E
P-47L	OH	Newbu	WASAC	Republic	Thunderbolt	Fuse Only
P-47M	CA	Chino	YACM	Republic	Thunderbolt	42-27385, N27385
P-47N	CO	CSpri	EJPSCM	Republic	Thunderbolt	44-89425
P-47N	NY	Garde	CoAM	Republic	Thunderbolt	44-89444
P-47N	TX	Dalla	CFM	Republic	Thunderbolt	44-89436, N47TB
P-47N	TX	Galveston	LSFM	Republic	Thunderbolt	42-25068, N47DG, "Little Demon"
P-47N	TX	Midla	CAFFM	Republic	Thunderbolt	
P-47N	TX	San A	LAFB	Republic	Thunderbolt	44-89348
P-51	AL	Ozark	USAAM	North American	Mustang	44-72990
P-51	AL	Troy	TMA	North American	Mustang	
P-51	CA	Camarillo	CAF-SCW	North American	Mustang	On loan
P-51	CA	Shafter	MFAM	North American	Mustang	N71FT, "Strega"
P-51	CA	Shafter	MFAM	North American	Mustang	"Huntress 3"
P-51	CA	Riverside	TLHM	North American	Mustang	
P-51	CT	Winds	NEAM	North American	Mustang	
P-51	FL	FtLau	WJAIS&L	North American	Mustang	
P-51	GA	Atlanta	ASG	North American	Mustang	
P-51	IA	CBluf	CAF-RU	North American	Mustang	N5428V
P-51	IL	Aurora	RH	North American	Mustang	
P-51	IL	Wheeling	94th Aero Sq	North American	Mustang	
P-51	IL	Sugar Grove	ACM	North American	Mustang	44-74813, N6301T, At Danville, IL (Restoration)
P-51	MN	StPau	CAF-SMW	North American	Mustang	N215CA, "Gunfighter"
P-51	MO	Branson	VMM	North American	Mustang	44-60356
P-51	NM	Albuquerque	KAFB	North American	Mustang	51-1400
P-51	NM	STere	WEAM	North American	Mustang	658, "Ghost Rider"
P-51	ND	Wahpe	TSA	North American	Mustang	
P-51	OH	Cleve	100thBGR	North American	Mustang	
P-51K-NT-10	OH	Cleve	FCAAM	North American	Mustang	"Second Fiddle"
P-51	ON-C	Ottaw	CAM	North American	Mustang	9298
P-51	OR	Tillamook	TAM	North American	Mustang	
P-51	TX	Galve	LSFM	North American	Mustang	
P-51	UT	Heber	HVAM	North American	Mustang	
P-51	WI	Madison	MWVM	North American	Mustang	
P-51 ½ Scale	IN	Auburn	HW	North American	Mustang	
P-51 Replica	GA	Savan	MEHM	North American	Mustang	
P-51(TF)	FL	Kissi	S51C	North American	Mustang	48-745, "Crazy Horse"
P-51(TF)	NM	STere	WEAM	North American	Mustang	48-4658, "Friendly Ghost"
P-51(XP)	WI	Oshko	EAAAAM	North American	Mustang	41-38, NX51NA
P-51A	AZ	Grand	PoFGCVA	North American	Mustang	43- 6251, NX4235Y
P-51A	CA	Chino	PoFAM	North American	Mustang	
P-51D(CF)	WA	Seattle	MoF	North American	Mustang	NL151X, CV-J, "Ho! Hun"
P-51A	MA	Stow	BCF	North American	Mustang	
P-51A-1	CA	Chino	YACM	North American	Mustang	43- 6274, N90358, HY
P-51C	ID	Nampa	WAM	North American	Mustang	Project
P-51C	TX	Midla	CAFFM	North American	Mustang	
P-51D(F)	AL	Mobil	BMP	North American	Mustang	44-74216
P-51D	AZ	Grand Canyon	PoFGCVA	North American	Mustang	
P-51D	AZ	Mesa	CFM	North American	Mustang	45-11582, N5441V, B6-Y, "Spam Cam, Glamorous Glen"
P-51D	CA	Chino	PoFAM	North American	Mustang	G4-U
P-51D-10	CA	Chino	YACM	North American	Mustang	44-74910, N74920
P-51D-5NA	CA	Los Angeles	CSC	North American	Mustang	44-13704, B7-H, "Ferocious Frankie"
P-51D	CA	PalmS	PSAM	North American	Mustang	44-74908, N151BP, Side # E2S, "Button Nose"
P-51D	CA	S.Mon	MoF	North American	Mustang	N51DP, 49, "Cotton Mouth"
P-51D-30NA	CA	S.Mon	MoF	North American	Mustang	44-74996, N5410V, 4, "Dago Red"
P-51D	CA	El Cajon	SDAMGF	North American	Mustang	
P-51D	CA	San Diego	SDAM	North American	Mustang	44-73683, N5551D, DGP
P-51D	CA	SRosa	PCAM	North American	Mustang	41-767, V-C5 A
P-51D	CO	Denver	CA	North American	Mustang	
P-51D	DC	Washi	NA&SM	North American	Mustang	569, #7, "Miss Kentucky State"
P-51D	DE	Dover	DAFB	North American	Mustang	
P-51D	FL	Miami	WOM	North American	Mustang	44-72145"Petie 3rd"
P-51D	FL	Lakeland	SNF	North American	Mustang	45-115-7, 41- 3321, NL 921PHO, "Cripes A Mighty 3"
P-51D-11	FL	Shali	USAFAM	North American	Mustang	41- 3571
P-51D	IL	Belvi	PW	North American	Mustang	44-63701, Owner: Bengt Kuller
P-51D-25NA	IL	Springfield	ACM	North American	Mustang	44-73287, N5445V "Worry Bird"
P-51D	IN	Hunti	WoF	North American	Mustang	44-72922, L2W, "Scat VII", Gen Olds, 434FS, 479FG
P-51D	IN	Valparaiso	IAM	North American	Mustang	45-11549
P-51D	KY	Louisville	CCA	North American	Mustang	44-73206, NL-375D, "Hurry Home Honey"
P-51D	KY	Louisville	CCA	North American	Mustang	44-11553, NL-51VF, "Shangrila"
P-51D	LA	Bossi	BAFB	North American	Mustang	"Moonbeam McSwine"
P-51D-30-NA	MI	Belleville	YAF	North American	Mustang	44-74474, N6341T, "Old Crow"
P-51D	MI	Kalam	KAHM	North American	Mustang	Winter Only
P-51D	MN	Minne	MAGM	North American	Mustang	47-5024, 489
P-51D	ND	Fargo	FAM	North American	Mustang	44-74404, Yellow, Blue & Silver, B-CH
P-51D	ND	Fargo	FANG	North American	Mustang	

152

Model	State	City	Code	Manufacturer	Name	Notes
P-51D	OH	Dayto	USAFM	North American	Mustang	44-74936
P-51D	OH	N Canton	MAM	North American	Mustang	44-13016, NL5551D, "Dove of Peace"
P-51D	OR	Mc Minnville	EAEC	North American	Mustang	122 31302, N51DH
P-51D	PA	Pitts	PANG	North American	Mustang	
P-51D	TX	Breck	BAM	North American	Mustang	
P-51D-20-NA	TX	Dalla	CFM	North American	Mustang	44-72339, N251JC, WD-C
P-51D	TX	Midla	CAFFM	North American	Mustang	
P-51D	UT	Ogden	HAFBM	North American	Mustang	41-3, OP-V, "Audrey"
P-51D	WA	Bellevue	AM	North American	Mustang	44-72364
P-51D-30NT	WA	Eastsound	HFM	North American	Mustang	44-11525, "Val-Halla" Racer
P-51D	WA	Olympia	OFM	North American	Mustang	
P-51D	WI	CDoug	WNGML&M	North American	Mustang	WIS-NG
P-51D	WVA	Charl	CANG	North American	Mustang	
P-51D(FP)	WI	Oshko	EAAAM	North American	Mustang	44-75007, N, "Paul I"
P-51H	IL	Ranto	OCAM	North American	Mustang	41-4265, MASS ANG
P-51H	TX	San A	LAFB	North American	Mustang	44-64376
P-51K	OH	Newbu	WASAC	North American	Mustang	
P-51K	SC	McEnt	MEANGB	North American	Mustang	
P-55(XP)	MD	Silve	PEGF	Curtiss	Ascender	
P-55(XP)	MI	Kalamazoo	KAHM	Curtiss	Ascender	42-78846
P-56(XP)	MD	Silve	PEGF	Northrop	Black Bullet	
P-56(XP)	WVA		Northrop	Northrop	Black Bullet	
P-59	NE	Minde	HWPV	Bell	Airacomet	
P-59(XP)	DC	Washi	NA&SM	Bell	Airacomet	
P-59A-1	CA	Riverside	MFAM	Bell	Airacomet	44-22614, Side 88
P-59A(YP)	CA	Chino	PoFAM	Bell	Airacomet	
P-59B	CA	Rosam	EAFB	Bell	Airacomet	44-22633
P-59B	OH	Dayto	USAFM	Bell	Airacomet	44-22650
P-61 Nose	MD	Ft Meade	QM	Northrop	Black Widow	
P-61B-1	PA	Readi	MAAM	Northrop	Black Widow	42-39445
P-61C	MD	Silve	PEGF	Northrop	Black Widow	
P-61C	OH	Dayto	USAFM	Northrop	Black Widow	43-8353
P-63	FL	Lakeland	SNF	Bell	Kingcobra	
P-63	MO	SChar	CAF-MW	Bell	Kingcobra	N191H
P-63	NJ	Atlanta	DWFFA	Bell	Kingcobra	
P-63	TX	Houst	CAF-MC	Bell	Kingcobra	N6763
P-63	VA	Suffolk	FF	Bell	Kingcobra	N6763 Storage in Virginia Beach
P-63	WA	Olympia	OFM	Bell	Kingcobra	Project
P-63A	CA	Chino	PoFAM	Bell	Kingcobra	Model 309
P-63A	CA	Chino	Sq 1 Avi	Bell	Kingcobra	N 90805,Model 309
P-63A	CA	Chino	YACM	Bell	Kingcobra	42-8740, N94501, Model 309
P-63A	MD	Silve	PEGF	Bell	Kingcobra	Model 309
P-63A	CA	Palm SPrg	PSAM	Bell	Kingcobra	NX163BP, 268864, "Pretty Polly"
P-63A	OH	Newbu	WASAC	Bell	Kingcobra	Model 309
P-63A	TX	Midla	CAFFM	Bell	Kingcobra	Model 309
P-63C	AZ	Mesa	GU	Bell	Kingcobra	
P-63E	AZ	Mesa	GU	Bell	Kingcobra	
P-63E	AZ	Tucso	PAM	Bell	Kingcobra	43-11727, N9003A, Model 309 (P-39)
P-63E	OH	Dayto	USAFM	Bell	Kingcobra	43-11728, Model 309
P-63G(RP)	TX	San A	LAFB	Bell	Kingcobra	45-57295, Model 309, Target Plane
P-75A	OH	Dayto	USAFM	Fisher	Eagle	44-44553
P-80(XP)	OH	Dayton	USAFM			
P-81(XP)	OH	Dayton	USAFM			
P1Y1-C	MD	Silve	PEGF	Kugisho	Frances (Ginga)	
P2B-1S	CA	Richm	AMS			
P2B-1S	FL	Polk	FoF			
P2V	AZ	Tucso	PAM	Lockheed	Neptune	N14448, 147957
P2V	HI	Kaneohe	MB	Lockheed	Neptune	
P2V	NY	Brooklyn	NARF	Lockheed	Neptune	210
P2V	WY	Greyb	H&PA	Lockheed	Neptune	
P2V-1(P-2)	FL	Pensa	USNAM	Lockheed	Neptune	89082
P2V-1(XP)	FL	Pensa	USNAM	Lockheed	Neptune	
P2V-3	FL	Clear	FMAM	Lockheed	Neptune	Underwater in Ocean
P2V-3	ME	Bangor	MAM	Lockheed	Neptune	
P2V-5	CO	Puebl	FWAM	Lockheed	Neptune	128402
P2V-5	FL	Jacks	NASJ	Lockheed	Neptune	131410 LN-4
P2V-5	HI	Kaneohe	KBMCAS	Lockheed	Neptune	150279, VP-17 / VP-6
P2V-5	ME	Bruns	BNAS	Lockheed	Neptune	
P2V-7	AZ	Tucso	PAM	Lockheed	Neptune	135620
P2V-7	IN	India	IMoMH	Lockheed	Neptune	
P2V-7	NS-C	Greenwood	GMAM	Lockheed	Neptune	Side # VN101
P2V-7	OH	Newbu	WASAC	Lockheed	Neptune	140436
P2V-7	OR	Tillamook	TAM	Lockheed	Neptune	
P2V-7	PA	Beave	AHM	Lockheed	Neptune	
P2V-7	PA	Readi	MAAM	Lockheed	Neptune	144683
P2V-7(SP-2H)	FL	Pensa	USNAM	Lockheed	Neptune	141234, PG 6, VP-65
P5M(SP-5B)	FL	Pensa	USNAM	Martin	Marlin	5533, QE, 10, VP-40
P6M (Fuse/Tail)	MD	Middl	GLMAM	Martin	Marlin	
P8MU-3	MD	Silve	PEGF			
PA- 5	DC	Washi	NA&SM	Pitcairn		
PA-11	FL	Kissi	FTWAM	Piper	Cub Special	
PA-12	CA	Hayward	VAM	Piper	Super Cruiser	
PA-12	MD	Silve	PEGF	Piper	Super Cruiser	"City of Washington"
PA-18	MD	Silve	PEGF	Piper	Super Cub	
PA-18	MI	Dearb	HFM	Pitcairn	Autogiro	
PA-18	NE	Minde	HWPV	Pitcairn	Autogiro	
PA-18	NY	Rhine	ORA	Pitcairn	Autogiro	
PA-18	TX	RioHo	TAM	Piper	Super Cub	SN18-15, N5424H
PA-20	IL	Harva	BA	Piper	Pacer	
PA-20	NY	Bayport	BA	Piper	Pacer	
PA-20	WI	Oshko	EAAAM	Piper	Pacer	N3762P
PA-22	IL	Harva	BA	Piper	Tri Pacer	
PA-22	KS	Liber	MAAM	Piper	Tri Pacer	
PA-22	OK	Fredi	AAM	Piper	Tri-Pacer	
PA-22-125	PA	Readi	MAAM	Piper	Tri-Pacer	
PA-22-150	WI	Oshkosh	EAAAM	Piper	Tri-Pacer	
PA-23	DC	Dulle	DA	Piper	Apache	
PA-23	KS	Liber	MAAM	Piper	Apache	
PA-23	NE	Minde	HWPV	Piper	Apache	
PA-23	OK	Fredi	AAM	Piper	Apache	
PA-23(U-11)	KS	Liber	MAAM	Piper	Aztec	
PA-23(U-11A)(O-1)	AZ	Tucso	PAM	Piper	Aztec	149067, Model 250
PA-23-250	CA	Hayward	VAM	Piper	Aztec	
PA-23-250	OK	Fredi	AAM	Piper	Aztec	
PA-23-250	PA	Readi	MAAM	Piper	Aztec	N14281
PA-24	KS	Liber	MAAM	Piper	Commanche	

PA-28-140	AL	Birmingham	SMoF	Piper		
PA-28-140	WI	Oshkosh	EAAAAM	Piper		
PA-34-200	PA	Readi	MAAM	Piper	Seneca II	N5297T
PA 36-7	OH	Groveport	MMM	Higgins	Patrol Boat	
PA-38-112	PA	Readi	MAAM	Piper	Tomahawk	N382PT
PA-39	WI	Oshko	EAAAAM	Pitcairn-Larsen	Autogiro	N3908
PA-44	FL	Dayto	ERAU	Piper	Cheyenne II	
PA-44	MN	Winoma	WTI	Piper	Cheyenne II	N23MW
PA-48	CA	Rosam	EAFB	Piper	Enforcer	48-35010 2
PA-48	OH	Dayto	USAFM	Piper	Enforcer	48-83011
Pacific Airwave Kiss 89	AZ	Tucson	PAM	Pacific Airwave	Kiss	Man Sn KM92514
Packard LePere LUSAC	OH	Dayton	USAFM	Packard LePere	LUSAC	
Panavia Tornado	OH	Dayton	USAFM	Panavia	Tornado	
Paramount Cabinair	FL	Delan	OHA	Paramount	Cabinair	
Paramount Cabinaire	WY	Jackson	GWFM	Paramount	Cabinaire	
Paramotor FX-1	NY	Garden	CoAM	Paramotor	FX-1	
Parker JP-001	WI	Oshko	EAAAAM	Parker	American Special	N113JP
Parker Pusher	OK	Oklah	KCASM	Parker	Parker Pusher	
Parker Sailplane	CA	S.Mar	SMMoF	Parker	Sailplane	
Parsons Autogyro	PA	WChester	AHM	Parsons	Autogyro	
Passett Ornithopter	NY	Rhine	ORA	Passett	Ornithopter	
PB-1W	TX	Midla	CAFFM	Boeing		
PB2M-1(XP)	BC-C	P.Alb	Spoat Lk	Martin	Mars	
PB2Y-5R	FL	Pensa	USNAM	Consolidated	Coronado	57 N 69003 7099
PB4Y*1 Tail ver of B-24*	CA	Chino	PoFAM	Consolidated	Privateer	
PB4Y-2	FL	Pensa	USNAM	Consolidated	Privateer	66304 F 202
PB4Y-2	TX	Galve	LSFM	Consolidated	Privateer	59819, N3739G
PB4Y-2	WY	Greyb	H&PA	Consolidated	Privateer	
PB4Y-2G(P4Y-2G)	MI	Belleville	YAF	Consolidated	Privateer	59876, N6319D
PBM	MD	Balti	BMoI	Martin	Mariner	
PBM	TX	Hawki	RRSA	Martin	Mariner	
PBM-5A	AZ	Tucso	PAM	Martin	Mariner	N3190G 122071
PBR	AL	Mobile	BMP		River Boat	31RP7331
PBR	WI	Kenosha	KMM		River Boat	NSN 1940000BOAT, Movie "Apocalypse Now"
PBR	WI	Kenosha	KMM		River Boat	2 at this location
PBY	AZ	Mesa	CAFM	Consolidated	Catalina	
PBY	NC	CPoin	CPMB	Consolidated	Catalina	
PBY	NY	Brooklyn	NAAM	Consolidated	Catalina	
PBY	NF-C	Gander	NAAM	Consolidated	Catalina	
PBY	TX	Brown	CAFRGVW	Consolidated	Catalina	
PBY-5	FL	Pensa	USNAM	Consolidated	Catalina	8317
PBY-5A	AK	Ancho	AAHM	Consolidated	Catalina	
PBY-5A	CA	San Diego	SDAM	Consolidated	Catalina	N5590V 48406
PBY-5A	FL	Jacks	NASJ	Consolidated	Catalina	6882 J1-P 17
PBY-5A	FL	Miami	WOM	Consolidated	Catalina	
PBY-5A	NM	Albuq	KAFB	Consolidated	Catalina	
PBY-5A	NS	Halifax	ACAM	Consolidated	Canso	
PBY-5A	ON-C	Ottaw	CAM	Consolidated	Catalina	11087
PBY-5A	NF-C	Botwood	CAM	Consolidated	Catalina	
PBY-5A	NS-C	Greenwood	GMAM	Consolidated	Catalina	
PBY-5A	OR	Tillamook	TAM	Consolidated	Catalina	N2172N
PBY-5A	TX	Brown	RGVW-CAF	Consolidated	Catalina	N68756
PBY-5A	TX	C Christi	NAS	Consolidated	Catalina	
PBY-5A	TX	Galve	LSFM	Consolidated	Catalina	N68740 407
PBY-5A	VA	Suffolk	FF	Consolidated	Catalina	48294, N9521C, VP-82
PBY-5A(OA-10A)	NM	Albuq	KAFB	Consolidated	Catalina	
PBY-6A	MN	Duluth	CAF-LSS	Consolidated	Catalina	N7179Y
PBY-6ACF	MN	Duluth	CAF-LSS	Consolidated	Catalina	N324FA
PBY-6A	NY	Horseheads	NWM	Consolidated	Catalina	64072, N7057C, Side 62-P
PBY-6A	TX	Midla	CAFFM	Consolidated	Catalina	
PCA-1A	MD	Silve	PEGF	Pitcairn	Autogiro	
PCA-1A	PA	WChester	AHM	Pitcairn	Autogiro	
PCA-2	ON-C	Ottaw	CAM	Pitcairn	Autogiro	NC 2624
Pearson-Williams	CA	Chino	PoFAM	Pearson-Williams	W-7 Racer	"Mr Smooth"
Peacekeeper RV Bus	OH	Dayton	USAFM	Peacekeeper	RV Bus	
Pedal Plane	WI	Oshko	EAAAAM	Pedal	Pedal Plane	
Peel Z-1	CA	Santa Martin	WoHAM	Peel	Glider Boat	15-822, W
Pembroke C.51	NJ	Fairf	YAFDCWA	Hunting-Percival	Pembroke	K66B-4001, N51973
Penaud Planaphore	ME	Owls Head	OHTM	Penaud	Planaphore	
Penguin Ground Trainer	CA	Santa Martin	WoHAM	Penguin	Ground Trainer	
Pentercost E.III	AZ	Tucson	PAM	Pentercost	Hoppicopter	269
Pentercost E.III	MD	Silve	PEGF	Pentercost	Hoppicopter	
Pfalz D.III	AL	Gunte	LGARFM	Pfalz	Pfalz	
Pfalz D.III	AZ	Mesa	CFM	Pfalz	Pfalz	
Pfalz D.III	NV	Carso	YF	Pfalz	Pfalz	
Pfalz D.XII	WA	Seattle	MoF	Pfalz	Pfalz	3498, n43c
Pfalz D.XII	DC	Washi	NA&SM	Pfalz	Pfalz	
Pfalz D.XII	MD	Silve	PEGF	Pfalz	Pfalz	
PG-1 Explorer	WI	Oshko	EAAAAM	Sklier Aquq	Explorer	N6498D, "Bayou Bird"
PG-185	CA	SCarl	HAM	Nelson	Hummingbird	
PG-185	MD	Silve	PEGF	Nelson	Hummingbird	
PGM-17	AZ	Tucso	PAM	Douglas	Thor	
PGM-17A	CA	Rosamond	EAFB	Douglas	Thor	
PGM-17	OH	Dayton	USAFM	Douglas	Thor	
PGM-19	OH	Dayton	USAFM	Douglas	Jupiter	
Pheasant H-10	SK-C	MJaw	WDM	Pheasant		
Pheasant H-10	WI	Oshko	EAAAAM	Pheasant		NC151N
Phoenix 6	MD	Silve	PEGF	Phoenix		
Phoenix Hang Glider	KS	Liber	MAAM	Phoenix		
Phoenix Streak	MD	Silve	PEGF	Phoenix	Streak	
Phoenix Vipper	MD	Silve	PEGF	Phoenix	Vipper	
PHSC Scout	NY	Rhine	ORA		Scout	
Piel-Emeraude	AL	Birmingham	SMoF	Piel	Emeraude	
Pietenpol	GA	Woodstock	NGWS	Pietenpol	Aerial	
Pietenpol B4A	AB-C	Wetas	RM	Pietenpol	Aircamper	
Pietenpol B4A	BC-C	Sidne	BCAM	Pietenpol	Aircamper	
Pietenpol B4A	CA	Santa Martin	WoHAM	Pietenpol	Aircamper	
Pietenpol B4A	CA	El Cajon	SDAMGF	Pietenpol	Aircamper	
Pietenpol B4A	CA	San Carlos	HAM	Pietenpol	Aircamper	001, N3133
Pietenpol B4A	CA	San Diego	SDAM	Pietenpol	Aircamper	N37680
Pietenpol B4A	FL	Lakeland	SNFAM	Pietenpol	Aircamper	
Pietenpol B4A	IA	Ottumwa	AAA	Pietenpol	Aircamper	N4716
Pietenpol B4A	IL	Sprin	SA	Pietenpol	Aircamper	
Pietenpol B4A	IN	LaPorte	DPAM	Pietenpol	Aircamper	
Pietenpol B4A	KS	Liber	MAAM	Pietenpol	Aircamper	N2NK
Pietenpol B4A	MN	Minne	MAGM	Pietenpol	Aircamper	

Model	State	City	Code	Manufacturer	Type	Notes
Pietenpol B4A	MN	Fountain	FCM	Pietenpol	Aircamper	N1932A
Pietenpol B4A	ND	Minot	DTAM	Pietenpol	Aircamper	N12072
Pietenpol B4A	NY	Niagara Falls	NAM	Pietenpol	Aircamper	
Pietenpol B4A	NY	Rhine	ORA	Pietenpol	Aircamper	N6262
Pietenpol B4A	OK	Fredi	AAM	Pietenpol	Aircamper	
Pietenpol B4A	PA	Bethel	GAAM	Pietenpol	Aircamper	NX54N
Pietenpol B4A	PA	Readi	MAAM	Pietenpol	Aircamper	
Pietenpol B4A	RI	NKing	QAM	Pietenpol	Aircamper	N86404, CMK-1
Pietenpol B4A	VA	Sands	VAM	Pietenpol	Aircamper	Sn 410, N86404
Pietenpol B4A	WI	Fond du Lac	WAM	Pietenpol	Aircamper	N44162
Pietenpol B4A	WI	Oshko	EAAAAM	Pietenpol	Aircamper	N12937
Pietenpol B4A	WI	Oshko	EAAAAM	Pietenpol	Aircamper	N7533U
Pietenpol P-9	IA	Ottumwa	APM	Pietenpol	Sky Scout	SC1, N12942
Pietenpol P-9	TX	Kingbury	VAHF	Pietenpol	Sky Scout	
Pietenpol P-9	WI	Oshko	EAAAAM	Pietenpol	Sky Scout	N12941
Pigeon Fraser	NY	Rhine	ORA	Pigeon	Fraser	
Pilatus P-3	NC	Asheboro	PFAC	Pilatus		
Pioneer Flightstar	CT	Winds	NEAM	Pioneer	Flightstar	
Piper Commanche	IL	Elliot	CFF	Piper	Commanche	
Piper PT	WI	Oshko	EAAAAM	Piper	PT N	X4300
Piper Vegabond	MO	Maryland Hts	HARM	Piper	Vegabond	
Pitcairn AC-35	MD	Silve	PEGF	Pitcairn		
Pitcairn C-8	MD	Silve	PEGF	Pitcairn	C-8	
Pitcairn PA-5	VA	Sands	VAM	Pitcairn	Mailwing	Sn 9
Pitts P-6	WI	Oshko	EAAAAM	Pitts	Special	N58P
Pitts Racer 190	WI	Oshko	EAAAAM	Pitts	Racer 190	N8JD, "Little Monster"
Pitts S-1	AL	Birmi	Southe	Pitts	Special	
Pitts S-1	AZ	Grand Canyon	PoFGCVA	Pitts	Special	
Pitts S-1	AZ	Scott	SA	Pitts	Special	
Pitts S-1	AZ	Tucso	PAM	Pitts	Special	Man Sn 66, N2RB
Pitts S-1	WI	Oshko	EAAAAM	Pitts	Special	N58J
Pitts S-1	WI	Oshko	EAAAAM	Pitts	Special	NX528
Pitts S-1	WI	Oshko	EAAAAM	Pitts	Special	N442X
Pitts S-1-C	MD	Silve	PEGF	Pitts	Special	"Little Stinker"
Pitts S-1-C	NS-C	Halifax	ACAM	Pitts	Special	
Pitts S-1-C	VA	Hampt	VA&SC	Pitts	Special	
Pitts S-1-C	WI	Oshko	EAAAAM	Pitts	Special	N66Y
Pitts S-1-S	CA	San Diego	SDAM	Pitts	Special	N4HS
Pitts S-1-S	MD	Silve	PEGF	Pitts	Special	"Maryann"
Pitts S-1-S	TX	Dalla	CFM	Pitts	Special	N215JC
Pitts S-1-S	WI	Oshko	EAAAAM	Pitts	Special	N9J
Pitts S-2	WI	Oshko	EAAAAM	Pitts	Special	N22Q, "Big Stinker"
Pitts S-2-A	FL	KeyWe	FWIA	Pitts	Special	
Pitts S-2-B	AZ	Grand	PoFGCVA	Pitts	Special	N25CH, "Double Take"
Pitts S-2-B	FL	Miami	WOM	Pitts	Special	N21MM
Pitts S-2-B	OR	McMinnville	EAM	Pitts	Special	5105, N5352E
PL-4A	AL	Birmingham	SmoF	PL-4A		
Platt-LePage XR-1	MD	Silve	PEGF	Platt-LePage		
Player Sportplane	WI	Oshko	EAAAAM	Player	Sportplane	N21778
Pliska 1911	TX	Midla	PAM	Pliska	1911	
Po-2(U-2)	VA	Suffolk	FF	Polikarpov	Mule	641543, N46GU
Pober Jr. Ace	WI	Oshko	EAAAAM	Pober	Junior Ace	NX16PP
Pober P-5 Sport	WI	Oshko	EAAAAM	Poberenzy	Sport	N51G
Pober P-9 Pixie EAA	WI	Oshko	EAAAAM	Pober	Pixie	N9PH
Pober Super Ace	WI	Oshko	EAAAAM	Poberenzy	Super Ace	N113PP
Polan Special	WA	Vancouver	PAM	Polan	Racer	
Poude Ceil	KS	Wichita	KAM	Poude	Ceil	Homebuilt
PQ-14 (TD2C-1)	FL	Pensa	USNAM	Culver	Target Drone	120082
PQ-14 (TD2C-1)	MD	Silve	PEGF	Culver	Cadet	
PQ-14 (TDC-1)	AZ	Tucso	PAM	Culver	Cadet	44-21819, N1063M
PQ-14 (TDC-1)	CA	Chino	PoFAM	Culver	Cadet	
PQ-14B(TDC-2)	IA	Ottumwa	APM	Culver	Cadet	N-917, N5526ANR-D
PQ-14B(TDC-2)	OH	Dayto	USAFM	Culver	Cadet	44-68462, TDC-1, 2
PQ-14B(TDC-2)	WI	Oshko	EAAAAM	Culver	Cadet	N999ML, 68334
Pratt-Read Line-1	CT	Winds	NEAM	Pratt-Read	Line	
Primary	NY	Elmir	NSM			
Princeton Air Scooter	MD	Silve	PEGF	Princeton	Air Scooter	
Princeton Air Cycle	PA	WChester	AHM	Princeton	Air Cycle	
Provost Jet	WA	Everett	MoF	British Aerospace	Provost	NX4107, XW307
PS-2	FL	Pensa	USNAM	Franklin		9617
PS-2	MD	Silve	PEGF	Franklin		"Texaco Eaglet"
PT- 6A	CA	Riverside	MFAM	Cunningham-Hall		30-385, "Riverside"
PT- 6	CA	S. Monica	MoF	Cunningham-Hall		N1238V, Side # 8
PT- 6F	WY	Jackson	GWFM	Cunningham-Hall		
PT-1	CA	San Diego	SDAM	Consolidated	Trusty	"Husky"
PT-1	OH	Dayto	USAFM	Consolidated	Trusty	26- 233
PT-1	PA	Lock Haven	PAM	Consol;idated	Trusty	
PT-12	OH	Colum	CoS&I			
PT-13	CA	Oakla	OWAM	Boeing-Stearman	Kaydet	Model 73
PT-13	FL	Pompa	PAC	Boeing-Stearman	Kaydet	Model 73
PT-13	KS	Liber	MAAM	Boeing-Stearman	Kaydet	Model 73
PT-13	OK	Oklan	CAF-OW	Boeing-Stearman	Kaydet	Model 73, N51583
PT-13	OR	Mc Minnville	EAM	Boeing-Stearman	Kaydet	75-5300, n450ur
PT-13	TX	Burnet	HLS-CAF	Boeing-Stearman	Kaydet	Model 73
PT-13	TX	Odessa	CAFDS	Boeing-Stearman	Kaydet	Model 73
PT-13	WA	Eastsound	HFM	Boeing-Stearman	Kaydet	Model 73
PT-13A	WA	Seatt	MoF	Boeing-Stearman	Kaydet	75-055, n8fl
PT-13D	CA	Riverside	MAFB	Boeing-Stearman	Kaydet	Model 73, 42-16388
PT-13D(N-2S5)	MI	Kalam	KAHM	Boeing-Stearman	Kaydet	61614
PT-13D	NC	Asheboro	PFAC	Boeing-Stearman	Kaydet	Model 73,
PT-13D	OH	Dayto	USAFM	Boeing-Stearman	Kaydet	Model 73, 42-17800
PT-13D	PA	Readi	MAAM	Boeing-Stearman	Kaydet	Model 73
PT-16(YPT)(ST-A)	OH	Dayto	USAFM	Ryan		Model 73, 40-44, NC18922
PT-17	AL	Ozark	USAAM	Stearman	Kaydet	Model 73
PT-17	AR	Fayet	AAM	Stearman	Kaydet	Model 73
PT-17	AZ	PBluf	RWCAF	Stearman	Kaydet	Model 73, 41-8882
PT-17	AZ	Tucso	PAM	Stearman	Kaydet	Model 73, 41-869, N58219
PT-17	CA	Atwater	CAM	Stearman	Kaydet	Model 73
PT-17	AZ	Grand	PoFAM	Stearman	Kaydet	Model 73
PT-17	CA	Shafter	MFAM	Stearman	Kaydet	
PT-17	DE	Dover	DAFB	Stearman	Kaydet	Model 73, # 13
PT-17	FL	Jacks	MoS&H	Stearman	Kaydet	Model 73
PT-17	FL	Kissi	FTWAM	Stearman	Kaydet	Model 73
PT-17	FL	Miami	WOM	Stearman	Kaydet	Model 73
PT-17	FL	Titusville	VACM	Stearman	Kaydet	Model 73

PT-17	GA	Pooler	M8AFHM	Stearman	Kaydet	Model 73,
PT-17	GA	Woodstock	AAM	Stearman	Kaydet	Model 73,
PT-17	GA	Woodstock	NGWS	Stearman	Kaydet	Model 73,
PT-17	GA	Woodstock	NGWS	Stearman	Kaydet	Model 73,
PT-17	IN	India	IMoMH	Stearman	Kaydet	Model 73
PT-17	IN	Valparaiso	IAM	Stearman	Kaydet	41-8311, "Delta Airlines"
PT-17	KS	Topek	CAM	Stearman	Kaydet	N-5764, Model 73
PT-17	KS	New Century	CAF-HoAW	Stearman	Kaydet	#34, N234x
PT-17	MA	Stow	BCF	Stearman	Kaydet	Model 73
PT-17	CA	Palm SPrg	PSAM	Stearman	Kaydet	Model 73, N9955H
PT-17	MO	Missoula	MMF	Stearman	Kaydet	Model 73
PT-17	MS	Petal	MWHMM	Stearman	Kaydet	Model 73
PT-17	NC	Durham	CB	Stearman	Kaydet	N79500
PT-17	ND	Wahpe	TSA	Stearman	Kaydet	Model 73
PT-17	NY	Ghent	POMAM	Stearman	Kaydet	Model 73,
PT-17	NY	Horseheads	NWM	Stearman	Kaydet	Model 73, 07190, N64606
PT-17	OR	Tillamook	TAM	Stearman	Kaydet	Model 73, N65727
PT-17	SK-C	MJaw	WDM	Stearman	Kaydet	Model 73
PT-17	TX	Bealt	FCA	Stearman	Kaydet	Model 73
PT-17	TX	Burnet	HLSCAF	Boeing	Kaydet	Model 73, N5805V
PT-17	TX	Burnet	HLSCAF	Boeing	Kaydet	Model 73, N65355
PT-17	TX	FWort	BCVintag	Stearman	Yellow Peril	Model 73,
PT-17	TX	Ft Wort	Slanton	Stearman	Yellow Peril	Model 73,
PT-17	TX	Midla	CAFFM	Stearman	Kaydet	Model 73
PT-17	TX	SMarc	CTWCAF	Stearman	Kaydet	Model 73
PT-17A	UT	Ogden	HAFBM	Stearman	Kaydet	Model 73, 41-25284
PT-17	UT	SLake	CAF-UW	Stearman	Kaydet	Model 73, N1387V
PT-17	VA	Bealt	FCA	Stearman	Kaydet	Model 73
PT-17	WA	Vashon	OTA	Stearman	Kaydet	Model 73, N68462
PT-17(A75N1)	ME	OwlsH	OHTM	Boeing-Stearman	Kaydet	Model 73
PT-17(A75N1)	TX	Burnet	HLSCAF	Boeing	Kaydet	Model 73, N49943, 75-4645
PT-17(B75N1)(N2S-3)	KS	Liber	MAAM	Stearman	Kaydet	Model 73
PT-17(B75N1)(N2S-3)	OK	Fredi	AAM	Stearman	Kaydet	Model 73
PT-17 (See N2S)						
PT-17D	GA	Warner Robin	MoF	Stearman	Kaydet	Model 73, 42-16365, 365, C302
PT-18	AR	Fayet	AAM	Boeing Stearman	Super Kaydet	N55562, "Golliath"
PT-18	CA	Palm Springs	PoFAM	Boeing Stearman	Super Kaydet	41-61042, N1391V
PT-19	AB-C	Edmonton	AAM	Fairchild	Cornell	
PT-19	AB-C	Nanton	NLSAM	Fairchild	Cornell	
PT-19	AL	Birmi	SMoF	Fairchild	Cornell	
PT-19	AZ	PBluf	RWCAF	Fairchild	Cornell	
PT-19	BC-C	Langley	CMoF&T	Fairchild	Cornell	
PT-19	CA	Fairf	TAFB	Fairchild	Cornell	
PT-19	ID	Zellw	BWA	Fairchild	Cornell	
PT-19	KS	New Century	CAF-HoAW	Fairchild	Cornell	33, N50303
PT-19	KS	New Century	CAF-HoAW	Fairchild	Cornell	44
PT-19	MB-C	Brandon	CATPM	Fairchild	Cornell	
PT-19	ND	Fargo	FAM	Fairchild	Cornell	N51437, No 21, Yellow & Blue
PT-19	OH	Newbu	WASAC	Fairchild	Cornell	
PT-19	OH	N Canton	MAM	Fairchild	Cornell	
PT-19	OK	Fredi	AAM	Fairchild	Cornell	
PT-19	TX	Brown	RGVW-CAF	Fairchild	Cornell	
PT-19	TX	Burnet	HLSCAF	Ryan	Cornell	N274351, 42-2767
PT-19	TX	Midla	CAFFM	Fairchild	Cornell	
PT-19	TX	RioHo	TAM	Fairchild	Cornell	
PT-19	WA	Eastsound	HFM	Fairchild	Cornell	
PT-19	WY	Jackson	GWFM	Fairchild	Cornell	
PT-19 Cockpit	CA	Chino	PoFAM	Fairchild	Cornell	
PT-19A	AZ	Tucso	PAM	Fairchild	Cornell	41-14675, N53963
PT-19A	GA	Warner Robin	MoF	Fairchild	Cornell	43-7220
PT-19A	MD	Silve	PEGF	Fairchild	Cornell	
PT-19A	MI	Ypsil	YAF	Fairchild	Cornell	
PT-19A	NY	Horseheads	NWM	Fairchild	Cornell	5203AE, N49830, #32
PT-19A	OH	Dayto	USAFM	Fairchild	Cornell	43-34023
PT-19A	PA	Toughkenamon	CFCM	Fairchild	Cornell	42-83641, N51324, Nose # 65
PT-19A	TX	Dalla	CFM	Fairchild	Cornell	N58307, 44 217
PT-19A-AE	MI	Belleville	YAF	Fairchild	Cornell	43-31550, N9884
PT-19A-FA	KS	Liber	MAAM	Fairchild	Cornell	
PT-19B	KS	New Century	CAF-HoAW	Fairchild	Cornell	AE6103, N50481
PT-19B	WA	Vancouver	PAM	Fairchild	Cornell	
PT-19B	CA	Riverside	MFAM	Fairchild	Cornell	43-5598, Side 29
PT-19B	NY	Horseheads	NWM	Fairchild	Cornell	42-47871, Side # 65
PT-19B (2ea)	PA	Readi	MAAM	Fairchild	Cornell	40-2594, N119EC, 39
PT-19B	PA	Toughkenamon	CFCM	Fairchild	Cornell	N60112, Nose # 60
PT-19B(M-62A)	WI	Oshko	EAAAAM	Fairchild	Cornell	43-7240
PT-21(NR-1)	FL	Pensa	USNAM	Ryan	Recruit	1541, 49086
PT-22	AZ	Tucso	PAM	Ryan	Recruit	41-15736, N1180C
PT-22	CA	Atwater	CAM	Ryan	Recruit	
PT-22	CA	Corno	CAF-IES	Ryan	Recruit	N48742
PT-22	CA	Palm Springs	PoFAM	Ryan	Recruit	41-15550, N441V, Side # 634
PT-22	CA	San Diego	SDAM	Ryan	Recruit	1901, N47483
PT-22	CO	Denve	JWDAS	Ryan	Recruit	
PT-22	FL	Kissi	FTWAM	Ryan	Recruit	
PT-22	FL	Miami	WOM	Ryan	Recruit	
PT-22	GA	Warner Robin	MoF	Ryan	Recruit	41-21039, 66
PT-22	IA	Ottumwa	APM	Ryan	Recruit	1254, N50644
PT-22	KS	Liber	MAAM	Ryan	Recruit	
PT-22	IL	Paris	HAAM	Ryan	Recruit	
PT-22	IL	Springfield	ACM	Ryan	Recruit	41-20796, 2005
PT-22	MI	Kalam	KAHM	Ryan	Recruit	41-20652
PT-22	OH	Dayto	USAFM	Ryan	Recruit	41-15721
PT-22	OH	Madis	CFR	Ryan	Recruit	
PT-22	OK	Fredi	AAM	Ryan	Recruit	
PT-22	TX	Brown	RGVW-CAF	Ryan	Recruit	N22AL
PT-22	TX	Dalla	CFM	Ryan	Recruit	N46217, 4847AAF
PT-22	TX	Midla	CAFFM	Ryan	Recruit	
PT-22 (ST3KR)	AK	Fairb	APAM	Ryan	Recruit	N50880
PT-23	CA	Atwater	CAM	Fairchild	Cornell	
PT-23	KS	Liber	MAAM	Fairchild	Cornell	
PT-23	KS	Witch	CAF-JW	Fairchild	Cornell	N64176
PT-23HO	MI	Kalam	KAHM	Fairchild	Cornell	
PT-23	MN	Blaine	GH	Fairchild	Cornell	
PT-23	OK	Fredi	AAM	Fairchild	Cornell	
PT-23	PA	Readi	MAAM	Fairchild	Cornell	
PT-23	WI	Oshko	EAAAAM	Fairchild	Cornell	
PT-23A	WY	Jackson	GWFM	Fairchild	Cornell	

Model	State	City	Museum	Manufacturer	Type	Notes
PT-23A	CT	Winds	NEAM	Fairchild	Cornell	
PT-26	AB-C	Wetas	RM	Fairchild	Cornell	
PT-26	AB-C	Nanton	NLS	Fairchild	Cornell	
PT-26	AR	PineB	CAF-RW	Fairchild	Cornell	N6072C
PT-26	AZ	Tucso	PAM	Fairchild	Cornell	Sn 10530, N127O, CF-FLY
PT-26	CA	Chino	YAM	Fairchild	Cornell	
PT-26	CA	Shafter	MFAM	Fairchild	Cornell	
PT-26	CO	Denve	JWDAS	Fairchild	Cornell	
PT-26	GA	Atlan	CAF-DW	Fairchild	Cornell	N26GA
PT-26	IN	India	CAF-IW	Fairchild	Cornell	N60535
PT-26	KS	Liber	MAAM	Fairchild	Cornell	
PT-26	NM	Albuq	CAF-LW	Fairchild	Cornell	N5519N
PT-26	NY	Albion	VAG	Fairchild	Cornell	
PT-26	NY	Bayport	BA	Fairchild	Cornell	
PT-26	OH	Dayto	USAFM	Fairchild	Cornell	N2039A
PT-26	OK	Fredi	AAM	Fairchild	Cornell	
PT-26	PA	Readi	MAAM	Fairchild	Cornell	
PT-26	PA	Toughkenamon	CFCM	Fairchild	Cornell	N75463, Side # FH950
PT-26	TX	Brown	RGVW-CAF	Fairchild	Cornell	N940H
PT-26	TX	Brown	RGVW-CAF	Fairchild	Cornell	N4732G
PT-26	TX	Midla	CAFFM	Fairchild	Cornell	
PT-26	WY	Jackson	GWFM	Fairchild	Cornell	
PT-26A	BC-C	Langley	CMoF&T	Fairchild	Cornell	
PT-26A	ON-C	Ottaw	CAM	Fairchild	Cornell	10738
PT-26B	ON-C	Hamilton	CWH	Fairchild	Cornell	
PT-27	ON-C	Hamilton	CWH	Boeing-Stearman	RCAF Kaydet	
PT-27-BW	BC-C	Langley	CMoF&T	Boeing-Stearman	RCAF Kaydet	42-15683, N56773
PT-617	MA	Fall	USSMM		Patrol Boat	
Pterodactyl Fledgling	MD	Silve	PEGF	Manta Products	Fledgling	
Pulsar	KY	Lexington	AmoK	Pulsar	Ultralight	N156KB
PV-2 Piasecki	IN	Indianapolis	AMHF	Piasecki	Harpoon	37396, N2697C
PV-2 Piasecki	MD	Silve	PEGF	Piasecki	Helicopter	
PV-2	AZ	Tucso	PAM	Lockheed	Harpoon	N7255C, 37257
PV-2	CA	Chino	PoFAM	Lockheed	Harpoon	
PV-2	NM	Las Cruces	SA	Lockheed	Harpoon	
PV-2	OR	Tillamook	TAM	Lockheed	Harpoon	
PV-2	PA	WChes	AHM	Lockheed	Harpoon	
PV-2	SC	N Myrtle Beach	M	Lockheed	Harpoon	
PV-2	TX	SAnto	CAF-YRS	Lockheed	Harpoon	N25YR
PV-2	VA	Quantico	MCAGM	Lockheed	Harpoon	34807
PV-2D	TX	C Christi	USS Lexi	Lockheed	Harpoon	
PV-2D	TX	Galve	LSFM	Lockheed	Harpoon	N6655D 37634
PV-2D	WI	Wauke	CAF/WW	Lockheed	Harpoon	N86493, "Empire Express"
Q-200	FL	Lakel	SFAF	Rutan	Quickie	N150CS
Q-3A(YQ)	AL	Ozark	USAAM			
Q-4(XQ)	CO	Monte	ALP53	Sikorsky		
Q-4(XQ)	NM	Alamo	CityPark	Sikorsky		
QH-50C	GA	Warner Robin	MoF	Gyrodyne	Dash Drone	DS-1045
QH-50C	NY	Garde	CoAM	Gyrodyne	Dash Drone	1235
QH-50C	WA	Seatt	MoF	Gyrodyne	Dash Drone	
QH-50C/DSN-3	AZ	Tucso	PAM	Gyrodyne	Dash Drone	DS-1045
Quadraplane	KY	Lexington	AVoK	Sellers	Quadraplane	
QU-22B	OH	Dayton	USAFM	Beech	Beech 36	
Quick Kit Seaplane	NY	River	TFAC	Quick	Seaplane	
Quick Monplane	AL	Hunts	AS&RC	Quick	Monoplane	
Quick Silver	CA	San Diego	SDAM	Quick	Silver	Glider 1980
Quick Silver MX	AK	Fairb	APAM	Quick	Silver MX	
Quick Silver MX	TX	RioHo	TAM	Quick	Silver MX	
R-3(M-B)	CT	Winds	NEAM	Keith Rider		
R-4(XR)(VS-300)Cockpit	PA	WChes	AHM	Sikorsky	Hoverfly	
R-4(XR)(VS-316)	MD	Silve	PEGF	Vought-Sikorsky	Hoverfly	346514
R-4B	AZ	Tucson	PAM	Sikorsky	Hoverfly	43-46521
R-4B	CT	Winds	NEAM	Sikorsky	Hoverfly	
R-4B	OH	Dayto	USAFM	Sikorsky	Hoverfly	43-46506
R-5(XR)	MD	Silve	PEGF	Sikorsky	Dragonfly	VS-317
R-85(XR)	MD	Silve	PEGF			
R.H. Northcutt Aircamper	TX	RioHo	TAM	Northcutt	Aircamper	SN RN-1, N36RN
R3C-2	DC	Washi	NA&SM	Curtiss		
R4B(HNS)	AZ	Tucson	PAM	Sikorsky	R4B Helicopter	Sn 43-46521
R4B(HNS)	CA	Chino	YACM	Sikorsky	R4B Helicopter	Sn 43-46534
R4B(HNS-1)	FL	Pensa	USNAM	Sikorsky		104, N75988, 39047
R4D-6(DC-3)	CA	Atwater	CAM	Douglas	Skytrooper	90407
R4D-5	NY	Horseheads	NWM	Douglas	Skytrooper	39091
R4D-6(DC-3)	PA	Readi	MAAM	Douglas	Skytrooper	26819, N68AH, GB50819, "NATS 1945"
R4D-6(DC-3)	VA	Quant	MCAGM	Douglas	Skytrooper	17278
R4D-6Q(DC-3)	AL	Birmingham	SMoF	Douglas	Skytrooper	
R4D-8(C-117)	CA	Miramar	FLAM	Douglas	Super Gooney Bird	708,MCAS, MCASIWAKUNI
R4D-8(C-117D)	AZ	Tucso	PAM	Douglas	Super Gooney Bird	50826, Skytrain, 43363, 26924
R4D-8(C-117D)	AZ	Tucso	PAM	Douglas	Super Gooney Bird	43-49663
R4D-8(C-117D)	FL	Pensa	USNAM	Douglas	Super Gooney Bird	50821, 821, Gooney Bird
R50-5	AZ	Tucso	PAM	Lockheed	Lodestar	12481, N15SA, Model 18
R50-5	CA	Riverside	MFAM	Lockheed	Lodestar	12473
RA-5C	CA	Ridgecrest	CLNWC	North American	Vigilante	
RA-5C	CO	Puebl	FWAM	North American	Vigilante	
RA-5C	FL	Pensa	USNAM	North American	Vigilante	
RA-5C	MD	Lexin	PNA&EM	North American	Vigilante	156624
RA-5C	NV	Fallon	NASF	North American	Vigilante	
RA-5C	NY	NYC	ISASM	North American	Vigilante	
RA-5C(A3J-3)	AZ	Tucso	PAM	North American	Vigilante	149289
Rabbit Model A	WI	Oshko	EAAAAM	Welsh	Rabbit	N3599G
Rally 3	KS	Liber	MAAM	Rally	Ultralight	
Ranchero	FL	Lakel	SFAF	Ranchero		N4659S, "Spirit of Ft Myers"
Rand KR-1	AL	Birmingham	SMoF	Rand	Robinson	
Rand KR-1	FL	Lakel	SFAF	Rand	Robinson	N12NS
Rand KR-1	KS	Liber	MAAM	Rand	Robinson	
Rand KR-1	OK	Fredi	AAM	Rand	Robinson	
Rand KR-1	WI	Oshko	EAAAAM	Rand	Robinson	N1436
Rand Robin KR-2	CA	Santa Maria	SMMoF	Rand Robin	KR-2	
Rand Robin KR-2	IA	SBluf	MAAM	Rand Robin	KR-2	
Rasor 21	WI	Oshko	EAAAAM	Rasor		
Raven Hang Glider	WI	Oshko	EAAAAM	Raven	Hang Glider	F28AO
Raven S-50	AK	Fairb	APAM	Raven	S-50	N24061
RB-1	AZ	Tucso	PAM	Budd	Conestoga	39307, XB-DUZ
RB-1	PA	Pitts	FI	Budd	Conestoga	
RB-1 Racer	MI	Dearb	HFM	Dayton-Wright	Racer	
RC-3	AL	Birmi	SMoF	Republic	Seabee	

RC-3	BC-C	Sidne	BCAM	Republic	Seabee	
RC-3	BC-C	Langley	CMoF&T	Republic	Seabee	
RC-3	Ont-C	Sault Ste Marie	CBHC	Republic	Seabee	Sn 822, C-FDKG
RC-3	CA	SCarl	HAM	Republic	Seabee	N87482
RC-3	CT	Winds	NEAM	Republic	Seabee	
RC-3	FL	KeyWe	HTC&C	Republic	Seabee	N87596
RC-3	MD	Silve	PEGF	Republic	Seabee	
RC-3	NY	Garde	CoAM	Republic	Seabee	N6461K
RC-3	PA	Readi	MAAM	Republic	Seabee	
RC-12G	AZ	Ft Huachuca	HMS	Beech	Crazyhorse	80-23372
Rearwin	WA	Vancouver	PAM	Rearwin	Sportster	
Rearwin 2000C	TX	Kingbury	VAHF	Rearwin		Project Ken-Royce
Rearwin 7000	IA	Ottumwa	APM	Rearwin	Sportster	
Rearwin 7000	KS	Liber	MAAM	Rearwin	Sportster	NC187
Rearwin 7000	OK	Fredi	AAM	Rearwin	Sportster	
Rearwin 8135	CA	San Diego	SDAM	Rearwin	Cloudster	N25553
Rearwin 8135	CT	Winds	NEAM	Rearwin	Cloudster	
Rearwin 8135	IA	Ottumwa	APM	Rearwin	Cloudster	832, N25555
Rearwin 8135	NY	River	TFAC	Rearwin	Cloudster	
Rearwin Skyranger	KS	Liber	MAAM	Rearwin	Skyranger	
Redstone Booster	OH	Dayton	USAFM	Redstone	Booster	
Renegade Spirit	MI	Kalamazoo	KAHM	Murphy	Spirit	
Resures 500	WA	Seatt	MoF	Resures	Space Capsule	
Revolution Mini 500	FL	Lakeland	SNF	Revolution	Mini 500	
Rheintocher	MD	Aberd	APG	Rheintocher		
Rigid Midget	NY	Elmir	NSM			1001, N90871
Ritter Special	FL	Lakel	SFAF	Russ Ritter	Ritter Special	N1017Z
Ritz 1983	IA	Ottumwa	APM	Ritz	Pusher	
RJ-4 Ric-Jet	CA	Chino	PoFAM			
RK-86F	OH	Dayton	USAFM	North American		
RLU-1	KS	Liber	MAAM	RLU	Breezy	
RLU-1	ND	Minot	DTAM	RLU	Breezy	
RLU-1	OK	Fredi	AAM	RLU	Breezy	
RLU-1	WI	Oshko	EAAAM	RLU	Breezy	N59Y
RLU-1	WI	Oshko	EAAAM	RLU	Breezy	N555JS
RLU-1	WI	Oshko	EAAAM	RLU	Breezy	N3915
SS Queen Mary	CA	Long	QM&SG		Ocean Liner	
Rocket Honest John	WI	Kenos	KMM		Honest John Rocket	
Rockets	AL	Hunts	AS&RC			
Rockets	FL	Cocoa	USAFSM			
Rockets	FL	Merri	KSC			
Rockets	MD	Green	NASAGVC			
Rockets	MI	Jacks	MSCJCC			
Rockets	NM	Las Cruces	WSMP			
Rockets	NM	Roswe	RM&AC			
Rocket Launcher M139C	IN	Atterbury	CAM&MC		Honest John	762mm, 22 Miles
Rocket Launcher XM33	IN	Atterbury	CAM&MC		Honest John	762mm, 22 Miles
Rockwell	NY	Garde	CoAM	Rockwell	Command Module 002	
Rockwell HiMat	DC	Washi	NA&SM	Rockwell	HiMat	
Rockwell Ranger 2000	OK	Tulsa	TA&SM	Rockwell	Ranger 2000	
RODA	OR	McMinnville	EAM	Homebuilt		
Rogallo Wing	CA	Hawth	WMoF	Rogallo	Wing	
Rogallo Wing	NC	Ralei	NCMoH	Rogallo	Wing	
RON-1(X)	MO	SLoui	NMoT	Gyrodyne	Rotorcycle	
RON-1(Y)	VA	Quant	MCAGM	Gyrodyne	Rotorcycle	4012
RON-1(YR)	FL	Pensa	USNAM	Gyrodyne	Rotorcycle	4013
Rose Parakeet A-1	IA	Ottumwa	APM	Rose	Parakeet A-1	N-13676
Rotec Rally IIIB	AL	Birmi	SMoF	Rotec	Rally IIIB	
Rotec Rally IIIB	PA	Readi	MAAM	Rotec		
Rotec Rally IIIB	WA	Seatt	MoF	Rotec	Rally IIIB	
Roton	CA	Ramona	CR	Roton		
Rotor Cycle Hiller	MD	Lexin	PNA&EM	Hiller	Rotorcycle	
Rotorway Exec 152	AL	Birmingham	SMoF	Rotorway	Executive	
Rotorway Exec 152	PA	Readi	MAAM	Rotorway	Executive	
Rotorway Exec 152	WI	Oshko	EAAAM	Rotorway	Executive	N3WN
Rotorway Exec 162	TX	Ladero	Airport	Rotorway	Executive	
Rotorway Scorpion I	PA	WChester	EAAAM	Rotorway	Scorpion	
Rotorway Scorpion I	WI	Oshko	EAAAM	Rotorway	Scorpion	N6165
Rotorway Scorpion 133	AK	Fairb	APAM	Rotorway	Scorpion 133	
Rotorway Scorpion 133	CA	Ramona	CR	Rotorway	Scorpion 133	
Rotorway Scorpion II	MD	Silve	PEGF	Rotorway	Scorpion	
Rotorway Scorpion II	NJ	Teterboro	AHoF&MNJ	Rotorway	Scorpion	N96328
Rotorway Scorpion II	PA	WChester	AHM	Rotorway	Scorpion	
Rotorway Scorpion II	WA	Seatt	MoF	Rotorway	Scorpion	75rjm, n65229
Rotorway Scorpion II	WI	Oshkosh	EAAAM	Rotorway	Scorpion	
RQ-1A	OH	Dayton	USAFM	General Atomics	Predator	
RQ-3A	OH	Dayton	USAFM	Lockheed Martin-Boeing	Dark Star	
RQ-3A	OH	Dayton	USAFM	Northrop Grumman	Global Hawk	
RP- 5A Drone	AZ	Grand	PoFAM	Radioplane	Drone	
RP- 5A Drone	CA	Hawthorne	WMoF	Radioplane	Drone	
RP-76B Drone	AZ	Grand Canyon	PoFGCVA	Radioplane	Drone	
RP-76B Drone	CA	Hawthorne	WMoF	Radioplane	Drone	
RT-14	MD	Silve	PEGF	Turner	Meteor	
Rumpler Taube	AZ	Mesa	CFM	Rumpler	Taube	
Rumpler Taube	WA	Seattle	MoF	Rumpler	Taube	
Rutan	FL	Tittusville	VACM	Rutan		
Rutan 354	CA	Rosam	EAFB	Rutan	Model 354	N309V
Rutan Grizzly	WI	Oshko	EAAAM	Rutan	Grizzly	N80RA, "Griz"
Rutan Quickie	AB-C	Calga	AMoC	Rutan	Quickie	
Rutan Quickie	AZ	Tucso	PAM	Rutan	Quickie	N 80EB
Rutan Quickie	CT	Winds	NEAM	Rutan	Quickie	
Rutan Quickie	FL	Lakel	SFAF	Rutan	Quickie	N303Q
Rutan Quickie	IA	Des M	ISHD	Rutan	Quickie	
Rutan Quickie	KS	Liber	MAAM	Rutan	Quickie	
Rutan Quickie	MD	Silve	PEGF	Rutan	Quickie	
Rutan Quickie	OR	Tillamook	TAM	Rutan	Quickie	
Rutan Quickie	NF-C	Gander	NAAM	Rutan	Quickie	
Rutan Quickie	WA	Seatt	MoF	Rutan	Quickie	1, n77q
Rutan Quickie	WA	Vancouver	PAM	Rutan	Quickie	
Rutan Quickie	WI	Oshko	EAAAM	Rutan-Herron	Quickie	N2WX
Rutan Quickie (2ea)	BC-C	Langley	CMoF&T	Rutan	Quickie	
Rutan Quickie II	AZ	Grand Canyon	PoFGCVA	Rutan	Quickie	
Rutan Quickie II	CA	S.Mon	MoF	Rutan	Quickie II	N635AB
Rutan Quickie II	MB-C	Winni	WCAM	Rutan	Quickie	USAAF as C-8 or UC-96
Rutan Quickie Q1	CA	Santa Martin	WoHAM	Rutan	Quickie	
Rutan Solitair Glider	RI	NKing	QAM	Rutan	Sailplane	N8114J

Rutan Vari-eze	AL	Birmingham	SMoF	Rutan	Vari-eze	
Rutan Vari-eze	AK	Fairb	APAM	Rutan	Vari-eze	N37840
Rutan Vari-eze	CA	Chino	PoFAM	Rutan	Vari-eze	
Rutan Vari-eze	CT	Winds	NEAM	Rutan	Vari-eze	
Rutan Vari-eze	FL	Lakel	SFAF	Rutan	Vari-eze	
Rutan Vari-eze	KS	Liber	MAAM	Rutan	Vari-eze	
Rutan Vari-eze	MD	Silve	PEGF	Rutan	Vari-eze	
Rutan Vari-eze	ND	Minot	DTAM	Rutan	Vari-eze	
Rutan Vari-eze	OK	Fredi	AAM	Rutan	Vari-eze	
Rutan Vari-eze	PA	Readi	MAAM	Rutan	Vari-eze	
Rutan Vari-eze	VA	Hampt	VA&SC	Rutan	Vari-eze	
Rutan Vari-eze	WA	Seatt	MoF	Rutan	Vari-eze	300, n300ez
Rutan Vari-eze	WI	Oshko	EAAAAM	Rutan	Vari-eze	N7EZ
Rutan Varigiggen	AL	Birmingham	SMoF	Rutan	Varigiggen	
Rutan Varigiggen	CA	S.Mon	MoF	Rutan	Varigiggen	
Rutan Varigiggen	FL	Lakel	SFAF	Rutan	Variggen	
Rutan Varigiggen	WA	Seatt	MoF	Rutan	Varigiggen	115, n27ms
Rutan Variviggen 50-160	WI	Oshko	EAAAAM	Rutan	Varigiggen	N27VV
Rutan Voyager	CA	S.Mon	MoF	Rutan	Voyager	
Rutan Voyager	DC	Washi	NA&SM	Rutan	Voyager	
RV-4 Homebuilt Monoplane	CA	San Diego	SDAM	Homebuilt	Monoplane	N32KM
RV-6 Homebuilt	FL	Zellw	BWA	Homebuilt	Monoplane	
RV-6 Homebuilt	WI	Fond du Lac	WAM	Homebuilt	Monoplane	
Ryan D-16	AZ	Tucso	PAM	Ryan	Twin Navion	N5128K
Ryan D-16	KS	Liber	MAAM	Ryan	Twin Navion	
Ryan D-16	OK	Fredi	AAM	Ryan	Twin Navion	
Ryan G Drone	CA	El Cajon	SDAMGF	Ryan	Firebee Drone	
Ryan G Drone	SC	FLore	FA&MM	Ryan	Firebee Drone	
Ryan M-1	CA	San Diego	SDAM	Ryan		
Ryan Navion A	OK	Fredi	AAM	Ryan	Navion	
Ryan NYP	CA	San Diego	SDAM	Ryan	NYP, NX-211	"Spirit of St. Louis"
Ryan NYP	DC	Washi	NA&SM	Ryan	NYP, NX-211	"Spirit of St. Louis"
Ryan NYP	IL	Rantoul	OCAM	Ryan	NYP, NX-211	"Spirit of St. Louis"
Ryan NYP	MI	Dearb	HFM	Ryan	NYP, NX-211	"Spirit of St. Louis"
Ryan NYP	MN	Bloom	SPMIA	Ryan	NYP, NX-211	"Spirit of St. Louis"
Ryan NYP	MN	Minne	MSPIA	Ryan	NYP, NX-211	"Spirit of St. Louis"
Ryan NYP	MO	SLoui	MHM	Ryan	NYP, NX-211	"Spirit of St. Louis"
Ryan NYP	NY	Garde	CoAM	Rutan	NYP, NX-211	"Spirit of St Louis" B-1 Brougham
Ryan NYP	NY	Rhine	ORA	Ryan	NYP, NX-211	"Spirit of St. Louis"
Ryan NYP	OK	Weatherford	GTSM	Ryan	NYP, NX-211	"Spirit of St. Louis"
Ryan NYP	WI	Oshko	EAAAAM	Ryan	NYP, NX-211	"Spirit of St. Louis"
Ryan SCW-145	WI	Oshko	EAAAAM	Ryan		NC17372
Ryan SCW-147	CA	San Diego	SDAM	Ryan		
Ryan STA	CA	Hayward	VAM	Ryan	Special	N14954
Ryan STA	CA	San Diego	SDAM	Ryan	Special	NC17361
Ryan STA	IA	Ottumwa	APPM	Ryan	Special	198, N18902
Ryan STA	WA	Vancouver	PAM	Ryan	Special	
S- 2	FL	Kissi	FTWAM	Grumman	Tracker	
S- 2	HI	Kaneohe	KBMCAS	Grumman	Tracker	147870, #22
S- 2(CP-121)	MB-C	Winnipeg	WRCAFB	Grumman	Tracker	
S- 2(CP-121)	NS	Halifax	SAM	Grumman	Tracker	Side # 157
S- 2(S2F-1)	AZ	Tucso	PAM	Grumman	Tracker	136468
S- 2(S2F-1)	CA	S.Mon	MoF	Grumman	Tracker	
S- 2(CS)	ON-C	Toronto	TAMD	Grumman	Tracker	
S- 2A	FL	Jacks	NASCF	Grumman	Tracker	148730, AU, 32 ,VS-27
S- 2A	KS	Liber	MAAM	Grumman	Tracker	
S- 2A	MI	Mt Clemens	SMAM	Grumman	Tracker	144721
S- 2A	OK	Fredi	AAM	Grumman	Tracker	
S- 2A	ON-C	Sault Ste Marie	CBHC	Grumman	Tracker	577
S- 2A	TX	RioHo	TAM	Grumman	Tracker	SN1025, N4982C
S- 2A(S2F-1)	KS	Topek	CAM	Grumman	Tracker	486
S- 2A(TS)	NY	NYC	ISASM	Grumman	Tracker	
S- 2B(E-1B)(WF-2)	AZ	Tucso	PAM	Grumman	Tracker	Sn 147227, "Willie Fudd"
S- 2B(E-1B)	CT	Winds	NEAM	Grumman	Tracker	147217
S- 2B(E-1B)	NY	NYC	ISASM	Grumman	Tracker	
S- 2B(E-1B)(WF-2)	FL	Pensa	USNAM	Grumman	Tracker	48146, AE 711, VAW-121
S- 2B(US-2B)	CA	Alameda	USSHM	Grumman	Tracker	136691
S- 2D(US)(E-1B)	CA	Paso Robles	EWM	Grumman	Tracker	44-17944, N45CV
S- 2E	NY	NYC	ISASM	Grumman	Tracker	
S- 2E(S2F)	MD	Lexin	PNA&EM	Grumman	Tracker	
S- 2E(S2F)	NY	Garde	CoAM	Grumman	Tracker	151664
S- 2E(S2F)	PE-C	Summe	PEIHAS	Grumman	Tracker	Model 131
S- 2E(S2F)	TX	Dalla	CFM	Grumman	Tracker	
S- 2E(S2F) Fuse	TN	Memph	LS	Grumman	Tracker	
S- 2E(S2F)	MD	Lexin	PNA&EM	Grumman	Tracker	
S- 2E(S2F-1)	FL	Pensa	USNAM	Grumman	Tracker	151647, AW-334, 27, VS-73
S- 2E(S2F-1)	KS	Liber	MAAM	Grumman	Tracker	
S- 2E(S2F-1)	OK	Fredi	AAM	Grumman	Tracker	
S- 2E(TS)	NY	NYC	ISASM	Grumman	Tracker	
S- 2F(CS2F)	FL	Titusville	VAC	Grumman	Tracker	
S- 2F(CS2F-3)	MB-C	Winnipeg	CFB	Grumman	Tracker	12155
S- 2F(CS2F-3)	NS-C	Shear	CFBS	Grumman	Tracker	
S- 2F(CS2F)	OH	N Canton	MAM	Grumman	Tracker	
S- 2F(CS2F)	ON-C	CFB Borden	BHT	Grumman	Tracker	1506
S- 2F(CS2F-3)	PEI-C	Summerside	CFB	Grumman	Tracker	12131
S- 2F(US-2A)	AZ	Tucso	PAM	Grumman	Tracker	N8225E, 147552, "Stoof"
S- 2F1T	AZ	Mesa	MAC	Grumman	Tracker	Firefighter
S- 2R	AZ	Mesa	MAC	Grumman	Tracker	Firefighter
S- 3A	CA	San Diego	NINAS	Lockheed	Viking	Tail NH, Side VS29, 700
S- 3A(US)	CA	San Diego	SDACM	Lockheed	Viking	
S- 3A	FL	Jacks	NASCF	Lockheed	Viking	157993, AA, 700, VS-30
S- 4B	NY	Rhine	ORA	Thomas-Morse	Scout	
S- 4B	VA	Quant	MCAGM	Thomas-Morse	Scout	NR66Y
S- 4B(T-4M)	FL	Polk	FoF	Thomas-Morse	Scout	
S- 4C	CA	San Diego	SDAM	Thomas-Morse	Tommy	
S- 4C	CT	Washi	TFC	Thomas-Morse	Tommy	
S- 4C	FL	Pensa	USNAM	Thomas-Morse	Tommy	A5858
S- 4C	NY	Garde	CoAM	Thomas-Morse	Tommy	38934
S- 4C	OH	Dayto	USAFM	Thomas-Morse	Tommy	SC-38944
S-39	CT	Winds	NEAM			
S-43	AK	Ancho	AAHM	Sikorsky		
S-51(H-5)	AB-C	Calga	AMoC	Sikorsky	Dragonfly	
S-51(H-5)	CT	Winds	NEAM	Sikorsky	Dragonfly	
S-51(H-5)	ON-C	Hamilton	CWH	Sikorsky	Dragonfly	9601
S-51(H-5)	ON-C	Ottaw	CAM	Sikorsky	Dragonfly	9601
S-51(R-5)	PA	WChes	AHM	Sikorsky	Dragonfly	

Model	State	City	Museum	Manufacturer	Name	Notes
S-55	AB-C	Calga	AMoC	Sikorsky	Chickasaw	
S-55	FL	Sandf	VAT	Sikorsky	Chickasaw	
S-55	TX	FtBli	TCRM	Sikorsky	Chickasaw	
S-56	NY	Garde	CoAM	Sikorsky		NC349N
S-58D	BC-C	Langley	CMoF&T	Sikorsky	Seabat	
S-58D	NY	NYC	ISASM	Sikorsky	Seabat	
S-58(SH-34G)	PA	Willo	WGNAS	Sikorsky	Seabat	
S-60	CT	Winds	NEAM	Sikorsky		
S-61	MN	Winoma	WTI	Sikorsky	Houston	46008, "Disposal"
S-62A	NJ	Teter	AHoFNJ	Sikorsky		
S-64E	CT	Winds	NEAM	Sikorsky	Skycrane	
S.P. 3	AK	Fairb	APAM	Pereira	Osprey II	N345JD
SA- 2A	WI	Oshko	EAAAAM	Stits	SA-2A	N5K
SA- 3A	WI	Oshko	EAAAAM	Stits	Playboy	N8KK
SA- 8	WI	Oshko	EAAAAM	Stits	Skeeto	N6048C
SA- 11A	WI	Oshko	EAAAAM	Stits	Playmate	N9681Z
SA-100	AL	Birmingham	SMoF	Stolp	Starduster	
SA-100	CA	S.Mon	MoF	Stolp	Starduster	
SA-102-5	KS	Liber	MAAM		Cavalier	
SA-102-5	OK	Fredi	AAM		Cavalier	
SA-300	MI	Belleville	YAF	Stolp	Starduster Too	SN 001, N693DH
SA-300	NV	Carso	YF	Stolp	Starduster Too	
SA-300	WA	Vanco	PAM	Stolps	Starduster Too	
SA-300	WI	Oshko	EAAAAM	Stolp	Starduster Too	N32CH
SA-500L Starlet	WI	Oshko	EAAAAM	Stolp	Starlet	N2300
SA-700	WI	Oshkosh	EAAAAM	Hayes-Greffenius-Green	Acroduster-1	
Santa Clara Glider	CA	San Carlos	HAM	Santa Clara	Glider 1905	
Saturn V Boat Tail	NY	Coron	NYHoS	Saturn	Flying Boat	
Saunders ST-27	MB-C	Winni	WCAM	Saunders	Commuter	
Saunders ST-28	MB-C	Winni	WCAM	Saunders	Commuter	
Saunders ST-28 Simulator	ON-C	Sault Ste Marie	CBHM	Saunders	Commuter	Sn 009, G-GCML,
SB2C-1A (A-25)	OH	Dayton	USAFM	Curtiss	Helldiver	
SB2C-3	CA	Chino	YACM	Curtiss	Helldiver	19075, 19075
SB2C-3 Replica	NY	NYC	ISASM	Curtiss	Helldiver	
SB2C-5	FL	Pensa	USNAM	Curtiss	Helldiver	83479, 212
SB2C-5	TX	Midla	CAFFM	Curtiss	Helldiver	
SBD	CA	Alameda Pt	USSHM	Douglas	Dauntless	
SBD	CA	El Cajon	SDAMGF	Douglas	Dauntless	
SBD(3/4 Scale)	CA	S.Mon	MoF	Douglas	Dauntless	
SBD	GA	Atlan	CAF-DW	Douglas	Dauntless	N54532
SBD-3	MI	Kalam	KAHM	Douglas	Dauntless	06624
SBD	SC	MtPleasant	PPM	Douglas	Dauntless	36173, Side # 2
SBD	TX	Breck	BAM	Douglas	Dauntless	
SBD(A-24B)	CT	Winds	NEAM	Douglas	Dauntless	
SBD-3	AL	Mobile	BMP	Douglas	Dauntless	06583
SBD-3	FL	Pensa	USNAM	Douglas	Dauntless	6508
SBD-3	FL	Pensa	USNAM	Douglas	Dauntless	132MSB7, 6583
SBD-3	OR	Tillamook	TAM	Douglas	Dauntless	N5254
SBD-3	TX	C Christi	USS Lexi	Douglas	Dauntless	6508
SBD-3	WI	Milwaukee	GMA	Douglas	Dauntless	06624
SBD-4	AZ	Tucson	PAM	Douglas	Dauntless	Sn 10508
SBD-4	CA	Chino	YACM	Douglas	Dauntless	10518, N4864J, 10518
SBD-4	FL	Pensa	USNAM	Douglas	Dauntless	6583, 25
SBD-5	CA	Chino	PoFAM	Douglas	Dauntless	
SBD-5	CA	San Diego	SDAM	Douglas	Dauntless	N4522
SBD-5	CA	Palm Sprg	PSAM	Douglas	Dauntless	36176
SBD-5	VA	Quant	MCAGM	Douglas	Dauntless	42-54582
SBD-5(A-24B)	TX	Galve	LSFM	Douglas	Dauntless	N93RW
SBD-6	DC	Washi	NA&SM	Douglas	Dauntless	
SBS 2- 8	WI	Oshko	EAAAAM	Schweizer	Glider	N10VV
Sceptre	WA	Yakima	MmoA	Sceptre	Pusher	Twin Tail Monoplane
Scheibe Bergfalke II	BC-C	Langley	CMoF&T	Scheibe-Bergfalke		
Schleiche ASW-12	VA	Hampt	VA&SC	Schleiche	Glider	N491V
Schmidt Helicopter	AZ	Grand Canyon	PoFGCVA	Schmidt	Helicopter	
Schmitt Commuter	AZ	Grand	PoFGCVA	Schmitt	Helicopter	N17RS
Schulgleiter SG. 38	MD	Silve	PEGF	Schulgleiter		
Schupal & Nylander	CA	Chino	PoFAM	Schupal-Nylander	Wing	
Schweitzer Secondary Glider	IA	Greenfield	IAM	Schweitzer	Glider	
Schweizer 1-23	NY	Niagara Falls	NAM	Schweizer	Glider	
Schweizer 1-26	NM	Hobbs	NSF	Schweizer	Glider	
Schweizer 2-22	MB-C	Winni	WCAM	Schweizer	Glider	
Schweizer 2-33	NM	Hobbs	NSF	Schweizer	Glider	
SE-5A	AL	Gunte	LGARFM	RAF	Farnborough	
SE-5A	AL	Ozark	USAAM	RAF	Farnborough	
SE-5A Rep	AR	Fayet	AAM	RAF	Farnborough	
SE-5A	AZ	Mesa	CFM	RAF	Farnborough	
SE-5A	WA	Seattle	MoF	RAF	Farnborough	
SE-5A	BC-C	Langley	CMoF&T	RAF	Farnborough	
SE-5A	FL	Lakel	SFAF	RAF	Farnborough	RAF
SE-5A	FL	Orlan	CSS	RAF	Farnborough	
SE-5A	FL	Orlan	OFW	RAF	Farnborough	
SE-5A	ID	Athol	NAM	RAF	Farnborough	
SE-5A	ME	Owls Head	OHTM	RAF	Farnborough	
SE-5A	NC	Hendersonville	WNCAM	RAF	Farnborough	
SE-5A	NY	NYC	ISASM	RAF	Farnborough	
SE-5A	OH	Dayto	USAFM	RAF	Farnborough	22-325
SE-5A	ON-C	Chelt	TGWFM	RAF	Farnborough	
SE-5A	TX	Kingbury	VAHF	RAF	Farnborough	
SE-5A 7/8 Scale	ON-C	Chelt	TGWFM	RAF	Farnborough	
Sea-Bee	FL	Key West	CRTC			N87596
Sea Prince	ON-C	Toronto	TAM		Sea Prince	
Seahawker	WA	Vanco	PAM		Biplane	
Security Airster	CA	Santa Martin	WoHAM	Security	Airster	Year 1939
Sellers Quadroplane	KY	Louis	MoH&S	Sellers	Quadroplane	
SG-1A	NM	Moriarty	SSM	Scanlon	Boom Glider	
SGS 1-19	NY	Elmir	NSM	Schweizer	Glider	14, N91806
SGS 1-19	NY	Mayvi	DA	Schweizer	Glider	
SGS 1-26	NY	Elmir	NSM	Schweizer	Glider	1, N91889
SGS 1-26B	CA	Calis	CG	Schweizer	Glider	
SGS 2-22EK	MD	Silve	PEGF	Schweizer	Glider	
SGS 2-32	CA	Calis	CG	Schweizer	Glider	
SGS 2-33	CA	Calis	CG	Schweizer	Glider	
SH- 2F(HH-2D)	PA	WChester	AHM	Kaman	Sea Sprite	
SH- 2F	CA	San Diego	NINAS	Kaman	Sea Sprite	Nose 33
SH- 2F	CA	San Diego	SDACM	Kaman	Sea Sprite	
SH- 2F	VA	Norfo	NNAS	Kaman	Sea Sprite	149029, HT 33, HSL-30

Aircraft	State	City	Code	Manufacturer	Model	Notes
SH- 2G	MD	Lexington	PRNAM	Kaman	Sea Sprite	161642,
SH- 3(HH-52)	AL	Mobile	BMP	Sikorsky	Sea King	1378
SH- 3	CA	S.Mon	MoF	Sikorsky	Sea King	
SH- 3	CA	San Diego	NINAS	Sikorsky	Sea King	Tail HC11, Side 727
SH- 3	NB	Omaha	FP	Sikorsky	Sea King	
SH- 3	NY	Brooklyn	NARF	Sikorsky	Sea King	
SH- 3B	FL	Jacks	NASJ	Sikorsky	Sea King	9696, AR 401
SH- 3D(H-3)	FL	Pensa	USNAM	Sikorsky	Sea King	148990, 156484
SH- 3H	RI	NKing	QAM	Sikorsky	Sea King	149738
SH-34	OH	Newbu	WASAC	Sikorsky	Sea Horse	
SH-34J	CO	Puebl	FWAM	Sikorsky	Sea Horse	17217
SH-60B	CA	San Diego	NINAS	Sikorsky		Tail T2, Side HSL 45
Sherpa C203A	MT	Misso	AFDSC	Sherpa		
Shober Willie II	KS	Liber	MAAM	Shober	Willie II	
Shober Willie II	OK	Fredi	AAM	Shober	Willie II	
Short S-29	NY	Rhine	ORA	Short		
Short Skyvan	IL	Cahok	PCUSL	Short	Skyvan	
Short Solent Mark 3	CA	Oakla	OWAM	Short	Solent	
Siemens-Schuckert D.III	NY	Rhine	ORA	Siemens-Schuckert		
Siemens-Schuckert D.IV	AL	Gunte	LGARFM	Siemens-Schuckert		
Siemens-Schuckert D.IV Rep	AZ	Grand	PoFGCVA	Siemens-Schuckert	Fliegertruppe D IV	N1094G
Siersma SRC-B7	MI	Kalamazoo	KAHM	Siersma		
Sikorsky	AR	Pocahontas	PMA	Sikorsky		3251
Sikorsky	NE	Minde	HWPV	Sikorsky		1944
Silver Dart	NS-C	Halifax	ACAM	A.E.A.	Silver Dart	Replica
Silver Dart	NY	Hammonds	CM	A.E.A.	Silver Dart	
Silver Dart	ON-C	Ottaw	CAM	A.E.A.	Silver Dart	
Silver Dart	ON-C	Sault Ste Marie	CBHC	A.E.A.	Silver Dart	
Simulator 2B13	FL	Titusville	VAC	Navy	Multi Engine	
Skycat	NC	Charl	CHAC		Skycat	
Skycat	NC	CPoin	CPMB		Skycat	
Skylab Command Module	FL	Pensa	USNAM	Skylab	Command Module	116
SL-4	WY	Greyb	H&PA			
SM-8A Jr.	FL	Titusville	VACM	Stinson	SMS-8A Junior	
SM-8A Jr.	WI	Oshko	EAAAAM	Stinson	SMS-8A Junior	NC408Y, "Spirit of EAA"
SM-8A Jr.	WI	Oshko	EAAAAM	Stinson	SMS-8A Junior	N1026
SM-6000-B	WY	Jackson	GWFM	Stinson	TriMotor	"Flagship Texas"
Smith DSA	FL	Zellw	BWA	Smith	Miniplane	
Smith DSA	IA	Ottumwa	APM	Smith	Miniplane	ES-1, N44ES
Smith DSA	IN	Auburn	HW	Smith	Miniplane	
Smith DSA	OH	Madis	CFR	Smith	Miniplane	
Smith DSA	ON-C	Collingwood	CCAF	Smith	Miniplane	
Smith DSA	WI	Green	GBPHoF	Smith	Miniplane	N358L
Smith DSA-1	WI	Oshko	EAAAAM	Smith	Miniplane	N90P
Smith Eroplane	IN	FWayn	GFWAM	Smith	Pusher	
Smith H1	OK	Fredi	AAM	Smith	Termite	
Smyth Playmate	FL	Lakel	SFAF	Smyth	Playmate	N77JA
Smyth Sidewinder	FL	Lakel	SFAF	Smyth	Sidewinder	N28Z
Smyth Sidewinder	WI	Oshko	EAAAAM	Smyth	Sidewinder	N55P
SNC-1	FL	Pensa	USNAM	Curtiss		5194
Soko Galeb	IL	Springfield	ACM	Soko	Galeb	23172
Solar Riser	WI	Oshko	EAAAAM	UFM	Solar Riser	
Solbrig Biplane	IA	Des M	ISHD	Solbrig	Biplane	
Solitaire Motor-Glider	WI	Oshko	EAAAAM	Rutan	Solitaire	N142SD
Sollar Challenger	VA	Richm	SMoV		Sollar Challenger	
Sopwith 1- Strutter	AL	Gunte	LGARFM	Sopwith	Strutter	
Sopwith 1- Strutter	FL	Polk	FoF	Sopwith	Strutter	
Sopwith Camel	AL	Gunte	LGARFM	Sopwith	Camel	
Sopwith Camel F.1	AR	Little Rock	AEC	Sopwith	Camel	
Sopwith Camel	AZ	Mesa	CFM	Sopwith	Camel	
Sopwith Camel	BC-C	Langley	CMoF&T	Sopwith	Camel	
Sopwith Camel	CA	SCarl	HAM	Sopwith	Camel	
Sopwith Camel	ID	Athol	NAM	Sopwith	Camel	
Sopwith Camel	MI	Kalamazoo	KAHM	Sopwith	Camel	
Sopwith Camel	NY	Rhine	ORA	Sopwith	Camel	
Sopwith Camel	OH	Dayto	USAFM	Sopwith	Camel	F6034
Sopwith Camel	TX	Dalla	CFM	Sopwith	Camel	
Sopwith Camel 2F.1	ON-C	Ottaw	CAM	Sopwith	Camel	N8156
Sopwith Camel F.1	WA	Seattle	MoF	Sopwith	Camel	NX6330
Sopwith Camel F.1	FL	Pensa	USNAM	Sopwith	Camel	A5658
Sopwith Camel F.1	PA	Beave	AHM	Sopwith	Camel	
Sopwith Dolphin	NY	Rhine	ORA	Sopwith	Dolphin	
Sopwith Pup	AL	Gunte	LGARFM	Sopwith	Pup	
Sopwith Pup	AZ	Mesa	CFM	Sopwith	Pup	
Sopwith Pup	WA	Seattle	MoF	Sopwith	Pup	A 635, NX6018
Sopwith Pup	CA	El Cajon	SDAMGF	Sopwith	Pup	
Sopwith Pup	DE	Dover	DAFB	Sopwith	Pup	
Sopwith Pup	FL	Polk	FoF	Sopwith	Pup	
Sopwith Pup	ME	OwlsH	OHTM	Sopwith	Pup	
Sopwith Pup	ON-C	DonMi	OSC	Sopwith	Pup	
Sopwith Pup	ON-C	Hamilton	CWH	Sopwith	Pup	
Sopwith Pup	ON-C	Ottaw	CAM	Sopwith	Pup	
Sopwith Pup	ON-C	Toronto	OSC	Sopwith	Pup	
Sopwith Pup	TX	Dalla	FoF	Sopwith	Pup	SN:NCH1, N914W
Sopwith Pup	WI	Madison	MWVM	Sopwith	Pup	
Sopwith Snipe	AZ	Mesa	CFM	Sopwith	Snipe	
Sopwith Snipe	DC	Washi	NA&SM	Sopwith	Snipe	
Sopwith Snipe	MD	Silve	PEGF	Sopwith	Snipe	
Sopwith Snipe	ON-C	Ottaw	CAM	Sopwith	Snipe	
Sopwith Snipe F.1	WA	Seattle	MoF	Sopwith	Snipe	NX67650
Sopwith Triplane	AL	Gunte	LGARFM	Sopwith	Triplane	
Sopwith Triplane	AZ	Mesa	CFM	Sopwith	Triplane	
Sopwith Triplane	WA	Seattle	MoF	Sopwith	Triplane	N318057
Sopwith Triplane	FL	Polk	FoF	Sopwith	Triplane	
Sopwith Triplane	ON-C	Ottaw	CAM	Sopwith	Triplane	N5492
Sorrell Bathtub	WA	Seatt	MoF	Sorrell	Bathtub	1, N5087K
SP-2E	CT	Winds	NEAM	Lockheed	Neptune	
SP-2E	NY	NYC	ISASM	Lockheed	Neptune	
SP-2H	PA	Readi	MAAM	Lockheed	Neptune	145915, N45309, VP 67
Space Capsule	NY	NYC	ISASM		GT-3	"Unsinkable Molly Brown"
Space Shuttle	AL	Huntsville	SC		Shuttle	
Space Shuttle	DC	Dulle	DA		Space Shuttle	"Enterprise"
Space Shuttle 1/3	CA	Moffe	NASAAVC			
Space Shuttle Cargo Bay	CA	LAnge	CMoS&I			
Spacecraft	AL	Hunts	AS&RC			
Spacecraft	CA	San F	TE			

161

Aircraft	State	City	Code	Mfr	Model	Notes
Spacecraft	FL	Cocoa	USAFSM			
Spacecraft	FL	Merri	KSC			
Spacecraft	FL	Orlan	JYM&P			
Spacecraft	MO	SLoui	MP			
Spacecraft (5 ea)	MA	Bosto	MoSP			
Spad IV	VA	Quant	MCAGM	Spad		
Spad VII	AL	Gunte	LGARFM	Spad		
Spad VII	CA	Santa Martin	WoHAM	Spad		
Spad VII	FL	Polk	FoF	Spad		
Spad VII	MI	Kalamazoo	KAHM	Spad	AS	
Spad VII	OH	Dayto	USAFM	Spad	AS	94099
Spad VII	ON-C	Ottaw	CAM	Spad		
Spad VII	VA	Sands	VAM	Spad		Sn 9913
Spad VII	WI	Oshko	EAAAAM	Spad		N9104A
Spad VII.c.1	CA	San Diego	SDAM	Spad		5334, S 3
Spad XIII	AL	Gunte	LGARFM	Spad		
Spad XIII	AZ	Mesa	CFM	Spad		
Spad XIII	AZ	Tucso	PAM	Spad		
Spad XIII	DC	Washi	NA&SM	Spad		"Smith IV"
Spad XIIIc.1	ME	OwlsH	OHTM	Spad		
Spad XIII	NY	Rhine	ORA	Spad		
Spad XIII	OH	Dayto	USAFM	Spad		
Spad XIII	OR	Tillamook	TAM	Spad		
Spad XIII	WA	Seattle	MoF	Spad		NX3883F
Spad XVI	OH	Dayto	USAFM	Spad		959
Spartan C-3	NY	Rhine	ORA	Spartan	Executive	
Spartan C2-60	WY	Jackson	GWFM	Spartan	Executive	
Spartan Executive 7W	WI	Oshko	EAAAAM	Spartan	Executive	N13993, "Mrs. Mennon"
Speedbird Air Car	IN	Auburn	HW	Speedbird	Air Car	
Spencer Air Car	AK	Ancho	AAHM	Spencer	Air Car	N14NX
Spencer Air Car S-14	WI	Oshko	EAAAAM	Spencer	Air Car	N31SA
Spinks Akromaster	WI	Oshko	EAAAAM	Spinks	Akromaster	
Spitfire	CA	Camarillo	CAF-SCW	Supermarine	Spitfire	on loan
Spitfire	LA	New Orleans	DDM	Supermarine	Spitfire	
Spitfire	VA	Suffolk	FF	Supermarine	Spitfire	MS730, N730MSJ
Spitfire Mk.VIIIc LF	TX	Dalla	CFM	Supermarine	Spitfire	N719MT, YB-J
Spitfire Mk.IA	IL	Chica	MoS&I	Supermarine	Spitfire	
Spitfire Mk.II	TX	Breck	BAM	Supermarine	Spitfire	DB
Spitfire Mk.II B	ON-C	Ottaw	CAM	Supermarine	Spitfire	
Spitfire Mk.V Rep	AZ	Grand Canyon	PoFGCVA	Supermarine	Spitfire	PA908
Spitfire Mk.V	OH	Dayto	USAFM	Supermarine	Spitfire	PA908
Spitfire Mk.VII	DC	Washi	NA&SM	Supermarine	Spitfire	
Spitfire Mk.VII	ON-C	Ottawa	CWM	Supermarine	Spitfire	
Spitfire Mk.VIII	OR	Tillamook	TAM	Supermarine	Spitfire	TE 356, N58JE
Spitfire Mk.IX Replica	ON-C	N Kitchener	SE	Supermarine	Spitfire	Replica
Spitfire Mk.IX	TX	Midla	CAFFM	Supermarine	Spitfire	MK923, MJ772, N8R
Spitfire Mk.IX	WA	Seattle	MoF	Supermarine	Spitfire	C8AF-1X-1886, N521R
Spitfire Mk.IX L.F.	ON-C	Ottaw	CAM	Supermarine	Spitfire	
Spitfire Mk.IXe	WI	Oshko	EAAAAM	Supermarine	Spitfire	N62EA
Spitfire Mk.IXe	CA	Chino	PoFAM	Supermarine	Spitfire	
Spitfire Mk.XI	OH	Dayto	USAFM	Supermarine	Spitfire	PA908
Spitfire Mk.XIV	CA	Palm Sprg	PSAM	Supermarine	Spitfire	P-WZ
Spitfire Mk.XIV	TX	Galve	LSFM	Supermarine	Spitfire	TZ138, N5505A
Spitfire Mk.XVI	CA	San Diego	SDAM	Supermarine	Spitfire	WK-W
Spitfire Mk.XVI	ON-C	Ottaw	CAM	Supermarine	Spitfire	
Spitfire Mk.XVI	OR	McMinnville	EAM	Supermarine	Spitfire	TE 356, NX356EV
Spitfire Parts	SK-C	MJaw	WDM	Supermarine	Spitfire	
Sport Fury	AL	Birmingham	SmoF	Sport Fury		
SR-71A See Also A-12				Loockheed	Blackbird	
SR-71	LA	Bossier City	BAFB	Lockheed	Blackbird	61-7967
SR-71	CA	Palmd	PAFB	Lockheed	Blackbird	61-7973
SR-71	CA	Sands	VAM	Lockheed	Blackbird	61-7968
SR-71	DC	Dulle		Lockheed	Blackbird	61-7972
SR-71A	AZ	Tucso	PAM	Lockheed	Blackbird	61-7951
SR-71A	CA	Atwater	CAM	Lockheed	Blackbird	61-7960
SR-71A	CA	Marys	BAFB	Lockheed	Blackbird	61-7963
SR-71A	CA	Riverside	MFAM	Lockheed	Blackbird	61-7975
SR-71A	OR	McMinnville	EAEC	Lockheed	Blackbird	61-7971
SR-71A	CA	Rosam	EAFB	Lockheed	Blackbird	67-1980
SR-71A	CA	Rosam	EAFB	Lockheed	Blackbird	61-7955
SR-71A	FL	Shali	USAFAM	Lockheed	Blackbird	61-7959
SR-71A	GA	Warner Robin	MoF	Lockheed	Blackbird	61-7958,"Ichi Ban", 958
SR-71A	KS	Hutch	KC&SC	Lockheed	Blackbird	61-7961
SR-71A	OH	Dayto	USAFM	Lockheed	Blackbird	61-7976
SR-71A	TX	San A	LAFB	Lockheed	Blackbird	61-7979
SR-71A	VA	Sandstrom	VAM	Lockheed	Blackbird	61-7968
SR-71A	WA	Everret	MoF	Lockheed	Blackbird	61-7977
SR-71A-LO	NE	Ashland	SACM	Lockheed	Blackbird	61-7964
SR-71B	CA	Rosam	EAFB	Lockheed	Blackbird	61-7956
SR-71C	UT	Ogden	HAFBM	Lockheed	Blackbird	61-7981
ST-34KR	PA	Tough	CFCM	Ryan		
Stahltaube	CA	Santa Martin	WoHAM	Stahltaube		
Staib LB-5	KS	Liberal	MAAM	Staib	Tiny	
Stampe SV4	NY	Rhine	ORA	Stampe		
Stan Hall Cherokee II	CA	Santa Martin	WoHAM	Stan Hall	Sherokee II	Glider
Stan Hall Safari	CA	Santa Martin	WoHAM	Stan Hall	Safari	Powered Glider
Stanley Nomad	MD	Silve	PEGF	Stanley	Nomad	
Stargazer Gondola	OH	Dayton	USAFM	Stargazer		
Starr Bumble Bee	AZ	Tucson	PAM	Starr	Bumble Bee	N83WS, Worlds Smallest Aircraft
Stearman	AB-C	Wetas	RM	Stearman		
Stearman	CA	Hayward	VAM	Stearman		
Stearman (8ea)	FL	Zellw	BWA	Stearman		
Stearman	LA	Patte	WWMAM	Stearman		"Delta Airlines"
Stearman	ON-C	Trenton	CAHS	Stearman		
Stearman	MO	Maryland Hts	HARM	Stearman		
Stearman	NY	Bayport	BA	Stearman		
Stearman	TX	Ft Worth	VFM	Stearman		
Stearman	UT	Heber	HVAM	Stearman	Kaydet	
Stearman	VA	Chesapeake	CAFODW	Stearman		555
Stearman	VA	Suffolk	FF	Stearman		75-2743
Stearman	WA	Vancouver	PAM	Stearman		
Stearman 4	CA	Chino	YAM	Stearman	Bull	4026, NC11224, Model 4
Stearman 4-CM-1	CA	Hayward	VAM	Stearman	Bull	
Stearman 4-D	CA	Chino	YACM	Stearman	Bull	4026, N11224
Stearman 4-E	NV	Carso	YF	Stearman	Bull	

Stearman 4-EM	ON-C	Ottaw	CAM	Stearman	Bull	
Stearman A-75 (8 ea)	VA	Bealt	FCA	Stearman		
Stearman C-2B	AK	Ancho	AAHM	Stearman		N5415
Stearman C-3B	WA	Seatt	MoF	Stearman		166, N7550
Stearman EC 75	OR	McMinnville	EAEC	Stearman		
Stearman Fr 24	FL	Arcia	AA Clark	Stearman		
Stearman Super	WI	Oshko	EAAAAM	Boeing	Super Stearman	N5051V
Stearman-Hammond Y	MD	Silve	PEGF	Stearman-Hammond		
Stearman-Hammond YS-1	CA	SCarl	HAM	Stearman-Hammond		
Steco 1911	MN	St Paul	MA&SM	Steco	Aerohydro-Plane	
Steen Skybolt	FL	Lakel	SFAF	Steen	Skybolt	N 47216
Steen Skybolt	KS	Liber	MAAM	Steen	Skybolt	
Steen Skybolt	NV	Carso	YF	Steen	Skybolt	
Steen Skybolt	WI	Fond du Lac	WAM	Steen	Skybolt	
Stephens Akro	WA	Seatt	MoF	Stephens	Akro	434, N78JN
Stinson 105	ON-C	Collingwood	CCAF	Stinson	Voyager	7055, Parts: 7102, 7246
Stinson 105	SK-C	MJaw	WDM	Stinson	Voyager	
Stinson 108	AB-C	Edmonton	AAM	Stinson	Voyager	
Stinson 108	AK	Ancho	AAHM	Stinson	Voyager	
Stinson 108	GA	Woodstock	NGWS	Stinson	Voyager	
Stinson 108	OH	Madis	CFR	Stinson	Voyager	
Stinson 108	WA	Everett	MoF	Stinson	Voyager	108-626, N97626
Stinson 108-3(150)	KS	Liber	MAAM	Stinson	Voyager	
Stinson 108-3	OK	Fredi	AAM	Stinson	Voyager	
Stinson 7-B	NV	Carso	YF	Stinson		
Stinson 7M-7A	WY	Jackson	GWFM	Stinson		
Stinson A Trimotor	AK	Ancho	AAHM	Stinson	Tri-Motor	NC15165, 15, "Pennsylvania Central"
Stinson A Trimotor	MN	Blaine	GH	Stinson	Trimotor	
Stinson Junior	IA	Ottumwa	APM	Stinson	Junior	8074, NC-12165
Stinson SA-10A	AL	Birmingham	SMoF	Stinson	Voyager	
Stinson SA-10A	AK	Palme	MOAT&I	Stinson	Voyager	
Stinson SA-10A	CA	Santa Martin	WoHAM	Stinson	Voyager	
Stinson SA-10A	IA	Ottumwa	APM	Stinson	Voyager	7655, N27710
Stinson SA-10A	MB-C	Brand	CATPM	Stinson	Voyager	
Stinson SA-10A	ME	Bangor	MAM	Stinson	Voyager	
Stinson SA-10A	MI	Oscoda	YAF	Stinson	Voyager	7883, N32235
Stinson SA-10A	NJ	Teter	AHoFNJ	Stinson	Voyager	
Stinson SA-10A	OK	Fredi	AAM	Stinson	Voyager	
Stinson SA-10A	OK	Oklah	KCASM	Stinson	Voyager	
Stinson SA-10A	WA	Tacoma	MAFB	Stinson	Voyager	43-43847
Stinson SA-10A(L- 9)	KS	Liber	MAAM	Stinson	Voyager	
Stinson SA-10A(L-9B)	RI	NKing	QAM	Stinson	Voyager	
Stinson SM-1	AR	Fayet	AAM	Stinson	Detroiter	NC12143
Stinson SM-1	CA	San Carlos	HAM	Stinson	Detroiter	
Stinson SM-1	CT	Winds	NEAM	Stinson	Detroiter	
Stinson SM-1	MI	Dearb	HFM	Stinson	Detroiter	
Stinson SM-1	NE	Minde	HWPV	Stinson	Detroiter	
Stinson SM-1B	WY	Jackson	GWFM	Stinson	Detroiter	
Stinson SM-6000B	OR	McMinnville	EAEC	Stinson	Detroiter	
Stinson SR	CA	S.Mar	SMMoF	Stinson	Reliant	
Stinson SR V-77	IN	Auburn	HW	Stinson	Reliant	
Stinson SR	NC	Morga	CWCAF	Stinson	Reliant	
Stinson SR	ON-C	Ottaw	CAM	Stinson	Reliant	
Stinson SR	PA	Latro	WCM	Stinson	Reliant	
Stinson SR	TX	Slanton	TAM	Stinson	Reliant	
Stinson SR 7AC	TX	RioHo	TAM	Stinson	Reliant	
Stinson SR Float Plane	WA	Seatt	MoF	Stinson	Reliant	8732, N13477
Stinson SR(AT19)V-77	KS	Liber	MAAM	Stinson	Reliant	
Stinson SR-5 Replica	AL	Birmingham	SMoF	Stinson	Junior	
Stinson SR-5A	ND	Minot	DTAM	Stinson	Junior	
Stinson SR-5E	OR	Eugen	OAM	Stinson	Junior	
Stinson SR-5JR	AK	Fairb	APAM	Stinson	Junior	N13482, "Spirit of Barter Island"
Stinson SR-8	MB-C	Winni	WCAM	Stinson	Reliant	
Stinson SR-9FM	AB-C	Edmonton	AAM	Stinson	Reliant	5732
Stinson SR-9	ON-C	Sault Ste Marie	CBHC	Stinson	Reliant	Sn 5702, CF-BGN
Stinson SR-9 CM	AK	Ancho	AAHM	Stinson	Reliant	
Stinson SR-9 CM	WI	Oshkosh	EAAAAM	Stinson	Reliant	
Stinson SR-10F	DC	Washi	USPM	Stinson	Reliant	NC2311, "Human Pick-Up"
Stinson SR-10F	MD	Silve	PEGF	Stinson	Reliant	
Stinson SR-10G	VA	Sandston	VAM	Stinson	Reliant	Sn 5903
Stits DS-1	WI	Oshko	EAAAAM	Stits		N4453H, "Baby Bird"
Stits SA-3A	ON-C	Ottaw	CAM	Stits		
Stolp Starduster II	RI	NKing	QAM	Stolp	Starduster II	N100LF
Stolp V Star	WI	Oshko	EAAAAM	Stolp	V Star	N9LS
Stout Skycar	MD	Silve	PEGF	Stout	Skycar	
Strechen Helicopter	BC-C	Langley	CmoF&T	Strechen	Helicopter	
Stuart M-5	WA	Tilli	CMANGP	Stuart		
Student Prince	WA	Vancouver	PAM	Acft Bldg Corp	Student Prince	"Ladt Summer"
Sud Aviation SE 210	AZ	Tucso	PAM	Sud Aviation	Caravelle	N1001U
Sun Standard Hang Glider	MI	Kalamazoo	KAHM	Sun Aircraft	Hang Glider	
Sundancer I Racer	CA	San Diego	SDAM	Sundancer	Racer	N1AE
Super Lancer Hang Glider	FL	Lakeland	SNF	Lancer	Hang Glider	
Supermarine F.1	NY	NYC	ISASM	Supermarine	Scimitar	
Supermarine S6B	CA	Chino	PoFAM	Supermarine		
Supermarine Seafire Mk.XV	AB-C	Calga	AMoC	Supermarine	Seafire	
Supermarine Stranraer	BC-C	Langley	CMoF&T	Supermarine	Stranraer	
Surca-Tempete Homebuilt	FL	Lakel	SFAF	Surca-Tempete	Homebuilt	
SV-4C	BC-C	Langley	CMoF&T	Stampe		
SV-5D	OH	Dayton	USAFM	Martin	PRIME	Lifting Body
SV-5J	CO	CSpri	USAFA	Martin	PRIME	Lifting Body
SVA-9	CT	Washi	TFC		Ansaldo	
Swallow 1926	NE	Minde	HWPV	Swallow		
Swallow	WA	Seattle	MoF	Swallow		
Swallow A	AZ	Tucso	PAM	Swallow		968, N6070
Swallow Model 1924	WI	Oshko	EAAAAM	Swallow	Three Seater	N4028
Swallow TP	CA	San Diego	SDAM	Swallow		N8761
SX-300	FL	Lakeland	SNFAM	Swearingen		
T- 1	IN	Ft Wayne	Mercury	Folland	Gnat	
T- 2	CA	Chino	PoFAM	North American	Buckeye	
T- 2	DC	Washi	NA&SM	North American	Buckeye	
T- 2	IN	India	IMoMH	North American	Buckeye	
T- 2A	NC	Charlotte	CAM	North American	Buckeye	148239
T2-B	ID	Driggs	TAC	North American	Buckeye	Sn 155226, Side # 300S, Tail B
T- 2	OH	Newbu	WASAC	North American	Buckeye	
T- 2	TX	Slato	TAMCC	North American	Buckeye	47, 5
T- 3	CA	San Carlos	HAM	Boeing		

Type	State	City	Org	Manufacturer	Model	Notes
T-11	IN	India	IMoMH			
T-11	LA	New Orleans	FJB			
T-18	BC-C	Langley	CMoF&T	Thorp	Tiger	
T-18	IA	SBluf	MAAM	Thorp	Tiger	
T-18	KS	Liber	MAAM	Thorp	Tiger	
T-18	OK	Fredi	AAM	Thorp	Tiger	1093, N1093
T-18	WA	Seatt	MoF	Thorp	Tiger	
T-18	WI	Oshko	EAAAM	Thorp	Tiger	N455DT, "Victoria 76"
T-28	CO	Denve	JWDAS	North American	Trojan	
T-28	DC	Washi	NHND	North American	Trojan	
T-28	DC	Washington	ANAS	North American	Trojan	
T-28	FL	Milto	CityPark	North American	Trojan	
T-28	FL	Tittusville	VACM	North American	Trojan	
T-28	ID	Driggs	TAC	North American	Trojan	Cowl # 249, Tail NATC
T-28	IL	Rockf	CRA	North American	Trojan	
T-28	IN	India	IMoMH	North American	Trojan	
T-28	KS	Liber	MAAM	North American	Trojan	
T-28	KS	New Century	CAF-HoAW	North American	Trojan	
T-28	LA	Reser	AMHFM	North American	Trojan	
T-28	MI	Ypsil	YAF	North American	Trojan	
T-28	MS	Bilox	KAFB	North American	Trojan	
T-28 Cockpit	NC	Charlotte	CAM	North American	Trojan	
T-28	NM	STere	WEAM	North American	Trojan	
T-28	NV	Carso	YF	North American	Trojan	
T-28	ON-C	Hamilton	CWH	North American	Trojan	
T-28	PA	Beaver Falls	AHM	North American	Trojan	
T-28	TX	Big Springs	H25	North American	Trojan	
T-28	TX	C Christi	NAS	North American	Trojan	
T-28	TX	FWort	PMoT	North American	Trojan	
T-28	TX	Ladero	Airport	North American	Trojan	
T-28	TX	W Houston	CAF-WH	North American	Trojan	
T-28	UT	Heber	HVAM	North American	Trojan	0-37799
T-28	VA	Chesapeake	CAFODW	North American	Trojan	
T-28	WI	Beloi	BA			
T-28	WI	Boscobel	BA			
T-28A	AL	Ozark	USAAM	North American	Trojan	51-3612
T-28A	GA	Warner Robin	MoF	North American	Trojan	51-3612, "Rocky Yates"
T-28A-NI	MI	Belleville	YAF	North American	Trojan	50-234, N234NA
T-28A	MI	Kalarn	KAHM	North American	Trojan	51-7700
T-28A	OH	Dayto	USAFM	North American	Trojan	49-1494
T-28A	OH	Newbu	WASAC	North American	Trojan	4021800
T-28A	OK	Enid	VAFB	North American	Trojan	
T-28A	OK	Fredi	AAM	North American	Trojan	
T-28A	TX	D Rio	LAFB	North American	Trojan	
T-28A	TX	San A	GAFB			
T-28A	TX	San A	RAFB	North American	Trojan	
T-28A(GT)	TX	San A	LAFB	North American	Trojan	49-1611
T-28B	CA	Paso Robles	EWM	North American	Trojan	138303
T-28B	CA	Rosam	EAFB	North American	Trojan	137702
T-28B	CA	S.Mon	MoF	North American	Trojan	
T-28B	CA	Sacra	McCelAFB	North American	Trojan	138327
T-28B	FL	Pensa	USNAM	North American	Trojan	136326, 2W, 341, VT-3
T-28B	IN	Valparaiso	IAM	North American	Trojan	140018
T-28B	KS	Topek	CAM	North American	Trojan	137759, N-759T
T-28B	NC	Asheboro	CHAC	North American	Trojan	
T-28B	NC	Charl	CHAC	North American	Trojan	
T-28B	OH	Dayto	USAFM	North American	Trojan	140048
T-28B	OR	Mc Minnville	EAEC	North American	Trojan	13 8334, N394W
T-28B	TN	Sevierville	TMoA	North American	Trojan	138129, N32257, "Showtime"
T-28B	TX	C Christi	USS Lexi	North American	Trojan	
T-28B	UT	Ogden	HAFBM	North American	Trojan	
T-28C	AL	Everg	MA	North American	Trojan	
T-28C	AL	Everg	MAE	North American	Trojan	
T-28C	AZ	Tucso	PAM	North American	Trojan	140481
T-28C	CA	SRosa	PCAM	North American	Trojan	7696, 2G, 133, VT-2
T-28C	CO	Puebl	FWAM	North American	Trojan	140064
T-28C	CT	Winds	NEAM	North American	Trojan	
T-28C	MA	Fall	USSMM	North American	Trojan	
T-28C	MI	Belleville	YAF	North American	Trojan	140531, N944SD, "Tough Old Bird"
T-28C	TX	Galveston	LSM	North American	Trojan	
T-28C	VA	Quantico	MCAGM	North American	Trojan	140557
T-28D	PA	Readi	MAAM	North American	Trojan	
T-28D(AT-28D-5)	VA	Suffolk	FF	North American	Trojan	1634
T-28D(AT)	FL	FtWal	HF	North American	Trojan	
T-28S	OH	N Canton	MAM	North American	Trojan	51-3565, N85227
T-28S	RI	NKing	QAM	North American	Trojan	51-3529, "Fennec"
T-29	VT	Burlington	NANG	Convair	Flying Classroom	
T-29 (C-131)	GA	Calho	Mercer A	Convair	Flying Classroom	
T-29A(C-131)	NE	Ashland	SACM	Convair	Flying Classroom	50-190
T-29A(C-131A)	AZ	Tucso	PAM	Convair	Flying Classroom	49-1918
T-29A(C-131A)	GA	Warner Robin	MoF	Convair	Flying Classroom	49-1938
T-29A(C-131A)	TX	Wichi	SAFB	Convair	Flying Classroom	
T-29A(GT)(C-131)	TX	Wichi	SAFB	Convair	Flying Classroom	
T-29B(VT)	AZ	Tucso	PAM	Convair	Flying Classroom	51-7906
T-29B(VT)	TX	San A	LAFB	Convair	Flying Classroom	51-5172
T-29C(C-131)	CA	Sacra	SWAM	Convair	Flying Classroom	
T-29C(C-131)	TX	Abile	DLAP	Convair	Flying Classroom	52-1175
T-29C(C-131)	UT	Ogden	HAFBM	Convair	Flying Classroom	
T-33	CA	Torrance	Airport	Lockheed	Shooting Star	
T-33	GA	Griffin	SCA	Lockheed	Shooting Star	
T-33	GA	Marietta	NASA	Lockheed	Shooting Star	
T-33	IA	SBluf	MAAM	Lockheed	Shooting Star	
T-33	IN	Hobar	DickBoyd	Lockheed	Shooting Star	
T-33	KS	Wichita	KAM	Lockheed	Shooting Star	
T-33	LA	Bossi	BAFB	Lockheed	Shooting Star	
T-33	MI	Jackson	EAAC	Lockheed	Shooting Star	
T-33	MN	Alexandria	Airport	Lockheed	Shooting Star	
T-33	MT	Helena	CoT	Canadair	Shooting Star	
T-33 Cockpit	NC	Charlotte	CAM	Lockheed	Shooting Star	
T-33	NC	Hickory	HRA	Lockheed	Shooting Star	52-9529
T-33	ND	Minot	DTAM	Lockheed	Shooting Star	
T-33	ON-C	Grand Bend	PAFM	Lockheed	Shooting Star	
T-33	NM	STere	WEAM	Lockheed	Shooting Star	
T-33	TX	Big Springs	H25	Lockheed	Shooting Star	
T-33	TX	Ft Worth	SAM	Lockheed	Shooting Star	
T-33	WA	Seatt	MoF	Lockheed	Shooting Star	

T-33	WI	Janesville	BHTSAC	Lockheed	Shooting Star	
T-33	WI	Stoughton	VFW	Loockheed	Shooting Star	
T-33 Cockpit Trainer	CA	S.Mon	MoF	Lockheed	Shooting Star	
T-33 Mk 3	TN	Sevierville	TMoA	Lockheed	Shooting Star	X-R CAF 21566
T-33 Mk 3	WI	Oshko	EAAAAM	Lockheed	Shooting Star	N72JR
T-33A	AK	Ancho	EAFB	Lockheed	Shooting Star	
T-33A	AK	Ancho	KANGB	Lockheed	Shooting Star	
T-33A	AL	Atmor	CityPark	Lockheed	Shooting Star	
T-33A	AL	Birmingham	SMoF	Lockheed	Shooting Star	
T-33A	AL	Flora	CityPark	Lockheed	Shooting Star	
T-33A	AL	Mobil	CityPark	Lockheed	Shooting Star	
T-33A	AL	Monro	CityPark	Lockheed	Shooting Star	
T-33A	AL	Tusca	CityPark	Lockheed	Shooting Star	
T-33A	AR	Grave	VWF	Lockheed	Shooting Star	
T-33A	AR	Helen	VWF	Lockheed	Shooting Star	
T-33A	AR	Littl	LRAFB	Lockheed	Shooting Star	51-9080
T-33A	AZ	Gila	GBAFAF	Lockheed	Shooting Star	
T-33A	AZ	Grand	PoFGCVA	Lockheed	Shooting Star	71-5262
T-33A	AZ	Mesa	WAFB	Lockheed	Shooting Star	
T-33A	AZ	Phoenix	DVA	Lockheed	Shooting Star	
T-33A	AZ	Tucso	PAM	Lockheed	Shooting Star	53-6145
T-33A	CA	Atwater	CAM	Lockheed	Shooting Star	58-0629
T-33A	CA	Chino	YAM	Lockheed	Shooting Star	
T-33A	CA	Shafter	MFAM	Lockheed	Shooting Star	
T-33A	CA	Fresn	FANG	Lockheed	Shooting Star	
T-33A	CA	Los G	VWF	Lockheed	Shooting Star	
T-33A	CA	Mader	VWF	Lockheed	Shooting Star	
T-33A	CA	Oakland	CAF-GGW	Lockheed	Shooting Star	16581, NX91242Z
T-33A	CA	Paso Robles	EWM	Lockheed	Shooting Star	52-9769
T-33A	CA	Richm	AMS	Lockheed	Shooting Star	
T-33A	CA	Riverside	MFAM	Lockheed	Shooting Star	58-0513
T-33A	CA	S.Mon	MoF	Lockheed	Silver Star	69330, Side # FT-330
T-33A	CA	Sacra	McCelAFB	Lockheed	T-Bird	53-5205
T-33A	CO	CSpri	EJPSCM	Lockheed	Shooting Star	57-0713
T-33A	CO	Denve	WOR	Lockheed	Shooting Star	
T-33A	CO	Flage	VWF	Lockheed	Shooting Star	
T-33A	CT	Winds	NEAM	Lockheed	Shooting Star	
T-33A	DE	Dover	AL P-2	Lockheed	Shooting Star	
T-33A	DE	Dover	DAFB	Lockheed	Shooting Star	TR-497
T-33A	FL	Clear	FMAM	Lockheed	Shooting Star	
T-33A	FL	De Fu	CityPark	Lockheed	Shooting Star	
T-33A	FL	Jacks	JIA	Lockheed	Shooting Star	35325, 27
T-33A	FL	Lakel	SFAF	Lockheed	Shooting Star	58-697
T-33A	FL	Panam	TAFB	Lockheed	Shooting Star	58-619
T-33A	FL	Shali	USAFAM	Lockheed	Shooting Star	53-5947
T-33A	GA	Calhoun	MAM	Lockheed	Shooting Star	29574, TR-574
T-33A	GA	Corde		Lockheed	Shooting Star	
T-33A	GA	Dougl	CityPark	Lockheed	Shooting Star	
T-33A	GA	Griff	CityPark	Lockheed	Shooting Star	
T-33A	GA	Thoma	CityPark	Lockheed	Shooting Star	
T-33A	GA	Warner Robin	MoF	Lockheed	Shooting Star	52-9633
T-33A	GA	Wayne	ALP120	Lockheed	Shooting Star	
T-33A	GA	Willa	CityPark	Lockheed	Shooting Star	
T-33A	HI	Oahu	HAFB	Lockheed	Shooting Star	
T-33A	IA	Burli	CityPark	Lockheed	Shooting Star	
T-33A	IA	Cedar Rapids	Vet Memorial	Lockheed	Shooting Star	53-5916
T-33A	IA	Oelwe	ALP19	Lockheed	Shooting Star	
T-33A	IA	Sheld	CityPark	Lockheed	Shooting Star	
T-33A	IA	Sigou	CityPark	Lockheed	Shooting Star	
T-33A	ID	Burle	CityPark	Lockheed	Shooting Star	
T-33A	ID	Lewis	CityPark	Lockheed	Shooting Star	
T-33A	ID	Malad	CityPark	Lockheed	Shooting Star	
T-33A	ID	Twin	CityPark	Lockheed	Shooting Star	
T-33A	IL	Sugar Grove	ACM	Lockheed	Shooting Star	58-0632
T-33A	IL	Bloom	PAM	Lockheed	Shooting Star	35979
T-33A	IL	Cahok	PCUSL	Lockheed	Shooting Star	
T-33A	IL	Centr	CityPark	Lockheed	Shooting Star	
T-33A	IL	Highl	CityPark	Lockheed	Shooting Star	
T-33A	IL	Linco	HIFM	Lockheed	Shooting Star	
T-33A	IL	Pinck	CityPark	Lockheed	Shooting Star	
T-33A	IL	Quicy	CityPark	Lockheed	Shooting Star	
T-33A(F-80)	IL	Ranto	OCAM	Lockheed	Shooting Star	55-797
T-33A	IL	Versa	CityPark	Lockheed	Shooting Star	
T-33A	IN	Covin	VFWP2395	Lockheed	Shooting Star	50-29326
T-33A	IN	Elkhart	NIAM	Lockheed	Shooting Star	70688, TCD17
T-33A	IN	Hunti	CityPark	Lockheed	Shooting Star	
T-33A	IN	Peru	GAFB	Lockheed	Shooting Star	52-9563
T-33A	KS	Indep	VFWP1186	Lockheed	Shooting Star	
T-33A	KS	Topek	CAM	Lockheed	Shooting Star	0-29632
T-33A-5-LO	KS	Wichi	K&HAP	Lockheed	Shooting Star	53-5998
T-33A	LA	Houma	CityPark	Lockheed	Shooting Star	
T-33A	LA	Mansf	VFWP4586	Lockheed	Shooting Star	
T-33A	LA	N.Orl	FoJBMM	Lockheed	Shooting Star	
T-33A	LA	Rusto	LTUD305	Lockheed	Shooting Star	
T-33A	LA	Sprin	CityPark	Lockheed	Shooting Star	
T-33A	MA	Bourne	HQMMR	Lockheed	Shooting Star	14335
T-33A	MA	Otis	OANG	Lockheed	Shooting Star	
T-33A	MA	Stow	BCF	Lockheed	Shooting Star	
T-33A	MD	Cumbe	CityPark	Lockheed	Shooting Star	
T-33A	MD	Middl	GLMAM	Lockheed	Shooting Star	
T-33A	MD	Pocom	ALP93	Lockheed	Shooting Star	52-9650, TR-650
T-33A	MD	Rockv	CityPark	Lockheed	Shooting Star	
T-33A	MD	Silve	PEGF	Lockheed	Shooting Star	
T-33A	MI	Breck	ALP295	Lockheed	Shooting Star	
T-33A	MI	Calum	CAFS	Lockheed	Shooting Star	
T-33A	MI	Grayl	ALP106	Lockheed	Shooting Star	
T-33A	MI	Hart	City Fog	Lockheed	Shooting Star	35073, 8436, T33-600-2282
T-33A	MI	Iron	CityPark	Lockheed	Shooting Star	
T-33A	MI	Roseb	ALP383	Lockheed	Shooting Star	
T-33A	MI	Sebew	CityPark	Lockheed	Shooting Star	
T-33A	MI	Mt Clemens	SMAM	Lockheed	Shooting Star	53-6099
T-33A	MI	Ypsil	YAF	Lockheed	Shooting Star	
T-33A	MN	Alber	CityPark	Lockheed	Shooting Star	
T-33A	MN	Buffa	CityPark	Lockheed	Shooting Star	
T-33A	MN	Hecto	CityPark	Lockheed	Shooting Star	
T-33A	MN	Minne	CityPark	Lockheed	Shooting Star	

Type	State	City	Org	Mfr	Name	Serial
T-33A	MN	Minne	MAGM	Lockheed	Shooting Star	52-9806
T-33A	MN	Winoma	WTI	Lockheed	Shooting Star	N86905
T-33A	MN	Under	VFW874	Lockheed	Shooting Star	
T-33A	MO	Carut	CityPark	Lockheed	Shooting Star	
T-33A	MO	Mount	CityPark	Lockheed	Shooting Star	
T-33A	MO	Richm	ALP237	Lockheed	Shooting Star	
T-33A	MO	SLoui	ALP179	Lockheed	Shooting Star	
T-33A	MO	SLoui	NMoT	Lockheed	Shooting Star	52-9446
T-33A	MO	StCha	CityPark	Lockheed	Shooting Star	
T-33A	MS	Bilox	KAFB	Lockheed	Shooting Star	
T-33A	MS	Colum	CityPark	Lockheed	Shooting Star	
T-33A	MT	Glasg	CityPark	Lockheed	Shooting Star	52-9564
T-33A	MT	Great Falls	CityPark	Lockheed	Shooting Star	
T-33A	MT	Great Falls	GFANG	Lockheed	Shooting Star	
T-33A	MT	Great Falls	MAFB	Lockheed	Shooting Star	52-9672
T-33A	MT	Great Falls	MAFB	Lockheed	Shooting Star	57-0574
T-33A	NC	Charl	CHAC	Lockheed	Shooting Star	
T-33A	NC	CPoin	CPMB	Lockheed	Shooting Star	
T-33A	ND	Dicke	CityPark	Lockheed	Shooting Star	
T-33A	ND	Hatto	CityPark	Lockheed	Shooting Star	
T-33A	ND	Minot	MAFB	Lockheed	Shooting Star	
T-33A	ND	Vela	CityPark	Lockheed	Shooting Star	
T-33A	NE	Beatr	CityPark	Lockheed	Shooting Star	51-8880
T-33A	NE	Fairb	CityPark	Lockheed	Shooting Star	
T-33A	NE	Frank	CityPark	Lockheed	Shooting Star	
T-33A	NE	Linco	LANG	Lockheed	Shooting Star	52-9264, Tail ANG 29264
T-33A	NM	Clovi	CAFB	Lockheed	Shooting Star	
T-33A	NM	Truth	CityPark	Lockheed	Shooting Star	
T-33A	NY	Albion	VAG	Lockheed	Shooting Star	
T-33A	NY	NYC	ISASM	Lockheed	Shooting Star	
T-33A	NS-C	Greenwood	GMAM	Lockheed	Silver Star	
T-33A	OH	Brook	CityPark	Lockheed	Shooting Star	
T-33A	OH	Dayto	USAFM	Lockheed	Shooting Star	53-5974
T-33A(NT)	OH	Dayto	USAFM	Lockheed	Shooting Star	51-4120
T-33A	OH	Lockb	RANGB	Lockheed	Shooting Star	58-586, Model 580
T-33A	OH	Marie	CityPark	Lockheed	Shooting Star	
T-33A	OH	Newar	NAFM	Lockheed	Shooting Star	
T-33A	OH	Newbu	WASAC	Lockheed	Shooting Star	
T-33A	OH	Wadsw	CityPark	Lockheed	Shooting Star	
T-33A	OK	Coman	CityPark	Lockheed	Shooting Star	
T-33A	ON-NF	Goose Bay	TH	Canadair	Silver Star	
T-33A	OK	Elk C	CityPark	Lockheed	Shooting Star	
T-33A	OK	Enid	VAFB	Lockheed	Shooting Star	
T-33A	OK	Musko	City	Lockheed	Shooting Star	
T-33A	OK	Oklah	45IDM	Lockheed	Shooting Star	58-0505
T-33A	OK	Oklah	A&SM	Lockheed	Shooting Star	
T-33A	OK	Oklah	KCASM	Lockheed	Shooting Star	
T-33A	OK	Tinke	TANG	Lockheed	Shooting Star	
T-33A	OR	Woodb	CityPark	Lockheed	Shooting Star	
T-33A	PA	New K	CityPark	Lockheed	Shooting Star	
T-33A	PA	NHunt	VFWP781	Lockheed	Shooting Star	
T-33A	PA	Phila	FI	Lockheed	Shooting Star	
T-33A	SC	Charl	CAFB	Lockheed	Shooting Star	
T-33A	SC	Flore	FA&MM	Lockheed	Shooting Star	
T-33A	SC	Harts	CityPark	Lockheed	Shooting Star	
T-33A	SC	Huron	VFWP1776	Lockheed	Shooting Star	
T-33A	SC	Lake	CityPark	Lockheed	Shooting Star	
T-33A	SC	McEnt	MEANGB	Lockheed	Shooting Star	
T-33A	SD	Rapid	SDA&SM	Lockheed	Shooting Star	57-0590
T-33A	SD	Sioux	SDANGSF	Lockheed	Shooting Star	
T-33A	TN	Johnson City	R/CF	Lockheed	Shooting Star	
T-33A	TN	Crossville	CCHS	Lockheed	Shooting Star	51-6756, "Miss Netie"
T-33A	TN	Dayto	CityPark	Lockheed	Shooting Star	
T-33A	TN	Johns	CityPark	Lockheed	Shooting Star	
T-33A	TN	Sevierville	TMoA	Lockheed	Shooting Star	53-6069
T-33A	TN	Pulas	CityPark	Lockheed	Shooting Star	
T-33A	TX	Abile	DLAP	Lockheed	Shooting Star	51-4300
T-33A	TX	D Rio	CityPark	Lockheed	Shooting Star	36124
T-33A	TX	D Rio	LAFB	Lockheed	Shooting Star	
T-33A	TX	Dalla	CFM	Lockheed	Shooting Star	8069
T-33A	TX	Dalla	CFM	Lockheed	Shooting Star	56-1747,
T-33A	TX	Eagle	ALP211	Lockheed	Shooting Star	
T-33A	TX	Ellin	EANGB	Lockheed	Shooting Star	
T-33A	TX	FWort	PMoT	Lockheed	Shooting Star	
T-33A	TX	FWort	SAM	Lockheed	Shooting Star	
T-33A-1	TX	Grand Prairie	TACM	Lockheed	Shooting Star	
T-33A	TX	Lubbock	LSS	Lockheed	Shooting Star	2920, ATC
T-33A	TX	Odessa	CAFDS	Lockheed	Shooting Star	
T-33A	TX	Plainview	HCA	Lockheed	Shooting Star	16753, TR-753
T-33A	TX	San A	RAFB	Lockheed	Shooting Star	
T-33A	TX	Slanton	TAMCC	Lockheed	Shooting Star	52-519
T-33A	TX	Sweet	CityPark	Lockheed	Shooting Star	
T-33A	TX	Sweetwater	CP	Lockheed	Shooting Star	
T-33A	TX	Texar	CityPark	Lockheed	Shooting Star	
T-33A	TX	Wichi	SAFB	Lockheed	Shooting Star	
T-33A	UT	Murra	CityPark	Lockheed	Shooting Star	
T-33A	UT	Ogden	HAFBM	Lockheed	Shooting Star	
T-33A	VA	Hampt	APM	Lockheed	Shooting Star	51-9086
T-33A-1	VA	Hampt	APM	Lockheed	Shooting Star	52-9734
T-33A	VT	Burli	BANG	Lockheed	Shooting Star	
T-33A	WA	Othel	CityPark	Lockheed	Shooting Star	
T-33A	WA	Spoka	CityPark	Lockheed	Shooting Star	
T-33A	WA	Spoka	FAFBHM	Lockheed	Shooting Star	
T-33A	WI	Brill	CityPark	Lockheed	Shooting Star	
T-33A	WI	Fall	VFWP2219	Lockheed	Shooting Star	
T-33A	WI	Madis	VFWP8483	Lockheed	Shooting Star	
T-33A	WI	Milwa	MANG	Lockheed	Shooting Star	TR476
T-33A	WI	Prentice	Vetrans Park	Lockheed	Shooting Star	0-18814
T-33A	WI	Oshko	EAAAAM	Lockheed	Shooting Star	51-8627
T-33A	WI	Oshko	EAAAAM	Lockheed	Shooting Star	53-5250
T-33A	WY	Cheye	WYANG	Lockheed	Shooting Star	
T-33A	WY	New R	ALP80	Lockheed	Shooting Star	
T-33A	WY	Reeds	ALP199	Lockheed	Shooting Star	
T-33A	WY	Sherw	ALP496	Lockheed	Shooting Star	
T-33A	WY	Stoug	VFWP328	Lockheed	Shooting Star	
T-33A (2 ea)	AL	Selma	CityPark	Lockheed	Shooting Star	

Model	State	City	Museum	Manufacturer	Name	Serial/Notes
T-33A (3ea)	CA	Chino	PoFAM	Lockheed	Shooting Star	
T-33A Last Built	WA	Tacoma	MAFB	Lockheed	Shooting Star	58-2106
T-33A(3ea)	CA	Rosam	EAFB	Lockheed	Shooting Star	58-669
T-33A(QT)	TX	Wichi	SAFB	Lockheed	Shooting Star	
T-33A-1-LO	MI	Belleville	YAF	Lockheed	Shooting Star	51-8786, N6570
T-33A-1-LO	MI	Belleville	YAF	Lockheed	Shooting Star	51-17445, N133CK, "Kalitta Bounty Hunter"
T-33A-1-LO	MI	Oscoda	YAF	Lockheed	Shooting Star	52-9843, N58417
T-33A-1-LO	WA	Tacom	G Spieth	Lockheed	Shooting Star	52-9646
T-33A-5-LO	MI	Oscoda	YAF	Lockheed	Shooting Star	53-5948
T-33A-5-LO	MI	Belleville	YAF	Lockheed	Shooting Star	53-5484, N1541
T-33A-5-LO	NE	Ashland	SACM	Lockheed	Silver Star	58-548
T-33A-5-LO	OR	Mc Minnville	EAEC	Lockheed	Shooting Star	53-5943
T-33A-5-LO	WI	Kenos	KMM	Lockheed	Shooting Star	0-29141
T-33AN	TN	Sevierville	TMoA	Canadair	Silver Star	T33-566, N307FS
T-33B	CO	Puebl	FWAM	Lockheed	Shooting Star	137936
T-33B	CT	Winds	NEAM	Lockheed	Shooting Star	53-5646
T-33B	IN	India	IMoMH	Lockheed	Shooting Star	
T-33B	NC	Charl	CHAC	Lockheed	Shooting Star	
T-33B	NC	CPoin	CPMB	Lockheed	Shooting Star	
T-33B	NV	Battl	BMAM	Lockheed	Shooting Star	1338064
T-33B(TV-2)	AZ	Tucso	PAM	Lockheed	Shooting Star	53-2704, 136810
T-33B(TV-2)	CA	Chino	PoFAM	Lockheed	Seastar (T-33)	
T-33B(TV-2)	CT	Winds	NEAM	Lockheed	Seastar (T-33)	138048
T-33B(TV-2)	KS	Wichita	KAM	Lockheed	Seastar (T-33)	
T-33B(TV-2)	MI	Kalam	KAHM	Lockheed	Shooting Star	53-5696, 138090
T-33B(TV-2)	NY	NYC	ISASM	Lockheed	Seastar (T-33)	
T-33(CT)	AB-C	Calga	AMoC	Lockheed	Silver Star	
T-33(CT)	AB-C	Calga	AMoC	Lockheed	Silver Star	
T-33(CT)	AB-C	Calga	NMoA	Lockheed	Silver Star	
T-33(CT)	AB-C	Cold Lake	CFB	Lockheed	Silver Star	133181
T-33(CT)	AB-C	Edson	CFB	Lockheed	Silver Star	21506, 21097
T-33(CT)	AB-C	Leduc	CFB	Lockheed	Silver Star	21518
T-33(CT)	AB-C	Lethbridge	CFB	Lockheed	Silver Star	21578
T-33(CT)	AB-C	Nanton	NLSAM	Lockheed	Silver Star	21500
T-33(CT)	AB-C	St Albert	CFB	Lockheed	Silver Star	Xx271
T-33(CT)	MB-C	Gimli	CFB	Lockheed	Silver Star	21239
T-33(CT)	NF-C	Goose Bay	CFB	Lockheed	Silver Star	
T-33(CT)	NS-C	Greenwood	GMAM	Canadair	Silver Star	133434, 434 Bluenose Squadron
T-33(CT)	NS-C	Halifax	ACAM	Canadair	Silver Star	
T-33(CT)	ON-C	Barrie	CFB	Lockheed	Silver Star	21100, Red Knight Colours
T-33(CT)	ON-C	CFB Borden	BHT	Lockheed	Silver Star	21079
T-33(CT)	ON-C	Campbellford	MMM	Lockheed	Silver Star	133303
T-33(CT)	ON-C	Cornwall	RCAFA	Lockheed	Silver Star	21347
T-33(CT)	ON-C	Cornwall	RCAFA	Lockheed	Silver Star	133423
T-33(CT)	ON-C	Dundas	CFB	Lockheed	Silver Star	21123
T-33(CT)	ON-C	Ft Erie	NP	Lockheed	Silver Star	21373, Red Knight Colours
T-33(CT)	ON-C	Hamilton	HAA	Lockheed	Silver Star	
T-33(CT)	ON-C	Picton	CFB	Lockheed	Silver Star	133238
T-33(CT) Mk III	ON-C	Trenton	RCAFMM	Lockheed	Silver Star	21435, Red Knight Colours
T-33(CT)	SK-C	Moose Jaw	CFB	Lockheed	Silver Star	21297
T-33(CT)	SK-C	Saskatoon	CFB	Lockheed	Silver Star	21630, Red Knight Colours
T-33A(CT)	AB-C	Wetas	RM	Lockheed	Silver Star	
T-33(CT)	MB-C	Brandon	BA	Canadair	Silver Star	21130
T-33(CT)	MB-C	Portage	S	Canadair	Silver Star	21277
T-33(CT)	MB-C	Winnipeg	WRCAFB	Canadair	Silver Star	133186
T-33(CT)	MB-C	Winnipeg	WRCAFB	Canadair	Silver Star	21232, Golden Hawks
T-33(CT)	MB-C	Dudas	HAA	Canadair	Silver Star	
T-33A(CT)	MB-C	Winni	WCAM	Lockheed	Silver Star	133401
T-33A(CT)	NS-C	Cornwallis	CFBS	Lockheed	Silver Star	
T-33A(CT)	NS-C	Shear	CFBS	Lockheed	Silver Star	
T-33A(CT)	ON-C	Hamilton	CWH	Canadair	Silver Star 3	21275, PP275
T-33A(CT)	ON-C	Ottaw	CAM	Canadair	Silver Star 3	21574
T-33A(CT)	SK-C	MJaw	WDM	Lockheed	Silver Star	
T-33AN(CT)	AB-C	Edmonton	AAM	Lockheed	Silver Star	21001
T-33AN(CT)	BC-C	Langley	CMoF&T	Lockheed	Silver Star 3	
T-34	AZ	Scott	SA	Beechcraft	Mentor	
T-34	CO	Denve	JWDAS	Beechcraft	Mentor	
T-34	CA	Palm Sprg	PSAM	Beechcraft	Mentor	N8662E
T-34	ON-C	Hamilton	CWH	Beechcraft	Mentor	
T-34	TX	Galve	LSFM	Beechcraft	Mentor	53- 4135, N134
T-34	TX	W Houston	CAF-WH	Beechcraft	Mentor	
T-34	VA	Suffolk	FF	Beechcraft	Mentor	55-0221, VT-6, Tail GP, #117
T-34(YT)	CA	Atwater	CAM	Beechcraft	Mentor	50-0735
T-34A	IL	Springfield	ACM	Beechcraft	Mentor	675
T-34A	MI	Kalamazoo	KAHM	Beechcraft	Mentor	140768
T-34A	MN	Blaine	AWAM	Beechcraft	Mentor	
T-34A	OH	Dayto	USAFM	Beechcraft	Mentor	53-3310
T-34A	TX	San A	LAFB	Beechcraft	Mentor	55-206
T-34B	CA	S.Mon	MoF	Beech	Mentor	
T-34B	FL	Pensa	USNAM	Beechcraft	Mentor	144040, F-4033, 41, VT-1
T-34B	GA	Atlan	SW	Beechcraft	Mentor	SW4130, 30
T-34B	IN	Valparaiso	IAM	Beechcraft	Mentor	BG-411
T-34B	OK	Altus	AAFB	Beechcraft	Mentor	
T-34B	TX	Abile	DLAP	Beechcraft	Mentor	140810
T-34B	TX	C Christi	USS Lexi	Beechcraft	Mentor	
T-34B	TX	D Rio	LAFB	Beechcraft	Mentor	
T-34B	TX	San A	RAFB	Beechcraft	Mentor	
T-34C	FL	Whitt	WNAS	Beechcraft	Mentor	
T-37	CA	Chino	YAM	Cessna	Tweedie Bird	
T-37	FL	Clear	FMAM	Cessna	Tweedie Bird	
T-37	FL	Tittusville	VACM	Cessna	Tweedie Bird	
T-37	KS	Liber	MAAM	Cessna	Tweedie Bird	
T-37	KS	Wichita	KAM	Cessna	Tweedie Bird	
T-37	OK	Tulsa	TA&SC	Cessna	Tweedie Bird	67-21469
T-37	TX	Big Springs	H25	Cessna	Tweedie Bird	
T-37	TX	Burnet	HLS-CAF	Cessna	Tweedie Bird	
T-37	TX	Waco	WRA	Cessna	Tweedie Bird	
T-37	UT	Ogden	HAFBM	Cessna	Tweedie Bird	
T-37A	TX	D Rio	LAFB	Cessna	Tweedie Bird	
T-37B	AL	Birmingham	SMoF	Cessna	Tweedie Bird	
T-37B	AZ	Tucso	PAM	Cessna	Tweedie Bird	57-2267
T-37B	CA	Riverside	MAFM	Cessna	Tweedie Bird	57-2316
T-37B	FL	Clearwater	FMAM	Cessna	Tweedie Bird	
T-37B	GA	Warner Robin	MoF	Cessna	Tweedie Bird	57-2261
T-37B	MI	Battl	BCANG	Cessna	Tweedie Bird	
T-37B	MS	Colum	CAFB	Cessna	Tweedie Bird	

Model	State	City	Location	Manufacturer	Name	Notes
T-37B	OH	Dayto	USAFM	Cessna	Tweedie Bird	
T-37B	TX	Abile	PSCAF	Cessna	Tweedie Bird	54-2734
T-37B	TX	San A	RAFB	Cessna	Tweedie Bird	
T-38	CA	Carls	CAJM	Northrop	Talon	
T-38	CA	LAnge	CMoS&I	Northrop	Talon	
T-38	IL	Bloom	PAM	Northrop	Talon	50-549
T-38(F-5B)	IL	Ranto	OCAM	Northrop	Freedom Fighter	Thunderbirds #1, Tiger II
T-38	IN	Edinburg	VFW 233	Northrop	Talon	00558
T-38	KS	Liber	MAAM	Northrop	Talon	
T-38	MN	Dulut	CityPark	Northrop	Talon	
T-38	NM	Gallup	GMA	Northrop	Talon	
T-38	NY	Moria	AL	Northrop	Talon	
T-38	OK	Weatherford	GTSM	Northrop	Talon	
T-38A(YT)	SD	Rapid	SDA&SM	Northrop	Talon	58-1192
T-38	TX	Big Springs	H25	Northrop	Talon	
T-38	TX	Burnet	HLS-CAF	Northrop	Talon	
T-38	TX	C Christi	USS Lexi	Northrop	Talon	
T-38	TX	D Rio	LAFB	Northrop	Talon	
T-38A	AL	Montg	MAFB	Northrop	Talon	
T-38A	AZ	Tucso	PAM	Northrop	Talon	61-854
T-38A	CA	Chino	YAM	Northrop	Talon	
T-38A	CA	Riverside	MFAM	Northrop	Talon	60-0593
T-38A	CA	Rosam	EAFB	Northrop	Talon	61-810
T-38A	CA	Sacra	McCelAFB	Northrop	Talon	60- 551
T-38A	CO	CSpri	USAFA	Northrop	Talon	
T-38A	KS	Hutch	KC&SC	Northrop	Talon	
T-38A	MS	Colum	CAFB	Northrop	Talon	
T-38A	NM	Santa Teresa	WEAM	Northrop	Talon	
T-38A(AT)	OH	Dayto	USAFM	Northrop	Talon	
T-38A	OR	Mc Minnville	EAEC	Northrop	Talon	63-8224
T-38A	TX	Abile	DLAP	Northrop	Talon	60-0592
T-38A	TX	San A	LAFB	Northrop	Talon	59-1605
T-38A	TX	Wichi	SAFB	Northrop	Talon	
T-38A(QT)	AZ	Mesa	WAFB	Northrop	Talon	
T-38B	KY	Lexington	AMoK	Northrop	Talon	64-13292
T-39A	CA	Riverside	MFAM	North American	Sabreliner	62-4465
T-39	MO	SLoui	SLUPC	North American	Sabreliner	
T-39	MT	Helena	CoT	North American	Sabreliner	
T-39 Parts	TX	Ladero	Airport	North American	Sabreliner	
T-39	UT	Ogden	HAFBM	North American	Sabreliner	
T-39A	CA	Fairf	TAFB	North American	Sabreliner	
T-39A	GA	Warner Robin	MoF	North American	Sabreliner	62-4461A
T-39A	OH	Dayto	USAFM	North American	Sabreliner	62-4478
T-39A	TX	Abile	DLAP	North American	Sabreliner	61-634
T-39A	WI	Milwa	MANG	North American	Sabreliner	
T-39A(CT)	AZ	Tucso	PAM	North American	Sabreliner	62-4449
T-39A(CT)	CA	Rosam	EAFB	North American	Sabreliner	60-3505
T-39A(CT)	CA	Sacra	McCelAFB	North American	Sabreliner	61-660
T-39A(CT)	CA	San B	NAFB	North American	Sabreliner	
T-39A(CT)	IL	Sugar Grove	ACM	North American	Sabreliner	60-3503
T-39A(CT)	IL	Belle	SAFB	North American	Sabreliner	
T-39A(CT)	IL	Cahokia	PCUSL	North American	Sabreliner	03504
T-39A(CT)	IL	Ranto	OCAM	North American	Sabreliner	62-4494
T-39A(CT)	TX	San A	LAFB	North American	Sabreliner	
T-39A-NA	NE	Ashland	SACM	North American	Sabreliner	62- 4487
T-39D	AL	Birmingham	SMoF	North American	Sabreliner	
T-39D	MD	Lexington	PRNAM	North American	Sabreliner	150987, USNTPS Tail
T-40	WI	Oshko	EAAAAM	Turner	TEDDE	N191T, "Ophelia Bumps"
T-41	FL	Clearwater	FMAM	Cessna	Mescalero	
T-41	IN	Peru	GAFB	Cessna	Mescalero	
T-41A	OH	Dayto	USAFM	Cessna	Mescalero	
T-41B	GA	Hampton	AAHF	Cessna	Mescalero	
T-41B	NC	Asheboro	PFAC	Cessna	Mescalero	
T-46A	CA	Rosam	EAFB	Fairchild/Republic	Demonstrator	N73RA
T-46(NGT)	NY	Garde	CoAM	Fairchild/Republic	Demonstrator	
T-20	AB-C	Nanton	NLSAM	Cessna	Crane 1	Bamboo Bomber
T-50	AB-C	Calga	AMoC	Cessna	Crane 1	Bamboo Bomber
T-50	AB-C	Wetas	RM	Cessna	Crane 1	Bamboo Bomber
T-50	AK	Ancho	AAHM	Cessna	Crane 1	Bamboo Bomber
T-50	CA	Shafter	MFAM	Cessna	Crane 1	Bamboo Bomber
T-50	CA	Chino	YACM	Cessna	Crane 1	Bamboo Bomber, N46617, 5193
T-50	FL	Pensa	USNAM	Cessna	Crane 1	Bamboo Bomber, N63426, 5515
T-50	IL	Harva	BA	Cessna	Crane 1	Bamboo Bomber
T-50(UC-78)	IN	Auburn	HW	Cessna	Crane 1	Bamboo Bomber
T-50D	KS	Liber	MAAM	Cessna	Crane 1	Bamboo Bomber
T-50(UC-78)	KS	Wichita	CAF-J	Cessna	Crane 1	Bamboo Bomber
T-50	MB-C	Brandon	CATPM	Cessna	Crane 1	Bamboo Bomber
T-50	MB-C	Winni	WCAM	Cessna	Crane 1	Bamboo Bomber
T-50	OH	Newbu	WASAC	Cessna	Crane 1	Bamboo Bomber, NC60145
T-50	OK	Fredi	AAM	Cessna	Crane 1	Bamboo Bomber
T-50	ON-C	Campbellford	MMM	Cessna	Crane 1	Bamboo Bomber
T-50	ON-C	Ottaw	CAM	Cessna	Crane 1	Bamboo Bomber
T-50	SK-C	MJaw	WDM	Cessna	Crane 1	Bamboo Bomber
T-50	TX	Galve	LSFM	Cessna	Crane 1	Bamboo Bomber, N51469, 6614
T-50	TX	Midla	CAF-Hq	Cessna	Crane 1	Bamboo Bomber, N1238N
T2C	TX	C Christi	USS Lexi			
T2V(T-1A)	AZ	Tucso	PAM	Lockheed	Seastar	144200
T8P-1	AB-C	Calga	AMoC	Barkley	Grow	Storage
T8P-1	AB-C	Calga	AMoC	Barkley	Grow	
Tacit Blue	OH	Dayto	USAFM	Northrop	Whale	"Tatic Blue",
Target Drone	NM	STere	WEAM			
Target Drone	NY	Hammo	CM			
Task Silhouette	WA	Seatt	MoF	Task	Silhouette	TR601, N84TR
Taylor Aerocar	WI	Oshko	EAAAAM	Taylor	Aerocar	N4994P
Taylor Aerocar	WY	Jackson	GWFM	Taylor	Aerocar	
Taylor Monoplane	BC-C	Langley	CMoF&T	Taylor		
Taylor Monoplane	MI	Kalamazoo	KAHM	Taylor	Monoplane	
Taylor Monoplane	WI	Fond du Lac	WAM	Taylor	Monoplane	
Taylor Monoplane HB	WI	Oshko	EAAAAM	Taylor		N5406E
Taylor Titsch	CA	Santa Martin	WoHAM	Taylor	Titsch	Homebuilt, Year 1980
Taylor Young	FL	Kissi	FTWAM	Taylor	Young	
Taylor Young A	IA	Ottumwa	APM	Taylor	Young	
Taylor Young Model A	PA	Readi	MAAM	Taylor Young	Model A	
Taylorcraft	MN	Winoma	WTI	Taylorcraft		N438RM
Taylorcraft	WA	Vancouver	PAM	Taylorcraft		
Taylorcraft A	OH	Allia	FBA	Taylorcraft		

Taylorcraft A	WA	Everett	MoF	Taylorcraft	Classic CG	398, NC19893
Taylorcraft BC	WI	Oshko	EAAAAM	Taylorcraft		N21292
Taylorcraft BC-12	IA	Greenfield	IAM	Taylorcraft		
Taylorcraft BC-12	WA	Seatt	MoF	Taylorcraft		8171, N95871
Taylorcraft BC-12D	NY	River	RE	Taylorcraft		
Taylorcraft BC-12D	NC	Hendersonville	WNCAM	Taylorcraft		
Taylorcraft BC-12D	TX	RioHo	TAM	Taylorcraft		SN9404, N95004
Taylorcraft BC-65	NY	Rhine	ORA	Taylorcraft		
Taylorcraft BC-65	OC-C	Ottawa	CAM	Taylorcraft		
Taylorcraft Model 20	ON-C	Sault Ste Marie	CBHC	Taylorcraft	Auster	CF-FTC
Taylorcraft Mk VII	AB-C	Calga	AMoC	Taylorcraft	Auster	
Taylorcraft TG-6	AZ	Tucson	PAM	Taylorcraft	TG-6	Sn 42-58662, N59134
TBF	CA	S.Mon	MoF	Grumman	Avenger	
TBF	LA	New Orleans	DDM	Grumman	Avenger	
TBF	ND	Fargo	FAM	Grumman	Avenger	# 89, CO
TBF	TX	C Christi	USS Lexi	Grumman	Avenger	
TBF-1	CA	Chino	YACM	Grumman	Avenger	5997, 5997
TBF-1	MD	Silve	PEGF	Grumman	Avenger	
TBM	AB-C	Wetas	RM	Grumman	Avenger	
TBM	AL	Troy	TMA	Grumman	Avenger	
TBM	FL	FtLau	WJAIS&L	Grumman	Avenger	
TBM	ID	Twin	NWWI	Grumman	Avenger	
TBM	MA	Stow	BCF	Grumman	Avenger	
TBM	MB-C	N Brunswick	NBM	Grumman	Avenger	14, C-GLEK
TBM	ND	Minot	DTAM	Grumman	Avenger	
TBM	ND	Wahpe	TSA	Grumman	Avenger	
TBM	NM	STere	WEAM	Grumman	Avenger	
TBM	NS-C	Halifax	ACAM	Grumman	Avenger	
TBM	NS-C	Shear	CFBS	Grumman	Avenger	
TBM	NY	E Garden City	CoA	Grumman	Avenger	
TBM	NY	NYC	ISASM	Grumman	Avenger	2
TBM	NY	Farmingdale	AAM	Grumman	Avenger	2, 401SL
TBM	OH	Newbu	WASAC	Grumman	Avenger	
TBM	TX	Frede	NMofPW	Grumman	Avenger	
TBM-3	WA	Olmypia	OFM	Grumman	Avenger	Side # T-88
TBM-3	CA	Alameda	UUSHM	Grumman	Avenger	69-375
TBM-3	CA	Palm Springs	PoFAM	Grumman	Avenger	7154, NX7835C, Side # 2, "Barbara"
TBM-3	CA	Oakla	OWAM	Grumman	Avenger	E2
TBM-3	CO	GJunc	CAF-RMW	Grumman	Avenger	N53503
TBM-3	FL	Miami	WOM	Grumman	Avenger	N9548Z
TBM-3	MN	Minne	JJ	Grumman	Avenger	
TBM-3	KS	Liber	MAAM	Grumman	Avenger	R8 123
TBM-3	MN	Minne	JJ	Grumman	Avenger	
TBM-3	NS-C	Halifax	HAM	Grumman	Avenger	
TBM-3	OK	Fredi	AAM	Grumman	Avenger	
TBM-3	TX	College Station	GBLM	Grumman	Avenger	
TBM-3	TX	C Christi	NAS	Grumman	Avenger	
TBM-3	TX	Hawki	RRSA	Grumman	Avenger	
TBM-3	TX	Midla	CAFFM	Grumman	Avenger	
TBM-3	VA	Quant	MCAGM	Grumman	Avenger	85890
TBM-3E	AZ	Tucso	PAM	Grumman	Avenger	N9593C, 69472
TBM-3E	CA	Palm Sprg	PSAM	Grumman	Avenger	NL7075C, JR 456
TBM-3E	CA	Miramar	FLAM	Grumman	Avenger	VMTB-242
TBM-3E	FL	Jacks	NASCF	Grumman	Avenger	91664, SM
TBM-3E	FL	Pensa	USNAM	Grumman	Avenger	N 6822C, 53593
TBM-3E	MD	Fredericks	CAFS&S	Grumman	Avenger	
TBM-3E	NC	Asheboro	PFAC	Grumman	Avenger	14, N6824C,
TBM-3E	NS-C	Halifax	HAM	Grumman	Avenger	91586
TBM-3E	NY	Garde	CoAM	Grumman	Avenger	91752, #64, 401SL
TBM-3E	NY	Horseheads	NWM	Grumman	Avenger	91726, N5260V
TBM-3E	OR	McMinnville	EAEC	Grumman	Avenger	91726, N6447C
TBM-3E	OR	Tillamook	TAM	Grumman	Avenger	53914
TBM-3E	RI	NKing	QAM	Grumman	Avenger	
TBM-3E	SC	Mt Pleasant	PPM	Grumman	Avenger	91453, N4170A, VMT232
TBM-3E	TN	Sevierville	TMoA	Grumman	Avenger	
TBM-3E	TX	C Christi	USS Lexi	Grumman	Avenger	N86280, CVE 54 109
TBM-3E	TX	Dalla	CFM	Grumman	Avenger	N700RW, 69329
TBM-3E	TX	Galve	LSFM	Grumman	Avenger	53454, VS-22/801
TBM-3E	VA	Suffolk	FF	Grumman	Avenger	
TDD-1	FL	Pensa	USNAM	Radioplane	Target Drone	43-2, A
TDD-2(PQ-14A)	FL	Pensa	USNAM	Radioplane	Target Drone	120082
TDD-2(PQ-14A)	MD	Silver Hill	PEGF	Radioplane	Target Drone	
TDR-1	FL	Pensa	USNAM	Radioplane		33529
TDU-25B	CA	Chino	YAM	Hayes Int'l	Tow Target Drone	
Teal Ruby Satellite	OH	Dayton	USAFM	Teal	Ruby	
Teasdale	NY	Elmir	NSM			
Temple Aero Sportsman	TX	Dallas	FoFM	Temple Aero Corp	Sportsma	C-987N, "Texas Temple"
Terrapin	NY	Garde	CoAM	Republic	Terrapin Rocket	
TG-1A	MD	Silve	PEGF	Frankfort	Cinema B	
TG-1A	NM	Moriarty	SSM	Frankfort	Cinema B	
TG-1A	WY	Jackson	GWFM	Frankfort	Cinema B	
TG-1A-FR	BC-C	Langley	CMoF&T	Frankfort	Cinema B	42-52, CF-MDZ Cinema
TG-2(LNS-1)	CA	Riverside	MFAM	Great Lakes	Martin TG-2	N54301
TG-2(LNS-1)	MI	Kalam	KAHM	Great Lakes	Martin TG-2	04383
TG-2(LNS-1)	NY	Horseheads	NWM	Great Lakes	Martin TG-2	
TG-3A	AZ	Tucso	PAM	Schweizer	Glider	Man Sn 15, N69064
TG-3A	AZ	Tucso	PAM	Schweizer	Glider	Man Sn 32, N63905
TG-3A	BC-C	Langley	CMoF&T	Schweizer	Glider	42-529, N33637
TG-3A	CA	Atwater	CAM	Schweizer	Glider	
TG-3A	CO	Denve	JWDAS	Schweizer	Glider	
TG-3A	NY	Elmir	NSM	Schweizer	Glider	43, N61279
TG-3A(LNE-1)	NY	Ghent	POMAM	Schweizer	Glider	
TG-3A(LNE-1)	OH	Dayto	USAFM	Schweizer	Glider	
TG-3A	TX	Midla	CAF-Hq	Schweizer	Glider	N87603
TG-4A	AL	Birmingham	SMoF	Laister-Kauffman	Glider	
TG-4A	CO	Denve	JWDAS	Laister-Kauffman	Glider	
TG-4A	GA	Warner Robin	MoF	Laister-Kauffman	Glider	42-43740, N43LK
TG-4A	MI	Kalam	KAHM	Laister-Kauffman	Glider	92
TG-4A	NM	Moriarty	SSM	Laister-Kauffman	Glider	
TG-4A	OH	Dayto	USAFM	Laister-Kauffman	Glider	
TG-5	TX	Slato	TAMCC	Aeronca	Glider	
TGM-13	CO	Flage	VWF			
Thaden Transporter	CA	SCarl	HAM	Thaden	Transporter	
Tharps	AR	Fayetteville	AAM	Tharps	Homebuilt	
Thomas Pidgeon	CA	Chino	YACM	Thomas	Pidgeon	1
Thomas Pusher	NY	Rhine	ORA	Thomas	Pusher	

Name	St	City	Museum	Mfr	Model	Notes
Tilbury Flash	IL	Bloom	McLCHS	Tilbury	Flash	NR12931
Tocan Ultrlight	AB-C	Edmonton	AAM	Tocan	Ultrlight	
Trains 6	OH	Dayto	CP			
Trains 60	MO	SLoui	NMoT			
Train K30 N Guage	CA	Inyo	INP		#18	
Transporter-Erector	ND	Grand	GFAFB			
Travel Air	IL	Urban	RFIA	Travel Air		
Travel Air 1000	CA	Lanca	BA	Travel Air	Mystery	
Travel Air 1000	IL	Chica	MoS&I	Travel Air	Mystery	
Travel Air 1000	TN	Tulla	SMF	Travel Air	Mystery	
Travel Air 2000	VA	Sands	VAM	Travel Air	Mystery	Sn 721 CAM Travel Air
Travel Air 2000	ON-C	Ottaw	CAM	Travel Air		
Travel Air 2000	WI	Oshko	EAAAAM	Travel Air		N241
Travel Air 4000	AR	Fayet	AAM	Travel Air		
Travel Air 4000	CA	Hayward	VAM	Travel Air		
Travel Air 4000(D4D)	KY	Lexington	AMoK	Travel Air		N434N
Travel Air 4000	MO	Maryland Hts	HARM	Travel Air		
Travel Air 4000	NY	Ghent	POMAM	Travel Air		
Travel Air 4000	NY	River	TFAC	Travel Air		
Travel Air 4000	TN	Tulla	SMF	Travel Air		
Travel Air 4000	WA	Vancouver	PAM	Travel Air		
Travel Air 4000E	ON-C	Hamilton	CWH	Travel Air		
Travel Air 4000E	WI	Oshko	EAAAAM	Travel Air		NC 648H
Travel Air 6000-A	WY	Jackson	GWFM	Travel Air		
Travel Air 6000A	AR	Fayet	AAM	Travel Air		N377M
Travel Air 6000A	TN	Tulla	SMF	Travel Air		
Travel Air 6000B	AK	Ancho	AAHM	Travel Air		
Travel Air 6000B	GA	Atlanta	DATHM	Curtiss-Wright	Sedan 6B	6B-2040, ATC 352, Reg 447W
Troyer VX	PA	Readi	MAAM	Troyer	Troyer VX	
TS-1	FL	Pensa	USNAM			A 6446
TS-11	CA	Chino	PoFAM	Polish	Iskra	
TS-11	MI	Belleville	YAF	Polish	Iskra	1H1019, N101TS
TS-11	TX	Dalla	CFM	Polish	Iskra	
Tu-2	FL	Polk	FoF	Tupolev	Bat	
Tu-2	NM	STere	WEAM	Tupolev	Bat	
TU-6	TX	Ft Worth	SAM	Charic		
U-2	CA	Moffe	NASAAVC			
U-2	MD	Silve	PEGF	Mitchell	Superwing	
U-2 Flying Wing	AB-C	Calga	AMoC	Mitchell	Flying Wing	
U-2A	OH	Dayto	USAFM			56-6722
U-2C	AZ	Tucso	DMAFB	Lockheed	Gray Ghost	
U-2C	DC	Washi	NA&SM	Lockheed	Gray Ghost	
U-2C	GA	Warner Robin	MoF	Lockheed	Dragon Lady	56- 6682
U-2C	TX	D Rio	LAFB	Lockheed	Gray Ghost	
U-2C-LO	NE	Ashland	SACM	Lockheed	Gray Ghost	56- 6701, "Dragon Lady"
U-2CT	CA	Rosam	EAFB	Lockheed	Gray Ghost	56- 6953
U-2D	CA	Rosam	EAFB			
U-2R	CA	Marys	BAFB			
U-3A	AL	Ozark	USAAM	Cessna	Blue Canoe	57- 5863
U-3A	CA	Atwater	CAM	Cessna	Blue Canoe	57-5849
U-3A	CA	Fairf	TAFB	Cessna	Blue Canoe	
U-3A	CO	Denve	JWDAS	Cessna	Blue Canoe	
U-3A	CO	Denve	WOR	Cessna	Blue Canoe	
U-3A	IN	Peru	GAFB	Cessna	Blue Canoe	57- 5922
U-3A	MI	Mt Clemens	SMAM	Cessna	Blue Canoe	58-2111
U-3A	OH	Dayto	USAFM	Cessna	Blue Canoe	58-2124
U-3A	SD	Rapid	SDA&SM	Cessna	Blue Canoe	57-5872
U-3A	UT	Ogden	HAFBM	Cessna	Blue Canoe	
U-3A(L-27A)	AZ	Tucso	PAM	Cessna	Blue Canoe	58- 2107
U-3B9D	GA	Warner Robin	MoF	Cessna	Blue Canoe	60- 6052
U-4A	AL	Ozark	USAAM	Aero	Commander	55-4640
U-4B	GA	Warner Robin	MoF	Aero	Commander	63- 7948, N37948
U-4B	OH	Dayton	USAFM	Aero	Commander	
U-505 German	IL	Chica	MoS&I		Submarine	
U-8	CO	Denve	JWDAS	Beech	Queen-Air	
U-8	KS	Wichita	KAM	Beech	Queen-Air	
U-8	GA	Hampton	AAHF	Beech	Queen-Air	
U-9A(YU)	AL	Ozark	USAAM	Aero Eng.	Commander	52- 6219
U-9A	CA	Riverside	MFAM	Aero	Commander	52-6218
U-9A	KS	Liberal	MAAM	Aero	Commander	
U-9A	WI	Kenos	KMM	Aero	Commander	
U-10	CO	Denve	JWDAS	Helio	Courier	
U-10(YU)(YL-24)	AL	Ozark	USAAM	Helio	Courier	52-2540
U-10A	FL	FtWal	HF	Helio	Courier	62- 3606, AH
U-10D	GA	Warner Robin	MoF	Helio	Super Courier	63-13096, N87743
U-10D	OH	Dayto	USAFM	Helio	Super Courier	
U-21	CO	Denve	JWDAS	Beech	Ute	
U-21(YU)	AL	Ozark	USAAM	Beech	Ute	63-12902
U-21G	GA	Hampton	AAHF	Beech	Ute	
UFM Easy Riser	WI	Oshko	EAAAAM	UFM	Easy Riser	
Ultra-Light	CA	Chino	PoFAM			
Ultimate 100	ON-C	Toronto	TAM	Ultimate	100	
Unident Atec	MN	Winoma	WTI	Unident	Aztec	
Unruh	WI	Oshko	EAAAAM	Unruh	Uhruh	N1473V, "Pretty Prairie Special III"
UTVA-66	FL	Titusville	VAC	YUGO	Trainer	
UAV	MD	Lexington	PRNAM	Israeli Aircraft Industry	Pioneer	101
UV-18	CO	Denver	69thB		Twin Turboprop	
V-1 * See Fi-103 * Flying Bomb						
V-1	FL	Shali	USAFAM	Vultee	Voland	
V-1	ON-C	Ottaw	CAM	Vultee	Voland	
V-1	UT	Ogden	HAM	Vultee	Voland	
V1-A	VA	Sands	VAM	Vultee	Voland	Sn 25
V-1(Fi-103)	VA	Suffolk	FF	Vultee	Voland	
V-1(XV)	AL	Ozark	USAAM	McDonnell	Convertiplane	53-4016
V-2	KS	Hutch	KC&SC	Peene Munde	Rocket	
V-2	MD	Aberd	APG	Peene Munde	Rocket	
V-2	NM	Las Cruces	WSMP	Peene Munde	Rocket	
V-2	OK	Oklah	KCASM	Peene Munde	Rocket	
V-2	OH	Dayton	USAFM	Peene Munde	Rocket	
V-6A(XV)	AL	Ozark	USAAM	Hawker-Siddley	Kestrel	64-19264
V-6A(XV)	OH	Dayto	USAFM	Hawker-Siddley	Kestrel	NASA 521
V-6A(XV)	VA	Hampton	HAP	Hawker-Siddley	Kestrel	64-18266, NASA 520
V-22 Osprey II	AZ	Tucso	PAM	Pereira	Osprey	105, N17EH, A
V-22 Osprey II	ON-C	Toronto	TAM	Pereira	Osprey	
V-22 Osprey II	PA	West Chester	AHM	Bell-Boeing	Osprey	
V-22 Osprey II	WI	Oshko	EAAAAM	Pereira	Osprey	N346JS

V-101B	AR	Roger				
V-173	MD	Silve	PEGF	Vought	Flying Pancake	
Valkyrie Hang Glider	MD	Silve	PEGF	Valkyrie	Hang Glider	
Van Dellen LH-2	IA	Ottumwa	APM	Van Dellen		
Vansgrunsven RV-3	FL	Lakel	SFAF	Vansgrunsven	Homebuilt	N920SR
Vansgrunsven RV-3	WI	Oshkosh	EAAAAM	Vansgrunsven	Homebuilt	
Vansgrunsven RV-4	WI	Oshkosh	EAAAAM	Vansgrunsven	Homebuilt	
Vector 27	WI	Oshko	EAAAAM	Vector		
Velie Model 70	CA	LAnge	CMoS&I	Velie	Monocoupe	
Veligdans Monerai	NY	Garde	CoAM	Veligdans	Monerai Glider	N525S
Venture 200	WI	Oshko	EAAAAM	Questair		N62V
Ventuier Airship	NY	Geneseo	1941AG	Ventuier	Airship	
Vertol 44	BC-C	Langley	CMoF*T	Vertol		
Vertol 44B	CA	Ramona	CR	Vertol		
Verville Sport Trainer	MD	Silve	PEGF	Verille	Sport	
Vickers Vedette V	MB-C	Winni	WCAM	Vickers	Vedette	
Vickers Viking Mk.IV Rep	AB-C	Edmonton	AAM	Vickers	Viking Mk.IV	
Vickers Viscount 744	AZ	Tucso	PAM	Vickers	Viscount 744	Sn 40, N22SN
Vickers Viscount	MB-C	Winni	WCAM	Vickers	Viscount 757	
Vickers Viscount	ON-C	Ottaw	CAM	Vickers	Viscount	
Vickers Viscount	PA	Readi	MAAM	Vickers	Viscount	
Vickers Viscount	WA	Seatt	MoF	Vickers	Viscount 724	
Viking Dragonfly	KS	Liber	MAAM	Viking	Dragonfly	
Viking Dragonfly	OK	Fredi	AAM	Viking	Dragonfly	
Viking Kittyhawk	CT	Winds	NEAM	Viking	Kittyhawk	
VJ-21	CA	Santa Martin	WoHAM	Volmer-Jensen	Powered Glider	
VJ-23	IA	Ottumwa	APM	Volmer-Jensen		
VJ-24	FL	Lakel	SFAF	Lazair	Ultralight	
Voisin Model 8	DC	Washi	NA&SM	Voisin	Model 8	
Voisin Model 8	MD	Silve	PEGF	Voisin	Model 8	
Voisin Model 8	NY	NYC	ISASM	Voisin	Model 8	
Voisin Model 8	NY	Rhine	ORA	Voisin	Model 8	
Volmer Jensen	CA	S.Mar	SMMoF	Volmer-Jensen	Hang Glider	
VP-1	AZ	Tucso	PAM	Evans	Volksplane	N 47188
VP-1	FL	Kissimmee	SNFAM	Evans	Volksplane	
VP-1	IA	Ottumwa	APM	Evans	Volksplane	
VP-1	ND	Minot	DTAM	Evans	Volksplane	
VPS Hu-Go Craft	WI	Oshko	EAAAAM	Hugo	VPS Hu-Go Craft	N29H
VS-300A	DC	Washi	NA&SM	Sikorsky		
VS-300A	MI	Dearborn	HFM	Sikorsky	Helicopter	
VS-300A Cockpit	PA	WChester	AHM	Sikorsky		
VS-316(R-4B)	ON-C	Ottaw	CAM	Sikorsky	Hoverfly	43-46565
VS-44A	CT	Windsor Locks	NEAM	Sikorsky	Excambian	
VZ-2A Vertol	MD	Silve	PEGF	Boeing	Vertol	
VZ-3RY	AL	Ozark	USAAM	Ryan	Vertiplane	56- 6941
VZ-4-DA Doak	VA	FtEus	USATM	Doak		
VZ-8P	PA	WChes	AHM	Piasecki	Airgeep	
VZ-8P	PA	Willo	WGNAS	Piasecki	Airgeep	
VZ-8P-1	VA	FtEus	USATM	Piasecki		
VZ-8P-2	VA	FtEus	USATM	Piasecki		
VZ-9V	MD	Silve	PEGF	Avro-Canada	Avrocar	
VZ-ZAP	AL	Ozark	USAAM			
VZ1 Hiller 1031	CA	SCarl	HAM	Hiller	Flying Platform	
VZ1 Hiller 1031	MD	Silve	PEGF	Hiller	Flying Platform	
Waco	AK	Palme	MOAT&I	Waco		
Waco	AZ	Scott	SA	Waco		
Waco	IL	Urban	RFIA	Waco		
Waco	ND	Minot	DTAM	Waco		
Waco	NY	Rhine	ORA	Waco		
Waco	TX	Houston	1940ATM	Waco		
Waco Model F	MO	Maryland Hts	HARM	Waco	Model F	
Waco 4	OH	Troy	WHS	Waco		
Waco 9	ID	Athol	NAM	Waco		
Waco 9	MD	Silve	PEGF	Waco		
Waco 9	NY	Rhine	ORA	Waco		
Waco 10	CA	San Carlos	HAM	Waco		
Waco 10	CA	Santa Martin	WoHAM	Waco		
Waco 10	FL	Ameli	IAT	Waco		
Waco 125	MN	Bloom	SPMIA	Waco		
Waco 128	MN	Minne	MSPIA	Waco		NC 4576, "Northwest Airways"
Waco AQC-6	BC-C	Langley	CMoF&T	Waco		
Waco Arisocraft "W"	OH	Troy	WHS	Waco	Arisocraft	
Waco ATO	PA	Reading	WAM&ALC	Waco		Sn A118
Waco Cabin UIC	MD	Silve	PEGF	Waco	Cabin	
Waco CTO	OH	Troy	WHS	Waco		
Waco CTO	WI	Oshko	EAAAAM	Waco		NC75527
Waco CUC-1	WY	Jackson	GWFM	Waco	Custom Cabin	
Waco EQC-6	AB-C	Calga	AMoC	Waco	Custom	
Waco Glider	MD	Silve	PEGF	Waco	Glider	
Waco Glider	OH	Troy	WHS	Waco	Glider	
Waco GXE	CA	S.Mon	MoF	Waco	Model 10	
Waco INF	BC-C	Langley	CMoF&T	Waco		
Waco INF	MI	Kalam	KAHM	Waco	INF	NC644V
Waco RNF	AZ	Tucson	PAM	Waco	RNF	Man Sn 3392, NC11206
Waco RNF	WI	Oshkosh	EAAAAM	Waco	RNF	
Waco UBF-2	ME	OwlsH	OHTM	Waco		
Waco UEC	CA	S.Mon	MoF	Waco	Cabin	C Cabin
Waco UIC	AB-C	Edmonton	AAM	Waco		
Waco UPF-7	AB-C	Wetas	RM	Waco		
Waco UPF-7	AZ	Tucso	PAM	Waco		N30135
Waco UPF-7	FL	KeyWe	FWIA	Waco		
Waco UPF-7	ND	Minot	DTAM	Waco		
Waco UPF-7	OH	Troy	WHS	Waco		
Waco UPF-7	VA	Bealt	FCA	Waco		
Waco UPF-7	WA	Vashon	OTA	Waco		Sn 5540, NC30143
Waco UPF-7	WA	Vashon	OTA	Waco		Sn 5871, NC39738
Waco YKS	AK	Ancho	AAHM	Waco		
Waco YKS	AL	Birmi	Southe	Waco		
Waco YKS	SK-C	MJaw	WDM	Waco		
Waco YKS-6	WA	Vashon	OTA	Waco	Trainer	NC16241
Waco YKS-6	ID	Athol	NAM	Waco		
Waco YKS-6	MB-C	Winni	WCAM	Waco		
Waco YKS-7	CA	San Diego	SDAM	Waco		N48980
Waco YKS-7	WI	Oshkosh	EAAAAM	Waco		
Waco YMF	OH	Troy	WHS	Waco		
Waco YPF-7	NC	Durham	CB	WACO	YPF-7	5644

Aircraft	State	City	Museum	Manufacturer	Model	Notes
Waco YOC	AL	Birmi	Southe	Waco		
Waco YOC	VA	Sands	VAM	Waco		Sn 4279
Waco ZKS-6	AZ	Tucso	PAM	Waco		N16523
Wag-Aero CUBy	WI	Oshko	EAAAAM	Brugioni	CUBy	
Wallis Model 3	MI	Belleville	YAM	Wallis	Redwing Black Bird	N65022
Warwick W-4	WI	Oshko	EAAAAM	Warwick		N4777W, "Hot Canary"
Wasol Racer	WA	Vancouver	PAM	Wasol	Formula 1 Racer	Reno
Waspair Tomcat Tourer	WI	Oshko	EAAAAM	Waspair	Tomcat Tourer	"Feeline Fokker IV"
Waterman Aeromobile	MD	Silve	PEGF	Waterman	Aeromobile	
Waterman Whatsit	MD	Silve	PEGF	Waterman	Whatsit	
WD-A	WI	Oshko	EAAAAM	Estupinan Hovey	Wing Ding	N6272
WE-1	WI	Oshko	EAAAAM	Evans	Volksplane	N6414
Weddell-Williams	LA	Patte	WWMAM	Weddell-Williams	Racer	44
Weddell-Williams	OH	Cleve	FCAAM	Weddell-Williams	Special	Model 44
Wee Bee	CA	San Diego	SDAM		Wee Bee	
Weedhopper	NE	Minde	HWPV	Gypsy	Weedhopper	
Weeks Solution	FL	Polk	FoF	Weeks	Solution	
Weeks Special	FL	Polk	FoF	Weeks	Special	
Westland Lysander Rep	AB-C	Edmonton	AAM	Westland	Lysander	
Westland Mk.II	FL	Lakeland	SNF	Westland	Lysander	
Westland Mk.III	BC-C	Langley	CMoF&T	Westland	Lysander	
Westland Mk.III	ON-C	Hamilton	CWH	Westland	Lysander	2361
Westland Mk.III	ON-C	Ottaw	CAM	Westland	Lysander	
Whirlwind	NY	River	TFAC			
Whitaker Centerwing	WI	Oshko	EAAAAM	Whitaker	Centerwing	N121LW
White 1912 Monoplane	TX	McAll	MIA	White	Monoplane	
Wiley Post Biplane	OK	Oklah	KCASM	Wiley	Post Biplane	
Wills Wing XC	ON-C	Ottaw	CAM	Wills	Wing XC	
Windecker Eagle I	MD	Silve	PEGF	Windecker	Eagle	
Windstead Special	PA	Bethel	GAAM	Windstead	Special	2297
Wiseman-Cooke	DC	Washi	USPM	Wiseman-Cooke		
Wiseman-Cooke	MD	Silve	PEGF	Wiseman-Cooke		
Wisman-Prescott	KS	Wichita	KAM	Wittman	Pusher	
Wisman-Prescott	WI	Oshko	WRA	Wittman	Pusher	
Wittman W	WI	Oshko	EAAAAM	Wittman	Midwing	N4486E, "Bonzo"
Wittman Buster	DC	Washi	NA&SM	Wittman	Buster	
Wittman DFA	WI	Oshko	EAAAAM	Wittman		N1292, "Little Bonzo"
Wittman W-8C	NC	Hendersonville	WNCAM	Wittman	Tailwind	
Wittman W-8C	WI	Oshko	WRA	Wittman	Tailwind	N5747N
Woodstock Glider	WI	Fond du Lac	WAM	Woodstock	Glider	
Woody Pusher	FL	Lakel	SFAF	Woody	Pusher	N100FQ
Woolaroc Airplane	OK	Bartl	WM	Woolaroc		NX- 869
Wright 1903	NE	Minde	HWPV	Wright Brothers		
Wright Brothers B	CA	SCarl	HAM	Wright Brothers		
Wright Brothers B	MD	College Park	CPAM	Wright Brothers		
Wright Brothers B	OH	Dayto	USAFM	Wright Brothers		
Wright Brothers B	PA	Phila	FI	Wright Brothers		
Wright Brothers B	VA	Suffolk	FF	Wright Brothers		
Wright EX Vin Fiz	CA	Oakla	OWAM	Wright Brothers	Vin Fiz	
Wright EX Vin Fiz	CA	San Diego	SDAM	Wright Brothers	Vin Fiz	
Wright Ex Vin Fiz	DC	Washi	NA&SM	Wright Brothers	Vin Fiz	
Wright EX Vin Fiz	MA	Stow	BCF	Wright Brothers	Vin Fiz	
Wright EX Vin Fiz	ME	OwlsH	OHTM	Wright Brothers	Vin Fiz	
Wright Flyer	AR	Little Rock	AEC	Wright Brothers	Kitty Hawk Flyer	
Wright Flyer	AZ	Tucso	PAM	Wright Brothers	Kitty Hawk Flyer	
Wright Flyer	CA	San Diego	SDAM	Wright Brothers	Kitty Hawk Flyer	
Wright Flyer	CA	Santa Martin	WoHAM	Wright Brothers	Kitty Hawk Flyer	
Wright Flyer	DC	Washi	NA&SM	Wright Brothers	Kitty Hawk Flyer	
Wright Flyer	FL	Dayto	ERAU	Wright Brothers	Kitty Hawk Flyer	
Wright Flyer	FL	Polk	FoF	Wright Brothers	Kitty Hawk Flyer	
Wright Flyer	IL	Rantoul	OCM	Wright Brothers	Kitty Hawk Flyer	
Wright Flyer	IN	Hagerstown	WWBP	Wright Brothers	Kitty Hawk Flyer	
Wright Flyer	MI	Kalamazoo	KAHM	Wright Brothers	Kitty Hawk Flyer	
Wright Flyer	NC	Mante	WBNM	Wright Brothers	Kitty Hawk Flyer	
Wright Flyer	NC	Ralei	NCMoH	Wright Brothers	Kitty Hawk Flyer	
Wright Flyer	NY	Rhine	ORA	Wright Brothers	Kitty Hawk Flyer	
Wright Flyer	OH	Dayto	CP	Wright Brothers	Kitty Hawk Flyer	
Wright Flyer	OH	Dayto	USAFM	Wright Brothers	Kitty Hawk Flyer	
Wright Flyer	OH	Miamisburg	WBF	Wright Brothers	Kitty Hawk Flyer	Flyable Replica
Wright Flyer	OK	Wetherford	GTSM	Wright Brothers	Kitty Hawk Flyer	
Wright Flyer	OR	McMinnville	EAM	Wright Brothers	Kitty Hawk Flyer	
Wright Flyer	WA	Vancouver	PAM	Wright Brothers	Kitty Hawk Flyer	
Wright Flyer	WI	Oshko	EAAAAM	Wright Brothers	Kitty Hawk Flyer	
Wright Glider	CA	LAnge	CMoS&I	Wright Brothers	Wright Glider	
Wright Glider	NC	Charl	CHAC	Wright Brothers	Wright Glider	
Wright Glider	NC	Mante	WBNM	Wright Brothers	Wright Glider	
Wright Glider	NY	Elmir	NSM	Wright Brothers	Wright Glider	5
Wright Glider	NY	Rhine	ORA	Wright Brothers	Wright Glider	
Wright Glider	VA	Richm	SMoV	Wright Brothers	Wright Glider	
Wright Glider 1900	VA	Sands	VAM	Wright Brothers	Glider	
Wright Glider 1901	VA	Sands	VAM	Wright Brothers	Glider	
Wright Glider 1902	VA	Sands	VAM	Wright Brothers	Glider	
Wright Glider	WA	Seatt	MoF	Wright Brothers	Wright Glider	
Wright Model G Aeroboat	OH	Wapak	NAA&SM	Wright	Aeroboat	
WSA-1	WA	Vancouver	PAM			
WWI Biplane	TX	RioHo	TAM			
X- 1	CA	Chino	PoFAM	Bell	Research	
X- 1	DC	Washi	NA&SM	Bell	Research	"Glamorous Glennis"
X- 1B	OH	Dayto	USAFM	Bell	Research	
X- 1E	OH	Dayton	USAFM		Princeton	46-63
X- 2	CA	Chino	PoFAM			
X- 2	PA	Willo	WGNAS			
X- 3	OH	Dayto	USAFM	Douglas	Stiletto	
X- 4	CA	Rosamond	EAFB	Northrop	Skylancer	
X- 4	CO	CSpri	USAFA	Northrop	Skylancer	
X- 4	OH	Dayto	USAFM	Northrop	Skylancer	
X- 4	WVA		Northrop	Northrop	Skylancer	
X- 5	OH	Dayto	USAFM	Bell	Swept Wing	
X- 7	CA	Chino	PoFAM	Lockheed		
X- 7	OH	Dayton	USAFM	Lockheed		
X- 10	OH	Dayton	USAFM	North American		
X- 13	CA	San Diego	SDAM	Ryan	Vertijet	41619
X- 13	OH	Dayto	USAFM	Ryan	Vertijet	
X- 15A-1	DC	Washi	NA&SM	North American	Research	
X- 15A-2	AZ	Tucso	PAM	North American		56- 6671
X- 15A-2	OH	Dayto	USAFM	North American		

X-17	OH	Dayton	USAFM	Lockheed		
X-21	CA	Rosam	EAFB			55- 408
X-21	OH	Dayton	USAFM	Bell		
X-22	NY	Niagara Falls	NAM	Bell		151521
X-24A(SV-5J)	OH	Dayto	USAFM	Martin	Marietta	
X-24B	OH	Dayto	USAFM	Martin	Marietta	
X-25A	CA	Hawthorne	WMoF	Benson	Gyrocopter	
X-25A	GA	Warner Robin	MoF	Benson	Gyrocopter	N 61CN
X-25A	OH	Dayton	USAFM	Benson	Gyrocopter	
X-25B	CA	Sacra	SWAM			
X-26B	AL	Ozark	USAAM	Lockheed	Quiet One	67-15345
X-28	KS	Liber	MAAM	Sopery	Air Skimmer	
X-28	MI	Kalam	KAHM	Pereira	Air Skimmer	
X-28A	MI	Ypsil	YAF	Sopery	Air Skimmer	
X-29	DC	Washi	NA&SM	Grumman		
X-29A	OH	Dayto	USAFM	Grumman		
X-32	OH	Dayton	USAFM	Boeing	Fighter	
X-112	WI	Oshko	EAAAM	Lippisch	Aerofoil Boat	N 5961V
XB-25B	CA	Rosam	EAFB	Bensen	Gyro-Chute	
XC-99	TX	San A	TA	Convair		
XC-124A	OH	Dayton	USAFM			Tilt Wing 1964
XF-81	OH	Dayton	USAFM	Consolidated	Vultee	44-91000
XF-81	OH	Dayton	USAFM	Consolidated	Vultee	44-91001
XF15C-1	CT	Winds	NEAM	Curtiss-Wright	Stingaree	
XF15C-1	RI	NKing	QAM	Curtiss-Wright	Stingaree	01215
XF2Y-1	MD	Balti	OMA	Convair	Sea Dart	
XF2Y-1	MD	Silve	PEGF	Convair	Sea Dart	
XF2Y-1	PA	Willo	WGNAS	Convair	Sea Dart	135764
XF2Y-1	WA	Seatt	MoF	Convair	Sea Dart	135765
XF2Y-1(SF)	FL	Lakel	SFAF	Convair	Sea Dart	135765
XF2Y-1(YF)	CA	San Diego	SDAM	Convair	Sea Dart	135763
XFV-1	FL	Lakel	SFAF	Lockheed	Salmon	138657
XFV-1	FL	Pensa	USNAM	Lockheed	VTO	
XFY-1	MD	Silve	PEGF	Convair		
XJL-1	AZ	Tucso	PAM	Columbia	Columbia	31400 N 54205
XO-60	MD	Silve	PEGF	Kellett	Autogiro	
XR-8	MD	Silve	PEGF	Kellett	Autogiro	
XRG-65	PA	WChes	AHM	Glaticopter	Helicopter	
XROE	CA	SCarl	HAM			
XROE	MD	Lexington	PRNAM	Goodyear	Inflatoplane	
XROE-1	AL	Ozark	USAAM			4004
XRON-1	NY	Elmira	B&ECN&SP	Gyrodyne	Rotorcycle	
XRON-1	NY	Garde	CoAM	Gyrodyne	Rotorcycle	4014
XV-1	MD	Silve	PEGF		Conovertiplane	
Yak 3	CA	Camarillo	CAF-SCW	Yakovlev		On loan
Yak 3	ID	Nampa	WAM	Yakovlev		
Yak 3U	TX	RioHo	TAM	Yakovlev		
Yak 3UA	CA	Santa Monica	MoF	Yakovlev		NX854DP
Yak 9	WA	Seattle	MoF	Yakovlev		
Yak 11	CA	Chino	PoFAM	Yakovlev	Moose	
Yak 11	FL	Miami	WOM	Yakovlev	Moose	N 111K
Yak 11	TX	RioHo	TAM	Yakovlev	Moose	
Yak 18	CA	Chino	PoFAM	Yakovlev	Max	
Yak 18	MD	Silve	PEGF	Yakovlev	Max	
Yak 18	VA	Suffolk	FF	Yakovlev		1160314
Yak 50	OR	Mc Minnville	EAEC	Yakovlev		832604
Yak 52	CA	S.Mon	MoF	Yakovlev		
Yak 52	CA	Santa Rosa	PCAM	Yakovlev		
Yak 52	FL	Miami	WOM	Yakovlev		
Yak 55	VA	Suffolk	FF	Yakovlev		
YF-12A(YF)	OH	Dayto	USAFM	Lockheed		60- 6935 Model A-11
YF-22	OH	Dayto	USAFM			
YIM-99B	WA	Brews	CityPark			
YCGM-121B	OH	Dayton	USAFM	Boeing	Brave 200	"Seek Spinner"
YO3A	CA	SanCarlos	HAM	Lockheed	Quiet Star	
Yokosuka P1Y1c	MD	Silver Hill	PEGF	Yokosuka	Frances	
Youngsters Simulator	KY	Lexington	AmoK	Youngsters	Simulator	
YPT-9B	CA	Chino	YACM			6004 N 795H
YQM-94A RPV	OH	Dayton	USAFM	Boeing	Compass Cope B	
YQM-98A Drone	AZ	Tucso	PAM			72- 1872
YS-11A-600	TX	Ladero	Airport	Nihon		N-173RV
Zenair Zenith	MO	Maryland Hts	HARM	Zenair	Zenith	
Zenair Zenith	ON-C	Toronto	TAM	Zenair	Zenith	
Zephyr Zal	CT	Winds	NEAM	Zephyr	Zal	
Zimmerman	MD	Silve	PEGF	Zimmerman	Flying Platform	
Zlin 526M	CA	Santa Rosa	PCAM	Zlin		
Zoegling Glider Rep	NM	Moriarty	SSM	Zoegling	Glider	
Zoegling Glider	SK-C	MJaw	WDM	Zoegling	Glider	
ZPG Rudder	FL	Pensa	USNAM	ZRG	Rudder	141561
Zugvogel III-B	AZ	Tucso	PAM	Zugvogel		N 111MG

Armored Vehicles

Personnel Carrier:

Fort T-16	OH	Norwalk	FmoMH		Armored Personel	
Mark VII Ferrett	OH	Norwalk	FmoMH	British	Armored Car	
M75 APC	AL	Mobil	BMP		Armored Personel	16196782
M84 APC	NY	Buffa	B&ECNP		Armored Personel	

Tanks:

Tank	IL	Sprin	S.ArmyNG			
Tank	IN	Van Buren	VFW			
Tank	IN	Warsaw	City Square			
Tank	TX	Harli	MMA			
Tanks	IA	Des Moines	ING			6 Different Tanks
Tank M-1A	WI	Kenosha	KMM	Abrams		In Movie "Curage Under Fire"
Tank M-3	NJ	Dover	PAAM			
Tank M-3	TX	Frede	NMofPW			
Tank M-4	AL	Mobile	BMP	Stuart	Sherman Light	D51011
Tank M-4	AL	Starke	CBM	Stuart	Sherman Light	
Tank M-4	CA	Chino	PoF	Stuart	Sherman Light	
Tank M-4	IN	Scottsburg	INGC	Stuart	Sherman Light	
Tank M-4	LA	Many	VFW	Stuart	Sherman Light	
Tank M-4	ON-C	Oshaw	OAM&IM	Stuart	Sherman Light	
Tank M-4	WI	Kenos	KMM	Stuart	Sherman Light	D706

173

Tank M-4	WI	Kenos	KMM	Stuart	Sherman Light	70676A, Training Turret
Tank M-4A1	IL	Wheat	Cantigny	Stuart	Sherman Light	
Tank M-4A1	IN	Atterbury	CAM&MC	Stuart	Sherman Light	2-2084
Tank M-4A1	IN	Atterbury	CAM&MC	Stuart	Sherman Light	1-2451
Tank M-4A1E8	OH	Hubbard	WWIIVM	Stuart	Sherman Light	
Tank M-4A3E8	IL	Wheaton	FDM	Stuart	Sherman Light	
Tank M-4A3(75)VVSS	IN	Sunman	AM	Stuart	Sherman Light	
Tank M-4A3	LA	New Orleans	DDM	Stuart	Sherman Light	
Tank M-4A3	OH	Hubbard	WWIIVM	Stuart	Sherman Light	
Tank M-4A3	SC	Citadel	CC	Stuart	Sherman Light	
Tank M-4A3	TX	FtBli	TCRM	Stuart	Sherman Light	
Tank M-5	IL	Wheaton	FDM	Stuart	Sherman Light	C105826
Tank M-5A	WI	Kenos	KMM	Stuart	Sherman Light	M5058147
Tank M-5A1	OH	Carroll	HAS	Stuart	Sherman Light	
Tank M-7B1	OH	Hubbard	WWIIVM	Stuart	105 mm	
Tank M-7	WI	Kenos	KMM	Stuart	105 mm	
Tank M-8	PA	Tough	CFCM	Barlett	Hovercraft	
Tank M-18C	MD	Silve	PEGF	Mooney	Mite	
Tank M-19	OH	Hubbard	WWIIVM		Duster	
Tank M-24	ON-C	Oshaw	OAM&IM			
Tank M-26	AL	Mobile	BMP		Pershing	E10609
Tank M-31	NJ	Dover	PAAM			
Tank M-37	WI	Kenos	KMM	Stuart	105 mm	
Tank M-38	WI	Kenos	KMM	Stuart	105 mm	
Tank M-38A1	WI	Kenos	KMM	Stuart		
Tank M-41	IL	Wheaton	FDM	Walker	Walker Bulldog	254
Tank M-41	IN	Atterbury	CAM&MC	Stuart	Walker Bulldog	38-1-1, 138
Tank M-41	IN	Atterbury	CAM&MC	Stuart	Walker Bulldog	
Tank M-41	NY	Buffa	B&ECNP	Walker	Walker Bulldog	
Tank M-41	WA	Tilli	CMANGP	Walker	Walker Bulldog	
Tank M-41	WI	Kenosha	KMM	Walker	Walker Bulldog	#26
Tank M-42A1	AL	Mobile	BMP	General Motors	Duster	112L729
Tank M-42 Twin	IN	Atterbury	CAM&MC	General Motors	Duster	
Tank M-42 Twin	NY	NYC	ISASM	General Motors	Duster	
Tank M-42 Twin	OH	Groveport	MMM	General Motors	Duster	40 mm
Tank M-42 Twin	OH	Norwalk	FMoMH	General Motors	Duster	40 mm
Tank M-42 Twin	PA	Smethport	AAAM	General Motors	Duster	40 mm
Tank M-42 Twin	WI	Kenosha	KMM	General Motors	Duster	40 mm
Tank M-46	IL	Wheat	Cantigny	Chrysler	Patton	J26E4
Tank M-46	IN	Cromw	City	Chrysler	Patton	
Tank M-46	WI	Kenos	KMM	Chrysler	Patton	
Tank M-47	WI	Kenos	KMM	Chrysler	Patton	Korean
Tank M-47	IL	Wheat	FDM	Chrysler	Patton	2313
Tank M-47	IN	Atterbury	CAM&MC	Chrysler	Patton	A00193, 753710338
Tank M-47	IN	Atterbury	CAM&MC	Chrysler	Patton	38-11, 138, K7389955 Ser 4
Tank M-47	OH	Groveport	MMM	Chrysler	Patton	331
Tank M-48	IL	Wheat	FDM	Chrysler	Patton	2650
Tank M-48	NC	C Lejeune	CL	Chrysler	Patton	
Tank M-48A1	AL	Mobil	BMP	Chrysler	Patton	8369684
Tank M-48A1	PA	Smethport	AAAM	Chrysler	Patton	
Tank M50	IN	Atterbury	CAM&MC		OWTOS	Six 106mm's
Tank M-51	NJ	Dover	PAAM	Douglas		
Tank M-60	AL	Starke	CBM	Chrysler	Patton	
Tank M-60	AL	Tuscaloosa	I-20/59	Chrysler	Patton	
Tank M-60	AR	Littl	LRAFB	Chrysler	Patton	
Tank M-60	CA	Imperial	PM	Chrysler	Patton	
Tank M-60	D.C.	Washington	USS&AH	Chrysler	Patton	
Tank M-60	IL	Wheaton	FDM	Chrysler	Patton	280
Tank M-60	IN	Atterbury	CAM&MC	Chrysler	Patton	1201 (7953748) 105mm
Tank M-60	IN	South Bend	MHP	Chrysler	Patton	
Tank M-60	KY	Middleboro	LS	Chrysler	Patton	
Tank M-60	NY	NYC	ISASM	Chrysler	Patton	
Tank M-60	NC	C Lejeune	CL	Chrysler	Patton	
Tank M-60	OH	Norwalk	FMoMH	Chrysler	Patton	
Tank M-60A1	AL	Mobile	BMP	Chrysler	Patton	8208
Tank M-60A-1	MI	Sterling Hts	FHCMP	Chrysler	Patton	
Tank M-60A-3	TN	Caryville	I-75 & US25W	Chrysler	Patton	
Tank M-60	WI	Kenos	KMM	Chrysler	Patton	
Tank M551	IL	Wheaton	FDM		Sheridan	725
Tank M551A	NC	Charlotte	CAM		Sheridan	1447 Airborne
Tank MK3	TX	Frede	NMofPW			
Tank T-55	AL	Mobile	BMP			1184 USATTU
Tank T-26E4	IL	Wheat	FDM		Pershing	
Tanks	WA	Tacom	FL			
Tanks	VA	Quantico	MCAGM			

Missiles

Missile	AZ	Green	TMM		Missile	
Missile	CA	Point	PMMP		Missile	
Missile	FL	Cocoa	USAFSM		Missile	
Missile	GA	Cochr	CityPark		Missile	
Missile	WA	Tacom	FL		Missile	
Missile Silo	AZ	Green Valley	TMM		Titan II	571-7
Missile Silo	SD	Rapid	SDA&SM		Minuteman	
AGM-12	AZ	Tucso	PAM	Maxson	Bullpup	D79
AGM-12C	NY	Garde	CoAM	Maxson	Bullpup	
AGM-22A	NJ	Dover	PAAM			
AGM-28A(GAM-77)	AZ	Tucso	PAM	North American	Hound Dog	59-2866
AGM-28A(GAM-77)	AZ	Tucso	PAM	North American	Hound Dog	60-2092
AGM-28A(GAM-77)	CA	Sacra	SWAM	North American	Hound Dog	
AGM-28A(GAM-77)	IL	Rantoul	OCAM	North American	Hound Dog	20796
AGM-28A(GAM-77)	OK	Oklah	CityPark	North American	Hound Dog	
AGM-28A(GAM-77)	TX	Abilene	DLAP	North American	Hound Dog	
AGM-28A(GAM-77)	WY	Buffa	S&SHome	North American	Hound Dog	
AGM-28A(GAM-77)	WY	River	ALP121	North American	Hound Dog	
AGM-28B(GAM-77)	ME	Blain	ALP118	North American	Hound Dog	
AGM-28B(GAM-77)	OH	Dayto	USAFM	North American	Hound Dog	
AGM-28C(GAM-77)	CA	Atwater	CAM	North American	Hound Dog	
AGM-65	UT	Ogden	HAM	Hughes	Maverick	
AGM-86(ALCM)	NY	Rome	GAFBM	Boeing		
AGM-86B(ALCM)	OH	Dayton	USAFM	Boeing	ALCM	
AGM-86B(ALCM)	UT	Ogden	HAM	Boeing	ALCM	
AGM-86B(ALCM)	WA	Seattle	MoF	Boeing	ALCM	
AGM-129	CA	El Cajon	SDAMGF		Missile	
AGM-129	OH	Dayton	USAFM		Missile	

AGM-136	OH	Dayton	USAFM	Tatic	Rainbow	
Atlas	CA	El Cajon	SDAMGF		Atlas Missile	
CGM-13	FL	Panam	TAFB		Mace Missile	
CGM-13B	FL	Wildw	ALP-18		Mace Missile	
CGM-13B	GA	Warner Robin	AFASSOC		Mace Missile	
CGM-13B	OH	Dayton	USAFM		Mace Missile	
CIM-10A	CO	CSpri	EJPSCM	Boeing	Bomarc	59-2051
CIM-10A	GA	Warner Robin	MoF	Boeing	Bomarc 59-1953	
CIM-10A	OH	Dayton	USAFM	Boeing	Bomarc	
CIM-10A	UT	Ogden	HAM	Boeing	Bomarc	
CIM-10B	VA	Hampt	APM	Boeing	Bomarc Missile	
Convair Atlas	OH	Dayton	USAFM	Convair	Atlas Missile	
Corporal M2	KS	Topeka	CAM	Firestone Tire-JPL	Missile	From Ft Riley, KS
Corporal M2	VA	Hampton	HAP	Firestone Tire-JPL	Missile	
Corporal M2	WI	Kenos	KMM	Firestone Tire-JPL	Missile	
Drone Missile	WI	Kenos	KMM		Drone Missile	
GAM-54	AZ	Grand Canyon	PoFGCVA	Northrop	Crossbow	
GAM-63	CA	Atwater	CAM	McDonnell	Quail	
GAM-63	OK	Midwe	ALP170			
GAM-63(X)	OH	Dayton	USAFM	Bell	Rascal	
GAM-67(X)	CA	Banni	VWF			
GAM-67(X)	WA	Bridg	CityPark			
GAM-72	AL	Montg	GAFB	McDonnell	Quail	
GAM-72	CA	Oakland	WAM	McDonnell	Quail	
GAM-77	CA	Fairf	TAFB		Hound Dog Missile	
GAM-77	FL	Shali	USAFAM		Hound Dog Missile	
Grumman Rigel	NY	Garde	CoAM	Grumman	Rigel Missile	
Hawk Missile	WI	Kenos	KMM		Hawk Missile	
HGM-25A	OH	Dayton	USAFM		Titan I	Missile
IM-99	FL	Shali	USAFAM	Boeing	Bomarc Missile	
JB-1	CA	Hawth	WMoF	Northrop	Bat Bomb	
JB-2	AL	Wasilla	MoAT&I	Republic	Loon Missile	
JB-2	CT	Winds	NEAM	Republic	Loon Missile	
JB-2	IL	Milford	LC	Republic	Loon Missile	
JB-2	NY	Garde	CoAM	Republic	Loon Missile	Buzz Bomb
KD2G-2	FL	Pensa	USNAM	Globe	Target Drone	1268
KD6G-2	AZ	Tucso	PAM	Globe	TargetDrone	633
KD6G-2	CA	Chino	YAM	Globe	Target Drone	
KDB-1	CA	Chino	YAM	Beech	Target Missile Drone	
KDB-1	FL	Pensa	USNAM		Bug Torpedo	
Kettering Bug Torpedo	OH	Dayton	USAFM	Kettering	Bug Torpedo	
Lacrosse Missile	WI	Kenos	KMM		Lacrosse Missile	
LGM-25C(N-10)	AZ	Tucso	PAM	Martin Marietta	Titan II Missile	60- 8817, 9510003, "Small Paul's Pocket Rocket"
LGM-25C(N-10)	NY	Coron	NYHoS	Martin Marietta	Titan II Missile	Gemini
LGM	UT	Ogden	HAM	Boeing	Minuteman	
LGM-30	CA	Riverside	MAFM	Boeing	Minuteman II	
LGM-30	OH	Dayton	USAFM	Boeing	Minuteman II	
LGM-30A	OH	Dayton	USAFM	Boeing	Minuteman I	
LGM-30G	OH	Dayton	USAFM	Boeing	Minuteman III	
LTV	NC	Hickory	HRA			
LTV	OH	Dayton	USAFM		AST Missile	
Martin Marietta MX	OH	Dayton	USAFM	Martin	Peacekeeper Missile	
MGM-1	GA	Hawki	CityPark			
MGM-13A	FL	Shali	USAFAM	Martin	Mace	
MGM-13B	AR	Pocah	VWF	Martin	Mace	
MGM-13B	GA	Calhoun	MAM	Martin	Mace	62863
MGM-13B	GA	Warner Robin	I-75 E45	Martin	Mace	
MGM-13B	GA	Warner Robin	MoF	Martin	Mace	58-1465
MGM-13B	PA	Mildr	ALP452	Martin	Mace	
MGM-109	AZ	Tucson	PAM	General Dynamics	Cruise Missile	
Minuteman I	IL	Ranto	OCAM		Minuteman Missile	
Minuteman II	AZ	Tucso	PAM		Minuteman Missile	
Minuteman II	ND	Grand	GFAFB		Minuteman Missile	
Minuteman II	OH	Dayton	USAFM		Missile Trainer	
Minuteman Missile	SD	Rapid	SDA&SM		Minuteman	
Nike Missile	WI	Kenos	KMM		Nike Missile	
Nike-Ajax Missile	SD	Rapid	SDA&SM		Nike-Ajax	
NIM Missile	CO	CSpri	EJPSCM	Western Electric	Nike Ajax	
NIM Missile	MD	Handc	VFW	Western Electric	Nike Ajax	
NIM Missile	VA	Hampt	APM	Western Electric	Nike Ajax	
NIM-14 Missile	CO	CSpri	EJPSCM	Western Electric	Nike Hercules	
NIM-14 Missile	VA	Hampt	APM	Western Electric	Nike Hercules	
NIM-14 Missile	WA	FtLew	FtLewis	Western Electric	Nike Hercules	
Posedon Missile	DC	Washi	NM		Posedon	
SAM S-2A	OH	Dayton	USAFM	Soviet	Missile	
SAM S-2A	TX	Paris	FTAM	Soviet		
SAM AT Replica	NY	Garde	CoAM	Sperry		
SAM M1 Replica	NY	Garde	CoAM	Sperry		
SAM-N-7(SM-2)	NY	Garden	CoAM	Sperry	Terrier	Missile
SAM-N-8	NC	Surf City	TIM	Bendiz/McDonnell	Talos	# 114
SAM-N-8	SC	MtPleasant	PPM	Bendiz/McDonnell	Talos	
SICM	OH	Dayton	USAFM	Boeing	Midgetman Missile	
SM-62	OH	Dayton	USAFM	Northrop	Snark	
SM-62	UT	Ogden	HAM	Northrop	Snark	
SM-65	OH	Dayton	USAFM	Northrop	Atlas	
SM-68(B-68)	AZ	Tucso	PAM	Martin Marietta	Titan I Missile	4515
SM-68(B-68)	FL	Kissi	HJFPPH	Martin Marietta	Titan I Missile	Lox/Kerosene Fuel
SM-68(B-68)	GA	Corde	I-75 E32	Martin Marietta	Titan I Missile	
SM-68	OH	Dayton	USAFM	Northrop	Titan II Missile	N2O4/Aerozine Fuel
SM-68(B-68)	NE	Kimba	CityPark	Martin Marietta	Titan I Missile	
SM-68(B-68)	SC	FLore	FA&MM	Martin Marietta	Titan I Missile	
SM-78(PGM-19)	VA	Hampt	APM	Chrysler	Jupiter Missile	58-5282
Talos Rocket	SC	Topsail Beach	TIM			
Tartar	KS	Topeka	CAM		Missile	Navy
Titan II Missile	CA	Paso Robles	EWM		Upper Stage	Titan I
Titan I Missile	SD	Rapid	SDA&SM		Titan I	
TM-61	AZ	Grand Canyon	PoFGCVA	Martin	Matador	
TM-61A	FL	Titusville	VACM	Martin	Matador	
TM-61A	GA	Warner Robin	MoF	Martin	Matador	52-1891
TM-61A	OH	Dayton	USAFM	Martin	Matador	
TM-61C	SC	FLore	FA&MM	Martin	Matador	
Tomahawk II	PA	Phila	FI		Tomahawk Missile	
Tomahawk Missile	CA	Ridgecrest	CLNWC	Convair	Tomahawk Missile	
Tomahawk Missile	CA	San Diego	SDAM	Convair	Tomahawk Missile	
Torpedo Mk.14	MI	Sterling Hts	FHCMP	US Navy	Torpedo	

Naval Ships

CSS Neuse	NC	Kinston	CSS N&GCM	Confederate Navy	Ironclad Gunboat	"Ram" 1862, 1 of 3 survor out of 22
German Seehund	DC	Washi	NM	German WWII	Submarine	
HMCS Haida	ONT	Hamilton	OP	Vickers Armstrong	Destroyer	Tribal Class, # G63
Japanese Kaiten II	NJ	Hackensack	SMA-NJNM	Japanese WWII	Submarine	
SS American Victory	FL	Tampa	AVMM&MS		Liberty Ship	
USCG Taney	MD	Baltimore	BMM		Cutter	
USD-4	GA	Agust	FG			
USD-5	GA	Agust	FG			
USF Constitution	MA	Boston			Frigate	
USF Constellation	MD	Baltimore	BIH		Frigate Sister Ship	
USS Airzona	HI	Honol	AM		Battleship	BB- 39
USS Alabama	AL	Mobil	BMP		Battleship	BB- 60
USS Becuna	PA	Philadelphia	ISM		Submarine	
USS Blueback	OR	Portland	OmoS&I		Submarine	SS-581
USS Bowfin	HI	Honol	AM		Submarine	SS-287
USS Cassin Young	MA	Boston	USSC		Destroyer	DD-793, DestroyerDD-793
USS Chesapeake	MD	Baltimore	BMM		Lightship	
USS Clamagore	SC	Mt Pl	PPM		Submarine	SS-343
USS Cobia	WI	Manit	WMM		Submarine	SS-245
USS Cod	OH	Cleveland	SUSSC		Submarine	SS-224
USS Croaker	NY	Buffa	B&ECN&SP		Submarine	SSK-246
USS Drum	AL	Mobil	BMP		Submarine	SS-228
USS Edson	NY	NYC	ISASM		Destroyer	DD-946
USS Fall River	MA	Fall River	BC		Cruiser	
USS Forrestal	MD	West River	USSFNM		Aircraft Carrier	#"59"
USS Growler	NY	NYC	ISASM		Submarine	SS-215
USS Guadalcanal	NY	NYC	ISASM		Helicopter Carrier	LPH- 7
USS Hazard	NB	Omaha	FP		Mine Sweeper	AM-240
USS Helena Parts	OH	Newcomerstown	NNM			CL50
USS Hornet	CA	Alameda	USSH		Aircraft Carrier	
USS Ingham	SC	Mt Pl	PPM		Coast Guard Cutter	35
USS Intelligent Whale	NJ	Sea Grit	NJNGMM		Submarine	
USS Intrepid	NY	NYC	ISASM		Aircraft Carrier	CVA-11
USS Jeremiah O'Brian	CA	SFransico	SF		Liberty Ship	
USS JP Kennedy	MA	Fall	USSMM		Destroyer	DD-850
USS John Brown	MD	Baltimore	PLS		Liberty Ship	
USS Kidd	LA	BRoug	LNWM		Destroyer	DD-661
USS LSM-45	NB	Omaha	FP			Landing Ship
USS Laffey	SC	Mt Pl	PPM		Destroyer	DD-724
USS Lane Victory	CA	San Diego			Liberty Ship	
USS Lexington	TX	C Christi	USS Lexi		Aircraft Carrier	CV- 16
USS Lionfish	MA	Fall	USSMM		Submarine	SS-298
USS Ling	NJ	Hackensack	SMA-NJNM		Submarine	SS-297
USS Little Rock	NY	Buffa	B&ECNP		Cruiser	CLG-4
USS Maiale SSB	DC	Washi	NM		Submarine	
USS Marlin	NB	Omaha	FP		Submarine	SST-2, T-2
USS Massachusetts	MA	Fall	USSMM		Battleship	BB- 59
USS Misouri	HI	Honolua	AM		Battleship	BB- 63
USS New Jersey	NJ	Camden	PSNS		Battleship	BB- 62
USS North Carolina	NC	Wilmi	USSNCBC		Battleship	BB- 55
USS Olympia	PA	Philadelphia	ISM			
USS Orleck	TX	Orange	STWM		Destroyer	DD-886
USS Pamanito	CA	San Franciso	USSC		Submarine	
USS Pinato Tower	TX	Frede	NMotPW		Submarine	SS-387
USS Radford Parts	OH	Newcomerstown	NNM		Battleship	DD-446
USS Requin	PA	Pittsburg	CSC		Submarine	SS-481
USS Roncador Tower	CA	San Francisco	MPA		Submarine	SS-301
USS Salem	MA	Quincy	USN&SM		Battleship	CA-139, Flagship, Graf Spee Movie
USS Savannah	VA	Newpo				
USS Silversides	MI	Muske	USS SILV		Submarine	SS-236
USS Slater	NY	Albarry	USS S		Destroyer	DE-766
USS Sullivans	NY	Buffa	B&ECNP		Destroyer	DD-537
USS Texas	TX	LaPor	USS Texa		Battleship	BB- 35
USS Towers	NB	Omaha	FP		Captains Gig	DDG-9
USS Torsk	MD	Baltimore	BMM		Submarine	
USS Turner Joy	WA	Breme	PSNS		Destroyer	DD-951
USS Turtle	DC	Washi	NM		Submarine	
USS Wisconsin	VA	Norfolk	TBW		Battleship	BB- 64
USS Yorktown	SC	Mt Pleasant	PPM		Aircraft Carrier	CV- 10

Engine Displays:

OX-5	FL	Kissi	FTWAM
OX-5	PA	Harri	SMoP